Visual Studio LightSwitch 2012

Tim Leung

Visual Studio LightSwitch 2012

ISBN-13 (pbk): 978-1-4302-5071-5

ISBN-13 (electronic): 978-1-4302-5072-2

President and Publisher: Paul Manning
Lead Editor: Ewan Buckingham
Developmental Editor: Tom Welsh
Technical Reviewers: Stephen Provine and Fabio Claudio Ferracchiati
Editorial Board: Steve Anglin, Mark Beckner, Ewan Buckingham, Gary Cornell, Louise Corrigan, Morgan Ertel, Jonathan Gennick, Jonathan Hassell, Robert Hutchinson, Michelle Lowman, James Markham, Matthew Moodie, Jeff Olson, Jeffrey Pepper, Douglas Pundick, Ben Renow-Clarke, Dominic Shakeshaft, Gwenan Spearing, Matt Wade, Tom Welsh
Coordinating Editor: Katie Sullivan
Copy Editor: Roger LeBlanc
Compositor: SPi Global
Indexer: SPi Global
Artist: SPi Global
Cover Designer: Anna Ishchenko

Distributed to the book trade worldwide by Springer Science+Business Media New York, 233 Spring Street, 6th Floor, New York, NY 10013. Phone 1-800-SPRINGER, fax (201) 348-4505, e-mail orders-ny@springer-sbm.com, or visit www.springeronline.com. Apress Media, LLC is a California LLC and the sole member (owner) is Springer Science + Business Media Finance Inc (SSBM Finance Inc). SSBM Finance Inc is a Delaware corporation.

For information on translations, please e-mail rights@apress.com, or visit www.apress.com.

Apress and friends of ED books may be purchased in bulk for academic, corporate, or promotional use. eBook versions and licenses are also available for most titles. For more information, reference our Special Bulk Sales–eBook Licensing web page at www.apress.com/bulk-sales.

Any source code or other supplementary materials referenced by the author in this text is available to readers at www.apress.com. For detailed information about how to locate your book's source code, go to www.apress.com/source-code/.

Nutrition and Growth

Human Nutrition
A COMPREHENSIVE TREATISE

General Editors:
Roslyn B. Alfin-Slater, University of California, Los Angeles
David Kritchevsky, The Wistar Institute, Philadelphia

Contents at a Glance

Contents

About the Author

Tim Leung is a professional software developer based in England. For the past 15 years, he has specialized in enterprise application development using products from the Microsoft technology stack. In particular, he possesses deep knowledge of Microsoft LightSwitch, the Microsoft .NET Framework and SQL Server. He is an active member of the U.K. developer community and often delivers presentations on technical topics. He is also a chartered member of the British Computer Society. He is passionate about the concept of rapid application development and was awarded the Microsoft Community Contributor Award in 2011 for contributions to the LightSwitch community.

About the Technical Reviewers

Stephen Provine is a principal software design engineer on the Microsoft Visual Studio LightSwitch team. He has 12 years of experience working across many aspects of the Visual Studio rapid-application-development (RAD) experiences, including the Server Explorer, SQL database tooling and overall data designer extensibility in the Visual Studio IDE. Most recently, he has focused on the architecture and design for the LightSwitch HTML client introduced in Visual Studio 2012 Update 2. Prior to working at Microsoft, Stephen received a bachelor's degree in Computer Science from Harvard University.

Fabio Claudio Ferracchiati is a senior consultant and a senior analyst/developer using Microsoft technologies. He works for Brain Force (`www.brainforce.com`) in its Italian branch (`www.brainforce.it`). He is a Microsoft Certified Solution Developer for .NET, a Microsoft Certified Application Developer for .NET, a Microsoft Certified Professional, and a prolific author and technical reviewer. Over the past ten years, he's written articles for Italian and international magazines and coauthored more than ten books on a variety of computer topics.

Acknowledgments

I'd like to thank everyone who supported me during the writing of this book. In particular, I'd like to thank my development editor Tom Welsh for all the help he's given me throughout this project. Stephen Provine spent a lot of time reviewing this book and went out of his way to answer my technical questions. I highly appreciate all the help that he gave me. Beth Massi at Microsoft has helped me countless times in the past, and I'm very grateful for her support. Last but not least, I'd like to thank Katie Sullivan, Ewan Buckingham, and everybody at Apress for making this book possible.

Foreword

Every business uses software to automate their business functions. At their heart, such applications are about gathering, storing, and processing data, so such applications could involve what we typically think of under the rubric of "business applications"—for example, tracking finances or assets (as in ERP software). But it also includes the process of software development, systems management, or anything else involving data. There is a lot of this business software out there, a lot more being written, and even more that people wish they had the time, budget, and skill to write.

Building such software involves two concerns: the business problem to be solved (the domain) and the technology into which a solution is rendered. First you have to have one person who understands both the domain and the technology necessary to render it into software, or you have to have a team with a mix of skills. That's enough to kill many small projects.

Assuming you can get the right people together, the technologist then spends a great deal of time on issues that have nothing to do with the business problem being solved, including UI, protocols, business logic mechanism, security, integration with Microsoft Office, and much, much more. One needs a good deal of skill, time, inclination, and budget to get a project accomplished.

To help people write business applications faster, we created Microsoft Visual Studio LightSwitch, the simplest way for developers of all skill levels to develop business applications for the desktop and cloud. Using LightSwitch, the core technical problems are solved and a lot of projects—that without LightSwitch would have never seen the light of day—are now in production.

Visual Studio LightSwitch 2012 provides a conceptual and practical introduction to many core LightSwitch building blocks, including importing and defining data schema, designing queries and screens, validating data, authenticating and authorizing application users, and deploying the final product.

However, the challenge with rapid application development environments is that they're great at solving the problems they anticipated, but what if you need to do more? Happily, LightSwitch was designed without the glass ceiling that constrains the tools of the 4GL generation, so the full power of Visual Studio is available to you if you want it—the limit is your imagination.

Tim has a lot of imagination and has explored many ways to supplement LightSwitch in this book. He offers solutions for a number of problems that LightSwitch does not address but that you may encounter as you write your applications. His is a cookbook. Some recipes won't have ingredients you like, some you'll season to fit your taste, some will open possibilities you hadn't even considered, and some you'll use as is. A sampling includes sending e-mail, creating reports, and implementing auditing.

He shares a passion with the LightSwitch team and with their readers: to build great business applications, fast. Together we can make businesses more successful through software.

Steve Anonsen, Distinguished Engineer, Microsoft Visual Studio

Introduction

It's possible to see many things in life as a journey, and writing a business application is no exception. On this particular journey, your goal is to build an application that fully works and meets the expectations of your users. Let's imagine, for a moment, that the tool that builds your application represents your journey's mode of transport. Using this analogy, I like to think of LightSwitch as a high-speed train because it allows you to reach your destination a lot faster than usual.

Speaking of trains, journeys are much more comfortable today than they were in the past. Modern carriages are Wi-Fi enabled and include tables and electrical sockets that you can plug your laptop into. There are even touch-screen displays that you can use to watch television or to view a map that shows you exactly where you are, and how much further there is to go. The ride itself is smooth enough for you to leave your hot coffee on the table without fear of it spilling. Everything is much cleaner than in the age of steam; and you never risk getting a hot cinder in your eye if you open a window!

The fascinating thing is that your railway journey might follow exactly the same route as it would have 150 years ago. However, the experience itself is quicker, cleaner, and more convenient. Just like the railways, LightSwitch has evolved during its short lifespan. The improvements in the latest version help to keep it fresh, relevant, and purposeful.

When LightSwitch first came out, it created applications based on Microsoft Silverlight. Today, you can support mobile and touch-screen tablet devices by extending your application to include an HTML front end. A big benefit of this approach is that you can reuse all of your existing data and business logic. This technical change is the railway equivalent of swapping all the carriages on a train for modern replacements.

Likewise, the first version of LightSwitch employed RIA services as the communication channel between the client and server. Today's LightSwitch uses the OData protocol instead. Applying the railway analogy once more, this is like replacing the railway tracks with smoother rails. If LightSwitch doesn't totally meet your requirements, you can easily integrate your application with other systems and platforms—like completing the final leg of the journey by car, bus, or foot.

The point of this analogy is to highlight one of the beauties of LightSwitch. It's possible for LightSwitch to evolve and improve because it's built in a modular way that allows individual pieces to be replaced. This modular architecture ensures that LightSwitch will remain relevant for a long time to come.

You can also consider this book as a journey—a tour that shows you how to build a LightSwitch application from start to finish. As with most journeys, there'll be highlights and features along the way. I'm really pleased that you've chosen to take the LightSwitch journey. It's sure to save you time and make your life easier; so I'm certain it'll be a journey that you won't regret taking!

Who This Book Is For

This book is designed for readers who want to build data-driven business applications quickly. You don't need to have any prior knowledge of LightSwitch, but it helps if you know a little about .NET and database development in general.

How This Book Is Organized

If learning LightSwitch seems like an enormous task, don't worry! You might have heard of the Pareto Principle, which also goes by the name of the 80/20 rule. This rule states that in most situations, 20% of something causes 80% of the results.

If you apply the Pareto Principle to this book, it suggests that you can accomplish 80% of what you want to accomplish by reading less than four chapters! And, in fact, the first three chapters highlight the key topics that are all you need to build an application that's almost 80% complete.

By the end of Chapter 3, you'll understand how to create data tables and attach to external data. You'll know how to build a Silverlight web or desktop application that includes screens and navigation controls. You'll see how to open child records from a parent record and how to assign parent records to child records by using controls like the autocomplete box (a picker control that's similar to a drop-down box). In short, you'll know how to build a working business application with enough functionality to perform most basic tasks.

The next part of the book shows you how to write code and queries. After that, you'll learn how to create screens that contain advanced features and support mobile devices by adding an HTML client.

Unless you want to create an application that's completely isolated from other systems, it's useful to know how you can attach to unusual data sources and how to share your LightSwitch data with other applications. You'll discover how to do this through RIA services and OData.

You can extend your Silverlight applications through custom controls and extensions, and you'll find an entire section of the book devoted to this topic.

The remaining chapters of the book show you how to build reports, integrate with e-mail systems, and deploy your application.

The Sample Application

Most of the chapters include code samples that refer to a HelpDesk application. The purpose of this application is to relate the technical content in the book to a real-life scenario that you can understand.

The HelpDesk application is typical of the applications that you can build with LightSwitch. Its features are simple enough to understand, yet complex enough to show off the more advanced features of LightSwitch. It is designed to help companies manage problems, and it's especially suitable for departments that deal with technical support issues. It allows users to record the actions they carry out to resolve a problem, while giving managers an overview of all current issues.

Figure 1 shows a screen from this application and illustrates some of the features that you'll learn about in this book.

Figure 1. *A typical screen from the HelpDesk manager*

Figure 1 shows the data-entry screen through which users can enter help desk issues. They can set the user that the issue relates to and allocate an engineer to the record. The data-entry screen allows users to respond to the issue, attach documents, register feedback, and record the time that engineers spend on the task. To help you re-create this application, you can find a summary of the application's tables in Appendix E.

Code Samples

LightSwitch supports C#, VB.NET, and JavaScript. This book includes code samples in all three languages. To make life simple, LightSwitch hides much of the complexity that's associated with application design. When you want to write some code, you do this by clicking on a *write code* button that LightSwitch shows in its graphical designers. The write code button shows a list of events that you can handle. When you select one of the options in the list, LightSwitch opens a code editor window that you can use to author your code.

When you're starting out with LightSwitch, it isn't always obvious where your code is stored. To add some clarity, each code listing includes a file location, as shown in Listing 1.

Listing 1. Hello World Example

VB:
File: HelpDeskVB\Server\UserCode\ApplicationData.vb

```
Imports System.Text.RegularExpressions

'REM VB Code appears here                                    ❶
Dim message = "Hello World"                                  ❷
```

C#:
File: HelpDeskCS\Server\UserCode\ApplicationData.cs

```
using System.Text.RegularExpressions;

//REM C# Code appears here                                   ❶
var message = "Hello World";                                 ❷
```

For both the VB and C# examples in Listing 1, the File heading specifies the file name and path. In this example, HelpDeskVB and HelpDeskCS refer to the name of your LightSwitch application. The name Server refers to the Server project. This piece of information is useful because it informs you that the code runs on the server rather than the client. (You'll learn all about this in Chapter 1.) The next part of the file heading, UserCode, indicates a subfolder in the Server project. Finally, ApplicationData.vb and ApplicationData.cs refer to the name of the VB or C# file that the listing shows.

If a piece of code requires you to reference a .NET namespace, the code listing will show the necessary Imports (VB.NET) or using (C#) statement. Be sure to add these statements to the top of your code file.

Many of the code samples include numeric symbols to help you locate specific lines in a code listing. For example, line ❶ defines a comment, whereas line ❷ declares a variable. There's obviously no need to enter these numeric symbols when you re-create this code for real!

As in all books, the length of a code line can exceed the width of this book. In most cases, I've put line breaks in places that still allow the code to compile. But in some circumstances, this isn't always possible. Notable examples include namespace declarations in XAML files and VB.NET keywords like inherits and implements. If your application doesn't compile, it's worth checking your code for extraneous line breaks.

Tips/Notes/Cautions

This book includes callouts with tips, notes, and cautions. Tips are helpful hints or pieces of information that may be particularly interesting. Notes provide you with nonessential, yet interesting additional information about a particular topic. Cautions alert you to anything that might be detrimental to your work or could cause damage.

Exercises

Some readers prefer to learn kinesthetically (that is, in a touchy-feely way). If you fall into this category, you can try the exercises that you'll find throughout this book. These exercises provide you with ideas to try out in LightSwitch to help you further understand the content that's described in the book.

Comments and Errata

Although my editors and I have tried to be as accurate as possible, mistakes do sometimes happen (particularly with a book of this length). If you have any feedback or want to report any bugs, please visit the official page for this book at the Apress website:

http://www.apress.com/9781430250715

This page also shows any mistakes that we've found following the publication of this book.

■ ■ ■

CHAPTER 1

Introducing LightSwitch

Do you ever feel that software development is too complicated? If you're building business applications already, do you feel frustrated by the amount of time that it takes to build an application? Or if you've never built a modern-day web application, does the thought of doing so frighten you? If you're starting from scratch, where exactly do you begin? And are you really confident that you can build a robust application that meets the expectations of your users and isn't susceptible to "falling over" or getting hacked?

If any of this sounds familiar, LightSwitch will come as a breath of fresh air. It's a rapid software development tool that helps you to work faster, better, and smarter. It allows you to build data-centric business applications that can run on the desktop or on the web.

But despite LightSwitch's simplicity, there's no need to compromise on functionality. You can build applications with all the features that you'd expect to find in a typical business application, and this book will show you exactly how.

The first chapter teaches you the core LightSwitch principles that will help you throughout the rest of this book. The key topics that you'll cover in this chapter include

- The three-tier architecture that LightSwitch uses

- How LightSwitch uses a model-centric architecture, and applies the MVVM pattern

- What exactly happens when you build and compile a LightSwitch application

Let's begin by taking a look at LightSwitch's architecture.

Understanding LightSwitch's Architecture

In keeping with best practices, LightSwitch applications consist of three layers. This architecture enforces the logical separation of your application and provides better maintainability and scalability. The biggest advantage is that it allows Microsoft to rewrite or replace entire layers in response to changes in requirements or technology. Every time you create a new application, LightSwitch creates multiple projects in your LightSwitch solution. Each project is designed to run on a specific layer in this architecture.

This automation of the project layout itself is a major timesaver. If you built an application without LightSwitch, you could spend days on getting the architecture correct.

Figure 1-1 illustrates the parts that make up a LightSwitch application. It highlights the way that applications are separated into data, logic, and presentation layers. It also illustrates how the layers communicate with each other.

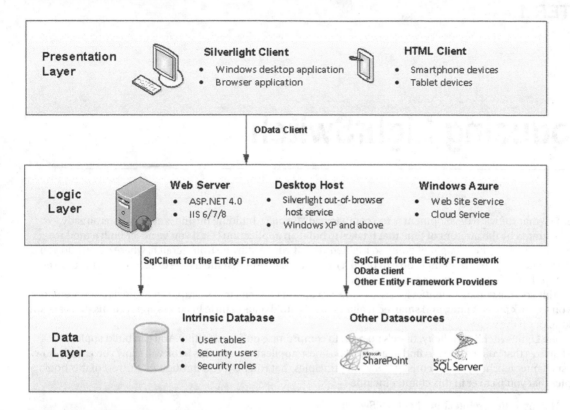

Figure 1-1. *LightSwitch's architecture*

The Data Layer

LightSwitch's architecture defines a separate logical data layer. This means that LightSwitch stores your data separately from the rest of your application, and allows you to run the data-storage processes on a platform that's separate from the rest of your application.

The advantage of this *data independence* is that it doesn't tie you to a specific database or datasource. If you're not happy with using Microsoft SQL Server, for example, you can more easily configure your application to store its data in Oracle instead.

Delegating the responsibility of data storage to a separate layer also improves scalability and performance. It allows you to take advantage of database-engine features such as mirroring, clustering, and indexes, and you can also upgrade your database engine without affecting the rest of your application.

In practical terms, LightSwitch allows you to read and write data from SQL Server, SQL Azure, SharePoint, and many other data sources. In fact, your data-storage options are almost limitless. This is because you can connect to almost any data source by creating your own custom RIA (Rich Internet Applications) service.

A special database that LightSwitch uses is the Intrinsic (or Application Data) database. LightSwitch uses this database to store the tables that you create through the built-in table designer.

LightSwitch allows you to define users and to apply security access control. To manage your users and roles, it uses the ASP.NET SQL membership provider. This membership provider relies on database tables and, by default, LightSwitch adds these tables to your Intrinsic database.

During design time, LightSwitch hosts your Intrinsic database using LocalDB (the successor to Microsoft SQL Server Express). But when you deploy your application, you can host your Intrinsic database on any version of SQL Server 2005 or above.

The Logic Layer

LightSwitch's architecture defines a separate logic layer that contains application services. A big advantage of this separation is that it allows Microsoft to rewrite parts of LightSwitch without impacting either the client or data tiers.

The application services are responsible for carrying out business rules, validation, and data access. LightSwitch creates a *Data Service* for each data source in your application and exposes it through an OData end point at the logic layer boundary. OData is a data-access protocol, which you'll learn more about in Chapter 10.

When your LightSwitch client needs to access some data, it doesn't communicate directly with your underlying database or data store. Instead, it accesses data by making an OData call to the data service that's hosted in your logic layer.

There are three places where you can host your application services. The most common place is through an ASP. NET application that's hosted on an IIS (Internet Information Services) server. But you can also host your application services on Windows Azure, or you can host the services on the client workstation in the case of a desktop application.

Note that the word *layer* describes the logical separation of your application, whereas *tier* refers to the physical place where you deploy a layer. Therefore, later chapters in this book use the term 'middle tier' to describe the machine that hosts your logic layer's end point.

Data-retrieval process

The data service exposes operations that return data to the client. By default, these operations include queries that return all records in a table or single records that are filtered by a primary key value. LightSwitch also exposes the queries you create as OData methods.

Figure 1-2 illustrates a typical data operation. When the LightSwitch UI requires data, it calls a query operation on the data service. In this example, the query operation refers to a search query that we've created ourselves to allow users to search for customers by surname. This query allows the client to supply an argument to define the surname to search for.

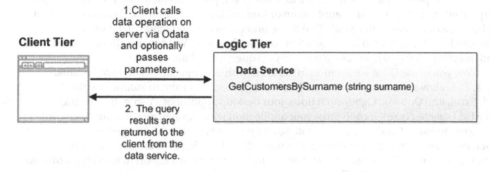

Figure 1-2. Calling a query that returns customers filtered by surname

When the data service executes the query, it passes through the *Query Pipeline*. This opens up various phases where you could inject your own custom code. During the pre-processing phase, for example, you can tailor the results of a query by adding extra filter conditions using LINQ (Language Integrated Query) code.

Data-saving process

The data service provides an operation called SaveChanges. As the name suggests, this method starts the process that saves any updated data. Let's see how this save process works.

At the very beginning (before SaveChanges is called), the client calls a query that returns an initial set of data. The client caches this data using an object called a *Change Set*. This object maintains a record of any records that the user adds, updates, or deletes.

When the user clicks on the save button, the LightSwitch client calls the SaveChanges operation and supplies the Change Set. Before the data service commits the changes to the database (or underlying data store such as SharePoint), the processing enters the Save Pipeline.

Just like the Query Pipeline, the Save Pipeline provides places where you intercept the save operation by writing custom code. For example, you can prevent certain users from updating data by including code in the Save Pipeline.

Another feature of LightSwitch is that it prevents users from overwriting changes that have been made by other users. If LightSwitch detects a conflicting data change, it won't allow the save operation to succeed. Instead, it shows what the current and proposed values are and allows the user to choose what to do.

LightSwitch also maintains the consistency of your data by applying all updates inside a transaction. For example, any proposed change to a parent record won't be applied if an update to a child record fails.

Without LightSwitch, you could spend ages writing this type of boring, repetitive boilerplate code. This is an ideal example of how LightSwitch can help you save time.

The Presentation Layer

The presentation layer is the part of LightSwitch that runs on the user's computer or device. This layer actually performs a lot of work. It shows data to the user, allows data entry to happen, and controls all other tasks that relate to human interaction.

Importantly, it also performs business logic such as data validation, keeps track of data changes, and interacts with the Data Services in the logic layer.

You can build your user interface (or client) by using either Silverlight or HTML. In fact, the choice isn't mutually exclusive. You can include both Silverlight and HTML clients in a single LightSwitch application.

Silverlight Client

The advantage of Silverlight is that it provides a rich experience for both developers and end users. You can configure your project so that your application runs as a desktop application or from within a web browser. You can easily switch your application type by clicking a radio button that you'll find in the properties of your LightSwitch project.

An advantage of Silverlight is that it's easier to write code that runs on the client. You can use strongly typed C# or Visual Basic (VB) code and use .NET language features such as LINQ to query your data.

Desktop applications allow you to use COM automation to integrate with the applications that are installed on your end user's machine. This allows you to export the results of data grids to Excel and to automate Office applications such as Word, Excel, and Outlook. LightSwitch hosts your desktop applications using the Silverlight out-of-browser host service (`sllauncher.exe`). It configures your application with elevated permissions to give it access to features such as Export to Excel, COM-based automation, and greater access to the file system.

LightSwitch web applications are hosted by the Silverlight runtime that's installed in your user's web browser. Silverlight browser applications execute inside a sandbox, and access to features such as Export to Excel is prohibited. Silverlight also restricts access to certain parts of the file system.

LightSwitch Shell

You can customize the appearance of a Silverlight application by applying a Shell and a Theme. A Shell controls the location of all of the major UI elements in your application. It also contains the logic that logs users in to your application, and it generates and activates the screens that LightSwitch displays.

Themes define a set of styles that specify the fonts and colors that your application uses. Unlike Shells, Themes apply presentational changes that are much more subtle. Themes are usually designed to work with a specific shell, but it's entirely possible for you to mix and match different Shells and Themes.

Themes and Shells allow you to apply a consistent look and feel throughout your entire application. New developers often struggle to set control attributes (such as fonts and colors) because many of these attributes are designed to be controlled by a Theme, rather than set for each individual control. LightSwitch applies good practice by encouraging you to apply style settings at an application level.

You can set the Shell and Theme for each application through the properties pane of your project. (See Chapter 3.) The two default shells that ship with LightSwitch are called Standard and Cosmopolitan. Figure 1-3 illustrates the same application, but with different Shells applied.

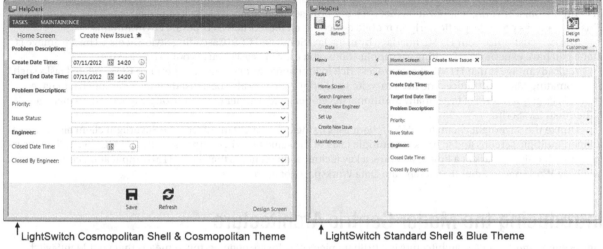

LightSwitch Cosmopolitan Shell & Cosmopolitan Theme   LightSwitch Standard Shell & Blue Theme

Figure 1-3. *The Cosmopolitan Shell (on the left) and the Standard Shell (on the right)*

If you don't like the Shells or Themes that LightSwitch provides, you can choose to write your own. (This is covered in Chapter 13.)

Understanding Silverlight Screens

A Screen represents a piece of user interface that allows users to view or enter data (just like a Form in an Access application, or a Web Form in an ASP.NET application).

Developers create screens with prebuilt functions by using Templates. For example, there are templates that allow you to create search, editable grid, and data entry screens. You can also create your own screen templates—this is yet another extensibility point that LightSwitch offers.

Users can open multiple screens in a Silverlight LightSwitch application, but there can be only one single active screen at any time.

Each screen contains an object called a *Data Workspace* that is responsible for fetching and managing data. The Data Workspace manages the state of the data in the Change Set that is submitted to the *Data Service* on the logic tier when the user initiates a save.

Because each screen contains its own Data Workspace, the data changes that a user makes in one screen won't be visible in other screens. You can't share data changes between screens because each screen maintains an independent view of the data.

When you're writing Screen code, you'll need some way to reference objects such as data, controls, or screen parameters. LightSwitch exposes these objects through a *Screen Object*, and you'll learn how to use this in Chapter 7.

5

HTML Client

The *HTML client* is new to LightSwitch 2012. This client is highly recommended for applications that run on mobile or touch-screen devices.

The advantage of using the HTML client is that your application will work on a wider range of devices. In comparison, a Silverlight application that runs in a browser requires the user to install the Silverlight runtime. This isn't always possible, particularly on mobile devices or on locked-down corporate environments.

You can customize your HTML interface by using JavaScript and CSS (Cascading Style Sheets). The advantage is that if you have experience of writing web applications, you can very easily reuse your existing skills.

A disadvantage is that HTML clients are less rich in functionality, and you can't perform COM-related tasks such as automating Microsoft Office. The need to write JavaScript code may also be a disadvantage. Although language choice is largely a matter of taste, many traditional developers find it easier to use a strongly typed .NET language, rather than JavaScript.

Unlike the Silverlight client, the HTML client uses a single document interface. The Silverlight client allows users to open multiple screens and to work on multiple tasks at the same time. In comparison, the HTML client allows users to carry out only one task at a time. Therefore, a key technical difference is that each HTML application contains only one Data Workspace, rather than a separate Data Workspace for each screen.

Introducing the Model-Centric Architecture

LightSwitch's *model-centric* architecture is a brilliant piece of software engineering. It means that your LightSwitch application (data items, screens, queries) is defined and saved in XML files that are named with an LSML extension. When you run your LightSwitch application, the *LightSwitch runtime* processes this XML data and transforms it into a working application.

As a very loose analogy, think of the LightSwitch runtime as a copy of Microsoft Word. Using this analogy, your LightSwitch application would be a Microsoft Word document. In the same way that Word opens Word documents and makes them readable and editable, the LightSwitch runtime opens LightSwitch applications and makes them functional.

The advantage of this architecture is that LightSwitch isn't strongly tied to any specific technology. If Microsoft wants LightSwitch to run on a different platform or device, they can do this by simply writing a new runtime.

Building Your Application

Figure 1-4 shows the parts that make up a LightSwitch application, from design time through to run time. LightSwitch solutions consist of three projects: the Client, Common, and Server projects. These are shown as columns in the diagram. To further explain what happens, let's begin at the bottom.

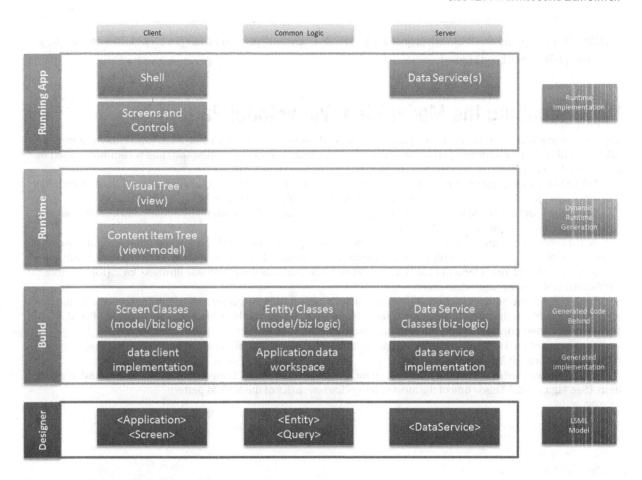

Figure 1-4. *LightSwitch build process*

As part of the model-centric architecture, LightSwitch constructs your applications from building blocks. Think of these as XML representations of the objects that are available in the LightSwitch designer. Let's say that you add a data source to your application. When you do this, LightSwitch expresses your data source as an XML element within the LSML file in your Server project. When you've finished in Visual Studio, your application will be defined entirely in XML, and this is known as the *LSML Model*.

When you build your application, LightSwitch compiles the .NET code that's present in your application. This includes the user code that you've written, in addition to the classes that LightSwitch autogenerates to support your application. The autogenerated code includes the DataWorkspace classes and Screen object classes. These are core API objects that allow you to access your data through code.

The interesting thing about the LightSwitch clients is that they don't contain any UI that's specific to your application. Instead, the LightSwitch runtime dynamically generates your screens and UI at runtime.

In the case of the Silverlight client, the LightSwitch runtime composes the screens, controls, and shell using the Managed Extensibility Framework (MEF). This dynamic generation prevents you from customizing your Silverlight application by hand-crafting the Extensible Application Markup Language (XAML). This is something that experienced Silverlight developers might be interested in doing. If you want to build your own UI elements using XAML, you can do so by creating your own custom controls (as you'll see in Chapter 11).

In the case of the HTML client, you can customize the HTML that's shown to the user by writing JavaScript that generates custom HTML.

■ **Note** You can create a LightSwitch project in C# or VB.NET. However, you can't change a project from one language to the other after it has been created.

Understanding the Model-View-ViewModel Pattern

LightSwitch applications follow a design pattern called Model-View-ViewModel, or M-V-VM (also known simply as MVVM). This pattern was developed by John Gossman (a technical architect at Microsoft) and is commonly used by Silverlight developers.

MVVM keeps the presentation, logic, and data elements of your application logically distinct. This pattern helps you produce applications that are cleaner, more maintainable, and more testable.

The *Model* part of MVVM refers to the conceptual representation of your data. The entities and queries that you define in your application make up the model.

At runtime, LightSwitch constructs a *screen layout* by interpreting the LSML model. The screen layout consists of a tree of content items, which can represent data items, lists, commands, or parent items. A content item at runtime represents the *View Model* element of MVVM. The View Model controls the client-side business logic (for example, validation) and also manages data access.

In the case of the Silverlight client, the LightSwitch runtime builds the *visual tree*, which contains the actual tree of Silverlight controls that are presented on screen. These Silverlight controls make up the *View* part of MVVM. Views are designed only to display data—nothing more.

In the case of the HTML client, LightSwitch binds HTML controls (the view) to content items that are implemented through JavaScript.

Because views are designed only to display data, it allows you to easily change the control that's bound to a data item. (See Figure 1-5.) This is one of the most striking characteristics of the MVVM pattern.

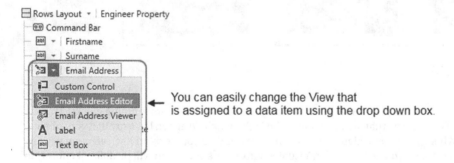

Figure 1-5. Changing the views that are bound to a data item

Examining LightSwitch Projects

When you open a project in LightSwitch, you can view your project in one of two ways: Logical View or File View. The default view that LightSwitch presents is the *Logical View*. This basic view organizes your project into various folders such as Data Sources, Entities, and Screens. The Logical View enables you to add and edit items such as screens, queries, and data sources.

File View allows you to see and work on the individual projects that make up your LightSwitch solution. Importantly, it allows you to add references to external dynamic-link libraries (DLLs) and to add your own custom code files.

A button in Solution Explorer allows you to switch between these two views. (See Figure 1-6.) In File View, some files might be hidden by default. Click on the Show All Files button to view all items.

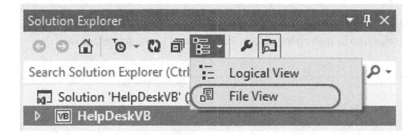

Figure 1-6. Switching to File View

EXERCISE 1.1 – EXAMINING LIGHTSWITCH'S SOLUTION STRUCTURE

Start LightSwitch and create a new project. Notice how Solution Explorer shows two folders: Data Sources and Screens. Now switch to File View and examine the underlying projects and files. From Visual Studio's Build menu, select the Build Solution option. After Visual Studio builds your project, use Windows Explorer to view your project files. Notice how LightSwitch generates your build output into a folder called Bin. Notice how this folder contains a subfolder called Data that contains your design-time Intrinsic database.

After you complete Exercise 1.1, the contents of Solution Explorer will appear as shown in Figure 1-7.

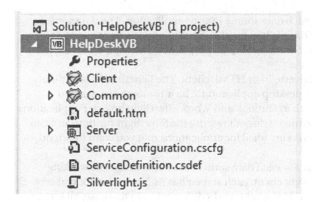

Figure 1-7. File View of Project

Notice the Client, Server, and Common projects that make up your solution.

The Client project contains the Silverlight client project, the Server project contains the ASP.NET code that runs on the server, and the Common project contains the logic that runs on both the client and server. Custom validation code is an example of something that belongs in the Common project. This is because LightSwitch executes the same code on both the presentation and logic tiers. In keeping with good practice, LightSwitch validates data on the client to provide instantaneous feedback to the user. It then revalidates on the server to ensure security.

If you create an HTML client project (as discussed in Chapter 8), your project will contain two projects: a Server project, and an HTML Client project. In this scenario, the HTML Client project contains the content that runs on the user's browser. If you add an HTML client to an existing LightSwitch project, LightSwitch no longer uses the code that's in your Common project. Instead, it adds the shared code into the Server project and adds links to the shared code files from the Client project.

■ **Tip** Logical View doesn't allow you to organize your screens, queries, and tables into subfolders. If you're working on a large project, you can keep your project organized by naming the objects that you want to group together with a common prefix.

Reducing Project Sizes

Even the smallest LightSwitch project consumes over 180 MBs in hard disk space. The large project sizes make it difficult to back up, share, or email your LightSwitch projects.

If you want to reduce the amount of space your projects take up on disk, you can safely delete the contents of the \Client\Bin and \Server\Bin folders. This will reclaim around 130 MBs of space. LightSwitch re-creates these contents when you next compile your application, so there's no need to worry about permanently damaging your project.

Summary

LightSwitch is a rapid development tool that's built with modern technologies, well-known patterns, and best practices. It allows you to easily build data-centric applications that run on the desktop and on the web. LightSwitch applications employ a three-layer architecture and apply the MVVM software design pattern.

LightSwitch relies on a special database called the Intrinsic database. This database stores the tables that you create inside LightSwitch, as well as the login details for your users.

The LightSwitch client application doesn't talk directly with your data sources. Instead, it accesses data by communicating with the logic layer via the OData protocol.

At the logic layer, LightSwitch creates a Data Service for each data source in your application. The data service exposes methods that allow your client to access and update data. When the data service updates or retrieves data for the client, the server-side data operation passes through either the Save or Query Pipelines. These pipelines expose points where you can inject your own custom code.

You can develop LightSwitch user interfaces by using a Silverlight or HTML client. The benefits of a Silverlight client are that it provides a richer experience and can run as a desktop application. The advantage of a desktop application is that it can interact with desktop applications such as Outlook and Word. Silverlight browser applications are unable to do this. The benefits of an HTML application are that it doesn't require the Silverlight runtime and can therefore run on a far wider range of devices. HTML applications are ideal for applications that you want to run on mobile or tablet devices.

LightSwitch uses a Data Workspace object to access data. For each data source, the client caches its working data in an object called a Change Set. In the case of the Silverlight client, each screen has its own Data Workspace; therefore, data changes cannot be shared across screens. The HTML client works differently—in this case, all screens share the same data workspace.

In a Silverlight application, Shells and Themes allow you to re-clothe or skin your application. Changing the Shell allows you to radically change the appearance of your application, whereas changing the Theme allows you to apply more subtle changes, such as changing the font colors and sizes.

LightSwitch solutions consist of three projects. You can see these by switching your solution into File View. This view allows you to add custom classes and references to other .NET assemblies.

LightSwitch applications are defined using XML building blocks, and this XML content is persisted in files with an LSML extension. When you build your application, your LightSwitch clients don't contain any UI that's specific to your application. Instead, LightSwitch autogenerates your application's UI at runtime by interpreting your LSML model.

LightSwitch applies the MVVM pattern throughout your application. A big advantage of this pattern is that it keeps everything logically distinct and allows you to easily change the controls that are bound to data items.

CHAPTER 2

■ ■ ■

Setting Up Your Data

LightSwitch's greatest strength is how easy it makes working with data. So to get the most out of the product, it's vital that you learn how to do that!

This chapter teaches you how to

- Design tables and attach external data sources to your application

- Define relationships between tables

- Create computed properties and apply business types

This chapter traces the genesis of an application that manages help desk issues. It provides a real-life demonstration of a typical application that you'll find in everyday business, and includes sufficient complexity to demonstrate most of the features in LightSwitch.

In this chapter, you'll find out how to create tables that store help desk issues and engineer details. You'll learn how to associate engineers with multiple issues and how to define a manager/engineer hierarchy by defining relationships. To help users identify engineers in lists of data, you'll learn how to create a computed property and define a summary property. The computed property summarizes the first name and surname of each engineer, and provides a friendly record descriptor for each engineer record.

Choosing Where to Store Your Data

There are two approaches for storing data in LightSwitch. You can create your own tables in the Intrinsic database by using the built-in table designer, or you can attach to an external data source. Of course, these two approaches are not mutually exclusive. You can create your own tables and also attach as many external data sources as you want.

When you build tables using the built-in table designer, LightSwitch persists any data that you add at design time. So if you add some data to a table during a debug session, your data will still be there during the next debug session. For this to work, LightSwitch creates a LocalDB development database in the location \Bin\Data\Temp\ApplicationDatabase.mdf.

The advantage of creating tables in the Intrinsic database is that your project is self-contained. If you share your LightSwitch project with other users, they'll be able to run your project without having to reattach the external data.

The difficulty arises when you deploy your application. The deployment wizard doesn't allow you to deploy your development data into your live environment. This can be frustrating if you've spent a lot of time entering data during the design process. So if design time data is important to you, you should consider building your tables externally in a Microsoft SQL Server database rather than building it internally within LightSwitch.

What Are Entities and Properties?

Database developers often use the terms *tables* and *rows*. However, LightSwitch regularly refers to *entities* and *properties* instead. An entity represents the data from a single row in a database table, whereas a property is analogous to a field or column from a database table.

LightSwitch uses Microsoft's Entity Framework internally to provide object relational mapping. Entity and Property are terms that the Entity Framework uses, and are more appropriate given that LightSwitch can connect to nonrelational data sources. For example, if you connect to a SharePoint data source, list items map to LightSwitch entities, and list columns are exposed as LightSwitch properties.

In this book, I use the words *tables* and *fields* interchangeably because it's often clearer to use the database terms. For example, a property in the screen designer can mean a local instance of an entity or something that you can find in Visual Studio's property sheet. And once you start talking about the properties of a property, things can quickly become quite confusing.

Creating Tables (Entities)

Let's start by creating a new table and adding some fields. We'll create a table called Engineers that stores details about the engineers.

In Solution Explorer, right-click the Data Sources folder and choose the Add Table option. Once you've added your table, you can modify the properties using the Properties sheet. (See Figure 2-1.)

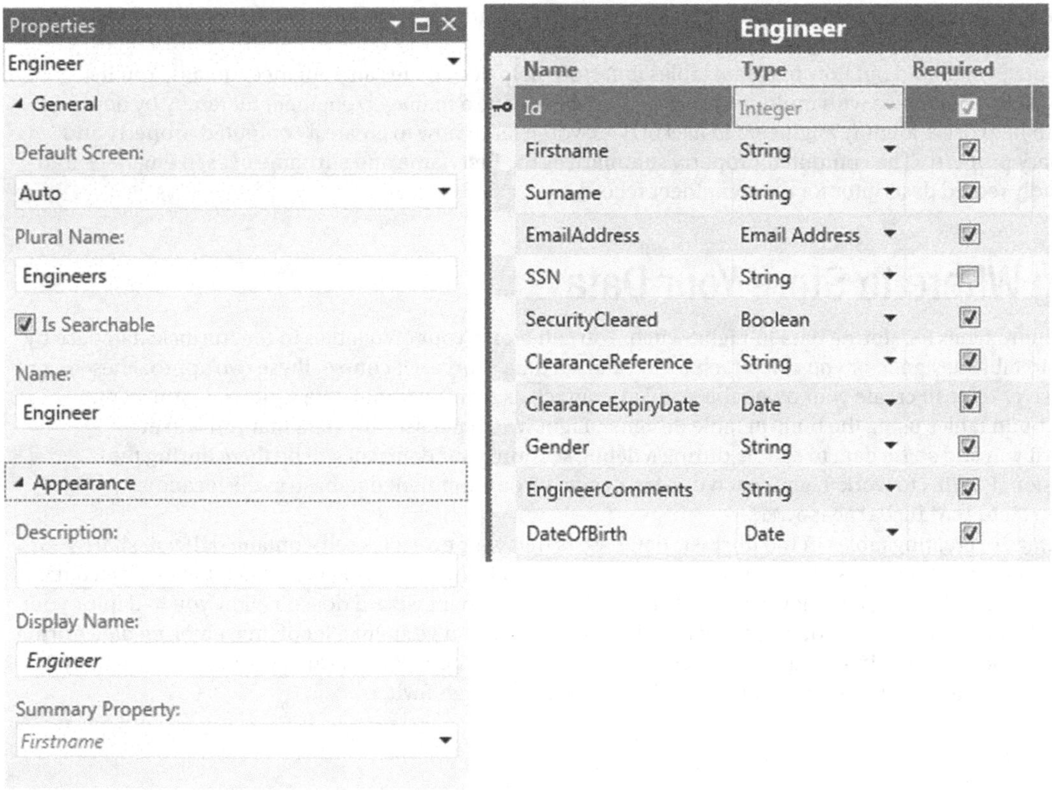

Figure 2-1. *Creating a table and editing its properties*

Some of the table properties that you can set include

- **Name:** The name uniquely identifies your table. The name must begin with an alphabetic character and can contain only alphanumeric characters and the underscore character. Other special characters, such as spaces or the period character, are not permitted.

- **Display name:** This is the friendly name that describes your table—it can contain spaces.

- **Description:** The description field provides a long description of the table.

- **Plural Name:** LightSwitch uses the value that you enter here to name the collections of entities that you add to a screen. You would also use the plural name to refer to collections of entities when you're writing code.

- **Summary Property:** this allows you to specify the property that identifies a data row to a user. You can add a control to your screen called a Summary Control that exposes the value of this property to the user.

- **Default Screen:** The Summary Control renders itself as a link. When a user clicks on this link, it opens the default screen that's specified here. There is an option to select Auto from the drop-down list. If you select Auto, LightSwitch displays an autogenerated screen.

- **Is Searchable:** Checking this defines that the text properties in the table will be searchable.

Creating Fields (Properties)

After creating the Engineer table, add the fields (or properties) that are shown in Figure 2-1. When you add a field to a table, you'll need to specify the type of data that'll be stored in the field. Let's take a look at some of the data types that you can use.

■ **Caution**   Try not to name your fields using words that are reserved keywords in SQL Server or the Entity Framework. Prefixing field names with the word *Entity* (for example, EntityKey) caused unexpected errors in LightSwitch 2011. Although Microsoft has fixed this particular bug, it's safer never to name your fields after reserved keywords because you never know what unexpected errors might occur.

Storing String Data

The string data type includes support for international character types (for example, Arabic, Chinese, and Japanese). For maximum performance, it's a good idea to set the maximum field size to a value that's appropriate for the data that you want to store.

If you want to store unlimited length or multiline text, clear the contents of the maximum field text box and leave it blank, as shown in Figure 2-2.

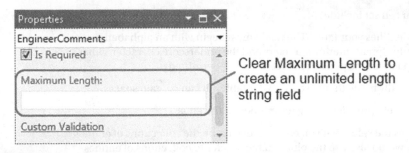

Figure 2-2. Setting a string field to store text with unlimited length

Storing Numbers (Double and Decimal Types)

If you want to store numbers with decimal places, LightSwitch provides a choice of either double or decimal data types.

The practical difference between the two types is that doubles can store a wide range of numbers in a smaller amount of memory. However, doubles are less precise and are subject to rounding errors when calculations are performed against them.

Decimals don't suffer from such rounding errors but take up more space and are slower to compute. Sums of money should always be based on the decimal data type.

Other important attributes that relate to decimals are precision and scale. *Precision* defines the total number of digits in a number. *Scale* defines the number of digits after the decimal place. Figure 2-3 illustrates precision and scale using the example number 123456.789.

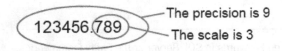

Figure 2-3. Precision and scale

When you create a new decimal field, LightSwitch defaults the precision and scale values to 18 and 2, respectively. In keeping with good practice, you should shorten these values if you don't require that level of accuracy.

Formatting Numeric Fields

This is a new feature in LightSwitch 2012. You can specify a display format for each numeric property that you define in LightSwitch. This means that LightSwitch formats the number on the user's screen using the format that you've specified.

Figure 2-4 shows a field that stores a feedback rating. A format string of N2 means that the number is shown to 2 decimal places.

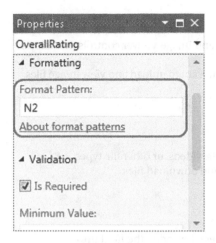

Figure 2-4. *Setting the format*

.NET format strings begin with a Format Specifier, followed by a number that indicates the desired number of decimal places. Table 2-1 shows the Format Specifiers that you can use.

Table 2-1. *.NET format specifiers*

Format Specifier	Description
C or c	Currency
D or d	Decimal
E or e	Scientific (exponential)
F or f	Fixed-point
G or g	General
N or n	Number
P or p	Percent
R or r	Round-trip
X or x	Hexadecimal

■ **Note**   LightSwitch 2011 didn't allow you to format numeric fields with .NET format strings. In March 2011, I submitted this idea on Microsoft Connect, a web site that allows you to provide feedback on how to improve Microsoft products: https://connect.microsoft.com/VisualStudio/feedback/details/654220/lightswitch-allow-data-to-be-formatted.

I'm very pleased that Microsoft has added this useful feature. This goes to show that if you have any ideas on how to improve LightSwitch, it's worth recording them through Connect or the Uservoice web site (http://visualstudio.uservoice.com/).

Storing Images

The Image Type allows you to store images. LightSwitch includes Image Editor and Image Viewer controls that allows users to upload and view images.

Note that these controls support only images in JPG and PNG format. If you want to upload and view image files in other formats, you'll need to write or purchase a third-party custom control.

Storing Binary Data

You can use the binary data type to store binary large objects such as documents, videos, or other file types. Chapters 7 and 8 show you how to design a screen that allows users to upload and download files.

Ensuring Unique Values

Each field contains an Include In Unique Index check box. Selecting this check box adds the field into a combination index.

It's not possible to create individual unique fields through the designer. If you want to do this, you can write validation to enforce uniqueness at a field level. Chapter 5 contains sample code that shows you how to do this.

Alternatively, you could create unique indexes on your SQL Server table if you're using an attached SQL database.

Changing Data Types

If you're working on tables in your Intrinsic database and make some major table changes, LightSwitch can discard the data in your tables. At worst, it can even destroy and re-create your entire development database. However, it generally warns you before any data loss occurs. (See Figure 2-5.)

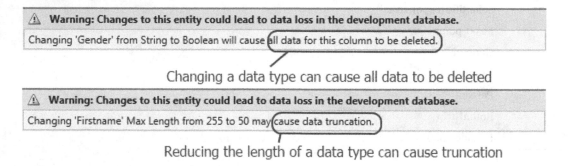

Figure 2-5. *Warnings that appear before data loss occurs*

Using LightSwitch Business Types

You'll find some special data types that you won't find in other database management systems. These include Email, Money, Phone Number, Web Address, and Percent. These data types are called *business types*. They're specially designed to store specialized data and provide built-in validation and data entry controls. These business types include properties that control how LightSwitch displays your data on screen, as well as data entry and validation characteristics. Let's take a closer look at some of these business types.

Storing Email Addresses

As its name suggests, the Email business type provides storage for email addresses.

When you add an Email field, you'll find two properties that you can set (as shown in Figure 2-6):

- **Default Email Domain:** If the user leaves out the email domain, LightSwitch appends the default email domain that you specify to the end of the email address. This setting is ideal for internal systems that are used by a single company.

- **Require Email Domain:** If this is checked, the user must enter an email domain when entering an email address.

Figure 2-6. *The two Email business type properties*

Storing Money Values

When you add a Money field to a table, the additional properties that you can set are shown, as you can see in Figure 2-7. These are

- **Currency Code:** Use this field to specify the locale for the currency. For example, if you want to specify United States Dollars, specify USD. Appendix A shows a list of valid codes that you can use.

- **Is Formatted:** If you check this, LightSwitch applies formatting when you use the currency control on a screen to display your money value. The formatting that the control applies includes the currency symbol, the grouping separator, and decimal places.

Figure 2-7. *Properties that you can set on a Money field*

The following options apply only if you check the Is Formatted check box:

- **Is Grouped:** If checked, LightSwitch shows digit-grouping separators. For example, it displays 1,234,567.89 rather than 1234567.89.

- **Symbol Mode:** The symbol mode dropdown allows you to select Currency Symbol, ISO Currency Symbol, or No Currency Symbol. Here are some examples of how LightSwitch would format a money value using the available symbol modes:

  - Currency Symbol: $123.45

  - ISO Currency Symbol: 123.45 USD

  - No Currency Symbol: 123.45

- **Decimal Places:** This defines the number of decimal places that LightSwitch shows when it formats a money value.

Storing Phone Numbers

The Phone Number business type is designed to store phone numbers, and it validates data by making sure that users can enter only phone numbers that match a list of predefined formats.

You can define formats by using the dialog that's shown in Figure 2-8. The symbols that you can use to define a format are

- C – Country Code

- A – Area or City Code

- N – Local number

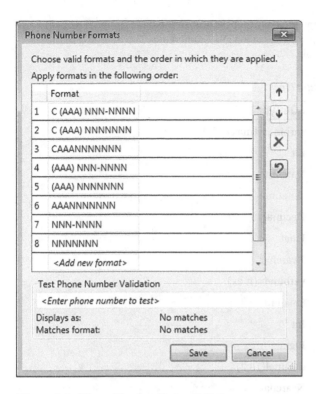

Figure 2-8. *Phone Number Formats dialog*

Other additional symbols that you can use include the following: +, –, (,), .

When a user enters a phone number through the Phone Number control, the control attempts to validate the phone number against the first format in the list. If the digits match the format, LightSwitch displays the phone number using that format. Otherwise, the control attempts to validate the phone number against all remaining formats in the list until a match is found. If it doesn't find a match, LightSwitch prevents the record from being saved.

When LightSwitch saves the phone number in the database, it does so without any formatting. If you want to create reports or use the phone number data outside of LightSwitch, you'll need to write your own procedure to format the data.

Unfortunately, it isn't possible to specify additional formats on a global or application basis. They must be specified each time a Phone Number field is used in a table.

Storing Web Addresses and Percentage Values

The Web Address business type is new to LightSwitch 2012. It allows you to store Web addresses, and it allows users to add and edit data using the Web Address Editor and Web Address Viewer controls.

Also new to LightSwitch 2012 is the Percent business type. This Business Type allows you to store percentage values. Just like the other business types, LightSwitch provides a Percent Editor and Percent Viewer control for data entry.

Examining What Happens in SQL Server

When you create a table in the table designer, LightSwitch creates the actual table in your Intrinsic SQL Server database. If you create a string property of 255 characters, LightSwitch creates a 255 length nvarchar column (a data type that stores variable length unicode data) in the underlying SQL Server table.

LightSwitch provides an API that allows you to access any property that's visible in the table designer through code. When you're writing code, LightSwitch exposes table properties using .NET data types. The mapping between LightSwitch, .NET, and SQL Server data types is shown in Table 2-2.

Table 2-2. *Mappings between LightSwitch, .NET, and SQL data types*

LightSwitch Type	VB.NET Type	C# Type	SQL Type
Binary	Byte()	byte[]	varbinary(max)
Boolean	Boolean	bool	Bit
Date	DateTime	DateTime	Datetime
DateTime	DateTime	DateTime	Datetime
Decimal	Decimal	decimal	Decimal
Double	Double	double	Float
Email Address	String	string	Nvarchar
Image	Byte()	byte[]	varbinary(max)
Short Integer	Short	short	Smallint
Integer	Integer	int	Int
Long Integer	Long	long	Bigint
Money	Decimal	decimal	decimal(18,2)
Phone Number	String	string	Nvarchar
Percent	Decimal	decimal	decimal(18,2)
String	String	string	Nvarchar
Web Address	String	string	Nvarchar

In Table 2-2, notice the business type mappings. LightSwitch uses SQL nvarchar and numeric types as the underlying storage type for business types.

■ **Tip**   Notice how LightSwitch Date and DateTime fields map to the SQL DateTime data type. The minimum date value that you can store is 01-Jan-1753. If you need to store earlier dates (for example, if you're writing genealogy software), create your tables in an external SQL database and create columns using the DateTime2 datatype (a data type that offers more precision and a greater range of date values).

Creating Choice Lists

Choice Lists allow you to use the Auto Complete Box or Modal Window Picker control to restrict the data values that users can enter. You can specify choice lists on fields from external data sources, as well as on tables that you create yourself in the Intrinsic database.

A choice list is a set of name value pairs, and you can configure these for most data types, including Boolean and numeric types. For example, you can create a choice list for a Boolean field with the choice values of Yes and No. The data types that don't support choice lists are the image and binary types.

To create a choice list, click the Choice List link on the properties sheet for your field and enter a list of Value and Display Name pairs. When the choices are shown on screen, they'll appear in the order in which they're entered. You can re-order the choices by right-clicking the item and selecting the Move Up or Move Down option, as illustrated in Figure 2-9.

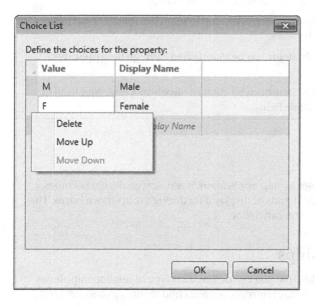

Figure 2-9. *Reorder items using the right-click context menu*

LightSwitch saves your choice list settings in the following file: `Common\My Project\Common.lsml`. It's possible to maintain your choice list entries by editing this file manually in Notepad. This could be useful if you want to speed up data entry by adding multiple choices using copy and paste, rather than adding them one by one through the Choice List dialog.

___

■ **Caution** Always back up and take care before you manually modify an LSML file. You can irreparably damage your LightSwitch solution if you make a mistake. Without a recent backup, you can end up having to re-create your entire LightSwitch solution and redo all of your work.

___

Choice Lists vs. Related Tables

If you want your users to enter data by choosing from a list of available choices, the choice values can either come from a choice list or a related table.

A choice list is ideal for data items that are relatively static. The disadvantage of using a choice list is that adding or deleting items requires you to recompile and redeploy your application, which can be cumbersome. Table 2-3 summarizes the pros and cons of choice lists and related tables.

Table 2-3. *Choice List and Related Table Pros and Cons*

Choice List	Related Table
✓ Very simple to create.	✗ More complex setup. The choice tables need to be created and relationships need to be set up.
✓ Choice list values are deployed with your application.	✗ An extra step is needed to populate the database table with values.
✗ Adding or deleting requires a rebuild and redeployment of the application	✓ List items can be maintained through the application.
✗ Choice list items must be duplicated if you want to use them in more than one field.	✓ List items can be entered once into a table and used in multiple fields.

Defining Relationships

It's important to set up relationships between the sets of tables in your application. If not, screen design becomes very difficult, particularly when you want to create parent-child grids or display data through drop-down boxes. The following section describes the various types of relationships you can define.

Defining One-to-Many Type Relationships

One-to-many relationships are a common type of relationship that you can define. This type of relationship allows you to define a data model where a parent record in one table may reference several child records in another table. The following example shows you how to set up your tables so that engineers can be assigned to multiple help desk issues.

To begin, create the Issue and Engineer tables as shown in Figure 2-10. At this point, no relationships have been defined.

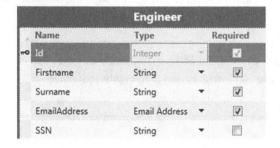

Figure 2-10. *Issue and Engineer tables without relationships*

To create the relationship, click the Relationships button in the screen designer toolbar and set up the relationship as shown in Figure 2-11.[1]

---

[1]Notice how it produces the sentence 'a engineer (sic)', rather than 'an engineer'. If this annoys you too, you could rename your tables so that they don't begin with vowels. However, I'd recommend that you spend your time doing something else more meaningful!

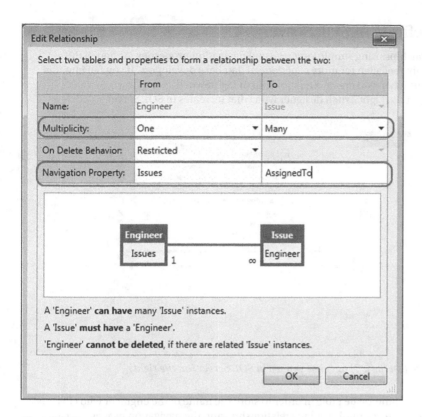

Figure 2-11. *Creating a one-to-many relationship*

The Multiplicity row allows you to define the type of relationship between the two tables—in this case, we've created a one-to-many relationship. This means that when a help desk operator creates an issue, they must assign an engineer.

The last row of the dialog allows you to set the Navigation Property names for each table. These allow you to give a meaningful name to the relationship. In our case, we've named the Navigation Property on the Issue table AssignedTo.

If you want to add another relationship to the Engineer table (for example, to store the name of the engineer who closes the issue), you can rename the Navigation Property to ClosedBy to distinguish it clearly from the other relationships that might exist between the two tables. The default Navigation Name in this example would be Engineers1, which isn't very meaningful.

The purpose of a Navigation Property is to give you a way to navigate related entities. When you're writing code, these properties appear as objects that you can use to reference child and parent entities. You can also query navigation properties by constructing Language Integrated Query (LINQ) expressions in code.

How Relationships Are Defined in SQL Server

With LightSwitch, you can define relationships using simple language and navigation properties. Although this simplifies the process for a novice, it might feel alien for more experienced database developers. If you fall into this category, let's take a look at what happens when you create a relationship in LightSwitch.

Figure 2-12 compares what you see in the LightSwitch designer with what it creates in SQL Server.

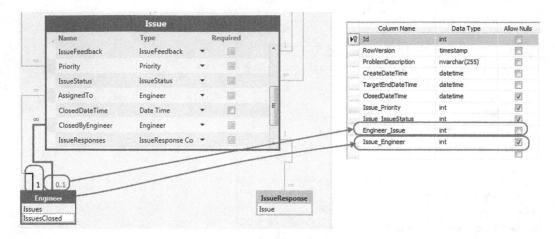

Figure 2-12. *What you see in LightSwitch (on the left) vs. what you see in SQL Server (on the right)*

This diagram shows how we've adapted the Issue table in order to store the name of the engineer who closes the issue. This relationship is defined as a (zero-or-one)-to-many relationship, and the navigation property is called ClosedByEngineer. A (zero-or-one)-to-many relationship means that for an issue, specifying a value for "closed by engineer" isn't mandatory.

For the AssignedTo relationship, notice how LightSwitch creates a column in the issue table called Issue_Engineer. And for ClosedByEngineer, it creates a nullable column called Engineer_Issue. This allows SQL Server to support the (zero-or-one)-to-many relationship that we've defined. For both these columns, LightSwitch also creates a SQL Server foreign key relationship to the Id column in the Engineer table.

So when you create relationships in the table designer, LightSwitch carries out the same keying that you would need to carry out if you were to create the tables manually.

Defining Self-Referencing Relationships

Self-referencing or recursive relationships are relationships where entities reference themselves. You'll often find these when modeling hierarchies. To illustrate this type of relationship, let's modify the Engineer table so that it stores the name of the engineer's manager.

To create a self-join, open the relationship dialog and select the same table name in the To side of the relationship, as shown in Figure 2-13. Rename the Navigation Properties to Subordinates (in the From column) and Manager (in the To column). This will result in two navigation properties for the engineer entity, each representing one end of the relationship.

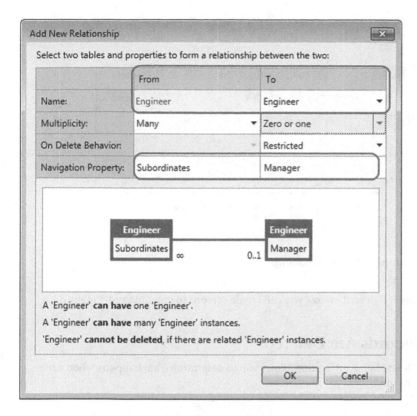

Figure 2-13. *Setting up a self join in the relationships dialog*

Defining Many-to-Many Relationships

In the relationship designer, many-to-many type relationships are not natively supported. If you want to create a many-to-many relationship, you'll need to create an intermediary table that contains two one-to-many relationships.

In this example, we'll create a set of tables for storing engineer skills. An engineer can have many skills and a skill can be assigned to one or more engineers.

After creating the Engineer and Skill tables, create an EngineerSkill table to store the many-to-many relationship. In the table designer for the EngineerSkill table, create a one-to-many relationship between the Engineer and EngineerSkill tables. Next, create a one-to-many relationship between the Skill and EngineerSkill tables. Figure 2-14 illustrates the table structure that we have created.

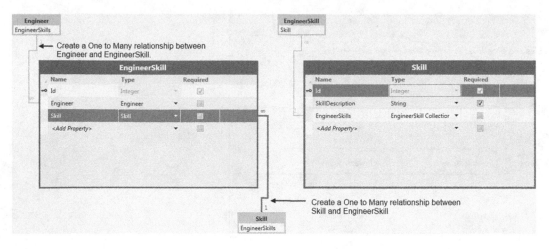

Figure 2-14. *The data structure behind a many-to-many relationship*

This completes the table design; Chapter 7 describes how you can create screens to enter many-to-many data.

Determining How Child Records Are Deleted

When you create a relationship, the 'On Delete Behavior' setting allows you to determine what happens when a user deletes a record. The three possible options are

- Cascade delete

- Restricted

- Disassociate

In the engineer and issue example, setting the deletion behavior to cascade delete will delete all related issue records when a user deletes an engineer.

If you set the behavior to restricted, engineers can't be deleted until all related issues have been deleted.

The disassociate option sets all engineer references to null on related issues prior to the deletion of an engineer. The disassociate option is valid only on (zero-or-one)-to-many relationships.

The deletion behavior option is not available and is grayed out if you attempt to create a relationship between two separate data sources. Furthermore, these deletion options are available only for tables that belong in the Intrinsic database. They aren't available for external data sources.

EXERCISE 2.1 – CREATING TABLES AND RELATIONSHIPS

Open the project that you created in Exercise 1.1, and use the table designer to create some of the tables that are described in this chapter. Appendix E shows a list of tables that you can re-create. For the Engineer table, try adding a property called Engineer. Does LightSwitch allow you to do this? Create the Issue table, and create a one-to-many relationship between the Engineer and Issue tables. After you create these tables, notice how you can view and modify the tables and relationships in the table designer. For these two tables, LightSwitch automatically sets the plural name of your tables to Engineers and Issues. Try creating a table called IssueStatus. What plural name does LightSwitch give this table?

Attaching Existing Data

The other way to use data in LightSwitch is to connect to an existing data source.

LightSwitch allows you to connect a wide range of data sources. When you choose the option to attach to existing data, LightSwitch provides you with four choices. You can attach to a database, a SharePoint list, an OData Service, or a WCF RIA service (Windows Communication Foundation Rich Internet Application service).

The list doesn't end there, however. As long as there's an entity framework provider for your data source, LightSwitch can consume your data. This enables you to connect to data sources such as Oracle and MySQL (as shown in Figure 2-15). By downloading third-party data-source providers, you can even attach to social networks such as Facebook.

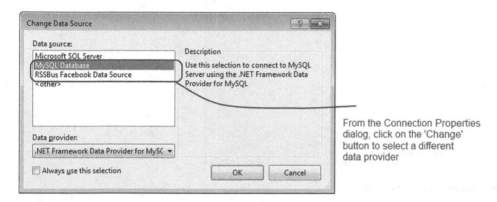

Figure 2-15. *Connecting to a MySQL data source*

If there isn't an entity framework provider for your data, you can write your own RIA service, OData service, or even custom data-source extension. These options allow you to connect to data sources that are not natively supported by LightSwitch.

When you attach to an external data source, you can't add new tables or new fields. You also can't rename existing fields or modify the schema of other database objects.

However, you can change the data type of an attached field so that it uses a LightSwitch business type. For example, you can configure a SQL Server nvarchar field to use the Phone Number business type rather than a string data type.

■ **Tip**   If you attach a table that contains an image column, LightSwitch sets the data type for that column to binary. If you want the column to behave as an image column and to use the built-in LightSwitch image controls, be sure to open the table in the designer and change the data type from binary to image.

Attaching to an Existing Database

To attach to an existing SQL Server database, right-click the Data node in Solution Explorer and select the Add A Datasource option. Select the Database option, and follow the steps in the wizard.

You'll eventually reach the dialog that's shown in Figure 2-16. This allows you to choose the tables and views that you want to use in your LightSwitch application.

Figure 2-16. *Choose Your Database Objects dialog*

Stored procedures, user-defined functions, and other SQL objects are not supported and don't appear in the dialog that's shown. If you want to use stored procedures, you can do so by writing a custom RIA service.

■ **Note** After attaching to an external table, you can use the table designer to reorder the columns. Although this will not affect the underlying SQL table, any new screens that you create will have their data-entry controls ordered in the sequence that you've specified.

Dealing with missing tables

If you find that some of your tables are missing from the dialog shown in Figure 2-16, make sure that you've defined primary keys on those tables. Tables won't appear unless primary keys are set up.

If an identity column has been specified but a primary key is not defined, the table will appear but can be added only in read-only mode. (See Figure 2-17). If you're unfamiliar with SQL Server, identity columns are auto-incrementing fields similar to Sequences in Oracle or Auto Numbers in Access.

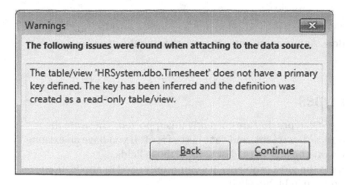

Figure 2-17. *Table attached in read-only mode*

Likewise, any views that you want to add must contain a derivable primary key column and can be added only in read-only mode.

Refreshing data sources

If the location of your database server changes, or if the schema of your tables changes, you can refresh your LightSwitch model by right-clicking your data source and choosing the Refresh Data Source option.

When the wizard appears, you can update your database connection details by returning to the very first page in the wizard. Although you can change the connection string from one database server to another, you can't change the underlying data provider. For example, you can't change from SQL Server to MySQL without deleting the tables in your application and reimporting.

If the wizard finds any table changes, it indicates these by using a red cross or exclamation point (as shown in Figure 2-18).

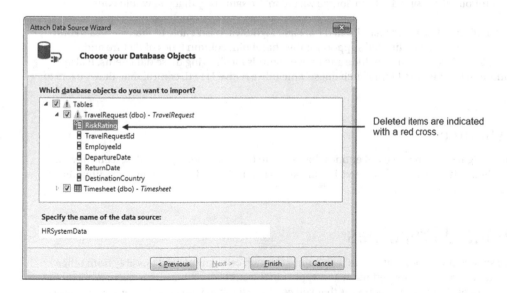

Figure 2-18. *Choose Your Database Objects dialog showing changed items*

When you click the Finish button, the wizard updates all screens and removes controls that are bound to the deleted fields. However, any references to these fields in code will not be updated. If references exist in code, they'll become invalid and will show up in the Error List window. At this point, you can work through the error list and resolve any remaining errors.

DataTime offset and unsupported data types

When you connect to an existing database, there are five SQL types that are currently unsupported. These are the spacial data types geography and geometry, `hierarchyid`, `sql_variant`, and `datetimeoffset`. If you have an existing database that uses any of these data types, LightSwitch won't be able to read or write to those fields.

`Datetimeoffset` is the data type that gives developers the most problems. It's commonly used in applications that span multiple time zones, but it is currently unsupported in LightSwitch.

If you want to create an application that supports multiple time zones, the simplest solution is to save all datetime values in UTC (Coordinated Universal Time). You can use server-side code to ensure that all dates are saved in this format (Chapter 4 shows you how to write code that runs on the server). The .NET `datetime` class contains a `DateTime.ToUniversalTime` method that you can use to convert times.

■ **Tip** If you save your date values in UTC, you'll never encounter daylight saving problems. For example, if you create an application that calculates employee working hours by storing the start and end dates and times, you won't incorrectly pay an employee for an extra hour if they choose to work when the clocks go forward.

Attaching to SharePoint Data

You can connect your application to a SharePoint 2010 data source. LightSwitch uses a custom OData provider, so it doesn't support versions prior to SharePoint 2010.

You can attach to SharePoint lists using the Data Source wizard in the same way that you would connect to a SQL Server database.

There are various limitations when using SharePoint data. First, LightSwitch isn't able to manage SharePoint attachments or documents. Second, there's limited support for the SharePoint column types of Picture and Hyperlink. This is because LightSwitch doesn't include any native controls for showing these data items. It also doesn't fully support multiline text because LightSwitch doesn't include a native HTML control that allows users to edit the content.

Deleting a Data Source

If you delete a data source, LightSwitch removes all entities that relate to that data source from all screens in your application. The screens themselves will not be deleted, but instances of entities and related controls within those screens will be removed.

Creating Computed Properties

Computed properties are special properties that derive their values through calculations and possibly from other fields. Computed properties are read-only by definition and appear in the entity designer with a calculator icon next to the field. A slight limitation of computed properties is that you can't use them in your HTML client applications.

Computed properties are very versatile. The code that you write belongs in your Common project, and LightSwitch executes this code both on the Silverlight client and server. From a practical point of view, this means that LightSwitch can immediately recalculate a computed property and show the result on screen without requiring any intervention that triggers a server event, such as clicking on the Save button on the screen.

You'll now see several examples of computed properties. This will give you a flavor of the type of code that's involved in constructing a computed property.

■ **Tip**　There's nothing to prevent you from creating a computed property on an attached table. Computed properties are not just limited to tables that you create in the Intrinsic database.

Creating Summary Properties

Each table allows you to specify a summary property through the properties sheet in the table designer. Summary properties are designed to summarize the contents of a data row for display purposes. To show a summary property on a screen, you'd use a summary control. This control is most often used in grids and autocomplete boxes.

In the example that follows, we'll create a computed property in the Engineer table called FullName that concatenates the first name and surname of an engineer.

Open the Engineer table, and create a new property called FullName. In the General section of the properties sheet for the new property, check the Is Computed check box. Click on the Edit Method hyperlink, and enter the code that's shown in Listing 2-1.

Listing 2-1. Formatting Strings in a Computed Property

VB:
File: HelpDeskVB\Common\UserCode\Engineer.vb

```
Private Sub FullName_Compute(ByRef result As String)
    result = String.Format("{0} - {1}", Surname, Firstname)
End Sub
```

C#:
File: HelpDeskCS\Common\UserCode\Engineer.cs

```
partial void FullName_Compute(ref string result)
{
    result = String.Format("{0} - {1}", this.Surname, this.Firstname);
}
```

This code demonstrates how to format strings using .NET's String.Format method. This method accepts two parameters. The first parameter specifies the string to be displayed and includes placeholders in the format {0}, {1} and so on. The second parameter accepts a comma-separated list of data items, which are then substituted into the display string.

To set this as the summary property, open the properties sheet for the Engineer table and choose FullName from the Summary Property drop-down list (as shown in Figure 2-19 ❶).

Figure 2-19 ❷ shows the FullName summary property on a screen that's designed for entering new issues.

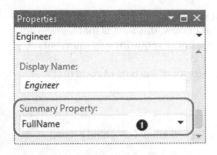

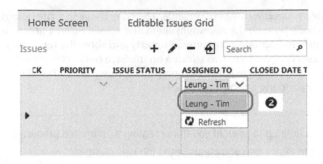

Figure 2-19. *Summary Property set to a computed field*

Calculating Dates with Computed Properties

You can use computed properties to calculate dates. This example shows you how to calculate the difference between two dates. The Engineer table contains a date of birth field. By using a computed property, you can calculate the age of a person in years.

To do this, create an integer computed property called Age and enter the code that's shown in Listing 2-2.

Listing 2-2. Calculating Date Differences

VB:
File: HelpDeskVB\Common\UserCode\Engineer.vb

```
Private Sub Age_Compute(ByRef result As Integer)
    result = DateDiff(DateInterval.Year, DateOfBirth, Now)
End Sub
```

C#:
File: HelpDeskCS\Common\UserCode\Engineer.cs

```
partial void Age_Compute(ref int result)
{
    DateTime now = DateTime.Today;
    int age = now.Year - DateOfBirth.Year;
    if (DateOfBirth > now.AddYears(-age)) age--;
    result = age;
}
```

This code illustrates the use of the VB.NET DateDiff function. This function allows you to calculate date and time differences accurately, and also takes leap years into consideration. C# doesn't have an equivalent method, and the calculation is therefore slightly more complex.

■ **Caution**   Computed property values are cached by the Silverlight client. This can result in incorrect results if you decide to use computed properties to calculate real-time data (for example, the number of minutes since a support issue was opened).

Summarizing Child Records with Computed Properties

You can easily refer to related records through navigation properties. In this example, we'll create a computed property in the Engineer table that returns the number of help desk issues that are assigned to each engineer.

To do this, create a computed property called IssueCount and enter the code that's shown in Listing 2-3.

Listing 2-3. Using Navigation Properties in a Computed Property

VB:
```
File: HelpDeskVB\Common\UserCode\Engineer.vb

Private Sub IssueCount_Compute(ByRef result As Integer)
    result = Issues.Count()
End Sub
```

C#:
```
File: HelpDeskCS\Common\UserCode\Engineer.cs

partial void IssueCount_Compute(ref int result)
{
    result = this.Issues.Count();
}
```

The code in Listing 2-3 demonstrates how to refer to child items in a computed property. Specifically, it shows you how to use the aggregate count operator against a navigation property. Other aggregate operations that you can use include Sum and Average.

Returning Images with Computed Properties

You're not just limited to returning string and numeric data in a computed property. This example shows you how to create a computed property that returns an image. If the current date exceeds the target end date, the computed property returns a warning icon. Otherwise, it returns a blank white image.

To create this example, create a computed image property called icon and enter the code that's shown in Listing 2-4.

Listing 2-4. Creating a Computed Property That Returns an Image

VB:
```
File: HelpDeskVB\Common\UserCode\Issue.vb

Private Sub Icon_Compute(ByRef result As Byte())
    If TargetEndDateTime < DateTime.Now Then
        ' this string has been truncated for brevity
        Dim base64EncodedImage = "/9j/4A..."
        result = Convert.FromBase64String(base64EncodedImage)
    Else
        result = Nothing
    End If
End Sub
```

C#:
```
File: HelpDeskCS\Common\UserCode\Issue.cs
```

```
partial void Icon_Compute(ref byte[] result)
{
    if (TargetEndDateTime < DateTime.Now)
    {
        // this string has been truncated for brevity
        string base64EncodedImage = @"/9j/4A...";
        result = Convert.FromBase64String(base64EncodedImage);
    }
    else
    {
        result = null;
    }
}
```

The computed property returns a hardcoded, base 64 encoded image. There are various web sites that allow you to upload an image and to find out its base 64 encoding. Alternatively, you can retrieve the image from a table, and Chapter 4 shows you how to access data from code. Figure 2-20 shows an example of how this computed property appears on a data grid.

Issue Search All

	ISSUE SUMMARY	TARGET END DATE TIME		ENGINEER
⚠	(1) - quorum esset gravis imagine	05/10/2012	09:33	Alvarado
	(2) - nomen pladior estum. estis \	04/06/2013	08:24	O'Connell
	(3) - habitatio in non rarendum p	03/09/2013	09:12	Lawrence
⚠	(4) - fecit, e gravum dolorum si a|	25/05/2012	04:39	Holland
⚠	(5) - non et quo in cognitio, glave	05/01/2013	03:57	Hutchinson

Figure 2-20. *A computed column that returns an image*

Sorting and Filtering by Computed Properties

A slight limitation of computed properties is that you can't sort or filter by these fields. If you create a query that uses a table with computed properties, these fields will not appear in the drop-down list of available fields when you're creating a filter or sort.

If you need to sort grids by computed properties, a possible workaround is to use a SQL Server computed field rather than a LightSwitch computed property. This approach will work only with data in an external SQL data source. Furthermore, SQL Server computed columns are less powerful because you can't refer to data in other tables.

If you want to sort a table by a computed value, you can do this by creating a query and writing code in the PreProcessQuery method. Chapter 6 shows you how to do this.

Summary

To work with data, you can create tables in the Intrinsic database or connect to existing data sources. A single LightSwitch application can consume multiple data sources, and you can pretty much work with any data source that you want. If LightSwitch doesn't support your data source, you can write an RIA service or Custom Data Source extension to access your data. The data sources that LightSwitch natively supports include SQL Server, SharePoint, OData, and RIA services.

During development, LightSwitch hosts your Intrinsic database using LocalDB (the successor to SQL Server Express). LightSwitch persists any data you add at design time between debug sessions. However, you should be aware that there isn't a built-in way to deploy your design-time data into your live SQL Server environment.

LightSwitch uses the term *entity* to refer to a row of data from a table, and the term *property* to refer to a field or column in a table.

You can store your data using standard data types, such as strings and integers. But unlike other databases, you can also store rich data types like web addresses, phone numbers, and email addresses. These data types are called *business types*. They provide you with custom validation and specialized data-entry controls, and you can take advantage of these features by simply setting the type of a field to a business type.

Business types use native data types for their underlying storage. This means that they're not limited to fields in your Intrinsic database. You can also apply business types to table fields that belong in attached data sources.

You can set up relationships between tables, even if your tables belong in different data sources. It's important to define relationships on your tables; otherwise, you'll find it very difficult to design screens later on.

If you want your users to enter data by choosing from a list of predefined selections, you can either use a related table or create a choice list. Choice lists are ideal for storing static lists of data that rarely change.

To carry out math and logic at an entity level, you can attach computed properties to your tables. These allow you to define row-level calculations that you can make available throughout your application. Computed properties aren't just limited to tables in your Intrinsic database. You can also create them against tables in attached databases. One caveat is that you can't sort or filter collections of entities using computed columns.

CHAPTER 3

■ ■ ■

Introducing Silverlight Screen Design

Users of your application will spend most of their time interacting with it through screens. So no matter how well you've designed other aspects of your application, screen design is the single factor that determines how users perceive your application.

In this chapter, you'll learn how to

- Create screens, lay out controls, and configure screen navigation

- Present data using built-in controls

- Modify the appearance of screen items

This chapter shows you how to create a search screen in the HelpDesk application that allows users to find records about engineers. Once a user finds a record, you'll learn how to enable the selected record to be opened in a new screen. This parent/child navigation is a common scenario that you'll likely want to implement in most of your applications.

This chapter intentionally contains no code and highlights how much you can achieve without having to write a single line of .NET code.

Choosing a Screen Template

When you create a new screen, the initial dialog prompts you to choose a template. LightSwitch uses templates to create screens with an initial layout and purpose. In general, you would use these screens as a starting point for further customization.

The standard templates that ship with LightSwitch are shown in the Add New Screen dialog. (See Figure 3-1.) The descriptions in this dialog explain the purpose of each template.

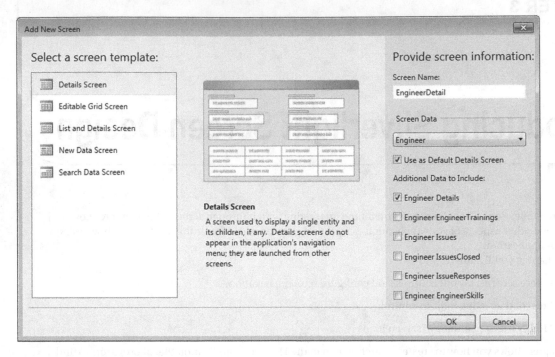

Figure 3-1. *Creating a new screen*

The Details Screen and New Data Screen templates are designed to work with a single record. The remaining templates create screens that show multiple records.

The Screen Data area includes a drop-down menu that shows a list of tables, queries, and other options you use to define the data source for your screen. If the data source that you choose includes related records, you can choose to include the related data on your screen.

If you want to create a screen that isn't bound to any data, choose the New Data Screen template and leave the Screen Data drop-down empty.

Showing a Single Record

The Details Screen template creates a screen that shows a single record. If the record that you're showing is a parent of child records, you can choose to include the child records on your details screen. Details screens are launched from other screens and can't be opened directly. For example, a user can open a details screen by clicking on the results of a search screen.

When you create a details screen, you can choose to mark it as the default screen for the underlying table. This means that your application uses this screen whenever it needs to display a record of that particular type.

The absence of a details screen for any given table doesn't prevent LightSwitch from displaying data. If a default screen doesn't exist, LightSwitch displays the data using an autogenerated screen. However, you can't customize the autogenerated screens in any way. Therefore, the advantage of creating a custom details screen is that you can modify the appearance of your screen.

Organizing Your Screen

After creating your Engineer details screen, the LightSwitch screen designer allows you to modify the layout and carry out further customization.

Unlike the WYSIWYG designers that you may have used in other development applications (such as Microsoft Access or Windows Forms), the screen designer shows the UI elements as a series of tree nodes. Technically, this is called the Screen Content Tree. (See Figure 3-2.)

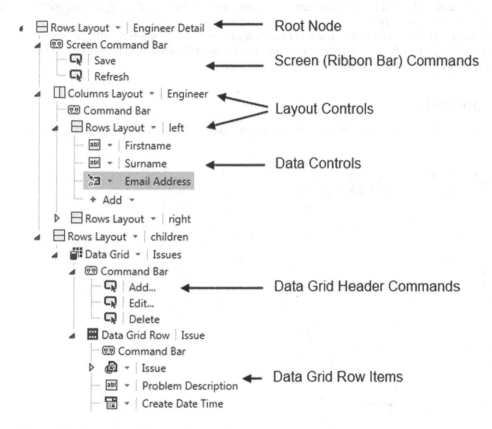

Figure 3-2. *Example of a Screen Content Tree*

A couple of important nodes that you should note are the Root node and Screen Commands node. The Root Node allows you to set screen attributes such as your screen title. The items within the Screen Command Bar node are shown in the Ribbon Bar section of your application (when you apply the Standard shell). By default, LightSwitch shows Save and Refresh buttons on every screen that you create. If you want to rename or delete these items, you can do it by editing or deleting the items that are shown in the Screen Command Bar node.

The remaining nodes contain a mixture of layout controls and data controls, and you'll find out exactly how to use these controls later in this chapter.

Introducing the Screen Designer Toolbar

You'll find the Screen Designer command bar at the top of the screen designer. It has six buttons, which are shown in Figure 3-3.

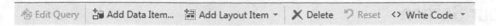

Figure 3-3. *Screen Designer command bar*

The Edit Query button opens the query editor and allows you to edit the underlying query.

You can use the Add Data Item button to add additional properties, queries, and commands to your screen.

You can modify the items that are shown in the Screen Content Tree by using the Add Layout Item and Delete buttons. The options that you'll find in the Add Layout Item button are a subset of the options that appear within the Add button for a node in the Screen Content Tree.

The Reset button provides a really useful feature. If you add extra fields to your table, the Reset button resets the controls within a container back to their default state. It automatically creates controls for the new fields that you've added and saves you from having to create them manually.

Setting Screen Properties

The properties for the first node in the tree (the Root node) allow you to configure various attributes that apply to your screen. (See Figure 3-4.)

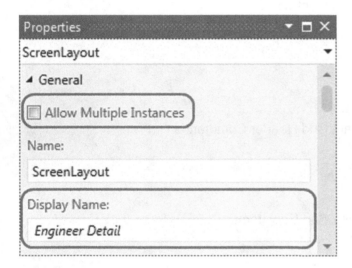

Figure 3-4. *Root-node properties*

Most notably, it lets you set the display name for your screen. LightSwitch shows this piece of text in the screen's tab title and uses it to identify your screen in your application's navigation pane.

The Allow Multiple Instance check box controls the ability of users to open multiple instances of your screen. If this is unchecked and the user attempts to open more than one instance, LightSwitch displays the screen that's already open.

Grouping and Laying Out Your Screen

You can organize the appearance of your screen by using group controls. There are five layout types that you can choose: Rows Layout, Columns Layout, Tabs Layout, Group Box Layout, and Table Layout.

These group controls allow you to position the data controls (for example, text boxes, labels, and check boxes) on your screen. You can nest these controls inside one another, and you can create as many levels of nesting as you want.

For any given node, you can change the group control that's used by using the drop-down menu that appears next to the node.

Figure 3-5 shows the screen designer and how the formatting looks at run time.

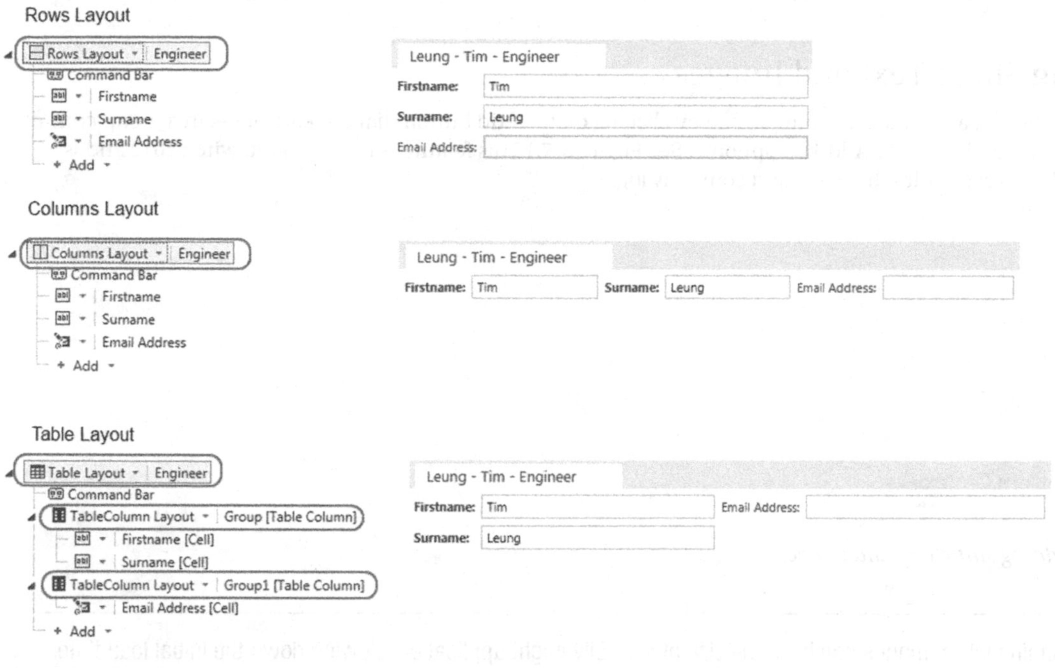

Rows Layout

Columns Layout

Table Layout

Figure 3-5. *Rows, Columns, and Table layout controls*

The Rows Layout container lays out controls one below another. The Columns Layout container places the controls side by side. The Table Layout container allows you to arrange your controls in a tabular fashion by placing them inside child TableColumn Layout groups.

Figure 3-6 shows the Tabs Layout and Group Box Layout controls. LightSwitch renders each group beneath the Tabs Layout control as a separate tab. It sets the tab title using the value you specified in the Display Name property setting for the group.

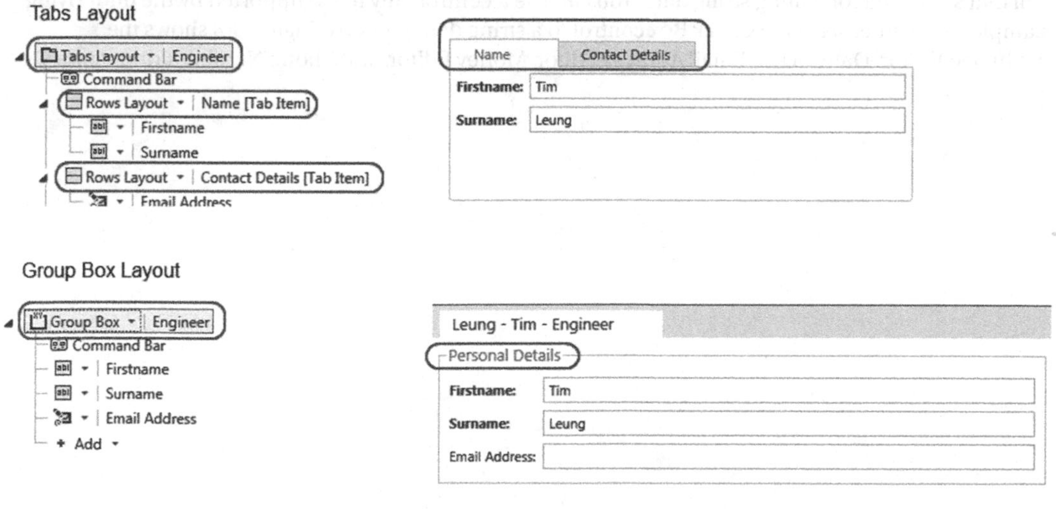

Tabs Layout

Group Box Layout

Figure 3-6. *Tabs and Group Box layout controls*

The Group Box Layout control is new to LightSwitch 2012 and places a border around the child controls. The Display Name property of the Group Box Layout control sets the title that appears on the control.

Displaying Static Text and Images

You can add static text and images to your screen by clicking on the Add button that appears beneath a group control, and choosing the Add Image, or Add Text options. (See Figure 3-7.) This feature is new in LightSwitch 2012 and is perfect for adding screen titles, headers, and company logos.

Figure 3-7. *Adding static text and images*

■ **Caution**   Adding large images can bloat the size of your Silverlight application, slowing down the initial load time.

Choosing Data Controls

Data controls are the UI elements that allow users to view or edit your data. There are many controls that you can use, but if you can't find a built-in control that suits your needs, you can create your own custom control instead (as explained in Chapter 11).

Table 3-1 shows the controls that you can use to edit data. In many cases, you'll use the Text Box control. This is the default control that's selected for editing string data. You can use a control only if it's supported by the underlying data type. For example, you can't assign the Check Box control to a string data property. Figure 3-8 shows the appearance of the Image Editor, Date Picker, Email Address Editor, Money Editor, and Phone Number Editor controls at run time.

Table 3-1. *Editable Data Controls*

Name	Description	Supported Data Types
Text Box	You can edit the data by typing into this control.	All LightSwitch data types
Check Box	Allows you to edit Boolean values.	Boolean
Date Picker	A control that you can use to type or select a date from a calendar view.	Date
Date Time Picker	Allows you to edit a date and time value using a calendar view and a time drop-down list.	Date, Date Time
Email Address Editor	Allows you to edit an email address. Includes validation to ensure that only valid email addresses can be entered.	Email
Image Editor	Displays an image and allows you to upload an image by using a file-browser dialog.	Image
Phone Number Editor	Allows you to enter a phone number using predefined formats.	Phone Number
Money Editor	Allows you to edit a monetary value.	Money

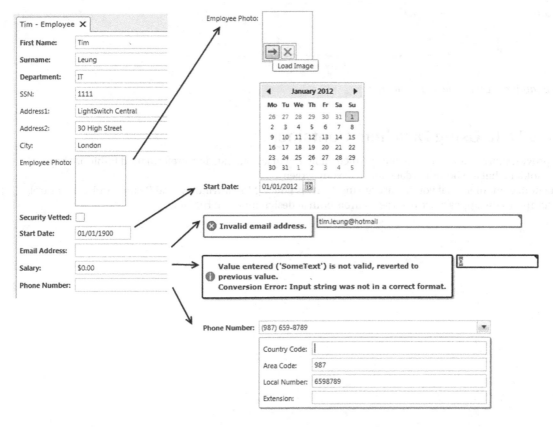

Figure 3-8. *Editable data controls at run time*

The Image Editor control allows users to upload an image. When the user clicks on the control, it shows a Load Image button that opens a file-browser dialog.

The Date Picker control displays a pop-up calendar that allows users to select a date.

The Email Address Editor and Money Editor controls enable data entry and validate the data that the user enters.

When users click the Phone Number Editor control, it reveals a drop-down panel that contains separate data-entry controls for each part of a phone number. The formats that you want to allow are defined in the table designer. Figure 2-8 in Chapter 2 shows the dialog that you use to specify the valid formats.

Displaying Multiline Text Using the Text Box Control

By default, the Text Box control renders text using a single-line text box. If you want to allow multiline text and enable the user to enter line breaks, set the Lines property of your Text Box control to a value greater than 1. (See Figure 3-9.)

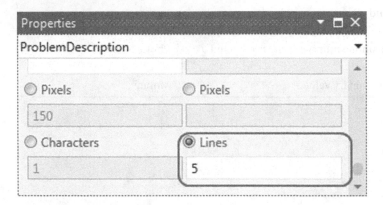

Figure 3-9. *Enabling multiline text to be entered*

Displaying Data Using Data Item Containers

LightSwitch provides three data item containers which allow you to lay out data in a preformatted fashion. They contain placeholders that are bound to data items on your screen.

The data item containers that you can use are the Address Editor, Modal Window, and Picture And Text controls. Figure 3-10 compares the appearance of these controls both at design time and run time.

Address Editor Control

▲ ⊟ Rows Layout ▾ | Employee Property
　├ ▣ Command Bar
　├ 🔠 ▾ | Firstname
　├ 🔠 ▾ | Surname
　▲ 🔲 Address Editor ▾ | Group
　　├ 🔠 (STREET LINE 1) ▾ | Address1 ▾
　　├ 🔠 (STREET LINE 2) ▾ | Address2 ▾
　　├ 🔠 (CITY) ▾ | Town ▾
　　├ 🔠 (STATE) ▾ | County ▾
　　├ 🔠 (ZIP CODE) ▾ | Postcode ▾
　　└ 🔠 (COUNTRY) ▾ | Country ▾

Firstname:	
Surname:	
Employee Address: Address1:	
Address2:	

| Town: | County: | Postcode: |

| Country: | |

Modal Window Control

▲ ⊟ Rows Layout ▾ | Employee Property
　├ ▣ Command Bar
　├ 🔠 ▾ | Firstname
　├ 🔠 ▾ | Surname
　▲ 🖼 Modal Window ▾ | Employee Address
　　├ 🔠 ▾ | Address1
　　├ 🔠 ▾ | Address2
　　├ 🔠 ▾ | Town
　　├ 🔠 ▾ | County
　　├ 🔠 ▾ | Postcode
　　├ 🔠 ▾ | County
　　├ 🔠 ▾ | Country
　　└ ✛ Add ▾

Firstname:	
Surname:	
	Employee Address

Employee Address ✕
Address1: [ ]
Address2: [ ]
Town: [ ]
County: [ ]
Postcode: [ ]
County: [ ]
Country: [ ]

Picture and Text Control

▲ ⊟ Rows Layout ▾ | Employee Property
　├ ▣ Command Bar
　▲ 🖼 Picture and Text ▾ | Group
　　├ 🖼 (PICTURE) ▾ | Employee Photo ▾
　　├ A (TITLE) ▾ | Fullname ▾
　　├ ☒ (SUBTITLE) | Choose Content
　　└ ☒ (DESCRIPTION) | Choose Content

Tim　- Employee

Tim　Leung

Figure 3-10. *Data item containers at design and run time*

The Address Editor control contains placeholders that you can assign to the address fields that you've defined in your table. LightSwitch shows the display name for your control in the Address Editor control's label at run time.

The Modal Window control displays a button on the screen. When the user clicks on this button, LightSwitch opens a modal window popup that contains the controls that you've added beneath the Modal Window control.

The Picture And Text and Text And Picture controls allow you to display an image and various pieces of associated text.

EXERCISE 3.1 – CREATING A DETAILS SCREEN

Open your project from Exercise 2.1, and create New Data and Details screens for your Engineer entity. Notice the controls that LightSwitch uses, and try changing some of your data items so that they use different controls. Use the Add Text option to add a title to your Details screen. Run your application, and use your New Data screen to create a new record. After you save a record, notice how LightSwitch automatically opens the new record in your Details screen.

Including Related Data Items

You can customize a details screen so that it shows related records. In the Details screen that you created in Exercise 3.1, take a look at the screen query that appears in the Screen Members list (the left hand part of the screen designer). You'll find a link that's titled 'Add Issues - click this to add the related Issues collection' (See Figure 3-11.)

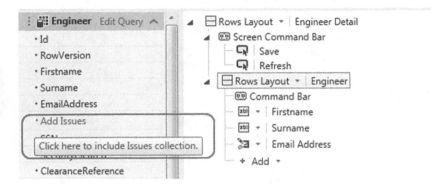

Figure 3-11. *Adding related items*

When you click this link, LightSwitch adds the Issues collection and you'll see it appear in the Screen Member list. You can then add a data grid of issues by dragging the Issues collection onto your details screen. (See Figure 3-12.)

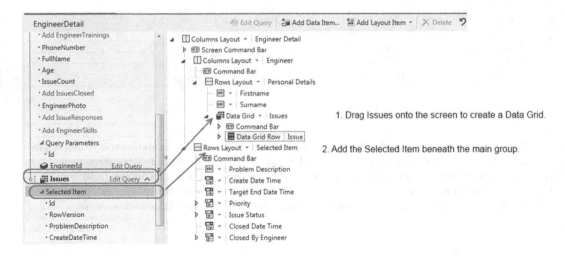

Figure 3-12. *Design-time view of your details screen*

Beneath the top level Rows Layout for Engineer Detail, click on the Add button and select the Issues ➤ Selected Item option. Note that the option to add the selected issue item only appears outside of the main Engineer Detail group.

By adding the selected item, users can select an issue from the data grid and view the selected issue detail in a separate part of the screen. As soon as a user selects an issue, the data controls that are bound to the selected item will automatically refresh. Figure 3-13 shows the runtime view of this screen. Notice that this example sets the parent layout to a Columns Layout, so that LightSwitch shows the selected issue in the right hand part of the screen.

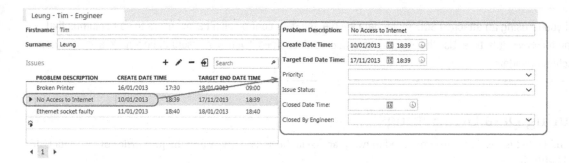

Figure 3-13. *Runtime view of screen*

This example demonstrates how LightSwitch keeps track of the currently selected data item whenever you work with collections of data. It also shows how you can bind the selected item to data controls on your screen. At design time, LightSwitch exposes the selected item as an entity property. This allows you to use the properties of the selected item or to bind them to additional data controls.

Showing Collections of Records

LightSwitch includes two controls that allow you to display collections of records: the Data Grid and Data List controls (you've already seen the Data Grid control in the earlier example). The main difference between the two controls is that the Data List control is designed to show read-only data.

The Data Grid control displays editable data in a grid. It allows users to sort data by clicking on the column header. You can add or remove the columns that are shown on your data grid by adding or deleting the child nodes that are shown beneath the Data Grid node.

At run time, a user can sort the rows in a Data List control by using a drop-down box that appears in the header. By default, a Data List control uses a Summary control to display each entry in the list. But if you want to display additional properties, you can change the Summary control to a Rows Layout control and use that to add your additional fields.

These two controls are shown in Figure 3-14.

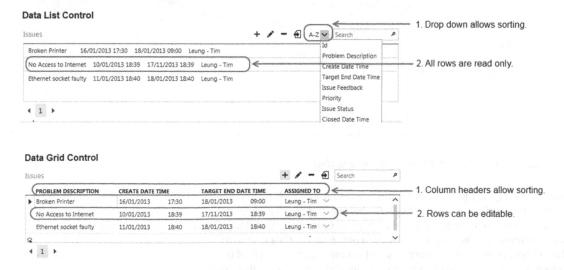

Figure 3-14. *Data Grid and Data List controls*

■ **Note** If you're using an attached SQL Server data source, the data controls don't allow users to sort columns that are based on the text data type. Use the varchar or nvarchar data types if you want users to be able to sort their data using the column headers.

Configuring Data Grid Settings

Data Grid and Data List settings are configured in two places: via the screen query and the properties of the Data Grid or Data List control.

It's useful to remember where these settings are configured. Otherwise, you could spend a considerable amount of time hunting around in the properties sheet of a Data Grid control trying to find a setting that actually belongs to the query.

The screen query represents a data source and is an object of type VisualCollection<T>. Figure 3-15 shows the properties that you can set.

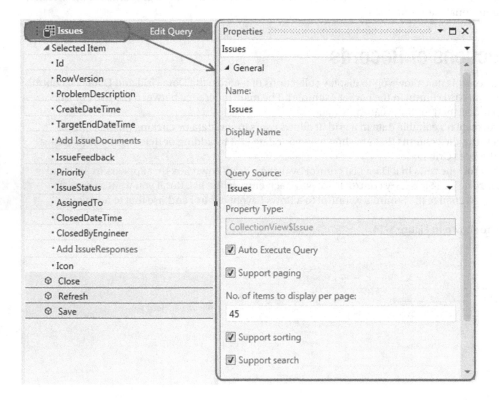

Figure 3-15. *Data grid paging, sorting, and searching options*

The Auto Execute Query property indicates whether or not LightSwitch executes your query when the screen first opens. To demonstrate this property, Figure 3-16 shows a data-entry screen that allows engineers to make time sheet entries. It's designed as a data-entry screen that displays only the entries that an engineer makes during a session. When the screen initially loads, it isn't necessary to populate the data grid with any previous time-sheet entries. You can achieve this behavior by setting the Auto Execute Query property of the time-sheet query to false. Appendix E shows the schema of the TimeTracking table that allows you to recreate this example.

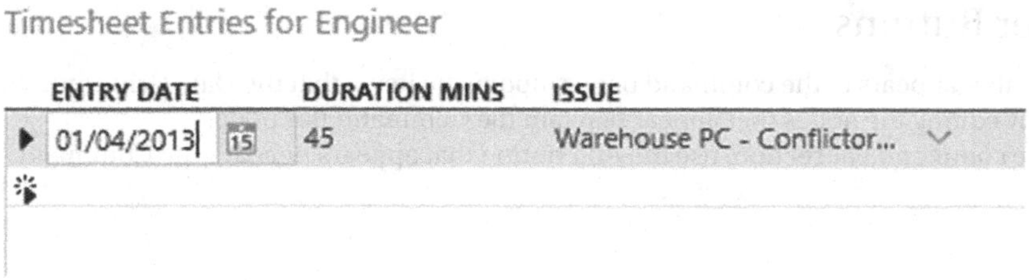

Timesheet Entries for Engineer
ENTRY DATE
DURATION MINS
ISSUE
01/04/2013
45
Warehouse PC - Conflictor...

Figure 3-16. Hiding existing records by deselecting the Auto Execute Query check box

The paging, sorting, and search check boxes control whether or not LightSwitch shows these options on the data grid.

The properties of the data grid (shown in Figure 3-17) allow you to hide or show the Export To Excel button, which appears in the data grid toolbar (for desktop applications only).

Properties
Issues
Label Position:
None
Disable Export to Excel
Show Add-new Row

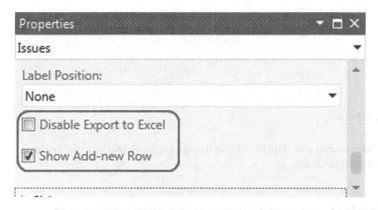

Figure 3-17. Data grid properties

You can also uncheck the Show Add-new Row check box to hide the empty row placeholder that appears at the bottom of the data grid. However, unchecking this option doesn't disable the option to add new records altogether. Users can still add records by clicking the Add button that appears in the command bar section of the data grid. (See Figure 3-18.)

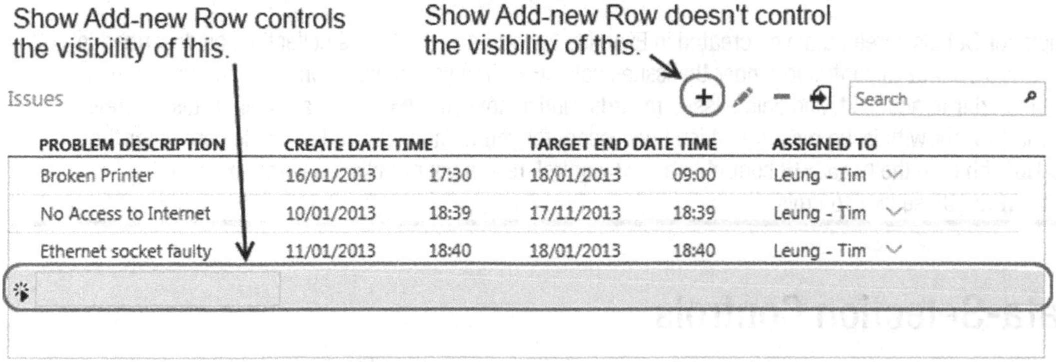

Show Add-new Row controls the visibility of this.
Show Add-new Row doesn't control the visibility of this.
Issues
Search
PROBLEM DESCRIPTION
CREATE DATE TIME
TARGET END DATE TIME
ASSIGNED TO
Broken Printer
16/01/2013 17:30
18/01/2013 09:00
Leung - Tim
No Access to Internet
10/01/2013 18:39
17/11/2013 18:39
Leung - Tim
Ethernet socket faulty
11/01/2013 18:40
18/01/2013 18:40
Leung - Tim

Figure 3-18. Show Add-new Row property

Setting Data Grid Header Buttons

If you want to remove the Add button that appears in the command bar or modify the items that the Data Grid control shows in this section, you can do so by editing the nodes that appear beneath the Command Bar node.

If you want to add a button to the command bar section, use the Add button that appears beneath the Command Bar node, as shown in Figure 3-19.

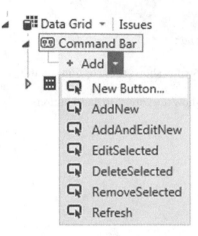

Figure 3-19. *Editing the Data Grid command bar buttons*

In this figure, you see the command types that you can add. The New Button option is particularly useful because it allows you to write your own code to perform a custom task.

■ **Note** When a user clicks on a data grid's Add or Edit button, LightSwitch displays the selected record using an autogenerated window. By default, these autogenerated windows aren't customizable, but Chapter 7 shows you how to work around this limitation.

```
EXERCISE 3.2 – SHOWING RELATED DETAILS
```

Take the Engineer Details screen that you created in Exercise 3.1 and add the Issues collection, as described in this section. Use a `DataGrid` control to render the Issues collection. Run your application, and use the controls in the `DataGrid` header to add, edit, and delete issue records. Notice how your `DataGrid` autogenerates a screen that allows you to work with issue records—it isn't necessary for you to manually add a details screen for the Issue entity. Now change the `DataGrid` control to a `List` control, re-run your application, and examine the differences between these two controls.

Using Data-Selection Controls

LightSwitch provides a couple of controls that allows users to view or select related entities. These are the Auto Complete Box and Modal Window Picker controls.

Using the Auto Complete Box Control

The Auto Complete Box is a control that's similar to a drop-down box, in that it allows users to select from a list of drop-down values. However, it also allows users to type into the control and filters the items by the text that's entered.

When a user types into this control, LightSwitch searches against all records in the underlying table. You can restrict the records that LightSwitch searches by writing your own query and assigning it to the Auto Complete Box's Choices property. (See Figure 3-20.) The Filter Mode property controls the way that the matching works.

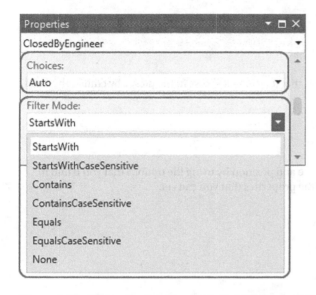

Figure 3-20. *Setting the Auto Complete Box Choices and Filter Mode values*

The Auto Complete Box shows a summary for each row that's shown through a Summary control. But if you want to show additional properties, change the Summary control to a Columns Layout control and add the additional properties that you want to show. (See Figure 3-21.)

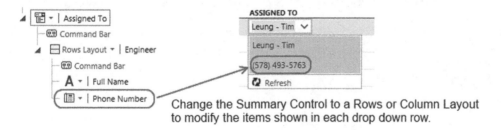

Figure 3-21. *Setting the items shown in an Auto Complete Box*

Using the Modal Window Picker Control

The Modal Window Picker control renders a button on the screen. When the user clicks on this button, LightSwitch opens a pop-up window that allows the user to search and select a record. (See Figure 3-22.)

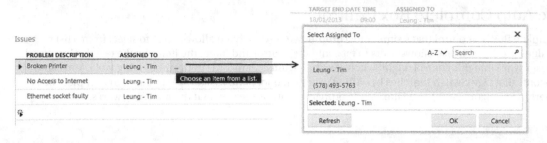

Figure 3-22. *Modal Window Picker control*

As with the Auto Complete Box, you can control the fields that the control shows in the picker by editing the child items of the Modal Window Picker control.

Setting Control Appearances

For each control that you add to a screen, you can adjust its size and position by using the options that you'll find in the Sizing section of the Properties sheet. Figure 3-23 shows the properties that you can set.

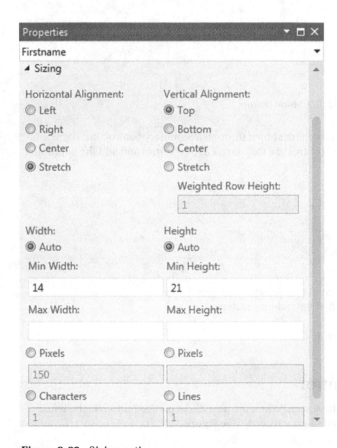

Figure 3-23. *Sizing options*

Depending on the control you choose, additional sizing options may also be available. For example, you'll find an Is Resizable option in some of the layout controls. This allows your user to resize the contents using a splitter control.

Most of these sizing options are self-explanatory. The Width and Height settings default to Auto. This means that LightSwitch chooses an optimal width and height based on the space available. If you want to specify a definite size, the units that you can use are pixels or characters and lines.

Depending on the control you choose, additional appearance options may also be available. If you choose the Date Time Picker control, for example, you can configure whether or not to show the time component.

Positioning Control Labels

For each data control that you add to your screen, LightSwitch automatically displays a label. If you add a Surname text box to your screen, for example, LightSwitch displays a Surname label next to the text box. The text that it uses for the label comes from the Display Name property that you set in the table designer.

Figure 3-24 shows the label position drop-down. Once again, most of these options are self-explanatory. An interesting pair of options you'll find are None and Collapsed.

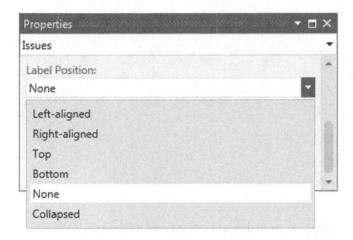

Figure 3-24. *Label Position drop-down*

If you want to hide a label, you can set the Label Position to None. However, the label will still take up space on the screen, even though it's not shown. If you choose the Collapsed option, the label doesn't take up any space. This is illustrated in Figure 3-25.

Figure 3-25. *The difference between the Collapsed and None options*

Styling Labels and Static Text Controls

In general, you can't change the fonts that individual LightSwitch controls use. This is because the font settings are designed to be configured using the theme you've defined for your application. The benefit of a theme is that it allows you to easily maintain a consistent look and feel throughout all the screens in your application.

A nice feature about the Label control is that you can set the font style to one of six predefined styles. Figure 3-26 shows the available font styles, and illustrates how they look at run time.

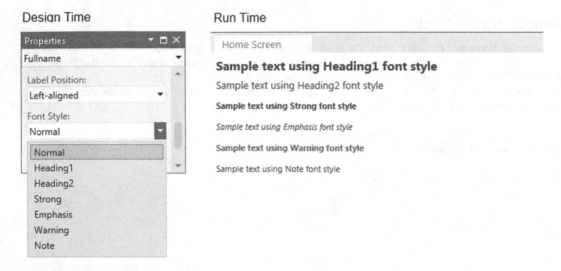

Figure 3-26. *The available font label styles*

Making Controls Read-Only

If you want to make parts of your screen read-only, the easiest way to do this is to replace your text boxes with labels.

Group controls include a Use Read-Only Controls check box. If you set this to true, LightSwitch replaces all child data controls with labels or their read-only equivalents.

The other read-only controls that LightSwitch provides are described in Table 3-2. This table also shows their supported data types.

Table 3-2. *Read-Only Controls*

Name	Description	Supported Data Types
Label	This displays a read-only copy of the data value.	All LightSwitch data types
Date Viewer	Displays a date value.	Date
Date Time Viewer	Displays a date/time value.	Date, Date Time
Email Address Viewer	Displays an email address.	Email
Image Viewer	Displays an image.	Image
Phone Number Viewer	Displays a phone number.	Phone Number
Money Viewer	Displays a monetary value.	Money

In Table 3-2, notice how there isn't a read-only check box. If you want to make a check box read-only, you'll need to write some code. You'll see how to do this in Chapter 7.

Creating a Search Screen

The Search Screen template allows you to create screens that allow users to carry out searches.

Figure 3-27 demonstrates a screen that's been created with the Search template. The key feature of this screen is that it includes a Search text box.

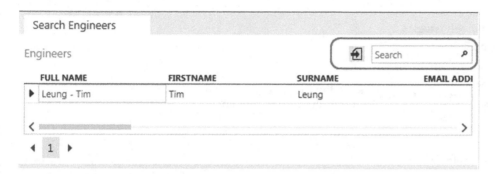

Figure 3-27. Example Search screen

The search operation matches all records that contain the value that the user enters into the text box. It searches all string fields in the underlying table where the Is Searchable check box is selected. Figure 2-1 in Chapter 2 shows where you can set this property.

Behind the scenes, LightSwitch uses the Search operator, which is exposed via the IDataServiceQueryable query property of your data source.

The search screen doesn't allow you to change the type of search LightSwitch performs. If you want to return all records that begin with (rather than contain) the text-box value that's entered, you'll need to create a custom search screen.

LightSwitch only searches against string properties. It won't search against numeric or navigation properties, even if you've chosen to show string data from a navigation property on your search screen's data grid. To perform a more advanced search, you'll need to create a search screen that uses a custom query.

EXERCISE 3.3 – CREATING A SEARCH SCREEN

Use the Search Screen template to create a search screen for your Engineer table. Run your application, and use the Search box to search for engineer records. Notice how LightSwitch matches the text that you enter in the Search text box against all properties where you selected the Is Searchable check box in the table designer. Return to the screen designer, select the Data Grid Row check box for your Engineers data grid, and use the Properties sheet to deselect the Use Read-only Controls check box. Select the Command Bar for your Engineers data grid, and click the Add button to add the AddAndEditNew, EditSelected, and DeleteSelected items. Run your application, and notice how your search screen now allows you to fully add and edit records.

Launching Child Screens

In this section, you'll find out how to allow users to launch child screens from the engineer search screen that you created in Exercise 3-3. The child screen will show the issues that have been assigned to the selected engineer.

First, create a screen that shows the issues that have been assigned to an engineer. This is the screen that you'll launch from your search screen.

To do this, create a new details screen called EngineerIssues. Choose Engineer from the Screen Data drop-down, and check the Engineer Issues checkbox in the Additional Data to Include section. Delete the engineer details so that only the Issues data grid remains. (See Figure 3-28.)

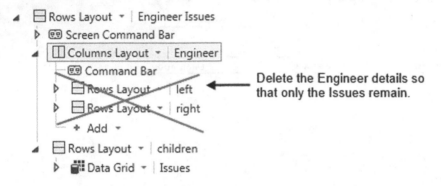

Figure 3-28. *EngineerIssues screen*

Now open the engineer search screen that you created in Exercise 3.3. In the Data Grid Row for the Engineer data grid, find the IssueCount label. Check the Show As Link check box, and choose EngineerIssues from the Target Screen drop-down list. (See Figure 3-29.)

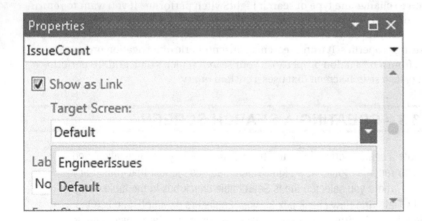

Figure 3-29. *The Target Screen options on the Properties sheet*

This means that LightSwitch will render each Issue Count cell in the grid as a link. When the user clicks on this link, LightSwitch opens the record using the EngineerIssues screen.

Figure 3-30 shows how the screen looks at run time. Notice that the Full Name link still opens the engineer details screen. Therefore, it's possible to launch multiple instances of different screen types from a single data grid.

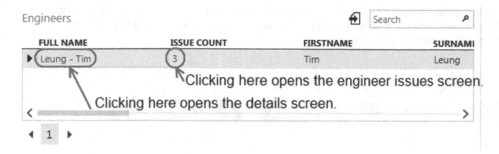

Figure 3-30. The search screen at run time

Setting Application Properties

The General Properties tab of your project (shown in Figure 3-31) allows you to control application-level settings.

Figure 3-31. General Properties tab

This tab enables you to change the shell and theme of your application. As you learned in Chapter 1, changing the shell and theme alters the look and feel of your application.

You can also set your application name on the General Properties tab. LightSwitch shows the text that you enter here in the title bar of your application. In a desktop application, LightSwitch shows the server name in the title bar after your application name. This is a security feature that Silverlight imposes, and it isn't possible to hide the server name.

The Icon settings allow you to assign icons to your application. The icons that LightSwitch displays depend on the application type and shell you choose. For example, if you've chosen the Cosmopolitan shell, your logo image will appear in the banner of your application. In a desktop application that uses the Standard shell, the application icon appears in the title bar of your application and the logo image appears in the desktop shortcut that starts your application.

Changing the Language and Culture Settings

To change the primary language of your application, use the culture drop-down box in the General Properties tab of your project and select one of the 42 available cultures. If Microsoft decides to add support for the English (British) culture in a future release, it would make one particular author very happy.

Figure 3-32 shows a running application with the culture setting set to Spanish. As shown in this illustration, LightSwitch automatically localizes the built-in messages and menu items that the user sees. LightSwitch also provides support for right-to-left languages such as Arabic and Chinese.

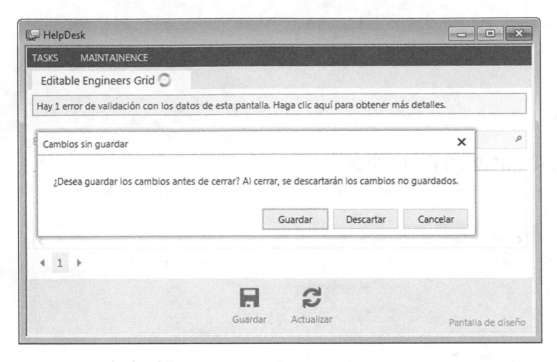

Figure 3-32. *Localized application*

Until very recently, LightSwitch applications supported only a single language and culture. But if you install Visual Studio 2012 Update 2 and upgrade your project (see Chapter 8 for details), you can make your application fully multilingual. If you've ever localized an ASP.NET, you'll recognize that localizing a LightSwitch application works in a very similar way.

It involves adding localized resource files into both your Client and Server projects. So if the primary language of your application is English and you want your application to also support Spanish, switch to File View and use Visual Studio's Add New ➤ Item option to create two resource files in the root folder of your Client and Server projects. You should name the files in your Client project Client.resx and Client.es-ES.resx, and name files in your Server project Service.resx and Service.es-ES.resx. es-ES is the culture code for the Spanish (Spain) locale, and Appendix A shows a full reference list of culture codes. If you want your application to support additional languages, you'll need to add additional resource files and name them with your desired language code.

The resource files allow you to create name/value pairs of string values. Let's suppose that you want to localize the Surname property's label on an Engineer screen. To do this, you'd add an entry to your Client.resx file with a name/value pair of SurnameDisplayName and Surname. SurnameDisplayName is a user-defined key that allows you to identify the word "Surname." Next, you'd add the name/value pair SurnameDisplayName and Apellido to your Client.es-ES.resx file. (*Apellido* is the Spanish word for *surname*.) You'd then open your Engineer screen, and change the Surname property's Display Name value from *Surname* to $(SurnameDisplayName). The $() notation prompts LightSwitch to retrieve the localized version of the value from the resource file at run time. If a user runs a Spanish version of Windows, or sets their computer to Spanish by installing and enabling the Spanish Windows language pack, your application will automatically show the Spanish version of the Surname label.

To complete the localization task, you'll need to repeat the same process for the remaining text values in your application and localize any text that you've assigned to entity and property descriptions through the table designer. To localize table settings, you'd create the name/value pairs in your Server resource file. To find out more about localizing an application, take a look at the help file by visiting the following Microsoft web page:

`http://msdn.microsoft.com/en-us/library/vstudio/xx130603(v=vs.110).aspx`

This page also shows you how to retrieve resource values in .NET code, and how to localize HTML Client applications.

Configuring Screen Navigation

The Screen Navigation menu allows users to open the screens that you've created in your application. The menu appears along the left hand side of your application, but it can appear elsewhere depending on the shell that you select.

The Screen Navigation tab allows you to manage the items that LightSwitch shows in your navigation menu. In particular, you can create groups to help better organize your screens.

Figure 3-33 shows the Screen Navigation tab in the designer, alongside the screen navigation menu in running applications with both the Cosmopolitan and Standard shells applied.

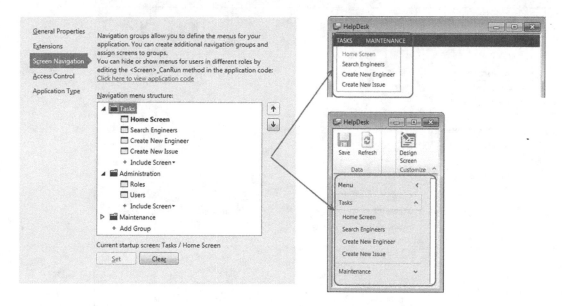

Figure 3-33. *Screen navigation at design time and run time*

LightSwitch automatically adds any new screen that you create to the navigation menu. This, however, excludes any screens that are based on the Details Screen template.

You can add multiple menu items that refer to the same screen. If you want to prevent all users from opening a specific screen, right-click the screen and select the Delete option.

The Include Screen drop-down menu allows you to add two built-in screens called Users and Roles. These screens allow you to manage the security of your application. By default, LightSwitch adds these screens into the Administration group.

At debug time, LightSwitch doesn't show the Administration group. This group appears only in deployed applications and is shown only to application administrators.

LightSwitch recognizes the permissions of the logged-on user when it builds the navigation menu at run time. If a user doesn't have sufficient permission to access a screen, LightSwitch doesn't show it in the navigation menu. (Chapter 17 shows you how to set screen-level permissions.) This makes your life really easy because you don't need to do any extra work to configure menu-item permissions.

Finally, you can set the initial screen that's shown to your user by specifying the startup screen. But if you don't want any screens to be shown at startup, you can click the Clear button to unset your startup screen.

Designing Screens at Run Time

It's difficult to visualize how your screen might look at run time when you're designing it through a series of tree nodes.

To simplify this task, LightSwitch provides a runtime designer that allows you to design screens at debug time. This is particularly useful for setting the sizing and appearance of controls, because it allows you to see immediately the changes that you're making.

To use the runtime designer, start up your application (by pressing F5) and click on the Design Screen link or button (depending on the shell that you've chosen). This opens the runtime designer, as shown in Figure 3-34.

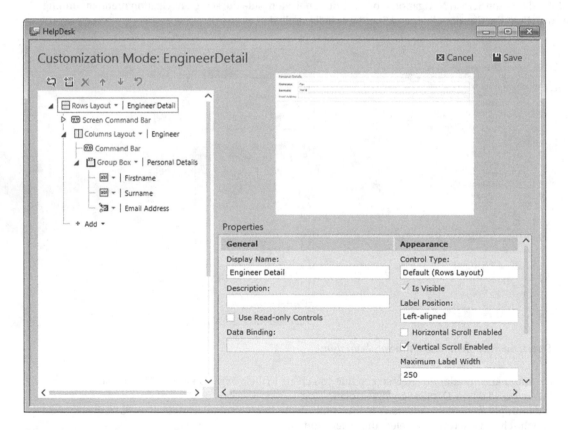

Figure 3-34. *Runtime screen designer*

The runtime designer allows you to add and delete controls, and to change the appearance properties of the controls on your screen. You can even add and delete group controls.

Although the runtime designer provides a great way to visually design your screens, it has some slight limitations. You can't add new data items such as local screen properties, queries, or methods. Also, you can't move items out of their layout containers or modify the underlying Visual Basic or C# code on your screen.

One last caveat—when you deploy your application, don't forget to change your build configuration from Debug to Release. If you forget, the link to the runtime designer will appear in your deployed application.

■ **Tip**   If you spend most of your time in Visual Studio, it's easy to overlook the runtime screen designer. The top tip for this chapter is to remember to use the runtime designer. It definitely makes screen design much easier.

Summary

This chapter has showed you how to create and design screens for the Silverlight client. To create a screen, you'd use one of the five built-in template types: Details, New Data, Search, Editable Grid, and List/Details.

Templates allow you to build screens with a prebuilt layout and function. The template names intuitively describe the purpose of each template, but a template type that warrants further explanation is the Details screen template. Details screens are designed to show a single record and can optionally display related data. Details screens must be opened from other screens and cannot be opened directly. A common use-case scenario is to create a search screen that allows users to open the selected record in a details screen.

LightSwitch includes a screen designer that allows you to build a screen by adding *content items* to a tree view. Each content item might represent a group or a data item. LightSwitch allows you to change the control that it uses to render a content item. In the case of a group, the Rows and Columns layout controls are two common controls that you can use. These controls allow you to display the group's child items in a horizontal or vertical stack.

The controls that allow you to display data include text box, label, check box, and a whole range of other controls. If you want to allow users to select a record, you can use either an Auto Complete Box or Modal Window Picker control. To display lists of related child records, you can use either the Data Grid or Data List control. The difference between these two controls is that the Data List control is designed to show data in read-only mode.

When you add a label to your screen, you can set the label to "show as a link" and specify a target screen. This allows users to click on the label and to open a related record in a new details screen.

All controls have appearance properties that allow you to set attributes such as the height and width. It's quite difficult to visualize your screen when you're developing it through a series of tree nodes. To simplify this task, LightSwitch provides a runtime designer that allows you to design screens in a WYSIWYG fashion.

Finally, the General Properties window allows you to set your application title and icon. It also allows you to configure your application's navigation menu and to specify the primary language of your application.

CHAPTER 4

■ ■ ■

Accessing Data with Code

It's entirely possible to create functional applications without writing any code. But to go further, you'll need to understand the event model and data Application Programming Interfaces (APIs) that LightSwitch exposes.

In this chapter, you will learn how to

- Access data with code and understand the event model
- Work with the save pipeline
- Understand transactions and concurrency

This chapter extends the HelpDesk application and shows you how to add features that are possible only through code. For example, you'll find out how to allow administrators to configure the system for first-time use by autocreating issue status records. You'll also find out how to allow managers to close multiple issues or to purge all issue records in the database by clicking on a button.

The system maintains a history of issue status changes by recording the old status, the new status, and the date that the change occurred. You'll learn how to create this feature by using change sets and writing code in the save pipeline.

For compliance purposes, the system can also audit changes by creating records in a separate SQL Server database. You'll learn how to carry out this process inside a transaction. If the auditing fails, the data changes that the user made in LightSwitch will be rolled back.

■ **Note**   This chapter focuses on writing .NET data-access code for Silverlight applications. HTML client applications (discussed in Chapter 8) rely on a JavaScript data-access model that looks very similar to the .NET API that's covered in this chapter.

Performing Application Tasks in Code

Let's begin this chapter by looking at the `Application` object. This object allows you to carry out application-specific functions in code. It allows you to open screens, access active screens, work with user data, and create data workspaces.

You can reference the `Application` object in both client-side and server-side code. Because screens are part of the client and don't exist on the server, the properties and methods that the `Application` object exposes will depend on where you call it.

Figure 4-1 shows the IntelliSense options that Visual Studio shows when you write screen code, compared to those that it shows when you write code in the `common` or `server` projects.

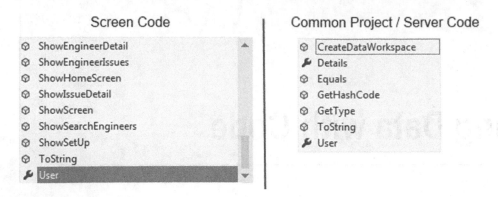

Figure 4-1. *The* Application *object properties and methods*

LightSwitch automatically generates a Show method for each screen in your application. You can open your screens in code by calling these methods. Figure 4-1 shows some example Show methods in the Screen Code section.

The ShowDefaultScreen method allows you to pass in any entity and opens the entity by using the default screen. Another method that exists is the ShowScreen method. This allows you to open a screen by passing in a screen definition (an IScreenDefinition object). However, in general, you'd use the strongly typed Show methods that LightSwitch exposes for each screen.

The Application object also exposes a collection called ActiveScreens. This collection contains a reference to each screen that's currently open in your application. As an example of how you would use this collection, you could create a button on your screen to refresh all other screens that are currently open. Chapter 7 shows you the code that does this, and you'll also find additional code samples that show you how to use the Application object to open screens.

Working with Data

LightSwitch provides an API that allows you to access your data, and Figure 4-2 illustrates the objects that make up this API. These objects allow you to create, retrieve, update, and delete records in code. This section contains examples that show you how to carry out these tasks.

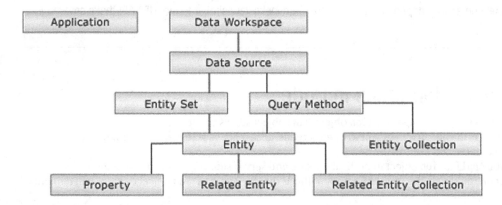

Figure 4-2. *Data access objects*

Creating Records

In this first example, you'll find out how to add records in code. You'll create a screen that contains a button. When a user runs your application and clicks on this button, the code behind the button prepopulates the IssueStatus table with data. This feature allows an administrator to initialize your application with data during first use.

To create this example, add a new screen called Setup. In the Add New Screen dialog, choose the New Data Screen template; from the Screen Data drop-down menu, choose None. Add a Rows Layout control to your screen, and add a new button. To create a button, right-click your Rows Layout control and select the Add Button option. (See Figure 4-3.) When the Add Button dialog appears, choose the Write My Own Method option, and name your method SetupData.

***Figure 4-3.** The Add Button dialog*

When you click the OK button in the Add Button dialog, LightSwitch adds a SetupData method to your Screen Member list. Select this method and right-click the Edit Execute Code option to open the code editor. Now enter the code that's shown in Listing 4-1.

Listing 4-1. Creating a New Record

VB:
File: HelpDeskVB\Client\UserCode\Setup.vb

```
Dim statusRaised =
    Me.DataWorkspace.ApplicationData.IssueStatusSet.AddNew()          ❶
statusRaised.StatusDescription = "Raised"                            ❷
Me.DataWorkspace.ApplicationData.SaveChanges()                       ❸
```

C#:
File: HelpDeskCS\Client\UserCode\Setup.cs

```
var statusRaised =
    this.DataWorkspace.ApplicationData.IssueStatusSet.AddNew();       ❶
statusRaised.StatusDescription = "Raised";                          ❷
this.DataWorkspace.ApplicationData.SaveChanges();                    ❸
```

Let's take a closer look at this code. LightSwitch generates entity types for each entity in your application. These types represent a single row in a table. For each entity type, LightSwitch also creates properties you can use to get and set the value of each field in the table.

The IssueStatus class is an example of an entity type thatLightSwitch automatically generates for you.

The first line of code ❶ refers to a DataWorkspace. This is an object that allows you to access the data sources in your project.

LightSwitch creates a Data Source class for each data source in your project, and the names of these classes match the data source names that you see in Solution Explorer. (See Figure 4-4.) Therefore, the ApplicationData object ❶ refers to your intrinsic database. SecurityData is a special data source that allows you to work with your application's users, and you'll find out more about this later on.

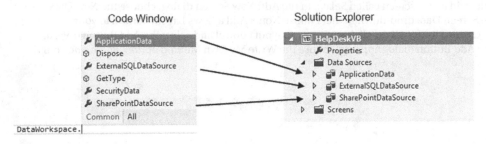

Figure 4-4. *Data sources*

You can use the Data Source class to access *entity sets*. LightSwitch generates Entity Set classes for each table in every data source. An Entity Set object represents a set of data on the server. By using the static AddNew method, you can create a new instance of an entity—in this case, a new issue status.

Once you've created an Issue Status object, you can set the description property by using the code shown in ❷. The final part of the code commits the record to the database by calling the data source's SaveChanges method ❸. Note that this code references your screen's data workspace, and because of this, the SaveChanges method will save all other data changes that a user might have made on your screen.

■ **Note**   The source code for this book includes a screen called Setup that extends the code in Listing 4-1. The extra code encapsulates this logic in a method, and includes additional code that checks that the status code doesn't exist before adding it.

Finding Single Records by ID Value

The Data Source object provides two query methods, called _Single and _SingleOrDefault, for each entity in your data source. (See Figure 4-5.) These methods return a single record by ID or primary key value.

Figure 4-5. *Returning a single record*

The difference between `Single` and `SingleOrDefault` is that `Single` throws an exception if the record doesn't exist. `SingleOrDefault` returns null rather than throwing an exception.

Updating Records

This example shows you how to update records in code by adding a button a user can click to set the status of all issues in the database to "closed."

Open your Setup screen, and add a button called `CloseAllIssues`. Open this method in the code editor, and enter the code that's shown in Listing 4-2.

Listing 4-2. Retrieving and Updating Records

VB:
File: HelpDeskVB\Client\UserCode\Setup.vb

```
Private Sub CloseAllIssues_Execute()

    Dim statusClosed =
        DataWorkspace.ApplicationData.IssueStatusSet_SingleOrDefault(1)      ❶

    For Each issue As Issue In
            Me.DataWorkspace.ApplicationData.Issues                          ❷
        issue.IssueStatus = statusClosed                                     ❸
    Next
    Me.DataWorkspace.ApplicationData.SaveChanges()

End Sub
```

C#:
File: HelpDeskCS\Client\UserCode\Setup.cs

```
partial void CloseAllIssues_Execute()
{
    var statusClosed =
        DataWorkspace.ApplicationData.IssueStatusSet_SingleOrDefault(1);     ❶

    foreach (Issue issue in
        this.DataWorkspace.ApplicationData.Issues)                           ❷
    {
        issue.IssueStatus =
            statusClosed;                                                    ❸
    }
    this.DataWorkspace.ApplicationData.SaveChanges();

}
```

The first part of this code uses the `SingleOrDefault` method to return an instance of an `IssueStatus` object that represents a closed state ❶. The code assumes that the issue status record in the database with an Id of 1 represents a closed issue status. You might choose instead to retrieve the issue status by its description, and you can do this by writing a query. (See Chapter 6.)

The next part of this code loops over the Issues entity set ❷. This allows you to access each issue record in your database and to set the IssueStatus to "closed" ❸. In most cases, you'll likely want to work with a smaller subset of data rather than the entire issue table, and you can do this by using a query. You can access queries by name. For example, if you create a query called OldIssues that returns issues that are older than 30 days, you can access this query through the Data Source object by using the syntax DataWorkspace.ApplicationData.OldIssues. This returns an entity collection of issues that you can enumerate, and you can work with the child items in the same way. Chapter 6 shows you exactly how to create such a query.

Deleting Records

The final example in this section shows you how to delete records in code. It shows you how to create a delete button that allows a user to delete all of the issue records in your database.

Open your Setup screen, and add a button called DeleteAllIssues. Open this method in the code editor, and enter the code that's shown in Listing 4-3.

Listing 4-3. Deleting Records

VB:
File: HelpDeskVB\Client\UserCode\Setup.vb

```
For Each issue As Issue In
  Me.DataWorkspace.ApplicationData.Issues                     ❶
    issue.Delete()                                            ❷
Next
Me.DataWorkspace.ApplicationData.SaveChanges()                ❸
```

C#:
File: HelpDeskCS\Client\UserCode\Setup.cs

```
foreach (Issue issue in
    this.DataWorkspace.ApplicationData.Issues){              ❶
        issue.Delete();                                       ❷
}
this.DataWorkspace.ApplicationData.SaveChanges();            ❸
```

Just like the previous example, this code loops over all the issue records in your database ❶. But rather than update the issue status, the code calls the Delete method on the Issue entity ❷. As usual, the code finishes with a call to the Data Source object's SaveChanges method ❸.

The main purpose of this code is to illustrate the Delete method and it's important to note the overall process that's shown in this example isn't the most efficient. The screen code pulls the issue records onto the client just to carry out the deletion. So, in practice, you'll find that this code will run slowly. A Rich Internet Application (RIA) service can help you improve performance, and Chapter 9 covers this in further detail.

Working with Properties and Nullable Data Types

Entity types allow you to refer to data properties in code. For example, issue.StatusDescription is the kind of syntax that would allow you to reference an issue's status description.

The data type of each property matches the data type that you've defined in the table designer. If you've unchecked the required check box for a property in the table designer, LightSwitch defines the property using a nullable data type (except for String and Binary, which are reference types and are able to accept a null value).

Figure 4-6 shows the additional members that you'll see with nullable properties. These include Value, HasValue, and GetValueOrDefault.

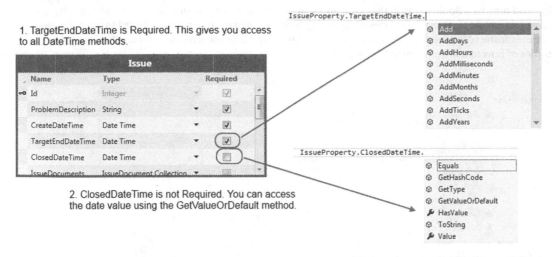

1. TargetEndDateTime is Required. This gives you access to all DateTime methods.

2. ClosedDateTime is not Required. You can access the date value using the GetValueOrDefault method.

Figure 4-6. *Nullable data types in IntelliSense*

If you try to access the value of a nullable property that's set to null, LightSwitch throws an exception. It's therefore much safer to access nullable properties using the GetValueOrDefault method.

■ **Note**   If you receive a compilation error along the lines of *Cannot implicitly convert type decimal to decimal*, it is likely to be caused by nullable variables. The GetValueOrDefault method can help you fix these errors.

Working with User Details

There are a couple of places where you can access user-related details in LightSwitch. As mentioned earlier, the Application object provides access to the currently logged-on user. The code in listing 4-4 shows you the syntax that allows you to retrieve the logged-on user.

Listing 4-4. Accessing the Currently Logged-On User

VB:
```
Me.Application.User
```

C#:
```
this.Application.User;
```

LightSwitch allows you to manage users and permissions through a built-in data source called SecurityData. The underlying data store that LightSwitch uses is the ASP.NET membership provider.

The SecurityData data source allows you to access membership and security features, such as the ChangePassword and IsValidPassword methods. You use the ChangePassword method to change the password for a user by supplying the user name, old password, and new password values. The IsValidPassword method accepts a password string and returns a Boolean result that indicates whether the password is sufficiently strong enough.

You can also access role and permission details by using the Role, Permission, and RolePermission collections. Figure 4-7 illustrates some of the methods that you'll see through the IntelliSense window. You can find some practical examples of how to use this code in Chapter 17.

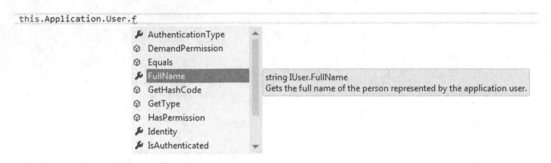

Figure 4-7. *IntelliSense options that relate to the user*

Working with Screen Data

You'll probably spend a lot of time in the screen designer, so now's a good time to learn about the data objects that you can find there.

When you create a screen, LightSwitch adds a data object to the Screen Member list (the left hand part of the screen designer). The object that it adds depends on the screen template that you've chosen. This is shown in Figure 4-8.

Figure 4-8. *Screen Member list*

When you create a screen that contains a data grid, LightSwitch adds a query to your screen. In Figure 4-8, this query is called Engineers. Notice that LightSwitch uses the plural name Engineers—this is because the query returns one or more engineers. LightSwitch determines this name using the plural name value that you've defined in the table designer.

When you create a details screen, LightSwitch adds an object called Engineer. Once again, this is a query, but unlike the previous example, it returns only a single engineer.

If you create a new data screen, LightSwitch adds a property to your screen. In this example, it names the property EngineerProperty.

The important distinction is that although the details screen and new data screen are both designed to show a single record, details screens are based on a query, whereas new data screens are not. This distinction is important because an engineer query is very different from an engineer property. The distinction is apparent both visually through the designer and in code.

Working with Screen Events

LightSwitch exposes various screen events that you can handle. For example, if you want to perform some additional logic when your user saves a screen, you can do so by writing code in the Saving method.

To handle these events, click the Write Code button that appears in the toolbar of your screen designer. This produces a drop-down list of methods, which can vary depending on the screen template type that you've chosen. (See Figure 4-9.) When you click on one of these methods, Visual Studio opens the method in the code editor window.

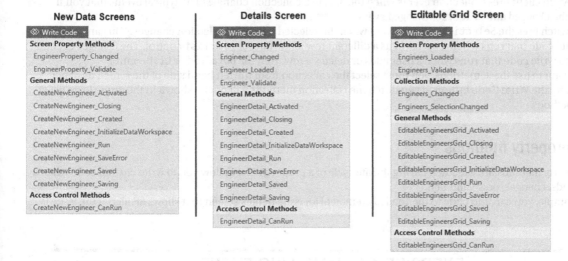

Figure 4-9. *Screen events*

As the figure shows, the available methods are grouped into sections, and I'll now describe the methods that you'll find in each section.

General methods

The LightSwitch client triggers *general events* throughout the life cycle of a screen. You can handle these events in order to write custom code that executes when your screen loads, closes, or carries out a save.

The InitializeDataWorkspace method allows you to write custom code just before the client initializes your screen (and data workspace). You'll see examples of why you would want to do this in Chapter 7.

You can use the Saving method to run your own code just before the client saves the data on the screen. When you click on the Write Code button and select the Saving method, LightSwitch creates a method stub and opens the code editor window. This method stub includes a parameter called handled. If you set this to true, LightSwitch will not perform the save operation. This allows you to carry out your own custom save logic. The "Handling Conflicts in Code" sample later in this chapter demonstrates this concept.

The client fires the Closing event just before it closes a screen. The Closing method includes a parameter called cancel. If you set this to true, LightSwitch prevents the screen from closing.

Access control methods

The LightSwitch client fires the CanRun method just before it opens a screen. This allows you to write security code that controls who can view a screen. You'll find example code in Chapter 17.

With some imagination, you can write code in the CanRun method to carry out tasks that are outside the intended security purpose of this method. For example, you can create a dummy screen so that LightSwitch creates an entry in your application's navigation panel. This gives you an entry point into the dummy screen's CanRun method and allows you to execute Silverlight code outside the context of your screen object. In Chapter 17, the "Opening Screens Conditionally at Login" example demonstrates this technique.

Collection methods

The LightSwitch client fires Collection events when the data in a collection changes. The typical events that you'll handle are the Changed and SelectionChanged events.

LightSwitch fires the SelectionChanged event when the selected item in a collection changes. You can use this event to write code that runs when a user selects a different row in the DataGrid or List control. The Changed event allows you to write code that runs when a user adds or deletes a row from the DataGrid or List control.

If you want to use these methods, you must select the collection from the left hand side of the screen designer before clicking the Write Code button. If you don't, the collection methods will not be shown in the drop-down list of available methods.

Screen property methods

Screen property methods are executed during the life cycle of a property. They allow you to write custom code when a property loads, changes, or is validated.

For example, you can add code to the loaded method of an issue details screen that shows an alert if the issue is overdue.

EXERCISE 4.1 – HANDLING EVENTS

Open the Engineer Detail screen that you created in Exercise 3.1. Select the Root node of your screen, and click the Write Code button. Notice the methods that appear in the Write Code button. Now select the Engineer property in the Screen Member list, click the Write Code button, and examine the extra methods that appear. Select the Engineer_Loaded method, and take a look at the code that LightSwitch autogenerates for you. Notice how LightSwitch executes code to update the screen's display name whenever the Engineer property loads or changes, or whenever the user saves the screen. Now open the Search screen that you created in Exercise 3.3. In the screen designer, select the Engineers collection and click on the Write Code button. Notice the collection methods that appear in the Write Code button.

Working with the Save Pipeline

The screen methods you've just seen are executed by your Silverlight client. In this section, you'll learn about the methods LightSwitch executes on the server. The key component that allows you to execute server side code is the save pipeline. This includes various interception points where you can inject custom code.

When the user triggers a save operation, the client serializes the change set and passes it to the data source's save method. The change set then enters the save pipeline. Figure 4-10 shows you the full process.

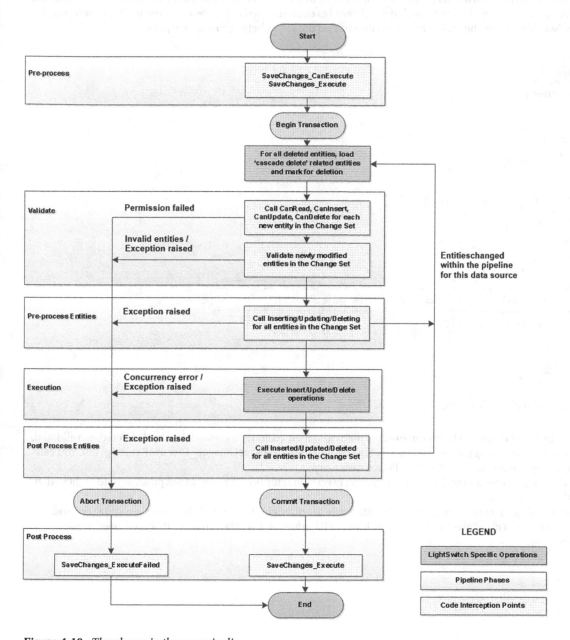

Figure 4-10. *The phases in the save pipeline*

Some of the reasons why you might want to write code in the save pipeline include

- Performing permission checks and, optionally, preventing changes from being saved

- Carrying out validation

- Carrying out additional tasks after a successful save (for example, auditing)

You'll see code examples of these tasks later in this book.

To access the methods in the save pipeline, open a table in the table designer and click on the Write Code button. As you hover the mouse over the methods that are shown (as demonstrated in Figure 4-11), the tooltip shows you where LightSwitch executes the code. The events that run on the server belong to the save pipeline.

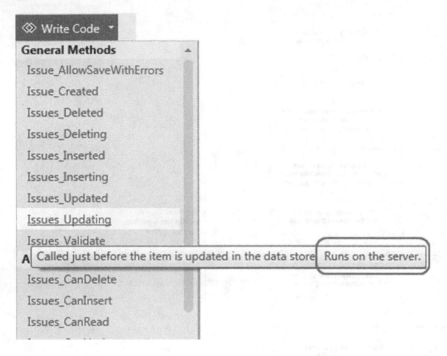

Figure 4-11. *Writing code in the save pipeline*

As you can see in Figure 4-11, you can execute methods when an entity is created, inserted, deleted, or validated.

If an error occurs during the save operation, LightSwitch raises the SaveChanges_ExecuteFailed event. You can capture this exception and handle it on the client if necessary.

If you change any entities inside the save pipeline, execution returns to the start of the pipeline, and LightSwitch will rerun the validation methods.

If the processing succeeds, any changes that are made to entities in the original change set are serialized and returned to the client. This allows the client to retrieve the ID values or any other changes that have been made during processing.

It's important to note that any entities that you've added in the save pipeline are not returned to the client. To retrieve items that have been added, you'll need to handle the Screen_Saved event and manually call code to refresh the data. You can perform a refresh by calling the refresh method on the screen's visual collection—for example, Issues.Refresh() on an issues grid screen. An alternative is to refresh the entire screen by calling the screen's refresh method—Me.Refresh() in VB.NET or this.Refresh() in C#.

■ **Tip**   When you're writing code in the save pipeline, you can use the methods in the Entity Functions class. This class contains useful functions that allow you to calculate date differences and perform aggregate calculations, such as standard deviation, variances, and averages. You'll find this class in the System.Data.Objects namespace. To use this class, you'll need to add a reference to the System.Data.Entity dynamic-link library (DLL) in your server project.

Calling Server-Side Code from the Client

You can run server-side code only by calling the save operation on a data source. This is awkward because, at times, you might want to trigger a server-side operation from the client. For example, you might want to create a screen button that backs up a database, calls a web service, or sends an email.

One technique for triggering server-side code is to create a dummy table that exists purely for the purpose of running server code. Chapter 15 shows you how to use this technique to send email from the server.

Working with Change Sets

When a user works with a screen, LightSwitch keeps track of data changes and can revert a record back to its initial state. It does this through the magic of change sets.

The good news is that you can access LightSwitch's change sets in code, which allows you to carry out clever things in your application. For example, you can determine the data items that have changed, retrieve their original values, or discard any specific changes that a user makes.

Retrieving Original Values

To show you how to use a change set to retrieve the original value of a record, here's a demonstration of how to create audit records whenever a user changes an issue record. You'll learn how to write code in the save pipeline that audits the change by recording the new and original status of an issue and the time that the change took place.

Let's begin by creating a table that stores the status history. Create a table called IssueStatusChange, and create a property called ChangeDate. Now create two (zero-or-one)-to-many relationships between the IssueStatus and IssueStatusChange tables. Name your navigation properties OldStatus and NewStatus.

Next, create a (zero-or-one)-to-many relationship between the Issue and IssueStatusChange tables. Figure 4-12 shows how your table looks in the designer.

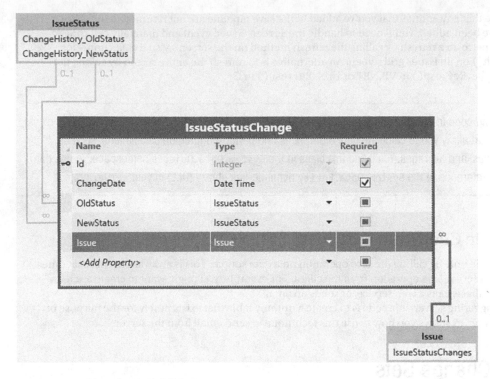

Figure 4-12. *Issue change table*

Open the Issue table in the table designer, and click on the Write Code button. Select the Issues_Updated method, and enter the code that's shown in Listing 4-5.

Listing 4-5. Retrieving Original Values in Code

VB:
File: HelpDeskVB\Server\UserCode\ApplicationDataService.vb ❶

```
Private Sub Issues_Updated(entity As Issue)                        ❷

    Dim issueHistory As IssueStatusChange =
    Me.DataWorkspace.ApplicationData.IssueStatusChanges.AddNew()

    issueHistory.OldStatus =
        entity.Details.Properties.IssueStatus.OriginalValue          ❸

    issueHistory.NewStatus = entity.IssueStatus
    issueHistory.Issue = entity
    issueHistory.ChangeDate = DateTime.UtcNow                        ❹

End Sub
```

C#:
File: HelpDeskCS\Server\UserCode\ApplicationDataService.cs   ❶

```
partial void Issues_Updated(Issue entity)                           ❷
{
    IssueStatusChange issueHistory =
        this.DataWorkspace.ApplicationData.
        IssueStatusChanges.AddNew();

    issueHistory.OldStatus =
        entity.Details.Properties.IssueStatus.OriginalValue;        ❸

    issueHistory.NewStatus = entity.IssueStatus;
    issueHistory.Issue = entity;
    issueHistory.ChangeDate = DateTime.UtcNow;                      ❹

}
```

Now run your application and modify an existing issue. When you do this, the code adds a record to the IssueStatusChange table.

The first thing to notice is the file location of the code file that LightSwitch creates when you click on the Write Code button ❶. LightSwitch creates your code file in the server project because the code relates to logic in the *server*-side save pipeline. Because the Issues table belongs in your Intrinsic database, LightSwitch names the file ApplicationDataService (after the name of your data source).

The signature of the updated method includes a parameter called entity ❷. This allows you to reference the item that's currently being saved.

The key part of this code is shown in ❸. The Details member of the entity object allows you to retrieve additional information about the entity, which allows you to find the original value of the IssueStatus property.

The final part of the code ❹ records the change time using UTC (Coordinated Universal Time). It's good practice to use UTC, particularly if you want to calculate time differences later on. It means that you don't need to consider the effects of Daylight Savings Time whenever you carry out calculations.

Notice that you don't need to call SaveChanges at the end of this code. As the save pipeline diagram (in Figure 4-10) shows, execution returns to the start of the save pipeline whenever you add entities from within the pipeline. If you trigger this code from a screen that shows issues and change records, remember that your application won't show the newly added change records when you save the screen. You'll have to call one of the Refresh methods, as explained earlier.

Discarding Items That Have Changed

You use change sets to determine which data items have changed and to write code that reverts data values back to their original state. The ability to do this is very powerful. You can make your application react to changes in data, or simplify the workflow of some process by creating tasks based on some data condition.

To put this into practice, the next example shows you how to write code that discards the changes that a user makes. Let's imagine that you've created an Issue details screen that allows users to edit issues and their related issue response records. By writing code that accesses the change set, you can add an Undo button that discards any changes that a user makes to the issue record but retain any changes to the child issue response records.

To create this example, add a new table to your application, name it IssueResponse, and create a one-to-many relationship between the Issue and IssueResponse tables. Appendix E shows the full definition of the IssueResponse table.

Create a details screen for your Issue table, and name it IssueDetail. In the Add New Screen dialog, select the IssueReponses check box in the Additional Data To Include section. Once Visual Studio opens the screen designer, select the Screen Command Bar section, and use the Add drop-down box to add a new button. When the Add Button dialog appears, choose the option to add a new method, and name your method DiscardIssueRespChanges. Open this method in the code editor, and enter the code that's shown in Listing 4-6.

Finally, use the Search Data Screen template to create a new screen that's based on the Issue table. Configure this screen so that it opens the selected issue in your IssueDetail screen.

Listing 4-6. Discarding Screen Changes

VB:
File: HelpDeskVB\Client\UserCode\IssueDetail.vb

```
Private Sub DiscardIssueRespChanges_Execute()
    For Each resp As IssueResponse In _
        DataWorkspace.ApplicationData.Details.GetChanges()          ❶
          .OfType(Of IssueResponse)()                               ❷
              resp.Details.DiscardChanges()                         ❸
    Next
End Sub
```

C#:
File: HelpDeskCS\Client\UserCode\IssueDetail.cs

```
partial void DiscardIssueRespChanges_Execute()
{
    foreach (IssueResponse resp in
    DataWorkspace.ApplicationData.Details.GetChanges().             ❶
      OfType<IssueResponse>())                                      ❷
    {
        resp.Details.DiscardChanges();                             ❸
    }
}
```

The GetChanges method ❶ returns a collection of entities that have been modified. By specifying the type IssueResponse ❷, you can find just the issue response records that have changed. This allows you to loop through a collection of issue responses and to undo the changes by calling the DiscardChanges method ❸.

Because LightSwitch makes it easy for you to carry out complex tasks in screen code, it's useful to consider exactly what you're trying to do before you write screen code. For example, it's relatively simple to write business logic in the Saving method that prevents a user from modifying closed issues by discarding their changes. However, this type of logic really should be added to methods that run on the server-side save pipeline. This is because server code is more reusable (you can call it from multiple screens and clients) and isn't susceptible to malicious users bypassing your business logic by accessing your data directly via the OData end point.

Managing Transactions in LightSwitch

Many computer systems rely on transactions to maintain data integrity and consistency. One of the key characteristics of a transaction is atomicity. Often known as the "all or nothing" rule, this means that operations in a transaction must either all succeed or all fail. The typical example of a transaction involves a bank payment. If you move $100 from your checking account into a savings account, two distinct data operations occur. The first operation subtracts $100 from your checking account, and the second operation adds $100 into your savings account. Both operations must succeed, or both must fail. What must never happen is for one operation to succeed and the other to fail.

There's no reason why LightSwitch shouldn't process your data with the same care as this banking example. So you'll be pleased to know that LightSwitch maintains the integrity of your data by supporting the use of transactions. In this section, you'll find out exactly how transactions work in LightSwitch.

■ **Note**   LightSwitch supports transactions against the intrinsic data source, attached SQL Server databases, and transaction-aware RIA services. It won't apply transactions against SharePoint or non-transaction-aware data sources.

Applying Transactions on Screens

The thought of using transactions might sound complicated, but in reality, this couldn't be further from the truth. If you create a screen that uses data from the intrinsic or attached SQL Server data sources, LightSwitch performs the save operation inside a transaction. The good news is that LightSwitch does this automatically for you, without you needing to do anything at all.

To illustrate this behavior, let's consider the issue details screen that you created earlier on. Let's suppose that a user edits an issue and creates an issue response record. If LightSwitch fails to create the issue response record, it won't apply the data changes to the issue record. In other words, LightSwitch applies all data changes on a screen atomically.

This is how it works technically. When the user clicks on the save button on a screen, the client calls the server's SaveChanges operation and supplies a change set. This call to SaveChanges starts the save pipeline process. The server creates a new data workspace and loads the change set that it receives from the client. It creates a SQL Server connection and starts a SQL Server transaction. During this process, LightSwitch applies a transaction isolation level of RepeatableRead. This means that other processes can't modify the data that's being read until the transaction completes. At the end of the save pipeline process, LightSwitch commits the SQL Server transaction if all the data operations succeed. If not, it rolls back the transaction.

This design imposes a restriction that you must be aware of when you're creating screens. The restriction is that, by default, LightSwitch prevents users from updating multiple data sources on the same screen. To illustrate this behavior, Figure 4-13 shows a screen that includes issue data from the Intrinsic database and the audit data from the external SQL Server data source. If LightSwitch were to allow users to update two data sources on the same screen, it would need to update both data sources independently by calling the SaveChanges operation for both data sources. Because LightSwitch can't guarantee the transactional integrity of the screen as a whole, it prevents users from updating multiple data sources on the same screen. It does this by allowing users to modify the data only in a single data source and rendering any controls that are bound to other data sources as read-only.

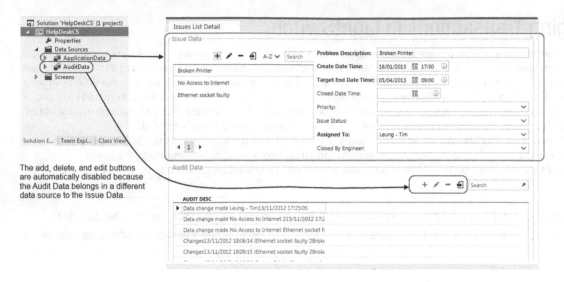

Figure 4-13. Screen sections are read-only when multiple data sources are used

Creating Transactions in the Save Pipeline

Although LightSwitch configures your screens to stop users from updating multiple data sources, it doesn't completely prohibit you from writing functionality that spans data sources. The restriction that prevents you from working with multiple data sources applies only at the screen. Once the code execution reaches the save pipeline, you can work with as many data sources as you like. To demonstrate this, the following example shows you how to work with multiple data sources in the save pipeline, and also shows you how to enlist data operations from multiple data sources into a single transaction.

This example shows you how to create an audit record in a second (SQL Server) data source called AuditDataSource when a user saves an engineer record in the Intrinsic database. If the update to the intrinsic database fails, the audit record must not be created (and vice versa). Figure 4-14 shows the schema of the audit table.

Column Name	Data Type	Allow Nulls
AuditID	int	☐
AuditDesc	nvarchar(MAX)	☑
LoginName	nvarchar(255)	☑
AuditDate	datetime	☑
		☐

Figure 4-14. Schema of the AuditDetail table

If you need some help creating an external database and table, SQL Server Books Online (BOL) is a great place to look. Here are links to the sections in BOL that will help you:

- **Creating a database:**
  http://msdn.microsoft.com/en-us/library/ms186312.aspx

- **Creating a table:**
  http://msdn.microsoft.com/en-us/library/ms188264.aspx

After you create your database and AuditDetail table, you'll need to attach it to your LightSwitch project, using the instructions from Chapter 2. Next, switch your project to File View and add a reference to the System.Transactions.dll in your server project.

Now open the Engineer table in the table designer and write code in the Executing and Executed methods as shown in Listing 4-7.

Listing 4-7. Creating Your Own Transaction Scope

VB:
File: HelpDeskVB\Server\UserCode\ApplicationDataService.vb

```
Imports System.Transactions
Imports System.Text

Namespace LightSwitchApplication

    Public Class ApplicationDataService

        Dim transaction As TransactionScope                              ❶

        Private Sub SaveChanges_Executing()

            Dim transactionOptions = New TransactionOptions()
            transactionOptions.IsolationLevel = IsolationLevel.ReadCommitted

            'Create an audit record as part of the transaction           ❷
            Me.transaction = New TransactionScope(
                TransactionScopeOption.Required, transactionOptions)

            Dim auditDesc As StringBuilder =
                New StringBuilder("Changes " + DateTime.Now.ToString() + " :")   ❸
            For Each changedEntity In
                Me.DataWorkspace.ApplicationData.Details.GetChanges()

                    auditDesc.AppendLine(changedEntity.Details.Entity.ToString())
            Next

            Using dataworkspace2 = Me.Application.CreateDataWorkspace()   ❹
                Dim auditRecord = dataworkspace2.AuditDataSource.AuditDetails.AddNew
                auditRecord.AuditDesc = auditDesc.ToString()
                    dataworkspace2.AuditDataSource.SaveChanges()
            End Using

        End Sub
```

```vb
        Private Sub SaveChanges_Executed()                                    ❺
            'Commit the transaction
            Me.transaction.Complete()
            Me.transaction.Dispose()
        End Sub

        Private Sub SaveChanges_ExecuteFailed(exception As System.Exception)
            'Rollback the transaction on an error                             ❻
            Me.transaction.Dispose()
        End Sub

    End Class

End Namespace
```

C#:
File: HelpDeskCS\Server\UserCode\ApplicationDataService.cs

```csharp
using System.Text;
using System.Transactions;

namespace LightSwitchApplication
{
    partial  class ApplicationDataService
    {
        TransactionScope transaction;                                         ❶

        partial void SaveChanges_Executing()
        {
            TransactionOptions transactionOptions = new TransactionOptions();
            transactionOptions.IsolationLevel = IsolationLevel.ReadCommitted;

            //Create an audit record as part of the transaction              ❷
            this.transaction = new TransactionScope(
                TransactionScopeOption.Required, transactionOptions);

            StringBuilder auditDesc =
                new StringBuilder("Changes " + DateTime.Now.ToString() + " :");  ❸
            foreach (var changedEntity in
                this.DataWorkspace.ApplicationData.Details.GetChanges())
            {
                auditDesc.AppendLine (changedEntity.Details.Entity.ToString());
            }
            using (var dataworkspace2 = this.Application.CreateDataWorkspace())  ❹
            {
                AuditDetail auditRecord =
                    dataworkspace2.AuditData.AuditDetails.AddNew();
                auditRecord.AuditDesc = auditDesc.ToString();
                dataworkspace2.AuditData.SaveChanges();
            }
        }
```

```
        partial void SaveChanges_Executed()
        {
            //Commit the transaction                                                ❺
            this.transaction.Complete();
            this.transaction.Dispose();
        }

        partial void SaveChanges_ExecuteFailed(System.Exception exception)
        {
            //Rollback the transaction on an error                                  ❻
            this.transaction.Dispose();
        }
    }
}
```

This code works by creating an ambient transaction in the Executing phase of the save pipeline and committing it in the Executed phase. Ambient transactions were introduced in .NET 2.0 and help simplify the task of working with transactions. Operations that are based on transaction-aware providers can enlist in ambient transactions. Therefore, you could also add transaction-aware RIA service data sources into your transactional logic.

The code first declares a class-level TransactionScope object ❶, and then sets it to a new instance of a TransactionScope object ❷ in the SaveChanges_Executing method. The TransactionScope constructor allows you to pass in a TransactionOption object. This object allows you to set the transaction isolation level.

The next piece of code builds up a string that summarizes the changes that have been made to the issue ❸. Next, it creates a new data workspace and uses this to create a record in the audit table ❹.

If the data changes in the Intrinsic database succeeds, the code commits the transaction in the SaveChanges_Executed method ❺. Otherwise, it disposes of the transaction scope in the SaveChanges_ExecuteFailed method, thus rolling back the transaction ❻. This means that the audit record that was created in the SaveChanges_Executing method will not be persisted to the data store, along with any other data changes that were attempted in the save pipeline.

For this code to work, you'll need to start the Distributed Transaction Coordinator service on your machine.

Understanding Concurrency

If two users modify the same record, LightSwitch prevents the second user from overwriting any changes made by the first user.

When this condition occurs, LightSwitch shows a data-conflict screen that allows the second user to resolve the conflict. For more-complex scenarios, you can even write your own code to resolve data conflicts.

Displaying a Data-Conflict Screen

LightSwitch checks for data conflicts whenever a user performs a save. If it detects a conflict, it displays a screen that allows the user to fix the data. (See Figure 4-15.)

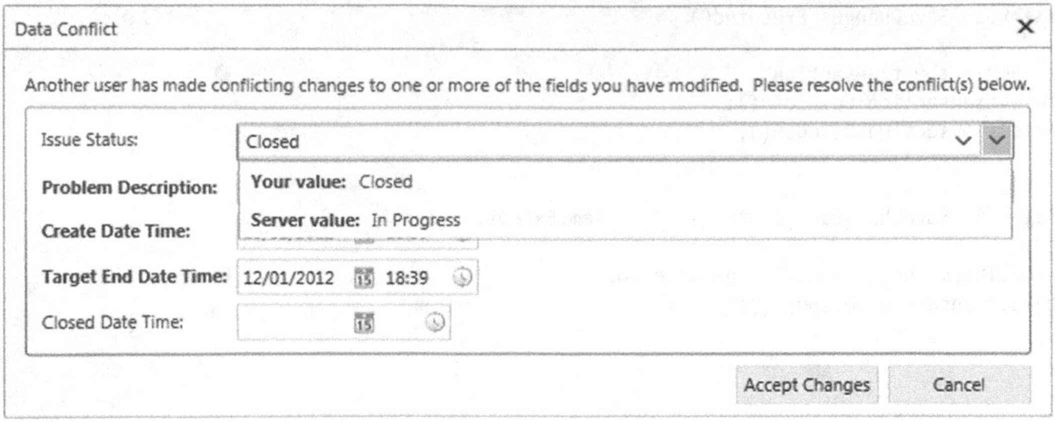

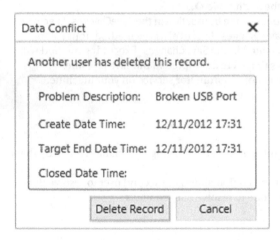

Figure 4-15. *Autogenerated data-conflict screen*

This screen shows the data when the record was first opened, the current data, and the proposed changes. This allows the user to make an informed choice before re-saving the record.

If you attempt to update a record that's been deleted by another user, LightSwitch displays the error message that's shown in Figure 4-16. In this case, it isn't possible for LightSwitch to recover the deleted record.

Figure 4-16. *Dialog box shown to the user when a record is deleted*

LightSwitch detects data conflicts by applying a row version number to each record. When the data service updates the database, it uses this to detect whether another user has modified the record by comparing the version numbers.

■ **Caution**   Because the data-conflict screens are autogenerated, the dialog that LightSwitch shows might contain data fields that you don't want the user to see. If this concerns you, make sure to carry out data-conflict tests on your screens so that you can see exactly the fields that LightSwitch exposes on your data-conflict screen.

EXERCISE 4.2 – VIEWING THE CONFLICT SCREEN

You can view the conflict screen by modifying the same record in two separate screens. Open the Engineer Search screen that you created in Exercise 3.3, and search for some engineers. Choose a record from the search results, and open it in the Details screen that you created in Exercise 3.1. Make a change to your record and save it. Without refreshing the results in your Search screen, edit the record in your Search screen and try saving your change. Examine the data-conflict screen that LightSwitch now shows you.

Handling Conflicts in Code

Aside from using LightSwitch's built in data-conflict screen, you can also perform data-conflict resolution manually in code. In this example, you'll build an issue details screen that's designed for managers. It allows a manager to always update an issue, even if it overwrites another user's changes.

To re-create this example, create a details screen for the Issue table and name it IssueDetailManager. When the screen designer opens, click on the Write Code button and select the saving method. Now enter the code that's shown in Listing 4-8.

Listing 4-8. Resolving Conflicts in Code

VB:
File: HelpDeskVB\Client\UserCode\IssueDetailManager.vb

```
Private Sub IssueDetailManager_Saving(ByRef handled As Boolean)

    handled = True                                                        ❶

    Try
        Me.DataWorkspace.ApplicationData.SaveChanges()                    ❷
    Catch ex As ConcurrencyException

                                                                          ❸
        For Each entityConflict In ex.EntitiesWithConflicts.OfType(Of Issue)()
            entityConflict.Details.EntityConflict.ResolveConflicts(
                Microsoft.LightSwitch.Details.ConflictResolution.ClientWins)    ❹
        Next

        Try
            Me.DataWorkspace.ApplicationData.SaveChanges()
            ShowMessageBox(
                "Your record was modified by another user. Your changes have
                    been kept.")
        Catch ex2 As Exception
            ' A general exception has occurred
            ShowMessageBox(ex2.Message.ToString())
        End Try

    End Try

End Sub
```

85

C#:
File: HelpDeskCS\Client\UserCode\IssueDetailManager.cs

```csharp
partial void IssueDetailManager_Saving(ref bool handled)
{
    handled = true;                                                           ❶

    try
    {
        DataWorkspace.ApplicationData.SaveChanges();                          ❷
    }
    catch (ConcurrencyException ex)
    {
        foreach (var entityConflict in ex.EntitiesWithConflicts.OfType<Issue>())   ❸
        {
            conflictingStatus.EntityConflict.ResolveConflicts(
                Microsoft.LightSwitch.Details.ConflictResolution.ClientWins);      ❹
        }

        try
        {
            this.DataWorkspace.ApplicationData.SaveChanges();
            this.ShowMessageBox(
              "Your record was modified by another user. Your changes have
                been kept.");
        }
        catch (Exception ex2)
        {
            // A general exception has occurred
            this.ShowMessageBox(ex2.Message.ToString());
        }
    }
}
```

When a data conflict occurs, the data service throws a ConcurrencyException. Handling this exception is the key to handling data conflicts in code.

The Saving method on the client includes a handled parameter. If you set this to true ❶, LightSwitch doesn't call the data service's save operation. This allows you to manually call the SaveChanges method ❷ and to catch the ConcurrencyException.

When the data service raises a ConcurrencyException, it returns the conflicting data in a collection called EntitiesWithConflicts ❸. LightSwitch represents conflicts by using an EntityConflict object. Figure 4-17 shows the methods that this object exposes.

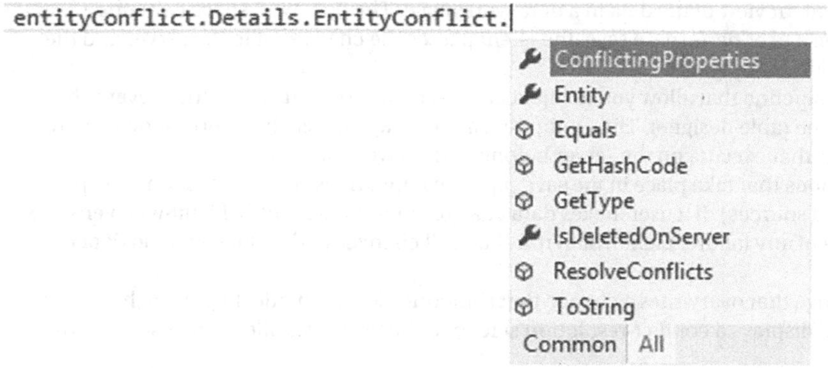

```
entityConflict.Details.EntityConflict.|
```

🔧	ConflictingProperties
🔧	Entity
⊗	Equals
⊗	GetHashCode
⊗	GetType
🔧	IsDeletedOnServer
⊗	ResolveConflicts
⊗	ToString

Common | All

Figure 4-17. *EntityConflict object*

If you need to, you can also find the exact properties that are in conflict by examining the ConflictingProperties collection. The IsDeletedOnServer property returns true if another user has deleted the record.

The last part of the code resolves the conflict by calling the ResolveConflicts method ❹. This method accepts the argument ConflictResolution.ClientWins or ConflictResolution.ServerWins. ClientWins overwrites the server copy with the out-of-date client version. ServerWins replaces the client version with the up-to-date server version.

To conclude this section, note that it isn't possible to handle concurrency exceptions on the server by using a method such as SaveChanges_ExecuteFailed. This is because you can't reinitiate a save from within the save pipeline. So even if you correct any data conflicts by writing code in the SaveChanges_ExecuteFailed method, there isn't any way for you to save those changes.

■ **Caution** Calling ResolveConflicts(ConflictResolution.ClientWins) will overwrite the server record in its entirety rather than just the properties that are in conflict. For example, if user A modifies the issue status and priority of an issue, and user B subsequently modifies just the issue status, ResolveConflicts(ConflictResolution.ClientWins) also overwrites the priority, even though the priority property is not in conflict.

Summary

LightSwitch provides APIs that allow you to create, read, update, and delete data through code. It generates data-access objects with names that match the tables and fields that you've defined in your project. This makes it intuitive for you to access your data in code. LightSwitch exposes the nonrequired fields you defined using nullable data types. To prevent null value exceptions, use the GetValueOrDefault method to retrieve the property values.

When you write client-side screen code, you can use the Application object to access the logged-on user and to call methods to open and access screens.

Screens raise events during their life cycle. You can handle these events by choosing a method from the list that appears when you click the Write Code button. For example, you can write code in the CanRead method to apply access control, or write code in the Saved method to carry out additional tasks after a user saves a screen. If you've added a collection of data and want to handle the Changed or SelectionChanged events, make sure to select the collection before clicking the Write Code button. If you don't, these methods won't appear.

Each screen contains an independent view of the data in a data workspace. The data workspace contains a change set for each data source. When a user performs a save, the client passes the change set to the server and the processing continues via the server-side save pipeline.

There are various phases in this pipeline that allow you to inject custom code. You can access these events by clicking on the Write Code button in the table designer. The tooltip that appears against each method shows where LightSwitch executes the code. Events that execute on the server belong to the save pipeline.

For each data source, the operations that take place in the save pipeline happen inside a transaction (except when working against SharePoint data sources). If a user makes data changes in multiple tables, LightSwitch ensures that all changes succeed. In the event of any failure, LightSwitch rolls back all changes and ensures that no data is modified.

If a user attempts to make a change that overwrites a change that someone else has made, LightSwitch automatically detects the conflict and displays a conflict-resolution screen to the user. This allows the user to correct their data and to resubmit the change.

CHAPTER 5

■ ■ ■

Validating Data

There's an old saying in IT: *garbage in, garbage out.* In essence, it means that if you enter nonsense data into a computer system, the results of any processing will also be rubbish. Fortunately, LightSwitch makes it easy for you to ensure that users can enter only clean data.

In this chapter, you'll learn how to do the following:

- Define data rules by using the table designer

- Write validation code that runs on the server

- Create validation code that runs only on the client

This chapter extends the HelpDesk application and shows you examples of how to apply validation rules. When a manager attempts to save an engineer record with an empty email address, the application shows a warning, but it still allows the user to save the record. You'll learn how to create these types of validation warnings.

You'll also learn how to create validation rules that apply to the HelpDesk issues. These include conditional rules (for example, if the user enters a closing date, "closed-by engineer" becomes mandatory) and comparison rules (such as "closing date can't be earlier than create date"). Users can upload issue documents, and you'll learn how to restrict file sizes and file numbers. If a user tries to delete an issue, the system prevents the deletion if there are outstanding responses.

When a manager edits an engineer record, the system ensures that the engineer's Social Security number (SSN) adheres to a valid format (using regular expressions). It also ensures that SSN and security reference numbers are unique for each engineer.

Understanding Validation in LightSwitch

LightSwitch allows you to apply validation and business rules in several places throughout your application. First, you can apply predefined validation by using the table designer. Any screens that you create in LightSwitch will then automatically validate the data type and data length that you've defined. If you change the data length of a property afterward, LightSwitch handles all changes to the validation without you having to do any extra work.

For more complex scenarios, you can write your own custom validation rules. You can define custom validation rules on tables and fields.

You can also define validation at a screen level. This allows you to perform validation that's specific to a particular screen. Finally, LightSwitch enforces any validation that's defined at the storage layer (for example, Microsoft SQL Server check constraints).

LightSwitch performs the validation on the client and server tiers. Figure 5-1 illustrates the workflow and shows the type of validation that's carried out on each tier.

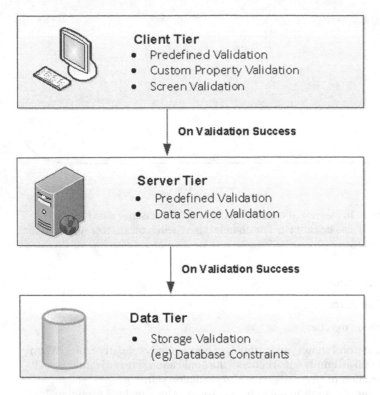

Figure 5-1. *The type of validation that runs on each tier*

On the client, LightSwitch performs screen and entity validation. It applies all predefined entity rules on the client as soon as any data change occurs. This allows your screen to show validation errors immediately to the user. For example, if the user enters text that exceeds the maximum length, LightSwitch alerts the user as soon as the focus leaves the text box.

Users must correct all validation errors before the client calls the server-side save operation. When the server receives the change set data, it repeats the validation that was carried out on the client. However, it won't repeat any custom screen validation because the screen object doesn't exist on the server. Therefore, LightSwitch won't re-validate any rules that you've defined on local screen properties. During server-side execution, LightSwitch also applies any custom rules that you might have defined in the save pipeline.

When LightSwitch completes the server validation, it submits the change to the data-storage layer (such as SQL Server for Intrinsic data). If the data fails any validation that's defined at the data store, the data store returns an exception to the server. The server then rolls back any data changes that have been applied, executes the code in the SaveChanges_ExecuteFailed method, and returns the data store error to the client. You can refer to the save pipeline diagram in Chapter 4, Figure 4-10 to remind yourself of this path through the save pipeline.

How Client Validation Works

LightSwitch uses an efficient client-side validation engine that caches the results after they are first derived. When the validation runs again, it saves the client from having to rerun all validation rules if just one single rule fails validation. Behind the scenes, LightSwitch uses a system of dependency tracking.

Let's suppose that you create a validation rule on a field/property called EndDate. This rule specifies that EndDate must be greater than StartDate. When the validation engine first processes this rule, it registers StartDate as a *validation dependency* of the EndDate validation rule. If the StartDate property changes afterward, LightSwitch schedules the EndDate validation rule for re-evaluation.

The validation engine tracks entities, properties, and most of the properties that are exposed by the LightSwitch API. Specifically, this includes the members that it exposes via the Details class. As you'll remember, this is the class that allows you to access the change set (as discussed in Chapter 4).

To further reduce overhead, the validation engine does not compute results for unmodified properties. For example, say you've created an engineer entity and set the surname property to Is Required. If you open a new data screen based on this entity, the screen won't report the surname as missing, even though it is. This is because LightSwitch evaluates the rule only when the surname property has changed. You'll need to type something into the surname text box and modify the value before LightSwitch checks the rule.

How MVVM Applies to Validation

If a user enters data that fails validation, LightSwitch summarizes the errors in a validation summary control. It also surrounds any offending controls with a red border to highlight the error (as shown in Figure 5-2).

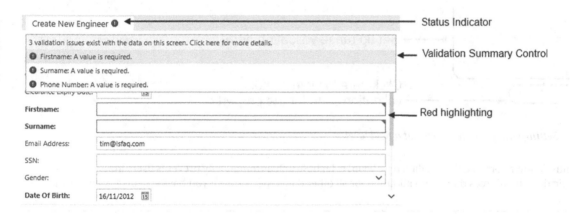

Figure 5-2. *Validation summary control*

These red borders are generated by the Silverlight control. Silverlight controls are bound to content items that are autogenerated by LightSwitch at runtime. These content items expose validation errors to the controls by implementing the INotifyDataErrorInfo interface.

So in keeping with the MVVM principles that were explained in Chapter 1, the View (Silverlight Control) performs only the red highlighting, and the actual validation logic is carried out by the View Model (the content item).

Defining Validation Rules

The simplest way to apply validation is to specify your rules declaratively through the table designer. Figure 5-3 highlights the validation rules that you can define for a table field, using the properties sheet.

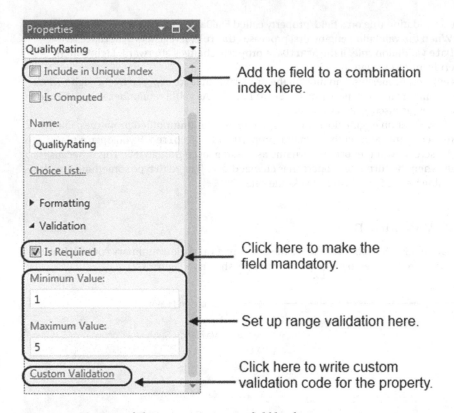

Figure 5-3. *Setting validation properties at a field level*

This illustration refers to a field of data type Double. LightSwitch automatically prevents users from entering non-numeric data. It enforces data type validation for all other data types without you having to do any extra work.

■ **Note**   LightSwitch creates storage constraints for many of these settings. This enables your database engine to enforce the same validation rules. For example, if you check the Include In Unique Index check box, LightSwitch creates a unique index in your SQL Server database.

Other property validation rules that you can specify through the property sheet for various data types include the following:

- **Data Length Validation:** The String data type allows you to specify the maximum amount of text that a user can enter.

- **Range Validation:** The Numeric and Date data types allow you to perform range validation by specifying the Minimum Value and Maximum Value properties. This type of range validation applies to the data types Date, DateTime, Decimal, Double, Money, and all Integer types.

- **Required Field Validation:** You can make a field mandatory by checking the Is Required check box. When you do this in the Intrinsic data source, LightSwitch also creates a NOT NULL constraint on the database column.

Note that many of the declarative validation settings apply only to your intrinsic database. If you attach an external SQL Server database table and view the properties of a numeric column, LightSwitch won't give you the option to set minimum and maximum values. You'll need to apply this rule in your SQL Server database by adding a check constraint to your database.

EXERCISE 5.1 – USING PREDEFINED VALIDATION

Open your Engineer table in the designer, and examine the validation options that you can set for each property. Select the firstname property, and set the Maximum Length property to 15. Run your application, open any of your engineer screens, and try entering a first name that exceeds 15 characters. How exactly does LightSwitch apply the maximum-length validation and prevent users from entering text that exceeds 15 characters? Now return to the table designer and increase the Maximum Length property to 20. Notice how LightSwitch automatically applies the new Maximum Length setting on all of your screens.

Writing Custom Validation

Although predefined validation works well for simple scenarios, you might want to enforce more complex validation rules. You can achieve this by writing custom validation, which you can apply at a property or entity level (as part of the save pipeline).

■ **Note**   Several of the code samples in this chapter contain LINQ (Language Integrated Query) syntax that might be unfamiliar to you. Don't worry if you struggle to understand this code—Chapter 6 will explain the syntax in further detail.

Identifying Where Validation Runs

LightSwitch can carry out validation on the client, on the server, or on both the client and server. It's important to target the validation at the right tier. For example, if you want to write validation that relies heavily on data, it wouldn't be efficient to download lots of data onto the client just to perform this task.

Custom validation requires you to click on the Write Code button and to write .NET code that applies your validation rules. To help you understand where validation takes place, Figure 5-4 illustrates the table and screen designers, highlights the three validation methods that you can choose, and shows you where LightSwitch carries out the validation.

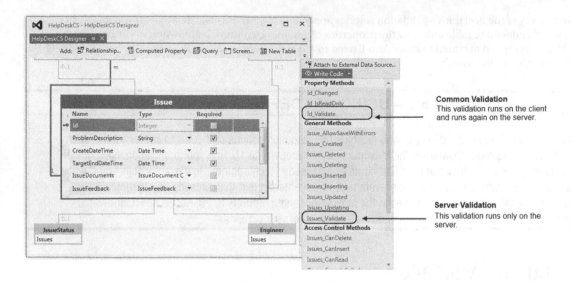

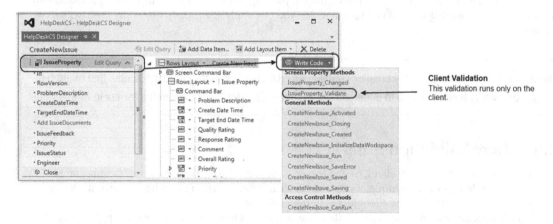

Figure 5-4. *Where validation is performed in relation to the designer*

Creating Validation Rules and Warnings

You can use custom validation to enforce mandatory rules or to simply provide optional warnings. The method for creating both types of validation is similar, so let's begin by creating a validation warning.

The engineer table includes an optional email address field. To encourage users to enter email addresses for engineers, this example creates a validation rule that prompts the user to supply an email address if the user leaves it blank.

To begin, open the engineer table and select the EmailAddress property. Open the properties sheet, and click on the Custom Validation link that appears in the Validation Group. This opens the code window and reveals a method stub that contains the commented-out line results.AddPropertyError("<Error-Message>"). Uncommenting this line produces a validation error when LightSwitch validates the email address. So the key to building custom validation is to build conditional logic around this line of code.

To complete this sample, replace your code with the code that's shown in Listing 5-1.

Listing 5-1. Creating a Validation Warning

VB:
File: HelpDeskVB\Common\UserCode\Engineer.vb

```vb
Private Sub EmailAddress_Validate(results As EntityValidationResultsBuilder)
    ' results.AddPropertyError("<Error-Message>")
    If String.IsNullOrEmpty(EmailAddress) Then                              ❶
        results.AddPropertyResult(
            "Providing an Email Address is recommended",
            ValidationSeverity.Informational)                              ❷
    End If
End Sub
```

C#:
File: HelpDeskCS\Common\UserCode\Engineer.cs

```csharp
partial void EmailAddress_Validate(EntityValidationResultsBuilder results)
{
    // results.AddPropertyError("<Error-Message>");

    if (System.String.IsNullOrEmpty (EmailAddress))                        ❶
    {
        results.AddPropertyResult(
            "Providing an Email Address is recommended",
            ValidationSeverity.Informational);                             ❷
    }
}
```

Now run your application. Use the engineer screens that you created in Chapter 3 to create an engineer record without an email address. When you attempt to save the record, LightSwitch displays a validation warning that prevents you from saving. (See Figure 5-5.) Because this is just a warning, LightSwitch allows the user to save the record by clicking on the Save button again.

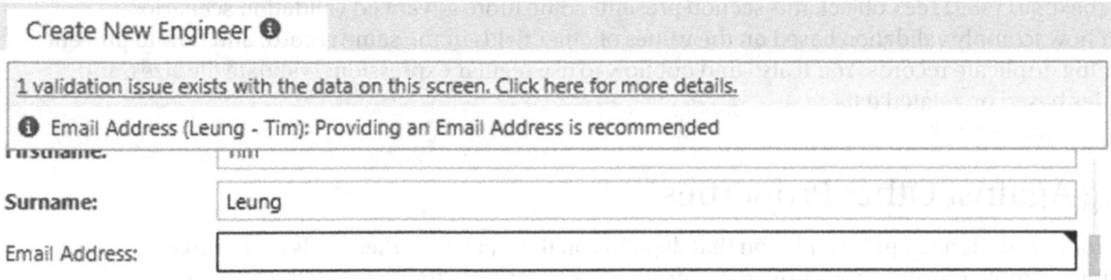

Create New Engineer ❶

1 validation issue exists with the data on this screen. Click here for more details.

❶ Email Address (Leung - Tim): Providing an Email Address is recommended

Firstname: Tim

Surname: Leung

Email Address:

Figure 5-5. *Validation warning*

Let's examine the code in Listing 5-1. The first part ❶ tests for an empty or null email address. If this condition is true, the code raises a validation warning by calling the result object's AddPropertyResult method ❷. The first parameter allows you to supply the error that's shown to the user.

The results object is of type EntityValidationResultsBuilder, and the methods that you can call are shown in Table 5-1.

Table 5-1. EntityValidationResultsBuilder Methods

Method	Description
AddPropertyError	Generates a validation error that refers to a property
AddPropertyResult	Produces a validation warning that refers to a property
AddEntityError	Generates a validation error that refers to an entity
AddEntityResult	Produces a validation warning that refers to an entity

The AddPropertyResult method that's used in this example allows users to save their changes after viewing the validation warning. The AddEntityResult method also behaves in the same way.

Both methods allow you to supply a severity level that can be either ValidationSeverity.Informational or ValidationSeverity.Warning. If you choose the ValidationSeverity.Informational option, LightSwitch displays a blue information icon in the validation summary, whereas choosing the warning level produces a red exclamation point icon. (These icons may not be shown if you've chosen a nonstandard Shell.)

If you use the AddPropertyError or AddEntityError methods instead, users will not be able to save their changes until they enter data that conforms to the validation rules.

■ **Tip**   Screen validation occurs immediately, as soon as a user leaves a text box or control. If you want to perform a task that runs as soon as a user leaves a control, you could add the logic to the property's validate method. For example, you could write code in the Surname_Validate method that changes the surname characters to uppercase, and this code will run as soon as the user leaves the surname text box. But before you apply this technique, you should read the section on using INotifyPropertyChanged in Chapter 7. This technique provides a better approach for running custom code when data changes.

Custom Validation Examples

Now that you understand how to write validation code and how to call the methods that belong to the EntityValidationResultsBuilder object, this section presents some more advanced validation scenarios.

You'll learn how to apply validation based on the values of other fields in the same record, and how to prevent users from entering duplicate records. You'll also find out how to use regular expressions, validate file sizes, and validate properties based on related data.

Comparing Against Other Properties

You can use custom validation to apply validation that depends on the values of other fields in the table.

The following example prevents users from entering an issue Close Date that's earlier than the Create Date.

To create this rule, open the Issue table in the table designer and select the ClosedDateTime property. Open the properties sheet, click on the Custom Validation link, and enter the code that's shown in Listing 5-2.

Listing 5-2. Compare Validation

VB:
File: HelpDeskVB\Common\UserCode\Issue.vb

```
Private Sub ClosedDateTime_Validate(results As EntityValidationResultsBuilder)
   If CreateDateTime > ClosedDateTime Then
      results.AddPropertyError("Closed Date cannot be before Create Date")
   End If
End Sub
```

C#:
File: HelpDeskCS\Common\UserCode\Issue.cs

```
partial void ClosedDateTime_Validate(EntityValidationResultsBuilder results)
{
    if (this.CreateDateTime > this.ClosedDateTime )
    {
        results.AddPropertyError("Closed Date cannot be before Create Date");
    }
}
```

If you now run any screen that uses the Issue table, you'll be unable to set the Closed Date field to a value that's earlier than the Create Date.

■ **Caution** If you want to create a validation rule by using the Write Code button, rather than the Custom Validation link, you must select the property (for example, ClosedDateTime) before clicking the Write Code button. If you don't, the property's validate method (ClosedDateTime_Validate) will not appear in the drop-down menu of available options.

Mandating Data Using Conditions

You can very easily make fields mandatory: just select the Is Required check box for your property in the table designer. However, you might want to make a field mandatory based on some other condition, and to do this, you need to write custom validation.

The Issue table contains a ClosedDateTime field and a ClosedByEngineer field. If the user enters a ClosedByEngineer value, the ClosedDateTime field becomes mandatory. Otherwise, the CloseDateTime field can be left blank.

In the previous example, the properties sheet for the ClosedDateTime property shows a Custom Validation link that opens the code window and creates a method stub. The properties sheet for the ClosedByEngineer field doesn't include a Custom Validation link. This is because ClosedByEngineer refers to a related item. It belongs on the many side of a (zero-or-1)-to-many relationship between the engineer table.

So to access the code window, you'll need to select the ClosedByEngineer navigation property in the table designer and click on the Write Code button. When the drop-down menu appears, you'll be able to validate ClosedByEngineer by selecting the ClosedByEngineer_Validate method that appears. (See Figure 5-6.) Now enter the code that's shown in Listing 5-3.

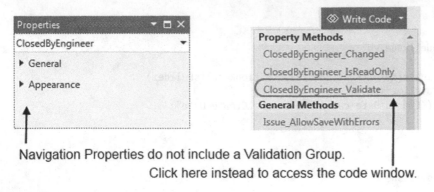

Navigation Properties do not include a Validation Group.
Click here instead to access the code window.

Figure 5-6. *Creating validation on navigation properties*

Listing 5-3. Making Fields Mandatory Based on Some Condition

VB:
File: HelpDeskVB\Common\UserCode\Issue.vb

```
Private Sub ClosedByEngineer_Validate(
     results As EntityValidationResultsBuilder)
   If ClosedByEngineer IsNot Nothing And
     ClosedDateTime.HasValue = False Then
        results.AddPropertyError("Closed Date must be entered")
   End If
End Sub
```

C#:
File: HelpDeskCS\Common\UserCode\Issue.cs

```
partial void ClosedByEngineer_Validate(
    EntityValidationResultsBuilder results)
{
    if (ClosedByEngineer != null &&
      ClosedDateTime.HasValue == false)
    {
        results.AddPropertyError("Closed Date must be entered");
    }
}
```

Validating Patterns with Regular Expressions

Regular expressions (regexes) allow you to carry out validation that involves matching string patterns. You might use regexes to validate the formats of Social Security numbers, bank sort codes, postal codes, or domain names.

This technique uses the Regex class in the System.Text.RegularExpressions namespace. Listing 5-4 shows the code that you would use to validate the format of the Social Security Number field in the Engineer table.

Listing 5-4. Regex Validation to Check Social Security Numbers

VB:
File: HelpDeskVB\Common\UserCode\Engineer.vb

```vb
Imports System.Text.RegularExpressions

Private Sub SSN_Validate_Validate(
    results As EntityValidationResultsBuilder)

    Dim pattern As String =
        "^(?!000)([0-6]\d{2}|7([0-6]\d|7[012]))([ -]?)(?!00)\d\d\3(?!0000)\d{4}$"
    If (Not SSN Is Nothing) AndAlso
        (Regex.IsMatch(SSN, pattern) = False) Then              ❶
            results.AddPropertyError(
                "Enter SSN in format 078-05-1120")
    End If

End Sub
```

C#:
File: HelpDeskCS\Common\UserCode\Engineer.cs

```csharp
using System.Text.RegularExpressions;

partial void SSN_Validate(
    EntityValidationResultsBuilder results)
{
    string pattern =
        @"^(?!000)([0-6]\d{2}|7([0-6]\d|7[012]))([ -]?)(?!00)\d\d\3(?!0000)\d{4}$";
    if (SSN !=null && !Regex.IsMatch(SSN, pattern))             ❶
    {
        results.AddPropertyError(
            "Enter SSN in format 078-05-1120");
    }
}
```

This code highlights the use of the IsMatch method ❶. This method allows you to pass in an expression, and the method returns a Boolean result that indicates whether a match is found.

■ **Tip**   There's a famous quote by Jamie Zawinski that illustrates how difficult using regular expressions can be:

Some people, when confronted with a problem, think, "I know, I'll use regular expressions." Now they have two problems.'

To make life easy for yourself, visit web sites such as http://regexlib.com or http://www.regular-expressions.info. There, you'll find libraries of prebuilt expressions that you can easily reuse.

Validating File Sizes

If you have tables that store image or binary data, it's useful to restrict the size of the files that users can upload into your application. You can do this by writing code that checks the size of the image or file that the user uploads.

The Engineer table contains a field called EngineerPhoto that stores a photo of the engineer. Listing 5-5 shows the code that ensures that users cannot upload images that are greater than 512 kilobytes (KBs).

Listing 5-5. Validating File Sizes

VB:
File: HelpDeskVB\Common\UserCode\Engineer.vb

```
Private Sub EngineerPhoto_Validate(
    results As EntityValidationResultsBuilder)
  If Me.EngineerPhoto IsNot Nothing Then
     Dim sizeInKB = Me.EngineerPhoto.Length / 1024
     If sizeInKB > 512 Then
        results.AddPropertyError("Image Size cannot be > 512kb")
     End If
  End If
End Sub
```

C#:
File: HelpDeskCS\Common\UserCode\Engineer.cs

```
partial void EngineerPhoto_Validate(
    EntityValidationResultsBuilder results)
{
    if (EngineerPhoto != null)
    {
        var sizeInKB = EngineerPhoto.Length / 1024;
        if (sizeInKB > 512)
        {
            results.AddPropertyError("Image Size cannot be > 512kb");
        }
    }
}
```

LightSwitch exposes Binary and Image properties in code as *byte arrays*. The code that's shown here calculates the file size in KBs by dividing the byte array length by 1,024. If you want to calculate the size in megabytes (MBs), you would divide by 1,048,576. Table 5-2 shows the conversion values that you would use. If you need to carry out lots of conversions, you can make this code more reusable by adding it to a helper class and method.

Table 5-2. Converting a Byte Array Length

Unit of Measurement	Divisor
Kilobyte (KB)	1,024
Megabyte (MB)	1,048,576 (1,024 × 1,024)
Gigabyte (GB)	1,073,741,824 (1,024 × 1,024 × 1,024)
Terabyte (TB)	1,099,511,627,776 (1,024 × 1,024 × 1,024 × 1,024)

Checking Against Child Collections

When you're writing custom validation, you can use code to access child collections and records. In this example, the HelpDesk system stores documents that are related to each issue. Each issue can have many documents, and the documents are stored in a table called IssueDocument.

You can write custom validation that enforces a maximum of ten documents per issue. This allows you to preserve storage space on the server.

Just like the Closed Engineer example earlier in the chapter, the IssueDocument property is a navigation property. But unlike the earlier example, the Issue table belongs on the zero-or-1 end of a (zero-or-1)-to-many relationship.

For these types of navigation properties, LightSwitch doesn't allow you to write property-level navigation that runs on both the client and server. Instead, you need to create entity (or data-service) validation that runs only on the server.

To create this validation, open the Issue table and click the Write Code button. Select the Issues_Validate method that belongs in the General Methods group (as shown in Figure 5-7). Now enter the code that's shown in Listing 5-6.

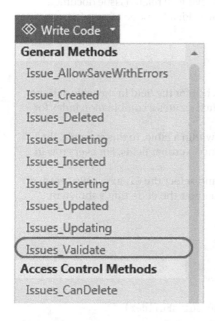

Figure 5-7. *Creating entity validation that runs on the server*

Listing 5-6. Validating the Counts of Child Items

VB:
File: HelpDeskVB\Server\UserCode\ApplicationDataService.vb

```
Private Sub Issues_Validate(
    entity As Issue, results As EntitySetValidationResultsBuilder)

  If entity.IssueDocuments.Count() > 10 Then
    results.AddEntityError(
        "Issues can only contain a maximum of 10 documents")
  End If
```

```
End Sub
```

C#:
File: HelpDeskCS\Server\UserCode\ApplicationDataService.cs

```csharp
partial void Issues_Validate(Issue entity, EntitySetValidationResultsBuilder results)
{
    if (entity.IssueDocuments.Count() > 10)
    {
        results.AddEntityError(
            "Issues can only contain a maximum of 10 documents");
    }
}
```

The code in Listing 5-6 shows how you can apply an aggregate function to a child collection. When you call the Count function on a navigation property, LightSwitch produces the count by retrieving all related issue document records. Because each issue document record can be large, this type of validation is ideally suited to running on the server.

Enforcing Uniqueness and Preventing Duplicates

LightSwitch allows you to define a unique field by selecting the Is Unique check box for the field in the table designer. If you select the Is Unique check box for more than one field in a table, LightSwitch creates a combination index for the set of fields that you've selected.

You may want to enforce uniqueness on two or more fields independently within a table. In this example, the Engineer table contains Social Security Number and Security Clearance Reference Number fields. For every row in the Engineer table, both of these fields must be unique.

To apply this validation, open the Engineer table in the table designer and select the ClearanceReference property. From the properties sheet, click on the Custom Validation link and enter the code that's shown in Listing 5-7.

Listing 5-7. Enforcing Unique Records

VB:
File: HelpDeskVB\Common\UserCode\Engineer.vb

```vb
Private Sub ClearanceReference_Validate(results As EntityValidationResultsBuilder)

    If Len(Me.ClearanceReference) > 0 Then
        Dim duplicateOnServer = (
            From eng In
            Me.DataWorkspace.ApplicationData.Engineers.Cast(Of Engineer)()
            Where
            eng.Id <> Me.Id AndAlso
            eng.ClearanceReference.Equals(Me.ClearanceReference,
                StringComparison.CurrentCultureIgnoreCase)
            ).ToArray()                                                      ❶

        Dim duplicateOnClients = (
            From eng In
            Me.DataWorkspace.ApplicationData.Details.GetChanges().
                OfType(Of Engineer)()
```

```vbnet
        Where
        eng IsNot Me AndAlso
        eng.ClearanceReference.Equals(Me.ClearanceReference,
            StringComparison.CurrentCultureIgnoreCase)
        ).ToArray()                                                          ❷

    Dim deletedOnClient = Me.DataWorkspace.ApplicationData.Details.GetChanges().
        DeletedEntities.OfType(Of Engineer)().ToArray()                      ❸
    Dim anyDuplicates = duplicateOnServer.Union(duplicateOnClients).Distinct().
        Except(deletedOnClient).Any()

    If anyDuplicates Then
        results.AddPropertyError("
            The clearance reference already exists")                         ❹
    End If

  End If

End Sub
```

C#:
File: HelpDeskCS\Common\UserCode\Enginner.cs

```csharp
partial void ClearanceReference_Validate(EntityValidationResultsBuilder results)
{
    if (ClearanceReference!=null &&
        ClearanceReference.Length > 0)
    {
        var duplicatesOnServer = (
            from eng in
                this.DataWorkspace.ApplicationData.Engineers.Cast<Engineer>()
            where (eng.Id != this.Id ) &&
            eng.ClearanceReference.Equals(this.ClearanceReference,
                StringComparison.CurrentCultureIgnoreCase)
            select eng
                ).ToArray();                                                 ❶

        var duplicatesOnClient = (
            from eng in
                this.DataWorkspace.ApplicationData.Details.GetChanges().
                OfType<Engineer>()
            where (eng != this) &&
            eng.ClearanceReference.Equals(this.ClearanceReference,
                StringComparison.CurrentCultureIgnoreCase)
            select eng
                ).ToArray();                                                 ❷

        var deletedOnClient =
            this.DataWorkspace.ApplicationData.Details.GetChanges().
                DeletedEntities.OfType<Engineer>().ToArray();                ❸
```

```
    var anyDuplicates =
      duplicatesOnServer.Union(duplicatesOnClient).
        Distinct().Except(deletedOnClient).Any();

    if (anyDuplicates)
    {
        results.AddPropertyError(
            "The clearance reference already exists");     ❹
    }
  }
}
```

This code might seem trickier than you first expect. This is because you need to check for duplicates on the client (the user might enter several new engineers in a datagrid) in addition to checking for duplicates on the server.

First, the code checks that no server records match the clearance reference number that's been entered by the user ❶. It uses a where clause that excludes the ID of the current record—if not, the query would return a match for the identical record on the server.

Next, it checks for duplicate clearance reference numbers that have been entered by the user on the client ❷. It then performs a query that returns any deleted records ❸.

If duplicate records were found on the server or client but are also marked as deleted, the clearance number passes validation. If not, the code raises a property error that prevents the user from saving the record ❹.

EXERCISE 5.2 – CREATING CUSTOM VALIDATION

Use the code editor to add some custom validation rules on some of the HelpDesk tables. Here are some rules that you can add: Engineer date of birth—must not be in the future; Engineer Age—must be 17 or above; Login Name—cannot contain special characters; App Settings Mail Server—must be a valid IP address, or fully qualified server name.

Performing Screen Validation

A big advantage of the validation that you've seen so far is that LightSwitch applies the validation rules globally throughout your application. Once you define table or field validation, LightSwitch applies the rules to every screen in your application and every screen that you might create in the future.

However, you might want to perform validation that applies to only a single screen. To do this, you need to apply validation on the screen property.

In this example, we'll make the priority field mandatory on the issue detail screen. By validating at a screen level, you can later extend the system to allow end users to raise their own issues, but not allow users to prioritize their own issues.

To begin, open the issue detail screen from Chapter 4 and select the issue property in the screen member list. Click on the Write Code button, and select the validate method from the Screen Property Methods group, as shown in Figure 5-8.

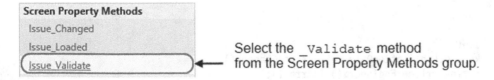

Figure 5-8. *Creating screen validation*

Now enter the code as shown in Listing 5-8.

Listing 5-8. Performing Screen-Level Validation

VB:
File: HelpDeskVB\Client\UserCode\IssueDetail.vb

```
Private Sub Issue_Validate(
    results As ScreenValidationResultsBuilder)                    ❶

    If Issue.Priority Is Nothing Then
        results.AddScreenError("Priority must be entered")
    End If

End Sub
```

C#:
File: HelpDeskCS\Client\UserCode\IssueDetail.cs

```
partial void Issue_Validate(ScreenValidationResultsBuilder results)    ❶
{
    if (this.Issue.Priority == null)
    {
        results.AddScreenError("Priority must be entered");
    }
}
```

■ **Caution**   The main purpose of this example is to show you that it's possible to carry out client-side screen validation, and to illustrate the code that produces the validation warnings. Screen validation isn't secure because malicious users can circumvent your validation rules by directly accessing your data service through the OData endpoint. Where possible, you should always try to enforce your validation rules by writing code that LightSwitch executes on the server. Screen validation is more suitable for validating local properties to support some process that runs locally on your screen. You'll find out more about local properties in Chapter 7.

This code looks similar to the earlier examples, but one difference is that the results object is of type ScreenValidationResultsBuilder ❶. This object includes two methods that are called AddScreenError and AddScreenMessage. These methods allow you to assign a validation error or warning that targets the whole screen. Another method you can call is AddPropertyError. This method allows you to raise a validation error and, optionally, associate it with a specific screen property by supplying a screen property name.

Validating Deletions

The examples so far have shown you how to validate data when users insert or update records. In some circumstances, you might also want to control the rules that govern the deletion of data.

In this section, you'll learn how to create a validation rule that prevents users from deleting issues where the issue status is still set to open. There are two places where you can perform this validation: on the client or on the server. The advantage of performing the validation on the client is that it involves much simpler code. But the disadvantage is that it's less secure because users can circumvent your rule by accessing your data service directly.

To create this example, open the issue detail from the previous example. When the screen designer opens, carry out the following tasks:

1. Select the Screen Command Bar, click the add drop-down, and select the New Button option. When the Add Button dialog appears, choose the Write My Own method and name it DeleteIssue.

2. Select the Issue property in the screen member list, click the Add Code button, and select the Issue_Validate method.

3. When the code editor opens, add the DeleteIssue_Execute and Issue_Validate code that's shown in Listing 5-9.

4. If you haven't done so, create a search screen or an editable grid screen that allows you to open your issue details screen at runtime.

Listing 5-9. Validating Deletions

VB:
File: HelpDeskVB\Client\UserCode\IssueDetail.vb

```
Private Sub DeleteIssue_Execute()
    Issue.Delete()                                              ❶
End Sub

Private Sub Issue_Validate(
    results As ScreenValidationResultsBuilder)

    If Issue.Details.EntityState = EntityState.Deleted AndAlso  ❷
       (Not Issue.IssueStatus Is Nothing) AndAlso
          (Issue.IssueStatus.StatusDescription = "Open") Then

       results.AddScreenError("Unable to delete open issue")    ❸

    End If

End Sub
```

C#:
File: HelpDeskCS\Client\UserCode\IssueDetail.cs

```
partial void DeleteIssue_Execute()
{
    Issue.Delete();                                            ❶
}

partial void Issue_Validate(ScreenValidationResultsBuilder results)
{
    if (Issue.Details.EntityState == EntityState.Deleted &&    ❷
        Issue.IssueStatus != null
          && Issue.IssueStatus.StatusDescription == "Open")
```

```
    {
        Issue.Details.DiscardChanges();
        results.AddScreenError ("Unable to delete open issue");        ❸
    }
}
```

The first part of this code contains the logic that's behind the `DeleteIssue` button. This code deletes the issue by calling its `Delete` method ❶.

The code in the `Validate` method checks the issue entity's `EntityState` ❷. If the issue is marked as deleted, the code checks the issue status. If the status is set to open, the code undeletes the issue and adds a screen error ❸ to inform the user that the record can't be saved.

Validating Deletions on the Server

Validating deletions by using screen validation is relatively simple. I included the last example to highlight its simplicity, but it's far from ideal. Relying on the client to perform validation isn't good practice. If you want to apply the deletion rule throughout your application, you'll need to write code in every single place where users can delete an issue. But if you want to validate deletions on the server, the process can be quite complex.

This complexity arises because LightSwitch doesn't apply validation rules on deleted entities during the save pipeline process. If it did, your users would be forced to fill in all mandatory fields, even just to delete a record!

In this example, you'll learn how to apply a slightly different deletion rule that includes a check on child records. The HelpDesk system allows engineers to respond to issues by adding records into a table called `IssueResponse`. If the response requires some input from the user, the engineer would set a field called `AwaitingClient` to true.

The following example shows you how to prevent issues from being deleted if there are responses that are awaiting client. This process consists of at least two parts (and optionally three):

1. Carry out the validation check in the entity set's `Validate` method.

2. If errors are found, raise an exception in the entity set's `Deleting` method.

3. On the client, undelete the records that have failed validation (Optional).

To create the code in your entity set's `validate` method, open the `Issue` table in the table designer, click on the Write Code button, and select the `Validate` method. Enter the code that's shown in the first part of Listing 5-10.

Next, create a screen that's based on the `Issue` table. Choose the Editable Grid Screen template, and name your screen `EditableIssuesGrid`. When the screen designer opens, click the Write Code button, and select the `SaveError` method. Enter the code that's shown in the second part of Listing 5-10.

Listing 5-10. Validating Deletions on the Server

VB:
File: HelpDeskVB\Server\UserCode\ApplicationDataService.vb

```
Private Sub Issues_Validate(entity As Issue,
    results As Microsoft.LightSwitch.EntitySetValidationResultsBuilder)

    ' Check for validation errors for deletions
    If entity.Details.EntityState = EntityState.Deleted Then          ❶
        If entity.IssueResponses.Where(
            Function(s) s.AwaitingClient).Any() Then                  ❷
            results.AddEntityError(
                "Cannot delete issues with responses awaiting client.")  ❸
        End If
    End If
```

```vb
End Sub

Private Sub Issues_Deleting(entity As Issue)

    ' Check for validation errors for deletions
    If entity.Details.ValidationResults.Errors.Any Then
      Throw New ValidationException(Nothing,
          Nothing, entity.Details.ValidationResults)          ❹
    End If

    ' Cascade delete children because delete rule is Restricted
    For Each resp In entity.IssueResponses
      resp.Delete()                                            ❺
    Next

End Sub
```

File: HelpDeskVB\Client\UserCode\EditableIssuesGrid.vb

```vb
' This is the screen code
Private Sub EditableIssuesGrid_SaveError(
    exception As Exception, ByRef handled As Boolean)

    ' Un-delete deleted records that had server-side validation errors
    Dim validationExc = TryCast(exception, ValidationException)

    If validationExc IsNot Nothing Then
      Dim entities = From v In validationExc.ValidationResults
          Let e = TryCast(v.Target, IEntityObject)
            Where e IsNot Nothing AndAlso
                e.Details.EntityState = EntityState.Deleted
      Select e
      For Each e In entities
          e.Details.DiscardChanges()
      Next
    End If

End Sub
```

C#:
File: HelpDeskCS\Server\UserCode\ApplicationDataService.cs

```csharp
partial void Issues_Validate(Issue entity, EntitySetValidationResultsBuilder results)
{
    if (entity.Details.EntityState == EntityState.Deleted)          ❶
    {
        if (entity.IssueResponses.Where(s => s.AwaitingClient).Any())  ❷
        {
            results.AddEntityError(
                "Cannot delete issues with responses awaiting client.");  ❸
        }
    }
}
```

```
partial void Issues_Deleting(Issue entity)
{
    // Check for validation errors for deletions
    if (entity.Details.ValidationResults.Errors.Any())
    {
        throw new ValidationException(
            null, null, entity.Details.ValidationResults);          ❹
    }

    // Cascade delete children because delete rule is Restricted
    foreach (var childResp in entity.IssueResponses)
    {
        childResp.Delete();                                         ❺
    }
}
```

File: HelpDeskCS\Client\UserCode\EditableIssuesGrid.cs
// This is the screen code

```
partial void EditableIssuesGrid_SaveError(
    Exception exception, ref bool handled)
{
    ValidationException validationExc =
        (exception as ValidationException);
    if (validationExc != null)
    {

        var entities = from v in validationExc.ValidationResults
                       let e = (v.Target as IEntityObject)
                       where (e != null &&
                           e.Details.EntityState == EntityState.Deleted)
                       select e;

        foreach (IEntityObject e in entities)
        {
            e.Details.DiscardChanges();
        }
    }
}
```

The server-side Validate method checks the EntityState to see whether the issue is marked as deleted ❶. If this condition is true, the code queries the IssueResponses navigation property to find any related issue-response records that have their AwaitingClient ❷ property set to true. If one or more records exist, the code calls the AddEntityError method to record the fact that the entity has failed validation ❸. Chapter 6 will explain the LINQ syntax and Any operator in more detail.

Because LightSwitch ignores validation errors on deleted entities, code execution continues into the pre-process entities phase of the save pipeline. (See Figure 4-10.) Here, the save pipeline executes the code in the Deleting method, and the code raises an exception if the AddEntityError method was called in the Validate method ❹. By raising an exception here, the save pipeline aborts the transaction and executes the SaveChanges_ExecuteFailed method. This prevents the record from being deleted.

An important point is that if you want to perform validation against child records during a delete, you need to turn off the Cascade Delete option on the relationship (that is, set it to Restricted). If not, the save pipeline deletes any related child records prior to calling the validate method and you won't be able to access any issue-response records in the validate method of your issue entity.

Because of this, the code manually carries out the cascade delete behavior by deleting the child records in the deleting method ❺.

The second part of the code in Listing 5-10 refers to screen code that handles the save error event. This code finds the deleted entities and undeletes those entities. This allows the user to clearly see that the deletion has failed. Note that if you allow users to delete items other than issues, you should modify the screen code so that it checks that the deleted item is an issue before undeleting it.

■ **Note**   You can refer to the Save Pipeline diagram in Figure 4-10 to help you follow the workflow in this example.

Accessing Validation Results in Code

If you need to access validation results in code, you can do so by using the details API. Listing 5-11 provides some example syntax.

Listing 5-11. Accessing Validation Results in Screen Code

VB:
```
' Examples of calling the IsValidated and HasErrors properties
Dim firstnameValid As Boolean = Me.Details.Properties.Firstname.IsValidated
Dim firstnameHasErrors As Boolean =
    Me.Details.Properties.Firstname.ValidationResults.HasErrors

' Get a count of all results with a severity of 'Error'
Dim errorCount As Integer = Me.Details.ValidationResults.Errors.Count

' Concatenate the error messages into a single string
Dim allErrors As String = ""
For Each result In Me.Details.ValidationResults
    allErrors += result.Message + " "
Next
```

C#:
```
// Examples of calling the IsValidated and HasErrors properties
bool firstnameValid = this.Details.Properties.Firstname.IsValidated;
bool firstnameHasErrors = this.Details.Properties.Firstname.ValidationResults.HasErrors;

// Get a count of all results with a severity of 'Error'.
int errorCount = this.Details.ValidationResults.Errors.Count();

// Concatenate the error messages into a single string.
string allErrors="";
foreach (ValidationResult result in  this.Details.ValidationResults ){
    allErrors += result.Message  + " ";
}
```

You can use the Details.Properties object to return only those errors for a specific field (for example, Details.Properties.Firstname).

LightSwitch validates properties only when they are modified, and the IsValidated property indicates whether a property is validated. The HasErrors property indicates whether or not any validation errors have been found.

The ValidationResults collection allows you to view the detail of each validation error. When you access ValidationResults, LightSwitch validates all objects that have not already been validated.

Database Validation

You can create your own validation rules at the database when working with an external SQL Server database. For example, you could create a SQL Server *check constraint* that validates your data against a T-SQL expression. If a user attempts to enter data that conflicts with the database rules you defined, LightSwitch will return the error to the user.

Earlier in this chapter, I showed you how to prevent users from entering duplicate records. If you were using an attached SQL Server database, you could apply this validation using a SQL Server unique constraint instead. To create a unique constraint, open your table in SQL Server Management Studio. Open the Indexes/Keys dialog box by clicking on the toolbar's Index button.

In the General section of this dialog, choose the column that you want to apply the index on, set the Is Unique option to Yes, and select the type Unique Key.

Figure 5-9 illustrates a unique constraint on the SSN column in the engineer table. If you attempt to enter a duplicate SSN, LightSwitch displays the database constraint error in summary panel, as shown in Figure 5-10. Notice that the error message includes a heading that indicates that the error originates from the server. If the server returns any other errors, those errors are also grouped into the same block.

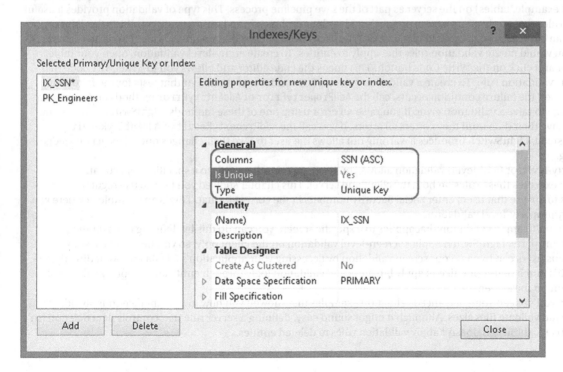

Figure 5-9. *Creating a unique index*

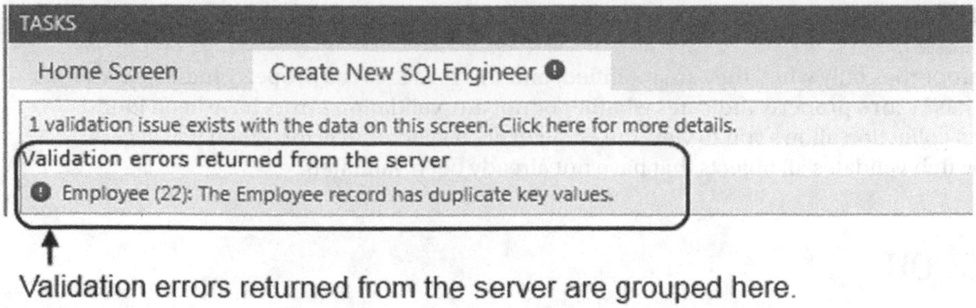

Validation errors returned from the server are grouped here.

Figure 5-10. *Unique constraint violation error*

Summary

LightSwitch allows you to apply validation in two ways: predefined validation, and custom validation. Predefined validation allows you to define rules by using the table designer. They allow you to make fields mandatory, set maximum field lengths, and set minimum and maximum values for numeric data types.

LightSwitch applies predefined validation without you needing to carry out any extra work. If, for example, you increase the length of a text field, LightSwitch's validation takes account of this change automatically.

For more-complex scenarios, you can apply custom validation by writing custom code. This allows you to define validation rules on entities, properties, and screens. LightSwitch executes the validation rules that you apply to entities (for example, tables) on the server as part of the save pipeline process. This type of validation provides a useful way to add rules that apply to navigation properties. This chapter showed you how to create conditional validation that makes an issue's "close date" field mandatory if the user selects a "closed by engineer" rule. This is an example of where you would create validation rules that apply to entities. To create entity-level validation, open your table in the designer and click on the Write Code button. This opens the code editor and allows you to write .NET code that applies your validation rule. To create a validation rule, write a conditional statement that tests for the failure of your rule. When the failure condition occurs, call the `AddPropertyError` or `AddEntityError` methods and supply an error message to raise a validation error. If you raise an error using one of these methods, LightSwitch won't allow the user to save their data until they correct all errors. If you call the `AddPropertyResult` or `AddEntityResult` methods instead, LightSwitch produces a warning but allows the user to save their changes once they acknowledge the warning.

Property-level (or field-level) validation allows you to create rules that apply to a specific property, and LightSwitch executes these rules on both the client and server. This chapter showed you how to use regular expressions to ensure that users enter Social Security numbers in the correct format. This is an example of where you would apply property-level validation.

If you want to apply validation that applies to a specific screen, you can do this by defining rules on the local screen property. LightSwitch applies screen-level validation on the client only, so you need to be aware that malicious users can bypass your screen validation by accessing your application's OData endpoint directly. Therefore, it's much better practice to apply business and validation logic through entity and property validation rules that run on the server.

Finally, you've seen some advanced validation examples that showed you how to prevent deletions, avoid duplicates, and validate files sizes. Although it might sound easy, defining a server rule that controls data deletion isn't trivial because LightSwitch doesn't apply validation rules to deleted entities.

CHAPTER 6

■■■

Querying Your Data

Along with tables and screens, queries play an important role in LightSwitch application design. They allow you filter records, display a subset of records, build search screens, and to show other significant pieces of information.

In this chapter, you'll learn how to

- Filter and sort data by using the graphical designer
- Write server-side and client-side queries using .NET and LINQ code
- Create global filter values that you can reuse in multiple queries

LightSwitch provides a designer that allows you to build a query graphically. If the graphical designer isn't able to produce your desired output, you can apply filters in code. This allows you to use LINQ and the many methods in the .NET Framework to customize your query output.

The four main query types are default queries, user-defined data service queries (queries that you define in the graphical designer), screen queries, and code-based queries. This chapter covers all of these query types.

The HelpDesk application includes an Engineer Dashboard screen, and you'll find out how to write code queries to support the retrieval of statistical information. This includes whether the engineer has outstanding high-priority issues, and whether or not all issues that have been open more than seven days are closed.

You'll learn how to apply filter operations that are not supported by the graphical designer. For example, you'll find out how to create a query that returns all issue records that don't have related issue-response records. (This is an example of a Not Exists type of query.) You'll also learn how to filter issues by the month and year they were created (an example of filtering by date parts).

Introduction to Data Retrieval

I'll begin by reminding you how the data-retrieval process works. Every data source in your application has a corresponding data service that runs on the server. When you define a query by using the graphical designer, LightSwitch creates a *query operation* on the data service. It exposes this query operation as an OData service endpoint.

When a user wants to retrieve some data, your LightSwitch client calls the query operation method via an OData call. If you've defined parameters on your query, the client will supply the necessary arguments. When the server completes the query, the query operation will return either a single entity or multiple entities to the client.

LightSwitch Queries Always Return Entities

Because query operations return entities from an entity set, the *shape* of the query results cannot be modified. For example, a query could return a single engineer or a collection of engineers. Alternatively, it could return a single issue or a collection of issues. However, a query can't return just the first name from a set of engineers, nor can it return some sort of combined object that's created by joining engineers and issues. Equally, you can't

113

perform a union on data from two different tables and return a combined data set. LightSwitch's data service isn't capable of returning non-entity data from a query. And even if it could, you wouldn't be able to consume this data from a screen, anyway. You'll remember that the 'Add New Screen' dialog only allows you to set the underlying data source of a screen to entities that you've defined in the table designer.

This behavior might seem strange, particularly for Access or SQL developers who are accustomed to selecting just the columns they need or returning results that are joined to other tables.

At this point, you may wonder how to retrieve additional data that isn't part of the underlying data set. Provided that you've set up correct relationships between entities, you can retrieve related data by using the navigation properties that you've defined.

Once you start thinking in the LightSwitch way, you'll soon realize that it isn't necessary to return joined data from queries.

Understanding the Query Pipeline

When you call a query in LightSwitch, the server-side execution passes through the query pipeline. Just like the save pipeline (which was discussed in Chapter 4), the query pipeline consists of phases that include points where you can inject your own custom server-side code.

Figure 6-1 shows the phases in the query pipeline, and highlights the points where you can add custom code.

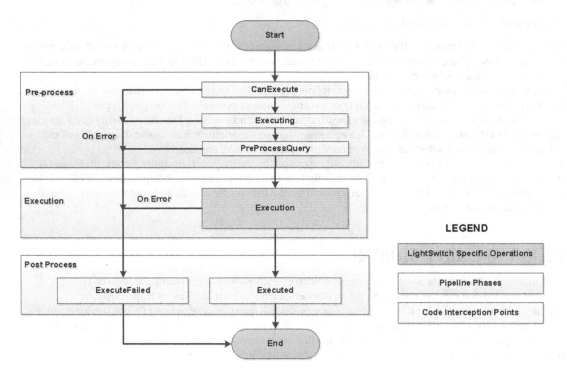

Figure 6-1. *The query pipeline*

At the start of the query pipeline, the CanExecute method allows you to carry out security checks and apply access control rules. You can find more details on writing authorization code in Chapter 17.

You'll most likely spend much of your time writing code in the PreProcessQuery method. This area allows you to customize your query by writing LINQ code, and you'll see plenty of examples toward the end of this chapter.

During the Execution phase, LightSwitch transforms the query into one that the data provider understands. (Examples of data providers are the ADO.NET Entity Framework provider for SQL Server and the OData data provider for SharePoint.) During the Execution phase, LightSwitch also translates *business types* between their underlying storage type and business type representation.

If the query succeeds, the query pipeline executes the code in the Executed method. For example, you could write custom code here to audit the users who have read some data.

If the query fails, you can perform additional error handling by writing code in the ExecuteFailed method.

■ **Tip**   If your query fails to return data, handle the ExecuteFailed event and place a breakpoint in this method. This allows you see the details of the full exception by examining the queryDescriptor object.

Using LightSwitch's Default Queries

LightSwitch automatically generates two queries, called *All* and *Single*, for each entity set in your application. Taking the engineers example, LightSwitch generates a query called Engineers_All that returns all engineers, and a query called Engineers_Single that returns a single engineer by ID value.

You can use these queries in several ways. If you create an editable grid screen and select Engineers from the Add New Screen dialog's screen data drop-down list, LightSwitch uses the Engineers_All query as the data source. If you create a details screen for an engineer, LightSwitch uses the Engineers_Single query as the data source.

Another place where you'll see default queries is if you add additional data items to a screen by opening the screen designer and clicking the Add Data Item button, as shown in Figure 6-2.

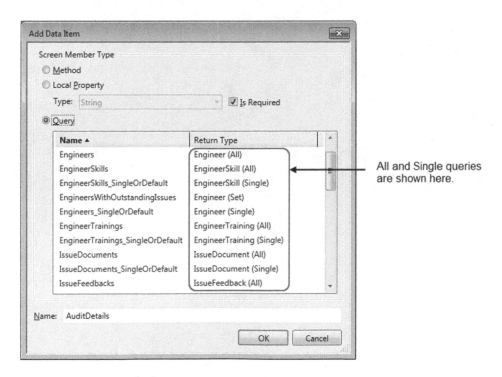

Figure 6-2. *Adding default queries to your screen*

An important concept is that queries that return collections are *composable*. This means that you can create queries based on other queries. Once you've created a query, you can right-click your query in Solution Explorer and create a query that's based on the one that you've selected.

Another important point is that the _ALL query will always be the base query for any user query that you define. For example, if you create a query by right-clicking your Engineer table in Solution Explorer and choosing the Add Query menu item, LightSwitch bases your query on the Engineers_All query.

Filtering and Sorting Data

The graphical query designer allows you to sort and filter data in several different ways. For example, you can filter by hard coded values, other property values, or by global values. This section describes all of these options in further detail.

Creating Queries Based on Entities

To create a user-defined query, right-click a table in Solution Explorer and choose the Add Query menu option. Because queries are composable, you can extend existing queries by right-clicking and selecting the Add Query item for the query.

When you add a query, the properties sheet allows you to set various attributes. (See Figure 6-3.) Let's take a look at some of these settings in more detail.

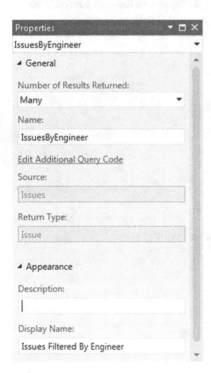

Figure 6-3. *Query properties*

- **Name:** The name uniquely identifies your query in Solution Explorer and appears in the screen data drop-down box in the Add New Screen dialog.

- **Number Of Results Returned:** This displays a drop-down box with the options One and Many.

- **Description:** You can use the Description text box to add a comment about your query at design time. The description text isn't exposed elsewhere in LightSwitch during design time or runtime.

- **Display Name:** This allows you to specify a friendly name, which appears in the query source drop-down list in the screen designer (as shown in Figure 6-4).

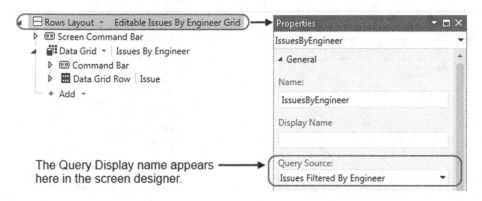

Figure 6-4. Query display name shown on a screen

By default, any new query that you create returns multiple records. This is controlled by the Number Of Results option.

Selecting the *one* option from this drop-down list defines the query as a singleton query. This is a query that returns a single record or is null. Singleton queries are not composable and can't be further modified. If you designate a query as a singleton query and define a query that returns more than one record, LightSwitch will *not* generate a compile-time error. Instead, it throws an exception at run time when it executes the query.

The Number Of Results Returned option also specifies where LightSwitch shows your query in the Add New Screen dialog. You can use singleton queries to create New Data and Details screens. Queries that return multiple records allow you to create Editable Grid, List And Details, and Search Data screens.

Applying Filters

Once you create your query, you can use the graphical designer to filter your data. Figure 6-5 illustrates the controls that you can use to set up filters. LightSwitch applies the filters that you define here on the server, as part of the query pipeline.

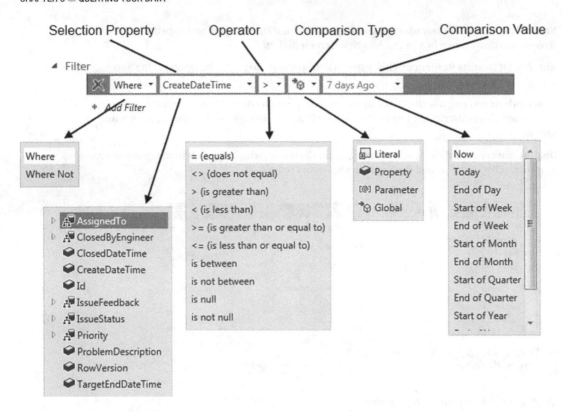

Figure 6-5. *The parts that make up a filter*

The operator drop down allows you to choose the operator that you want to apply. Some of these operators will depend on the data type of the selection property and whether the property is defined as a required property.

The comparison type drop down allows you to select from the options literal, property, parameter, or global.

The literal option allows you create a filter that uses a hard-coded value. For example, Figure 6-6 shows you how to create a query that returns issues with a status of Open. Because the status description is held in a separate table, this query shows how you can use the IssueStatus navigation property to filter by related parent records.

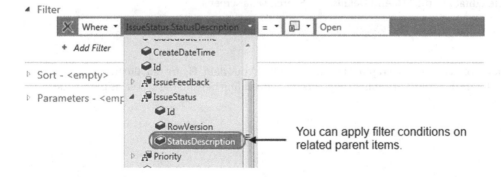

Figure 6-6. *Filtering by parent items using literal values*

Comparing Against Other Fields/Properties

The comparison type drop-down allows you create a filter that compares by property. This lets you compare two fields from the same record. After you choose the Property option, LightSwitch displays a second drop-down box that allows you to specify the comparison property.

Figure 6-7 shows a query that allows you to find issues that have overrun by returning issues where the close date exceeds the target end date.

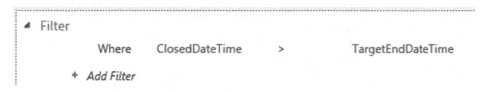

Figure 6-7. *Comparing against another property*

Passing Arguments into a Query

Rather than using a hard-coded literal value, you can make queries more reusable by creating parameters. To create a parameter, choose the Parameter option from the comparison type drop-down list. After you select the parameter option, a second drop-down box appears that allows you to either create a new parameter or select an existing parameter (if one exists).

If you choose to create a new parameter, the parameter appears in the Parameter section in the lower part of the query designer.

You can make parameters optional by checking the Is Optional check box. If the user doesn't set the value of an optional parameter at run time, LightSwitch won't apply the filters that use the parameter. Optional parameters are ideal for creating search queries that filter on multiple fields. If the user doesn't supply search criteria for any given field, LightSwitch simply omits the filter clause during execution.

■ **Note**   Refer to Chapter 7 to find out how to set parameter values on a screen, and how to display the data that the query returns.

Filtering by Global Values

If you filter by the Date or DateTime property, you can choose to filter by a set of global values that LightSwitch provides. These include Today, Start Of Week, End Of Week, and several others. (See Figure 6-8.)

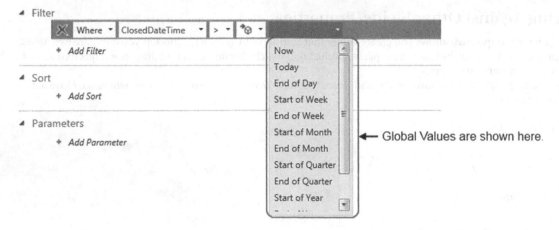

Figure 6-8. *Global value options when filtering by Date/DateTime*

If you filter on a DateTime property, take care when applying the equals operator with the Today global value. For example, the Issue table contains a field called ClosedDateTime. If you want to create a query that returns all queries that are closed today, the filter ClosedDateTime=Today won't work.

This is because Today returns today's date with a time of 12:00:00am. To apply the correct filter, you have to use the is between operator and filter the ClosedDateTime property between Today and End Of Day.

Therefore, the Start Of Day option is perhaps a better description for the value that's returned by the Today global value.

EXERCISE 6.1 – CREATING QUERIES

To familiarize yourself with the query designer, create a query that's based on the Issue table and name it IssueSearchAll. You'll use this query in Chapter 7 to build a custom search screen.

Create a filter that matches the Issue Engineer's Id against a new parameter called EngineerId. Select your EngineerId parameter, and use the Properties sheet to select the Is Optional check box.

Return to the Selection Property drop-down list, select the Engineer property, and take a look at the other properties that you can filter by. Does LightSwitch allow you to filter by computed properties, such as the Engineer Age property that you created in Chapter 2? Does LightSwitch allow you to filter against properties in the IssueResponse table? (There's a one-to-many relationship between the Issue and IssueResponse table.) To complete your query, add additional parameters to optionally filter your results by IssueStatus.Id, Priority.Id, and ProblemDescription.

Sorting Data

The graphical query designer allows you sort the output of your query by multiple properties. (See Figure 6-9.)

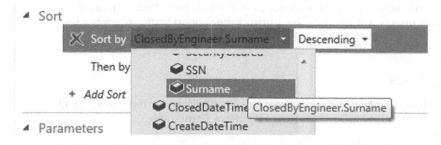

Figure 6-9. *Sorting a query*

The first drop-down list allows you to select a property. The second drop-down list allows you choose from the sort orders Ascending and Descending. After you specify a sort order, you can sort on additional properties by clicking on the Add Sort button.

A new feature in LightSwitch 2012 is the ability to sort queries by related parent properties. In Figure 6-9, notice how you can sort issues by the related engineer's surname.

It isn't possible to sort queries by related child records. For example, users and engineers can add multiple issue-response records to each issue. It isn't possible to create a query on the issue table that sorts the output using the response date that's held in the issue-response table. (This would allow you to return issues in the order that they've been most recently been worked on.) To perform this type of sort, you'll need to extend your query by writing code in the PreprocessQuery method. You'll see an example of how to do this later in this chapter.

Sorting Data Grids

When you display data on a grid, users can toggle the sort order by clicking on the column headings. The column header includes an arrow that indicates the sort order that's currently in use (as shown in Figure 6-10).

Users

Click on the column header to sort.

FIRSTNAME	SURNAME ▲	PHONE NUMBER	USERNAME
▶ Tabatha	Acevedo	(034) 219-5591	Neil905
Ira	Acevedo	(732) 851-2940	Leonard
Debra	Acosta	(273) 681-4479	Jose945
Melisa	Acosta	(320) 791-5209	Marjorie347
Orlando	Acosta	287259-9064	Heidi4

Figure 6-10. *Sorting a query*

LightSwitch retains the column header sort sequence between sessions, and it even restores the sort sequence after the user closes and reopens your application.

The problem with this behavior is that a user can't clear the grid sort order and return to the initial sort sequence that you intended.

To give an example, let's say you've created an Editable Engineer Grid screen that uses a query that sorts the data by surname followed by first name. If the user opens this screen and sorts the data by priority, there isn't any way for the user to return to the initial sort sequence of surname followed by first name.

Therefore, if you create grid screens that use queries that are sorted by multiple properties, it makes sense to disable sorting to prevent this problem from occurring. To do this, uncheck the Support Sorting check box for your query in the screen designer.

Examining User Setting Files

To explain the grid sort behavior, LightSwitch retains the user settings for your application in the following path, which appears below your Documents folder (or My Documents on a Windows XP machine): `Microsoft\LightSwitch\Settings\`

In this folder, there'll be a subfolder for every LightSwitch application that you've run on your computer. Inside each application folder, you'll find a `.SortSettings` file for each screen in your application. (See Figure 6-11.) This is an XML file that contains the user sort orders for the screen. Users could manually clear their sort settings by deleting this file.

Name	Type	Size
Application.OutOfBrowser.WindowSettings	WINDOWSETTINGS File	1 KB
EditableEngineersGrid.Engineers.SortSettings	SORTSETTINGS File	1 KB
EditableEngineersGrid.grid.ColumnSettings	COLUMNSETTINGS File	2 KB
EditableIssuesGrid.grid.ColumnSettings	COLUMNSETTINGS File	1 KB
EditableIssuesGrid.Issues.SortSettings	SORTSETTINGS File	1 KB

Figure 6-11. *File listing of C:\Users\Tim\Documents\Microsoft\LightSwitch\Settings\HelpDesk.1.0.0.0*

In this folder, you'll find various other files. If a user resizes the widths of the columns on a data grid, LightSwitch persists these settings between sessions in the `.ColumnSettings` file. LightSwitch uses the remaining files to retain the state of the application, navigation, and ribbon settings. To illustrate one of these XML files, Listing 6-1 shows you the contents of the `Application.OutOfBrowser.WindowSettings` file. LightSwitch uses the data in this file to reopen your application in the same screen position as your last session.

Listing 6-1. Contents of Application.OutOfBrowser.WindowSettings

```xml
<?xml version="1.0" encoding="utf-8"?>
<OutOfBrowserWindowSettings
  xmlns:xsi="http://www.w3.org/2001/XMLSchema-instance"
  xmlns:xsd="http://www.w3.org/2001/XMLSchema">
  <Top>10</Top>
  <Left>360</Left>
  <Width>1077</Width>
  <Height>604</Height>
  <WindowState>Normal</WindowState>
</OutOfBrowserWindowSettings>
```

Modifying Screen Queries

When you create a screen that's based upon a collection of data (an editable grid screen or search screen, for example), you can define additional parameters, filtering, and ordering at the screen level.

To do this, click on the Edit Query link that appears next to your data collection. (See Figure 6-12.) This opens the graphical query designer and allows you to apply filter and sort conditions.

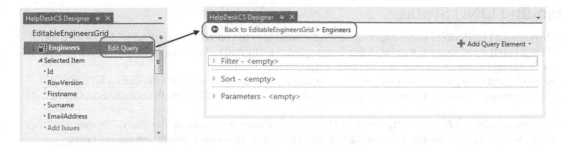

Figure 6-12. Editing a screen query

A disadvantage of this approach is that you can't reuse your filter conditions on other screens. Also, you can't further customize your query by writing code. However, the advantage of modifying the screen query is that it's simple. It's the perfect way to apply a different sort order for a collection of data that you want to show on a screen. By now, you'll know that you can't organize the queries and objects that LightSwitch shows in Solution Explorer into subfolders. So screen queries save you from cluttering up your view of Solution Explorer with lots of one-off queries.

You're not just limited to modifying the main underlying query for a screen. In fact, if you add other collections of data to your screen by using the dialog that's shown in Figure 6-2, LightSwitch gives you the option to edit the query for the data collection that you've added.

Writing Queries in Code

Although you can easily create queries in the graphical designer, LightSwitch allows you to create more powerful queries by writing custom code.

There are a couple of places where you can write custom query code. First, you can extend the queries that you've created in the graphical designer by applying extra filtering in code.

Second, you can query data entirely in code by using the data APIs that you saw in Chapter 4. To give you an illustration of what you can do, Figure 6-13 shows an Engineer Dashboard screen.

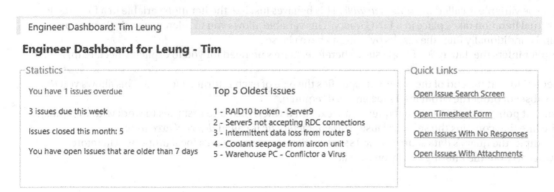

Figure 6-13. Engineer Dashboard page

The examples in this section will show you how to retrieve the statistical details that are shown on this screen. But before moving on further, let's take a closer look at how LINQ works.

Understanding LINQ Syntax

LINQ is used throughout LightSwitch, so it's important to understand how to construct a query with LINQ. Once you start learning LINQ, you'll soon discover that you can express queries using two different types of syntax: Query Syntax and Method (or Lambda) Syntax.

You'll commonly find Query Syntax in documentation, and it's generally more readable. (It looks a bit like SQL.) You've already seen some examples of Query Syntax in this book. The screen code that undeletes records in Listing 5-10 is one example.

Figure 6-14 shows a snippet of Query Syntax code and highlights the parts that make up the query. The query belongs in an engineer details screen and is designed to return a collection of open issues sorted in date descending order.

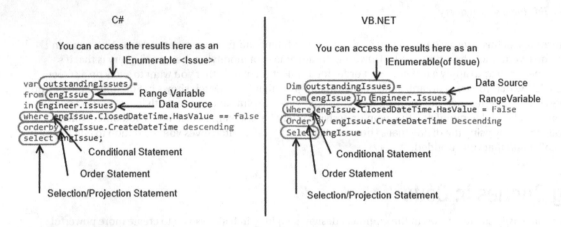

Figure 6-14. *Parts that make up a query expressed using Query Syntax*

Every query needs a data source, and in this sample, the `Engineer.Issues` navigation property is the data source. Because the code belongs in a details screen, `Engineer` refers to the Engineer query that's created by the details screen template.

The `engIssue` variable is called the *range variable*. This behaves just like the iteration variable in a for-each loop, although no actual iteration takes place in a LINQ query. This variable allows you to reference each element in the data source and conditionally filter the results by using a `where` clause.

The compiler infers the data type of `engIssue.` Therefore, there's no need for you to explicitly declare this as an `Issue` object.

The `select` clause at the end of the statement specifies the type of each returned element. This allows you to return only a subset of properties from the `Issue` entity, if required.

An important point about LINQ is that queries are executed when the code first tries to work with the query, and not on the line that contains the `select` clause. This characteristic is called *deferred execution*.

In this example, the query's data source is the `Issues` navigation property on a local property. Therefore, LightSwitch will carry out the filtering locally on the client.

Understanding Method (Lambda) Syntax Code

Although Query Syntax is generally easier to read and write, there are certain operations that you can perform only with Method Syntax. Retrieving the element with the maximum value in a source sequence is an example.

Method Syntax queries are characterized by lambda expressions, and you've already seen a few examples in this book.

Figure 6-15 illustrates the same query as before, but expressed using Method Syntax rather than Query Syntax.

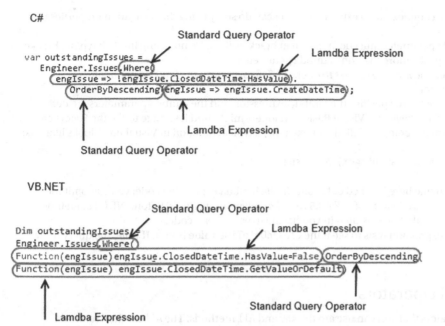

C#

Figure 6-15. *Parts that make up a query expressed using Method Syntax*

Standard Query operators define the operations you want to perform, such as filtering or ordering. You can control the way that many of these operators work by supplying a lambda expression.

Using Standard Query Operators

Standard Query operators are extension methods on top of the objects that implement the `IEnumerable` or `IDataServiceQueryable` interface. The operators you can use depend on the data source that you've chosen.

There are over 50 Standard Query operators you can apply when you're working with navigation properties. As well as the `where` and `orderby` operators, there are many other useful operators that you can use. For example, you can apply various aggregate operators, such as `count`, `min`, `max`, and `average`.

Filtering Data with Lambda Expressions

Let's take a closer look at the `where` operator and lambda expression from Figure 6-15:

C# `Where(engIssue => !engIssue.ClosedDateTime.HasValue)`
VB `Where(Function(engIssue) engIssue.ClosedDateTime.HasValue= false)`

The `where` operator expects you to pass in a `Func` delegate that returns a Boolean. The return value indicates whether the supplied value (`engIssue`) meets the criteria for inclusion in the `where` clause.

`engIssue` is called the *lambda parameter*. This represents a single issue in the collection of issue responses that you're working against. This code uses .NET's implicit data-typing feature, which saves you from having to define the data type of `engIssue`. You could equally write the expression like this:

C# `Where((Issue engIssue )=> !engIssue.ClosedDateTime.HasValue)`
VB `Where(Function(engIssue As Issue) engIssue.ClosedDateTime.HasValue= false)`

If you want to construct more complex query expressions, you can do so by using the navigation properties that your lambda parameter exposes.

In the C# version, the lambda parameter must be enclosed in brackets if you're not using implicit typing. Brackets must also be used if you want to specify more than one lambda parameter.

In C#, the => operator is called the *lambda* or *goes to* operator. This separates the lambda parameter or parameters from the actual expression.

In Visual Basic, the Function keyword specifies the lambda expression and the lambda parameters are defined inside brackets following the Function keyword. Visual Basic developers might find it strange to see the Function keyword used without a function name being specified. For example, a typical function in Visual Basic looks like this:

```
Public Function GetIssue (issueId  As Integer) As Issue
```

As you can see, the function name here is called GetIssue. In the lambda expression code, you can omit the function name because the syntax uses a feature of .NET 3.5 called *anonymous methods*. Before .NET 3.5, methods had to be explicitly named, which would have resulted in you having to write more code.

The final part of the lambda expression tests to see if the ClosedDateTime value is null. If true, the query returns the record in the results.

Using the Any and All Operators

Two useful Standard Query operators that you can use are the Any and All methods. The All method returns a Boolean that indicates whether or not all elements of a sequence match a condition, whereas the Any method returns whether or not any element satisfies a condition.

The code in Listing 6-2 finds whether or not there is at least one issue in the database with a priority set to high. Because the data source is the outstandingIssues query (shown in Figure 6-15), the query searches only open issues.

If you want to run the code that's shown in this section, the first part of Chapter 7 will give you more detail. In Chapter 7, you'll find out how to display your query results on your screen by adding local screen properties.

Listing 6-2. Using the Any Standard Query Operator

VB:
File: HelpDeskVB\Client\UserCode\EngineerDashboard.vb

```
Dim highPriorityExists As Boolean =
    outstandingIssues.Any(
        Function(engIssue) engIssue.Priority.PriorityDesc = "High")
```
C#:
File: HelpDeskCS\Client\UserCode\EngineerDashboard.cs

```
bool highPriorityExists =
   outstandingIssues.Any(
        engIssue => engIssue.Priority.PriorityDesc == "High");
```

The code in Listing 6-3 returns whether or not all issues that have been open for more than seven days are closed, and it demonstrates the use of the All query operator.

Listing 6-3. Using the All Standard Query Operator

VB:
File: HelpDeskVB\Client\UserCode\EngineerDashboard.vb

```
Dim oldIssueExists As Boolean =
    Engineer.Issues.Where(
        Function(engIssue) engIssue.CreateDateTime < DateTime.Now.AddDays(-7)).All(
            Function(engIssue) engIssue.ClosedDateTime.HasValue)
```
C#:
File: HelpDeskCS\Client\UserCode\EngineerDashboard.cs

```
bool oldIssueExists =
    Engineer.Issues.Where(engIssue =>
        engIssue.CreateDateTime < DateTime.Now.AddDays(-7)).All(
            engIssue => engIssue.ClosedDateTime.HasValue);
```

Performing For Each Logic

A neat little method that you can use is the ForEach extension method. This allows you to supply an Action delegate that defines some logic that you want to carry out against each element in a sequence.

Listing 6-4 shows you how to build a string that shows the top-5 oldest issues.

Listing 6-4. Using the ForEach Operator

VB:
File: HelpDeskVB\Client\UserCode\EngineerDashboard.vb

```
Imports System.Text

Dim sb As StringBuilder = new StringBuilder()

outstandingIssues.OrderByDescending(
    Function(engItem) engItem.CreateDateTime).Take(5).ToList().ForEach(
        Function(engItem) sb.AppendLine(engItem.ProblemDescription))
```
C#:
File: HelpDeskCS\Client\UserCode\EngineerDashboard.cs

```
using System.Text;

StringBuilder sb = new StringBuilder();

outstandingIssues.OrderByDescending(
    engItem => engItem.CreateDateTime).Take(5).ToList().ForEach(
        engItem => sb.AppendLine(engItem.ProblemDescription));
```

The first part of the code retrieves the top-five oldest records by ordering the issues in date descending order and calling the Take method to retrieve the first five records in the sequence.

The ForEach extension method belongs to the type List<T>, so you need to call the ToList method to return a list of issues.

The code inside the ForEach method then builds a list of the issue descriptions by using a StringBuilder object. At the end of this process, the code would display the contents of the StringBuilder object on the Engineer Dashboard screen.

Querying Data Remotely

When you're writing queries, it's important to consider where the query executes. Take a look at the code that's shown in Listing 6-5.

Listing 6-5. Querying Data Collections

VB:
File: HelpDeskVB\Client\UserCode\EngineerDetail.vb

```
Dim startOfYear = New DateTime(DateTime.Now.Year, 1, 1)

'Query 1
Dim issuesLastMonth =
    Engineer.Issues.Where(
        Function(issueItem) issueItem.CreateDateTime > startYear).
            Count()

'Query 2
Dim issuesLastMonth2 =
    Engineer.IssuesQuery.Where(
        Function(issueItem) issueItem.CreateDateTime > startYear).
            Execute().Count()
```

C#:
File: HelpDeskCS\Client\UserCode\EngineerDetail.cs

```
DateTime startOfYear = new DateTime(DateTime.Now.Year, 1, 1);

//Query 1
var issuesLastMonth =
    Engineer.Issues.Where(
        issueItem => issueItem.CreateDateTime > startOfYear).Count();

//Query 2
var issuesLastMonth2 =
    Engineer.IssuesQuery.Where(
        issueItem => issueItem.CreateDateTime > startOfYear).
            Execute().Count();
```

This code exists on an Engineer details screen, and both queries are designed to return engineer issues that have been created since the start of the year. Although query 1 looks very similar to query 2, there's a big difference between the two code samples.

The data source for query 1 is a navigation property. Navigation properties are of type EntityCollection<T>, and any queries that you perform on a navigation property are executed by LightSwitch locally.

The code in query 2 calls the <CollectionName>Query method. This returns an IDataServiceQueryable, and LightSwitch remotely executes any filtering that you define against this object.

Considering that each engineer could be associated with hundreds or even thousands of issues, it's much more efficient to perform this specific query remotely. However, a common pitfall with remote queries is that they won't include any entities that have been added locally. Therefore, you'll need to consider this behavior when you're writing remote queries.

Figure 6-16 shows you the actual SQL that's executed by SQL Server by highlighting the output from SQL Server Profiler. This output proves that when you use <CollectionName>Query as a data source, SQL Server carries out the filtering, not LightSwitch.

Querying a Navigation Property

```
SELECT
[Extent1].[Id] AS [Id],
[Extent1].[RowVersion] AS [RowVersion],
[Extent1].[TargetEndDateTime] AS [TargetEndDateTime],
[Extent1].[Subject] AS [Subject],
[Extent1].[ClosedDateTime] AS [ClosedDateTime],
[Extent1].[CreateDateTime] AS [CreateDateTime],
[Extent1].[ProblemDescription] AS [ProblemDescription],
[Extent1].[Issue_Engineer] AS [Issue_Engineer],
[Extent1].[Issue_Engineer1] AS [Issue_Engineer1],
[Extent1].[Issue_Priority] AS [Issue_Priority],
[Extent1].[Issue_IssueStatus] AS [Issue_IssueStatus],
[Extent1].[Issue_User] AS [Issue_User]
FROM [dbo].[Issues] AS [Extent1]
WHERE 1 = [Extent1].[Issue_Engineer]
```
⟵ SQL Server doesn't filter by CreateDateTime.

Querying an IDataServiceQueryable

```
SELECT
[Extent1].[Id] AS [Id],
[Extent1].[RowVersion] AS [RowVersion],
[Extent1].[TargetEndDateTime] AS [TargetEndDateTime],
[Extent1].[Subject] AS [Subject],
[Extent1].[ClosedDateTime] AS [ClosedDateTime],
[Extent1].[CreateDateTime] AS [CreateDateTime],
[Extent1].[ProblemDescription] AS [ProblemDescription],
[Extent1].[Issue_Engineer] AS [Issue_Engineer],
[Extent1].[Issue_Engineer1] AS [Issue_Engineer1],
[Extent1].[Issue_Priority] AS [Issue_Priority],
[Extent1].[Issue_IssueStatus] AS [Issue_IssueStatus], |
[Extent1].[Issue_User] AS [Issue_User]
FROM [dbo].[Issues] AS [Extent1]
WHERE (1 = [Extent1].[Issue_Engineer]) AND ([Extent1].[CreateDateTime] > convert(datetime, '2013-01-01
00:00:00.000', 121))
```
SQL Server filters the output by CreateDateTime.

Figure 6-16. *The SQL Profiler result of querying navigation properties and IDataServiceQueryables*

Querying Data Locally

Although it might seem more efficient to perform your querying remotely, there are good reasons to query your data locally. If the data that you want to use is already loaded on the client, it's quicker to query the data that's already loaded.

Also, not all standard query operators support remote execution, or there might be application features that you want to create that can be achieved only with a local query.

To demonstrate such a feature, here's a screen that allows engineers to enter the time that they've spent on issues. This screen includes a button that merges time entries that refer to the same issue. Figure 6-17 illustrates how the screen functions.

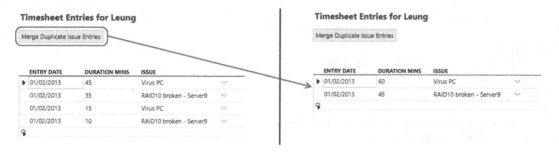

Figure 6-17. *Merging duplicate issues*

To create this example, carry out the following steps:

1. Add the TimeTracking table to your project. You'll find the schema of this table in Appendix E.

2. Create a detail screen, and base it on the Engineer table. In the Add New Screen dialog, make sure to include the TimeTracking data collection.

3. When the screen designer opens, add a new button and bind it to a new method called MergeDuplicateIssues. Add the code that's shown in Listing 6-6 to this method.

Listing 6-6. Querying an EntityCollection

VB:
File: HelpDeskVB\Client\UserCode\EngineerTimeTracking.vb

```
Dim duplicates =
    From timeEntry In Engineer.TimeTracking
    Group timeEntry By timeEntry.Issue Into issueGroup = Group, Count()
    Where issueGroup.Count() > 1
    Select issueGroup                                                    ❶

For Each dup In duplicates
    Dim totalDuration = dup.Sum(Function(timeEntry) timeEntry.DurationMins)
    Dim firstLine = dup.First
    firstLine.DurationMins = totalDuration                               ❷
    dup.Except(New TimeTracking() {firstLine}).ToList().ForEach(
        Sub(timeEntry) timeEntry.Delete())                               ❸
Next
```

C#:
File: HelpDeskCS\Client\UserCode\EngineerTimeTracking.cs

```
var duplicates =
    from TimeTracking timeEntry in this.Engineer.TimeTracking
    group timeEntry by timeEntry.Issue into issueGroup
    where issueGroup.Count() > 1
    select issueGroup;                                                   ❶

foreach (var dup in duplicates)
{
    var totalDuration =
        dup.Sum(timeEntry => timeEntry.DurationMins);
    var firstEntry = dup.First();
    firstEntry.DurationMins = totalDuration;                             ❷
    dup.Except(
        new TimeTracking[] { firstEntry }).ToList().ForEach(
        timeEntry => timeEntry.Delete());                                ❸
}
```

This code uses several of the features that you've covered in this section. The TimeTracking table stores the amount of time that an engineer has spent on an issue. The first part of the code groups the TimeTracking records by issue and selects groups that contain more than one time-tracking record ❶.

The second part of the code loops through the collection of grouped records, sums the total duration into the first record ❷, and deletes the remaining records in the group ❸.

Notice how the code uses the Except operator, along with the ForEach operator that you saw earlier.

Performing Advanced Filtering

In this section, you'll find out how to apply filter operations that are not supported by the graphical designer. This allows you to carry out more complex filtering by adding LINQ code to your query's PreprocessQuery method. All the queries in this section are server based and are executed by LightSwitch through the query pipeline. You can run the queries in the section by adding new screens that are based on the query.

Filtering by Related Child Items

If you create a query that uses the issue table, the graphical designer allows you to filter the results by engineer. In other words, the graphical designer allows you to filter by parent records. Working in the other direction, however, a query that's based on the engineer table can't be filtered by a property in the issue table. Figure 6-18 illustrates how the drop-down box in an Engineer query doesn't contain an entry for Issue.

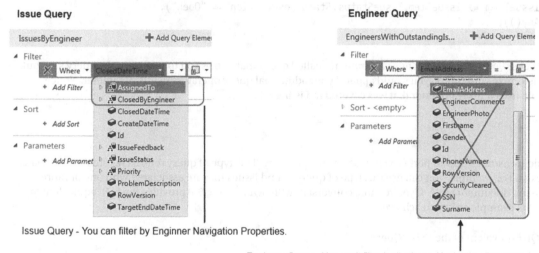

Figure 6-18. You cannot filter by child items in the graphical designer

To filter by child items, you'll need to write some custom code. To demonstrate this, here's how to create a query that returns engineers with outstanding issues.

Right-click on the Engineer table in Solution Explorer, and create a query called EngineersWithOutstandingIssues. Click on the Write Code button, and select the PreprocessQuery method. When the code editor opens, enter the code that's shown in Listing 6-7.

Listing 6-7. Filtering by Child Items

VB:
File: HelpDeskVB\Server\UserCode\ApplicationDataService.vb

```
Private Sub EngineersWithOutstandingIssues_PreprocessQuery(
    ByRef query As IQueryable(Of Engineer))

      query = query.Where(Function(engItem) engItem.Issues.Where(
         Function(issueItem) issueItem.IssueStatus.StatusDescription = "Open").Any())
End Sub
```

C#:
File: HelpDeskCS\Server\UserCode\ApplicationDataService.cs

```
partial void EngineersWithOutstandingIssues_PreprocessQuery(
    ref IQueryable<Engineer> query)
{
    query = query.Where
        (engItem => engItem.Issues.Where(
            issueItem => issueItem.IssueStatus.StatusDescription == "Open").
            Any());
}
```

The PreprocessQuery method includes a parameter called query that allows you to reference the query's output. So to further customize your query, you would append your additional query operators to this parameter. Notice how this example uses the Any operator that was covered in Listing 6-2.

Exists, In

This example demonstrates how to perform an *exists* or *in* type query. This type of query returns records where related child records exist. For example, you can use this type of query to find issues that are associated with one or more records in the issue document table. If you're more conversant with SQL, Listing 6-8 provides the SQL equivalent to illustrate what this example strives to achieve.

Listing 6-8. SQL Equivalent of the Exists Query

```
SELECT  *
 FROM Issues
WHERE IssueID IN (
    SELECT IssueID FROM IssueDocuments)
```

To create this example, create a query called IssuesWithAttachments. Click on the Write Code button, select the PreprocessQuery method, and enter the code that's shown in Listing 6-9.

Listing 6-9. Returning All Issues with Related Issue Document Records

VB:
File: HelpDeskVB\Server\UserCode\ApplicationDataService.vb

```
Private Sub IssuesWithAttachments_PreprocessQuery(
    ByRef query As IQueryable(Of Issue))
      query = query.Where(Function(issueItem) issueItem.IssueDocuments.Any())
End Sub
```

C#:
File: HelpDeskCS\Server\UserCode\ApplicationDataService.cs

```
partial void IssuesWithAttachments_PreprocessQuery(
    ref IQueryable<Issue> query)
{
    query = query.Where (issueItem => issueItem.IssueDocuments.Any());
}
```

Not Exists, Not In

As a natural progression of the previous example, this example shows you how to perform a *not exists* or *not in* type query. This type of query returns records where no related child records exist.

This example demonstrates a query that returns all issues without any issue-response records. Just like before, Listing 6-10 shows the equivalent SQL that you would use to perform this query.

Listing 6-10. SQL Equivalent of a Not In Query

```
SELECT   *
 FROM Issues
WHERE IssueID NOT IN (
    SELECT IssueID FROM IssueResponses)
```

To carry out this example, create a query called `IssuesWithNoResponse` and add the code shown in Listing 6-11 to the `PreprocessQuery` method of your query.

Listing 6-11. Returning Issue Records Without Any Issue Responses

VB:
File: HelpDeskVB\Server\UserCode\ApplicationDataService.vb

```
Private Sub IssuesWithNoResponse_PreprocessQuery(
    ByRef query As System.Linq.IQueryable(Of LightSwitchApplication.Issue))
       query = query.Where(Function(issueItem) Not issueItem.IssueResponses.Any())
End Sub
```

C#:
File: HelpDeskCS\Server\UserCode\ApplicationDataService.cs

```
partial void IssuesWithNoResponse_PreprocessQuery(ref IQueryable<Issue> query)
{
    query = query.Where(issueItem => !issueItem.IssueResponses.Any());
}
```

Filtering by Date Elements

The ability to filter by date elements is a common scenario. Finding people who were born on a given day and month is a typical example.

This example shows you how to create a query that allows users to find all issues that were raised during a specified month and year.

To allow your user to specify the month and year, create a query on the Issue table called IssuesByMonthAndYear and create two integer parameters, called IssueMonth and IssueYear. (See Figure 6-19.) Set the Is Optional property of both of these parameters to true.

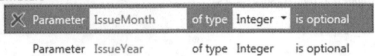

Figure 6-19. *IssueMonth and IssueYear parameters*

Now add the code that's shown in Listing 6-12 to the PreprocessQuery method of your query.

Listing 6-12. Filtering by Month and Year Parameter Values

VB:
File: HelpDeskVB\Server\UserCode\ApplicationDataService.vb

```vb
Private Sub IssuesByMonthAndYear_PreprocessQuery(
    IssueMonth As System.Nullable(Of Integer),
    IssueYear As System.Nullable(Of Integer),
    ByRef query As System.Linq.IQueryable(Of LightSwitchApplication.Issue))

    If (IssueMonth.HasValue And IssueYear.HasValue) Then
        query = query.Where(
            Function(item) item.CreateDateTime.Month = IssueMonth.Value AndAlso
                item.CreateDateTime.Year = IssueYear.Value)

    End If

End Sub
```

C#:
File: HelpDeskCS\Server\UserCode\ApplicationDataService.cs

```csharp
partial void IssuesByMonthAndYear_PreprocessQuery(
    int? IssueMonth, int? IssueYear, ref IQueryable<Issue> query)
{
    if (IssueMonth.HasValue && IssueYear.HasValue)
    {
        query = query.Where(
            item => item.CreateDateTime.Month == IssueMonth.Value &&
            item.CreateDateTime.Year == IssueYear.Value);
    }
}
```

To create a screen that uses this query, you can simply create an editable grid screen that's based on this query. As with all other parameterized queries, LightSwitch automatically creates text boxes that allow the user to supply the required values.

Top N Records

This final example shows you how to create a query that returns the top *n* records from an entity set. To demonstrate this technique, this example shows you how to create a query that returns the top five issues with the highest feedback rating.

If you've not done so, create a (zero-or-1)-to-many relationship between the Issue and IssueFeedback tables. (You'll find the schema for the IssueFeedback table in Appendix E.) Create a query based on the Issue table called IssuesWithHighestFeedback. Now add the code that's shown in Listing 6-13 to the query's PreprocessQuery method.

Listing 6-13. Query to Return Issues with the Highest Feedback

VB:
File: HelpDeskVB\Server\UserCode\ApplicationDataService.vb

```
Private Sub IssuesWithHighestFeedback_PreprocessQuery(
    ByRef query As System.Linq.IQueryable(Of LightSwitchApplication.Issue))

    query = query.OrderByDescending(
        Function(issueItem) issueItem.IssueFeedback.Average(
            Function(feedback) feedback.OverallRating)).Take(5)
End Sub
```

C#:
File: HelpDeskCS\Server\UserCode\ApplicationDataService.cs

```
partial void IssuesWithHighestFeedback_PreprocessQuery(
    ref IQueryable<Issue> query)
{
    query = query.OrderByDescending(
    issueItem => issueItem.IssueFeedback.Average(
        feedback => feedback.OverallRating)).Take(5);
}
```

Each issue item can have multiple issue-feedback records. So to calculate a value that the query can use to sort the issues, the code works out the average feedback that's assigned to each issue. The important part of this code is the take method—this is a method that allows you to retrieve the top five records.

To improve this code further, you could add a parameter to allow the user to choose the number of records to return, rather than use a hard-coded value of 5.

Creating Global Values

Let's imagine that you want find all issues that were raised within the last seven days. To do this, you could create a query and write some code in the pre-process query method. However, this is more difficult than it should be because it involves having to write code.

A much neater approach is to create a global value that you can reuse in multiple queries. This example shows you exactly how to do this by creating a global value called 7 Days Ago. At the end of this section, you'll have a global value that you can reuse in the query designer, as shown in Figure 6-20.

▲ Filter

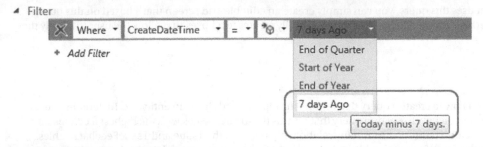

Figure 6-20. *Using global parameters*

The task of creating a global value involves two things:

- Editing your project's LSML file
- Creating a class and writing the code that performs the calculation

Note that if you're working on an HTML client application, or a project that's been upgraded after installing Visual Studio 2012 Update 2, you need to follow the modified instructions that are shown at the end of this section.

■ **Caution**   Make sure to back up your project before manually editing your LSML file. You can easily corrupt and damage your project if you make mistakes during this process.

Adding Your Global Value to Your LSML File

First, you need to append the global value definition to your Common project's LSML file. Switch to File View, and open the file Common ➤ Properties ➤ Common.lsml.

Add the code in Listing 6-14 to the end of your file, just before the </ModelFragment> tag.

Listing 6-14. Global Value Definition to Add to the LSML file

```
<GlobalValueContainerDefinition
  Name="GlobalDates">
  <GlobalValueDefinition
    Name="SevenDaysAgo"
    ReturnType=":DateTime">
    <GlobalValueDefinition.Attributes>
      <DisplayName Value="7 days Ago" />
      <Description Value="Today minus 7 days." />
    </GlobalValueDefinition.Attributes>
  </GlobalValueDefinition>
</GlobalValueContainerDefinition>
```

The name of the GlobalValueContainerDefinition needs to match the name of the class that you're about to create. In this example, it's been named GlobalDates.

Each global value is defined within a GlobalValueDefinition element. The ReturnType attribute specifies the data type for your global value. The acceptable values that you can use include :String, :Int32, :Decimal, and :Boolean. Appendix B shows a full list.

Note that these values are case sensitive. Visual Studio will not load your project if you get the casing wrong.

Creating the Global Value Class

The next thing to do is to write the code that does the computation. Switch to File View, and create a new class in your Common project. An ideal place to create this class is in the User Code folder (if it exists). LightSwitch creates this folder if you've written any entity code.

The name of your class needs to match the name that's defined in your GlobalValueContainerDefinition element (GlobalDates in this example). Enter the code that's shown in Listing 6-15.

Listing 6-15. Code to Return Date

VB:
File: HelpDeskVB\Common\UserCode\GlobalDates.vb

```
Imports System

Namespace LightSwitchCommonModule

    Public Class GlobalDates

        Public Shared Function SevenDaysAgo() As DateTime
            Return DateTime.Now.AddDays(-7)
        End Function

    End Class

End Namespace
```

C#:
File: HelpDeskCS\Common\UserCode\GlobalDates.cs

```
using System;

namespace LightSwitchCommonModule
{
    public class GlobalDates
    {
        // The name of the GlobalValueDefinition
        public static DateTime SevenDaysAgo()
        {
            return DateTime.Now.AddDays(-7);
        }
    }
}
```

The new class contains Visual Basic shared or C# static methods for each GlobalValueDefinition element that you defined in your LSML. The method name needs to match the name that you've defined in the GlobalValueDefinition element, and the namespace of your class must be set to LightSwitchCommonModule.

Your new global value is now ready for use. Whenever you filter a query on a date-time property, you'll be able to select 7 Days Ago as a global value.

■ **Note**   If you're curious as to how the default DateTime global values work, the equivalent logic for the built-in global values can be found in the Microsoft.LightSwitch.RelativeDates namespace.

Using Global Values in Upgraded Projects

If you've added an HTML client application (as discussed in Chapter 8) or have upgraded your project after installing Visual Studio 2012 Update 2, the instructions that you'll need to follow are slightly different. Upgraded projects no longer include a `Common` project. Therefore, the LSML file that you'll need to modify will exist in the following locations, depending on your project's language:

- VB Projects: `YourApp.server\My Project\service.lsml`

- C# Projects: `YourApp.Server\Properties\service.lsml`

Locate your `service.lsml` file, and add the `GlobalValueContainerDefinition` block from Listing 6-14 to the end of your file, just before the `</ModelFragment>` tag. After you do this, create a folder called `UserCode\Shared` in your `server` project, and add your `GlobalDate` class file to this folder. When you create your `GlobalDate` class, you need to modify the code in Listing 6-14 by changing the namespace of your class from `LightSwitchCommonModule` to `LightSwitchApplication`.

Summary

Queries allow you to find records by applying filters. They allow you to display a subset of records, build search screens, or show other significant pieces of information. LightSwitch queries can return a single entity or multiple entities. Because LightSwitch queries always returns entities, you can't add or remove properties (for example, table columns) from the output of a query. If you've developed applications using systems other than LightSwitch, you'll notice that this chapter doesn't show you how to join data. This is because LightSwitch allows you to access related data through navigation properties, so if you've properly designed your application, there's no need for you to create joins.

You can easily create *data service* queries that run on the server by using LightSwitch's graphical designer. This allows you to filter a query by hard-coded values, parameters, and other fields in the same table. You can filter date fields by global values. These include Today, Start Of Week, Start Of Month, and many more. It's possible to create your own global values, and you've seen an example of how to create a 7 Days Ago global value.

By default, LightSwitch creates two queries that return all entities or a single entity by ID value. Queries that return multiple entities are composable, meaning that you can build queries upon other queries.

At a screen level, you can customize the sort and filter criteria that the screen applies by clicking on the Edit Query link that appears against the relevant collection in the screen designer. However, you can't reuse any filter settings that you've defined like this in other queries, and you can't extend these queries using code.

When the server executes a query, the process passes through the query pipeline. This pipeline includes phases that allow you to attach custom code. It allows you to apply filter operations that are not supported by the graphical designer by writing code in a query's `PreprocessQuery` method. You've learned how to write LINQ code in the `PreprocessQuery` method to filter a query by child records and date parts, and how to carry out Exists and Not Exists type queries. Another useful query pipeline method is the `CanExecute` method. This allows you to carry out security checks to prevent certain users from running a query.

You can express a LINQ query syntactically in one of two ways: Method Syntax or Query Syntax. Query Syntax looks a bit like SQL and is simple to read. When .NET compiles your code, it converts your Query Syntax into the Method Syntax equivalent. Although Query Syntax is easy to read, there are certain operations that you can perform only by using Method Syntax. Method Syntax LINQ is characterized by Standard Query operators (the `Where` and `OrderBy` operators are examples) and lambda expressions. A lambda expression is an anonymous function that you can supply as an argument to a standard query operator.

This chapter has showed you how to define LINQ queries on a Silverlight client screen. The output of these queries allows you to show statistical details to your users. Every LINQ query requires a data source. If the data source for your query is a collection or navigation property, LightSwitch performs your query locally. If the data source for your query uses your screen collection's `<CollectionName>Query` method, LightSwitch applies any query conditions that you define remotely on the server.

CHAPTER 7

■ ■ ■

Mastering Silverlight Screen Design

Chapter 3 introduced you to the basics of screen design. It showed you how to create screens, display data, and set up screen navigation. This chapter builds on what you've learned, and it shows you how to enrich your application by adding features you'll commonly find in business applications.

In this chapter, you'll learn how to

- Use local properties and set the value of data items in code

- Set query parameters and pass arguments into screens

- Make your UI react to data changes by handling the PropertyChanged event

This chapter shows you how to extend the HelpDesk application by adding rich screen features. You'll find out how to create a custom search screen, and how to add a button that toggles the visibility of the search criteria options. If there are issues that are overdue, you'll find how to highlight these details by changing the label color. You'll also learn how to create a label that keeps a running count of the number of remaining characters that an engineer can enter when replying to an issue.

You'll also learn how to create a combined screen for creating and editing issues - this saves you from having to maintain two separate screens for this purpose. Other handy techniques that you'll learn include customizing data grid dialogs, creating nested autocomplete boxes, and bulk updating records. Finally, you'll find out how to create a screen that allows engineers to upload and download supporting documents.

Working with Screen Data

The first section of this chapter focuses on how to work with screen data. You'll find out how to work with screen properties, and learn how to add a custom search screen to your application. This example teaches you how to bind a screen to a query and how to set query parameters.

The initial set of examples is based on the Engineer Dashboard screen, as shown in Figure 7-1.

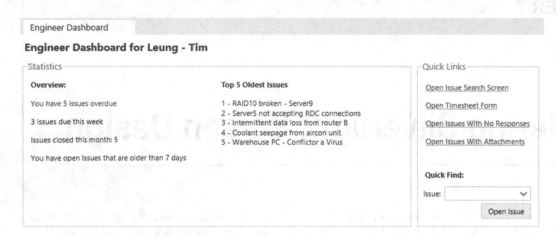

Figure 7-1. *Engineer Dashboard screen*

Displaying Custom Text and Information

The first part of the Statistics section shows the number of overdue cases. The technique you use to add custom text to a screen relies on local string properties, and you'll now find out how to create these.

To create a string property that shows overdue issues, create a details screen that's based on the Engineer entity and name your screen EngineerDashboard. Click the Add Data Item button, and add a new string property called IssuesOverdueLabel (as shown in Figure 7-2).

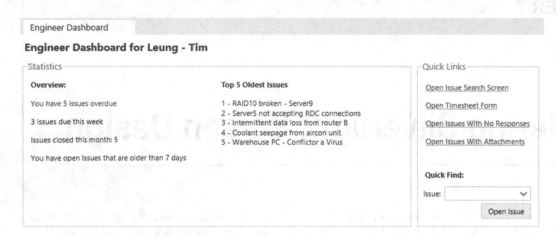

Figure 7-2. *Adding a new data item*

You can then set the text of this property by writing code in the `InitializeDataWorkspace` method. (See Listing 7-1.) This code uses the `outstandingIssues` query from Chapter 6 to return the issue count.

Listing 7-1. Building Text to Display on a Screen

VB:
File: HelpDeskVB\Client\UserCode\EngineerDashboard.vb

```
IssuesOverdueLabel = String.Format(
    "You have {0} issues overdue",
    outstandingIssues.Where(
        Function(item) item.TargetEndDateTime < Date.Today).
            Count().ToString()
)
```

C#:
File: HelpDeskCS\Client\UserCode\EngineerDashboard.cs

```
IssuesOverdueLabel = String.Format(
    "You have {0} issues overdue",
    outstandingIssues.Where(
        item => item.TargetEndDateTime < Date.Today).
            Count().ToString()
);
```

To display this text on your screen, simply drag the `IssuesOverdueLabel` property from the Screen Member list onto your Screen Content Tree. By default, LightSwitch renders `IssuesOverdueLabel` as a text box, so you need to change the control type to a label to render a read-only version of the data.

Local properties are a key part of screen design. Any content you want to add to a screen must be bound to a property, so you use local properties to work with data that's disconnected from the main data on your screen.

Adding Data Controls to a Screen

The Engineer Dashboard screen includes a Quick Find feature engineers can use to quickly find and open issue records by using an autocomplete box. Therefore, you need to add an autocomplete box that's not connected to the main data shown on your screen.

As with the string property example, you can add additional data controls by using the Add Data Item button. Because you want to add an autocomplete box that shows issues, select `Issue` from the type drop-down box and name your property `IssueSelectionProperty`.

To create the autocomplete box, simply drag `IssueSelectionProperty` from the Screen Member list onto your Screen Content Tree.

By default, the autocomplete box searches all records in the issue table. If you want to restrict the autocomplete box choices, create a query on the issue table and apply some filters. Add the query to your screen using the Add Data Item dialog and amend the Choices property of your autocomplete box using the Properties sheet.

To open the issue the user selects in a new screen, write code that calls the `show` method that relates to your issue details screen, and pass in the issue ID of the `IssueSelectionProperty`. You'll see an example of how to do this later on. (See Listing 7-4.)

Setting Control Values and Default Values

You'll often need to set the value that's displayed on text boxes, date pickers, and other controls. In LightSwitch, you don't set control values by accessing the Silverlight controls directly. If you recall the Model-View-ViewModel (MVVM) principles described in Chapter 1, controls are views that bind to the view model. So to set the value that's shown on a control, you should update the value on the underlying property.

The new issue screen allows users to set a priority by using an autocomplete box. To default the priority to medium when the screen loads, add the code from Listing 7-2 to the InitializeDataWorkspace method of your screen.

Listing 7-2. Setting Control Values

VB:
File: HelpDeskVB\Client\UserCode\CreateNewIssue.vb

```
Me.IssueProperty.Priority =
   DataWorkspace.ApplicationData.Priorities.Where(
      Function(item) item.PriorityDesc = "Medium").
        FirstOrDefault()
```

C#:
File: HelpDeskCS\Client\UserCode\CreateNewIssue.cs

```
this.IssueProperty.Priority =
   DataWorkspace.ApplicationData.Priorities.Where(
      (item => item.PriorityDesc == "Medium").
        FirstOrDefault();
```

The properties you can access in code correspond to the items that the screen designer shows in the Screen Member list. (See Figure 7-3.)

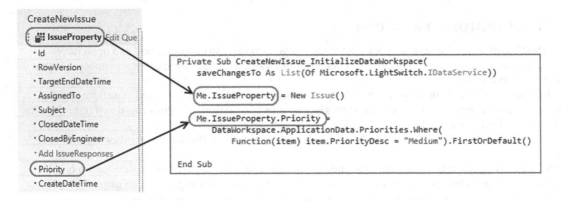

Figure 7-3. *The names in code match the names in the screen designer*

Notice that you cannot set the priority value by simply setting a string value of medium. Priority is a related item, so you need to assign an object that represents a medium priority to the IssueProperty.Priority property. The LINQ query shown in Listing 7-2 retrieves the medium priority by priority description, and it enables you to make this assignment.

Accessing grid and list values

If you need to reference the items shown in a data grid or data list, you can reference the underlying data collection in code. Just as before, the collection name you call in code matches the name you see in the Screen Member list. (See Figure 7-4.)

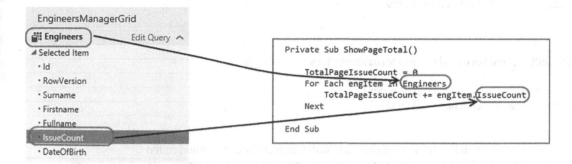

Figure 7-4. Accessing a screen collection property in code

LightSwitch exposes your data collections as *visual collections* (of type `Microsoft.LightSwitch.Framework.Client. VisualCollection`). This object contains the records LightSwitch currently shows in the data grid or list. An important point is that if you loop over the items in a visual collection, you'll loop only through the items that are shown on the screen. The data items you can access are limited by the pagination options you configured.

Visual collections include some useful properties and methods you can use, such as adding new records and opening records in a modal window. These are shown in Table 7-1.

Table 7-1. Visual Collection Members

Member	Description
SelectedItem	Gets or sets the record that is currently selected in the visual collection.
AddAndEditNew	Adds a new record to the visual collection, and opens a modal window to edit it. You can optionally supply a `completeAction` argument. This specifies a method to be run when the modal window is closed.
AddNew	Adds a new record to the visual collection.
EditSelected	Opens a modal window for the currently selected item.
DeleteSelected	Marks the currently selected record for deletion, and removes it from the visual collection. The actual deletion happens when the data workspace is saved.

Setting the Screen Title in Code

The Engineer Dashboard screen shows a custom title rather than the engineer summary property. To set a screen title in code, you set the `DisplayName` property as shown in Listing 7-3.

Listing 7-3. Setting the Screen Title in Code

VB:
File: HelpDeskVB\Client\UserCode\EngineerDashboard.vb

```
Private Sub Engineer_Loaded(succeeded As Boolean)
    Me.DisplayName = "Engineer Dashboard"
End Sub
```

C#:
File: HelpDeskCS\Client\UserCode\EngineerDashboard.cs

```
partial void Engineer_Loaded(bool succeeded)
    this.DisplayName = "Engineer Dashboard";
End Sub
```

Figure 7-5 shows the screen tab title at runtime. LightSwitch also includes a method called SetDisplayNameFromEntity. You use this method to pass in an entity and to set the screen title using the summary property of the entity you supplied. By default, LightSwitch uses this method on any screens that you created based on the Details Screen template.

Engineer Dashboard

Figure 7-5. *Setting the screen title in code*

Creating an Advanced Search Screen

The HelpDesk application includes an advanced search screen engineers can use to search for issues by using multiple combinations of search criteria. This screen uses the IssueSearchAll query you created in Exercise 6.1. An important topic you'll work with in this section is how to set query parameters.

Begin by creating an editable grid screen that uses the IssueSearchAll query, and name your screen IssueSearchAll. When you create a screen that uses a query with parameters, LightSwitch automatically creates properties and controls that allow the user to enter the parameter values.

You'll notice that LightSwitch creates an EngineerId property and renders it as a text box onto the search screen. In terms of usability, be aware that your users won't thank you for making them search for issues by the numeric engineer ID. A much better approach is to show the engineer names in an autocomplete box, and to bind the selected engineer ID to your query parameter.

To do this, create an autocomplete box in the same way as in the earlier example by adding a local engineer property called EngineerSelectionProperty. Now use the Properties sheet to set the Parameter Binding value to the ID value of EngineerSelectionProperty, as shown in Figure 7-6. You can now delete the autogenerated EngineerId property because it's no longer needed.

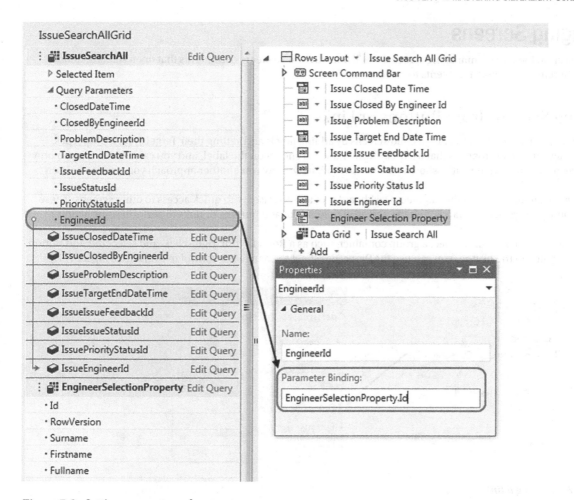

Figure 7-6. *Setting parameter values*

When you run this screen, you'll be able to use the autocomplete box to filter the issues by engineer. (You'll extend this screen in the "Hiding and Showing Controls" section later in this chapter.)

EXERCISE 7.1 – CREATING A SEARCH SCREEN

Extend your Search screen to allow users to find issues that were created between a user-specified start date and end date. To build this feature, you need to modify the IssueSearchAll query so that it includes StartDate and EndDate parameters. You need to create query filters to return issues where the create date is greater than or equal to the StartDate parameter, and less than or equal to the EndDate parameter. After you edit your query, modify your Search screen to allow users to enter the start and end dates. Write some screen-validation code to prevent users from entering a start date that's greater than the end date. To make it easier for the user, write code that defaults the end date to five days after the start date if the end date is empty.

Managing Screens

This next section focuses on managing screens. You'll find out how to create commands that open screens, define screen parameters, and pass arguments to screens.

Opening Screens from Buttons or Links

In Chapter 3, you learned how to launch child screens by adding labels and setting their Target Screen properties. A disadvantage of this approach is that it's tricky to alter the text shown on the label, and you can choose to open only details screens that match the entity shown on your label. I'll now show you another approach you can use to open screens.

The Quick Links section in the Engineer Dashboard provides the user with quick access to other screens. These links are bound to screen commands. You use screen commands to add buttons or links to perform some action in code.

To create a new command, select a group container, such as a Rows Layout, right-click, and select the Add Button option. After you add the button, you can use the Properties sheet to change the control to a link. (See Figure 7-7.)

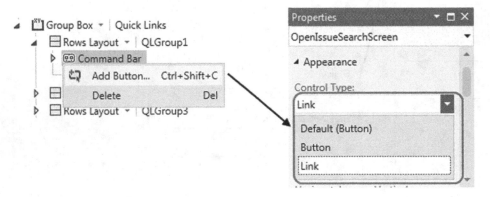

Figure 7-7. *Creating a link*

Although it's fairly simple to add a button or link, the actual screen layout takes a bit of effort. Figure 7-8 shows you how this layout looks at design time compared with how it looks at runtime. Notice how the layout uses sets of groups, each containing one command. To make sure all your links line up, you need to verify that the horizontal alignment settings are all set to left rather than stretch.

Design Time

- ◢ ⬚ Columns Layout ▾ | Group1
  - ▷ ⬚ Group Box ▾ | Statistics
  - ◢ ⬚ Group Box ▾ | Quick Links
    - ◢ ⊟ Rows Layout ▾ | QLGroup1
      - ◢ ⊡ Command Bar
        - └ **A** ▾ | Open Issue Search Screen
    - ◢ ⊟ Rows Layout ▾ | QLGroup2
      - ◢ ⊡ Command Bar
        - └ **A** ▾ | Open Highest Feedback Screen
    - ◢ ⊟ Rows Layout ▾ | QLGroup3
      - ◢ ⊡ Command Bar
        - └ **A** ▾ | Open Issues With No Responses
    - ◢ ⊟ Rows Layout ▾ | QLGroup4
      - ◢ ⊡ Command Bar
        - └ **A** ▾ | Open Issues With Attachments
    - └ + Add ▾

Run Time

Quick Links

Open Issue Search Screen

Open Highest Feedback Screen

Open Issues With No Responses

Open Issues With Attachments

Figure 7-8. *Laying out your screen*

Laying out controls at design time is difficult because you can't visualize how your screen will appear. As I mentioned in Chapter 3, the trick to effective layout design is to use the runtime screen designer. By doing so, you can change the appearance settings and immediately see the effect the change has on your running screen.

Once you create your command, you can double-click it to open the code window. Here, you can write code that uses the `Application` object's `Show` methods to open your screens (as discussed in Chapter 4).

Another area where you'll want to open screens is through a cell on a data grid. Chapter 3 showed you how to do this by using labels and specifying the link settings. The problem with this approach is that you can open only details screens that match the entities shown in the grid. Another problem is that the data grid binds the display text to a property, which means you can't use static text.

The way around this problem is to use a grid row command. In the designer, expand the Command Bar group in the Data Grid Row, and click the Add button to add a new button. In this example, the grid row command is called `ViewDashboard`.

Figure 7-9 shows an engineer selection page that's used by managers. It includes two links that appear on the right side of the grid to allow a manager to view the dashboard and time-tracking screens for an engineer.

Figure 7-9. *Adding command buttons on a grid*

The code that opens the dashboard is shown in Listing 7-4. Notice how the code uses the SelectedItem property of the visual collection to return the ID of the engineer in the selected row.

Listing 7-4. Opening Screens from a Data Grid Command

VB:
File: HelpDeskVB\Client\UserCode\EngineersManagerGrid.vb

```
Private Sub ViewDashboard_Execute()
    Application.ShowEngineerDashboard(
        Engineers.SelectedItem.Id)
End Sub
```

C#:
File: HelpDeskCS\Client\UserCode\EngineersManagerGrid.cs

```
partial void ViewDashboard_Execute()
    this.Application.ShowEngineerDashboard(
        Engineers.SelectedItem.Id);
End Sub
```

Refreshing All Open Screens

The dashboard page includes a link to refresh all screens that are open in the application. The code that performs this refresh is shown in Listing 7-5.

Listing 7-5. Refreshing All Open Screens

VB:
File: HelpDeskVB\Client\UserCode\EngineerDashboard.vb

```
Dim screens = Me.Application.ActiveScreens()      ❶
For Each s In screens
    Dim screen = s.Screen
    screen.Details.Dispatcher.BeginInvoke(        ❷
        Sub()
            screen.Refresh()                      ❸
        End Sub)
Next
```

C#:
File: HelpDeskCS\Client\UserCode\EngineerDashboard.cs

```
var screens = this.Application.ActiveScreens;     ❶
foreach (var s in screens)
{
    var screen = s.Screen;
    screen.Details.Dispatcher.BeginInvoke(() =>   ❷
    {
        screen.Refresh();                         ❸
    });
}
```

This code uses the Application object's ActiveScreens ❶ collection to find all open screens. It then calls the Refresh method ❸ on each screen. The code needs to call the Refresh method on the same thread that owns the screen. The threading code in ❷ invokes the logic on the correct thread, and you'll learn more about this in the "Working with Threads" section.

Passing Arguments into Screens

You can use the screen designer to create screen parameters that accept arguments when you open a screen.

The first link in the Quick Links section opens the custom search screen you created earlier. This example shows you how to supply an engineer property to the Search screen when it opens. This allows you to default the engineer autocomplete box to the value that's passed to it from the Engineer Dashboard screen.

To turn your Search screen's engineer property into a parameter, select the engineer property and select the Is Parameter check box as shown in Figure 7-10.

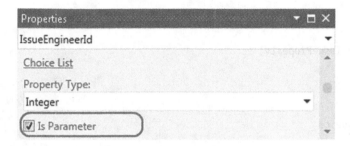

Figure 7-10. Defining screen parameters

To pass an engineer to the Search screen, you can simply call the screen's show method and provide the engineer you want to use. The code in Listing 7-6 passes to the Search screen the engineer that's represented by the dashboard screen's engineer property.

Listing 7-6. Passing Screen Parameters

VB:
File: HelpDeskVB\Client\UserCode\EngineerDashboard.vb

```
Private Sub OpenIssueSearchScreen_Execute()
    Application.ShowIssueSearchAll (Me.Engineer.Id)
End Sub
```

C#:
File: HelpDeskCS\Client\UserCode\EngineerDashboard.cs

```
partial void OpenIssueSearchScreen_Execute(){
    this.Application.ShowIssueSearchAll (this.Engineer.Id);
}
```

If you defined multiple parameters, IntelliSense shows you the correct order in which to pass in the arguments.

Creating a Continuous New Data Screen

The screens you create with the New Data Screen template behave in a specific way. When a user saves her record, LightSwitch closes the screen and reopens the record by using the Details Screen for your entity.

In some circumstances, you might want to allow the user to immediately enter another record rather than show the newly created record in a details screen.

To make this change, open the code file for your New Data Screen and delete the two lines in the Saved method that closes the screen and reopens the entity in the details screen. (See Listing 7-7.) To allow the entry of another new record, add a line that creates an instance of a new entity.

Listing 7-7. Reset the New Data Screen After a Save

VB:
File: HelpDeskVB\Client\UserCode\CreateNewIssue.vb

```
Private Sub CreateNewIssue_Saved()
    'Delete the auto generated lines below
    'Me.Close(False)
    'Application.Current.ShowDefaultScreen(Me.IssueProperty)
    Me.IssueProperty = New Issue
End Sub
```

C#:
File: HelpDeskCS\Client\UserCode\CreateNewIssue.cs

```
partial void CreateNewIssue_Saved(){
    //Delete the auto generated lines below
    //this.Close(false);
    //Application.Current.ShowDefaultScreen(Me.IssueProperty);
    this.IssueProperty = new Issue();
}
```

Showing MessageBox and InputBox alerts

You use the ShowMessageBox method to show an alert or to prompt the user to confirm an action. Listing 7-8 demonstrates this method.

Listing 7-8. Displaying a Message Box

VB:
File: HelpDeskVB\Client\UserCode\Setup.vb

```
Private Sub ArchiveIssues_Execute()
    If Me.ShowMessageBox(
            "Are you sure you want delete all issues older than 12 months?",
            "Confirm Delete", MessageBoxOption.YesNo) =
            System.Windows.MessageBoxResult.Yes Then
        DeleteOldIssues()
    End If
End Sub
```

C#:
File: HelpDeskCS\Client\UserCode\Setup.cs

```csharp
partial void ArchiveIssues_Execute()
{
    if (this.ShowMessageBox(
        "Are you sure you want delete all issues older than 12 months?",
        "Confirm Delete", MessageBoxOption.YesNo) ==
        System.Windows.MessageBoxResult.Yes)
    {
        DeleteOldIssues();
    }
}
```

This code refers to a button on a screen that allows a user to delete old issues. You use the ShowMessageBox method to pass in a message, a caption, and an argument that specify the buttons that are shown. You use the return value to control the logic flow in your application. So in this example, the code executes a user-defined method called DeleteOldIssues if the user clicks the message box's Yes button.

If you want to display a dialog that allows the user to enter some text, you can use the ShowInputBox method rather than the ShowMessageBox method. Figure 7-11 illustrates what these dialog boxes look like at runtime.

Figure 7-11. ShowMessageBox and ShowInputBox dialogs

Working with Controls

This section focuses on how to use controls in code. It includes information about how to toggle the visibility of controls, set the focus to a control, and obtain references in code to set other attributes and to handle events.

Finding Controls Using *FindControl*

The key to working with controls is to use the FindControl method. This returns an object of type IContentItemProxy, which represents LightSwitch's View-Model object. The IContentItemProxy members you can access are shown in Table 7-2.

Table 7-2. IContentItemProxy Methods and Properties

Methods/Properties	Description
Focus	LightSwitch sets the focus to the control when you call this method.
DisplayName	Allows you to change the display name of your control. LightSwitch uses the display name value to set the label text for your control.
IsEnabled	If you set this to `false`, LightSwitch disables the control. The control will still be visible, but it will be grayed out.
IsReadOnly	If you set this to `true`, the control becomes read-only and the user won't be able to edit the contents of the control.
IsVisible	LightSwitch hides the control if you set this to `false`.
SetBinding	This method allows you to perform data binding.

As you can see, there are some useful properties you can access, especially the IsVisible and IsEnabled properties.

A related method is the FindControlInCollection method. You use this to obtain an IContentItemProxy reference to a control that belongs inside a data grid (or any control that shows a collection of data, such as a list). You'll see an example of how to use this method later on.

Setting the focus to a control

By using IContentItemProxy's Focus method, you can set the focus to a specific control. Listing 7-9 shows you how to set the focus to the Problem Description field on a screen that allows users to enter new issues.

Listing 7-9. Setting the Focus to a Control

VB:
File: HelpDeskVB\Client\UserCode\CreateNewIssue.vb

```
Me.FindControl("ProblemDescription").Focus()
```

C#:
File: HelpDeskCS\Client\UserCode\CreateNewIssue.cs

```
this.FindControl("ProblemDescription").Focus();
```

The FindControl method requires you to pass in the name of the control, which you can find in the Properties sheet.

If your code doesn't work, double-check the name you pass into this method. Because you can add multiple controls that bind to the same property on a screen, the control you want to use might not match the name of your property. For example, your control might be named ProblemDescription1 if you've added more than one problem description control to your screen.

Hiding and showing controls

The issue search screen contains multiple search fields. This example shows you how to tidy up this screen by adding a button that toggles the view between *simple* and *advanced* modes. In advanced mode, the screen shows a full set of filter options, whereas in simple mode, several of the filter options are hidden.

To create this example, open the IssueSearchAll screen you created earlier in this chapter and carry out the following steps:

1. Create two Rows Layout controls called SimpleGroup and AdvancedGroup. In the Properties sheet for the AdvancedGroup layout, set the Is Visible property to false.

2. Add a new button in the command bar of SimpleGroup, and name your button ToggleVisibility. Set the Display Text property of this button to Show Advanced Filters.

3. Move the engineer and problem description controls into the simple group. Move the remaining controls into the advanced group. The layout of your screen should now appear as shown in Figure 7-12.

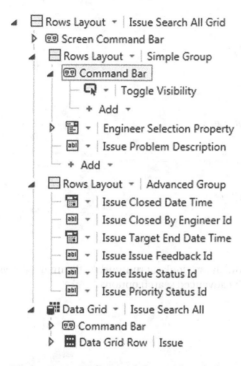

Figure 7-12. *Hiding and showing controls*

Add the code shown in Listing 7-10. Notice how it uses the FindControl method to toggle the visibility of the Rows Layout that contains the advanced controls ❶ and also sets the display text of the button depending on the mode that's selected ❷.

Listing 7-10. Hiding and Showing Controls

VB:
File: HelpDeskVB\Client\UserCode\IssueSearchAll.vb

```vb
Private Sub ToggleVisibility_Execute()
    Dim rowLayout = Me.FindControl("AdvancedGroup")
    rowLayout.IsVisible = Not (rowLayout.IsVisible)                    ❶
```

```
    If rowLayout.IsVisible Then
        Me.FindControl("ToggleVisibility").DisplayName =
            "Show Simple Filters"                              ❷
    Else
        Me.FindControl("ToggleVisibility").DisplayName =
            "Show Advanced Filters"                            ❷
    End If
End Sub
```

C#:
File: HelpDeskCS\Client\UserCode\IssueSearchAll.cs

```
partial void ToggleVisibility_Execute()
{
    var rowLayout = this.FindControl("AdvancedGroup");
    rowLayout.IsVisible = !(rowLayout.IsVisible);              ❶

    if (rowLayout.IsVisible)
        {
         this.FindControl("ToggleVisibility").DisplayName =
            "Show Simple Filters";                             ❷
        }
    else
        {
         this.FindControl("ToggleVisibility").DisplayName =
            "Show Advanced Filters";                           ❸
        }
}
```

You're now ready to run your screen, and Figure 7-13 shows how it looks at runtime. As the image shows, the ToggleVisibility button allows the user to hide and show the advanced search options.

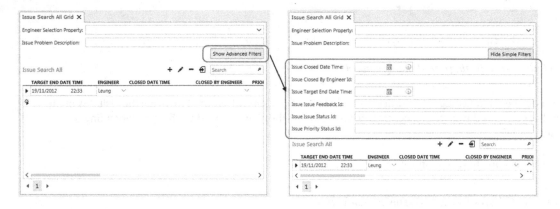

Figure 7-13. *Clicking the button toggles the visibility of the Advanced group*

■ **Caution**   For the sake of brevity, most of the code samples don't contain the checks and exception handling you'd normally add to a production application. In this example, it's a good idea to test that rowLayout isn't null before setting its properties.

Making check boxes read-only

Check boxes have an annoying problem: they don't honor the read-only setting you applied in the Properties sheet for your check box. To make them read-only, you need to write code.

This example features an editable grid screen that's based on the Engineer table, and shows you how to disable a check box called SecurityVetted. To create this example, add an editable grid screen, choose the engineer table from the screen data drop-down, and name your screen EngineersManagerGrid. Now add the code that's shown in Listing 7-11 to the InitializeDataWorkspace method of your screen.

Listing 7-11. Making Check Boxes Read-Only

VB:
File: HelpDeskVB\Client\UserCode\EngineersManagerGrid.vb

```
For Each eng In Engineers                              ❶
    Me.FindControlInCollection(
        "SecurityVetted", eng).IsEnabled = False       ❷
Next
```

C#:
File: HelpDeskCS\Client\UserCode\EngineersManagerGrid.cs

```
foreach (Engineer eng in Engineers)                    ❶
{
    this.FindControlInCollection(
        "SecurityVetted", eng).IsEnabled = false;       ❷
}
```

Because you need to make each check box in every row of your data grid read-only, the code begins by looping through the Engineers collection ❶. It obtains an IContentItemProxy object for each engineer in the collection by calling the FindControlInCollection method and supplying an engineer object. It disables the check box by setting the IsEnabled property to false ❷.

Reference the Underlying Silverlight Control

As you'll recall from Figure 7-1, the Engineer Dashboard screen displays the number of outstanding issues. If the number of outstanding issues exceeds 10, the label should be shown in red.

Although you can use the IContentItemProxy object to set the visibility, focus, and read-only state of a control, you cannot use it to access other control attributes. To do this, you need to reference the underlying Silverlight control.

Once again, this requires you to use the FindControl method to return an IContentItemProxy object. This provides you with two ways to access the Silverlight control. You can either handle the ControlAvailable event or data-bind your screen properties to dependency properties on your control by calling the SetBinding method. Chapter 9 shows you how to apply the SetBinding technique.

To use the ControlAvailable method, add the code in Listing 7-12 to the InitializeDataWorkspace method of your Engineer Dashboard screen.

155

Listing 7-12. Referencing a Control Using ControlAvailable

VB:
File: HelpDeskVB\Client\UserCode\EngineerDashboard.vb

```
AddHandler Me.FindControl("IssuesOverdueLabel").ControlAvailable,
    Sub(sender As Object, e As ControlAvailableEventArgs)
    Dim issueLabel = CType(e.Control,
        System.Windows.Controls.TextBlock)                          ❶
    issueLabel.Foreground = New SolidColorBrush(Colors.Red)         ❷
End Sub
```

C#:
File: HelpDeskCS\Client\UserCode\EngineerDashboard.cs

```
using System.Windows.Media;

var control = this.FindControl("IssuesOverdueLabel");

control.ControlAvailable +=
(object sender, ControlAvailableEventArgs e) =>
{
    var issueLabel =
        (System.Windows.Controls.TextBlock)e.Control;               ❶
    issueLabel.Foreground = new SolidColorBrush(Colors.Red);        ❷
};
```

When you handle the `ControlAvailable` event, the `ControlAvailableEventArgs` parameter allows you to access the underlying Silverlight control.

Because you know that LightSwitch labels are rendered as a Silverlight Text Blocks, you can simply declare a variable and cast `IssuesOverdueLabel` to an object of type `System.Windows.Controls.TextBlock` ❶. This allows you to access all of the text-block properties in code and to set the foreground color ❷.

If you want to access a LightSwitch control in code but don't know what the underlying Silverlight type is, you can handle the `ControlAvailable` event, set a breakpoint in this method, and query `e.Control.GetType()` in the immediate window.

As the name suggests, LightSwitch fires the `ControlAvailable` event when the control becomes available. This means that when you write code that handles this event, you won't encounter the errors that might occur if you try to access the control too early.

Handling Silverlight Control Events

When you write code in the `ControlAvailable` method, you can also add event handlers to handle the events raised by the Silverlight control.

To give you an example of the sorts of events you can handle, Table 7-3 shows you some of the events that the Silverlight text-box control raises. There are many more events you can use; this table shows only a subset, but it gives you a flavor of the sort of events you can handle.

Table 7-3. *Events Raised by the Silverlight Text-Box Control*

Event	Description
GotFocus	Occurs when the text box receives the focus.
KeyDown	Occurs when a user presses a keyboard key while the text box has focus.
KeyUp	Occurs when a user releases a keyboard key while the text box has focus.
LostFocus	Occurs when the text box loses focus.
SelectionChanged	Occurs when the text selection has changed.
TextChanged	Occurs when content changes in the text box.

The Issue Response screen allows engineers to respond to users. The maximum response text allowed is 1000 characters.

This example shows you how to provide the user with a running count of the number of remaining characters as soon as they're entered by the user.

To create this example, create a new screen based on the Issue Response table, add a new local integer property called ResponseTextCount, and enter the code shown in Listing 7-13.

Listing 7-13. Handling the Text Box KeyUp Event

VB:
File: HelpDeskVB\Client\UserCode\CreateNewIssueResponse.vb

```
Private Sub CreateNewIssueResponse_InitializeDataWorkspace(
    saveChangesTo As List(Of Microsoft.LightSwitch.IDataService))
    Me.IssueResponseProperty = New IssueResponse()

    Dim control = Me.FindControl("ResponseText")
    AddHandler control.ControlAvailable,
        AddressOf TextBoxAvailable                               ❶

    ResponseTextCount = 1000

End Sub

Private Sub TextBoxAvailable(
    sender As Object, e As ControlAvailableEventArgs)
    AddHandler CType(e.Control,
        System.Windows.Controls.TextBox).KeyUp,
            AddressOf TextBoxKeyUp                                ❷
End Sub

Private Sub TextBoxKeyUp(
    sender As Object, e As System.Windows.RoutedEventArgs)
    Dim textbox = CType(sender, System.Windows.Controls.TextBox)
    ResponseTextCount = 1000 - textbox.Text.Count()              ❸
End Sub
```

C#:
File: HelpDeskCS\Client\UserCode\CreateNewIssueResponse.cs

```csharp
partial void CreateNewIssueResponse_InitializeDataWorkspace(
    List<IDataService> saveChangesTo)
{
    this.FindControl("ResponseText").ControlAvailable += TextBoxAvailable;      ❶
    ResponseTextCount = 1000;

}

private void TextBoxAvailable(object sender, ControlAvailableEventArgs e)
{
    ((System.Windows.Controls.TextBox)e.Control).KeyUp += TextBoxKeyUp;         ❷
}

private void TextBoxKeyUp(object sender, System.Windows.RoutedEventArgs e)
{
    var textbox = (System.Windows.Controls.TextBox)sender;
    ResponseTextCount = 1000 - textbox.Text.Count();                            ❸
}
```

When the screen first loads, the code in the InitializeDataWorkspace method adds an event handler called TextBoxAvailable, which handles the ControlAvailable event of the ResponseText text box ❶. This initial code also initializes the ResponseTextCount to 1000.

When the ResponseText control becomes available, the code adds an event handler called TextBoxKeyUp that handles the KeyUp event of the control ❷.

The TextBoxKeyUp method runs whenever the user types a character into the response text text box, and it recalculates the number of remaining characters ❸. Figure 7-14 shows how the screen appears at runtime.

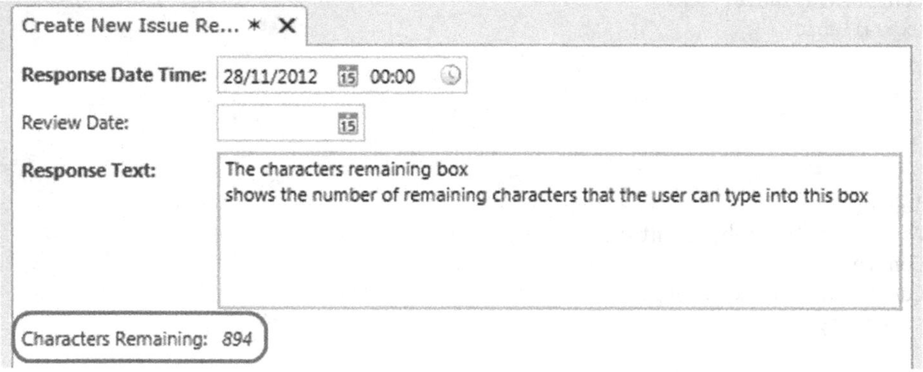

Figure 7-14. *Screen that shows the number of remaining characters*

Custom Examples

You now know how to work with data, screens, and controls. This section combines the content that you learned so far and presents some practical examples of screen design.

Designing an Add/Edit Screen

As you now know, you can create screens to view data by using the Details Screen template. For adding data, you can add a screen that uses the New Data template. However, LightSwitch doesn't include a screen template you can use to both edit and view data using the same screen.

In this example, you'll find out how to create a combined Add and Edit screen. If you need to create screens that look consistent for adding and viewing data, this technique saves you from having to carry out the same customization in two places. It'll also make your application more maintainable because there'll be fewer screens to maintain in your application.

Here are the steps to build a combined add/edit screen:

1. Create a details screen for the issue entity, and make it the default screen. Name your screen AddEditIssue.

2. LightSwitch creates an ID property called IssueId. Make this optional by deselecting the Is Required check box.

3. Click the Add Data Item button, and add a local property of data type issue. Name this IssueProperty.

4. Delete the content on the screen that's bound to the issue query.

5. Re-create the screen controls by dragging the IssueProperty property onto the Screen Content Tree. By default, LightSwitch creates IssueProperty as an autocomplete box. Change the control type to Rows Layout.

Now add the following code to the query's loaded method, as shown in Listing 7-14.

Listing 7-14. Issue Add and Edit Code

VB:
File: HelpDeskVB\Client\UserCode\AddEditIssue.vb

```
Private Sub Issue_Loaded(succeeded As Boolean)

    If Not Me.IssueId.HasValue Then
        Me.IssueProperty = New Issue()              ❶
    Else
        Me.IssueProperty = Me.Issue                 ❷
    End If

    Me.SetDisplayNameFromEntity(Me.Issue)

End Sub
```

C#:
File: HelpDeskCS\Client\UserCode\AddEditIssue.cs

```
partial void Issue_Loaded(bool succeeded)
{
    if (!this.IssueId.HasValue)
    {
        this.IssueProperty = new Issue();                          ❶
    }
    else
    {
        this.IssueProperty = this.Issue;                           ❷
    }
    this.SetDisplayNameFromEntity(this.IssueProperty);
}
```

When you create a screen that uses the Details Screen template, LightSwitch creates a query that returns a single issue using the primary key value. It creates a screen parameter/property called IssueId.

If all of your screen controls are bound to this query, your screen won't work in Add mode. Therefore, you need to create a local property called IssueProperty and bind the UI controls on your screen to this property.

You then need to make the IssueId screen parameter optional. If the code that opens the screen doesn't supply an IssueId value, the code sets IssueProperty to an instance of a new issue ❶ and allows the user to enter a new issue.

If the code that opens the screen supplies an IssueId, the code sets IssueProperty to the issue that's returned by the issue query ❷.

Because you set this screen as the default screen, any issue you display using the summary control will use this screen.

The code in Listing 7-15 shows the code that's used on the Engineer Dashboard screen to open the screen in Add mode.

Listing 7-15. Opening the Combination Screen to Add a New Record

VB:
File: HelpDeskVB\Client\UserCode\EngineerDashboard.vb

```
Private Sub OpenNewIssueScreen_Execute()
    Application.ShowAddEditIssue(Nothing)
End Sub
```

C#:
File: HelpDeskCS\Client\UserCode\EngineerDashboard.cs

```
partial void OpenNewIssueScreen_Execute()
{
    this.Application.ShowAddEditIssue(null);
}
```

■ **Tip** If you find yourself repeating the same tasks during screen design, you can save yourself time in the long run by creating extensions. Chapter 13 shows you how to create a screen template extension you use to create add/edit screens without having to carry out the tasks that are shown here every time.

Customizing Data Grid Dialogs

The Data Grid control includes buttons that enable users to add and edit records. But the data entry screens that LightSwitch shows are autogenerated and can't be modified. (See Figure 7-15.)

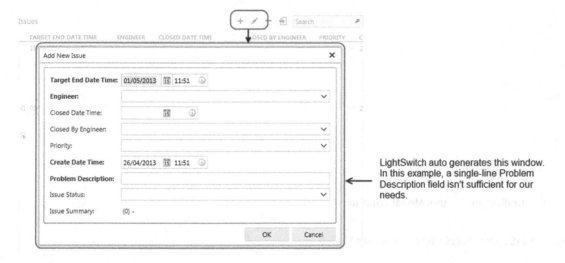

Figure 7-15. Data grid dialogs are not customizable

If you want to customize the data entry windows that open up from the data grid, remove the default Add and Edit buttons and build your own modal window.

In this example, you'll customize the data grid on the issue search screen. You'll modify the autogenerated window shown in Figure 7-15 to hide the issue closing details and make the Problem Description field multiline.

Here are the steps that you need to carry out to build a custom modal window screen:

1. Open your issues search screen (`IssueSearchAll`).

2. At the root level of the screen, add a new group and change the group type to Modal Window. Name this group `IssueWindow`.

3. Add the data items you want to show by dragging them from the `IssueSearchAll ➤ SelectedItem` property onto your modal window. Make the Problem Description field multiline by setting the lines property to a value greater than 1.

4. Add an OK button to your modal window by right-clicking the modal window group and choosing the Add Button option. Name your button `SaveItem`. Now add a Cancel button and call it `CancelItem`.

5. Hide the modal window's Show button by deselecting the Show Button check box in the Properties sheet. You'll be opening this modal window in code, so the default Show button isn't necessary.

6. Delete the data grid's Add, Edit, and Delete buttons in the command bar of your data grid (if they exist).

7. Add new Add, Edit, and Delete buttons in your data grid's Command Bar section. (Name these methods `AddItem`, `EditItem`, and `DeleteItem`.) Create their `Execute` methods.

You screen should now look like Figure 7-16. Now add the code that's shown in Listing 7-16.

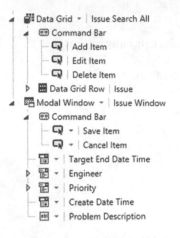

Figure 7-16. *Creating the modal window*

Listing 7-16. Controlling the Custom Modal Window

VB:
File: HelpDeskVB\Client\UserCode\IssueSearchAll.vb

```
Private Sub AddItem_Execute()
    Issues.AddNew()                                                        ❶
    Me.OpenModalWindow("IssueWindow")                                      ❷
End Sub

Private Sub EditItem_Execute()
    Me.OpenModalWindow("IssueWindow")                                      ❸
End Sub

Private Sub SaveItem_Execute()
    Me.CloseModalWindow("IssueWindow")
End Sub

Private Sub CancelItem_Execute()
    CType(Issues.SelectedItem, Issue).Details.DiscardChanges()             ❹
    Me.CloseModalWindow("IssueWindow")
End Sub
```

C#:
File: HelpDeskCS\Client\UserCode\IssueSearchAll.cs

```
partial void AddItem_Execute()
{
    Issues.AddNew();                                                       ❶
    this.OpenModalWindow("IssueWindow");                                   ❷
}

partial void EditItem_Execute()
{
    this.OpenModalWindow("IssueWindow");                                   ❸
}
```

162

```
partial void SaveItem_Execute()
{
    this.CloseModalWindow("IssueWindow");
}

partial void CancelItem_Execute()
{
    ((Issue)Issues.SelectedItem).Details.DiscardChanges();          ❹
    this.CloseModalWindow("IssueWindow");
}
```

LightSwitch includes two methods you use to work with modal windows (the `OpenModalWindow` and `CloseModalWindow` methods). Both of these methods require you to supply the name of the modal window you want to open or close.

The Add Item button creates a new issue by calling the visual collection's `AddNew` method ❶. Once you add a new issue, the new issue becomes the selected item. When the code opens your modal window ❷, it'll show the new record because the contents of the modal window are bound to the visual collection's selected item.

The Edit button simply calls the `OpenModalWindow` method ❸ and displays the issue that's currently selected in the data grid. Both the Save and Cancel buttons close the modal window by calling the `CloseModalWindow` method. The Cancel button calls the `DiscardChanges` method ❹ to undo any changes that have been made to the issue. This method restores the issue to the state it was in when the screen was first loaded. Unfortunately, it isn't simple to undo only the changes that the user made in the modal window without writing lots of extra code.

Figure 7-17 shows how the screen looks at runtime. As you can see, this is big improvement over the autogenerated window. (See Figure 7-15.)

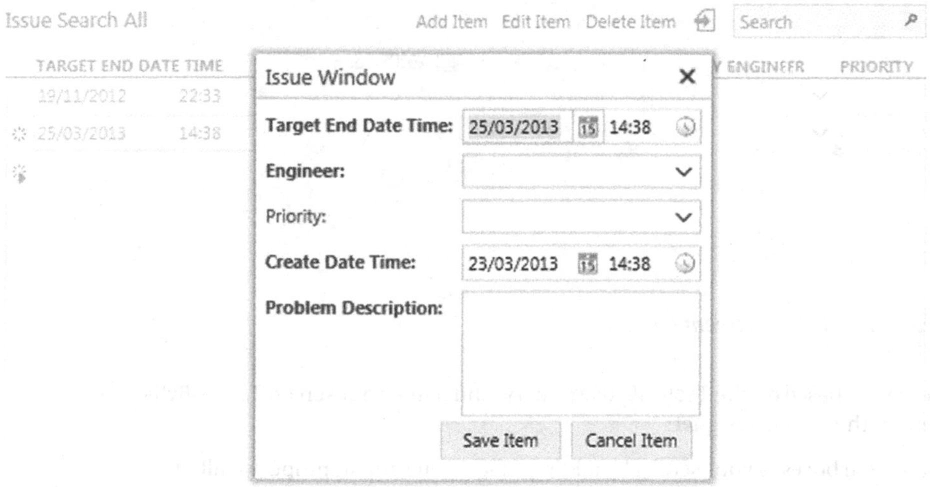

Figure 7-17. *Customized data grid dialog*

To extend this sample further, you can set the title of the modal window so that it shows the entity that's being edited. To do this, you set the `DisplayName` property of the modal window by calling the `FindControl` method. You can also change the text buttons to image buttons by using the option in the Properties sheet.

Nesting Autocomplete Boxes

Another scenario you might encounter is the need to create sets of nested autocomplete boxes.

In this example, you'll create an *editable grid screen* called IssuesByUser that allows managers to find issues filtered by user. This screen contains an autocomplete box that shows a list of departments. When the user selects a department, it populates a second autocomplete box that shows the users who belong in the department.

To carry out this example, you need to create a couple of queries. The first query returns a set of issues that are filtered by user. This query populates the main data grid that's shown on the screen. The second query returns a list of users filtered by department. It's used to populate the second autocomplete box.

Here are the steps you need to carry out to create these queries:

1. Create a query called IssuesByUsers that filters the User ➤ Id property by an integer parameter called UserId.

2. To allow the Users autocomplete box to be filtered by department, create a query called UsersByDepartment on the User table. Filter the Department ➤ Id property by a new parameter called DepartmentId. Both of these queries are shown in Figure 7-18.

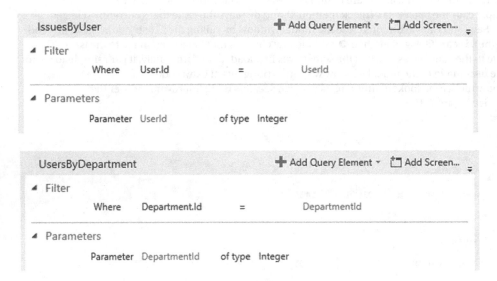

Figure 7-18. *IssuesByUser and UsersByDepartment queries*

Now create an editable screen based on the IssuesByUser query, and name your screen IssuesByUserGrid. Carry out the remaining steps in the screen designer:

1. Add two autocomplete boxes to your screen by adding a local department property called DepartmentProperty and a local user property called UserProperty.

2. Create autocomplete boxes by dragging these properties onto your screen.

3. Click the Add Data Item button, and add the UsersByDepartment query you created earlier.

4. Set the DepartmentId parameter value of your UsersByDepartment query to the value that's selected in the department AutoCompleteBox. To do this, select the DepartmentId parameter and set the parameter binding to DepartmentProperty.Id.

5. Select your Users autocomplete box, and view the Properties sheet. Use the Choices drop-down list to change the data source from Users to UsersByDepartment.

6. Change the parameter binding of the IssuesByUser ➤ UserId parameter so that it points to UserProperty.Id rather than the default binding of IssueUserId that LightSwitch sets up for you.

When you run your screen, the Users autocomplete box will be filtered by the value that the user selects in the department autocomplete box, as shown in Figure 7-19. As you'll notice, the presentation of this screen has been improved by placing the autocomplete boxes in a group and providing more friendly descriptions.

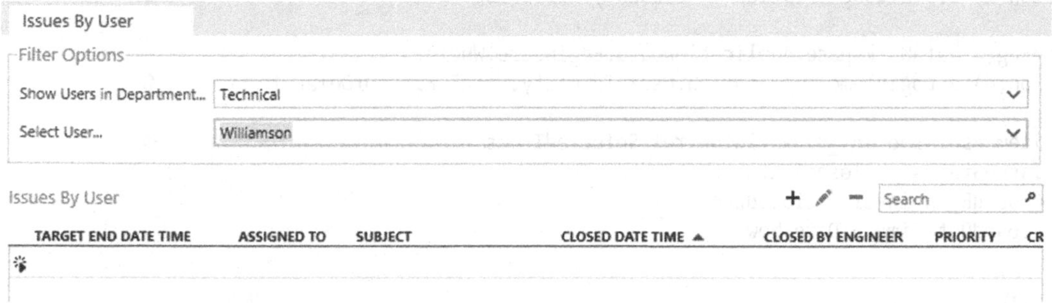

Figure 7-19. *Nested autocomplete box at runtime*

Bulk Updating Records by Using a Multiselect Grid

One of the limitations of the built-in data grid is that you can't select multiple records. In this example, you'll modify the IssuesManagerGrid so that it allows managers to close multiple issues.

To begin, you need to add a reference to the System.Windows.Controls.Data assembly. To do this, follow these steps:

1. Switch your project to File View and right-click your Client project.

2. Choose the Add Reference option, and select the System.Windows.Controls.Data assembly.

Now return to Logical View and carry out the following tasks:

1. Create an editable grid screen based on the issue entity, and name it IssuesManagerGrid.

2. Click the Add Data Item button, and add a new method called CancelSelectedIssues.

3. Create a button by dragging the CancelSelectedIssues method onto a suitable place in your screen.

4. Add the code that's shown in Listing 7-17.

Listing 7-17. Bulk-Closing Multiple Records

VB:
File: HelpDeskVB\Client\UserCode\IssuesManagerGrid.vb

```
Private WithEvents _datagridControl As DataGrid = Nothing

Private Sub IssuesManagerGrid_Created()
    '  1 Replace grid with the name of your data grid control          ❶
    AddHandler Me.FindControl("grid").ControlAvailable,
        Sub(send As Object, e As ControlAvailableEventArgs)
```

```
                _datagridControl = TryCast(e.Control, DataGrid)
                _datagridControl.SelectionMode =
                    DataGridSelectionMode.Extended                          ❷
        End Sub
End Sub

Private Sub CancelSelectedIssues_Execute()

    Dim closedStatus = DataWorkspace.ApplicationData.IssueStatusSet.Where(
        Function(i) i.StatusDescription = "Closed").FirstOrDefault          ❸

    Dim closedEng = DataWorkspace.ApplicationData.Engineers.Where(
        Function(e) e.LoginName=Application.User.Identity.Name).FirstOrDefault   ❹

    For Each item As Issue In _datagridControl.SelectedItems              ❺
        item.IssueStatus = closedStatus
        item.ClosedByEngineer = closedEng
        item.ClosedDateTime = Date.Now
    Next
End Sub
```

C#:
File: HelpDeskCS\Client\UserCode\IssuesManagerGrid.cs

```
using System.Windows.Controls;

private DataGrid _datagridControl = null;

partial void IssuesManagerGrid_Created()
{
    //1 Replace grid with the name of your data grid control            ❶
    this.FindControl("grid").ControlAvailable +=
        (object sender, ControlAvailableEventArgs e) =>
        {
            _datagridControl = ((DataGrid)e.Control);
            _datagridControl.SelectionMode =
                DataGridSelectionMode.Extended;                          ❷
        };
}

partial void CancelSelectedIssues_Execute()
{

    var closedStatus = DataWorkspace.ApplicationData.IssueStatusSet.Where(
        i => i.StatusDescription == "Closed").FirstOrDefault();          ❸

    var closedEng = DataWorkspace.ApplicationData.Engineers.Where(
        e => e.LoginName == Application.User.Identity.Name).FirstOrDefault();  ❹

    foreach (Issue item in _datagridControl.SelectedItems)               ❺
```

```
    {
        item.IssueStatus = closedStatus;
        item.ClosedByEngineer = closedEng;
        item.ClosedDateTime = DateTime.Now;
    }
}
```

When the screen first loads, the code in the Created method adds an event handler that handles the ControlAvailable event of the data grid. The code uses the FindControl method ❶ to return a reference to the data grid. By default, this called grid, so you might need to change this line of code if you named your data grid differently.

When the data grid becomes available, the code sets the SelectionMode of the data grid to Extended ❷. This setting allows the user to select multiple records.

When a user clicks the CancelSelectedIssues button, the code loops through the selected items ❺ on the grid and cancels the issues. The queries in this method retrieve the "closed state" ❸ and "closed by engineer" ❹ entities that are needed to close the issue.

The code in ❹ works on the assumption that you enabled authentication in your application. (See Chapter 16.) When you enable authentication, Application.User.Identity.Name returns the name of the logged-in user. The Engineer table is designed to store the login name of each engineer so that you can match engineer records with login names.

Figure 7-20 shows how the screen looks at runtime. Notice how you can select multiple rows by using the Ctrl key.

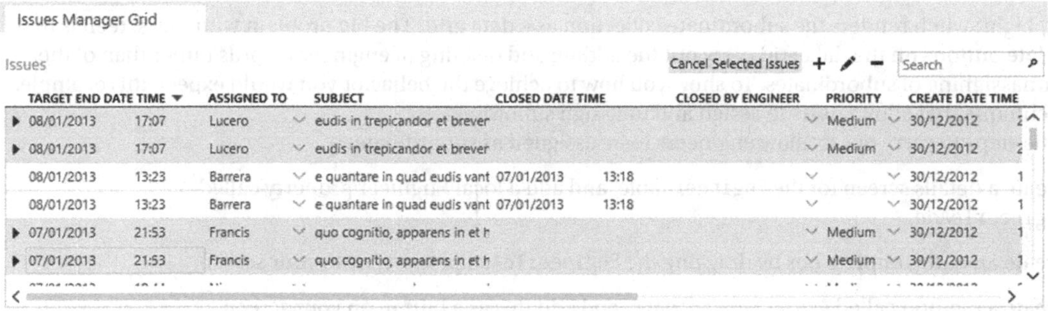

Figure 7-20. *Multiselect screen at runtime*

EXERCISE 7.2 – CUSTOMIZING SCREENS

This example allows users only to cancel selected issues. Try to adapt this screen so that it allows users to choose what to do with their selected records. For example, you could modify your screen to allow a user to bulk-update the target end date for all selected issues or to reassign all selected issues to a different engineer. To achieve this, add a button to your screen that opens a modal window control. Create check boxes to allow your user to choose how they want to update their selected records. If a user wants to set a new target end date, provide a date picker that allows the user to enter a new target end date. If the user wants to reassign the selected issues, provide an autocomplete box that allows the user to choose the new engineer. You can use local properties to create these controls. Finally, add a button to your modal window control to allow the user to apply his changes.

Assigning and Unassigning Self-Joined Data

The Engineer table includes a self-relationship that allows it to store the manager for each engineer (as shown in Figure 2-13 in Chapter 2). If you create a details screen for the Engineer table and include the Engineer subordinates data item, you end up with a screen that looks like Figure 7-21.

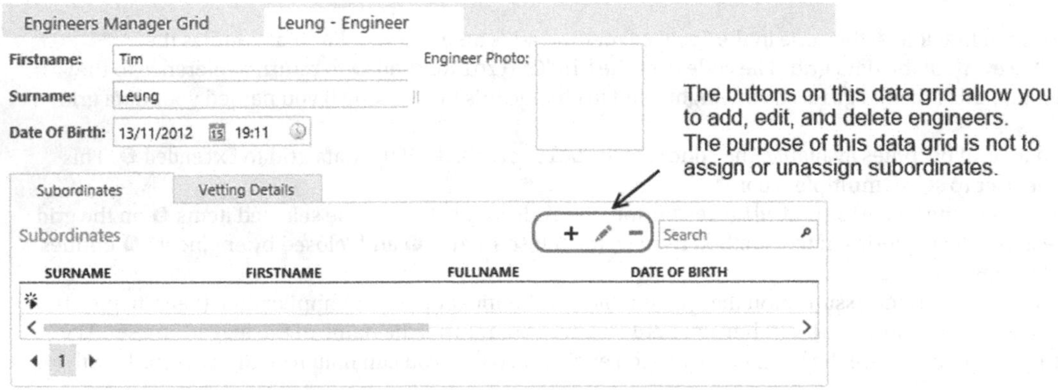

Figure 7-21. *Default subordinate data grid*

By default, LightSwitch renders the subordinate collection as a data grid. The big problem with this screen is that the add and delete buttons on the data grid carry out the adding and deleting of engineer records rather than of the assigning and unassigning of subordinates. To show you how to achieve the behavior you would expect, this example shows you a technique that allows users to assign and unassign subordinates.

Here are the steps to carry out to allow engineers to be assigned as subordinates:

1. Create a details screen for the Engineer table, and add a local Engineer property called EngineerToAdd.

2. Create an autocomplete box by dragging the EngineerToAdd property onto your screen.

3. Create a method called AssignSubordinate, and add this as a button on your screen.

4. Add the AssignSubordinate code, as shown in Listing 7-18.

Listing 7-18. Assigning and Unassigning Subordinates

VB:
File: HelpDeskVB\Client\UserCode\EngineerDetail.vb

```
Private Sub AssignSubordinate_Execute()
    Engineer.Subordinates.Add(EngineerToAdd)                       ❶
    Subordinates.Refresh()
End Sub

Private Sub UnassignSubordinate_Execute()
    Engineer.Subordinates.Remove(Subordinates.SelectedItem)        ❷
    Subordinates.Refresh()                                         ❸
End Sub
```

C#:
File: HelpDeskCS\Client\UserCode\EngineerDetail.cs

```
partial void AssignSubordinate_Execute()
{
    Engineer.Subordinates.Add(EngineerToAdd);                    ❶
    Subordinates.Refresh();
}

partial void UnassignSubordinate_Execute()
{
    Engineer.Subordinates.Remove(Subordinates.SelectedItem);     ❷
    this.Save();                                                 ❸
    Subordinates.Refresh();
}
```

To allow engineers to be unassigned as subordinates, carry out the following tasks:

1. Change the subordinate data grid to a data list. The default name that LightSwitch gives this collection is Subordinates.

2. Create a method called UnassignSubordinate, and add this as a button to your screen.

3. Add the UnassignSubordinate code, as shown in Listing 7-18.

The Assign Subordinate button adds the engineer who is selected in the autocomplete box to the engineer's subordinate collection ❶. (In practice, you'll want to write some extra code to check that the user hasn't left the autocomplete box blank.)

The Unassign Subordinate button removes the engineer who is selected in the subordinates data list from the engineer's subordinate collection ❷.

In both of these methods, you'll find that assigning engineers to and unassigning engineers from the subordinates collection doesn't automatically refresh the data list of subordinates. (Calling the refresh method on the subordinates collection won't work either.) Although it might not be ideal, the simple way to address this problem is to save and refresh your screen ❸. Because this saves all changes that have been made on the screen, you might want to add a confirmation message to check that the user wants to carry out the save.

When you now run your screen, you'll be able to assign and unassign subordinates as shown in Figure 7-22.

Figure 7-22. *Subordinate allocation screen*

Creating Screens to Work with Single Row Tables

Sometimes, you need to create a table that's designed to store just a single row of data. Typical examples are tables designed to store configuration or application settings. The HelpDesk application includes a table called AppOptions. This table allows administrators to control auditing and specify reporting and email settings.

To create a screen that works with just the first record in the AppOptions table, create a new data screen for the AppOptions table and name it AppOptionsEdit. Now add the code in Listing 7-19 to the InitializeDataWorkspace method.

Listing 7-19. Creating a Screen That Works Only with the First Record

VB:
File: HelpDeskVB\Client\UserCode\AppOptionsEdit.vb

```
Private Sub AppOptionsEdit_InitializeDataWorkspace(
    saveChangesTo As List(Of Microsoft.LightSwitch.IDataService))
    Me.AppOptionProperty =
        DataWorkspace.ApplicationData.AppOptions.FirstOrDefault()    ❶
    If AppOptionProperty Is Nothing Then
        AppOptionProperty = New AppOption                            ❷
    End If
End Sub
```

C#:
File: HelpDeskCS\Client\UserCode\AppOptionsEdit.cs

```
partial void AppOptionsEdit_InitializeDataWorkspace(
    List<IDataService> saveChangesTo)
{
    this.AppOptionProperty =
        DataWorkspace.ApplicationData.AppOptions.FirstOrDefault();   ❶

    if (AppOptionProperty == null){
        this.AppOptionProperty = new AppOption();                   ❷
    }
}
```

By default, the New Data Screen template creates a screen with controls that are bound to a property called AppOptionProperty. The first part of the code ❶ sets the property to the first record in the table by calling the FirstOrDefault method. If the method returns null, the table is empty. In this circumstance, the code assigns a new instance of an AppOption entity to the AppOptionProperty ❷.

You're now ready to run your application. Figure 7-23 shows how the screen looks at runtime.

Application Config	
Audit Changes On:	☐
Send Email On:	☑
SMTP Server:	
SMTP Port:	
SMTP Username:	
SMTP Password:	
Report Web Site Root URL:	

Figure 7-23. *Application options screen*

Working with Threads

So far, you've seen a few examples of code that includes threading syntax. I'll now explain how this works in more detail.

LightSwitch applications are multithreaded. This means that your application can perform multiple tasks at the same time, which results in better use of resources and a more responsive user interface.

Although each thread provides an independent execution path, threads are not completely isolated from one another. The threads in a LightSwitch application are able to share data and memory. This is the reason why multithreading is so useful. In a LightSwitch application, one thread can fetch data from the data service while another thread updates the UI as soon as the data arrives.

Threads can be categorized into two distinct types: UI threads and worker threads. *UI threads* are responsible for creating and controlling UI elements, whereas *worker threads* are generally responsible for carrying out long-running tasks such as fetching data.

Multithreaded applications start with a single thread (the main thread) that's created by the operating system and CLR (the .NET Common Language Runtime). LightSwitch creates additional threads off of the main thread, and your application thus becomes multithreaded.

When you write user code in LightSwitch, you can execute it in one of three threads. Certain tasks will work only on a specific thread. So if your code attempts to run on the wrong thread, you'll receive a runtime exception.

From a practical prospective, the key point to understand is that you must run code on the correct thread. .NET threading is a complex topic and beyond the scope of this book. But to help you choose the correct thread, here are three simple rules:

1. **UI Rule:** Any code that interacts with the user must be executed on the UI thread. If you try to perform UI tasks on a worker thread, you'll get an exception.

2. **Thread Affinity Rule:** Silverlight objects and controls inherit from the DependencyObject class. By doing so, these objects have *thread affinity*. This means that only the thread that instantiates the object can subsequently access its members. If you try accessing these members from a different thread, you'll get an exception.

3. **Worker Thread Rule:** If you want to perform data access or long-running tasks, you should carry out this work on a worker thread. If you carry out this work on the UI thread, you'll make your application unresponsive. This means that it'll be slow to respond to keystrokes and mouse clicks, or it might freeze for long periods of time.

Figure 7-24 illustrates the threads that make up a LightSwitch application. Your application starts execution on a main UI thread. The main thread spawns an application thread. This thread is responsible for opening screens and for performing global logic that isn't associated with any specific screen. The code in your Application class executes in this thread. You'll find the code file in the folder Client\Usercode.

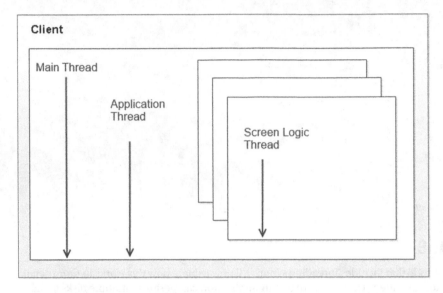

Figure 7-24. *Threads in a LightSwitch application*

Each screen in a LightSwitch application also has its own worker (or logic) thread. By default, LightSwitch executes any user code you write on the screen's logic thread. For example, if you click the Write Code button and write some code in the screen's `created` method, or if you write some custom code that handles the click of a button, that code will execute on the screen's logic thread. This is good news because you don't need to worry about inadvertently doing something that could freeze your UI.

If you need to run some code that updates your UI, you need to execute that code on the main UI thread. To do that, you use a `Dispatcher` object. The syntax you use to reference the three threads is as follows:

- **Main Dispatcher (UI thread):**

  `Microsoft.LightSwitch.Threading Dispatchers.Main`

- **Screen Dispatcher (screen logic thread):**

  `Screen.Details.Dispatcher`

  (Use the `Me.Details.Dispatcher` (VB) or `this.Details.Dispatcher` (C#)
  syntax in your screen code.)

- **Application Dispatcher (application thread):**

  `Application.Details.Dispatcher`

The `Dispatcher` object includes a method called `BeginInvoke`. You use this method to supply the code you want to execute on the thread and execute it asynchronously. This means that the calling code carries on executing, and the code you want to invoke will be queued for execution.

By adding an `imports` (VB) or `using` statement to the `Microsoft.LightSwitch.Threading` namespace at the start of your screen code file, you can access an extension method through the `Dispatcher` object called `Invoke`. The difference between `BeginInvoke` and `Invoke` is that the `Invoke` method executes your code synchronously, and the calling thread will wait for the code to complete before it continues. By calling `Invoke` rather than `BeginInvoke`, you can block your application while your code runs, and LightSwitch displays an hourglass to the user during this process. The advantage of using `Invoke` is that in some scenarios, you might want your application to show a 'wait state' in order to provide a positive indication that your process is in progress. Also, `Invoke` makes it easier for you to handle any return values from the code that you invoke, and can simplify any error handling code that you want to write.

Finding Out Which Thread Your Code Is Executing On

When you're debugging a piece of code, it's useful to know what thread your code is executing on. You can find this out by querying the Dispatcher's CheckAccess method in the Immediate Window (shown in Figure 7-25).

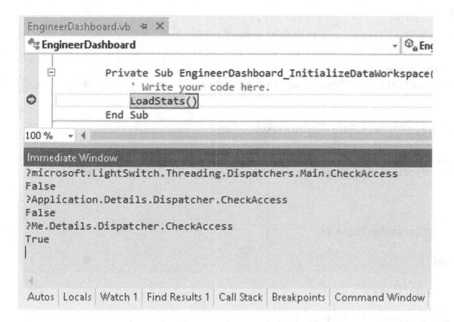

Figure 7-25. *Checking what thread you code runs on*

This figure illustrates a breakpoint on a line of code in the InitializeDataWorkspace method. This shows that when you query the CheckAccess method on the Main and Application dispatchers, the result is false. This indicates that the code isn't executing on any of those two threads. When you query the CheckAccess method on the screen logic dispatcher, the result is true. This confirms that the code is executing on the logic thread.

Understanding When to Execute Code on a Different Thread

The section you just read highlights an important characteristic about threading—you must execute any code that updates your UI on the main UI thread. You also learned that, by default, LightSwitch executes any screen code that you write on the logic thread. Given these two conflicting conditions, you might imagine that for any display-related task, you need to manually invoke your code on the UI thread. Thankfully, this isn't the case. In the vast majority of situations, LightSwitch takes care of updating your UI without you needing to write any custom threading code. This section shows you technically how this works.

Earlier in this chapter, you learned how to use the FindControl method to return an IContentItem object you use to set UI-related properties, such as DisplayName, IsVisible, and IsEnabled. An IContentItem object represents the View Model for a data item, and a screen consists of controls that data-bind to your View Model. So if you hide a control by setting the IsVisible property to false, you actually will not interact directly with the UI. Therefore, there's no need for you to write any special code that involves the UI thread.

Another interesting characteristic about LightSwitch objects is that, in most cases, you can update property values from any thread. Take a look at the code shown in Listing 7-20. This listing illustrates code that's been added to the initialize method of the Create New Issue screen from Listing 7-7.

Listing 7-20. Threading

VB:
File: HelpdeskVB\Client\UserCode\CreateNewIssue.vb

```
Me.IssueProperty = New Issue                                                    ❶

Me.Details.Dispatcher.BeginInvoke(
    Sub()
        'This code executes on the screen logic thread
        Me.IssueProperty.ProblemDescription = "Desc. (screen logic thread)"    ❷
    End Sub)

Microsoft.LightSwitch.Threading.Dispatchers.Main.BeginInvoke(
    Sub()
        //This code executes on the UI thread
        Me.IssueProperty.ProblemDescription = "Desc. (main thread)"            ❸
    End Sub)
```

C#:
File: HelpDeskCS\Client\UserCode\CreateNewIssue.cs

```
this.IssueProperty = new Issue();                                              ❶

this.Details.Dispatcher.BeginInvoke(() =>
    {
        //This code executes on the screen logic thread
        this.IssueProperty.ProblemDescription = "Desc. (screen logic thread)" ;  ❷
    }
);

Microsoft.LightSwitch.Threading.Dispatchers.Main.BeginInvoke(() =>
    {
        //This code executes on the UI thread
        this.IssueProperty.ProblemDescription = "Desc. (main thread)";         ❸
    }
);
```

In this example, IssueProperty ❶ is a local screen property. The purpose of this code is to demonstrate that you can set the Problem Description property from either the UI or logic thread without LightSwitch throwing a "cross-thread access exception." Let's imagine you place a breakpoint in this code and use the Immediate Window to find out who owns this object, by issuing the following command:

```
?Me.IssueProperty.Details.Dispatcher.ToString
```

The answer that the Immediate Window returns is this:

```
"Microsoft.LightSwitch.Threading.BackgroundDispatcher"
```

This basically tells you that the screen logic thread owns IssueProperty. Based on this result, you'd expect the assignment operator in ❷ to work. But the curious thing is this: why does LightSwitch allow you to update the IssueDescription property on the UI thread ❸ without throwing an exception?

The answer is that many LightSwitch objects inherit from a class called `DualDispatcherObject`. (You'll find this in the `Microsoft.LightSwitch.Threading` namespace.) An object that inherits from this class has affinity to not one, but two threads: the main thread and the screen logic thread. From a practical perspective, this means you can access these objects from either thread without causing an exception. However, the act of getting or setting a property behaves differently depending on the thread you use.

When you write code on the UI thread that tries to get the value of a property that hasn't been loaded, LightSwitch begins to load the value asynchronously, and it returns the current uninitialized value (for example, null). When the property value finally loads, it raises the property changed event to notify listeners that the property value has changed. This behavior works very well for LightSwitch's asynchronous UI data binding. If you run the same code that gets the property on the screen logic thread, LightSwitch blocks the execution of your code until the property loads.

Returning to the code in Listing 7-20, you'll find that synchronously setting the value on the screen logic thread works as expected ❷. Although setting the value on the UI thread ❸ appears to succeed and doesn't throw an exception, you'll discover that LightSwitch doesn't actually set the value. Place a breakpoint on ❸, and use the debugger to interrogate the value just after you step over that line of code—you'll notice that the debugger returns null (or nothing).

The reason for this is because the UI thread cannot directly *mutate* data because it could allow screen logic code to observe arbitrary changes in data. This would cause errors if the screen logic contains conditional logic and the condition changes between the time the condition was checked and the time the code dependent on that condition executes. To resolve this, the UI thread queues up the mutation on the screen logic thread. In comparison, LightSwitch applies the mutation synchronously in the code that uses the screen logic thread ❷.

The main conclusion is that, in the most cases, LightSwitch carries out the tricky job of managing threading issues for you. It's only when you're doing some UI work that's a bit out of the ordinary that you need to manually invoke the code on the UI thread. Here are some examples of where in this book you need to do this:

- Showing Silverlight file save and file open dialogs

- Generating PDF files

- Working with the Silverlight Web Browser control

If you forget to invoke your code on the UI thread or are unsure of when to do so, there's no need to worry too much. You'll soon find out because you'll receive an error when you execute your code. You can use the exception LightSwitch returns to identify the threading problem and modify your code so that it executes on the correct thread.

Reacting to Data Changes

In any advanced application, you'll want some way to make your UI react to changes in your data.

LightSwitch entities implement the `INotifyPropertyChanged` interface and raise an event called `PropertyChanged` whenever the value of any property in the entity changes. To make your application react to data changes, you can handle this event and carry out any UI changes in an event handler.

Although you can achieve similar results by handling Silverlight's `LostFocus` event, there are several advantages to using `PropertyChanged`. If you want to use the `LostFocus` technique to monitor multiple properties, you need to create an event handler for each control. By using the `PropertyChanged` method, you need to set up only one event handler and you can use that to detect changes in any number of properties.

Furthermore, the `LostFocus` method is more fragile because it assumes what your underlying Silverlight control will be. You could potentially break your application by changing the control type.

In the example that follows, you'll create a new data screen based on the `Engineer` table. This table includes properties that relate to security clearance, such as

- **SecurityVetted:** Required, Boolean field.

- **SecurityClearanceRef:** String field.

- **VettingExpiryDate:** Date field.

By default, the screen hides the security reference and vetting expiry date text boxes. When the user selects the security vetted check box, your screen will reveal the hidden controls.

The PropertyChanged method works differently on screens that are based on the New Data Screen and Details Screen templates. This section begins by describing the technique on a New Data Screen template.

Using *PropertyChanged* on a New Data Screen Template

To handle the PropertyChanged event for an entity on a New Data Screen template, create a new screen based on the Engineer table and name it CreateNewEngineer. Move the security properties into a new Rows Layout control called SecurityGroup, as shown in Figure 7-26.

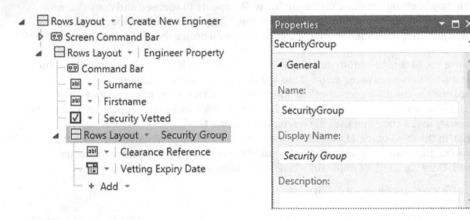

Figure 7-26. *Layout of the new data screen*

After creating your screen, enter the code as shown in Listing 7-21.

Listing 7-21. Using PropertyChanged on a New Data Screen

VB:
File: HelpDeskVB\Client\UserCode\CreateNewEngineer.vb

```vb
Imports System.ComponentModel

Private Sub CreateNewEngineer_Created()
    Microsoft.LightSwitch.Threading.Dispatchers.Main.BeginInvoke(
        Sub()
            AddHandler DirectCast(
              Me.EngineerProperty, INotifyPropertyChanged
            ).PropertyChanged, AddressOf EngineerFieldChanged        ❶
        End Sub)

    'Set the initial visibility here
    Me.FindControl("SecurityGroup").IsVisible =
        EngineerProperty.SecurityVetted
End Sub
```

```vb
Private Sub EngineerFieldChanged(
    sender As Object, e As PropertyChangedEventArgs)
    If e.PropertyName = "SecurityVetted" Then                          ❷
        Me.FindControl("SecurityGroup").IsVisible =
            EngineerProperty.SecurityVetted
    End If
End Sub
```

C#:
File: HelpDeskCS\Client\UserCode\CreateNewEngineer.cs

```csharp
using System.ComponentModel;

partial void CreateNewEngineer_Created()
{
    Microsoft.LightSwitch.Threading.Dispatchers.Main.BeginInvoke(() =>
    {
        ((INotifyPropertyChanged)this.EngineerProperty).PropertyChanged +=
            EngineerFieldChanged;                                      ❶
    });

    //Set the initial visibility here
    this.FindControl("SecurityGroup").IsVisible =
        EngineerProperty.SecurityVetted;
}

private void EngineerFieldChanged(object sender, PropertyChangedEventArgs e)
{
    if (e.PropertyName == "SecurityVetted")                            ❷
    {
        this.FindControl("SecurityGroup").IsVisible =
            EngineerProperty.SecurityVetted;
    }
}
```

The created method adds an event handler called EngineerFieldChanged that handles the PropertyChanged event of the EngineerProperty ❶. This event handler needs to be added using code that executes on the main UI thread. If you don't do this, you'll receive an error that says, "It is not valid to execute the operation on the current thread."

The EngineerFieldChanged method includes a parameter of type PropertyChangedEventArgs. You can find out the name of the property that has changed by referring to the PropertyChangedEventArgs's PropertyName property ❷.

If the SecurityVetted property changes, the code calls the FindControl method ❸ to hide or show the group that contains the controls related to security vetting. Figure 7-27 shows how the final screen looks at runtime.

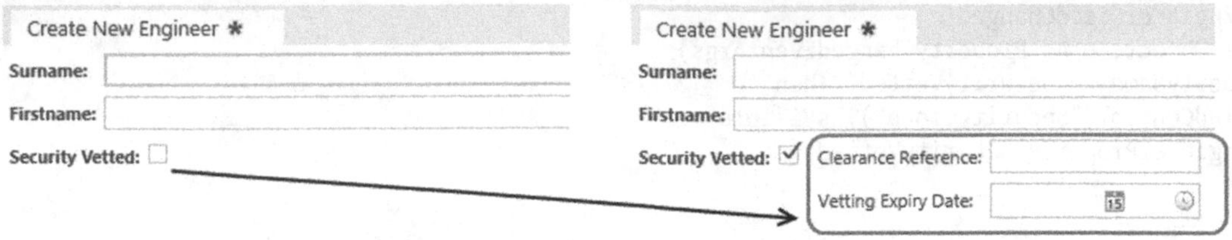

Create New Engineer ✳		Create New Engineer ✳	
Surname:		Surname:	
Firstname:		Firstname:	
Security Vetted: ☐		Security Vetted: ☑	Clearance Reference:
			Vetting Expiry Date:

Figure 7-27. *Selecting the SecurityVetted check box unhides the security vetting group*

Using *PropertyChanged* on a Details Screen

The code you use on a Details Screen template is different from the code you use on a New Data Screen template.

The reason for this is because a details screen uses a query that returns a single record filtered by the primary key value, whereas a new data screen contains a local property rather than a query. To monitor PropertyChanged on a details screen, you need to create a local property you can monitor.

In this example, you'll create a details screen that carries out the same function as before. The layout of this screen is identical to the layout shown in the New Data Screen example. Once you create the screen, add the code shown in Listing 7-22.

Listing 7-22. Using PropertyChanged on a Details Screen

VB:
File: HelpDeskVB\Client\UserCode\EngineerDetail.vb

```vb
Imports System.ComponentModel
Private monitoredEngineer As Engineer

Private Sub EngineerDetail_InitializeDataWorkspace(
    saveChangesTo As List(Of Microsoft.LightSwitch.IDataService))
    ' Write your code here.
    Microsoft.LightSwitch.Threading.Dispatchers.Main.BeginInvoke(
      Sub()
          AddHandler Me.Details.Properties.Engineer.Loader.ExecuteCompleted,
              AddressOf Me.EngineerLoaderExecuted                              ❶
      End Sub)
End Sub

Private Sub EngineerLoaderExecuted(
    sender As Object, e As Microsoft.LightSwitch.ExecuteCompletedEventArgs)

    If monitoredEngineer IsNot Me.Engineer Then
        If monitoredEngineer IsNot Nothing Then
            RemoveHandler TryCast(monitoredEngineer,
                INotifyPropertyChanged).PropertyChanged,
                    AddressOf Me.EngineerChanged
        End If

        monitoredEngineer = Me.Engineer                                        ❷
```

```vbnet
        If monitoredEngineer IsNot Nothing Then
            AddHandler TryCast(
                monitoredEngineer, INotifyPropertyChanged).PropertyChanged,
                    AddressOf Me.EngineerChanged

            'Set the initial visibility here
            Me.FindControl("SecurityGroup").IsVisible =
                monitoredEngineer.SecurityVetted

        End If
    End If
End Sub

Private Sub EngineerChanged(
    sender As Object, e As PropertyChangedEventArgs)
    If e.PropertyName = "SecurityVetted" Then
        Me.FindControl("SecurityGroup").IsVisible =
            monitoredEngineer.SecurityVetted                                    ❸
    End If
End Sub
```

C#:
File: HelpDeskCS\Client\UserCode\EngineerDetail.cs

```csharp
using System.ComponentModel;
private Engineer monitoredEngineer;

partial void EngineerDetail_InitializeDataWorkspace(
    List<IDataService> saveChangesTo)
{
    Microsoft.LightSwitch.Threading.Dispatchers.Main.BeginInvoke(() =>
    {
        this.Details.Properties.Engineer.Loader.ExecuteCompleted +=
            this.EngineerLoaderExecuted;                                        ❶
    });
}

private void EngineerLoaderExecuted(
    object sender, Microsoft.LightSwitch.ExecuteCompletedEventArgs e)
{

    if (monitoredEngineer != this.Engineer)
    {
        if (monitoredEngineer != null)
        {
            (monitoredEngineer as INotifyPropertyChanged).PropertyChanged -=
                this.EngineerChanged;
        }
```

```
        monitoredEngineer = this.Engineer;                                    ❷
        if (monitoredEngineer != null)
        {
            (monitoredEngineer as INotifyPropertyChanged).PropertyChanged +=
                this.EngineerChanged;

            //set the initial visibility here
            this.FindControl("SecurityGroup").IsVisible =
                monitoredEngineer.SecurityVetted;
        }
    }
}

private void EngineerChanged(
    object sender, PropertyChangedEventArgs e)
{
    if (e.PropertyName == "SecurityVetted")
    {
        this.FindControl("SecurityGroup").IsVisible =
            monitoredEngineer.SecurityVetted;                                  ❸
    }
}
```

This code adds an event handler in the InitializeDataWorkspace method that handles the ExecuteCompleted event of the query loader ❶. When the loader finishes executing the query, the code saves the engineer in a local property called monitoredEngineer ❷.

You can then handle the PropertyChanged event on the monitorEngineer property to detect any changes that have been made to the engineer. Just as before, the code that hides or shows the security vetting group uses the value of the SecurityVetted property ❸.

Working with Files

You can use the LightSwitch table designer to define properties with a data type of binary. By using this data type, you can allow users to store and retrieve files. However, LightSwitch doesn't include a built-in control that allows users to upload and download files. Instead, you need to write your own code that uses the Silverlight File Open and Save File dialog boxes.

Uploading Files

To demonstrate how to upload a file, create a new data screen that uses the IssueDocument table. Create a new button on your screen, and call your method UploadFileToDatabase. Add the code as shown in Listing 7-23.

Listing 7-23. Uploading a File

VB:
File: HelpDeskVB\Client\UserCode\CreateNewIssueDocument.vb

```
Imports System.Windows.Controls
Imports Microsoft.LightSwitch.Threading
```

```vb
Private Sub UploadFileToDatabase_Execute()
    '1 Invoke the method on the main UI thread                      ❶
    Dispatchers.Main.Invoke(
        Sub()

            Dim openDialog As New Controls.OpenFileDialog          ❷
            openDialog.Filter = "All files|*.*"
            'Use this syntax to only allow Word/Excel files
            'openDialog.Filter = "Word Files|*.doc|Excel Files |*.xls"

            If openDialog.ShowDialog = True Then
                Using fileData As System.IO.FileStream =
                    openDialog.File.OpenRead

                    Dim fileLen As Long = fileData.Length

                    If (fileLen > 0) Then
                        Dim fileBArray(fileLen - 1) As Byte
                        fileData.Read(fileBArray, 0, fileLen)      ❸
                        fileData.Close()

                        Me.IssueDocumentProperty.IssueFile = fileBArray    ❹
                        Me.IssueDocumentProperty.FileExtension =
                            openDialog.File.Extension.ToString()
                        Me.IssueDocumentProperty.DocumentName =
                            openDialog.File.Name

                    End If

                End Using
            End If

        End Sub)

End Sub
```

C#:
File: HelpDeskCS\Client\UserCode\CreateNewIssueDocument.cs

```csharp
using System.Windows.Controls;
using Microsoft.LightSwitch.Threading;

partial void UploadFileToDatabase_Execute()
{
    //1 Invoke the method on the main UI thread                     ❶
    Dispatchers.Main.Invoke(() =>
    {
        OpenFileDialog openDialog = new OpenFileDialog();          ❷
        openDialog.Filter = "Supported files|*.*";
        //Use this syntax to only allow Word/Excel files
        //opendlg.Filter = "Word Files|*.doc|Excel Files |*.xls";
```

```
        if (openDialog.ShowDialog() == true)
        {
            using (System.IO.FileStream fileData =
                openDialog.File.OpenRead())
            {
                int fileLen = (int)fileData.Length;

                if ((fileLen > 0))
                {
                    byte[] fileBArray = new byte[fileLen];
                    fileData.Read(fileBArray, 0, fileLen);                ❸
                    fileData.Close();

                    this.IssueDocumentProperty.IssueFile = fileBArray;    ❹
                    this.IssueDocumentProperty.FileExtension =
                        openDialog.File.Extension.ToString();
                    this.IssueDocumentProperty.DocumentName =
                        openDialog.File.Name;
                }
            }
        }

    });
}
```

Whenever you use the Silverlight File Open or File Save dialog, the code that invokes the dialog must be executed on the main UI thread ❶. This is because you're carrying out a UI task, and the logic must therefore run on the main UI thread.

The File Open dialog ❷ allows the user to choose a file. The code then reads the file data into a byte array by using a `FileStream` object ❸, and it assigns the data to the `IssueFile` property ❹. The code then saves the file name and file extension of the document in the same block of code.

You can set the File Open dialog's `Filter` property to limit the file types that the user can select. This example allows the user to select all files by setting the `*.*` filter, but you could supply a list of pipe-delimited file extensions and descriptions to apply the filter (as shown in the commented-out line of code).

Note that this code works only in desktop applications—it won't work in a browser application. If you try running this code in a browser application, you'll get the security exception "Dialogs must be user-initiated." This is because the button code runs on the screen logic thread, and by subsequently invoking the File Open dialog on the main UI thread, Silverlight loses the fact the action was indeed "user-initiated." Desktop applications don't suffer from this problem because the elevated trust of a desktop Silverlight application allows you to open the file dialog from any code.

In a browser application, the code that launches file dialogs must be at the top of the call stack. If you want to use the Silverlight file dialogs in a browser application, you can do this by creating a custom button control and handling the button's `click` event. Chapter 11 shows you how to use custom controls, and Chapter 15 shows you how to use the File Open dialog in a browser application to allow users to choose and send email file attachments. If you want to make this example work in a browser application, you can adapt the code you find in Chapter 15.

■ **Note**   If you're creating commands that work only in desktop applications, it's a good idea to disable your command in browser applications by writing code in your command's `CanExecute` method (`UploadFileToDatabase_CanExecute` in this example). Chapter 17 describes this process in more detail.

Downloading and Saving Files

Users need some way of downloading the issue documents that have been uploaded. You'll now find out how to allow users to retrieve a file and save it locally using the Silverlight File Save dialog. To create this example, create a details screen based on the IssueDocument table and name your screen IssueDocumentDetails.

Create a new button on your screen, and call your method SaveFileFromDatabase. Add the code as shown in Listing 7-24.

Listing 7-24. Downloading a File

VB:
File: HelpDeskVB\Client\UserCode\IssueDocumentDetails.vb

```
Imports System.Windows.Controls
Imports Microsoft.LightSwitch.Threading

Private Sub SaveFileFromDatabase_Execute()

    '1 Invoke the method on the main UI thread                        ❶
    Dispatchers.Main.Invoke(
        Sub()
            Dim ms As System.IO.MemoryStream =
                New System.IO.MemoryStream(IssueDocument.IssueFile)

            Dispatchers.Main.Invoke(
                Sub()
                    Dim saveDialog As New Controls.SaveFileDialog

                    If saveDialog.ShowDialog = True Then                ❷
                        Using fileStream As Stream = saveDialog.OpenFile
                            ms.WriteTo(fileStream)                      ❸
                        End Using
                    End If
                End Sub)
        End Sub)

End Sub
```

C#:
File: HelpDeskCS\Client\UserCode\IssueDocumentDetails.cs

```
using System.Windows.Controls;
using Microsoft.LightSwitch.Threading;

partial void SaveFileFromDatabase_Execute()
{
    //1 Invoke the method on the main UI thread                        ❶
    Dispatchers.Main.Invoke(() =>
    {
        System.IO.MemoryStream ms =
            new System.IO.MemoryStream(IssueDocument.IssueFile);
```

```
        Dispatchers.Main.Invoke(() =>
        {
            SaveFileDialog saveDialog = new SaveFileDialog();

            if (saveDialog.ShowDialog() == true)                         ❷
            {
                using (Stream fileStream = saveDialog.OpenFile())
                {
                    ms.WriteTo(fileStream);                              ❸
                }
            }
        });
    });
}
```

Just as before, the code needs to be executed on the main UI thread for the Save File dialog to work ❶. The Save dialog prompts the user to enter a file name and location ❷, and the final part of the code writes the data to the file using a MemoryStream object ❸.

Opening Files in Their Application

Instead of prompting users with a Save File dialog, you can display the standard dialog that prompts users to download the file and to open it using the default application.

Let's imagine that a user wants to retrieve a Word document from the IssueDocument table. In this example, you'll add a button to a LightSwitch screen that starts Microsoft Word and opens the document. Once again, this example works only in desktop applications.

The process you'll carry out is as follows:

- Save the file to an interim file location.

- Use the shell execute method to start Word and open the file that was saved above.

The first part of the process saves your file into a temporary location. There are some important points to consider when a user tries to save a file from a LightSwitch application. The security restrictions that Silverlight imposes means that you can't save files wherever you want. The limitations that it applies depends on the method you chose to save your file. These are described in Table 7-4.

Table 7-4. *Ways to Save a File Using LightSwitch*

Method	Description
Use the classes in the System.IO namespace	You can save files only in special locations. These include the My Documents, My Music, My Pictures, and My Videos folders of the current user.
Use the Silverlight SaveFileDialog dialog	You can save files to any location for which the user has read/write permissions.
Use isolated storage	This is a virtual file system that's provided by Silverlight.

If you want to save a file to a temporary location without any user intervention, you can choose from two options. You can create your file in the My Documents folder, or you can create the file in isolated storage.

Isolated storage is a virtual file system that Silverlight provides. The isolated storage location is a hidden folder that exists on the user's machine. This makes it an ideal place to save temporary files.

However, the disadvantage of using isolated storage is that Silverlight imposes a default storage quota, and administrators can also apply a more stringent quota. Therefore, there's no guarantee there'll be space for you to save your file.

This example shows you how to save your temporary file in the My Documents folder, but if you want to use isolated storage instead, the following MSDN web page shows you how (http://msdn.microsoft.com/en-GB/library/cc265154). Here's a brief summary of how to use isolated storage. You begin by using the IsolatedStorageFile class from the System.IO.IsolatedStorage namespace. This provides a static method called GetUserStoreForApplication you use to obtain the store for your application. You can then use an IsolatedStorageFileStream object to write your data to a file in isolated storage.

To create this example, open the IssueDocumentDetails screen and create a new method and button called OpenFileFromDatabase. Add the code that's shown in Listing 7-25.

Listing 7-25. Opening Files in Their Applications

VB:
File: HelpDeskVB\Client\UserCode\IssueDocumentDetails.vb

```vb
Imports System.Windows.Controls
Imports Microsoft.LightSwitch.Threading
Imports System.Runtime.InteropServices.Automation

Private Sub OpenFileFromDatabase_Execute()
    Try
        If (AutomationFactory.IsAvailable) Then
            'here's where we'll save the file
            Dim fullFilePath As String =
                System.IO.Path.Combine(
                    Environment.GetFolderPath(
                        Environment.SpecialFolder.MyDocuments),
                            IssueDocument.DocumentName)                  ❶

            Dim fileData As Byte() = IssueDocument.IssueFile.ToArray()
            If (fileData IsNot Nothing) Then
                Using fs As New FileStream(
                        fullFilePath, FileMode.OpenOrCreate, FileAccess.Write)
                    fs.Write(fileData, 0, fileData.Length)              ❷
                    fs.Close()
                End Using
            End If

            Dim shell = AutomationFactory.CreateObject("Shell.Application")
            shell.ShellExecute(fullFilePath)                            ❸

        End If
    Catch ex As Exception
        Me.ShowMessageBox(ex.ToString())
    End Try

End Sub
```

C#:
File: HelpDeskCS\Client\UserCode\IssueDocumentDetails.cs

```csharp
using System.Runtime.InteropServices.Automation;

partial void OpenFileFromDatabase_Execute()
{
    try
    {
        if ((AutomationFactory.IsAvailable))
        {
            //this is where we'll save the file
            string fullFilePath = System.IO.Path.Combine(
                Environment.GetFolderPath(Environment.SpecialFolder.MyDocuments),
                IssueDocument.DocumentName);                                        ❶

            byte[] fileData = IssueDocument.IssueFile.ToArray();

            if ((fileData != null))
            {
                using (FileStream fs =
                    new FileStream(
                        fullFilePath, FileMode.OpenOrCreate, FileAccess.Write))
                {
                    fs.Write(fileData, 0, fileData.Length);                         ❷
                    fs.Close();
                }
            }

            dynamic shell = AutomationFactory.CreateObject("Shell.Application");
            shell.ShellExecute(fullFilePath);                                       ❸
        }
    }
    catch (Exception ex)
    {
        this.ShowMessageBox(ex.ToString());
    }
}
```

The first part of this code builds the path where you'll save your file ❶. It then saves your data into this file ❷ and opens it using the Shell command ❸.

Summary

This chapter showed you how to enrich your Silverlight applications by employing advanced screen design techniques.

When you're building a LightSwitch application, you can't just add UI controls to a screen. A screen consists of controls that data-bind to properties. To display a new control that's unrelated to the main data on your screen, you have to first add a local property that *backs* your control. You can use the Add Data Item dialog to do this. In addition to adding local properties with this dialog, you also can add queries and methods. Adding a query to your screen allows you to show additional collections of data on your screen. You also can use queries to customize the choices that an autocomplete box or modal window picker shows. Another important feature of local properties is that you can set them up as parameters. This allows you to pass values to a screen when it opens.

Chapter 4 showed you the screen events you can handle. You use these events to run code when a screen opens, closes, or performs a save operation. If you want to run code when a change in data occurs, you can do this by handling the PropertyChanged event for your entity.

By using the LightSwitch API, you can access entity and property values by name. When you change the value of a property in code, LightSwitch automatically refreshes all controls bound to your property. With the FindControl method, you can access a specific control in code. This method returns an IContentItemProxy object that you can use to set the visibility and read-only properties of a control. Once you obtain a reference to an IContentItemProxy, you can add an event handler for the ControlAvailable event. The code that handles the ControlAvailable event allows you to access the underlying Silverlight control and add additional event handlers to handle the events that the Silverlight control raises. This allows you, for example, to handle a text box's KeyUp event.

LightSwitch applications are multithreaded. This improves your application's performance because it allows a screen logic thread to perform data operations, while a main UI thread deals with updating your user interface. In general, you don't need to worry too much about executing code on a specific thread. But on the rare occasions where this is necessary, you can achieve this by using a dispatcher object.

This chapter contains plenty of screen design examples. These examples include how to create a combined add/edit screen, how to create a custom search screen, and how to create a screen for managing single-row tables. You also saw demonstrations of how to create nested autocomplete boxes, how to work with recursive data, and how to allow users to upload and download files.

A combined data entry and edit screen saves you from having to create and maintain two separate screens. To create such a screen, you begin with a Details Screen template and use the default query to populate a local property. You then bind your screen controls to the local property.

By default, the data entry screens that open from the data grid are autogenerated and can't be modified. You can overcome this limitation by creating your own modal windows and attaching them to commands on your data grid. To allow users to select multiple rows in a data grid, you write code that sets the data grid's DataGridSelectionMode property to Extended.

Nested autocomplete boxes (ACBs) make it easier for users to find or enter data. For example, you could limit user choices in an ACB to the department that's been selected in a parent ACB. To do this, you set the data source of your users' ACB to a parameterized query that's bound to your parent ACB.

Finally, you learned how to upload and download files by using Silverlight's OpenFileDialog and SaveFileDialog controls. In a desktop application, you can allow users to open files in their native applications. To accomplish this, you save the file locally and use the Windows Shell command to open the file.

CHAPTER 8

■ ■ ■

Creating HTML Interfaces

Up until now, this book has focused on building user interfaces with LightSwitch's Silverlight client. By installing an update to Visual Studio, you can build applications that use an HTML interface. The biggest benefit is that it allows you to build applications that work well on mobile devices. In particular, the "HTML client" produces screens that are optimized for touch-screen devices.

In this chapter, you'll learn how to

- Add an HTML client, create screens, and build a navigation structure

- Show and edit data by using custom HTML controls

- Customize your application by adding CSS (Cascading Style Sheet) and JavaScript code

This chapter shows you how to build an HTML interface to the HelpDesk application. You'll find out how to build screens that allow engineers to add, view, and edit issues. You'll also find out how to allow users to upload and download files, replace the default Date/Time Picker control with a custom control, and apply different fonts and colors to your application by using themes.

Introducing the HTML Client

The ability to build HTML clients is a big step in the evolution of LightSwitch, allowing you to reach a far wider range of devices. In comparison, a Silverlight browser application requires the user to install the Silverlight runtime. This isn't always possible, particularly on mobile devices or locked-down corporate environments. A disadvantage of the HTML client is that it isn't suitable for all scenarios. If you're targeting your application at PC users and require rich features, such as output to Excel and COM automation, Silverlight is still the best choice.

One of the features of LightSwitch is that it builds applications that are based on industry standards and best practices. In Chapter 1, you learned how LightSwitch uses an n-tier architecture and is based on the MVVM pattern. The HTML client is also based on a "layered" architecture and uses libraries that are well known and popular with web developers.

As Figure 8-1 shows, LightSwitch HTML client applications are based heavily on jQuery. It uses the controls in the jQuery Mobile library, and it uses the datajs library to access your server through OData. It uses a small, cross-browser-compatible subset of the WinJS library. This is a JavaScript library that's primarily designed to help build browser applications that target Windows 8. Developing an HTML client application is very similar to developing a Silverlight application—the underlying concepts (such as screens, entities, content items, and controls) are identical. However, there are a few fundamental differences that you need to understand.

189

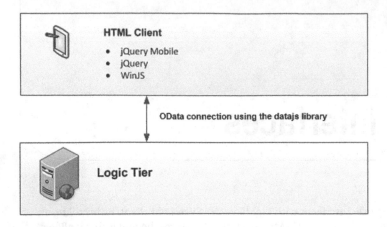

Figure 8-1. *HTML client architecture*

Whereas the Silverlight client allows users to open multiple screens and carry out multiple tasks at the same time, HTML clients are designed to carry out just a single task at any one time. In previous chapters, you learned how each screen includes a data workspace, and how each screen carries out data operations independently of other screens. This concept doesn't apply to the HTML client. The HTML client includes just one data workspace for your entire application.

Just like the Silverlight client, an HTML client application consists of screens. Each screen that you create centers on a unit of work and is generally based on an entity or a collection of data. Each screen can contain one or more tabs. Tabs allow you to split a screen into separate sections. At runtime, a user can switch between tabs by using links that appear at the top of your screen.

Compared to the Silverlight client, the HTML client makes it easier to share UI elements across multiple screens through dialogs. To create a dialog, you'd create a screen as normal, but configure it so that LightSwitch shows it as a dialog. When a user opens a dialog, LightSwitch displays the screen content in a floating panel and darkens the underlying screen area.

Another piece of UI that's new to the HTML client is the popup. A popup is a floating piece of UI that's perfect for showing messages or confirmations. Whereas a dialog takes up almost all of the available screen area, popups are generally smaller in size. When LightSwitch shows a popup, it doesn't darken the underlying screen, as in the case of a dialog. To dismiss a popup, a user would click on an area of the screen outside of the popup. Popups are screen-specific, so there's no way to share popups between screens.

Setting Up Visual Studio for HTML Development

To develop HTML client applications, you first need to install an update called "Visual Studio 2012 Update 2." You can download and install this from the following URL:

```
http://www.microsoft.com/en-us/download/details.aspx?id=38188
```

Once you install this update, you can begin to develop HTML client applications.

Adding an HTML Client

There are two ways for you to create an application that includes an HTML client. You can either create a brand new "LightSwitch HTML Application" by using Visual Studio's File ➤ New ➤ Project option, or you can add an HTML client to an existing Silverlight LightSwitch project.

To do the latter, right-click your LightSwitch project and choose the "Add Client" option. This opens the Add Client dialog, as shown in Figure 8-2.

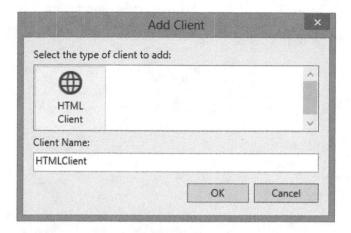

Figure 8-2. *Adding an HTML client*

Once you add an HTML client, Visual Studio upgrades your project. This process creates a new project file with an ls3proj extension and upgrades your application's model schema from v2 to v3.

Once the upgrade process finishes, your new HTML client project becomes your startup project. This means that when you debug your application by pressing F5, Visual Studio runs your HTML client project. If you want to debug and run your Silverlight client, right-click your Client project in Solution Explorer and select the "Set as StartUp Client" option.

If the "Add Client" dialog fails to add an HTML client, try upgrading your project independently, and then try adding an "HTML client" again. You can perform an independent upgrade by right-clicking your project in Solution Explorer and choosing the "Upgrade Project" option.

■ **Caution**   Make sure to back up your application. Upgrading a project rewrites the contents of your LSML file. You can lose data if you've customized your LSML file, for example, by creating global values (Chapter 6). Once you upgrade a project, you won't be able to share your work with other developers who haven't installed Visual Studio 2012 Update 2.

Adding Screens to Your Application

Once you add an HTML client, you can start to add screens to your application. To do this, right-click your HTMLClient in Solution Explorer and choose the "Add Screen" option. This opens the "Add New Screen" dialog, as shown in Figure 8-3.

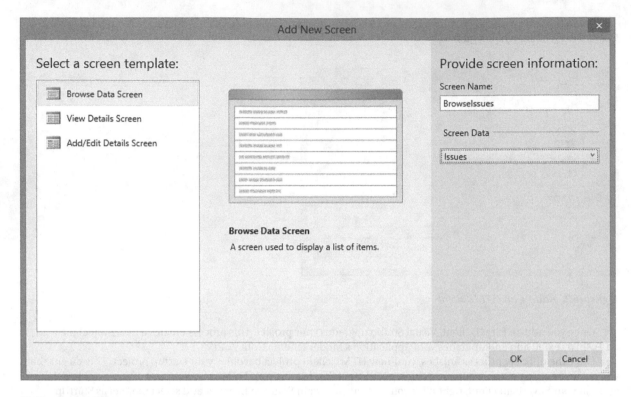

Figure 8-3. *Adding a new screen*

This dialog looks very similar to the Add New Screen dialog that you're familiar with, but notice how it contains fewer screen templates. The screen templates that appear are self-explanatory. The Browse Data Screen template creates a screen that shows a collection of entities through a List control.

The List control allows you to specify the action that occurs when a user selects an item in the control. It allows you to open the selected entity in a View Details Screen or Add/Edit Details Screen.

The View Details Screen template builds a screen that's designed to show a read-only view of data, whereas the Add/Edit Details Screen template creates a screen that allows users to edit data.

Designing Screens

Following on from Chapter 7, you won't have any difficulty in understanding how to design and customize HTML screens. This is because LightSwitch provides a screen designer that looks almost identical to the one that you've used before. Many of the concepts are the same—you still design screens using the hierarchical Screen Content Tree, Screen Members still appear in the left panel, and you can still add queries and local properties by clicking on the Add Data Item button.

Despite these similarities, the HTML designer introduces some different layouts and controls. This section describes the differences that you'll find in further detail.

Understanding the Top-Level Screen Layout

Let's begin by creating a Browse Data Screen that displays data from the Issue table. Open the "Add New Screen" dialog, select the "Browse Data Screen" template, and name your screen BrowseIssues. Once you do this, the template generates the screen layout that's shown in Figure 8-4. Beneath the root node, you'll find two folders: Tabs and Popups.

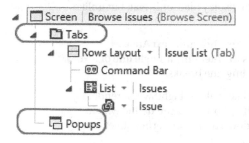

Figure 8-4. HTML screen layout, highlighting tabs and popups

Each data item that you add beneath the Tabs folder appears in a separate tab. The user can switch tabs simply by clicking the tab heading that appears at the top of the screen.

You can create popups by adding controls beneath the Popups folder. To show the contents of a popup, you can either write code or configure buttons or controls to open the popup.

Using Data List Controls

The Silverlight controls that you've seen in previous chapters include the DataGrid and DataList controls. You won't find these controls in the HTML client—instead, LightSwitch provides two controls that are called List and Tile List.

The difference between these two controls is that List renders data items from top to bottom, whereas Tile List renders data items from left to right and then top to bottom (Figure 8-5).

Figure 8-5. List View vs. Tile List

Using Data Controls

Just like the Silverlight client, data controls allow you to display individual data items. The controls that you'll find are intuitive, but following are several controls that you'll be unfamiliar with:

- **Text:** This control displays read-only text. It's the HTML client's equivalent of the Silverlight client's Label control.

- **Paragraph:** This is similar to the Text control. It allows you to display read-only text, but unlike the Text control, it allows you to set the height of the control.

- **Text Area:** There are two controls users can use to enter text: Text Box and Text Area. The difference between the two is that Text Boxes allow users to enter only a single line of text, whereas Text Areas allow users to enter multiple lines, including line breaks.

- **Flip Switch:** The Flip Switch control allows users to edit Boolean values. LightSwitch renders this control as a button that displays either Yes/No or On/Off options. You can define which set of options the control shows by setting the Options dropdown in the properties sheet.

- **Date/Time Picker:** The Date/Time Picker control allows users to enter and view dates and times. You can configure the Date/Time Picker through the properties sheet for your data item. The Date/Time Picker allows users to enter the date parts by choosing from a list of values. A useful setting is the minute increment setting, which defaults to 5 (Figure 8-6). This means that the minute picker shows the values 0, 5, 10, 15, 20, 25, 30 (and so on) rather than the values 0 through 60.

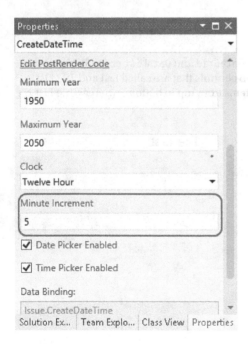

Figure 8-6. DateTime Picker control properties

Using Data-Picker Controls

The Silverlight client includes data-picker controls such as the AutoCompleteBox and Modal Window Picker controls. The HTML client comes with just a single data-selection control—the "Details Modal Picker." Just as with the AutoCompleteBox control, you can restrict the items that are shown in this control by setting the Choices property to a user-defined query.

To illustrate this control, Figure 8-7 shows a Details Modal Picker control that a user would use to allocate an engineer to an issue.

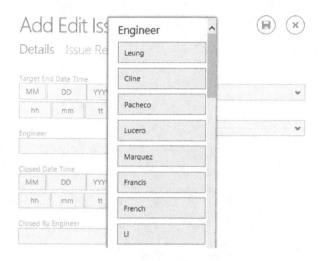

Figure 8-7. *Details Modal Picker*

You can modify the content that the control shows in each row by replacing the Details Modal Picker's Summary Control with a Rows Layout and adding data items beneath your Rows Layout. The principle of how this works is identical to the way that you would do it for the AutoCompleteBox. You can refer to the section "Using the Auto Complete Box Control" in Chapter 3 for further details.

Unlike the AutoCompleteBox or Modal Window Picker controls, the Details Modal Picker control doesn't allow users to search for records. For example, the AutoCompleteBox control filters the choices based on what the user types into the control. If your database contains hundreds of engineer records, your users could spend ages scrolling through the list until they find the correct engineer. You can improve this behavior by building a custom search dialog, and you'll find out how to do this later in this chapter.

Setting Screen Properties

The properties sheet for the root node of your screen allows you to set your screen's display name and control the visibility of tab titles (Figure 8-8).

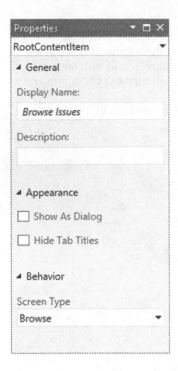

Figure 8-8. *Setting screen properties*

LightSwitch shows the Display Name that you specify as a title that appears at the top of your screen. If you choose the option to hide the tab titles, LightSwitch shows only the contents of the first tab. If you want to display a different tab, you'll need to write code or configure a button or control to show the tab.

The properties sheet allows you to define the Screen Type, and there are two options that you can choose: Browse and Edit. The main purpose of this setting is to control the navigation buttons that appear on your screen. If you set the Screen Type to Browse, LightSwitch shows only an OK button. If you set the Screen Type to Edit, LightSwitch also shows a Cancel button. This button allows the user to discard the changes that they've made on a screen. The exception to this is that LightSwitch shows a Save button, rather than an OK button, on the first Edit screen that the user encounters in an application.

Creating a Navigation Structure

Any serious application includes more than one screen, so you'll need to provide a way for users to navigate your application. In this section, you'll find out how to create a startup screen, how to allow users to open screens, and how to show popups and dialogs.

Creating a Startup Screen

When a user starts the HelpDesk application, the initial view that the user sees consists of a screen that contains a series of buttons. These buttons allow the user to open screens to carry out different tasks.

To create this screen, open the "Add Screen Dialog" and add a new screen to your application. Choose the Browse Data Screen template, set the Screen Data dropdown to None, and name your screen Startup. Once you do this, right-click the Startup screen in Solution Explorer and choose the "Set as Home Screen" option. This option sets the initial screen that LightSwitch displays when a user starts your application.

Return to the screen designer and, beneath the Tabs folder, add some Rows Layouts. Use the properties sheet to set the display name of the first Row Layout to "Issues." Beneath this group, add another Rows Layout. Use the Add button to add two buttons. When the Add Button dialog appears, choose the radio option to "Write my own method," and name your methods ViewIssues and CreateNewIssue.

Now select the root node of your screen and use the properties sheet to change the display name of your screen to "Main Menu." You can now run your application, and Figure 8-9 shows what your screen looks like at design time and runtime.

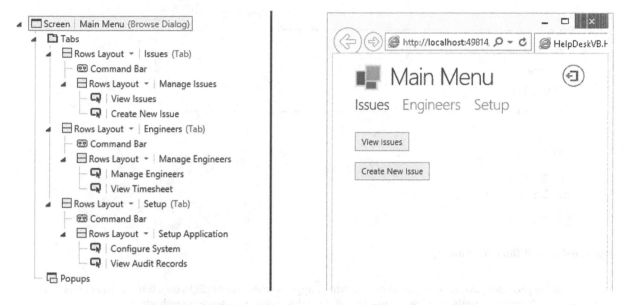

Figure 8-9. *Startup screen –Design time vs. runtime*

Notice that the screen includes a logout button. LightSwitch automatically adds this button to the screen that you've defined as your startup screen.

Navigating to Different Screens

The next step is to configure the "click action" of the buttons on your startup screen. Let's start with the first button, "View Issues." You'll now configure this button so that it opens your BrowseIssues screen.

In your StartUp screen, select the "View Issues" button and open the properties sheet. There, you'll find an Actions group that contains a "Tap" link. Click on this link to open the "Edit Tap Action" dialog that's shown in Figure 8-10.

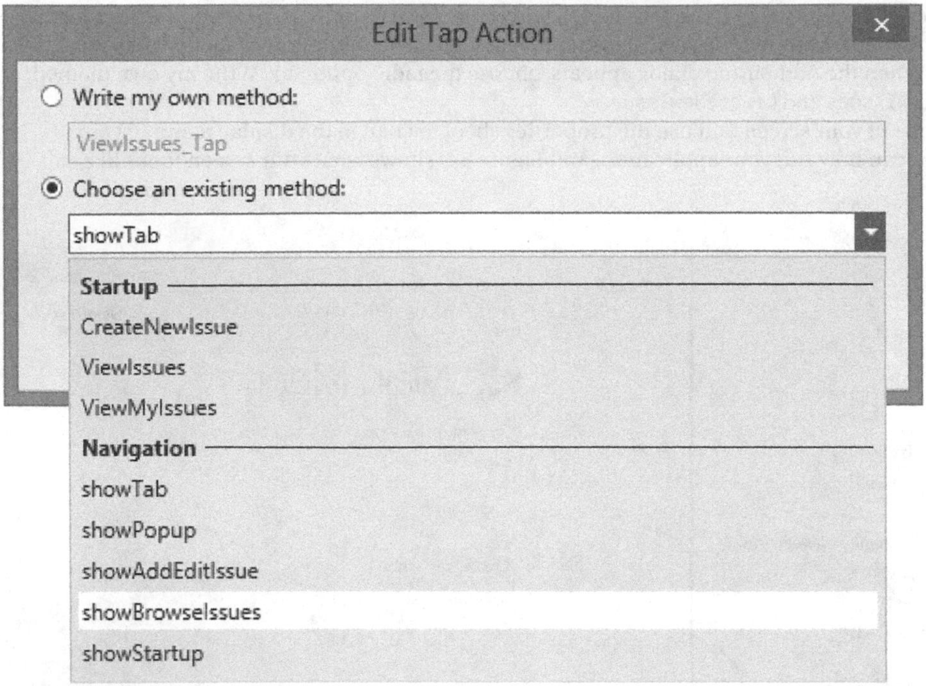

Figure 8-10. *Edit Tap Action dialog*

This dialog provides two ways for you to control what happens when a user clicks on a button. You can either write your own JavaScript method or choose one of LightSwitch's prebuilt navigation methods.

The "Choose an existing method" dropdown contains two main groups. The first group allows you to choose one of the local methods that you've defined on your screen. The second group contains show methods for each screen that you've created in your application. To open your "browse issues" screen, you can simply select the showBrowseIssues choice that you'll find in the Navigation group.

Adding New Records

Unlike the Silverlight client, there isn't a screen template that allows you to create screens for the sole purpose of adding records. Instead, you'll need to create a screen that uses the Add/Edit Screen Details template. So to add a screen that allows users to add records, create a screen that's based on the Issue table and name it AddEditIssue. In the "Add New Screen" dialog, use the check box to include the "Issue Response" data—you'll use this data collection in the next section.

Once you do this, you can configure the CreateNewIssue button on your setup screen to open your AddEditIssue screen by using the "Edit Tap Action" dialog (Figure 8-11). When this dialog opens, select the "Choose an existing method" radio button and choose the showAddEditIssue option from the "Navigation Group." LightSwitch detects that you've selected an Add/Edit screen and shows a text box that allows you to enter the entity that you want to work with. Enter "(New Issue)" into this text box to configure your button to open your Add/Edit screen in Add mode.

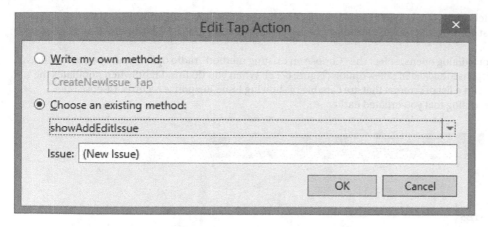

Figure 8-11. Adding new records

When you now run your application and click on your "Create New Issue" button, LightSwitch will open your Issue Detail screen in Add mode.

EXERCISE 8.1 – CREATING HTML SCREENS

Add an HTML client to your application, and create some HTML screens for your application. Create a Browse Screen for your Issue table. Experiment with the List and Tile List controls, and examine the differences between the two controls. Use the screen content tree to change the items that appear beneath these two controls. Create an Add/Edit Details screen for your Issue table, and configure your Browse screen so that it opens the selected issue in the Add/Edit Details screen. Now run your application and notice the navigation controls that LightSwitch displays at the top of your screen (for example, logout, save, discard, ok). Use the properties sheet to change the "Screen Type" for your Browse and Add/Edit Details screens, and notice the effect that it has on the navigation controls.

Using Dialogs

Dialogs are modal screens that "open up" and float above an existing screen. When LightSwitch shows a dialog, it darkens the existing screen, which is still visible beneath. Dialogs are perfect for adding UI elements that you can reuse on multiple screens. To create a dialog, simply create a screen and check the "Show as Dialog" check box in the properties sheet, as shown in Figure 8-8.

Dialogs are a great way to allow users to add and edit child records. This section shows you how to create a dialog that allows users to add and edit the child issue response records that relate to an issue record.

To create this example, add a new screen that uses the "Add/Edit Details Screen" template, and base it on the IssueResponse table. Name your screen AddEditIssueResponse. Once you create your screen, select the root node of your screen use the properties sheet to check the "Show As Dialog" check box.

Creating Child Records in a Dialog

To open your dialog, open your AddEditIssue screen in the screen designer. If you included the Issue Response data when you created your screen, the IssueResponses collection will appear in the screen member list. If not, don't worry. Simply select the "Add IssueResponses" link from the screen member list.

By default, LightSwitch adds your IssueResponses collection to a separate tab and renders the data using a List control. Find your List control, and add a new button beneath it by clicking on the Add dropdown and choosing "New Button."

When the "Add Button" dialog opens, select the "Choose an existing method" radio option and use the dropdown box to select the IssueResponse.addAndEditNew option (Figure 8-12). When you do this, LightSwitch populates the "Navigate To" dropdown with a list of screens that are capable of showing Issue Response records. Choose the "Add Edit Issue Response" dialog that you created earlier.

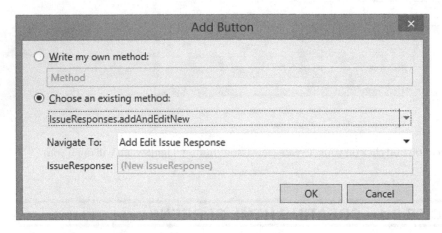

Figure 8-12. *Adding new records*

Editing Child Records in a Dialog

To allow users to open child records in a dialog, you can configure the "Tap Action" of your List control to open the selected record in a new dialog. To accomplish this, open your AddEditIssue screen, and select the list control for your issue responses collection. Click on the "Item Tap" link in the properties sheet and when the "Edit ItemTap Action" dialog opens, select the "Choose an existing method" radio option. Use the dropdown box to select the IssueResponse.editSelected option, and use the "Navigate To" dropdown to select your "Add Edit Issue Response" dialog (Figure 8-13).

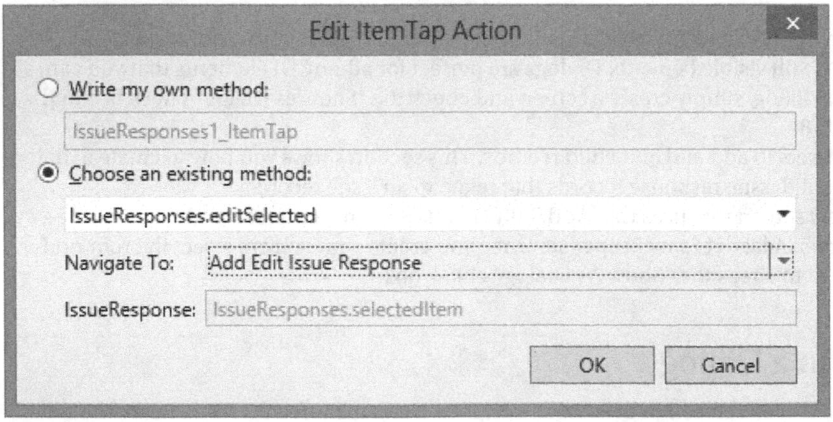

Figure 8-13. *Editing child records*

When you now run your application and view the Issue Response list for an issue, you can tap on a row to open the selected record in a dialog. Figure 8-14 shows how the dialog looks at runtime. This screenshot also illustrates the appearance of the default Date, Date/Time Picker, and Flip Switch controls. Notice how the Response Text field allows the user to enter multiline text. You can configure this by using a Text Area control that specifies a height in pixels.

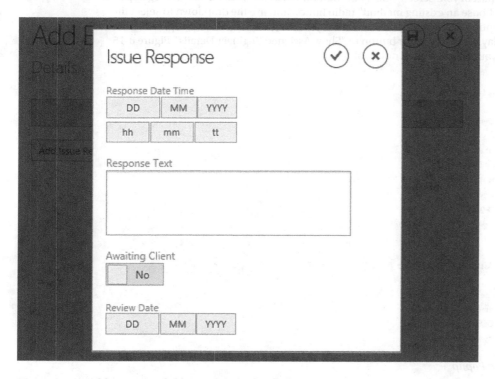

Figure 8-14. Adding a new child record through a dialog

Using Popups

Popups are similar to dialogs. They allow you to show UI controls in a modal panel that appears above an existing screen. The main difference between a popup and dialog is that popups are defined at a screen level and you can't share them across multiple screens. Unlike its treatment of dialogs, LightSwitch doesn't gray out the underlying screen when it shows a popup, nor does it show OK and Discard or Save buttons. To close a popup, a user would click on a screen area outside of the popup. Another characteristic is that LightSwitch doesn't center-align popups in the same way as dialogs.

To demonstrate how popups work, here's how to attach a popup to your issue screen that shows additional details about the engineer who has been assigned to the issue. To create this example, carry out the following steps:

1. Open your AddEditIssue screen in the screen designer, and create a new popup by clicking on the "Add Popup" button that appears beneath the popups folder. Open the properties sheet, and set the name of your popup to AssignedEngineerPopup.

2. Drag the Issue entity's AssignedTo property onto your popup. By default, LightSwitch renders the AssignedTo property as a "Details Modal Picker" control. Use the dropdown to change the control type to a Rows Layout.

3. Open the properties sheet for your Rows Layout, and check the "Use Read-only Controls" check box that you'll find in the General section. You can tidy up your popup view by deleting the engineer property controls that you don't want to show.

4. In the main part of your screen, add a new button. When the "Add Button" dialog appears, select the "Choose an existing method" radio button and use the dropdown to select the showPopup option. Use the dropdown to select the "Assigned Engineer Popup" choice. Set the display property of your button to "Show Assigned Engineer Details." Figure 8-15 shows how your screen should now look.

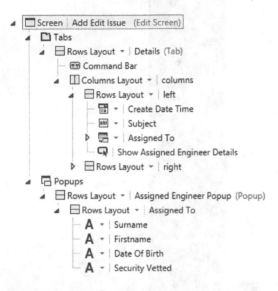

Figure 8-15. *Designing a Popup*

You can now run your screen, and Figure 8-16 shows how it looks. When a user edits an issue and sets an "Assigned To" engineer, the "Show Assigned Engineer Details" button allows the user to view the selected engineer in a popup.

Add Edit Issue

Figure 8-16. *Viewing a Popup*

This example demonstrates how popups are ideal for showing additional pieces of information on a screen. In Figure 8-16, also notice how the popup docks itself to the location of the button rather than aligning the content in the center of the screen (as in the case of a dialog).

Using Compact Margins

One of the property sheet options that you'll have noticed in group controls such as "Rows Layout" is the "Use Compact Margins" check box. According to the help, the purpose of this check box is to "display all child items with Compact Margins." This may not mean very much to you, so the best way to describe this feature is through the screenshot that's shown in Figure 8-17.

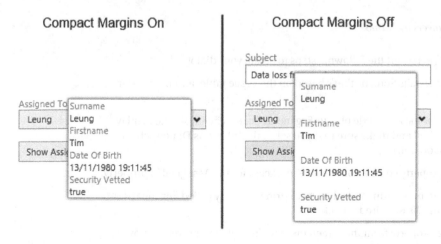

Figure 8-17. *Using Compact Margins*

Figure 8-17 shows the Add/Edit Issue screen with the "Compact Margins" setting enabled and disabled on the popup. With Compact Margins enabled, LightSwitch renders the child items much closer together. This "Compact" appearance looks much neater on pieces of UI that are designed to show summary data, such as the engineer popup.

Creating a Search Screen

Although LightSwitch doesn't include a search screen template, you can easily create a search screen by creating a Browse Data Screen that's based on a query. In fact, the process is identical to the "Creating an Advanced Search Screen" example that you saw in Chapter 7. You won't find it difficult to create a search screen, so this chapter focuses on showing you how to add search capabilities to your application by demonstrating how to allow users to filter the choices in the List control.

Filtering the List Control

Earlier in this chapter, you saw how difficult it is for users to assign an engineer to an issue by using the "Modal Window Picker" control. This is particularly the case if the control contains hundreds of engineers' records (Figure 8-7). This section shows you how to create a dialog that users can use to find engineers by name. You can then call this dialog from your AddEditIssue screen to make it easier for users to assign an engineer to an issue.

To begin, you'll need to create a query that returns engineer records where the surname or first name matches the value of a parameter called Name. Create the query that's shown in Figure 8-18, and name your query EngineersByName.

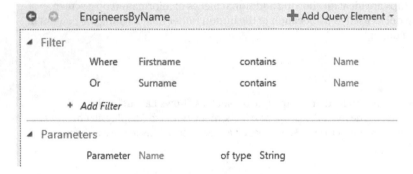

Figure 8-18. *Query that filters Engineers by Name*

Once you've added your query, carry out the following steps to create your dialog:

1. Create a new "Add/Edit Details Screen" that's based on the Issue table, and name your screen EngineerPicker.

2. In the properties sheet for the root node of your EngineerPicker screen, set the display property to "Find Engineer" and make sure that you select the "Show As Dialog" check box. (This is the default option.)

3. Delete all of the Issue property controls on the screen, except for the AssignedTo property.

4. Click on the "Add Data Item" button, and add a local string property called EngineerName. Make sure to uncheck the "Is Required" check box.

5. Drag the EngineerName property from the screen member list onto your screen, above the AssignedTo "Details Modal Picker."

6. Click on the "Add Data Item" button, and add your EngineersByName query.

7. Set the "Parameter Binding" for the EngineersByName query's Name parameter to the EngineerName property. (If you need some help on binding parameters, refer to the "Creating an Advanced Search Screen" section in Chapter 7.)

8. Open the properties sheet for your AssignedTo "Details Modal Picker." Change the Choices setting from Auto to EngineersByName.

9. Change the control that appears beneath your "Details Modal Picker" from a Summary Control to a Columns Layout. Delete the properties beneath the Columns Layout so that only the Firstname and Surname properties remain. This completes the design of your "Engineer Picker" dialog, and Figure 8-19 shows how your screen now looks.

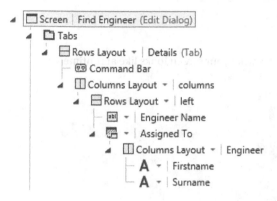

Figure 8-19. *Designing the EngineerPicker Dialog*

■ **Note** You might wonder why you've replaced the Summary Control with a Columns Layout that includes the engineer's first name and surname. Why not keep the Summary Control, and use it to show the full-name computed property that you defined in Chapter 2? The reason is because the HTML client doesn't support computed properties. Computed properties are defined with .NET code, and therefore, the JavaScript HTML client can't derive the result of a computed property value on the client.

Now that you've created your Engineer Picker dialog, you'll need to carry out the following step in your Issue screen to allow users to open your Engineer Picker dialog:

10. Open your AddEditIssue screen, and add a new button beneath the AssignedTo property. When the "Add Button" dialog appears, select the showEngineerPicker option and select Issue in the Issue text box (Figure 8-20). In this context, Issue refers to the local Issue property on your screen. Set the display name of your button to "Find Engineer."

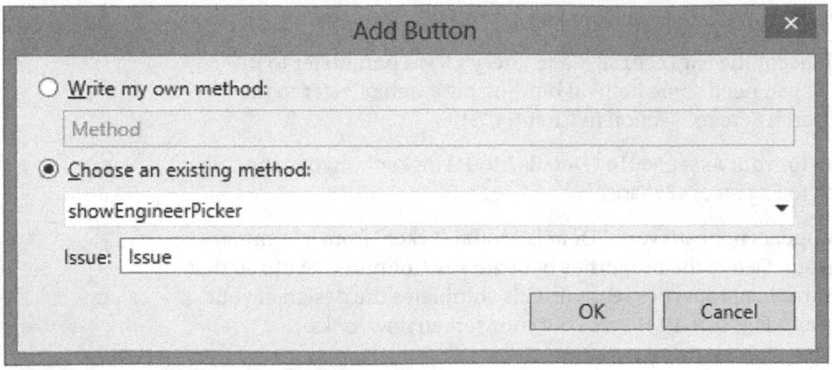

Figure 8-20. *Opening a Dialog*

You're now ready to run your application, and Figure 8-21 shows what your screen looks like at runtime.

Figure 8-21. *Engineer Picker screen at runtime*

When the user opens an issue and clicks on the "Find Engineer" button, LightSwitch opens the "Find Engineer" dialog that allows the user to enter a name. This allows the user to enter an engineer name, and Figure 8-21 illustrates a case where the user enters "el" into the engineer name search box. When the user clicks on the "Assigned To" control that's below the engineer name search box, LightSwitch shows a list of engineer records where the surname or first name contains the text that's been entered by the user (in this case, "el"). This filtered list makes it much easier to find an engineer, compared to forcing the user to find an engineer by scrolling through a list of hundreds of records.

This example also illustrates a case where a dialog works better than a popup or a tab. In this scenario, a dialog provides a center-aligned piece of UI that looks neater than a popup. When the user clicks on the "Assigned To" Details Modal Picker in the "Find Engineer" dialog, LightSwitch opens the list of available choices in a center-aligned panel that appears above everything else on the screen. By using a center-aligned dialog, you can be certain that the "Details Modal Picker" appears directly above the dialog, therefore drawing the user's attention to the "Assigned To - Details Modal Picker."

Another advantage is that dialogs include a cancel button. So if a user makes a mistake in the "Find Engineer" dialog and selects the wrong engineer, they can easily undo their change by clicking on the cancel button.

Extending Your Application with JavaScript

The HTML client allows you to customize your applications by writing JavaScript. This allows you to add custom logic (for example, client-side validation), customize the UI that's shown to the user, bind data to custom controls, and interact with data.

If you've used earlier versions of Visual Studio, you'll be pleasantly surprised at how well Microsoft has improved its support for JavaScript. The IDE provides full IntelliSense when you're writing JavaScript. It auto-completes and provides tooltip descriptions for most of the JavaScript objects that you'll encounter. This includes IntelliSense support for local screen properties and custom entities, as shown in Figure 8-22.

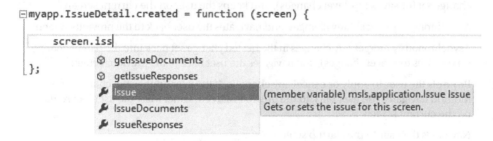

Figure 8-22. *IntelliSense provides support for custom entities*

Another improvement is that breakpoints now work as you'd expect them to work. In contrast to previous versions of Visual Studio, you don't need to mess about with enabling debugging in Internet Explorer or attach your Visual Studio debugger to your browser process. You can simply place breakpoints in your JavaScript code, press F5, and go!

Using the LightSwitch JavaScript API

Besides enhancements to the IDE and better debug support, LightSwitch also provides a JavaScript API that allows you to access data and carry out application tasks. The objects that you'll find in the JavaScript API work in very much the same way as the objects that exist in the .NET API.

The two objects that you'll most often use are the myapp and screen objects. The myapp object represents your LightSwitch application, and it allows you to open screens, access the data workspace, and save or cancel changes. myapp is actually an alias that you use to access the msls.application object, and msls refers to the LightSwitch API's top-level object.

Figure 8-23 shows some of the IntelliSense choices that apply to the myapp object. Notice the Show methods that allow you to open screens. This figure also highlights a method that you won't find in the Silverlight API, called navigateHome. This method moves the user back to the screen that you've defined as the home screen. Table 8-1 highlights some of the methods that you'll find through the myapp object.

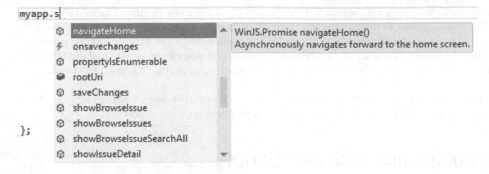

Figure 8-23. *Some of the methods that belong to the myapp object*

Table 8-1. *Application (myapp) Object Methods*

Method	Description
activeDataWorkspace	Gets the active data workspace
applyChanges	Asynchronously merges any changes in the nested change set back into the parent change set (or saves top-level changes), and keeps the user on the current screen
cancelChanges	Asynchronously cancels any changes, and navigates the user back to the previous screen
commitChanges	Asynchronously merges any changes in the nested change set back into the parent change set (or saves top-level changes), and navigates the user back to the previous screen
navigateBack	Prompts the user to apply or cancel any changes. If the user applies the change, this method navigates the user back to the previous screen. Otherwise, the user will remain on the current screen
navigateHome	Navigates the user to the startup screen
show<Screen>	Navigates the user to the specified screen

Attaching JavaScript Code

There are several "entry points" that allow you to write JavaScript code. First, you can create custom buttons and attach JavaScript code that executes when a user clicks on the button. Second, if you can't find a built-in control that suits your needs, you can author your own custom controls. JavaScript is the language that allows you to generate these controls. You can also create listeners that run custom code when, for example, the value of a control changes.

Finally, you can attach JavaScript to handle screen or content item events. As with the Silverlight client, you can use the Write Code button to create methods that handle these events. To illustrate this, select a Rows Layout and click on the "Write Code" button. This reveals the methods that are shown in Figure 8-24.

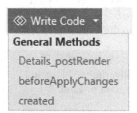

Figure 8-24. *Screen methods that allow you to add custom JavaScript code*

Compared to the "Write Code" button in the Silverlight client designer, there are far fewer methods. The JavaScript methods that you can use include

- **created:** The code that you write in this method executes when the HTML client creates your screen. It's the ideal place to set default screen values.

- **beforeApplyChanges:** This code runs just before the HTML client applies screen changes, and it is useful for adding validation code.

- **<control>_postRender:** For each control on your screen, the HTML client calls its postRender method after it generates the HTML for your control.

The created and beforeApplyChanges events are screen-wide events, whereas the postRender event is specific to each content item. The postRender event doesn't apply to custom controls, but you'll learn more about this later in this chapter.

Setting Default Screen Values

To show you how to apply JavaScript to your application, let's begin with a simple demonstration. This example customizes the Add/Edit Issue screen by defaulting the create date of the issue to today, when the user creates a new record.

To create this example, open your AddEditIssue screen in the designer, click on the "Add Code" button, and choose the created method. Visual Studio opens the code window and adds a method stub for the created method. Modify your code as shown in Listing 8-1.

Listing 8-1. Setting Default Values

File: HelpDeskVB\HTMLClient\UserCode\AddEditIssue.js

```
/// <reference path="../GeneratedArtifacts/viewModel.js" />

myapp.AddEditIssue.created = function (screen) {            ❶
    if (screen.Issue.Id == undefined) {                    ❷
        screen.Issue.CreateDateTime = new Date();          ❸
    }
};
```

The created method includes a screen parameter ❶ that allows you to access the screen object. The screen object allows you to access the local properties on your screen. This code detects whether the user is adding a new record by testing if the Issue.Id property is undefined ❷. If so, the code sets the CreateDateTime property to today's date by assigning to it a new instance of a JavaScript date object ❸.

■ **Caution** Your code file includes a reference to a file called viewModel.js. Make sure not to delete this line. If you do, IntelliSense's auto completion will no longer work in the code editor.

Setting the Screen Title

The screen object allows you to access your screen title through the displayName property. LightSwitch displays the screen title at the top of your screen and, by default, it shows the name of your screen.

This example shows you how to modify your AddEditIssue screen so that if a user opens an existing Issue, the screen title shows the Issue Subject text. Otherwise, it'll show the heading "New Issue" instead.

Open your screen in the designer, click on the "Add Code" button, choose the created method, and add the code that's shown in Listing 8-2.

Listing 8-2. Setting the Screen Title

File: HelpDeskVB\HTMLClient\UserCode\AddEditIssue.js

```
myapp.AddEditIssue.created = function (screen) {
    if (screen.Issue.Id == undefined) {                    ❶
        screen.details.displayName = "New Issue";          ❷
    } else{
        screen.details.displayName = screen.Issue.Subject; ❷
    }
};
```

Once again, the code tests whether the value of the Issue.Id property is undefined ❶. Depending on the result, it then sets the screen title by assigning a value to the screen.details.displayName property ❷.

The screen object exposes other useful properties and methods, and some of these are shown in Table 8-2.

Table 8-2. screen *Object Methods and Properties*

Method/Property	Description
closePopup	Closes the popup that's currently open
findContentItem	Finds a content item
showPopup	Allows you to specify a popup name, and opens the popup that you supply
showTab	Allows you to specify a tab name, and shows the tab that you supply
\<localProperty>	You can access the local properties that you've defined by name via the screen object
\<localMethod>	You can call the local methods that you've defined on your screen

Hiding Controls

In Chapter 7, you learned how to retrieve a reference to a content item (LightSwitch's representation of the View Model for your data item). The HTML client also allows you to access content item objects, and you can use these to access properties such as validation details and the underlying value of your data item.

The HelpDesk application allows users to store the date and time and the engineer who closes an issue. When a user enters a new issue, there's no point in wasting valuable screen space by showing the fields that relate to issue closure. In this example, you'll find out how to hide these controls when the user enters a new issue, but keep them visible when a user edits an issue.

To create this example, open the AddEditIssue screen in the designer, create a new group called ClosureDetails, and move the ClosedByEngineer and ClosedDateTime controls into this group. Click on the "Add Code" button, choose the created method, and add the code that's shown in Listing 8-3.

Listing 8-3. Hiding Controls

File: HelpDeskVB\HTMLClient\UserCode\AddEditIssue.js

```
myapp.AddEditIssue.created = function (screen) {
    if (screen.Issue.Id == undefined) {
```

```
        screen.findContentItem("ClosureDetails").isVisible = false;
    }
};
```

This code obtains a reference to a content item object for the ClosureDetails group by calling the screen's findConentItem method. If the screen is in add mode, the code hides the ClosureDetails group by setting the content item's isVisible property to false.

Accessing Data in Code

You can access data quite intuitively in code, and you've already seen how to access your Issue data in the "Setting Default Screen Values" section. Because you can easily work out the correct syntax through IntelliSense, this section won't go into too much detail. Instead, the following list shows you a brief summary of the syntax that you can use to carry out common data tasks:

- **Access the current data workspace**
  myapp.activeDataWorkspace

- **Access the Intrinsic data source**
  myapp.activeDataWorkspace.ApplicationData

- **Access the Engineer table**
  myapp.activeDataWorkspace.ApplicationData.Engineers

- **Create a new Engineer record**
  var newEng =
  myapp.activeDataWorkspace.ApplicationData.Engineers.addNew();

- **Delete the Engineer record that you've created**
  newEng.deleteEntity();

- **Save changes**
  myapp.activeDataWorkspace.saveChanges();

- **Create a new data workspace**
  var myWorkspace = new myapp.DataWorkspace;

Chapter 15 shows you a full example of how to create records in code. This includes a listing that shows you how to create a new data workspace and how to add new records by using the JavaScript API.

Deleting Records

If you create a button and bring up the "Tap Action" dialog, you'll notice that it doesn't include an option that allows you to delete records. Although the graphical dialog doesn't include a "delete" option, it's possible to delete records by writing custom JavaScript code. To demonstrate how to accomplish this, the following example shows you how to create a button with which users can delete Issue Response records. This button opens a popup that prompts the user for a confirmation prior to the actual deletion. To create this example, carry out the following steps:

1. Open your AddEditIssueResponse screen. Click on the "Add Data Item," and add a string property called PopupTitle. Make sure to uncheck the "Is Required" check box.

2. Click on the "Add Data Item," and add another string property called PopupText. Make sure to uncheck the "Is Required" check box.

3. Click on the "Write Code" button, select the created method, and enter the code that's shown in Part 1 of Listing 8-4.

Listing 8-4. Deleting Records

File: HelpDeskVB\HTMLClient\UserCode\AddEditIssueResponse.js

```
// Part 1 - Popup Display Code
myapp.AddEditIssueResponse.created = function (screen) {
    screen.PopupTitle = "Confirm Delete";                                        ❶
    screen.PopupText = "Are you sure you want to delete this record?";
};

// Part 2 - Popup Button Code
myapp.AddEditIssueResponse.CancelPopup_execute = function (screen) {
    screen.closePopup();                                                         ❷
};

myapp.AddEditIssueResponse.DoDelete_execute = function (screen) {
    screen.IssueResponse.deleteEntity();                                         ❸
    myapp.applyChanges();                                                        ❹
    myapp.navigateBack();                                                        ❺
};
```

4. Return to the screen designer. Create a new popup, and name it ConfirmDelete. Drag your PopupTitle property from the screen member list onto your popup, and change the control type from a TextBox to a Text control. In the properties sheet, set the Label Position to None, and set the Font Style to Large.

5. Drag your PopupText property from the screen member list onto your popup, and change the control type from a TextBox to a Text control. In the properties sheet, set the Label Position to None and set the Font Style to Normal.

6. Add a new Group beneath your PopupText control, and change the control type to a Columns Layout. Add a new button to your Columns Layout, and when the "Add Button" dialog opens, select the "Write my own method" radio button and name your method DoDelete. Set the Display Name of your button to "OK."

7. Add another button to your Columns Layout. When the "Add Button" dialog opens, select the "Write my own method" radio button and name your method CancelPopup. Set the Display Name of your button to "Cancel."

8. Add a button to the Command Bar section of the first tab on your screen. When the "Add Button" dialog opens, select the "Choose an existing method" radio button, select the showPopup option, and select the "Confirm Delete" popup from the popup dropdown. Use the dropdown in the Appearance section of the properties sheet to set the icon to "Trash." Set the Display Name of your button to "Delete Record."

9. Right-click the CancelPopup and DoDelete methods in the screen member list, click on the "Edit Execute Code" link, and enter the code that's shown in Part 2 of Listing 8-4. Figure 8-25 shows how your screen should now look.

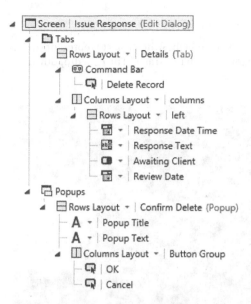

◢ ☐ Screen | Issue Response (Edit Dialog)
　　◢ ☐ Tabs
　　　◢ ⊟ Rows Layout ▾ | Details (Tab)
　　　　◢ 🎛 Command Bar
　　　　　└ ◳ | Delete Record
　　　　◢ ⊞ Columns Layout ▾ | columns
　　　　　◢ ⊟ Rows Layout ▾ | left
　　　　　　├ 📅 ▾ | Response Date Time
　　　　　　├ 🈸 ▾ | Response Text
　　　　　　├ ◲ ▾ | Awaiting Client
　　　　　　└ 📅 ▾ | Review Date
　◢ 🗗 Popups
　　◢ ⊟ Rows Layout ▾ | Confirm Delete (Popup)
　　　├ A ▾ | Popup Title
　　　├ A ▾ | Popup Text
　　　◢ ⊞ Columns Layout ▾ | Button Group
　　　　├ ◳ | OK
　　　　└ ◳ | Cancel

Figure 8-25. *Creating a Delete option*

You can now run your application and open your Issue Response screen by selecting an Issue Response record from your AddEditIssue screen. Figure 8-26 shows how your Issue Response dialog looks. If you click on the "Delete Record" button, LightSwitch opens the ConfirmDelete popup. The text that's shown in this popup is set by the code that you created in Listing 8-4 ❶. If the user clicks on the Cancel button, the code closes the popup by calling the screen's closePopup method ❷. The closePopup method closes the popup and keeps the user on the Issue Response screen. If the user clicks OK, the code deletes the Issue Response record by calling the property's deleteEntity method ❸. It then applies the change ❹ and navigates the user back to the calling screen (in this case, the AddEditIssue screen) by calling the navigateBack method ❺.

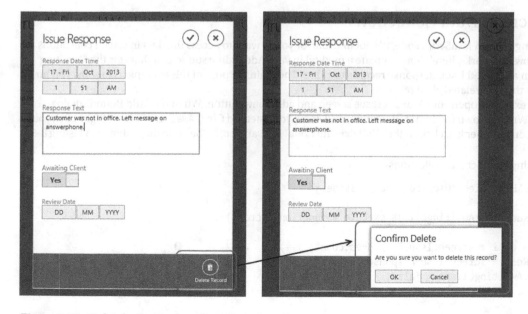

Figure 8-26. *Delete button and confirmation at runtime*

213

Setting a Custom Command Icon

When you add a button to the Command Bar section of a tab, you can set the icon LightSwitch uses to represent your button. In the previous example, you set the icon for the ShowConfirmDelete button to "Trash." The icon dropdown contains a list of 32 icons that you can use, and these are shown in Figure 8-27.

Figure 8-27. *Command Bar icon choices*

If you can't find an icon that suits your needs, you can configure your button to use a custom icon, and you can achieve this by writing code in your button's postRender method. You'll see an example of how to use this method later in the chapter.

Accessing Screen Data Collections

When you're writing custom JavaScript code, it's not unusual for you to want to access the data in screen collections. To demonstrate how this works, here's how to create a method in your Add/Edit Issue screen that sets the "Awaiting Client" property on all related Issue Response records to false. The main purpose of this example is to show you how to access and loop through related child records.

To create this example, open your AddEditIssue screen and add a new button. When the "Add Button" dialog opens, select the "Write my own method" radio button and name your method ClearAwaitingClient. Right-click your method in the screen member list, click on the "Edit Execute Code" link, and enter the code that's shown in Listing 8-5.

Listing 8-5. Working with Screen Collections

File: HelpDeskVB\HTMLClient\UserCode\AddEditIssue.js

```
myapp.AddEditIssue.ClearAwaitingClient_execute = function (screen) {

    for (var i = 0; i < screen.IssueResponses.count; i++) {          ❶
        var issResp = screen.IssueResponses.data[i];                 ❷
        issResp.AwaitingClient = false;                              ❸
    }
};
```

This completes the code, and you're now ready to build and run your screen. The first thing to highlight is the syntax that allows you to access your IssueResponses collection. You might imagine that screen.Issue.IssueResponses gives you access to the child collection, but in actual fact, screen.IssueResponses is the syntax that you should use. The for loop ❶ allows you to loop through the items in the collection that have loaded. The screen.IssueResponses.data member ❷ returns an array that allows you to access the individual IssueResponse records. The final part of the code sets the AwaitingClient property for each Issue Response record to false ❸.

Screen collection objects expose useful properties and methods that you can call, and Table 8-3 highlights some of the more useful methods.

Table 8-3. *Screen Collection Methods*

Method/Property	Description
addNew	Call this method to add a new item to the collection
canLoadMore	Returns true if the collection believes it can load more pages of data
count	Gets the number of items that are currently in the collection
data	Allows you to access the items in the collection
deleteSelected	Call this method to delete the currently selected item
isLoaded	Returns true if the collection has loaded one or more pages
load	Call this method to load the first page of data into the collection
loadError	Returns the last load error (if an error has occurred)
loadMore	Call this method to asynchronously load another page of data into the collection
selectedItem	Returns the currently selected item in the collection
state	Returns the state of the collection (the possible values are idle, loading, loadingMore)

You'll notice that Table 8-3 includes various "load" methods that you can call. This is because just as in the Silverlight client, data collections support pagination. If you select a data collection and open the properties sheet, you can enable or disable paging, and you can also specify the number of records that LightSwitch loads per page (Figure 8-28). In Listing 8-5, it's worth noting that the code loops through only the records that have loaded and you can call the canLoadMore and loadMore methods if you want to work through all of the related records.

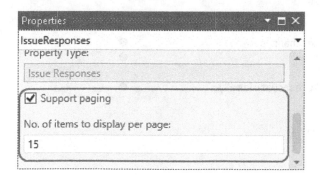

Figure 8-28. *Pagination settings*

Validating Data

You'll be pleased to know that it's very simple to perform basic validation. Chapter 5 showed you how to define predefined validation rules by using the table designer. As you'd expect, the HTML client enforces these predefined rules. It performs data type, data length, and mandatory field validation on the client. As soon as a user enters invalid data, LightSwitch highlights the offending field in red and prevents the user from applying the change. Figure 8-29 shows the screen error that appears when a user closes out of a screen and leaves a mandatory field empty.

Figure 8-29. *Example of required field validation*

Chapter 5 also showed you how to apply more advanced validation rules by writing .NET code. A problem is that the HTML client uses the JavaScript language, and not .NET. This means that LightSwitch won't apply your .NET rules on the client. It'll apply custom rules only through the server-side save pipeline when the user clicks on the save button.

This behavior can be frustrating for the user. Let's consider the validation rule that you saw in Chapter 5 (Listing 5-2). This rule specifies that an issue's close date cannot be earlier than the create date.

Let's imagine that a user opens the browse issues screen, finds an issue, and closes it with an invalid close date. The user then returns to the browse issues screen, finds another issue and closes it. This time, the user chooses a valid date. The difficulty is that the user won't discover the problem with the first record until they click on the Save button. Worst of all, LightSwitch only tells the user that 'Closed Date cannot be earlier than Create Date', but doesn't say which record the error relates to.

So to improve this behavior, it's important to provide more instant user feedback. In this example, you'll re-create this validation rule in JavaScript so that the HTML client shows a warning as soon as the user enters an invalid date.

To create this example, open your `AddEditIssue` screen, click on the "Add Code" button, choose the `created` method, and add the code that's shown in Listing 8-6.

Listing 8-6. Validating Data

File: HelpDeskVB\HTMLClient\UserCode\AddEditIssue.js

```
myapp.AddEditIssue.created = function (screen) {

    //1 add a change listener to the ClosedDateTime property          ❶
    screen.Issue.addChangeListener("ClosedDateTime",
       function (e) {

          //2 this code runs each time ClosedDateTime changes          ❷
          var issue = screen.Issue;                                    ❸

          var contentItem = screen.findContentItem("ClosedDateTime");   ❹

          if (issue.CreateDateTime != undefined &&
          issue.ClosedDateTime < issue.CreateDateTime) {

             contentItem.validationResults = [
                new msls.ValidationResult(
```

```
                screen.Issue.details.properties.ClosedDateTime,
                "Closed date can't be earlier than create date")];                    ❺
        }
    });
};
```

This code uses a method in the HTML client's API called addChangeListener ❶. This method calls JavaScript's addEventListener method and allows you to specify code that runs every time a property value changes.

The code inside the function ❷ runs each time the CloseDateTime property changes. This code includes logic that obtains a reference to the screen's issue property ❸ and the content item that represents the ClosedDateTime property ❹. The next piece of code checks whether the closed date is earlier than the create date. If so, it attaches a validation result to the ClosedDateTime content item ❺. LightSwitch will immediately show this warning to the user, as shown in Figure 8-30.

Create Date Time

26 - Sat	Jul	2013
10	33	AM

Closed Date Time

25 - Fri	Jul	2013
12	58	AM

Closed date can't be earlier than create date

Figure 8-30. *Conditional validation warning*

Adding Custom HTML to Screens

One of the beauties of HTML client applications is that you can customize almost all parts of your screen. The only exception is the heading section. To demonstrate this feature, this section shows you how to add custom images, text, and hyperlinks to a screen, as illustrated in Figure 8-31.

New Issue

Details   Issue Responses

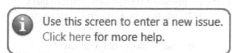
Use this screen to enter a new issue.
Click here for more help.

Target End Date Time

18 - Sun	May	2013
12	00	AM

Figure 8-31. *Adding custom HTML content*

217

To create this example, open your AddEditIssue screen in the designer and select the Rows Layout that corresponds to the first tab on your screen. By default, LightSwitch names this control Details. Click on the "Add Code" button, and choose the Details_postRender method. Now add the code that's shown in Listing 8-7.

Listing 8-7. Adding Custom HTML to a Screen

File: HelpDeskVB\HTMLClient\UserCode\AddEditIssue.js

```
myapp.AddEditIssue.Details_postRender =
    function (element, contentItem) {                                    ❶

        var helpText = $("<div style='padding-bottom:20px;'>" +          ❷
            "<img src='Content/Images/Info.png' style='float:left;padding-right:10px;'/>" +
        "Use this screen to enter a new issue.<br/>" +
        "<a href='http://intranet/help.htm' target='_blank'>Click here</a>" +
        " for more help.</div>");

    helpText.prependTo($(element));

};
```

The postRender method includes a parameter called element ❶. This represents the HTML markup that has been built by the HTML client. In this example, element contains the HTML markup that represents the Details group.

This code builds the new content that you want to add in a variable called helpText ❷. This content includes a DIV (an HTML *Division* element) that contains an image tag, help text, and a hyperlink. This HTML represents the content that's shown in Figure 8-31. For the image to display correctly, you'll need to create an image called Info.png and add it to your HTML client's Content\Images folder. You can add resources such as images by switching your project to File View and using the "Add" option in Solution Explorer. The final part of the code adds this HTML to the beginning of your Details Group by calling jQuery's prependTo method.

As you can see, the helpText contains a fair amount of presentational data in the style attributes. To improve this code, you could apply your own CSS classes and include the style definitions in a CSS file.

■ **Tip** jQuery's prependTo and appendTo methods are very useful for adding HTML content to your screens. You can read more about these methods at http://api.jquery.com/prepend/ and http://api.jquery.com/append/.

Using Custom Controls

As with the Silverlight Client, you're not limited to using the built-in controls that LightSwitch supplies. If there isn't a built-in control that looks or behaves exactly as you want, you can overcome this limitation by building your own custom control.

This section consists of two main parts. In the first part, you'll learn how to use custom controls to show data in a read-only format. In the second part, you'll learn how to create a fully interactive custom control that data-binds to your underlying data source. Technically, this two-way data binding requires you to carry out two distinct tasks. First, you need to run code that responds to changes in the value of your underlying data item. This allows you to write code that updates the display of your custom control. Second, you need to write code that reacts to user interaction and updates the value of your underlying data item.

Let's take a closer look at how you'd set up a custom control. To define a custom control, use the screen designer's dropdown to set the control type for a data item to "Custom Control" (Figure 8-32). The next step is to write JavaScript in your custom control's render method that defines the HTML for your control. The render method includes a parameter called ContentItem that allows you to access the data that your custom control binds to.

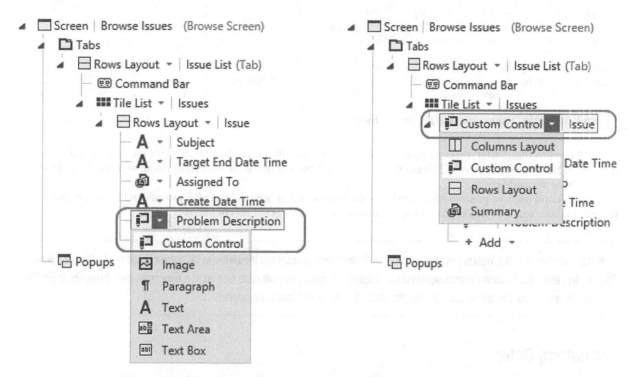

Figure 8-32. *Defining Custom Controls for properties and entities*

The "level" at which you create a custom control is very important because it determines the data that you can access in code. If, for example, you set the control type of the ProblemDescription property to a custom control, the ContentItem parameter gives you access to the ProblemDescription property only. If you want to create a custom control that shows both the Problem Description and the Target End Date, you wouldn't be able to accomplish this by using a custom control that binds to the ProblemDescription property. To access more than one property from an entity, you'd need to create a custom control that binds to the entity. So, in this example, you'd change the parent Rows Layout to Custom Control. This means that your custom control's ContentItem parameter gives you access to the Issue property, which in turn allows you to access both the Problem Description and Target End Date values.

Showing Data with Custom Controls

In the first custom control example, you'll find out how to customize the appearance of your browse issues screen. Figure 8-33 shows the default appearance of this screen.

Browse Issues

26/07/2013 22:33:34 Virus Infected Workstation	12/06/2013 14:47:13 Aircon leakage
12/06/2013 14:50:19 Data loss from router	13/06/2013 14:51:00 Server not accepting RDC connecti...

Figure 8-33. *Default appearance of the Browse Issues screen*

There a few things that you can improve in this screen. Each tile shows the create date of the issue, but the formatting isn't very easy to read. This example shows you how to remove the time component and how to display the month name in words.

The second improvement that you'll make will allow users to more easily identify issues that have exceeded the target end date. You'll do this by displaying a warning icon in the top left part of the tile.

■ **Note**   In Figure 8-33, notice how the Date/Time Picker control displays the dates in UK format (that is, day/month/year). The control uses the browser's language setting to apply the most suitable date format. If a user sets their browser to English (US), the screen would automatically format the dates in US format (month/day/year).

Formatting Dates

To make it easier to format dates, you'll use a utility called *momentjs*. Although you can use native JavaScript to format dates, a custom date library makes your life much simpler. It saves you (for example) from having to write your own custom method to convert the month number 2 to the month name "March." If you're unfamiliar with JavaScript, there's no mistake in the previous sentence. JavaScript months are zero based, but even more confusingly, day numbers are one based.

Although this example uses momentjs, you can choose to use other JavaScript date libraries instead. Another good library is datejs (http://www.datejs.com/), and a quick search on the Internet will reveal many more.

To begin, download momentjs from the following web site: http://momentjs.com/. You'll find two versions that you can download: a minified version, and a full version. The minified version doesn't contain comments or extra white space. The benefit of this version is that, because of its smaller size, browsers can download and parse the file more quickly.

Once you've downloaded momentjs, you'll need to carry out the following tasks:

1. The datejs library consists of a JavaScript file called moment.min.js. Switch your project to File View, and add this file to your HTMLClient project's scripts folder (HTMLClient\Scripts).

2. While still in File View, open the default.htm file that you'll find in the root of your HTMLClient project. The body section of the default.htm file contains links to script files. In the section of the file where the script links appear (just before the end of the body section), add a link to the moment.min.js file. Your link will look like this:

    ```
    <script src="Scripts/moment.min.js"></script>
    ```

CHAPTER 8 ■ CREATING HTML INTERFACES

3. Now switch back to Logical View, and open your BrowseIssues screen in the screen designer. Because you want to create a custom control that includes the CreateDateTime, TargetEndDateTime, and Subject fields, you'll need to change the Rows Layout beneath the Tile List to a custom control and make sure that no child items exist beneath your custom control (Figure 8-34).

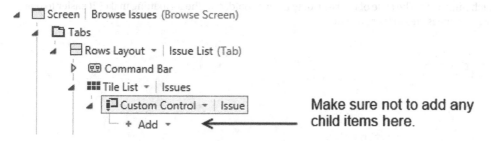

Figure 8-34. *Setting a Custom Control*

Select your custom control in the designer, and click on the "Edit Render Code" link in the properties sheet. When the code editor opens, enter the code that's shown in Listing 8-8.

Listing 8-8. Formatting Dates with Custom Controls

File: HelpDeskVB\HTMLClient\UserCode\BrosweIssues.js

```
myapp.BrowseIssue.IssuesTemplate_render =
    function (element, contentItem) {
    //RowTemplate
    var overdueAlert = "";
    var today = new Date();                                              ❶
    if (contentItem.value.TargetEndDateTime < today) {                   ❷
        overdueAlert =                                                   ❸
            "<img src='Content/Images/Warning.png' " +
            "style='float:left;padding-right:10px;'/>";
    }

    var customText = $("<div>" + overdueAlert + "<p><strong>" +          ❹
        moment(contentItem.value.CreateDateTime).format('ddd MMM DD YYYY') +
        "</strong></p></br>" +
        contentItem.value.Subject + "</div>");
    customText.appendTo($(element));
};
```

The render method for any custom control includes two parameters: contentItem and element. The contentItem object represents the view model that the custom control binds to—in this example, the Issue property. The element object represents the placeholder that you'll add your custom HTML to.

The code builds the custom control's HTML into a variable called customText. The first part of the code tests whether the issue's TargetEndDateTime is greater than today. The code determines today's date by declaring a variable and setting it to an instance of a new JavaScript Date object ❶. Because the ContentItem object's value is an Issue object, contentItem.value.TargetEndDateTime allows you to access the target end date value ❷. If the target end date is greater than today, the code creates an HTML image tag that shows a warning icon ❸. You'll need to create a warning image called warning.png and add it to your HTML client's Content\Images folder.

The next part of the code builds the HTML that's shown in the control . It begins by including the warning image, if it has been set. It then uses momentjs's format method to format the date as a string that looks like this: "Fri Mar 16 2012." You can find out more about the format strings that you can use on momentjs's web site. The final piece of code sets your custom control's HTML markup by assigning the contents of your customText variable to the element parameter.

You're now ready to run your application, and Figure 8-35 shows how your screen looks at runtime. As you can see, the appearance is now much improved. The style of the Issue date is set to bold, and the formatting makes it easier to read. The tiles also show icons next to the issues that are overdue.

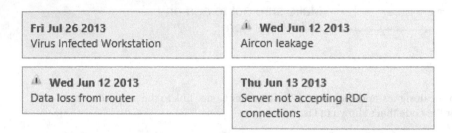

Figure 8-35. *Final screen*

Accessing Navigation Properties

In the example that you've just seen, you accessed the properties that belong to the Issue object (CreateDateTime, TargetEndDateTime, and Subject). You can also access the Issue object's navigation properties in code, but to do this, you need to make sure that LightSwitch loads your navigation property values. If not, your code will fail when it tries to retrieve data that isn't available.

You can configure the related data that the HTML client loads by clicking the "Edit Query" link that appears next to your query in the screen members list. When the query designer opens, click on the "Manage Included Data" link that appears in the properties sheet.

Figure 8-36 shows the Manage Included Data dialog. If, for example, you want to include the user's department in your custom control, you'll need to use this dialog to include the department data.

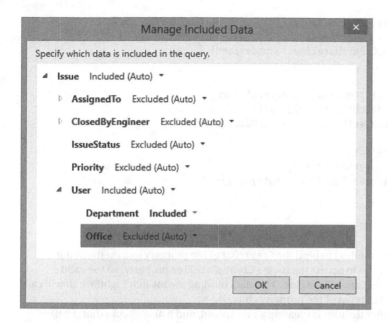

Figure 8-36. *Managing included data*

Running Code When Data Changes

The previous example showed you how to display data by using a custom control. If you want to do anything more sophisticated, you'll need to know how to update data in addition to showing it. You can accomplish this by calling a method that the contentItem object exposes called dataBind. This is a powerful method that allows you to bind JavaScript functions to data items.

To introduce how the dataBind method works, this section shows you how to run code when the value of a data item changes. The following example shows you how to modify your Add/Edit Issue screen so that when a user enters a new issue, it'll trigger custom code that sets the target end date of the issue to 3 days after its create date. The advantage of the data-binding technique is that the HTML client automatically updates the target end date as soon as the user changes the create date. And it'll do this every time that the user subsequently changes the create date.

To create this example, open your AddEditIssue screen and select the Rows Layout that contains the controls that relate to your Issue property. By default, this group is called Details. Click on the "Add Code" button, and choose the Details_postRender method. Now add the code that's shown in Listing 8-9.

Listing 8-9. Running Code When Data Changes

File: HelpDeskVB\HTMLClient\UserCode\AddEditIssue.js

```
myapp.AddEditIssue.Details_postRender = function (element, contentItem) {

    // 1 databind the createDateTime                                          ❶
    contentItem.dataBind("screen.Issue.CreateDateTime", function () {
        setTargetEndDate(contentItem);
    });

    function setTargetEndDate(contentItem) {
```

223

```
        // 2 only set the target date for new issues                          ❷
        if (contentItem.screen.Issue.Id == undefined
            && contentItem.screen.Issue.CreateDateTime != undefined) {

            // get the create date
            var createDate = contentItem.screen.Issue.CreateDateTime;
            var futureDate = new Date(createDate.getFullYear(),
                            createDate.getMonth(), createDate.getDate());

            // add 3 days onto the create date
            futureDate.setDate(futureDate.getDate() + 3);                      ❸
            contentItem.screen.Issue.TargetEndDateTime = futureDate;           ❹
        }
    };
};
```

The first part of this code uses the dataBind method to bind the CreateDateTime property to a method called setTargetEndDate ❶. The screen object allows you to access the issue's CreateDateTime property, so the valid binding path that you would use is screen.Issue.CreateDateTime. This data binding means that LightSwitch will call the setTargetEndDate method each time the CreateDateTime property changes.

The setTargetEndDate method tests whether the user is creating a new record, and it also checks that the user has set a create date ❷. If so, it creates a variable called futureDate and uses JavaScript's setDate method to set the value to three days after the create date ❸. Finally, the code sets the TargetEndDateTime to the future date ❹.

Replacing Default Controls with Custom Controls

Now you know how to use the dataBind method, you can begin to create even more sophisticated custom controls. This example shows you how to replace LightSwitch's Date/Time Picker with a third-party date-picker control that data-binds to your data item in both directions.

The third-party control that you'll use is provided by a company called Mobiscroll. However, you could use any other HTML control instead—the principles would remain the same.

In this example, you'll bind the Issue's CreateDateTime to an HTML input box and attach the Mobiscroll "Date & Time Scroller" control to this input box. Figure 8-37 shows what your screen looks like when you complete this example.

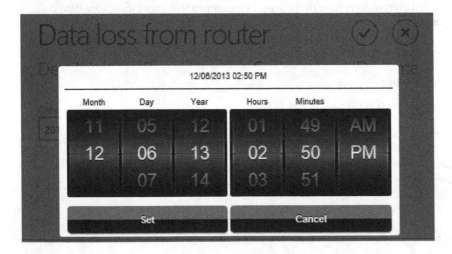

Figure 8-37. *Mobiscroll Control*

To create this example, carry out the following tasks:

1. Download the Mobiscroll control from the following web site:
    `http://download.mobiscroll.com/datetime`. At the time of writing, this control is free;
    however, the suite contains several other controls that you must pay for.

2. The Mobiscroll package includes two files: a CSS file and a JavaScript file. Switch to File
    View, and add these files to a new folder in the following location in your `HTMLClient`
    project: `HTMLClient\Content\mobiscroll`.

3. While you're still in File View, open the `default.htm` file that you'll find in the root of your
    `HTMLClient` project. The head section of this file contains links to CSS files. Before the end
    of the head section, add a link to the Mobiscroll CSS file. Your link will look like this:

    ```
    <link rel="stylesheet"
      href="Content/mobiscroll/mobiscroll.datetime-2.4.1.min.css" />
    ```

4. The body section of your `default.htm` file contains links to script files. Before the end of
    the body section, add a link to the Mobiscroll JavaScript file. Your link will look like this:

    ```
    <script src="Content/mobiscroll/mobiscroll.datetime-2.4.1.min.js">
    </script>
    ```

This completes all of the tasks that are needed in your `default.htm` file. If Mobiscroll releases a newer version
of its controls, or if you've saved the CSS and JS files in a different location, you can adapt the file names that are
specified in steps 3 and 4. Now switch your project to Logical View and carry the following steps:

1. Open your `AddEditIssue` screen in the screen designer.

2. Change your `CreateDateTime` control from a Date/Time Picker to a custom control.

3. Select your `CreateDateTime` control, click on the "Edit Render Code" link in the properties
    sheet, and add the code that's shown in Listing 8-10.

Listing 8-10. Adding the Mobiscroll Control

File: `HelpDeskVB\HTMLClient\UserCode\AddEditIssue.js`

```
myapp.AddEditIssue.CreateDateTime_render =
function (element, contentItem) {
    var CreateDateTime =
        $('<input id="CreateDateTime" type="datetime"/>');
    CreateDateTime.appendTo($(element));                          ❶

    // 2 Initialize the mobiscroll control                         ❷
    $(function () {
        var now = new Date();
        $('#CreateDateTime').mobiscroll().datetime({
            minDate: new Date(now.getFullYear() - 10,
            now.getMonth(), now.getDate()),
            dateFormat: 'yy-MM-dd HH:mm',
            theme: 'default',
            lang: ' ',
```

```
                display: 'modal',
                animate: ' ',
                mode: 'scroller'
        });
    });

    // 3 Listen for changes made in the view model                      ❸
    contentItem.dataBind("value", function (newValue) {
        // Update the HTML Input and Scroller Control
        CreateDateTime.val(moment(newValue).format('YYYY-MM-DD HH:mm'));    ❹
        $("#CreateDateTime").scroller('setDate', newValue , true);          ❺
    });

    // Listen for changes made via the custom control
    CreateDateTime.change(function () {
        // update the content item value
        var newDate = moment(CreateDateTime.val(), "YYYY-MM-DD HH:mm");

        if (contentItem.value != newDate.toDate()) {
            contentItem.value = newDate.toDate());                          ❻
        }
    });
};
```

After you've added this code, you can run your application. The code at the start of the render method creates a variable called CreateDateTime, and sets its value to the HTML markup that represents an HTML input control. It then renders it on screen by appending CreateDateTime to the render method's element parameter ❶. This piece of code is necessary because the Mobiscroll control technically works by attaching itself to an HTML input.

The next part of the listing contains code that's specific to the Mobiscroll control ❷. It initializes the Mobiscroll control by setting default attributes. This includes the minimum date that the user can select (it sets this to ten years before today's date), theme settings, and language settings. For more information, the Mobiscroll documentation shows you all of the attributes that you can use.

The code in the next section calls the content item's databind method ❸. This allows your control to react when the underlying value changes and to update the value of the HTML input control ❹ by calling a Mobiscroll method called scroller ❺. This method sets the value of the Mobiscroll control to the new value.

The next section adds code that executes when the value of the HTML input changes. When this happens, it sets the underlying value of the content item to the new value ❻. This section of code uses the momentjs library to test that the date has changed before updating the underlying content item value.

Executing Queries

Chapter 6 showed you several examples of how to query your data in code. In an HTML application, LightSwitch's JavaScript API allows you to carry out queries against your data. However, you'll find some important differences compared to the code that you've seen in previous chapters. The most obvious difference is that .NET objects such as EntityCollection<T>, IDataServiceQueryable, and LINQ don't exist in JavaScript. So to work with queries in JavaScript, you'll need to apply a different technique to access your data.

In this section, you'll find out how to modify the Browse Issues Screen so that it includes a summary of the issues that are due today and tomorrow. Figure 8-38 shows how your screen will look when you complete this example.

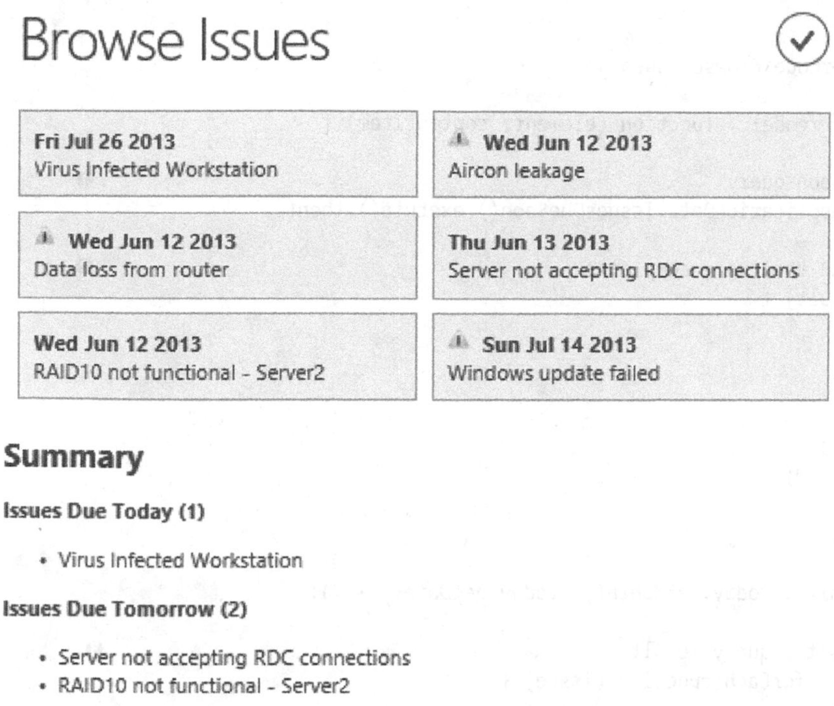

Browse Issues
Fri Jul 26 2013
Virus Infected Workstation
Wed Jun 12 2013
Aircon leakage
Wed Jun 12 2013
Data loss from router
Thu Jun 13 2013
Server not accepting RDC connections
Wed Jun 12 2013
RAID10 not functional - Server2
Sun Jul 14 2013
Windows update failed
Summary
Issues Due Today (1)
Virus Infected Workstation
Issues Due Tomorrow (2)
Server not accepting RDC connections
RAID10 not functional - Server2

***Figure 8-38.** Summary of Issues*

First, you'll need to create a query called `IssuesDueSoon` that returns Issues that are due between today and the following two days. The "Filtering by Date Elements" section in Chapter 6 shows you the type of code that you'd need to write to create such a query. If you simply want to run this example and aren't too concerned about the query returning correct data, you can create a query called `IssuesDueSoon` and not apply any filters.

Once you've created your query, open your `BrowseIssues` screen and add a new Rows Layout beneath your Tile View. Change it to a custom control, and name it `IssueSummary` (Figure 8-39).

Tabs
Rows Layout
Issue List (Tab)
Tile List
Issues
Custom Control
Issue Summary
Add

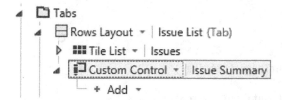

***Figure 8-39.** Adding a Summary Custom Control*

Select `IssueSummary`, click the "Edit Render Code" link in the properties sheet, and add the code that's shown in Listing 8-11.

Listing 8-11. Query Code

File: HelpDeskVB\HTMLClient\UserCode\BrowseIssues.js

```
myapp.BrowseIssues.IssueSummary_render = function (element, contentItem) {

    // 1 execute the IssuesDueSoon query                                              ❶
    myapp.activeDataWorkspace.ApplicationData.IssuesDueSoon().execute().then(

        // 2 this code runs when the query completes                                  ❷
        function (promiseObjResult) {

        var issuesToday = "";
        var issuesTomorrow = "";

        var issueCountToday = 0;
        var issueCountTomorrow = 0;

        var today = new Date();
        var tomorrow =
          new Date(today.getYear(), today.getMonth(), today.getDate() + 1);

        // 3 this code consumes the query result                                      ❸
        promiseObjResult.results.forEach(function (issue) {

            if (issue.TargetEndDateTime.getDate() == today.getDate()) {
                issuesToday = issuesToday + "<li>" + issue.Subject + "</li>";
                issueCountToday = issueCountToday + 1;
            }

            if (issue.TargetEndDateTime.getDate() == tomorrow.getDate()) {
                issuesTomorrow = issuesTomorrow + "<li>" + issue.Subject + "</li>";
                issueCountTomorrow = issueCountTomorrow + 1;
            }

        });

        // 4 this code creates the final HTML output                                  ❹
        var heading = $("<h2>Summary</h2>" +
            "<div><strong>Issues Due Today (" + issueCountToday.toString() +
            ")</strong><ul>" + issuesToday + "</ul></div>" +
            "<div><strong>Issues Due Tomorrow (" + issueCountTomorrow.toString() +
            ")</strong><ul>" + issuesTomorrow + "</ul></div>");

        heading.appendTo($(element));

    },
```

```
function (error) {                                                    ❺

    // 5 an unexpected error has occurred
    var heading = $("<h2>Summary</h2>" +
        "<div>Unexpected error - Summary data couldn't be retrieved because:" +
            error + "</div>");
    heading.appendTo($(element));
  }

  );
};
```

This completes the example, and you can now run your application. The code at the start of the render method calls the `IssuesDueSoon` query by calling the method `myapp.activeDataWorkspace.ApplicationData.IssuesDueSoon().execute()` ❶.

As you type the word `execute` into the code editor window, Visual Studio's IntelliSense informs you that the execute method is designed to "asynchronously execute your query." You'll notice that many of the other methods in the JavaScript API also work asynchronously—the data service's saveChanges method is one example. The advantage of asynchronous methods is that they allow you to carry out long-running processes without locking up your UI. LightSwitch provides asynchronous support by implementing the WinJS promise pattern (http://msdn.microsoft.com/en-us/library/windows/apps/br211867.aspx). A Promise object acts as a proxy for a result that's initially unknown. A query object's execute method is an example of an object that returns a promise.

Promise objects expose a method called then. You use this method to define the code that runs when the asynchronous work completes. In this example, the code executes a function that includes a parameter called `promiseObjResult` that represents the result of the query ❷. The first part of this code initializes some variables that help to build the HTML that's shown to the user. The next part of the code consumes the query result and loops through each issue record by using this syntax: `promiseObjResult.results.forEach` ❸. The code inside the forEach loop builds a list of issues that are due today and tomorrow, and it produces a count of issues for each day. The final piece of code ❹ builds the custom HTML output that's added to the screen.

The second function that you supply to the then method defines the code that runs if an error occurs ❺. The code in this function displays the error message that's returned by the request.

Working with Documents

As you'll remember from Chapter 7, the HelpDesk application includes a feature that allows users to upload multiple documents for each issue. In this section, you'll find out how to allow users to upload and download documents through your Add/Edit Issues screen.

Uploading Files

The HTML client doesn't include a file upload control, so you'll need to create a custom file-upload mechanism. An efficient way to provide this capability uses the File API capabilities that you'll find in HTML5 browsers. The HTML5 standard allows web browsers to interact with local files. This is a really powerful feature because it enables you to work with files on the client, before you send them to the server. For example, you could validate data or create thumbnails of images on the client. Figure 8-40 illustrates the process that you'll carry out in the form of a diagram.

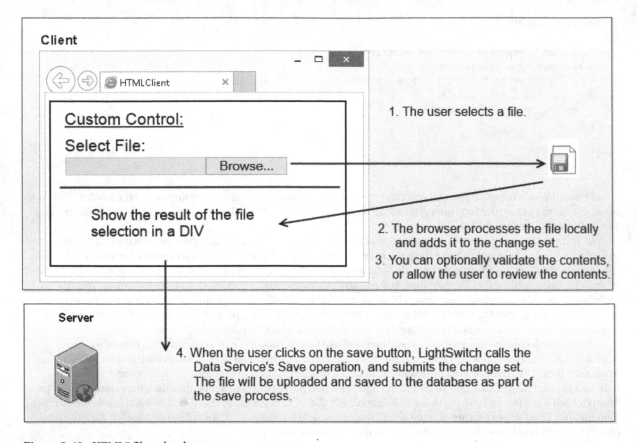

Figure 8-40. *HTML5 file upload process*

This process relies on a custom control that you'll create. This custom control consists of two elements: a file browse button (that is, an HTML Input of type file), and a DIV that shows the results.

When the user selects a file, the control uses the local file-processing feature of the HTML5 browser to read the file. It retrieves the contents as a base 64–encoded string, adds the data to the local change set, and shows the results in the DIV. When the user clicks on the save button, the HTML client calls the Data Service's Save operation. The file that the user adds will be included in the change set that the client sends to the server.

Despite the File API's ease of use, a big problem is that many users still don't use HTML5-compliant browsers. Therefore, you'll need a fallback method to make sure that users with older browsers can still upload files. Figure 8-41 shows how the non-HTML5 file-upload process works.

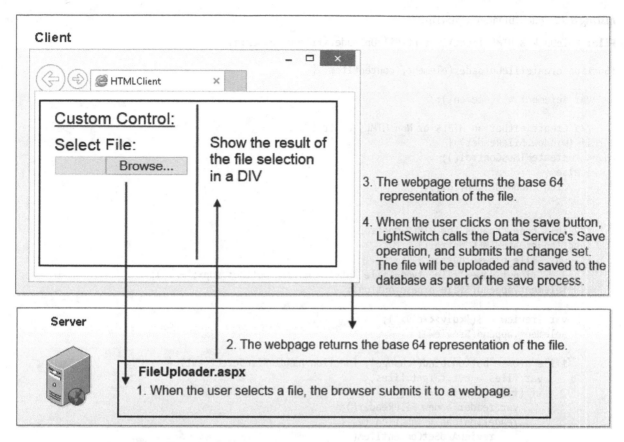

Figure 8-41. *Non-HTML5 file-upload process*

If the custom control detects that the user isn't using an HTML5 browser, it generates a control that contains three elements: a file browse button, a hidden iframe, and a DIV to display the progress details. (An iframe is an HTML control that you can use to display a web page inside another web page.)

Once the user selects a file, the control submits the file to an ASP.NET web page through the hidden iframe. The iframe allows the browser to submit the file to the server, without interrupting the user's ability to interact with the other parts of the screen. The ASPX page mimics the job that the HTML5 File API would carry out—it produces a base 64–encoded representation of the file and returns the result to the client. When the ASPX page finishes loading, the contents of the hidden iframe will contain the base-64 representation of the file. The custom control detects when the iframe finishes loading and displays the result in a DIV, in the same way as the HTML5 custom control.

Creating a Custom File-Upload Control

To create this example, the first step is to write the JavaScript methods that generate the custom control. To do this, switch your project to File View, go to your HTMLClient project, and add a new folder beneath the Content folder called FileUploader.

Now create a new file called file-uploader.js, and add the content that's shown in Listing 8-12.

Listing 8-12. File Uploader JavaScript

File: HelpDeskVB\HTMLClient\Content\FileUploader\file-uploader.js

```
function createfileUploader(element, contentItem) {

    var $element = $(element);

    //1 Create either an HTML5 or Non HTML5 control
    if (window.FileReader) {                                        ❶
        createHTML5Control();
    } else {
        createNonHTML5Control();
    }

    //2 This code creates the HTML5 control
    function createHTML5Control() {                                 ❷
        var $file_browse_button = $(
            '<input name="file" type="file" style="margin-bottom: 10px;" />');
        $element.append($file_browse_button);

        var $review = $('<div></div>');
        $element.append($review);

        $file_browse_button.bind('change', function handleFileSelect(evt) {
            var files = evt.target.files;
            if (files.length == 1) {
                var reader = new FileReader();
                reader.onload = function (e) {
                    reviewAndSetContentItem(
                        e.target.result, $review, contentItem);
                };
                reader.readAsDataURL(files[0]);
            } else {
                //  if no file was chosen, set the content to null
                reviewAndSetContentItem(null, $review, contentItem);
            }
        });
    }

    //3 This code creates the non HTML5 control
    function createNonHTML5Control() {                              ❸
        // Create a file submission form
        var $file_upload_form = $('<form method="post" ' +
                'action="../Web/FileUploader/FileUploader.aspx" ' +
                'enctype="multipart/form-data" target="uploadTargetIFrame" />');
        var $file_browse_button = $(
            '<input name="file" type="file" style="margin-bottom: 10px;" />');
        $file_upload_form.append($file_browse_button);
        $element.append($file_upload_form);
```

```javascript
    // The file contents will be posted to this hidden iframe
    var $uploadTargetIFrame = $('<iframe name="uploadTargetIFrame" ' +
        'style="width: 0px; height: 0px; border: 0px solid #fff;"/>');
    $element.append($uploadTargetIFrame);

    // This div shows the upload status and upload confirmation
    var $review = $('<div></div>');
    $element.append($review);

    // Submit the file automatically when the user chooses a file
    $file_browse_button.change(function () {
        $file_upload_form.submit();
    });

    // On form submission, show a "processing" message:
    $file_upload_form.submit(function () {
        $review.append($('<div>Processing file...</div>'));
    });

    // Once the result frame is loaded (e.g., result came back),
    $uploadTargetIFrame.load(function () {
        var serverResponse = null;
        try {
            serverResponse =
                $uploadTargetIFrame.contents().find("body").html();
        } catch (e) {
            // request must have failed, keep server response empty.
        }
        reviewAndSetContentItem(serverResponse, $review, contentItem);
    });
}

//4 This code shows the upload confirmation                              ❹
function reviewAndSetContentItem(fullBinaryString, $review, contentItem) {
    $review.empty();

    if ((fullBinaryString == null) || (fullBinaryString.length == 0)) {
        contentItem.value = null;
    } else {
        $review.append($('<div>File uploaded</div>'));

        //remove the preamble that the FileReader adds
        contentItem.value =
            fullBinaryString.substring(fullBinaryString.indexOf(",") + 1);
    }
}
}
```

The createfileUploader method is the method that you would call from the render method of a custom control that's bound to a binary property (for example, the IssueFile property from the IssueDocument table).

This code detects if the user is using an HTML5-compliant browser by calling the `Window.FileReader` method ❶. If so, the code creates the HTML5 custom control that's shown in Figure 8-40 by calling the `createHTML5Control` method ❷. Otherwise, it creates the non-HTML5 custom control that's shown in Figure 8-41 by calling the `createNonHTML5Control` method ❸. When the custom control processes the file during runtime, it calls the `reviewAndSetContentItem` method ❹. This method sets the value of the content item and generates a confirmation message in a DIV.

To use this file in your application, you'll need to add a link to `file-uploader.js` file in your `default.htm` file. Open your `default.htm` file, and add a link to this script just before the end of the body tag. If you completed the Mobiscroll example, you can add the link just beneath the link to the Mobiscroll JavaScript file. The link that you'll need to add will look like this:

```
<script src="Content/FileUploader/file-uploader.js"></script>
```

Supporting Non-HTML5 Browsers

To support non-HTML5 browsers, you'll need to create an ASP.NET page that accepts a file and returns the base-64 representation. To create this page, switch your project to File View and go to your Server project. Create a new folder beneath your Web folder, and name it `FileUploader`. Right-click your `FileUploader` folder, and select the Add ➤ New Item option. Create a new Web Form, name it `FileUploader.aspx`, and modify the contents as shown in Listing 8-13.

Listing 8-13. Creating a Page That Returns the base-64 Representation of a File

VB:
File: HelpDeskVB\Server\Web\FileUploader\FileUploader.aspx

```
<%@ Page Language="VB"%>

<script  runat="server">
   Sub Page_Load()
      If Request.Files.Count = 1 Then
         Dim file = Request.Files(0)
         If file.ContentLength > 0 Then
            Dim inputStream = file.InputStream
            Dim base64Block As Byte() =
               New Byte(inputStream.Length - 1) {}
            inputStream.Read(base64Block, 0, base64Block.Length)

            '1 Add the preamble of "data:{mime-type};base64,".          ❶
            Response.Write("data:" & file.ContentType & ";base64," &
                        Convert.ToBase64String(base64Block))
         End If
      End If
   End Sub
</script>
```

C#:
File: HelpDeskCS\Server\Web\FileUploader\FileUploader.aspx

```
<%@ Page Language="C#" %>
```

```
<script runat="server">
   void Page_Load(object sender, System.EventArgs e)
   {
      if (Request.Files.Count == 1)
      {
         var file = Request.Files[0];
         if (file.ContentLength > 0)
         {
            var inputStream = file.InputStream;
            byte[] base64Block = base64Block =
               new byte[inputStream.Length];

            inputStream.Read(base64Block, 0, base64Block.Length);

            //1 Add the preamble of "data:{mime-type};base64,".        ❶

            Response.Write("data:" + file.ContentType +  ";base64," +
                           Convert.ToBase64String(base64Block));
         }
      }
   }
</script>
```

The output from this web page creates the same response that the HTML5 FileReader produces by adding the preamble of "data:{mime-type};base64," to the start of the response ❶.

Attaching a File Upload Control to Your Screen

To complete this example, you'll need to create a dialog that allows users to add and edit IssueDocument records. Your dialog will contain the custom file upload control that allows the user to select a file. You'll then add a List Control to your Add/Edit Issue screen that shows the documents that belong to an Issue and a button that allows users to add new IssueDocument records.

To create the dialog that allows users to add and edit Issue Document details, carry out the following steps:

1. Create a new "Add/Edit Details Screen" that's based on the IssueDocument table, and name your screen AddEditIssueDocument.

2. In the properties sheet for the root node of your AddEditIssueDocument screen, set the "Display Name" property to "Issue Document" and make sure that you check the "Show As Dialog" check box. (This is the default option.)

3. By default, LightSwitch renders the IssueFile property using the Image control. Change the control type to a custom control. Click the "Edit Render Code" link in the properties sheet, and add the code that's shown in Listing 8-14.

   Listing 8-14. File Uploader JavaScript Code

   File: HelpDeskVB\HTMLClient\UserCode\AddEditIssueDocument.js

   ```
   myapp.AddEditIssueDocument.IssueFile_render =
       function (element, contentItem) {
       createfileUploader(element, contentItem);
   };
   ```

The next step is to modify your Add Edit Issue screen to allow users to edit Issue Documents or to upload a new Issue Document. Here are the steps that you'll need to carry out:

1. Open your `AddEditIssue` screen. If your screen doesn't contain the `IssueDocuments` collection, click on the "Add IssueDocuments" link in the screen member list.

2. Create a new tab, and name it `IssueDocumentsTab`. Set the Display Name of your tab to 'Issue Documents'. Drag the `IssueDocuments` collection from the screen member list onto this tab. This creates a List control for your `IssueDocuments` collection.

3. Select your `IssueDocuments` List control, open the properties sheet, and click the "Item Tap" link in the Actions section. When the "Edit ItemTap Action" dialog appears, select the "Choose an existing method" radio button, and use the dropdown box to select `IssueDocuments.editSelected`. Select "Issue Document" in the "Navigate To" dropdown (Figure 8-42).

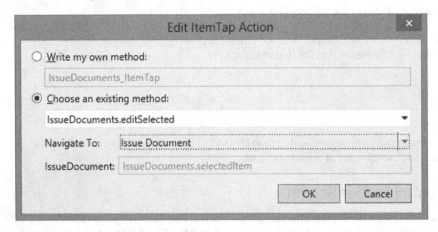

Figure 8-42. Opening the Add Edit Issue Document Dialog

4. Add a new button beneath your list control. When the "Add Button" dialog appears, select the "Choose an existing method" and use the dropdown to select `IssueDocuments.addAndEditNew`. Use the "Navigate to" dropdown to select your `AddEditIssueDocument` screen.

This completes the example, and you're now ready to run your application. Figure 8-43 shows what your screen looks like at runtime. The "Add Issue Document" button opens the "Issue Document" dialog that allows the user to upload a document. Once the user adds a document and clicks on the dialog's OK button, the newly added file will appear in the list control.

Figure 8-43. Document Uploader control at runtime

Downloading Files

The ability to upload files is just one half of this example. Users need some way to retrieve the files that have been uploaded, and you'll now find out how to implement this feature.

One way to do this is to write JavaScript that uses the LightSwitch's JavaScript API to retrieve the file content and write the data into a new file on the user's machine. Downloadify is a utility that can help you accomplish this (https://github.com/dcneiner/Downloadify). It's a free JavaScript library that allows you to create client-side files by using Adobe Flash.

However, a much easier way to retrieve files from your database is to take advantage of a new feature that the "Visual Studio 2012 Update 2" provides: the Server Application Context API. This is a powerful new feature that allows clients to communicate directly with the LightSwitch logic layer, without having to go through the save or query pipelines. Figure 8-44 shows how the download feature will work.

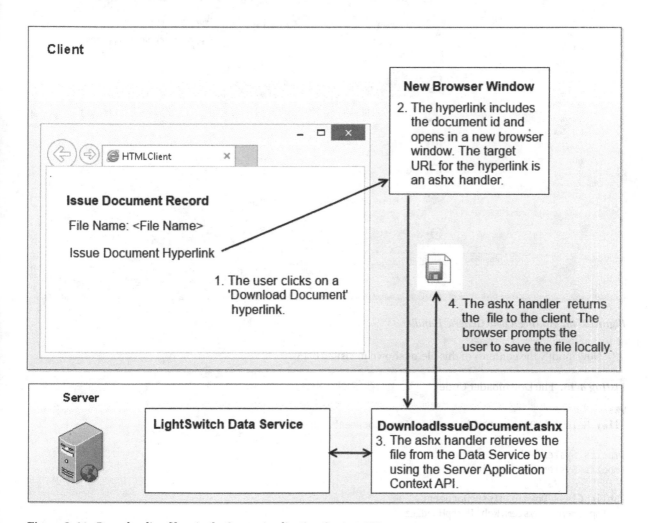

Figure 8-44. *Downloading files via the Server Application Context API*

The Server Application Context API allows you to access your data workspace from custom .NET applications. This, for example, allows you to create ASP.NET or MVC applications that can access your LightSwitch data. You can use the Server Application Context API to add custom functions to your application's Server project. This example creates a generic ASP.NET HTTP handler that uses the Server Application Context API. A generic handler provides an HTTP endpoint that serves HTTP responses without a UI.

To create a handler that returns the file contents, switch your project to File View. Navigate to your Server project, right-click on the Web folder, and add a new Generic Handler (Figure 8-45). Name your handler DownloadIssueDocument.ashx.

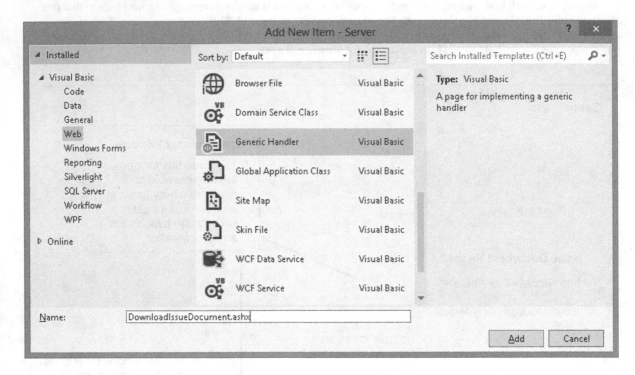

Figure 8-45. *Adding a new Generic Handler*

Now modify the contents of this file, as shown in Listing 8-15.

Listing 8-15. File Downloader Code

VB:
File: HelpDeskVB\Server\Web\DownloadIssueDocument.ashx.vb

```vb
Imports System.Web
Imports System.Web.Services

Public Class DownloadIssueDocument
    Implements System.Web.IHttpHandler

    Sub ProcessRequest(
        ByVal context As HttpContext) Implements IHttpHandler.ProcessRequest
```

```vb
        If context.Request.Params("id") IsNot Nothing Then
            context.Response.ContentType = "application/octet-stream"

        Using serverContext =
            LightSwitchApplication.ServerApplicationContext.CreateContext()

            Dim doc =serverContext.DataWorkspace.ApplicationData.
                IssueDocuments_SingleOrDefault(
                    context.Request.Params("id"))

            context.Response.AddHeader(
                "Content-Disposition",
                "attachment;filename=" & doc.DocumentName)
            context.Response.BinaryWrite(doc.IssueFile)

        End Using

        End If

    End Sub

    ReadOnly Property IsReusable() As Boolean Implements IHttpHandler.IsReusable
        Get
            Return False
        End Get
    End Property

End Class
```

C#:
File: HelpDeskCS\Server\Web\DownloadIssueDocument.ashx.cs

```csharp
using System;
using System.Collections.Generic;
using System.Linq;
using System.Web;

namespace LightSwitchApplication.Web
{
    public class DownloadIssueDocument : IHttpHandler
    {
        public void ProcessRequest(HttpContext context)
        {

            if (context.Request.Params["id"] != null)
            {
                context.Response.ContentType = "application/octet-stream";
                using (var serverContext =
                    LightSwitchApplication.ServerApplicationContext.CreateContext())
                {
                    var doc = serverContext.DataWorkspace.ApplicationData.
                        IssueDocuments_SingleOrDefault (
```

```
                        int.Parse (context.Request.Params["id"]));
                context.Response.AddHeader(
                    "Content-Disposition",
                    "attachment;filename=" + doc.DocumentName);
                context.Response.BinaryWrite(doc.IssueFile);
            }
        }
    }

    public bool IsReusable
    {
        get
        {
            return false;
        }
    }
}
}
```

The DownloadIssueDocument.ashx handler allows users to download issue documents by URL. For example, the URL http://WebServer/Web/DocumentIssueDocument.ashx?id=8 would return the document that's stored in the IssueFile property of an IssueDocument record with an id of 8.

To complete this example, you'll need to add a hyperlink to your AddEditIssueDocument dialog. In the screen designer, select the parent Rows Layout that contains the controls for your IssueDocument property—in this example, the default name of the group is left. In the properties sheet, click on the "Edit PostRender Code" link and add the code that's shown in Listing 8-16.

Listing 8-16. Button Code That Calls DownloadIssueDocument.ashx

File: HelpDeskVB\HTMLClient\UserCode\AddEditIssueDocument.js

```
myapp.AddEditIssueDocument.left_postRender =

function (element, contentItem) {

  if (contentItem.value.Id != undefined) {

    var downloadURL = '../Web/DownloadIssueDocument.ashx?id=' +      ❶
        contentItem.value.Id.toString();

    var downloadLink = $('<div><a target="_blank" ' +               ❷
        'href="' + downloadURL + '" style="margin-top: 10px;" >' +
        'Download Document File</a></div>');
    downloadLink.appendTo($(element));
  }
};
```

This code builds a hyperlink and appends it to the end of your Document dialog. The first part of this code creates the URL that points to the DownloadIssueDocument.ashx address and appends the Id value of the selected document record to the URL ❶. The code sets the target attribute to _blank ❷. This prompts the browser to open the hyperlink in a new window. If you didn't add this attribute, the hyperlink would navigate the user away from your LightSwitch application. The final piece of code appends the hyperlink to the end of the Rows Layout.

This code works on the basis that you deploy your HTML application to the following URL: `http://yourServer/HTMLClient`. The default address of your handler will be this: `http://yourServer/Web/DownloadIssueDocument.ashx`. The code in ❶ creates a hyperlink with a relative URL that uses the syntax `..` to refer to the parent folder. If the download link doesn't work when you deploy your application, you should check that you've deployed your `DownloadIssueDocument.ashx` file to the expected location. Figure 8-46 shows how your issue document dialog now looks at runtime.

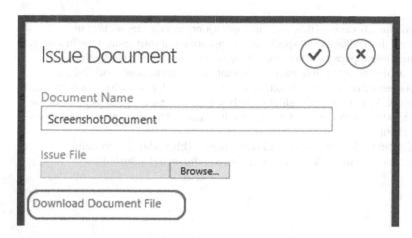

Figure 8-46. *Download link that appears*

You might wonder why you've added this code to the `postRender` method rather than create a custom control that's based on the `IssueDocument` Id. One of the reasons is because the HTML client applies the read-only and disabled properties of your content item when it renders custom controls (Figure 8-47). When the HTML client applies the disabled and read-only renderings to a custom control that includes a hyperlink, it makes the hyperlink nonclickable. You can't set the Id property of an entity to not be read only, so the simplest workaround is to append the custom HTML in the `postRender` method rather than use a custom control. Therefore, if you create a custom control and it doesn't work as you would expect it to work, it's worth checking these rendering options.

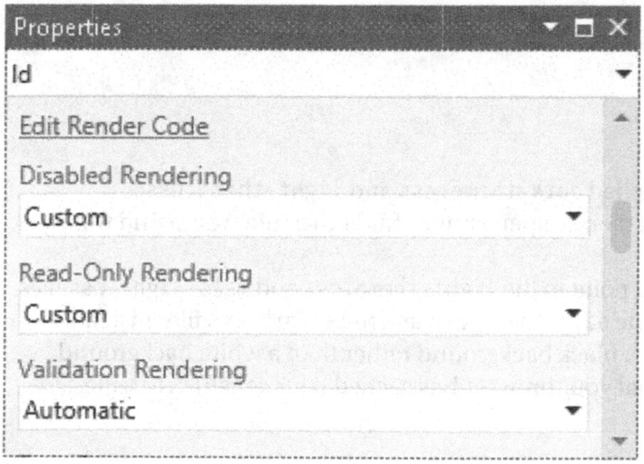

Figure 8-47. *Custom Control Rendering options*

Customizing the Appearance of Your Application

There are several ways that you can modify the icons, colors, and fonts that your application uses. This section shows you how to modify the appearance of your application by using themes.

Applying Themes

The HTML client uses jQuery mobile controls and, because of this, you can apply jQuery mobile themes to your application. The advantage of using a theme is that it allows you to package the appearance of your application in a single file. You can easily use the same theme in multiple applications, and even share your themes with other developers. A quick search for "jQuery mobile themes" on the Internet will reveal lots of themes that you can download and use.

By default, the HTML client applies a theme that uses a white background. However, it also includes a theme that consists of a black background with white text. When you're developing mobile applications, it's good practice to use the "dark theme" with a black background because it decreases the drain on the battery. This is because it minimizes the screen area that the device needs to light up.

LightSwitch stores its themes in the Content folder of your HTMLClient project. This folder also contains additional CSS files that define the appearance of your application. These files are shown in Figure 8-48.

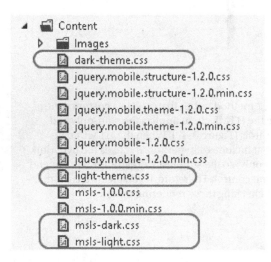

Figure 8-48. CSS Themes

The CSS files that contain the dark and light themes are called dark-theme.css and light-theme.css, respectively. To set up your application so that it uses the dark theme, open your default.htm file. You'll find this in the root folder of your HTMLClient project.

Near the top of this file, you'll find two style-sheet links that point to the light-theme.css and msls-light.css files. To use the dark theme, modify these links so that they point to the dark-theme.css and msls-dark.css files instead.

When you now run your application, LightSwitch applies a black background rather than a white background. If your application still shows a white background, it's likely that your browser has cached your default.htm file. You can fix this by problem by clearing your browser cache.

Creating Your Own Themes

The jQuery web site provides a tool called Theme Roller (Figure 8-49) that makes it very easy for you to create custom themes. To use Theme Roller, open your web browser and navigate to http://jquerymobile.com/themeroller/.

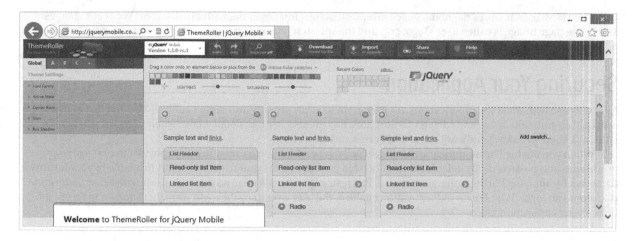

Figure 8-49. Using ThemeRoller

You can simplify the process of creating a theme by taking the light theme as a starting point for further customization. On the Theme Roller web site, click on the Import button that appears toward the top of the page. This opens a dialog that allows you enter a theme. Open your light-theme.css file, and copy and paste the contents into this dialog.

Once you've imported your theme, you can use the graphical designer to customize your theme. When you finish making your modifications, you can download your theme by clicking on the download button that appears at the top of the page. The download button creates a zip file that contains the CSS file for your theme. Extract the CSS file into your HTML client project's Content folder, and modify your default.htm file so that it points to your new theme file.

Changing the Application Icon and Title

The HTML client shows an icon that contains a mixture of blue squares while your application loads. Once your application loads, it shows a similar icon in the top left part of your home screen and sets the browser tab or window title to "<ProjectName>.HTMLClient" (Figure 8-50).

Figure 8-50. Changing the Title and Icon settings

The title tag in your default.htm file defines your page title. You can change this from "<ProjectName>.HTMLClient" to something more meaningful by modifying the value of the title tag. Near the top of the default.htm file, you'll find a div tag that contains the value "<ProjectName>.HTMLClient." This is the text that LightSwitch shows in the lower part of the screen when your application loads. Once again, you can modify this to a value that better describes your application.

The HTML client stores the home page and splash-screen images in the folder `HTMLClient\Content\Images`. The home page image is called `user-logo.png`, and the splash screen image is `user-splash-screen.png`. To use different images, you can replace these two files with new images.

Securing Your Application

As is the case with most web applications, it's important to apply security and access control. The first line of defense is to enable authentication, and Chapter 16 describes this process in more detail. LightSwitch supports two types of authentication: Windows authentication, and Forms authentication.

When you enable Forms authentication, LightSwitch uses the ASP.NET membership provider to manage your usernames and passwords. By default, the membership provider stores your user credentials in a table in your Intrinsic database. By applying Forms authentication, you can restrict your application so that only users with a username and password can login. With Forms authentication enabled, the user would see the login page that's shown in Figure 8-51 before your application loads.

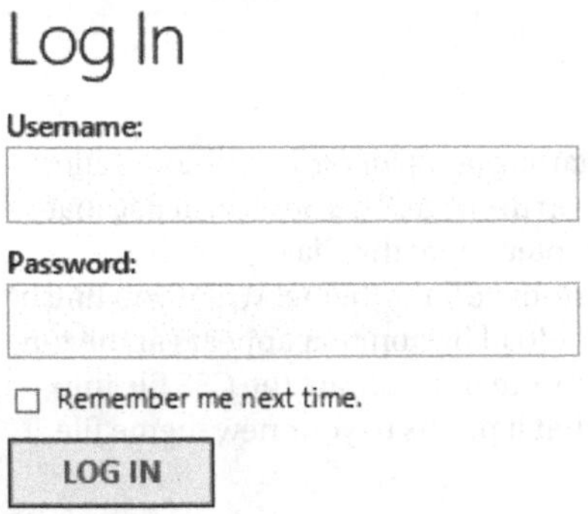

Log In

Username:

Password:

☐ Remember me next time.

LOG IN

Figure 8-51. Login Screen

The name of this login page is `LogIn.aspx`, and you'll find this file in the root folder of your `server` project. If you want to modify the appearance of this page (by adding a company logo, for example), you can simply open the `LogIn.aspx` file and make your amendments in Visual Studio.

Securing Methods

Each screen method that you create allows you to add JavaScript to a `CanExecute` method. Figure 8-52 shows the "Edit CanExecute Code" link that appears in the properties sheet for a method. You can prevent users from calling this method by setting the return value of the `CanExecute` method to `false`.

Figure 8-52. Securing a method by using the CanExecute Code

In Chapter 17, you'll discover that LightSwitch includes a security model that allows you to define permissions. The advantage of this system is that it allows you to apply access control at a granular level.

Unfortunately, LightSwitch's JavaScript API doesn't include the methods that allow you to determine whether the logged-in user has been granted a certain permission. This means, for example, that you can't easily restrict access to screens for editing and deleting engineers to only those users that you define as "managers."

If you need to apply access control based on group membership, a possible (but not ideal) workaround is to create separate applications for each group of users. Another option is to build your own authorization mechanism that ties into your CanExecute methods. If you choose to do this, it's important to remember that JavaScript is a text-based, uncompiled language that runs on the client. Because of this, users can easily view the source of your application and work out ways to compromise any custom security code that you've written.

Looking at the wider picture, the best place to implement security code is on the server. In Chapter 17, you'll learn how to prevent users from accessing or updating data by implementing access-control checks through the server and query pipelines. To help you apply server-side access control, LightSwitch allows you to obtain the logged-in user through server-side code, after you've enabled authentication in your application.

Summary

The HTML client allows you to create applications that work well on mobile and touch-screen devices. It uses industry-standard libraries that include jQuery, jQuery Mobile, datajs, and WinJS. To create an application that uses the HTML client, you need to install an update called "Visual Studio 2012 Update 2."

Unlike the Silverlight client (which uses a multidocument interface), HTML client applications are designed to perform one task at a time. If a user opens a child screen from an existing screen, LightSwitch bases the target screen on a nested change set. When the user returns to the calling screen, LightSwitch allows them to discard or accept their changes. If the user accepts the changes, LightSwitch merges the changes in the nested change set back into the main change set. A user can commit their changes to the database by clicking on a Save button. LightSwitch shows the Save button on the first Edit screen that the user encounters in your application.

LightSwitch allows you to design HTML screens by using a screen designer that's visually similar to the Silverlight designer that you're familiar with. There are three screen templates that you can use: the Browse Data, View Details, and Add/Edit Details Screen templates.

Browse Data Screens allow users to view and select records by using a List control. You can configure the tap action of the List control to open the record through a View Details or Add/Edit Details screen. View Detail screens are designed to show read-only data, whereas Add/Edit Detail screens are designed to enable users to edit data.

You can separate the contents of each screen into different tabs. Each screen includes a tab control that users can use to switch between tabs. You can prevent users from switching between tabs by hiding the tab header and controlling the visibility of tabs through buttons or code. Each screen also allows you to define popups. These are UI panels that appear on top of the current screen. Popups are perfect for showing details such as messages or confirmations. They appear next to the control that opens the popup, and a user can dismiss a popup by clicking on an area of the screen outside of the popup.

The properties sheet allows you to define a screen as a dialog. Dialogs open differently from normal screens. A normal screen fills up all of the available screen space, whereas a dialog opens on top of an existing screen. When a dialog opens, the background of the existing screen is still visible, but grayed out. Dialogs include OK and Cancel buttons. If your user clicks on the Cancel button, LightSwitch discards the changes the user has made and returns the user to the calling screen.

Just like the Silverlight client, the HTML client provides a set of controls that allow users to view and edit data. These controls include Text, Paragraph, Text Area, and the Date/Time Picker controls. The Modal Window Picker control allows users to select an entity. If there isn't a default control that does what you want, you can build your own custom HTML control.

To set up a custom control, you'd select a data item in the screen designer and change the control type to "custom control." Afterward, you can define your custom control's HTML by writing JavaScript in the control's render method. The render method includes a parameter called contentItem that you can use to access the data that your custom control binds to. In order for contentItem to give you access to the data that you need, it's important to define your custom control against the correct data item. If, for example, you set the control type of the firstname property to a custom control, contentItem will give you access to only the firstname data value. If you want a custom control that can access other property values, you should define a custom control for the entity rather than an individual property in an entity.

The contentItem object provides a method called databind that you can use to bind a custom control to your view model. databind allows you to specify a method that executes each time your property value changes. This allows you to implement the two-way data binding that enables custom controls to work.

There are several "entry points" that you can use to write custom JavaScript. You can call custom JavaScript methods from buttons or from the "tap" event of controls such as the List control. You can also define custom JavaScript that runs when the HTML client creates your screen, when the HTML client renders a screen control, or when a user initiates a save operation.

LightSwitch provides a JavaScript API that you can use to perform data and application tasks. The myapp object allows you to open screens, access the current data workspace, and cancel or apply changes. You can work with data by accessing local screen properties and collections, and by using the objects that the data workspace exposes.

LightSwitch executes many of its JavaScript API methods asynchronously. For example, it executes long-running data operations asynchronously, such as the data service's saveChanges method or a query's execute method. These asynchronous methods return a promise object. Promise objects expose a method called then that allows you to execute code when the asynchronous work completes.

You've learned how to create a custom control that users can use to upload files. You've also found out how to allow users to download files by using LightSwitch's Server Context API. This is a powerful feature that enables your client to communicate directly with LightSwitch's logic layer, without having to go through the save or query pipelines.

You can easily customize your application's fonts and colors by applying jQuery themes. LightSwitch supplies two built-in themes: a dark theme, and a light theme. You can change the theme that your application uses by editing your default.htm file. If you want to further customize your application's theme, you can use a tool that you'll find on the jQuery web site called ThemeRoller. If you switch your project to File View, you'll find all the CSS files and images that make up your application. You can modify the appearance of your application by editing the CSS or image files as you wish.

CHAPTER 9

■ ■ ■

Creating and Using RIA Services

LightSwitch allows you to connect to a wide range of data sources. But if you can't natively connect to the data source of your choice, you can still consume your data by writing a WCF RIA (Windows Communication Foundation Rich Internet Application) service.

In this chapter, you'll learn how to

- Consume an RIA service from your LightSwitch application

- Create an RIA service to retrieve and update data

- Call SQL Server stored procedures

Creating a custom RIA service enables you to connect to data sources that are not well supported. This could include nonrelational data or data sources that don't have an Entity Framework data provider. For example, you could create an RIA service that allows you to view XML files, Windows event logs, or even the Internet Information Services (IIS) log files on the server.

RIA services also allow you to create aggregated views of data or views that join multiple database tables. An aggregate view can provide counts, sums, averages, or totals of a group of data. RIA services can help you create views of your data for statistical or reporting purposes.

In this chapter, you'll find out how to create an RIA service to improve the performance of the HelpDesk application. You'll learn how to perform data operations, and also how to call a SQL Server stored procedure to delete engineer records.

Creating an RIA Services Project

Creating an RIA Service consists of the following four steps. We'll cover each of these in this chapter:

1. Create a class library project.
2. Write a class that represents your entity.
3. Add a domain service.
4. Write the data-access code.

In addition to helping you connect to nonstandard data sources, RIA services are an ideal way to improve your application's performance.

Let's take the Engineer table as an example. This table stores engineer details and includes a Photo field. Let's suppose you add a screen that includes a list of first names and surnames for engineers. Although you don't show the Photo field, the LightSwitch client still retrieves the photo data from the server. This is because the server can return only entity sets to the client, and entity sets can't exclude fields. If your average photo size is 500 KBs and you retained the default page size of 45 records, you could incur an additional 20 MBs of data-transfer between the client and server every time the page loads. By creating an RIA service that excludes the photo data, you'll end up with a screen that performs much better.

> ■ **Note** An RIA service is only one way to solve this problem. In practice, you'll find that it's quicker to split the employee photo data into a separate table.

Staying on the performance theme, this chapter shows how you can create an RIA service that improves the performance of a computed column. The HelpDesk application includes an engineers management screen that shows a count of issues for each engineer. (See Figure 9-1.)

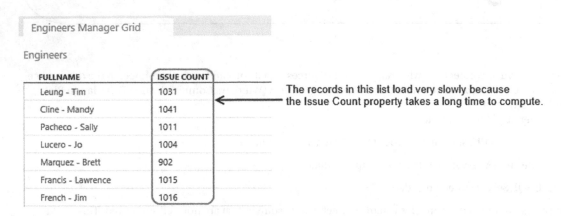

Figure 9-1. *The Engineers management screen*

Due to the high number of records in the system, this screen performs poorly because LightSwitch needs to retrieve every issue for each engineer to calculate the count. (You'll find the computed column code in Chapter 2, Listing 2-3.)

To get started, create a new RIA service project by opening Visual Studio and creating a new project using the Class Library template. Name your project HelpDeskDataService.

Creating an Entity Class

Your RIA service project needs a class that represents an engineer entity. The class doesn't need to contain every column in the Engineer table. As I mentioned earlier, returning a subset of columns is an ideal way to optimize performance.

In your project, create an EngineerRecord class and add the code shown in Listing 9-1.

Listing 9-1. Entity Class for Engineers

VB:
File: HelpDeskDataServiceVB\EngineerRecord.vb

```
Imports System.ComponentModel.DataAnnotations

Public Class EngineerRecord
    <Key(), Editable(False)>                              ❶
    Public Property Id As Integer
```

```
    <Required(ErrorMessage:="Surname required"),             ❷
        StringLength(50)>                                    ❸
    Public Property Surname As String

    <Required(ErrorMessage:="Firstname required"),
        StringLength(50)>
    Public Property Firstname As String

    <Required(ErrorMessage:="DateOfBirth required")>
    Public Property DateOfBirth As DateTime

    <Required(ErrorMessage:="SecurityVetted required")>
    Public Property SecurityVetted As Boolean

    <Editable(False)>
    Public Property IssueCount As Integer

End Class
```

C#:
File: HelpDeskDataServiceCS\EngineerRecord.cs

```
using System;
using System.ComponentModel.DataAnnotations;

namespace HelpDeskDataServiceCS
{
    public class EngineerRecord
    {
        [Key(), Editable(false)]                             ❶
        public int Id { get; set; }

        [Required(ErrorMessage = "Surname required"),        ❷
            StringLength(50)]                                ❸
        public string Surname { get; set; }

        [Required(ErrorMessage = "Firstname required"), StringLength(50)]
        public string Firstname { get; set; }

        [Required(ErrorMessage = "DateOfBirth required")]
        public DateTime DateOfBirth { get; set; }

        [Required(ErrorMessage = "SecurityVetted required")]
        public bool SecurityVetted { get; set; }

        [Editable(false)]
        public int IssueCount { get; set; }

    }
}
```

You'll need to add a reference to the `System.ComponentModel.DataAnnotations` DLL. The easiest way to do this is to add a Domain Service class (covered next). This automatically adds all the references that you'll need.

Your primary-key property (`Id`) must be decorated with the key attribute, and the `Editable` attribute needs to be set to `false` ❶. LightSwitch uses these attributes to prevent users from editing your engineer's `Id` property.

The `Required` attribute ❷ indicates that the property can't be null or empty. If a user fails to enter any of the required properties, LightSwitch triggers its built-in validation and prevents the user from saving the record.

The `StringLength` attribute ❸ allows you to specify the maximum length of a property. LightSwitch's built-in validation uses this value to prevent users from entering text that exceeds the maximum length that you specify.

It's important to apply the `StringLength` and `Required` attributes to stop users from entering invalid data.

In addition to the attributes that you've seen, you can also define relationships and navigation properties by using similar attributes. LightSwitch recognizes the relationships and navigation properties that you've specified when you attach to your RIA service.

■ **Tip**   The code that allows you to create a custom data source extension is very similar to the code that's shown in this section. Take a look at Chapter 13 if you want to see an example of how to create an entity class that includes navigation properties.

Creating a Domain Service Class

The next step is to create a new domain service class. To do this, right-click your project and choose the option to add a new Domain Service Class. (See Figure 9-2.) Name your class `EngineerDataService`.

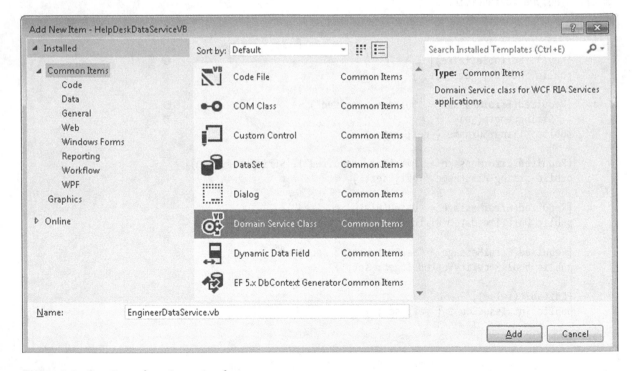

Figure 9-2. *Creating a domain service class*

In the next dialog that appears (shown in Figure 9-3), uncheck the Enable Client Access check box. Leaving this enabled can pose a security risk because it allows other external clients to call your service. If you disable client access, users can access your RIA service only through LightSwitch's service end point. This gives you the extra protection of any logic or security code that you might have added to the LightSwitch save and query pipelines.

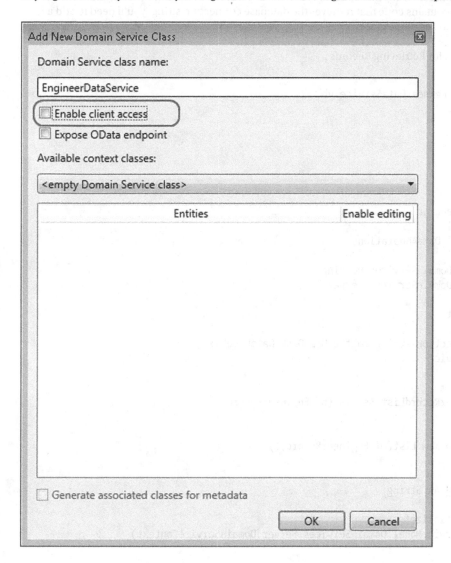

Figure 9-3. Uncheck the Enable Client Access check box

Retrieving Data

Now that you've added your domain service class, the next step is to write the code that performs the data access. The previous step created a class file called EngineerDataService. Modify this file by adding the code that's shown in Listing 9-2. Because this listing contains code that retrieves the database connection string, you'll need to add a reference to the System.Configuration namespace.

Listing 9-2. Domain Service Code for Retrieving Records

VB:
File: HelpDeskDataServiceVB\EngineerDataService.vb

```vb
Option Compare Binary
Option Infer On
Option Strict On
Option Explicit On

Imports System
Imports System.Collections.Generic
Imports System.ComponentModel
Imports System.ComponentModel.DataAnnotations
Imports System.Linq
Imports System.ServiceModel.DomainServices.Hosting
Imports System.ServiceModel.DomainServices.Server
Imports System.Configuration
Imports System.Data.SqlClient

<Description("Enter the connection string to the HelpDesk Database")>
Public Class EngineerDataService
    Inherits DomainService

    Private ReadOnly _EngineerRecordList As List(Of EngineerRecord)

    Public Sub New()
        _EngineerRecordList = New List(Of EngineerRecord)()
    End Sub

    Private _connectionString As String

    Public Overrides Sub Initialize(
        context As System.ServiceModel.DomainServices.Server.DomainServiceContext)

        _connectionString =
            ConfigurationManager.ConnectionStrings(
                Me.[GetType]().FullName).ConnectionString
        MyBase.Initialize(context)
    End Sub

    <Query(IsDefault:=True)>                                          ❷
    Public Function GetEngineerData() As IQueryable(
```

```
            Of EngineerRecord)                                              ❶
            _EngineerRecordList.Clear()

        Using cnn As New SqlConnection(_connectionString)                   ❸
            Using cmd As SqlCommand = cnn.CreateCommand()

                cmd.CommandText =
                    "SELECT Id, Surname, Firstname, DateOfBirth,
                    SecurityVetted, IssueCount
                    FROM dbo.Engineers eng
                    JOIN ( SELECT Issue_Engineer,
                             COUNT(Issue_Engineer) IssueCount
                           FROM  dbo.Issues GROUP BY Issue_Engineer)
                    AS iss ON eng.Id = iss.Issue_Engineer"             ❹

                cnn.Open()

                Using dr As SqlDataReader = cmd.ExecuteReader()
                    While dr.Read()
                        Dim Engineer As New EngineerRecord()
                        Engineer.Id = CInt(dr("Id"))
                        Engineer.Surname = dr("Surname").ToString()
                        Engineer.Firstname = dr("Firstname").ToString()
                        Engineer.DateOfBirth = CDate(dr("DateOfBirth"))
                        Engineer.SecurityVetted = CBool(dr("SecurityVetted"))
                        Engineer.IssueCount = CInt(dr("IssueCount"))

                        _EngineerRecordList.Add(Engineer)
                    End While
                End Using
                cnn.Close()
            End Using
        End Using

        Return _EngineerRecordList.AsQueryable()

    End Function

End Class
```

C#:
File: HelpDeskDataServiceCS\EngineerDataService.cs

```
namespace HelpDeskDataServiceCS
{
    using System;
    using System.Collections.Generic;
    using System.ComponentModel;
    using System.ComponentModel.DataAnnotations;
    using System.Configuration;
```

```csharp
using System.Data.SqlClient;
using System.Linq;
using System.ServiceModel.DomainServices.Hosting;
using System.ServiceModel.DomainServices.Server;

[Description("Enter the connection string to the HelpDesk DB")]
public class EngineerDataService : DomainService
{
    private readonly List<EngineerRecord> _EngineerRecordList;

    public EngineerDataService()
    {
        _EngineerRecordList = new List<EngineerRecord>();
    }

    string _connectionString;
    public override void Initialize
       (System.ServiceModel.DomainServices.Server.DomainServiceContext
          context)
    {
        _connectionString = ConfigurationManager.ConnectionStrings
          [this.GetType().FullName].ConnectionString;
        base.Initialize(context);
    }

    [Query(IsDefault = true)]                                            ❷
    public IQueryable<EngineerRecord> GetEngineerData()                  ❶
    {
        _EngineerRecordList.Clear();

        using (SqlConnection cnn = new SqlConnection(_connectionString)) ❸
        {
            using (SqlCommand cmd = cnn.CreateCommand())
            {
                cmd.CommandText  =
                  "SELECT Id , Surname , Firstname , DateOfBirth ,
                  SecurityVetted , IssueCount
                  FROM dbo.Engineers eng
                  JOIN ( SELECT Issue_Engineer,
                     COUNT(Issue_Engineer) IssueCount
                     FROM  dbo.Issues GROUP BY Issue_Engineer)
                  AS iss ON eng.Id = iss.Issue_Engineer";          ❹
                cnn.Open();

                using (SqlDataReader dr = cmd.ExecuteReader())
                {
                    while (dr.Read())
                    {
                        EngineerRecord Engineer = new EngineerRecord();
                        Engineer.Id = (int)dr["Id"];
                        Engineer.Surname = dr["Surname"].ToString();
                        Engineer.Firstname = dr["Firstname"].ToString();
```

```
                Engineer.DateOfBirth = (DateTime)dr["DateOfBirth"];
                Engineer.SecurityVetted = (bool)dr["SecurityVetted"];
                Engineer.IssueCount = (int)dr["IssueCount"];
                _EngineerRecordList.Add(Engineer);
            }
        }
        cnn.Close();
    }
}

return _EngineerRecordList.AsQueryable();
    }

}

}
```

The GetEngineerData method ❶ returns the engineer data. This method is decorated with the
Query(IsDefault=true) attribute ❷, which tells LightSwitch to use it as the default method for returning a collection.

If you don't decorate a method with this attribute and don't decorate any properties with the Key attribute,
LightSwitch won't allow you to import the entity or entity set.

The code uses ADO.NET to connect to your SQL data source. If you were writing an RIA service to connect to an
unsupported data source, you would need to adapt the code in this method to use a different data-access mechanism.

The pattern that's used here is to create a SqlConnection object ❸ and specify the SQL command that you want
to execute by using a SqlCommand object. The SQL that's specified in this method ❹ produces the issue count much
more efficiently than the native LightSwitch computed column code.

Retrieving a Connection String from web.config

The ADO.NET connection string your RIA service uses to connect to your database should be stored in the
web.config file of your LightSwitch application. By doing this, you can easily modify your connection string after
you deploy your application.

When you connect to an RIA service at design time, LightSwitch displays an automatic prompt that requests you
to enter a connection string. (You'll see this dialog later in the "Consuming Your RIA Service" section.)

LightSwitch saves your connection string in the ConnectionStrings section of your web.config file, and keys the
entry using the fully qualified name of your class.

You can obtain the connection string value in your RIA service code by using the methods in the
ConfigurationManager namespace, as shown here:

VB:
```
ConfigurationManager.ConnectionStrings(Me.[GetType]().FullName) ↪
.ConnectionString
```

C#:
```
ConfigurationManager.ConnectionStrings[this.GetType().FullName] ↪
.ConnectionString;
```

In practice, you might also want to write some additional error-checking code to make sure the connection string
setting exists, and that it isn't null or empty.

Also note how the name of the domain service class is decorated with the description attribute. (See Listing 9-2.)
LightSwitch shows this description when you attach to the RIA service from the Add Data Source Wizard.

Updating Data

So far, your RIA service only retrieves the engineer data but doesn't yet allow data to be updated. To allow users to update your engineer data from LightSwitch, add the code that's shown in Listing 9-3.

Listing 9-3. Updating and Inserting Data

VB:
File: HelpDeskDataServiceVB\EngineerDataService.vb

```
Public Sub UpdateEngineerData(Engineer As EngineerRecord)              ❶

    Using cnn As New SqlConnection(_connectionString)
        Using cmd As SqlCommand = cnn.CreateCommand()

            cmd.CommandText =
                "UPDATE Engineers SET [Surname] = @Surname,
                                     [Firstname] = @Firstname,
                                     [DateOfBirth] = @DateOfBirth,
                                     [SecurityVetted] = @SecurityVetted
                 WHERE Id=@Id"

            cmd.Parameters.AddWithValue("Surname", Engineer.Surname)
            cmd.Parameters.AddWithValue("Firstname", Engineer.Firstname)
            cmd.Parameters.AddWithValue("DateOfBirth", Engineer.DateOfBirth)
            cmd.Parameters.AddWithValue("SecurityVetted", Engineer.SecurityVetted)
            cmd.Parameters.AddWithValue("Id", Engineer.Id)

            cnn.Open()
            cmd.ExecuteNonQuery()
            cnn.Close()
        End Using
    End Using

End Sub

Public Sub InsertEngineerData(Engineer As EngineerRecord)              ❷

    Using cnn As New SqlConnection(_connectionString)
        Using cmd As SqlCommand = cnn.CreateCommand()

            cmd.CommandText =
                "INSERT INTO Engineers
                  (Surname, Firstname, DateOfBirth, SecurityVetted)
                    VALUES
                  (@Surname, @Firstname, @DateOfBirth, @SecurityVetted);
                  SELECT @@Identity "                                  ❸

            cmd.Parameters.AddWithValue("Surname", Engineer.Surname)
            cmd.Parameters.AddWithValue("Firstname", Engineer.Firstname)
            cmd.Parameters.AddWithValue("DateOfBirth", Engineer.DateOfBirth)
            cmd.Parameters.AddWithValue("SecurityVetted", Engineer.SecurityVetted)
```

```vbnet
            cnn.Open()
            Engineer.Id = CInt(cmd.ExecuteScalar())                    ❹
            cnn.Close()
        End Using
    End Using

End Sub
```

C#:
File: HelpDeskDataServiceCS\EngineerDataService.cs

```csharp
public void UpdateEngineerData(EngineerRecord Engineer)               ❶
{

    using (SqlConnection cnn = new SqlConnection(_connectionString))
    {
        using (SqlCommand cmd = cnn.CreateCommand())
        {
            cmd.CommandText =
                "UPDATE Engineers SET [Surname] = @Surname,
                                      [Firstname] = @Firstname,
                                      [DateOfBirth] = @DateOfBirth,
                                      [SecurityVetted] = @SecurityVetted
                WHERE Id=@Id";

            cmd.Parameters.AddWithValue("Surname", Engineer.Surname);
            cmd.Parameters.AddWithValue("Firstname", Engineer.Firstname);
            cmd.Parameters.AddWithValue("DateOfBirth", Engineer.DateOfBirth);
            cmd.Parameters.AddWithValue("SecurityVetted", Engineer.SecurityVetted);
            cmd.Parameters.AddWithValue("Id", Engineer.Id);
            cnn.Open();
            cmd.ExecuteNonQuery();
            cnn.Close();
        }
    }

}

public void InsertEngineerData(EngineerRecord Engineer)               ❷
{

    using (SqlConnection cnn = new SqlConnection(_connectionString))
    {
        using (SqlCommand cmd = cnn.CreateCommand())
        {
            cmd.CommandText =
                "INSERT INTO Engineers
                  (Surname, Firstname, DateOfBirth, SecurityVetted)
                    VALUES
                  (@Surname, @Firstname, @DateOfBirth, @SecurityVetted);
                SELECT @@Identity";                                   ❸
```

```
            cmd.Parameters.AddWithValue("Surname", Engineer.Surname);
            cmd.Parameters.AddWithValue("Firstname", Engineer.Firstname);
            cmd.Parameters.AddWithValue("DateOfBirth", Engineer.DateOfBirth);
            cmd.Parameters.AddWithValue("SecurityVetted", Engineer.SecurityVetted);
            cnn.Open();
            Engineer.Id = (int)cmd.ExecuteScalar();                              ❹
            cnn.Close();
        }
    }
}
```

The RIA service uses the UpdateEngineerData ❶ and InsertEngineerData ❷ methods to insert and update data. LightSwitch understands that these methods are responsible for inserting and updating through the presence of the Insert and Update prefixes in the method names. There isn't any more that you need to do to indicate that these methods are responsible for inserting or updating data.

The insert and update methods use ADO.NET code to update the database. The code uses named parameters to prevent rogue users from carrying out SQL injection attacks.

The SQL command that's used in the InsertEngineerData method includes an additional command that selects @@Identity ❸. This command retrieves the autogenerated identity value that SQL Server assigns to the newly added record. The code then executes the command by calling the command's ExecuteScalar method. This allows it to retrieve the ID value of the newly added engineer entity, which it then assigns to the engineer's Id property (❹). This allows your user to see the ID number of the record onscreen immediately after a save.

Calling SQL Stored Procedures

If you're working with existing SQL Server databases, the ability to call SQL Server stored procedures can be very useful. For security reasons, it's not uncommon for database administrators to block developers from accessing tables directly. The only way that you can often work with a SQL databases that you don't own is to retrieve data through views and update data through stored procedures.

Another scenario for using stored procedures is to improve performance. For certain data-intensive tasks, it can be more efficient to perform logic through a stored procedure rather than pull the data that's needed into the business logic layer.

To demonstrate how to call a stored procedure, this example shows you how to extend your domain service to delete engineers by using a stored procedure. In this scenario, using a stored procedure also helps you to perform an additional piece of functionality—It allows you to cascade-delete all related issue records when a user deletes an engineer.

Although LightSwitch provides this ability, there are some challenges that you need to overcome to make it work with the HelpDesk application. First, the Engineer table includes a self-relationship that allows you to store the manager for each engineer. Self-join navigation properties don't include the ability to disassociate related records on deletion. So if the engineer that you want to delete is the manager of other engineers, you can't automatically set the manager field for all subordinate engineers to null.

Second, there are two relationships between the Engineer and Issue tables. For each issue, the engineer can be the engineer assigned to the issue or the engineer who closes the issue. LightSwitch allows you to specify only a single cascade-delete rule on any pair of tables, so you'd need to manually carry out the cascade-deletion manually. Figure 9-4 illustrates these issues.

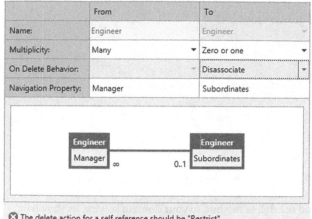

	From	To
Name:	Engineer	Engineer
Multiplicity:	Many	Zero or one
On Delete Behavior:		Disassociate
Navigation Property:	Manager	Subordinates

❌ The delete action for a self reference should be "Restrict".

↑ 1. The delete action for self references cannot be 'Disassociate'.

❌ 1 Association 'Issue_Engineer1' causes Entity Type 'Issue' to exist in more than one Cascade Delete Association Paths. Remove the association or fix its Delete Action.

↑ 2. You can specify a maximum of 1 Cascade Delete rule for each pair of tables.

❌ 1 .Net SqlClient Data Provider: Msg 1785, Level 16, State 0, Line 1 Introducing FOREIGN KEY constraint 'Issue_Engineer1' on table 'Issues' may cause cycles or multiple cascade paths. Specify ON DELETE NO ACTION or ON UPDATE NO ACTION, or modify other FOREIGN KEY constraints.

↑ 3. Although LightSwitch allows you to set the delete action for ClosedByEngineer to 'Disassociate', SQL Server doesn't allow LightSwitch to apply this rule.

Figure 9-4. Cascade-delete issues

When you set up a relationship to cascade-delete records, it's also important to consider performance. During this process, the save pipeline loads the records it needs to cascade-delete. In this example, LightSwitch loads all issue records that are related to the engineer before deleting the issues and the engineer.

For each issue record that LightSwitch deletes, it needs to load the issue response and document records to carry out the cascade-delete rules that are defined on the Issue table. And because each issue document record can be large, there'll be a noticeable delay in performance. In this scenario, a stored procedure provides an efficient alternative because it bypasses the need to load data prior to deletion.

To carry out this example, you'll need to create a stored procedure in your database. Listing 9-4 shows the stored procedure that carries out the deletion.

Listing 9-4. T-SQL Definition of the DeleteEngineer Stored Procedure

```
CREATE PROCEDURE DeleteEngineer
    @Id int
AS
BEGIN
    SET NOCOUNT ON;

    --Disassociate records where the engineer is the manager
    UPDATE Issues SET issue_engineer = NULL
    WHERE issue_engineer =@Id

    --Disassociate the issues that are closed by the engineer
    UPDATE Issues set Issue_Engineer1 = NULL
    WHERE issue_engineer=@Id

    --Delete issue document records
    DELETE IssueDocuments FROM IssueDocuments isd join issues iss
    ON iss.id = isd.IssueDocument_Issue
    WHERE iss.Issue_Engineer=@Id
```

```
  --Delete issue response records
  DELETE IssueResponses FROM IssueResponses isr join issues iss
  ON iss.id = isr.IssueResponse_Issue
  WHERE iss.Issue_Engineer=@Id

  --Delete Issues that are assigned to the engineer
  DELETE FROM Issues WHERE Issue_Engineer=@Id

  --Delete the engineer record
  DELETE FROM Engineer WHERE ID=@Id

END
GO
```

After creating your stored procedure, you'll need to add the delete method to your domain service, as shown in Listing 9-5.

Listing 9-5. Deleting Records

VB:
File: HelpDeskDataServiceVB\EngineerDataService.vb

```vb
Public Sub DeleteEngineerData(Engineer As EngineerRecord)
    Using cnn As New SqlConnection(_connectionString)
        Using cmd As SqlCommand = cnn.CreateCommand()

            cmd.CommandText = "DeleteEngineer"
            cmd.Parameters.AddWithValue("@Id", Engineer.Id)
            cmd.CommandType = System.Data.CommandType.StoredProcedure        ❶

            cnn.Open()
            cmd.ExecuteNonQuery()
            cnn.Close()
        End Using
    End Using
End Sub
```

C#:
File: HelpDeskDataServiceCS\EngineerDataService.cs

```csharp
public void DeleteEngineerData(EngineerRecord Engineer)
{
    using (SqlConnection cnn = new SqlConnection(_connectionString))
    {
        using (SqlCommand cmd = cnn.CreateCommand())
        {
            cmd.CommandText = "DeleteEngineer";
            cmd.Parameters.AddWithValue("@Id", Engineer.Id);
            cmd.CommandType = System.Data.CommandType.StoredProcedure;       ❶
            cnn.Open();
```

```
            cmd.ExecuteNonQuery();
            cnn.Close();
        }
    }
}
```

Just as with the update and insert methods, you'll need to prefix the delete method with the word `delete`. This indicates that the method is responsible for deleting the engineer entity.

The ADO.NET code is similar to the code that's shown earlier. An important difference is that you must set the `CommandType` property of the `SqlCommand` object to `StoredProcedure` ❶. Your SQL command will not run if don't do this.

You've now completed everything that's needed for your RIA service to work. Build your project, and make a note of the output DLL that your project produces—you'll need to refer to this in the next section.

EXERCISE 9.1 – CREATING AN RIA SERVICE

Try creating the RIA Service that's shown in chapter. You can try extending your project so that it includes tables other than the engineer table. If you need some help, you can refer to the entity class code in chapter 13 to see examples of how to set up navigation properties.

Consuming Your RIA Service

Once you've built your RIA Service, you can easily consume it from your LightSwitch application. To do this, open your LightSwitch project, right-click the Data Sources folder, select the Add Data Source Wizard, and choose the WCF RIA Service option.

When the Choose A WCF RIA Service dialog appears (as shown in Figure 9-5), click the Add Reference button. When the Reference Manager dialog appears, click the browse button and select the `HelpDeskDataService.dll` file that you built in the earlier exercise.

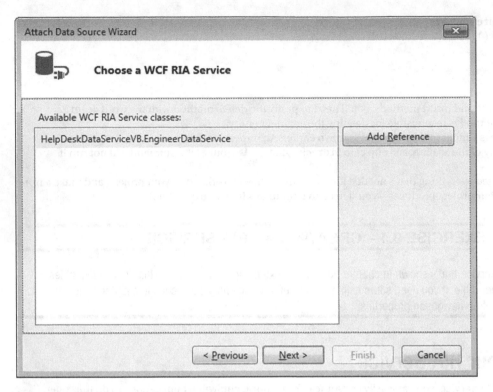

Figure 9-5. *Attaching a WCF RIA service*

The next step allows you to add entities and properties, just as you would for any other data source. (See Figure 9-6.) The name that you specify in this dialog appears in your list of data sources, so it's a good idea to keep it consistent with the names of your other data sources. For example, you could name your data source `EngineerData` to make it look similar to the intrinsic `ApplicationData` data source.

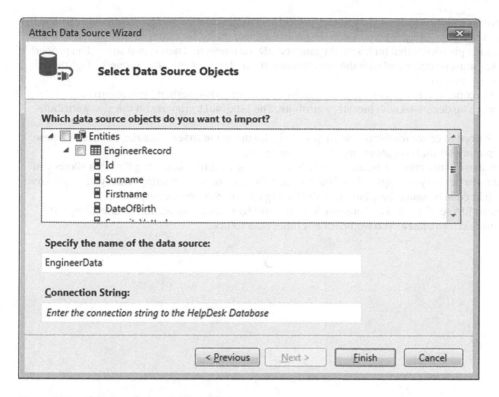

Figure 9-6. *Choosing the entities to include*

The dialog also contains the Connection String text box, that allows you to enter a connection string (as shown in Figure 9-6). Notice how the text box includes the following default text: "Enter the connection string to the HelpDesk Database." This help text comes from the Description attribute of the domain service class, which was shown in Listing 9-2.

Clicking the Finish button completes the addition of your RIA Service data source. You can now re-create the engineers management screen using your RIA service. You'll find that this new screen performs much quicker than the previous screen.

Summary

You can use RIA services to perform data-related operations that are not natively supported by LightSwitch. For instance, you could write an RIA service to allow your LightSwitch application to connect to data that's held in a Microsoft FoxPro or Access database, or even to connect to nonrelational data source.

You also can use RIA services to create views of your data. These can be aggregated views that contain counts, sums, and averages of your data, or they can even be views that contain joined-up data from multiple tables. Alternatively, you can create a view that returns a subset of columns from a table. This technique can help you optimize the performance of your application, particularly if you have a table that contains large rows (a table that contains images, for example).

Creating an RIA service involves creating a class library project and a domain service class. To do this, you need to create a class that represents your entity. If you want to return an engineer entity, for example, you'll need to create an engineer class and include properties that represent the engineer ID, surname, first name, and so on. The property that acts as the primary key must be decorated with the key attribute. If you don't specify a key property, LightSwitch won't allow you to import your entity.

Every RIA service must contain a method that returns a collection of data. This method must return an IQueryable object and has to be decorated with the query attribute. The IsDefault property on the query attribute must be set to true.

To update data, you'll need to create methods that are prefixed with the name Insert, Update, or Delete. These methods must include a parameter that accepts an instance of your entity.

You can store the database connection string that your RIA service uses in your web.config file. This allows you to change the setting after you deploy your application. You can easily set the connection string when you attach your RIA service, and retrieve it in code by using the methods in the ConfigurationManager namespace.

Once you've created an RIA service, you can consume it from your LightSwitch application by attaching to it using the Attach Data Source Wizard, just as you would for any other data source.

■ ■ ■

CHAPTER 10

Sharing Data with OData

There are many ways for you to work with external data. You can connect to external data sources by using the Add Data Source dialog, and for nonstandard data sources, you can create your own RIA service. OData (the Open Data protocol) provides you with yet another choice. A big advantage of using OData is that it allows you and other applications to access your LightSwitch data from outside of LightSwitch.

In this chapter, you'll learn how to

- Connect to third-party data by using OData

- Share your LightSwitch data with other applications

- Update LightSwitch data from outside of LightSwitch

This chapter extends the HelpDesk application by integrating travel advice data from an external data source for each office location. You'll learn how to allow managers to connect to your LightSwitch issue data from Microsoft Excel and how to allow users to update their issues through a custom ASP.NET web site.

What Is OData?

OData is an open standard that provides a common way to retrieve and update data via the Web, which makes it much easier to share data. It saves you from having to learn a new API each time you want to access a different type of data. For example, SAP (the enterprise resource-planning software product) publishes its data via OData. The great thing is that you can display your SAP data inside of LightSwitch without having to learn any complicated new API.

If you want to connect to your data from outside of LightSwitch, there are many languages and platforms that you can use. The languages that you can use include Java, PHP, Ruby, JavaScript, and many more.

In this first section, you'll learn to attach to an OData data source. Later in the chapter, you'll find out how to consume your LightSwitch data from Excel and .NET.

Using External Data Sources

A big benefit of OData is that it allows you consume the *silos* of data that are held within your organization. Microsoft products that support OData include SharePoint 2010, Microsoft Dynamics CRM 2011, and SQL Server Reporting Services 2012. If your company uses any of these products, you can use LightSwitch to connect to the data that's held in these applications.

In addition to OData data sources within your organization, there are plenty of third-party and external data sources that you can use. I'll now show you how to find public data sources that you can incorporate into your LightSwitch applications.

Finding Third-Party Data Sources to Use

A great place to find public data sources is the Ecosystem page on the official OData web site (http://www.odata.org/ecosystem). Here, you'll find a list of third-party OData providers that includes eBay, Windows Live, and various Government and public bodies.

Another great place is the Azure Data Market (http://datamarket.azure.com/). Here, you'll find many data sources, some of which are free.

To demonstrate how to consume an OData data source, I'll show you how to connect to a travel advisory service that's provided by the UK Foreign and Commonwealth Office. This enables the HelpDesk application to associate travel advice information with the office locations that are stored in your application. You can find this service by visiting http://datamarket.azure.com/dataset/uk.gov/traveladvisoryservice.

To use this service, you'll need to create an account on the Windows Azure Marketplace. Once you do this, the next step is to click on the Sign Up button that you'll find on the Travel Advisory Service's web page. (At the time of writing, it's free to sign up.) Once you sign up to a Marketplace service, you can use the web site's Explore This Dataset option to preview the data that's offered by the service.

Determining Connection Settings

To connect to an OData data source, you'll need to know the web address that identifies the data source and any authentication details that the service requires. The Travel Advisory Service displays these details on the Details tab of its web page. The OData address you need is labeled Service Root URL, as shown in Figure 10-1.

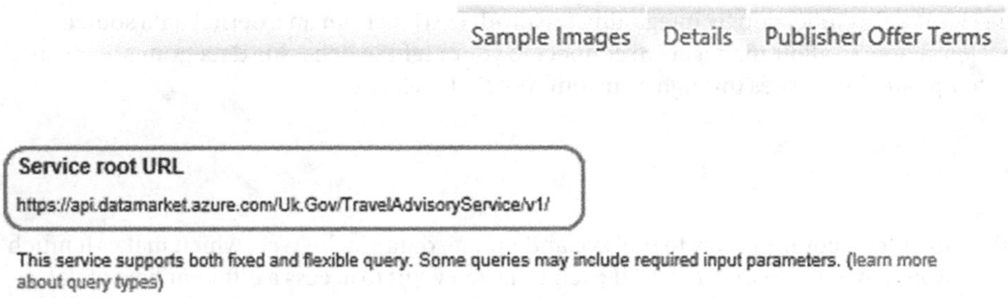

Figure 10-1. Finding the end point of an Azure Marketplace service

All the services from the Azure Marketplace require authentication. To find out your credentials, go to the My Account section of the Windows Azure Marketplace and note the Customer ID and Primary Account Key settings. (See Figure 10-2.) You'll need these details to authenticate to this service from LightSwitch.

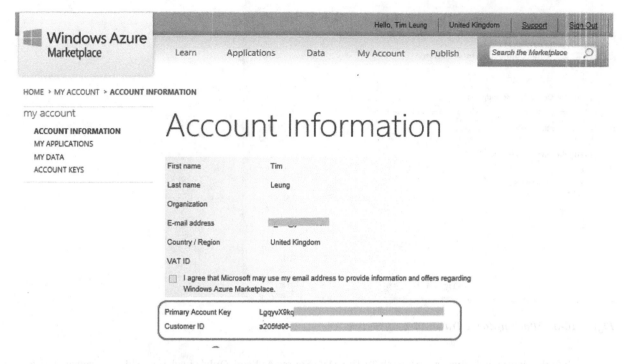

Figure 10-2. Finding your Azure Marketplace credentials

■ **Caution**   Because certain elements of the Windows Azure Marketplace are chargeable, you should protect your Primary Account Key in the same way as you would protect a credit card number.

Connecting to an OData Data Source

To connect to an OData data source from LightSwitch, right-click Solution Explorer, open the Attach Data Source Wizard, and choose the OData option. When the OData settings page appears, enter your OData URL in the Specify The OData Service Endpoint text box. (See Figure 10-3.) In the travel advisory example, the Customer ID is your user name and the Primary Account Key is your password.

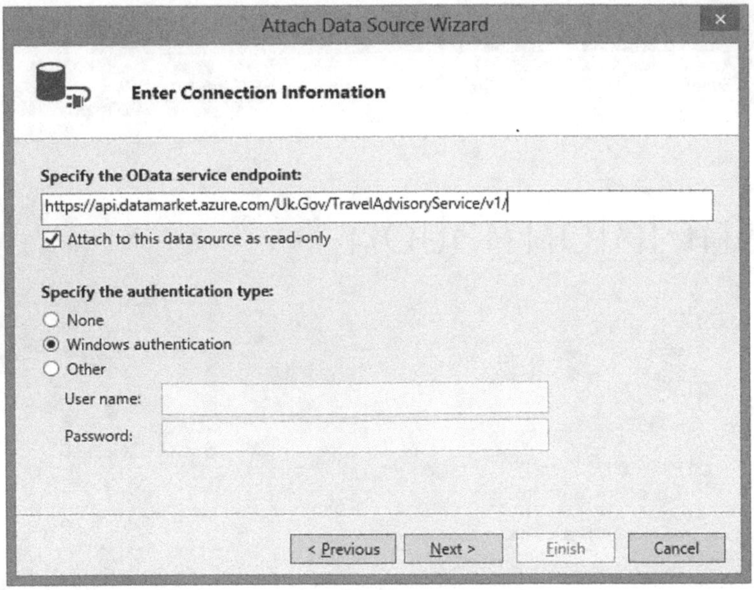

Figure 10-3. *Attaching to the Travel Advisory Service*

By default, LightSwitch checks the 'Attach To This Data Source As Read-Only' check box. This is because OData data sources are more likely to be non-updatable. This option disables the insert, update, and delete commands on screens and also prevents you from updating the data source through code.

Next, the wizard prompts you to select the entities you want to use in your application (as shown in Figure 10-4).

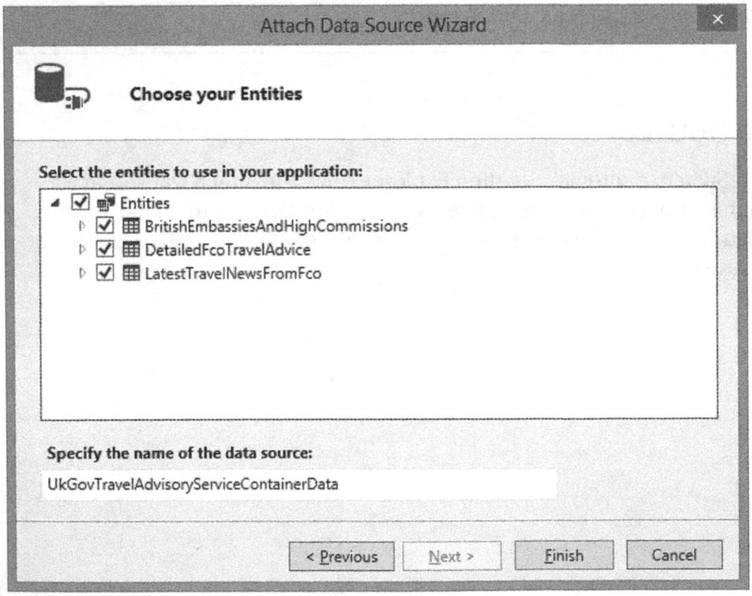

Figure 10-4. *Choosing the entities you want to use*

Once you complete the wizard, you can use the data source just as you would any other data source. Remember that you can also add relationships between entities in different data sources. Figure 10-5 shows the appearance of this data when you include it on a screen that includes department data.

Figure 10-5. *A screen that uses the OData data source*

EXERCISE 10.1 – FINDING ODATA DATA SOURCES

Visit the OData and Windows Azure Marketplace web sites, and try to find some interesting data sources. Once you find a data source you can use, use the Attach Data Source Wizard to attach it to your application and create an editable grid screen to view your data source.

Understanding Default Data Source Options

OData feeds from different sources behave differently. We used a data source that comes from the Foreign and Commonwealth Office (FCO). But the FCO might not have implemented all of the underlying OData query operators that LightSwitch supports. For example, some OData data sources don't support paging, sorting, or certain kinds of query filters.

To stop your application from breaking when LightSwitch tries to do something that isn't supported by your data source, LightSwitch applies application options that are more restrictive than normal. First, it switches off searching by setting the Is Searchable option to false at the entity level. Any collections of datathat you've added to a screen will also have their Support Search settings set to false. If you later discover that your OData data source supports searching, you can manually enable the setting in the table designer's property sheet. However, you should be aware that this can slow down your application.

To further help performance, LightSwitch disables eager loading if your screen contains multiple related tables that come from an OData data source. Finally, LightSwitch also turns off pagination on data grids and data lists if it isn't able to request an individual page of data or count how many pages of data there are.

Exposing Your LightSwitch Data via OData

Publishing your application's data is just as easy as consuming an OData data source. In fact, LightSwitch does this automatically for you without you having to carry out any extra work.

Finding Your Application's End Point URL

When you deploy your application, LightSwitch creates service end points for each data source in your application. You can access these end points in a web browser by entering the root URL for your application followed by the data source name with an .SVC extension, followed by the name of your entity set. Figure 10-6 shows some example URLs.

Figure 10-6. *OData end-point URLs*

To demonstrate the data that's returned by an OData end point, start up a LightSwitch web application and make a note of the root URL—it'll look something like this: `http://localhost:41155/HelpDesk`. Now open a new browser tab and enter `http://localhost:41155/HelpDesk/ApplicationData.svc/Engineers` into the address bar. This returns the raw data, as shown in Figure 10-7.

Figure 10-7. *Raw OData feed*

If you can't see the raw data as shown in Figure 10-7, you need to adjust your browser settings. In Internet Explorer, you do this by switching off the Turn On Feed Reading View option under Tools ➤ Internet Options ➤ Content ➤ Feeds and Web Sites (Settings).

■ **Tip**   If you try this technique on a table with a sizable number of rows, the amount of XML data that LightSwitch returns might be large enough to crash Internet Explorer. If this happens, you can request fewer records by specifying a query in the URL.

Querying OData

OData allows you to perform queries by appending query operators to your URL. To return records for the first engineer, you'd use this URL:

```
http://localhost:41155/ApplicationData.svc/Engineers(1)
```

The OData protocol allows you access related records by using similar syntax. So to return all issues that are assigned to the first engineer, you'd use the URL:

```
http://localhost:41155/ApplicationData.svc/Engineers(1)/Issues
```

If you want to find all engineers with a surname of Smith, you'd use

```
http://localhost:41155/ApplicationData.svc/Engineers?$filter=Surname eq 'Smith'
```

■ **Note**   LightSwitch OData queries are case sensitive. In this example, the URL includes the word Engineers rather than engineers. If you're interested in finding out more about the OData query operators that you can use, the official OData web site includes a full list of operators (http://www.odata.org/documentation/uri-conventions).

Securing OData Feeds

Following the previous example, seeing all your data exposed through OData might leave you feeling vulnerable. For instance, any user could easily view all your engineer records by typing this address into their browser:

```
http://localhost:41155/ApplicationData.svc/Engineers
```

If this concerns you, there sadly isn't a way to switch off OData end points. However, you can secure your data by using the security features that are built into LightSwitch. The first thing that you should do is to turn on authentication. This prevents someone from accessing the end point without a password or being Windows authenticated. Next, you can limit access to your data by writing code in your entity's CanRead, CanUpdate, CanDelete, and CanInsert methods. If you want to apply row-level access control, you can write code in your entity's Entity_Filter method. To find out more about securing your data, refer to Chapters 16 and 17.

■ **Note**   LightSwitch doesn't provide access control at a column level. For example, let's suppose that the Engineer table contains a Salary column. If you want all users to be able to view engineer names but only managers to be able to view the salary details, the salary data must to be split into a separate table. If not, your salary data can be exposed via the OData end point.

Consuming LightSwitch Data

Now that you understand how LightSwitch publishes your data using OData, I'll show you some examples of how to consume your data from outside of LightSwitch. You'll find out how to connect to your data from Microsoft Excel and from .NET.

Connecting to LightSwitch Data from Excel

Excel 2013 allows you to connect to your LightSwitch data via OData. The big advantage of using Excel is that it allows users to analyze their data by using custom formulas, charts, or PivotTables. To create a connection, select the OData option that you'll find in the Get External Data group in the ribbon's Data section. (See Figure 10-8.)

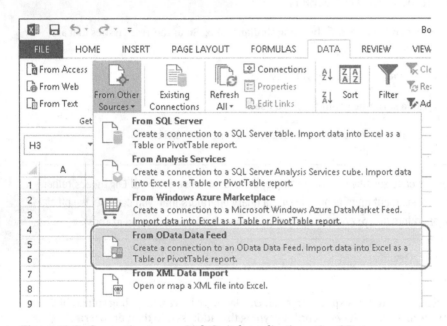

Figure 10-8. *Connecting to your LightSwitch application using OData*

Connecting to LightSwitch Data from .NET

Any application you create that uses .NET 3.5 or above can access your LightSwitch data through WCF (Windows Communication Foundation) Data Services. In this section, you'll find out how to extend the HelpDesk system by creating an ASP.NET application that allows users to create and view issues.

To create this application, start Visual Studio, create a new ASP.NET Web Forms application, and call it `HelpDeskPortal`. Right-click your project, and select the Add Service Reference option from Solution Explorer. This opens the dialog that's shown in Figure 10-9.

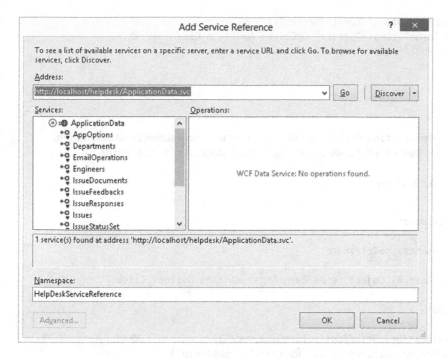

Figure 10-9. *Adding a service reference*

Enter the URL of your OData end point in the Address field (for example, `http://WebServer/YourAppName/ApplicationData.svc`), and click the Go button to populate the Services list box. Click the OK button to complete the addition of the service reference. You can use the service reference (also known as the *proxy* or *service client*) to access your LightSwitch entities in .NET code.

Adding data from ASP.NET

To add records to the HelpDesk system from outside of LightSwitch, we'll create a web page that allows users to add new issues. Add a new Web Form to your ASP.NET project, and name it `CreateIssue.aspx`. Listing 10-1 shows the markup for a page that includes data-entry controls and a button that performs the save.

Listing 10-1. Web Form for Adding a New Issue

File: HelpDeskPortal\CreateIssue.aspx

```
<html xmlns="http://www.w3.org/1999/xhtml">
<head runat="server">
    <title />
</head>
<body>
    <form id="form1" runat="server">
    <div>
        <asp:Label runat="server" Text="Issue Subject"/>
        <asp:TextBox ID="IssueSubject" runat="server"/>
        <asp:Label runat="server" Text="Description"/>
```

```
            <asp:TextBox ID="IssueDescription" runat="server"/>              ❷
            <asp:Button Text="Add Issue" runat="server" OnClick="AddIssue_Click" />  ❸
            <asp:Label ID="ConfirmLabel" runat="server" />
        </div>
        </form>
</body>
</html>
```

The IssueSubject ❶ and IssueDescription ❷ text boxes allow the user to enter a subject and description. The Add Issue button ❸ calls the code that adds the issue to your LightSwitch database. (See Listing10-2.)

Listing 10-2. Web Form Code That Adds a New Issue

VB:
File: HelpDeskPortalVB\CreateIssue.aspx.vb

```
Imports HelpDeskPortalVB.HelpDeskServiceReference

Protected Sub AddIssue_Click(sender As Object, e As EventArgs) Handles Button1.Click

    Dim srvRef As ApplicationData =
        New ApplicationData(
            New Uri("http://localhost/HelpDesk/ApplicationData.svc/"))       ❶
    'srvRef.Credentials = New Net.NetworkCredential("username", "password")

    Dim issue As HelpDeskServiceReference.Issue =
        New HelpDeskServiceReference.Issue()                                 ❷

    issue.Subject = IssueSubject.Text                                        ❸
    issue.CreateDateTime = DateTime.Now
    issue.TargetEndDateTime = DateTime.Now.AddDays(3)
    issue.ProblemDescription = IssueDescription.Text

    Try
        srvRef.AddToIssues(issue)                                            ❹
        srvRef.SaveChanges()
        ConfirmLabel.Text = "Issue Created"

    Catch ex As Exception
        ConfirmLabel.Text = ex.Message                                       ❺
    End Try

End Sub
```

C#:
File: HelpDeskPortalCS\CreateIssue.aspx.cs

```
using HelpDeskPortalCS.HelpdeskServiceReference;
```

274

```
protected void AddIssue_Click(object sender, EventArgs e)
{

    ApplicationData srvRef =
        new ApplicationData(
            new Uri("http://localhost/HelpDesk/ApplicationData.svc/"));      ❶
    //srvRef.Credentials =
    //      new System.Net.NetworkCredential("username", "password");

    HelpdeskServiceReference.Issue issue =
        new HelpdeskServiceReference.Issue();                                ❷

    issue.Subject = IssueSubject.Text;                                       ❸
    issue.CreateDateTime = DateTime.Now;
    issue.TargetEndDateTime = DateTime.Now.AddDays(3);
    issue.ProblemDescription = IssueDescription.Text ;

    try
    {
        srvRef.AddToIssues(issue);                                           ❹
        srvRef.SaveChanges();
        ConfirmLabel.Text = "Issue Created";
    }
    catch (Exception ex)
    {
        ConfirmLabel.Text = ex.Message;                                      ❺
    }
}
```

The first part of the code ❶ creates the service context you use to access your LightSwitch data. The constructor requires you to supply a URL for your OData end point. We hardcoded this URL, but in practice, it's a good idea to store this value in your application's web.config file. By doing this, you can change the end-point address after you deploy your application. If you sensibly secured your application by enabling authentication (as discussed in Chapter 16), the commented-out line of code shows you how to supply a user name and password.

The next part of the code creates a new instance of an issue entity ❷, and it sets several properties ❸ that include the subject, create date, target end date, and description properties. Visual Studio provides you with full IntelliSense—this makes it easy for you to set your entity's property values because there's no need for you to remember the exact names.

An AddTo method exists for each entity in your data source. To add a new record, you'll need to call the AddTo method that corresponds with your entity and supply the entity that you want to add. In this case, the method is called AddToIssues ❹. Finally, the SaveChanges method allows you commit your changes. If the data that your user enters fails validation, the SaveChanges method raises an exception, and you can handle this as you wish in the exception handler ❺.

With some extra styling, Figure 10-10 shows how this web page looks. This section highlights how easily you can work with LightSwitch data, and how the API objects that you use are very similar to those described in Chapter 4.

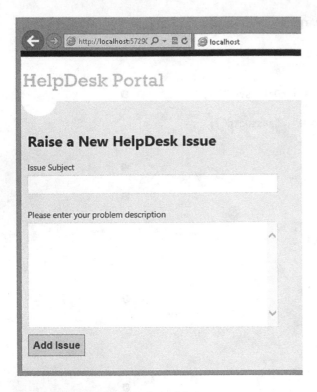

Figure 10-10. *Web page that adds issues*

Reading data from ASP.NET

To retrieve records from the HelpDesk system, we'll add a page that displays the issues that have been assigned to a user. Add a new Web Form to your ASP.NET project, and name it ViewIssues.aspx. From the toolbox, drag a GridView control onto your Web Form. Your markup will look like the code that's shown in Listing 10-3.

Listing 10-3. Web Form That Displays Records

File: HelpDeskPortal\ViewIssues.aspx

```
<html xmlns="http://www.w3.org/1999/xhtml">
<head runat="server">
    <title />
</head>
<body>
    <form id="form1" runat="server">
    <div>
        <asp:GridView ID="IssuesGrid" runat="server"/>
    </div>
    </form>
</body>
</html>
```

Now add the .NET code to the load method of your page, as shown in Listing 10-4.

Listing 10-4. Web Form Code That Populates a Grid View

VB:
File: HelpDeskPortalVB\ViewIssues.aspx.vb

```
Imports HelpDeskPortalVB.HelpDeskServiceReference

Protected Sub Page_Load
    (ByVal sender As Object, ByVal e As System.EventArgs) Handles Me.Load

    Dim srvRef As ApplicationData =
        New ApplicationData(
            New Uri("http://localhost/HelpDesk/ApplicationData.svc/"))        ❶

    Dim issues = srvRef.Issues.Where(Function(i) i.User.Username = "timl")     ❷

    IssuesGrid.DataSource = issues                                            ❸
    IssuesGrid.DataBind()

End Sub
```

C#:
File: HelpDeskPortalCS\ViewIssues.aspx.cs

```
using HelpDeskPortalCS.HelpDeskServiceReference;

protected void Page_Load(object sender, EventArgs e)
{
    ApplicationData srvRef =
        new ApplicationData(
            new Uri("http://localhost/HelpDesk/ApplicationData.svc/"));       ❶

    var issues = srvRef.Issues.Where(i => i.User.Username == "timl");         ❷

    IssuesGrid.DataSource = issues;                                          ❸
    IssuesGrid.DataBind();
}
```

Just like the previous example, the first part of the code ❶ creates the service reference context. The next line of code selects the issues that are assigned to the user timl ❷. In practice, you'd replace the hardcoded timl value with logic that determines the currently logged-in user. But the important point of this code is that you can query your data by using the same query syntax from Chapter 4. So if you want to return just a single issue, you can write code that uses the FirstOrDefault method.

The final piece of code sets the data source of your GridView control ❸, and data-binds the issues to the grid. Figure 10-11 shows how your final screen might look with some extra formatting.

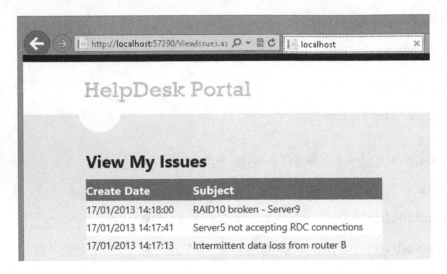

Figure 10-11. *Web page that shows issues*

Connecting to Use LightSwitch from Other Platforms

So far, you've seen how to consume LightSwitch data from a .NET /ASP.NET application. Fortunately, connecting to your LightSwitch data from other platforms or devices isn't very difficult. The main thing that you'll need to do is to find an appropriate OData client.

Table 10-1 shows a list of common platforms and links to suitable OData clients for those platforms. When you connect to a LightSwitch application from a different platform or language, the principles that you've learned will still remain the same. For example, you'd still use the same OData methods to access entities and to save your changes.

Table 10-1. *OData Platforms and Clients*

Platform	OData Client/Web Site
JavaScript	Datajs: http://datajs.codeplex.com/
Android/Java	OData4j: http://code.google.com/p/odata4j/
Windows Phone 7	Windows Phone 7 SDK: http://create.msdn.com/
iOS (Apple)	OData client for Objective-C: http://odataobjc.codeplex.com/
PHP	OData SDK for PHP: http://odataphp.codeplex.com/
Ruby	ruby_odata: http://github.com/visoft/ruby_odata

Summary

LightSwitch supports OData, a protocol that makes it easy to consume external data sources and share your data with other applications.

You can use OData to connect to data that's held in systems that you'll commonly find within businesses. This includes data that's stored in SharePoint 2010, Microsoft Dynamics CRM 2011, and SQL Server Reporting Services 2012. Externally, there are many other third-party data sources that you can use. This chapter shows you how to connect to a travel advisory service, but you'll find many other data sources through the official OData web site and the Windows Azure Marketplace.

To connect your application to an OData data source, you would use the Attach Data Source Wizard, just as you would for any other external data source. The connection process requires you to enter an *end point*—this is the web address that identifies the OData data source that you want to use. Depending on the service that you're connecting to, you may also need to enter a user name and password.

LightSwitch automatically creates service end points for each data source in your application. These end-point addresses consist of the root URL for your application, followed by the data source name with an `.SVC` extension, followed by the name of your entity set. For example, `http://WebSite/HelpDesk/ApplicationData.svc/Engineers` is the address that returns all engineer records. Because users can access your raw data through a web browser, it's a good idea to apply access control to your application. Chapters 16 and 17 show you how to do this.

OData allows you connect to your LightSwitch data from other applications. You've seen examples of how to do this with Excel and ASP.NET. In Excel, you can connect to OData data sources by using the Data Import feature. In .NET, you can add a WCF service reference to your LightSwitch data. This gives you strongly typed access to entities and allows you to query, add, and update records using much of the same syntax that you saw in Chapter 4.

Summary

■ ■ ■

CHAPTER 11

Creating and Using Custom Controls

The built-in Silverlight controls that you've seen so far include labels, text boxes, autocomplete boxes, and data grids. But if you can't find a control that suits your needs, there's no need to worry. When you're building Rich Client applications, you can customize the way that users enter and view data by using custom Silverlight controls. This opens up many extra ways for you to display your data. You can build your own Silverlight custom controls or use controls that other people have developed. In this chapter, you'll learn how to

- Display data using custom controls
- Bind screen data to custom controls
- Develop your own Silverlight custom controls

At the start of this chapter, you'll learn how to use the controls that you'll find in the Silverlight Software Development Kit (SDK). You'll find out how to customize the HelpDesk application by allowing administrators to enter password details through a masked input control. You'll learn how to apply a ComboBox box control to limit the priority values that a user can choose when entering an issue, how to allow users to set numeric values by using a Slider control, and how to display a web page on a screen. You'll also find out how to build a duration control that allows minutes to be split into hours and minutes. This control will allow engineers in our example to add timesheet records more easily.

Using Custom Controls

The easiest way to get started is to use the UI controls in the Silverlight SDK. You'll find these controls in the `System.Windows.Controls` namespace. Of course, you could use other third-party Silverlight controls. But the advantage of directly using the controls in the Silverlight SDK is that it quickly opens up a whole host of additional UI elements that you can use, such as the following:

- `PasswordBox`
- `WebBrowser`
- `TreeView`
- `RichTextBox`
- `MediaElement`
- `MultiScaleImage`
- `HyperLinkButton`
- `ComboBox`

An advantage of this technique is that you don't need to create a separate project, and you don't need to write very much code either. In the section that follows, you'll learn how to create a screen in the HelpDesk system that allows managers to specify email server settings (as shown in Figure 11-1).

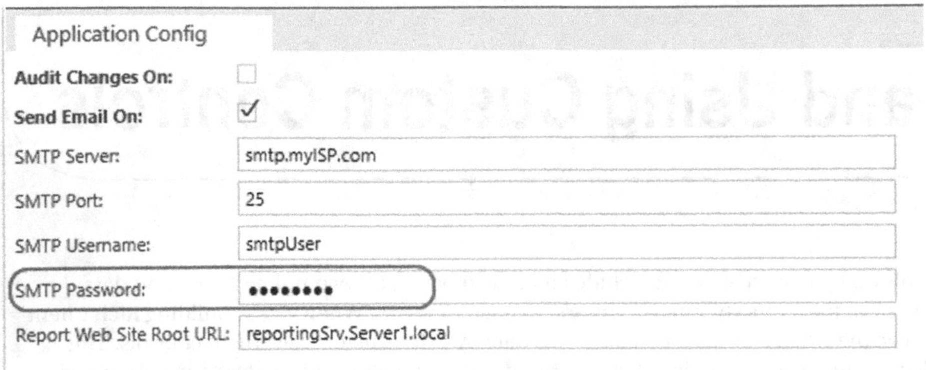

Application Config	
Audit Changes On:	☐
Send Email On:	☑
SMTP Server:	smtp.myISP.com
SMTP Port:	25
SMTP Username:	smtpUser
SMTP Password:	••••••••
Report Web Site Root URL:	reportingSrv.Server1.local

Figure 11-1. `PasswordBox` *control as it appears onscreen*

This screen uses the password box control that you'll find in the Silverlight SDK. The control provides a masked password input box, which replaces the characters that the user enters with a series of dots.

There are two parts to using a custom control. First, you need to specify a custom control for the data item that you want to use. Second, you'll need to write the code that binds the control to your underlying data. You'll now find out how to carry out both of these tasks.

Specifying a Custom Control

To use the password box control, use the New Data Screen template to create a screen based on the `AppOptions` table (or reuse the `AppOptionsEdit` screen that you created in Chapter 7, Listing 7-19). Now carry out the following steps in the screen designer:

1. Select the `SMTPPassword` data item, and change the control type from Text Box to Custom Control (as shown in Figure 11-2).

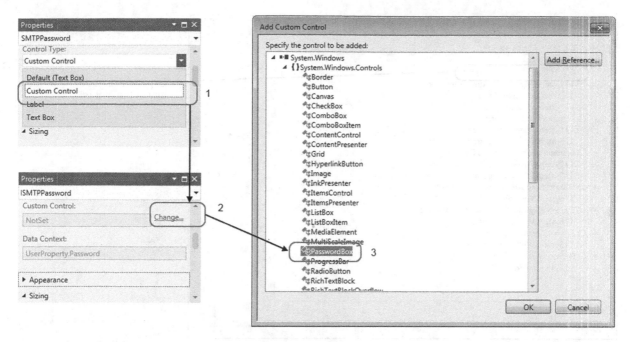

Figure 11-2. *Specifying a custom control of type* `PasswordBox`

2. Open the properties sheet, and click on the Change link.

3. When the Add Custom Control dialog appears, select System.Windows.Controls ➤ PasswordBox.

If the `PasswordBox` control doesn't appear in the Add Custom Control dialog, make sure that you've chosen the `System.Windows` DLL, rather than one of the other DLLs (as shown in Figure 11-3).

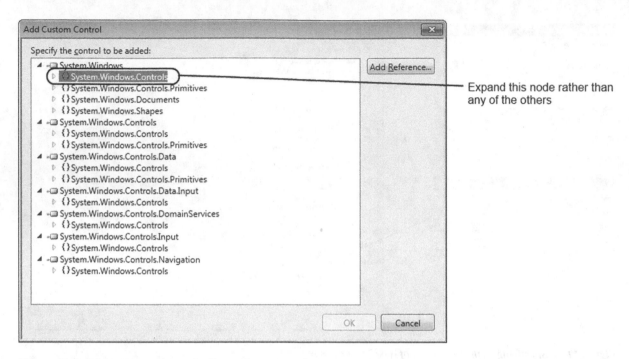

Figure 11-3. Make sure to choose the first node

Binding Data to Custom Controls

Once you set a data item to use a custom control, the next step is to bind the control to your underlying data item. In this example, you'll need to bind the password control's `PasswordProperty` to the `AppOption` entity's `SMTPPassword` property. To do this, click on the Write Code button, select the `InitializeDataWorkspace` method, and enter the code that's shown in Listing 11-1.

Listing 11-1. Calling the SetBinding Method

VB:
File: HelpDeskVB\Client\UserCode\AppOptionsEdit.vb

```
Private Sub AppOptionsEdit_InitializeDataWorkspace(
    saveChangesTo As List(Of Microsoft.LightSwitch.IDataService))

    Dim password = Me.FindControl("SMTPPassword")                              ❶
    password.SetBinding(
        System.Windows.Controls.PasswordBox.PasswordProperty,
        "Value",
        Windows.Data.BindingMode.TwoWay)

End Sub
```

C#:
File: HelpDeskCS\Client\UserCode\AppOptionsEdit.cs

```csharp
partial void CreateNewAppOption_InitializeDataWorkspace(
   List<IDataService> saveChangesTo)
{
    var password = this.FindControl("SMTPPassword");                    ❶
    password.SetBinding(
        System.Windows.Controls.PasswordBox.PasswordProperty,
        "Value",
        System.Windows.Data.BindingMode.TwoWay);
}
```

This code uses the FindControl method ❶ to return an IContentItemProxy object. (See Chapter 7 for more details.) IContentItemProxy's SetBinding method carries out the actual task of data binding. This method accepts three arguments.

The first argument specifies the dependency property to bind to. If you're not sure what a dependency property is, just think of it as a property that you can bind data to. To help you choose the correct dependency property, use the code editor's IntelliSense to view all the possible choices. You'll need to specify the control type that you've used, and in this example, the dependency property value is prefixed with the System.Windows.Controls.PasswordBox control type.

The second argument is the *binding path*. This is the most difficult part to get right because this method expects a string value, and Visual Studio provides no guidance as to what you should supply. If you get this wrong, the data binding fails to work without giving you any compile or runtime errors. This makes it difficult to trace the exact cause of a binding-path error.

You'll commonly see the string property Value used as a binding path. This binds your dependency property to the Data Context item that you'll find in the Properties sheet. (See Figure 11-4.) Table 11-1 shows the other binding paths that you can use.

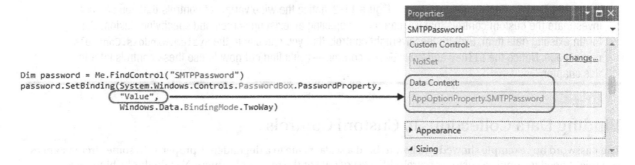

Figure 11-4. The Value data-binding path references the Data Context text box

Table 11-1. *Data-Binding Values*

Binding Path	Data binds to...
Value	The value specified in the Data Context text box in the Properties sheet
StringValue	The formatted version of the value specified in the Data Context text box in the Properties sheet
Details.Entity.Surname	Another property in the same entity (Surname in this example)
Screen.localPropertyName	A local property on your screen

You could also use the binding path StringValue rather than Value. StringValue reflects any specific formatting that's applied by the property, whereas Value simply returns the raw value. These property names (Value and StringValue) are public properties of Microsoft.LightSwitch.Presentation.Implementation.ContentItem.

The final argument is the binding mode. You can supply one of three values: OneTime, OneWay, or TwoWay. OneTime updates the control from the source data when your application creates the data binding. OneWay updates the control from the source data when the data binding is created, and also whenever the source data changes afterward. TwoWay updates the control and source in both directions whenever either of them changes.

This completes the example, and you're now ready to run your application. When you run your AppOptionsEdit screen, you'll be able to enter an SMTP password using the password control.

■ **Tip** Rather than using hard-coded binding paths, you could create a helper library that exposes a set of constants. The C# class would look something like this:

```
public static class ContentItemProperty
{
    public const string Value = "Value";
    public const string StringValue = "StringValue";
    public const string DisplayName = "DisplayName";
    public const string Details = "Details";
    // etc.
}
```

EXERCISE 11.1 – INVESTIGATING CUSTOM CONTROLS

In the Add Custom Control dialog shown in Figure 11-2, notice the wide variety of controls that you can use. Investigate the custom controls that you can use by opening an existing screen and specifying Custom Control for an existing data item. Explore the Silverlight controls that you can use in the System.Windows.Controls namespace. Notice the Slider and WebBrowser controls—you'll find out how to use these controls later in this chapter.

Binding Data Collections to Custom Controls

The password box example showed you how to bind a scalar value to a dependency property. In some circumstances, you might need to supply a custom control with a list of data or the results of a query. You do this by binding a collection of data to a dependency property on the custom control, and this example shows you how.

The new Issue screen allows engineers to enter a priority by using an autocomplete box. A disadvantage of this control is that engineers can type whatever text they choose into this control and if they enter invalid data, they won't be notified of their mistake until they attempt to save their record. To overcome this problem, you'll now find out how to use the ComboBox control. This control allows youto limit item selections to only those that are shown in the control. (See Figure 11-5.)

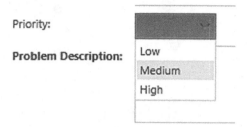

Priority:

Problem Description:

Figure 11-5. *Limiting item choices by using a ComboBox control*

Designing the screen

The steps that you need to carry out to use a ComboBox control are very much the same as those that you used to set up the PasswordBox control. However, there's one additional task that's required. LightSwitch doesn't know how to populate your ComboBox control with the item choices, so you'll need to add some code that sets your ComboBox's data source.

To create this example, use the New Data Screen template to create a screen based on the Issue table. Name your screen CreateNewIssue. Select the Priority data item, and change it from an autocomplete box to a custom control. From the Properties sheet, click on the Change link and use the Add Custom Control dialog to select System.Windows.Controls ➤ ComboBox.

Now click the Add Data Item button and create a new query called Priorities that returns all priorities. Click the Write Code button, select the screen's Activated method, and enter the code shown in Listing 11-2.

Listing 11-2. Data-Binding a ComboBox Control

VB:
File: HelpdeskVB\Client\UserCode\CreateNewIssue.vb

```
Private Sub CreateNewIssue_Activated()
    Dim comboControl As IContentItemProxy = Me.FindControl("Priority")
    comboControl.SetBinding(                                              ❶
        System.Windows.Controls.ComboBox.ItemsSourceProperty,
        "Screen.Priorities",                                             ❷
        Windows.Data.BindingMode.OneWay)

    comboControl.SetBinding(                                              ❸
    System.Windows.Controls.ComboBox.SelectedItemProperty,
    "Screen.IssueProperty.Priority",
    Windows.Data.BindingMode.TwoWay)

End Sub
```

C#:
File: HelpDeskCS\Client\UserCode\CreateNewIssue.cs

```
partial void CreateNewIssue_Activated()
{
    var comboControl = this.FindControl("Priority");
    comboControl.SetBinding(                                              ❶
        System.Windows.Controls.ComboBox.ItemsSourceProperty,
```

287

```
        "Screen.Priorities",                                                    ❷
        System.Windows.Data.BindingMode.OneWay);

    comboControl.SetBinding(                                                     ❸
        System.Windows.Controls.ComboBox.SelectedItemProperty,
        "Screen.IssueProperty.Priority",
        System.Windows.Data.BindingMode.TwoWay);
}
```

This code carries out two data-binding tasks by using the SetBinding method. First, it populates the items shown in the ComboBox by binding the ComboBox's ItemsSourceProperty to your Priorities query ❶. The binding path that allows you to reference the Priorities query is Screen.Priorities ❷. The next line of code sets the item that's selected in the combo box by binding the ComboBox's SelectedItemsProperty to the Issue property's Priority property ❸. This completes the example, and you're now ready to run your screen.

Converting Values When Data Binding

Sometimes, the data type of the dependency property that you want to use might not exactly match the data type of your data source. In this case, you'll need to create a value converter to enable the data binding to work.

The HelpDesk system stores details about each office location and includes the ability to record the office capacity of each location (that is, the maximum number of people that the building can hold). In this example, you'll find out how to allow users to enter the maximum capacity by using Silverlight's Slider control.

The Office table stores the capacity as an integer, but the Silverlight Slider control expects to be bound to a number that's of data type double. This mismatch means that in order to use the Slider control, you'll need to create a value converter that converts doubles to integers, and vice versa. To show you how to do this, this following example creates a new data screen that allows users to create entries for new offices and to set the capacity by using a Slider control. To complete this example, carry out the following tasks:

1. Create a new data screen that's based on the Office table, and name it CreateNewOffice.

2. Change the Building Capacity data item from Text Box to Custom Control.

3. In the Properties sheet, click the Change link. When the Add Custom Control dialog appears, select System.Windows.Controls ➤ Slider.

4. Set the Min Width value of the Slider control to 300. It's important to set this to a value other than Auto; otherwise, LightSwitch shows only the Slider button, and not the Slider section that allows the user to make a selection.

5. Create a new Columns Layout control beneath the main Rows Layout control for your Office Property. Set the Label Position setting of this group to Collapsed.

6. Drag your Slider control into the Columns Layout control. When you do this, make sure the Label Position setting is still set to Left-Aligned.

7. Add another Building Capacity data item into the Columns Layout control, and set the control type to Label. Set the Label Position setting of the label to Collapsed. This label is designed to show the selected integer value when the user uses the Slider control. Figure 11-6 shows how your screen now looks.

Figure 11-6. Screen layout in design view

8. Switch your project to File view. Create a new class in the UserCode folder of your Common project, and name it IntToDouble.

9. (Optional) If you've added an HTML client or upgraded your project, you won't have a Common project in your solution. Instead, create the IntToDouble class in the Client project's UserCode ➤ Shared folder.

10. Add a reference to the PresentationFramework.dll assembly in the project in which you've added your IntToDouble class. The default location of this file on a 64-bit machine is C:\Program Files (x86)\Reference Assemblies\Microsoft\Framework\ Silverlight\v5.0.

Now add the code that's shown in Listing 11-3 to your IntToDouble class.

Listing 11-3. Value Converter Code

VB:
File: HelpDeskVB\Common\UserCode\IntToDouble.vb

```vb
Imports System.Windows.Data

Public Class IntToDoubleConverter
    Implements IValueConverter                                          ❶

    Public Function Convert(                                            ❷
        value As Object,
        targetType As System.Type,
        parameter As Object,
        culture As System.Globalization.CultureInfo
    ) As Object Implements System.Windows.Data.IValueConverter.Convert

        Return CDbl(value)
    End Function
    Public Function ConvertBack(                                        ❸
        value As Object,
        targetType As System.Type,
        parameter As Object,
```

```
        culture As System.Globalization.CultureInfo
    ) As Object Implements System.Windows.Data.IValueConverter.ConvertBack

        Return CInt(value)
    End Function

End Class
```

C#:
File: HelpDeskCS\Common\UserCode\IntToDouble.cs

```
namespace LightSwitchApplication.UserCode
{
    public class IntToDoubleConverter : IValueConverter              ❶
    {
        public object Convert(object value, Type targetType,        ❷
            object parameter, System.Globalization.CultureInfo culture)
        {
            return Double.Parse(value.ToString());
        }

        public object ConvertBack(object value, Type targetType,    ❸
            object parameter, System.Globalization.CultureInfo culture)
        {
            return int.Parse(value.ToString());
        }
    }
}
```

The IntToDouble class implements the IValueConverter interface ❶, and contains the logic that carries out the data conversion. The Convert method ❷ converts an integer value to a double, whereas the ConvertBack ❸ method coverts a double to an integer. This example demonstrates a simple value converter that works well in this scenario. But in general, value converters should also use the culture parameter to provide better conversations. In particular, the culture information allows you to parse and format numbers and dates based on your user's language.

After you create your value converter, return to the screen designer, click the Write Code button, and select the screen's Activated method. Add the code shown in Listing 11-4.

Listing 11-4. Data-Binding the Slider Control

VB:
File: HelpDeskVB\Client\UserCode\CreateNewOffice.vb

```
Imports System.Windows.Controls
Imports System.Windows.Data

Private Sub CreateNewOffice_Activated ()
    Dim buildingCapacity As IContentItemProxy =
        Me.FindControl("BuildingCapacity")
    Dim converter As New IntToDoubleConverter
    buildingCapacity.SetBinding(
        Slider.ValueProperty,
        "Value",
```

```
        converter,
        BindingMode.TwoWay)
End Sub
```

C#:
File: HelpdeskCS\Client\UserCode\CreateNewOffice.cs

```
using System.Windows.Controls;
using System.Windows.Data;

partial void CreateNewOffice_Activated()
{
    var buildingCapacity = this.FindControl("BuildingCapacity");
    IntToDoubleConverter converter = new IntToDoubleConverter();
    buildingCapacity.SetBinding(
        Slider.ValueProperty,
        "Value",
        converter,
        BindingMode.TwoWay);
}
```

You're now ready to run your application. Figure 11-7 shows the appearance of the Slider control on the final screen.

Figure 11-7. *Illustration of the Slider control*

■ **Tip**   Value converters allow you to do much more than just basic type conversions, and you can use them in many other imaginative ways. For example, you could bind the background color of a text box or text block control to an integer value. If your data includes a priority field that stores numbers, say, from 1 to 5, you could set the background color of your control to green if the priority is 1, or set it to red if the priority is 5. Using a value converter, you can bind to the BackgroundProperty dependency property by converting the priority number into an object of type System.Drawing.Color.

Creating a Custom Silverlight Control

The examples that you've seen so far have used the controls from the System.Windows.Controls namespace. If there isn't a control in this namespace that suits your needs and if you can't use a third-party control that does what you need, another option is to create your own custom Silverlight control.

The time-tracking feature in the HelpDesk application allows engineers to record the time in minutes that they've spent on resolving issues. To improve the presentation of this screen, you'll now learn how to create a custom control that allows engineers to enter and view time durations in hours and minutes (as shown in Figure 11-8).

Figure 11-8. *Duration control*

Understanding Dependency Properties

The duration control that you'll create requires a dependency property you use to bind the data item on your LightSwitch screen to your control. But before you move on further, let's take a closer look at what dependency properties are and how they work.

Dependency properties are very often used in Silverlight and Windows Presentation Foundation (WPF). They're very similar to normal .NET properties, but they're more powerful. They use memory more efficiently, help support features like styles and animations, and also provide advanced features like coercion (I'll explain what this is later), validation, and change notification. Change notification is particularly important because it alerts your LightSwitch screen whenever a user makes a change to a custom control value.

Traditional .NET properties include two methods, called get and set. In the vast majority of cases, these methods retrieve and set the value of a private field. Unlike traditional .NET properties, dependency properties don't read their values from a private field. When you retrieve the value of a dependency property, .NET dynamically calculates the return value using a process called *dynamic value resolution*.

Let's imagine that you write some code that retrieves the background color of a Silverlight text box control. The background color might depend on various factors. It could be inherited from a parent control or could be set in styles and themes. Furthermore, the control might be involved in an animation that constantly changes the background color. To retrieve the correct value, Silverlight searches for the background color in the following places, in the order that's shown. It returns the first value that it finds.

1. Animations

2. Local Value

3. Styles

4. Property Value Inheritance

5. Default Value

Dynamic value resolution begins by checking whether the text box is involved in an animation. If so, it returns the background color that's applied by the animation. If not, it searches for a *local value*. This refers to the value that's explicitly set in code (for example, MyCtrl.BackColor = Colors.Green) or in XAML. If your background color is bound to data, the process also classifies a data-bound value as a locally set value. If you did not set a local value, dynamic value resolution searches for a value that has been set in a style or a template. If that doesn't return a match, it tries to find the value that was set at the parent control. It continues searching up the tree of parent controls until it reaches the root control. And if it doesn't find a value here, it returns the default value.

The big benefit of this approach is that it's highly efficient in terms of memory usage. Around 90% of the properties on a typical control stay at their initial value, so it's inefficient to allocate memory by storing the value of every property on a control. Dependency properties store only the value of properties that have changed, which is much more efficient. The local value of a dependency property isn't stored in a field of your object; instead, it's stored in a dictionary of keys and values that's provided by the base class DependencyObject. The dictionary uses the property name as the key value for the dictionary entry.

In summary, dependency properties don't hold a concrete value. Their value can be derived from many places—hence the name *dependency property*. They're important in LightSwitch because if you want to bind screen data to a property on a custom control, that property must be a dependency property.

Creating a New Control and Dependency Property

Now that you understand how dependency properties work, let's create the custom control that allows users to enter time durations. This process involves creating a Silverlight class library that contains a Silverlight user control. Your Silverlight user control contains the text boxes and UI elements that define your custom control. To create a custom control, carry out the following steps:

1. Start Visual Studio. Click File ➤ New ➤ Project. When the New Project dialog appears, select the Silverlight Class Library template and name your project ApressControls. If you're having trouble finding this template, you can use the search box that appears at the top of the New Project dialog.

2. The next dialog that appears prompts you to choose a Silverlight version. Choose Silverlight 5 (if it's available).

3. When your project opens, right-click your project in Solution Explorer and choose the Add ➤ New Item option.

4. When the Add New Item dialog appears, choose Silverlight User Control and name your control DurationEditorInternal.xaml.

5. Drag two TextBox controls from the toolbox into your user control. Name these controls HourTextbox and MinuteTextbox. Add two TextBlock controls to the right of each TextBox control, and set the text attribute of the controls to Hrs and Mins. Listing 11-5 shows the XAML for the control.

6. Right-click an area of your XAML file, click on the View Code option, and add the .NET code shown in Listing 11-6.

Listing 11-5. DurationEditorInternal.XAML Contents

File: ApressControlsVB\DurationEditorInternal.xaml

```
<UserControl x:Class="ApressControlsVB.DurationEditorInternal"              ❶
    xmlns="http://schemas.microsoft.com/winfx/2006/xaml/presentation"
    xmlns:x="http://schemas.microsoft.com/winfx/2006/xaml"
    xmlns:d="http://schemas.microsoft.com/expression/blend/2008"
    xmlns:mc="http://schemas.openxmlformats.org/markup-compatibility/2006"
    mc:Ignorable="d">

    <Grid x:Name="LayoutRoot" Background="White" Margin="0,0,0,0">
        <TextBox Name="HourTextbox"
            TextChanged="HourTextbox_TextChanged"/>                         ❷
        <TextBlock Text="Hrs" />                                            ❸
        <TextBox Name="MinuteTextbox"
            TextChanged="MinuteTextbox_TextChanged"/>
        <TextBlock Text="Mins"/>
    </Grid>
</UserControl>
```

Listing 11-5 shows the XAML for the Visual Basic version of the custom control. In this code, the project is named ApressControlsVB, so if you're re-creating this example, make sure that the Class setting ❶ matches the class name of your custom control.

The line of code in ❷ defines the TextBox that allows users to enter the number of hours in the time duration. The TextBlock control ❸ shows the text *Hrs* to the right of the TextBox. The following lines of code repeat the same thing with the minute component of the time duration.

If you dragged the controls onto your control (as described in step 5), Visual Studio adds formatting attributes to your controls, such as HorizontalAlignment, TextWrapping, VerticalAlignment, Width and Height. Listing 11-5 omits these attributes to make the code easier to read, but when you're re-creating this example, make sure to use the designer to include sizing and positioning details; otherwise, you'll find that all the controls overlap each other.

Listing 11-6. Code-Behind for the DurationEditorInternal Control

VB:
File: ApressControlsVB\DurationEditorInternal.xaml.vb

```
Partial Public Class DurationEditorInternal
    Inherits UserControl

    Public Sub New
        InitializeComponent()
    End Sub

    '1 Code that registers the Dependency Property                          ❶
    Public Shared ReadOnly DurationProperty As DependencyProperty =
        DependencyProperty.Register(
            "Duration",
            GetType(Integer),
            GetType(DurationEditorInternal),
            New PropertyMetadata(0, AddressOf OnDurationPropertyChanged))

    Public Property Duration As Integer
        Get
            Return MyBase.GetValue(DurationEditorInternal.DurationProperty)
        End Get
        Set(value As Integer)
            MyBase.SetValue(DurationEditorInternal.DurationProperty, value)
        End Set
    End Property

    '2 Code that runs when the underlying data value changes                ❷
    Public Shared Sub OnDurationPropertyChanged(
        re As DependencyObject, e As DependencyPropertyChangedEventArgs)

        Dim de As DurationEditorInternal = DirectCast(re, DurationEditorInternal)
        Dim ts As TimeSpan = TimeSpan.FromMinutes(CInt(e.NewValue.ToString))

        de.HourTextbox.Text = Math.Floor(ts.TotalHours).ToString
        de.MinuteTextbox.Text = ts.Minutes.ToString
    End Sub
```

```vbnet
'3 Code that runs when the user changes the value                              ❸
Private Sub HourTextbox_TextChanged(
    sender As Object, e As TextChangedEventArgs)
        Duration = CalculateDuration()
End Sub

Private Sub MinuteTextbox_TextChanged(
    sender As Object, e As TextChangedEventArgs)
        Duration = CalculateDuration()
End Sub

Private Function CalculateDuration() As Integer                                ❹
    Dim dur As Integer
    Try
        dur = (CInt(HourTextbox.Text) * 60) + CInt(MinuteTextbox.Text)
    Catch ex As Exception
    End Try
    Return dur
End Function

End Class
```

C#:
File: ApressControlsCS\DurationEditorInternal.xaml.cs

```csharp
using System;
using System.Windows;
using System.Windows.Controls;

namespace ApressControlsCS
{
    public partial class DurationEditorInternal : UserControl
    {
        public DurationEditorInternal()
        {
            InitializeComponent();
        }

        // 1 Code that registers the Dependency Property                       ❶
        public static readonly DependencyProperty DurationProperty =
            DependencyProperty.Register(
                "Duration",
                typeof(int),
                typeof(DurationEditorInternal),
                new PropertyMetadata(0, OnDurationPropertyChanged));

        public int Duration
        {
            get {
                return (int)base.GetValue(
                    DurationEditorInternal.DurationProperty);
            }
```

```
        set {
            base.SetValue(
                DurationEditorInternal.DurationProperty, value);
        }
    }

    // 2 Code that runs when the underlying data value changes                ❷
    public static void OnDurationPropertyChanged(
        DependencyObject re, DependencyPropertyChangedEventArgs e)
    {
        DurationEditorInternal de = (DurationEditorInternal)re;
        TimeSpan ts = TimeSpan.FromMinutes(int.Parse(e.NewValue.ToString()));
        de.HourTextbox.Text = Math.Floor(ts.TotalHours).ToString();
        de.MinuteTextbox.Text = ts.Minutes.ToString();
    }

    //  3 Code that runs when the user changes the value                      ❸
    private void HourTextbox_TextChanged(
        object sender, TextChangedEventArgs e)
    {
        Duration = CalculateDuration();
    }

    private void MinuteTextbox_TextChanged(
        object sender, TextChangedEventArgs e)
    {
        Duration = CalculateDuration();
    }

    private int CalculateDuration()                                          ❹
    {
        int dur = 0;
        try
        {
            dur = (int.Parse(HourTextbox.Text) * 60) +
                    int.Parse(MinuteTextbox.Text);

        }
        catch (Exception ex)
        {

        }
        return dur;
    }

    }
}
```

The code in this listing contains three distinct parts:

- The first part of the code ❶ registers the dependency property. The next section explains exactly how this code works.

- The code in ❷ runs when the underlying data value changes, and it updates the values of the Hour and Minute text boxes.

- The code in ❸ runs when the user updates the value of the Hour or Minute text box. It uses the CalculateDuration method ❹ to convert the duration that the user has entered back into minutes, and it updates the dependency property.

Creating a dependency property

There are two tasks that you need to carry out to create a dependency property:

1. Create a shared/static field of type DependencyProperty, and call the Register method to create an instance of a DependencyProperty object.

2. Create a normal .NET property that *backs* your dependency property. This property stores the dependency property value by using the GetValue and SetValue methods that are inherited from DependencyObject. The DependencyProperty acts as the *key* for the GetValue and SetValue methods.

Let's take a closer look at the code that registers your dependency property. To illustrate the arguments that you need to supply, here's the C# code from Listing 11-6:

```
public static readonly DependencyProperty DurationProperty =
    DependencyProperty.Register(
        "Duration",                                              ❶
        typeof(int),                                            ❷
        typeof(DurationEditorInternal),                         ❸
        new PropertyMetadata(0, OnDurationPropertyChanged));    ❹
```

This code defines a dependency property called DurationProperty. This name identifies your dependency property when you call the SetBinding method from your LightSwitch code. To adhere to .NET naming conventions, you should always make sure that the name of your dependency properties end with the word *Property*.

The Register method accepts four arguments, and returns an instance of a new dependency property object. The arguments that you need to supply to this method are as follows:

- ❶ The first argument specifies the .NET property that backs your dependency property. In this example, the .NET property is called Duration.

- ❷ The second argument specifies the data type of the .NET property.

- ❸ The third argument specifies the type that the dependency property belongs to.

- ❹ The fourth argument allows you to specify PropertyMetadata. The next section explains exactly what this does.

Specifying the behavior of dependency properties

The beauty of dependency properties is that you can specify default values, run code when the value of your dependency property changes, coerce values, and attach validation logic. The PropertyMetadata object is the key that makes all of this possible. As the following line shows, the PropertyMetadata constructor accepts four arguments:

```
new PropertyMetadata(0, OnDurationPropertyChanged, null, null)
```

- The first argument specifies the default value. The dependency property uses the default value only if it's unable to determine a value elsewhere. Dynamic value resolution chooses the default value as the very last resort. Therefore, it chooses the default value if a value hasn't been explicitly set or if it isn't able to find an inherited value. If you don't want to set a default value, you can pass in null (C#) or nothing (VB).

- The second argument specifies a *Value Changed Callback Method*. This is a method that's called each time your dependency property value changes. In this example, OnDurationPropertyChanged is the Value Changed Callback Method. This method contains the logic that updates the values of the hour and minute text boxes.

- The third argument allows you to specify a Coerce Callback Method. This allows you to run some code if a user attempts to set the value of your dependency property to a value that's beyond what you intend your dependency property to store. For example, you could create a method that sets the duration value to 0 if a user attempts to supply a negative value. Your method could also set the duration to a predefined maximum value if the user attempts to supply a value that is too large. The Coerce Callback Method executes before the Value Changed Callback Method.

- The fourth argument allows you to specify a Validation Callback Method. The method that you specify must return a Boolean, and allows you to write code that validates the value the user wants to set. If your method returns false, your dependency property will throw an ArgumentException.

Binding Dependency Properties to the Data Context

You almost have a custom control that you can use. Although you could now compile and use the duration control in your LightSwitch application, you'd need to write code on your LightSwitch screen that calls the SetBinding method, just like the code sample that you saw in Listing 11-1. You'll now improve the duration control so that it binds directly to the associated data item on your LightSwitch screen. This improvement saves you from having to write extra code on your LightSwitch screen every time that you want to use the duration control.

To bind your DurationProperty to the associated data item on your LightSwitch screen, you'll need to bind DurationProperty to the binding path of Value. The problem is that you have to specify the data-binding path in the XAML, but custom Silverlight controls don't allow you to set dependency property values in your XAML markup. The trick to get around this problem is to wrap a parent control around your custom control. This parent control acts as a conduit and exposes the XAML that allows the control to bind to the associated data item on your LightSwitch screen.

To complete the duration control, you'll need to carry out the following steps:

1. Right-click your project in Solution Explorer, and choose the Add ➤ New Item option.

2. When the Add New Item dialog appears, create a new Silverlight User Control and name it DurationEditor.xaml.

3. Drag the DurationEditorInternal control from your toolbox onto your DurationEditor control. If the control doesn't show on your toolbox, try rebuilding your project. Listing 11-7 shows what your XAML looks like.

Listing 11-7. Duration Editor Control

File: ApressControlsVB\DurationEditor.xaml

```
<UserControl
    xmlns="http://schemas.microsoft.com/winfx/2006/xaml/presentation"
    xmlns:x="http://schemas.microsoft.com/winfx/2006/xaml"
    xmlns:d="http://schemas.microsoft.com/expression/blend/2008"
    xmlns:mc="http://schemas.openxmlformats.org/markup-compatibility/2006"
    xmlns:local="clr-namespace:ApressControlsVB"                              ❶
    x:Class="ApressControlsVB.DurationEditor"
    mc:Ignorable="d">
    <Grid x:Name="LayoutRoot" Background="White">
        <local:DurationEditorInternal
            Duration="{Binding Value, Mode=TwoWay}"/>                        ❷
    </Grid>
</UserControl>
```

In the code that's shown, Visual Studio adds the local namespace ❶ when you drag the DurationEditorInternal control onto your screen. If you're re-creating this example by directly retyping the XAML that's shown in this book, you'll need to make sure that you enter the correct class names.

The definition of the DurationEditorInternal control ❷ within the XAML allows you to data-bind the "normal" Duration property by specifying the binding path Value.

You're now ready to build your ApressControls project. Save the output file (ApressControls.DLL) into a location that you can refer to later.

■ **Tip**   Creating a wrapper control provides a simple, declarative way to bind a custom control to the data context. If you prefer not to create two controls, another way to achieve this is to create a custom control that includes a call to SetBinding in its constructor.

Applying the Duration Control on a Screen

Your duration control is now ready for use. To demonstrate it, you'll now add it to a New Data Entry screen that allows engineers to enter timesheet records. To carry out this example, complete the following steps:

1. Create a New Data Entry screen for the TimeTracking table. By default, LightSwitch will name this screen CreateNewTimeTracking.

2. Change the DurationMins data item from Text Box to Custom Control.

3. Open the Properties sheet, and click on the Change link. When the Add Custom Control dialog appears, click on the Browse button and select the ApressControls.DLL file that you built earlier. This allows you to select the DurationEditor control.

You can now run your application. Figure 11-9 shows the result of this screen, both at design time and at runtime.

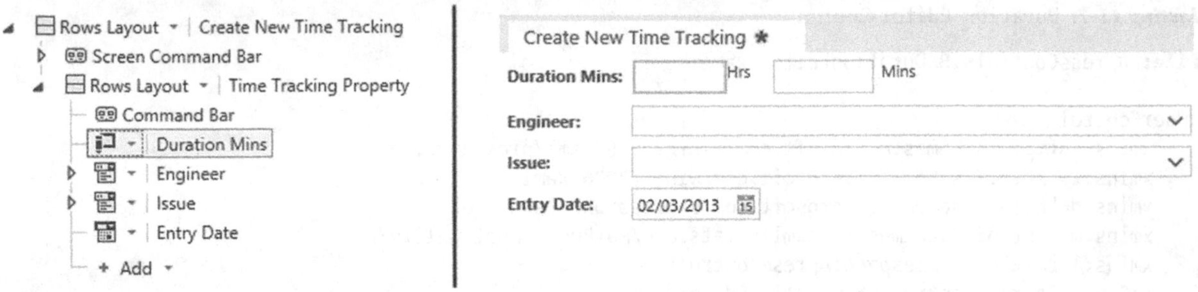

Figure 11-9. *Duration control*

Calling Custom Control Methods via Dependency Properties

Another practical reason for creating dependency properties is to use them as a trigger to call methods in your custom controls. As an example, let's take a look at the WebBrowser control that you'll find in the System.Windows.Controls namespace. As the name suggests, this control allows you to display web pages or HTML content on a screen. It's important to note that this control works only in LightSwitch desktop applications and won't work in browser applications.

The WebBrowser control includes a method called Navigate that allows you to supply a web address. When you call the Navigate method, the WebBrowser control will display the web page that you've specified. If you were to add the WebBrowser control to a LightSwitch screen, how exactly would you call the Navigate method? There isn't a simple way to call custom control methods from a LightSwitch screen, so a practical solution is to wrap the Navigate method in a dependency property. By doing this, you can bind a web address to the WebBrowser control and automatically refresh the page shown on the WebBrowser control whenever the underlying web address changes.

To create the custom web browser control, carry out the following steps:

1. Right-click your ApressControls project in Solution Explorer, and choose the Add ➤ New Item option.

2. When the Add New Item dialog appears, choose Silverlight User Control and name your control WebBrowser.xaml.

3. Amend the XAML for your WebBrowser control as shown in Listing 11-8.

Listing 11-8. WebBroswer Custom Control

File: ApressControlsVB\WebBrowser.xaml

```
<UserControl x:Class="ApressControlsVB.WebBrowser"
    xmlns="http://schemas.microsoft.com/winfx/2006/xaml/presentation"
    xmlns:x="http://schemas.microsoft.com/winfx/2006/xaml"
    xmlns:d="http://schemas.microsoft.com/expression/blend/2008"
    xmlns:mc="http://schemas.openxmlformats.org/markup-compatibility/2006"
    mc:Ignorable="d"
    d:DesignHeight="300" d:DesignWidth="400">

    <Grid x:Name="LayoutRoot" Background="White">
        <WebBrowser  Name="wb" HorizontalAlignment="Stretch"
            VerticalAlignment="Stretch" />
    </Grid>
</UserControl>
```

4. Right-click your XAML file, click on the View Code option, and add the .NET code that's shown in Listing 11-9.

Listing 11-9. WebBrowser Control .NET Code

VB:
File: ApressControlsVB\WebBrowser.xaml.vb

```
Partial Public Class WebBrowser
    Inherits UserControl

    Public Sub New
        InitializeComponent()
    End Sub

    '1 Code that registers the Dependency Property
    Public Shared ReadOnly URIProperty As DependencyProperty =          ❶
        DependencyProperty.Register(
            "uri",
            GetType(Uri),
            GetType(WebBrowser),
            New PropertyMetadata(Nothing, AddressOf OnUriPropertyChanged))

    Public Property uri() As Uri                                        ❷
        Get
            Return DirectCast(GetValue(URIProperty), Uri)
        End Get
        Set(value As Uri)
            SetValue(URIProperty, value)
        End Set
    End Property

    '2 Code that runs when the underlying URL changes
    Private Shared Sub OnUriPropertyChanged(
        re As DependencyObject, e As DependencyPropertyChangedEventArgs)

        If e.NewValue IsNot Nothing Then
            Dim web As WebBrowser =
                DirectCast(re, WebBrowser)
            web.wb.Navigate(DirectCast(e.NewValue, Uri))               ❸
        End If
    End Sub

End Class
```

C#:
File: ApressControlsCS\WebBrowser.xaml.cs

```
using System;
using System.Windows;
using System.Windows.Controls;

namespace ApressControlsCS
{
    public partial class WebBrowser : UserControl
    {
        public WebBrowser()
        {
            InitializeComponent();
        }

        // 1 Code that registers the Dependency Property
        public static readonly DependencyProperty URIProperty =      ❶
            DependencyProperty.Register(
                "uri",
                typeof(Uri),
                typeof(WebBrowser),
                new PropertyMetadata(null, OnUriPropertyChanged));

        public Uri uri                                                ❷
        {
            get { return (Uri)GetValue(URIProperty); }
            set { SetValue(URIProperty, value); }
        }

        // 2 Code that runs when the underlying URL changes
        private static void OnUriPropertyChanged(
            DependencyObject re, DependencyPropertyChangedEventArgs e)
        {

            if (e.NewValue != null)
            {
                WebBrowser web = (WebBrowser)re;
                web.wb.Navigate((Uri)e.NewValue);                     ❸
            }

        }

    }
}
```

Much of the code here is similar to the other samples that you've seen in this chapter. The .NET code includes the same dependency property logic that you saw earlier. The code creates a dependency property called URIProperty ❶, and bases it on a normal .NET property called uri ❷. The dependency property's metadata specifies a Value Callback Method that's called OnUriPropertyChanged. Whenever the underlying web address data changes, the OnUriPropertyChanged method executes and calls the WebBrowser control's Navigate method ❸ to update the web page that's shown in the control.

You're now ready to build and use your custom control. The custom web-browser control provides a useful tool when you're developing desktop applications. Chapter 14 explains how you can use this control to show HTML reports on LightSwitch screens.

Calling Screen Code from a Custom Control

As you might recall from Chapter 1, controls are simply views of the data and contain minimal business logic. In keeping with Model-View-ViewModel (MVVM) principles, it's good practice to place your business logic in screen methods and to call these from your custom controls, rather than placing it directly in the custom control.

In this example, you'll see how to create a stylized Save button. When the user clicks on this button, it calls business logic on your LightSwitch screen rather than logic on the control itself. To create this control, carry out the following steps:

1. Right-click your ApressControls project in Solution Explorer, and choose the Add ➤ New Item option.

2. When the Add New Item dialog appears, choose Silverlight User Control and create a control called SaveControl.xaml.

3. Amend the XAML for your SaveControl control as shown in Listing 11-10. This XAML applies a green style to your control, but you can use the designer to apply a different style.

    Listing 11-10. SaveControl XAML

    File: ApressControlsVB\SaveControl.xaml

    ```
    <UserControl x:Class="ApressControlsVB.SaveControl"
        xmlns="http://schemas.microsoft.com/winfx/2006/xaml/presentation"
        xmlns:x="http://schemas.microsoft.com/winfx/2006/xaml"
        xmlns:d="http://schemas.microsoft.com/expression/blend/2008"
        xmlns:mc="http://schemas.openxmlformats.org/markup-compatibility/2006"
        mc:Ignorable="d"
        d:DesignHeight="300" d:DesignWidth="400">

        <Grid x:Name="LayoutRoot" Background="White">
            <Button Content="Save Data" Height="125" HorizontalAlignment="Left"
                Margin="34,63,0,0"  Name="CustomButton1"
                VerticalAlignment="Top" Width="295" Background="#FF1FC453"
                Click= "CustomButton_Click" />
        </Grid>
    </UserControl>
    ```

4. Right-click your project in Solution Explorer, choose the Add Reference option, and add references to the Microsoft.LightSwitch.Client.dll and Microsoft.LightSwitch.dll files. The default location of these files on a 64-bit machine is C:\Program Files (x86)\Microsoft Visual Studio 11.0\Common7\IDE\LightSwitch\Client.

5. Right-click the contents of your SaveControl.xaml file, click on the View Code option, and add the .NET code that's shown in Listing 11-11.

Listing 11-11. Code to Call a Screen Method Called SaveData

VB:
File: ApressControlsVB\SaveControl.xaml.vb

```vb
Imports Microsoft.LightSwitch.Presentation

Partial Public Class CustomButton
    Inherits UserControl

    Public Sub New()
        InitializeComponent()
    End Sub

    Private Sub CustomButton_Click(
        sender As System.Object, e As System.Windows.RoutedEventArgs)          ❶

        ' Get a reference to the LightSwitch Screen
        Dim objDataContext = DirectCast(Me.DataContext, IContentItem)
        Dim clientScreen = DirectCast(
            objDataContext.Screen, Microsoft.LightSwitch.Client.IScreenObject)  ❷

        Me.CustomButton1.IsEnabled = False                                      ❸

        clientScreen.Details.Dispatcher.BeginInvoke(                            ❹
            Sub()
                Try
                    ' Call the Method on the LightSwitch screen
                    clientScreen.Details.Commands.Item("SaveData").Execute()    ❺
                Finally
                    SetEnabled()
                End Try
            End Sub)

    End Sub

    Private Sub SetEnabled()
        Me.Dispatcher.BeginInvoke(                                             ❻
            Sub()
                Me.CustomButton1.IsEnabled = True
            End Sub
        )
    End Sub

End Class
```

C#:
File: ApressControlsCS\SaveControl.xaml.cs

```csharp
using System.Windows;
using System.Windows.Controls;
using Microsoft.LightSwitch.Presentation;
```

```
namespace ApressControlsCS
{
    public partial class CustomButton : UserControl
    {
        public CustomButton()
        {
            InitializeComponent();
        }

        private void CustomButton_Click(System.Object sender,
            System.Windows.RoutedEventArgs e)                                    ❶
        {
            // Get a reference to the LightSwitch Screen
            var objDataContext = (IContentItem)this.DataContext;

            var clientScreen =
            (Microsoft.LightSwitch.Client.IScreenObject)objDataContext.Screen;   ❷

            this.CustomButton1.IsEnabled = false;                                ❸

            // Call the Method on the LightSwitch screen
            clientScreen.Details.Dispatcher.BeginInvoke(                         ❹
                () =>
                {
                    try
                    {
                        clientScreen.Details.Commands["SaveData"].Execute();     ❺
                    }
                    finally
                    {
                        this.SetEnabled();
                    }
                });
        }

        private void SetEnabled()
        {
            this.Dispatcher.BeginInvoke(() =>                                    ❻
            {
                this.CustomButton1.IsEnabled = true ;
            });
        }
    }
}
```

When a user clicks the custom button, the application executes the CustomButton_Click method ❶. All custom controls data-bind to objects that implement the IContentItem interface. This object allows you to access the control's parent screen via the Screen member ❷. The initial part of this code disables the custom button to prevent users from clicking on it further ❸.

The next block of code calls the method that you've defined on your LightSwitch screen. This could be a long-running data operation, so you'll need to execute this code on the screen's logic thread ❹. This prevents the process from locking up the UI and leaving your application unresponsive. The next line of code accesses a screen command called SaveData via the screen's `Details.Commands` collection, and runs the command by calling its Execute method ❺. If the command succeeds, the code in the `finally` block re-enables the custom button by calling a method called SetEnabled.

The code in the SetEnabled method needs to be invoked on the UI thread because it performs logic that modifies the UI ❻. You can now build your project.

To show you how to use this control on a screen, let's add it to the timesheet screen that you created earlier (as shown in Figure 11-9). To do this, you'll need to carry out the following steps:

1. Open the CreateNewTimeTracking screen that you created earlier in this chapter. (See Figure 11-9.)

2. Click on the Add Data Item button, and create new method called SaveData.

3. Click on the Add Data Item button, create a local property of data type String, and name it SaveDataButton. Uncheck the Is Required check box.

4. Add SaveDataButton to your screen, and change the control type from Text Box to Custom Control.

5. In the Properties sheet, click on the Change link. When the Add Custom Control dialog appears, click on the Browse button and select your `ApressControls.DLL` file. After you do this, choose the `CustomButton` control. Set the Label Style value for the data item to Collapsed. Figure 11-10 shows how your screen now looks.

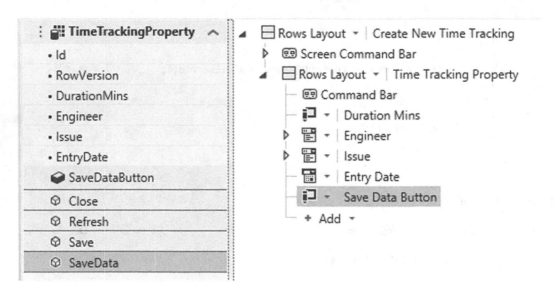

Figure 11-10. *Custom button screen in design view*

6. Right-click the SaveData method in the Screen Member list, and click on the Edit Execute Method option. Now enter the code shown in Listing 11-12.

Listing 11-12. Screen Code Called by the Custom Button

VB:
File: HelpDeskVB\Client\UserCode\CreateNewTimeTracking.vb

```
Private Sub SaveData_Execute()
    Me.Save()
    ShowMessageBox("Data Saved")
End Sub
```

C#:
File: HelpDeskCS\Client\UserCode\CreateNewTimeTracking.cs

```
partial void SaveData_Execute()
{
    this.Save();
    //Add additional screen logic here
    this.ShowMessageBox("Data Saved");
}
```

Note that the screen method that you want to call must be added using the Add Data Item dialog box in the screen designer, as described in step 2. If you directly create a method in your code file, your custom control won't find the method in the screen's Details.Commands collection and your code won't work. The name of the method shown in Listing 11-12 is SaveData_Execute. But when you access commands via the screen's Details.Commands collection, you would refer to the method without the _Execute suffix (as shown in Listing 11-11 ❺)

You can now run your application. Figure 11-11 shows how your screen looks at runtime. In case you're reading the 'black and white' print version of this book, Figure 11-11 illustrates how the Save button includes a bright green background color.

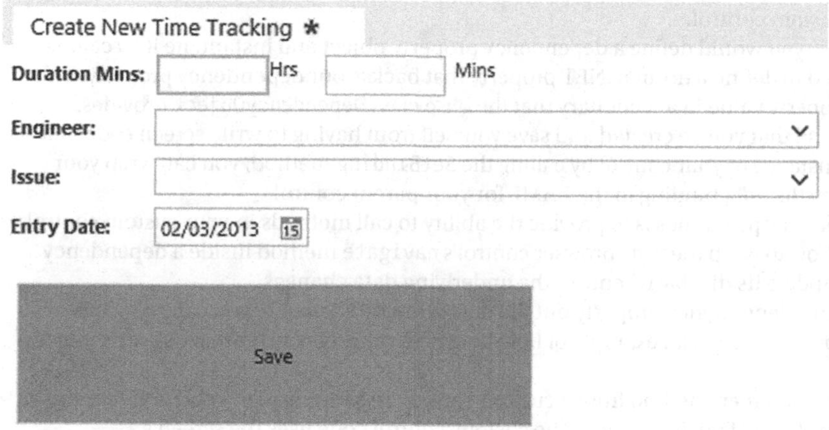

Figure 11-11. *Custom button control*

The custom control that we've created contains just a button, and the example is designed to show you how to call screen code from a custom control. More complex custom controls might feature multiple UI elements, and a button (or some other event) that calls screen code would make up part of the custom control. In this example, you'll notice how you've bound this control to local string property. In Chapter 12, you'll learn how to adapt this code sample to enable you to bind directly to your screen command.

■ **Tip**   In this example, we've hard-coded the name of the command (SaveData) into our custom control. You can make this example more reusable by passing the command name into the custom control rather than hard-coding it. Using the techniques that you've learned in this chapter, you could do this by creating a dependency property. By doing this, you can use the data-binding mechanisms that you've seen to bind your custom control to the command object names in LightSwitch.

Summary

In Rich Client applications, you can customize the way that users enter and view data by using custom Silverlight controls. This means that you're not just limited to using the standard set of controls that LightSwitch provides. For example, you could write your own controls to show data by using charts, Slider controls, or other more-sophisticated input-entry controls.

One of the simplest ways to enrich your application is to use the controls in the System.Windows.Controls namespace. The controls that you can use from this namespace include the combo box, password, and web browser controls. To apply a custom control to a data item on your screen, use the data item's drop-down box and set the control type to Custom Control. If you apply a control directly from the System.Windows.Controls namespace, you'll need to write code that binds your control to data by using the FindControl method and calling the SetBinding method on the IContentItem object that FindControl returns. This method requires you to supply a dependency property and a binding path. To bind a dependency property to the value that's stored by the data item, you would use the binding path of Value. Other binding path expressions enable you to bind your control to other entities, properties, or local screen properties.

If you want to bind screen data to a property on a custom control, that property must be a dependency property. Unlike normal properties, dependency properties don't hold a concrete value. .NET derives their values from multiple sources, and the benefit of this is that it enables your application to use memory more efficiently.

If you're creating your own custom control, you'll need to create a dependency property if you want to consume LightSwitch data from within your custom control.

To create a dependency property, you would define a dependency property object and instantiate it by calling the Register method. You'll also need to define a normal .NET property that backs your dependency property. This property stores your dependency property value in a dictionary that the base class DependencyObject provides.

If you want to use a custom control that you've created and save yourself from having to write screen code that performs the data binding for each instance of your control by calling the SetBinding method, you can wrap your control in a parent control and specify the data binding in the XAML for your parent control.

Another reason for using dependency properties is to provide the ability to call methods in your custom control. As a demonstration of this, you saw how to wrap the web-browser control's navigate method inside a dependency property. This allows the control to update its display whenever the underlying data changes.

If you want to bind a data item to a dependency property but the data types don't match, you can solve this problem by writing a value converter. You've seen an example of how to write a value converter that converts integers to doubles, and vice versa.

Finally, you've learned how to call a screen method from a custom control. In keeping with good practice, this allows you to keep your custom control free of business logic. The custom-control code uses the screen's Details.Commands collection to find the screen method. After it obtains a reference to the screen method, it can call its execute method to run the screen method.

■ ■ ■

CHAPTER 12

Creating Control Extensions

Custom controls provide a powerful way for you to customize the UI of your Silverlight application. However, a disadvantage is that they can be quite difficult to work with. Each time you want to use a custom control, you need to manually select the DLL that contains your control and write the .NET code that performs the data binding. By investing some time and wrapping your control in an extension, you can avoid all this effort and make it easier to work with your control. But that's not the only advantage. Control extensions allow you to customize your UI in ways that wouldn't be possible with stand-alone custom controls. For example, writing a layout control (like Rows Layout and Columns Layout) is something that you can accomplish only through a custom extension. And another advantage is that you can more easily share controls that are packaged as extensions, and even sell your work to other developers. The topics that you'll cover in this chapter include

- How to set up, build, and deploy extensions

- How to build control extensions and add control attributes

- How to extend the property sheets that appear in Visual Studio's screen designer

This chapter teaches you how to create control extensions and reuses some of the examples that you covered in the preceding chapter. You'll also learn how to allow developers to customize the behavior of your control by adding control attributes.

Using LightSwitch Extensions

To help you understand how LightSwitch extensions work, let's begin by looking at how to use extensions that other people have created. By the end of this chapter, you'll be able to create your own extensions that you can use in your LightSwitch projects.

Installing LightSwitch Extensions

To demonstrate how to install and use extensions, this section shows you how to use a control that was developed by Microsoft: the "Many-to-Many control." This control allows users to view and edit *Many-to-Many* data by using a check-box list control. To use this control, you'll need first to download it from the following web page:

http://code.msdn.microsoft.com/Many-to-Many-Control-for-52cd8c6c

LightSwitch extensions are packaged in Visual Studio Extension files—these are files that end with a VSIX file extension. To install the extension, simply double-click the VSIX file that you've downloaded in Windows Explorer. After the installer finishes, you can manage the extensions that you've installed by using Visual Studio's Extensions And Updates dialog. (You'll find a shortcut to this dialog in Visual Studio's Tools menu.) This dialog allows you to disable or uninstall extensions, as shown in Figure 12-1.

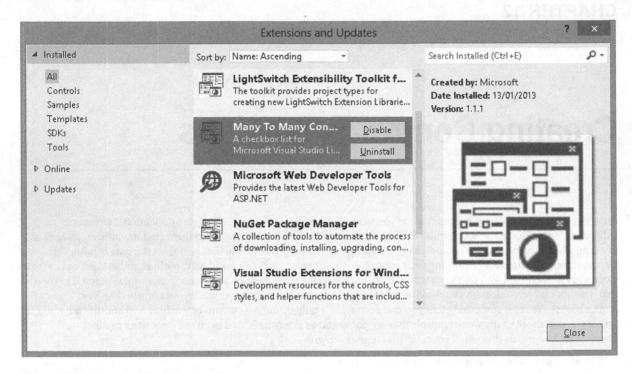

Figure 12-1. Extensions And Updates dialog

To use an extension in your LightSwitch project, you'll need to first enable it in the properties of your LightSwitch project. On the Extensions tab (shown in Figure 12-2), use the check boxes to enable the extensions that you want to use. You can also check the Use In New Projects check box to automatically enable the extension in any new projects that you create. This saves you from having to go to the Extensions tab and manually enable the extension each time you create a new project.

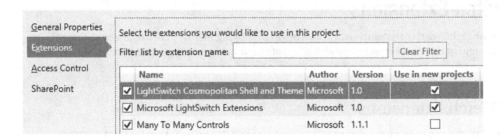

Figure 12-2. Enabling extensions in your LightSwitch project

Using the Many-to-Many Data Control

Once you install the Many-to-Many Control control, you can use it on your screens like any other built-in control. The HelpDesk system allows managers to enter skills and assign those skills to an engineer. To demonstrate this control, here's how to modify the Engineer Details screen to allow managers to assign skills to engineers. To set up your application, you'll need to carry out the following pre-requisites (you may have already completed some of these in earlier chapters):

1. Create the two tables: Skills and EngineerSkills. Create the relationships between these two tables, and also create the relationship between the EngineerSkills and Engineer tables. Refer to Chapter 2 (Figure 2-14) for full details.

2. Create an Editable Grid Screen for the Skills table. This will allow you to enter skill records at runtime.

Once you've set up your tables, you'll need to create an Engineer Details screen (if you haven't done so already). In the Add New Screen dialog, make sure that you've included the EngineerSkills data by checking the Engineer Skills check box in the Additional Data section. If you've already created an Engineer Details screen, you can click on the AddEngineerSkills link that appears inside your Engineer property in the screen member list.

In the screen designer, drag the EngineerSkills collection onto your screen. To lay out your screen more tidily, you can add the collection to a tab, as shown in Figure 12-3. By default, LightSwitch displays the data collection by using a Data Grid. Use the drop-down box to change the control type from a Data Grid to Checkbox List.

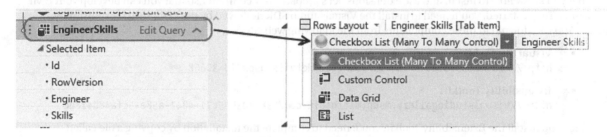

Figure 12-3. Using the Many-to-Many Control

That's all there is to using a custom control extension. You can now run your application. Figure 12-4 shows what the control looks like at runtime.

Figure 12-4. Many-to-Many Control as shown on screen at runtime

```
EXERCISE 12.1 – USING CUSTOM EXTENSIONS
```

Besides the Many-to-Many control, Microsoft has produced several other great extensions. Check out the following two extensions:

- **Filter Control:** This control makes it really simple for you to create a custom search screen:
  http://code.msdn.microsoft.com/Filter-Control-for-eb947bdc

- **Excel Importer:** This extension allows you to add a control to your screen that allows users to import data from an Excel spreadsheet:
  http://code.msdn.microsoft.com/Excel-Importer-for-Visual-61dd4a90

Preparing Your Computer to Develop Extensions

Now that you know how to install and use extensions, let's prepare your computer so that you can develop your own extensions. To get started, you'll need to install the Visual Studio SDK, followed by the LightSwitch Extensibility Toolkit. You can download these components from the following web sites:

- **Visual Studio SDK:**
  http://www.microsoft.com/en-us/download/details.aspx?id=30668

- **Extensibility Toolkit:**
  http://visualstudiogallery.msdn.microsoft.com/2381b03b-5c71-4847-a58e-5cfa48d418dc

Once you install the Extensibility Toolkit, you'll need to complete the installation by copying a file called `Microsoft.LightSwitch.Toolkit.targets` into your MSBuild folder. The Extensibility Toolkit's readme file provides full instructions. After you install both components, Visual Studio's File ➤ New Project dialog will include the C# and VB Extension Library Templates (as shown in Figure 12-5).

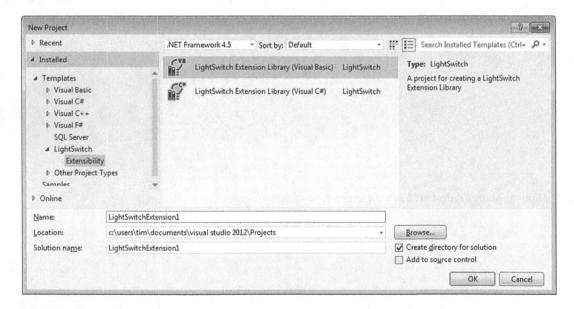

Figure 12-5. *Adding a new Extension Library project*

Once you create an Extension Library Project, you'll find that it contains seven individual projects. The starting point that allows you to extend your library is the LSPKG project. This allows you to create extension items by choosing the right-click Add New Item option (shown in Figure 12-6). This opens the Add New Item dialog, which allows you to create one of the six extension items. You'll use this dialog throughout the next two chapters to create extension items.

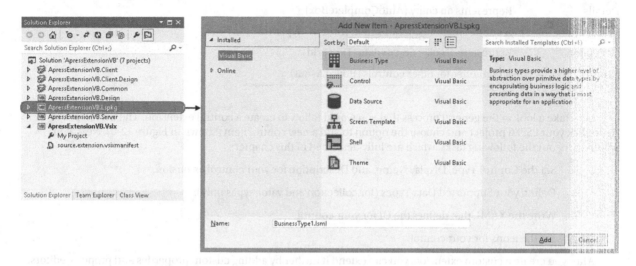

Figure 12-6. *Right-click the LSPKG project to create a new item*

In addition to the LSPKG project, the remaining projects and their purposes are as follows:

- **Client:** This contains the Silverlight custom control XAML and .NET code.

- **Client.Design:** This contains custom code that extends the Silverlight runtime designer.

- **Common:** This contains the lsml metadata that describes your extension and the common .NET code that runs on both the client and server.

- **Design:** This contains custom code that extends the Visual Studio design surface. Custom screen templates are also stored here.

- **Vsix:** This contains the build output that allows users to install your extension.

Understanding Custom Control Types

There are five custom control types that you can create, which are shown in Table 12-1. You'll be familiar with these control types because you'll have used controls that match these control types throughout your day-to-day use of LightSwitch.

Table 12-1. Custom Control Extension Types

Control Type	Purpose and Example Control
Value	Represents a single scalar value (text box, label)
Details	Represents an entity (AutoCompleteBox)
Command	A control that initiates an action (button, hyperlink)
Collection	Represents a collection of data (Datagrid)
Group	A container for other controls (RowsLayout)

Let's take a look at the general process that you would follow to create a control extension. The first step is to right-click your LSPKG project and choose the option to add a new control item (shown in Figure 12-6). Next, you would carry out the following tasks, which are fully described in this chapter:

1. Set the Control Type, Display Name, and Description for your control extension.

2. Define your Supported Data Types (for collection and value types only).

3. Write the XAML that defines the UI for your control.

4. Set the icons for your control.

After you create a custom extension, you can extend it further by adding custom properties and property editors. An example of a custom property is the Show As Link and Target Screen properties that you'll find in Visual Studio's property sheet for the label control. You can also add read only support, handle keyboard navigation, and allow developers to access your control in code.

Creating Value Controls

Value controls allow users to view or edit a single value. In this section, you'll find out how to wrap the duration control from Chapter 11 in a custom control extension. You'll learn how to allow developers to access your control in code and find how to optimize the performance of your control when it's used on a data grid.

To create the Duration Editor control extension, carry out the following steps:

1. Start Visual Studio, create a new Extension Library Project, and name it ApressExtension.

2. Right-click your LSPKG project, create a new Control item, and name it DurationEditor.xaml.

3. Right-click your Client project, select the Add Reference option, and add a reference to the ApressControls.dll assembly that you created in Chapter 11.

4. Modify your DurationEditor.xaml file as shown in Listing 12-1.

Listing 12-1. XAML Markup for a Value Control

File: ApressExtensionVB\ApressExtensionVB.Client\Presentation\Controls\DurationEditor.xaml

```
<UserControl
    x:Class="ApressExtensionVB.Presentation.Controls.DurationEditor"
    xmlns="http://schemas.microsoft.com/winfx/2006/xaml/presentation"
    xmlns:x="http://schemas.microsoft.com/winfx/2006/xaml"
```

```
xmlns:apControls="clr-namespace:ApressControlsVB;
    assembly=ApressControlsVB"                                    ❶
xmlns:converter="clr-namespace:ApressExtensionVB.Presentation.Controls"  ❷
xmlns:slu=
    "clr-namespace:Microsoft.LightSwitch.Utilities.SilverlightUtilities;
        assembly=Microsoft.LightSwitch.Client"
xmlns:framework="clr-namespace:Microsoft.LightSwitch.Presentation.Framework;
    assembly=Microsoft.LightSwitch.Client">                       ❸

    <UserControl.Resources>
        <converter:SplitMinutes x:Key="formatter"/>               ❹
    </UserControl.Resources>

    <framework:StatesControl HorizontalAlignment="Stretch" >      ❺
        <apControls:DurationEditorInternal
        Duration="{Binding Value, Mode=TwoWay}"                    ❻
            HorizontalAlignment="Stretch"
            Name="DurationControl"
            ToolTipService.ToolTip="{Binding Description}" />
    </framework:StatesControl>
</UserControl>
```

After you complete step one, Visual Studio opens your XAML file in the code editor window. The Add New Item dialog creates a custom control that includes a TextBox control. If you're in a hurry and want to skip some of the steps in this section, you can create a control extension that uses a TextBox control rather than the duration control from the ApressControls.dll assembly.

This XAML defines the presentation logic for your custom control and contains the following functionality:

- **Support for the duration control:** This code includes the duration control from Chapter 11, although as mentioned earlier, you can use a TextBox control instead to shortcut this example.

- **State Handling:** LightSwitch can *hook* into your control and show loading and error states. When a user enters invalid data in a screen, LightSwitch displays a red border around your control. This example includes the logic that supports this behavior.

- **Data Grid Optimization:** If you add this control to a data grid, the control appears in read-only mode and becomes active only when the user selects the cell that contains your control.

The first part of this code adds a namespace reference to the ApressControls assembly ❶. This allows you to use the duration control from Chapter 11 in your control extension. The second reference ❷ refers to a value converter that converts integer durations into their hour and minute representations. You'll create the value converter in Listing 12-5 so that, at this moment, Visual Studio will highlight the line as an error. The reference to the Microsoft.LightSwitch.Presentation.Framework assembly ❸ allows LightSwitch's State Handling mechanism to work. Note that namespace references mustn't contain line breaks—we've added these in the book to allow the code to fit the page. For LightSwitch's State Handling to work correctly, you must enclose the contents of your control inside a StatesControl element ❺.

The main part of this control defines an instance of a DurationEditorInternal control. It uses the data-binding path of Value to set the Duration dependency property ❻. Value represents the data context value of your custom control (that is, the value of the data item that your custom control binds to). The code also data binds the tooltip of the Duration Editor control to the description of your data item.

315

The UserControl.Resources tag ❹ defines the value converter that converts integer durations into a format that includes hours and minutes. At the moment, you won't find any XAML in the control that uses this value converter—you'll use this value converter later when you write the code that optimizes your control for data-grid use. You'll also receive an error on this line because it refers to the value converter that you'll create in Listing 12-5.

■ **Note**   The XAML examples in this book feature the VB version of the source code, and the listings refer to the namespace ApressExtensionVB. If you're re-creating these examples in C#, make sure to replace the references that include a VB suffix with the correct name.

Specifying Which Data Types to Support

Value custom controls are designed to work with specific data types and, in our case, the Duration Editor works only with numeric data. The supported data types for a custom control are defined in an LSML file that corresponds with your control. You'll find this file in the Metadata folder of your Common project.

To specify that your control should work only with integer data, open the DurationEditor.lsml file and modify the SupportedDataType element as shown in Listing 12-2 ❶.

Listing 12-2. Specifying Control Data Types

File: ApressExtensionVB\ApressExtensionVB.Common\Metadata\Controls\DurationEditor.lsml

```
<?xml version="1.0" encoding="utf-8" ?>
<ModelFragment
  xmlns="http://schemas.microsoft.com/LightSwitch/2010/xaml/model"
  xmlns:x="http://schemas.microsoft.com/winfx/2006/xaml">
  <Control Name="DurationEditor"
    SupportedContentItemKind="Value"
    DesignerImageResource="ApressExtensionVB.DurationEditor::ControlImage">
    <Control.Attributes>
      <DisplayName Value="DurationEditor" />
    </Control.Attributes>
    <Control.SupportedDataTypes>
      <SupportedDataType DataType=":Int32"/>                    ❶
    </Control.SupportedDataTypes>
  </Control>
</ModelFragment>
```

If you want your control to support additional data types, you can define this by adding additional SupportedDataType elements. The SupportedDataType values that you can use include :String, :Boolean, and :Date . Appendix B shows a full list of valid values that you can use.

Supporting the FindControl Method

Developers should be able to access the underlying Silverlight control in their screen code by calling the IContentItemProxy object's FindControl method. Refer to Chapter 7 if you want to remind yourself how this works.

To add support for the FindControl method, open the code file for your control. (You can do this by opening the DurationEditor.xaml file in the editor, and choosing the right-click View Code option.) Now edit your code by adding the code that's shown in Listing 12-3.

Listing 12-3. Adding Support for the FindControl Method

VB:

File: ApressExtensionVB\ApressExtensionVB.Client\Presentation\Controls\DurationEditor.xaml.vb

```
Partial Public Class DurationEditor
    Inherits UserControl
    Implements IContentVisual                                          ❶

    '1. Implement the Control property
    Public ReadOnly Property Control As Object ↵
        Implements Microsoft.LightSwitch.Presentation.IContentVisual.Control
        Get
            Return Me.DurationControl                                  ❷
        End Get
    End Property

    '2. Implement the Show method
    Public Sub Show() Implements ↵
        Microsoft.LightSwitch.Presentation.IContentVisual.Show
            Throw New NotImplementedException(
                "Show method not implemented")                        ❸
    End Sub

    'the rest of the DurationEditor class appears here...
```

C#:

File: ApressExtensionCS\ApressExtensionCS.Client\Presentation\Controls\DurationEditor.xaml.cs

```
public partial class DurationEditor : UserControl,
    IContentVisual                                                     ❶
{
    //1. Implement the Control property
    object IContentVisual.Control
    {
        get { return this.DurationControl;}                            ❷
    }

    //2. Implement the Show method
    void IContentVisual.Show()
    {
        throw new NotImplementedException(
            "Show method not implemented");                            ❸
    }
}

//the rest of the DurationEditor class appears here...
```

When you first add a control item, the Add New Item dialog creates two classes in your custom control's code file: a class that represents your user control, and a supporting factory class. The code that's shown in Listing 12-3 modifies your user control class so that it implements the IContentVisual interface ❶. The next block of code implements the Control property. This returns a reference to your Silverlight control and, in this example, DurationControl ❷ refers to the name of the `DurationEditorInternal` control that's defined in Listing 12-1. At this moment, Visual Studio will show a warning against the reference to `DurationControl` (if you're using VB). This is because you haven't yet built your project, and you can safely ignore this warning for the time being.

If you were writing a control that contained hidden UI elements (for example, an expander control), the `Show` method ❸ would include code that reveals the hidden content. Because this doesn't apply to this example, the code raises an exception if a developer attempts to call the `Show` method.

Setting the Control Icon

By default, LightSwitch's screen designer would identify your custom control with a green spherical icon (as shown in Figure 12-7). The Extension Toolkit's control template generates a PNG icon file for every custom control that you create and names it after the name of your control.

Figure 12-7. *Default green icon*

To change this icon, replace the `DurationEditor.png` file that you'll find in your `Design` project beneath the following path: `ApressExtensionVB.Design\Resources\ControlImages\`.

Optimizing Controls for Data-grid Use

If you add the control that you've built so far to a Data Grid, LightSwitch creates an editable instance of your control on every row. (See Figure 12-8.) There are three problems with this behavior. First, it doesn't match the default behavior of the standard LightSwitch controls. In Figure 12-8, notice how the grid displays the Entry Date as a read-only piece of text and makes the control editable only when the cell has the focus. The second relates to performance—it isn't efficient to show multiple editable controls on every row in a data grid. And the final problem relates to usability. Each editable control introduces a *tab stop*. If the user isn't using a mouse and attempts to navigate your screen by using the keyboard, the process can be very awkward. Let's suppose that your Data Grid contains 45 records (the default page size), and a user sets the focus to the first row in the grid. To get to the Save button that's shown after the grid, the user would have to press the tab key 90 times! (This assumes of course that unlike you, your user doesn't know how to use the <shift> <tab> key combination to navigate a screen in reverse order.)

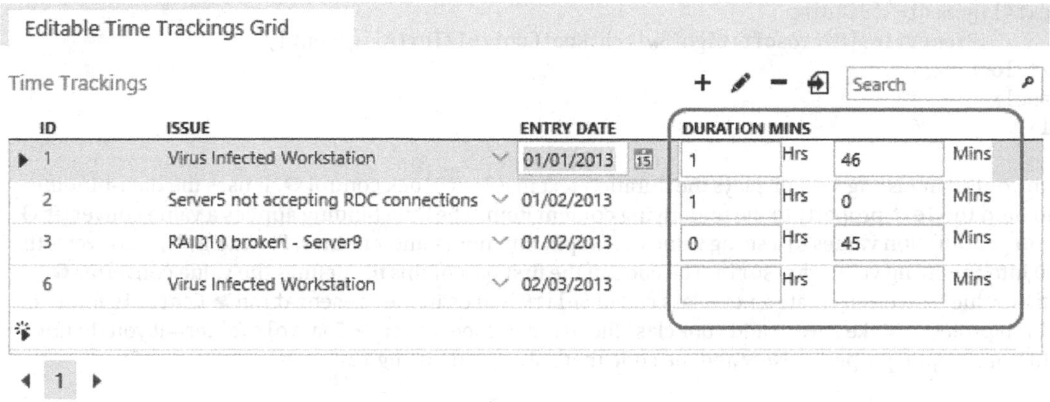

Figure 12-8. *The Duration Editor control is shown as Editable for each row*

Because of these problems, it's a good idea to write custom controls that display only the text value when they're rendered on a data grid. To do this, you'll need to create a display-mode template that contains the XAML that presents your data by using read-only controls. You would do this by modifying the return value of a method called GetDisplayModeDataTemplate, which you'll find in the factory class for your control. To make it simple for you to implement this logic, LightSwitch automatically creates a method stub that identifies where you need to write this code.

Before you write your display-mode template, you need to create a custom Silverlight control that displays your duration data using a Silverlight text-block control. In your Client project, add a new Silverlight User Control in your Presentation ➤ Controls folder and name it DurationViewer.xaml. Now modify the contents of this file, as shown in Listing 12-4.

Listing 12-4. Creating a Display Mode Control

File: ApressExtensionVB\ApressExtensionVB.Client\Presentation\Controls\DurationViewer.xaml

```
<UserControl x:Class="ApressExtensionVB.Presentation.Controls.DurationViewer"
    xmlns="http://schemas.microsoft.com/winfx/2006/xaml/presentation"
    xmlns:x="http://schemas.microsoft.com/winfx/2006/xaml"
    xmlns:d="http://schemas.microsoft.com/expression/blend/2008"
    xmlns:mc="http://schemas.openxmlformats.org/markup-compatibility/2006"
    xmlns:converter="clr-namespace:ApressExtensionVB.Presentation.Controls"
    mc:Ignorable="d"
    d:DesignHeight="300" d:DesignWidth="400">
    <UserControl.Resources>
        <converter:SplitMinutes x:Key="formatter" />                    ❶
    </UserControl.Resources>
    <StackPanel
        Width="{Binding Properties[Microsoft.LightSwitch:RootControl/Width]}"
        Height="{Binding Properties[Microsoft.LightSwitch:RootControl/Height]}"
        VerticalAlignment ="{Binding
            Properties[Microsoft.LightSwitch:RootControl/VerticalAlignment]}">

        <TextBlock                                                       ❷
            Text="{Binding Value, Mode=OneWay,                           ❸
                Converter={StaticResource formatter}}"
```

319

```
            TextAlignment="{Binding
                    Properties[Microsoft.LightSwitch:RootControl/TextAlignment]}">
        </TextBlock>
    </StackPanel>
</UserControl>
```

The custom control in Listing 12-4 displays the duration text in a TextBlock control ❷. It uses the data-binding path of Value to bind the Text property to the underlying content item. The data binding applies a value converter ❸ to convert the integer duration values to a string value that's split into hours and minutes. For example, it converts the integer value 90 into the string value 1hr 30min. The code in the first part of this file defines the value converter ❶.

To create this value converter, create a new class called SplitMinutes in the Presentation ➤ Controls folder of your Presentation project. (Make sure to add your class file to the Presentation ➤ Controls folder—if you do not, your code might not compile properly.) Now add the code that's shown in Listing 12-5.

Listing 12-5. Value Converter That Returns a String Representation of a Time Duration

VB:
File: ApressExtensionVB\ApressExtensionVB.Client\Presentation\Controls\SplitMinutes.vb

```vb
Imports System.Windows.Data
Namespace Presentation.Controls
Public Class SplitMinutes
    Implements IValueConverter

    Public Function Convert(
            value As Object, targetType As System.Type,
            parameter As Object, culture As System.Globalization.CultureInfo
        ) As Object Implements System.Windows.Data.IValueConverter.Convert

        Dim ts As TimeSpan = TimeSpan.FromMinutes(CInt(value))
        Return String.Format(
            "{0}hrs {1}mins", Math.Floor(ts.TotalHours), ts.Minutes)

    End Function

    Public Function ConvertBack(value As Object, targetType As System.Type,
        parameter As Object, culture As System.Globalization.CultureInfo) As ↩
        Object Implements System.Windows.Data.IValueConverter.ConvertBack
            Return Nothing
    End Function

End Class

End Namespace
```

C#:
File: ApressExtensionCS\ApressExtensionCS.Client\Presentation\Controls\SplitMinutes.cs

```csharp
using System;
using System.Windows.Data;
```

```
namespace ApressExtensionCS.Presentation.Controls
{
    public class SplitMinutes : IValueConverter
    {
        public object Convert(object value, Type targetType,
          object parameter, System.Globalization.CultureInfo culture)
        {
            TimeSpan ts = TimeSpan.FromMinutes(int.Parse(value.ToString() ));
            return String.Format(
                "{0}hrs {1}mins", Math.Floor(ts.TotalHours), ts.Minutes);
        }

        public object ConvertBack(object value, Type targetType,
            object parameter, System.Globalization.CultureInfo culture)
        {
            return null;
        }
    }
}
```

This code contains the standard logic that you'd find in a value converter. If you need help in understanding how this code works, Chapter 11 (Listing 11-3) provides further explanation.

Once you've created your DurationViewer control and SplitMinutes value converter, open the code file for your DurationEditor control. Now add the code that's shown in Listing 12-6 to the IControlFactory Members region of your file.

Listing 12-6. Returning a Read-Only Display-Mode Template

VB:
File: ApressExtensionVB\ApressExtensionVB.Client\Presentation\Controls\DurationEditor.xaml.vb

```
#Region "IControlFactory Members"

Private Const DisplayModeControlTemplate As String =                          ❶
"<DataTemplate" & _
  " xmlns=""http://schemas.microsoft.com/winfx/2006/xaml/presentation""" & _
  " xmlns:x=""http://schemas.microsoft.com/winfx/2006/xaml""" & _
  " xmlns:ctl=""clr-namespace:ApressExtensionVB.Presentation.Controls;
                assembly=ApressExtensionVB.Client"">" & _
  "<ctl:DurationViewer/>" & _
  "</DataTemplate>"

Private cachedDisplayDataTemplate As DataTemplate

Public Function GetDisplayModeDataTemplate(                                    ❷
  ByVal contentItem As IContentItem) As DataTemplate Implements ↵
    IControlFactory.GetDisplayModeDataTemplate

    ' provide the display mode template
    If Me.cachedDisplayDataTemplate Is Nothing Then
      Me.cachedDisplayDataTemplate =
        TryCast(XamlReader.Load(
```

```
                    DurationEditorFactory.DisplayModeControlTemplate),
                DataTemplate)
        End If
    Return Me.cachedDisplayDataTemplate

End Function

#End Region
```

C#:
File: ApressExtensionCS\ApressExtensionCS.Client\Presentation\Controls\DurationEditor.xaml.cs

```
#region IControlFactory Members

private const string DisplayModeControlTemplate =                    ❶
"<DataTemplate" +
    @" xmlns=""http://schemas.microsoft.com/winfx/2006/xaml/presentation""" +
    @" xmlns:x=""http://schemas.microsoft.com/winfx/2006/xaml""" +
    @" xmlns:ctl=""clr-namespace:ApressExtensionCS.Presentation.Controls;
                assembly=ApressExtensionCS.Client"">" +
    @"<ctl:DurationViewer/>" +
    @"</DataTemplate>";

private DataTemplate cachedDisplayDataTemplate;

public DataTemplate GetDisplayModeDataTemplate(IContentItem contentItem)    ❷
{
    // provide the display mode template
    if (null == this.cachedDisplayDataTemplate)
    {
        this.cachedDisplayDataTemplate =
            XamlReader.Load(
                DurationEditorFactory.DisplayModeControlTemplate) as DataTemplate;
    }
    return this.cachedDisplayDataTemplate;
}
```

The first part of this code defines a constant variable called DisplayModeControlTemplate ❶. This variable contains the data template that defines the Display Mode content of your custom control. The XAML in this data template presents your data by using the DurationViewer control that you created in Listing 12-4.

In simpler scenarios, you could create a DisplayModeControlTemplate that displays your data by using a TextBlock control and save yourself the effort of creating a custom *viewer* control. In this scenario, however, defining the logic in the DurationViewer control keeps your code more self-contained and allows you to more easily reference value converters.

GetDisplayModeDataTemplate ❷ is the method that LightSwitch uses to obtain the display-mode template. Your code file already includes this method, but by default, it returns a null. The code that you add creates a DataTemplate object based on the content of the DisplayModeControlTemplate variable. To further improve performance, the code caches the DataTemplate in a variable called cachedDisplayDataTemplate.

This completes the DurationEditor control. Figure 12-9 shows how it would look at runtime when you apply it to a data grid. Notice that if a row doesn't have the focus, the data grid shows the duration value by using the DurationViewer control. Otherwise, it uses the editable controls that you defined in your DurationEditor control.

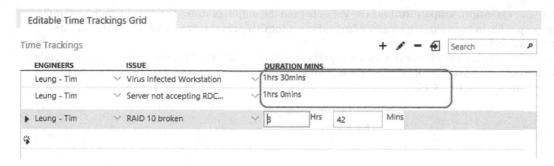

Figure 12-9. *Display-mode template at runtime*

Retrieving Height, Size, and Property Settings

You'll already be familiar with the appearance properties that you can set on LightSwitch controls. These properties include height, size, and alignment values. You can configure your custom controls so that they apply the appearance values that a developer supplies through Visual Studio's property sheet. Listing 12-4 already implements this and uses data binding to apply the settings that the developer supplies. Listing 12-7 highlights the specific code that does this.

Listing 12-7. Binding to Values That the Developer Enters in the Screen Designer

```
<StackPanel
    Width="{Binding Properties[Microsoft.LightSwitch:RootControl/Width]}"          ❶
    Height="{Binding Properties[Microsoft.LightSwitch:RootControl/Height]}"
    VerticalAlignment ="{Binding
        Properties[Microsoft.LightSwitch:RootControl/VerticalAlignment]}">


    <TextBlock
            Text="{Binding Value, Mode=OneWay,
                Converter={StaticResource formatter}}"
            TextAlignment="{Binding                                                 ❷
                Properties[Microsoft.LightSwitch:RootControl/TextAlignment]}">
```

This code data binds the text and vertical alignment settings that the `DurationViewer` control uses. To retrieve the width that the developer enters in the properties sheet, you would use the binding syntax `Properties[Microsoft.LightSwitch:RootControl/Width]` ❶.

`RootControl` refers to the control that every custom control inherits as its top-most base control. `Width` refers to the width value that the developer enters in the properties sheet. The remaining lines of code bind the height and alignment properties by using similar syntax. The code that defines the `TextBlock` control binds the `TextAlignment` setting to the value that the developer enters in the properties sheet, as shown in ❷. You can find a full list of data-binding keys that you can use in Appendix C.

Running and Deploying Your Extension

You've now completed all of the tasks that are needed to create a non-trivial control extension—well done! To run and debug your work, you can simply debug your project in the usual way by pressing F5. This starts an experimental instance of Visual Studio that allows you to create or open an existing LightSwitch application. You can then debug your extension as normal by placing break points in your extension code. If you need to modify the debug settings for this experimental instance, you can do so by opening the properties of your VSIX project and editing the details on the debug tab.

To deploy your extension, simply distribute the VSIX file from the output of your VSIX project. In this example, you'll find the output file in the following location: `ApressExtensionVB\ApressExtensionVB.Vsix\bin\Release\ApressExtensionVB.vsix`.

You can now install your VSIX file as you would any other extension. After you install your extension, remember to enable it in the properties window of your LightSwitch project. You can then use your Duration Editor control on your screens, as shown in Figure 12-10.

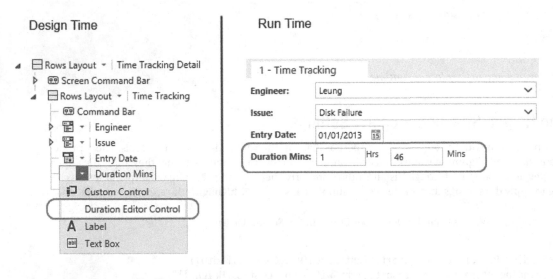

Figure 12-10. *Using the Duration Editor control*

Note that if you created your Duration Editor control in VB, you might need to carry out an additional step before you build your project for the first time. The problem is that the `DurationEditor` and `DurationViewer` controls depend on the `SplitMinutes` value converter class. Visual Studio refuses to build the `DurationEditor` and `DurationViewer` controls if the `SplitMinutes` class hasn't been built beforehand. The way to resolve this problem is to right-click the `DurationEditor.xaml` and `DurationViewer.xaml` files in Solution Explorer and choose the Exclude From Project item. Once you've excluded these two files, build your project. Once you've carried out your initial build (and compiled the `SplitMinutes` class in the process), re-enable the `DurationEditor.xaml` and `DurationViewer.xaml` files by choosing the right-click Include In Project item. You'll now be able to carry on as normal.

Setting Product/Installation Attributes

Your custom extension includes attributes that are shown during the installation of your VSIX file and that also appear in Visual Studio's Extensions And Updates dialog. These attributes include name, version, author, description, license details, icon, and a whole lot of other attributes. You can set these values through a file called `vsixmanifest` that you'll find in your VSIX project. Double-click this file to open the editor, as shown in Figure 12-11.

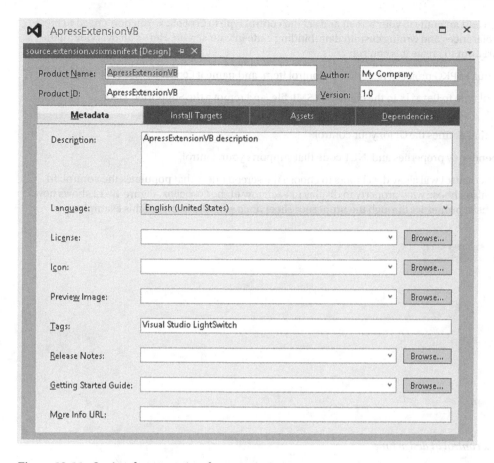

Figure 12-11. Setting the properties of your extension

EXERCISE 13.2 – CREATING A CUSTOM CONTROL

You now know how to create a value custom control, so try wrapping some of the other controls that you saw in Chapter 11 inside a custom control extension. For example, try creating a custom control extension for the PasswordBox or Slider controls.

Creating a Detail Control (ComboBox)

Now that you know how to create a value control and understand the principles of custom control design, let's move on and look at how to create detail controls. Value controls (like the Duration Editor control) are designed to work with single, scalar values. Unlike value controls, detail controls allow users to view and select entities. The best way to describe a detail control is to give an example from the standard controls that ship with LightSwitch. The default detail controls include the AutoCompleteBox and Modal Window Picker controls.

In this section, you'll learn how to create a ComboBox control extension that's based on the ComboBox example that you saw in Chapter 11. As you'll remember, the main benefit of a ComboBox control is that it restricts the values that users can choose (unlike the AutoCompleteBox control). And the advantage of an extension over a custom control is simplicity. It allows you to add an entity to your screen and set the control type to ComboBox. You don't need to mess about with adding DLL references and writing custom data-binding code in your screen. Here's an overview of the tasks that you need to carry out to create this control:

1. Right-click your LSPKG project, create a new Control item, and name it ComboBox.xaml.

2. Set the control type to Details in the control's LSML file, and remove the Supported Data Types setting.

3. Write XAML that defines the UI for your control.

4. Add the dependency properties and .NET code that supports your control.

The custom ComboBox control will allow developers to choose the screen query that populates the control. In addition, developers can also choose what property to display in each row of the ComboBox. Figure 12-12 shows how the developer can enter these properties through the properties sheet once you've completed this example.

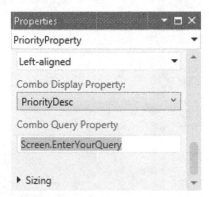

Figure 12-12. ComboBox control at design time

Setting the Control's Metadata

After you've added your ComboBox control item, open its corresponding LSML file (which you'll find in the Common project) and make the modifications that are highlighted in Listing 12-8.

Listing 12-8. LSML Settings for a Details Control

File: ApressExtensionVB\ApressExtensionVB.Common\Metadata\Controls\ComboBox.lsml

```
<?xml version="1.0" encoding="utf-8" ?>
<ModelFragment
  xmlns="http://schemas.microsoft.com/LightSwitch/2010/xaml/model"
  xmlns:x="http://schemas.microsoft.com/winfx/2006/xaml">

  <!--1 Set  SupportedContentItemKind to Details-->
  <Control Name="ComboBox"
    SupportedContentItemKind="Details"                                    ❶
    DesignerImageResource="ApressExtensionVB.ComboBox::ControlImage">
    <Control.Attributes>
      <DisplayName Value="ComboBox" />
    </Control.Attributes>
```

```
<!--2 Remove this block of code                                              ❷
<Control.SupportedDataTypes>
  <SupportedDataType DataType=":String"/>
</Control.SupportedDataTypes>-->

<!-- 3 - Add this block of code-->                                           ❸
<Control.Properties>
   <!-3.1 - Property that defines the display property-->
   <ControlProperty Name="ComboDisplayItemProperty"
                    PropertyType=":String"
                    CategoryName="Appearance"
                    EditorVisibility="PropertySheet">
    <ControlProperty.Attributes>
      <DisplayName Value="Combo Display Property" />
      <Description Value="Enter the Property that's shown on each row" />
    </ControlProperty.Attributes>

    <ControlProperty.DefaultValueSource>
      <ScreenExpressionTree>
        <ConstantExpression ResultType=":String" Value="PriorityDesc"/>
      </ScreenExpressionTree>
    </ControlProperty.DefaultValueSource>
   </ControlProperty>

   <!-3.2 - Property that defines the Query -->
   <ControlProperty Name="ComboQueryProperty"
                    PropertyType=":String"
                    CategoryName="Appearance"
                    EditorVisibility="PropertySheet">
    <ControlProperty.Attributes>
      <DisplayName Value="Combo Query Property" />
      <Description Value="Enter the Screen Query - eg Screen.Priorities" />
    </ControlProperty.Attributes>

    <ControlProperty.DefaultValueSource>
      <ScreenExpressionTree>
        <ConstantExpression ResultType=":String"
            Value="Screen.EnterYourQuery"/>
      </ScreenExpressionTree>
    </ControlProperty.DefaultValueSource>
   </ControlProperty>
  </Control.Properties>

 </Control>
</ModelFragment>
```

The first change that you need to make is to mark the control as a Details control. To do this, set the SupportedContentItemKind attribute to Details ❶. In value-type controls (such as the Duration Editor control), the Control.SupportedDataTypes element allows you to specify the data types that are supported by your control. Because detail controls are designed to work with entities, you'll need to delete the entire Control.SupportedDataTypes XML block ❷.

To create the custom properties that allow developers to enter the screen query and display properties, add the two Control.Property elements that are shown in ❸. Each Control.Property element includes additional attributes that you can set and the purposes of these attributes are shown in Table 12-2.

Table 12-2. *Property Attributes*

Attribute Name	Purpose of Attribute
Name	The name that uniquely identifies your property.
PropertyType	Defines the data type of your property. The list of values that you can use are shown in Appendix B.
CategoryName	Defines the Group where the property will be shown (for example, General, Appearance, Sizing).
Attributes – DisplayName	This defines the label text that's shown next to the data-entry control for your property in Visual Studio's property sheet.
Attributes – Description	This defines the text that appears when a developer hovers the mouse over the data-entry control for your property.

The next step is to define the user interface for your ComboBox control by adding the XAML that's shown in Listing 12-9 to your ComboBox.xaml file.

Listing 12-9. XAML Code for the ComboBox Control

File: ApressExtensionVB\ApressExtensionVB.Client\Presentation\Controls\ComboBox.xaml

```
<UserControl x:Class="ApressExtensionVB.Presentation.Controls.ComboBox"
    xmlns="http://schemas.microsoft.com/winfx/2006/xaml/presentation"
    xmlns:x="http://schemas.microsoft.com/winfx/2006/xaml"
    x:Name="DetailRoot">                                          ❶
    <ComboBox Name="Combo" />                                     ❷
</UserControl>
```

This XAML specifies the namespace DetailRoot ❶. This allows you to simplify your data-binding code later on. The next line of code defines the XAML that represents a System.Windows.Controls.ComboBox control ❷.

The next step is to write the .NET code that supports your custom control. The Extension Toolkit's Control item template automatically creates ComboBox and ComboBoxFactory classes in your Client project. Open your ComboBox control's code file, and modify the code as shown in Listing 12-10. Make sure to add the necessary Imports (VB) or using (C#) statements.

Listing 12-10. ComboBox Code File

VB:
File: ApressExtensionVB\ApressExtensionVB.Client\Presentation\Controls\ComboBox.xaml.vb

```
Imports System
Imports System.ComponentModel.Composition
Imports System.Windows
Imports System.Windows.Controls
Imports System.Windows.Markup
Imports System.Windows.Data
Imports Microsoft.LightSwitch.Presentation
Imports Microsoft.LightSwitch.Model
```

```vb
Partial Public Class ComboBox
    Inherits UserControl
    Implements IContentVisual
```

#Region "1. INITIALIZE CONTROL & RETRIEVE PROPERTY SHEET VALUES"

```vb
    Public Sub New()
        InitializeComponent()

        MyBase.SetBinding(ComboBox.ComboBoxQueryProperty,          ❶
          New Binding(
            "Properties[ApressExtensionVB:ComboBox/ComboQueryProperty]"))

        MyBase.SetBinding(ComboBox.ComboDisplayItemProperty,        ❷
          New Binding(
            "Properties[ApressExtensionVB:ComboBox/ComboDisplayItemProperty]"))

        MyBase.SetBinding(ComboBox.ContentItemProperty, New Binding())

    End Sub
```

#Region "2. DEFINE DEPENDENCY PROPERTIES"

```vb
    Public Property ComboDisplayItem As String
        Get
            Return MyBase.GetValue(ComboBox.ComboDisplayItemProperty)
        End Get
        Set(value As String)
            MyBase.SetValue(ComboBox.ComboDisplayItemProperty, value)
        End Set
    End Property

    Public Shared ReadOnly ComboDisplayItemProperty As DependencyProperty =    ❸
        DependencyProperty.Register(
            "ComboDisplayItem", GetType(String), GetType(ComboBox),
            New PropertyMetadata(AddressOf ComboBox.ComboDisplayItemChanged))

    Public Property ComboBoxQuery As String
        Get
            Return MyBase.GetValue(ComboBox.ComboBoxQueryProperty)
        End Get
        Set(value As String)
            MyBase.SetValue(ComboBox.ComboBoxQueryProperty, value)
        End Set
    End Property

    Public Shared ReadOnly ComboBoxQueryProperty As DependencyProperty =       ❹
        DependencyProperty.Register(
            "ComboBoxQuery", GetType(String), GetType(ComboBox),
            New PropertyMetadata(AddressOf ComboBox.ComboBoxQueryChanged))
    Public Property ContentItem As IContentItem
        Get
            Return MyBase.GetValue(ComboBox.ContentItemProperty)
        End Get
```

```vb
        Set(value As IContentItem)
            MyBase.SetValue(ComboBox.ContentItemProperty, value)
        End Set
    End Property

    Public Shared ReadOnly ContentItemProperty As DependencyProperty =
        DependencyProperty.Register("ContentItem",
            GetType(IContentItem), GetType(ComboBox),
            New PropertyMetadata(AddressOf ComboBox.ComboDisplayItemChanged))

#End Region

#Region "3. HANDLE PROPERTY SHEET CHANGES"

    Private Shared Sub ComboBoxQueryChanged(d As DependencyObject,
      e As DependencyPropertyChangedEventArgs)
            CType(d, ComboBox).SetComboContentDataBinding()
    End Sub

    Private Shared Sub ComboDisplayItemChanged(d As DependencyObject,
      e As DependencyPropertyChangedEventArgs)
            CType(d, ComboBox).SetContentDataBinding()
    End Sub

    Private Sub SetContentDataBinding()                              ❺

        If Not String.IsNullOrEmpty(Me.ComboDisplayItem) Then
            Dim str = "<DataTemplate
             xmlns=""http://schemas.microsoft.com/winfx/2006/xaml/presentation"">
                <TextBlock Text=""{Binding " & Me.ComboDisplayItem &
                 "}"" /> </DataTemplate>"

            Combo.ItemTemplate =
                CType(XamlReader.Load(str), DataTemplate)

            Dim selectedBinding As New Data.Binding("Value")
            selectedBinding.Mode = BindingMode.TwoWay
            Combo.SetBinding(                                        ❻
                System.Windows.Controls.ComboBox.SelectedValueProperty,
                selectedBinding)

        End If

    End Sub

#End Region

#Region "4. SET COMBO DATA SOURCE AND VALUE"

    Private Sub SetComboContentDataBinding()                         ❼
        If Not String.IsNullOrEmpty(Me.ComboBoxQuery) Then
            Dim dataSourceBinding As New Data.Binding(Me.ComboBoxQuery)
```

```
            dataSourceBinding.Mode = BindingMode.OneTime
            Combo.SetBinding(
                System.Windows.Controls.ComboBox.ItemsSourceProperty,
                dataSourceBinding)
        End If
    End Sub

#End Region

End Class
```

C#:
File: ApressExtensionCS\ApressExtensionCS.Client\Presentation\Controls\ComboBox.xaml.cs

```csharp
using System;
using System.ComponentModel.Composition;
using System.Windows;
using System.Windows.Controls;
using System.Windows.Markup;
using System.Windows.Data;
using Microsoft.LightSwitch.Presentation;
using Microsoft.LightSwitch.Model;
using System.Collections.Generic;
using System.Linq;

namespace ApressExtensionCS.Presentation.Controls
{
    public partial class ComboBox : UserControl
    {

        //1 . INITIALIZE CONTROL & RETRIEVE PROPERTY SHEET VALUES
        public ComboBox()
        {
            InitializeComponent();

            this.SetBinding(ComboBox.ComboBoxQueryProperty,                ❶
              new Binding(
               "Properties[ApressExtensionCS:ComboBox/ComboQueryProperty]"));

            this.SetBinding(ComboBox.ComboDisplayItemProperty,             ❷
             new Binding(
              "Properties[ApressExtensionCS:ComboBox/ComboDisplayItemProperty]"));

            this.SetBinding(ComboBox.ContentItemProperty, new Binding());
        }

        //2. DEFINE DEPENDENCY PROPERTIES
        public string ComboDisplayItem
        {
            get { return (string)GetValue(ComboDisplayItemProperty); }
            set { SetValue(ComboDisplayItemProperty, value); }
        }
```

```
    public static readonly DependencyProperty ComboDisplayItemProperty =    ❸
        DependencyProperty.Register("ComboDisplayItem", typeof(string),
            typeof(ComboBox), new PropertyMetadata(ComboDisplayItemChanged));

    public string ComboBoxQuery
    {
        get { return (string)GetValue(ComboBoxQueryProperty); }
        set { SetValue(ComboBoxQueryProperty, value); }
    }

    public static readonly DependencyProperty ComboBoxQueryProperty =       ❹
        DependencyProperty.Register("ComboBoxQuery", typeof(string),
            typeof(ComboBox), new PropertyMetadata(ComboBoxQueryChanged));

    public IContentItem ContentItem
    {
        get { return (IContentItem)GetValue(ContentItemProperty); }
        set { SetValue(ContentItemProperty, value); }
    }

    public static readonly DependencyProperty ContentItemProperty =
        DependencyProperty.Register("ContentItem",
            typeof(IContentItem), typeof(ComboBox),
            new PropertyMetadata(ComboDisplayItemChanged));

//3. HANDLE PROPERTY SHEET CHANGES
    private static void ComboDisplayItemChanged(DependencyObject d,
            DependencyPropertyChangedEventArgs e)
    {
        ((ComboBox)d).SetContentDataBinding();
    }

    private static void ComboBoxQueryChanged(DependencyObject d,
            DependencyPropertyChangedEventArgs e)
    {
        ((ComboBox)d).SetComboContentDataBinding();
    }

//4. SET COMBO DATA SOURCE AND VALUE
    private void SetContentDataBinding()                                     ❺
    {
        if (!String.IsNullOrEmpty(ComboDisplayItem))
        {
            string str = @"<DataTemplate
    xmlns=""http://schemas.microsoft.com/winfx/2006/xaml/presentation"">
    <TextBlock Text=""{Binding " + ComboDisplayItem + @"}"" />
    </DataTemplate>";

            Combo.ItemTemplate = (DataTemplate)XamlReader.Load(str);
```

```
        Binding selectedBinding = new Binding("Value");
        selectedBinding.Mode = BindingMode.TwoWay;
        Combo.SetBinding(                                              ❻
          System.Windows.Controls.ComboBox.SelectedValueProperty,
          selectedBinding);

    }
}

private void SetComboContentDataBinding()                              ❼
{
    if (!string.IsNullOrEmpty(this.ComboBoxQuery))
    {
        Binding dataSourceBinding = new Binding(this.ComboBoxQuery);
        dataSourceBinding.Mode = BindingMode.OneTime;
        Combo.SetBinding(
          System.Windows.Controls.ComboBox.ItemsSourceProperty,
          dataSourceBinding);
    }
}
}
}
```

Although this listing contains a lot of code, you can separate the logic into four distinct sections:

1. Initialization of the control, and the retrieval of property sheet values

2. The definition of dependency properties

3. Code that handles changes when the property sheet values change

4. Code that sets the ComboBox control's selected value and item choices

Let's begin by examining the first two sections. This code relies on the two dependency properties: ComboDisplayItemProperty and ComboBoxQueryProperty. The purpose of these dependency properties is to allow the control to access the *screen query* and display properties that the developer sets in Visual Studio's property sheet. You'll find out how to use the ContentItemProperty dependency property later in this chapter.

You might wonder why it's even necessary to use dependency properties. After all, you could simply retrieve your property sheet values without using any dependency properties, and save yourself a whole load of complexity, as well as reduce the code by about a third. The reason you need to use dependency properties is to support the Silverlight runtime designer. Developers can change the property sheet values at runtime, and dependency properties enable your control to react to the changes that a developer makes at runtime.

Let's take a closer look at these two dependency properties:

- **ComboDisplayItemProperty:** This dependency property stores the Display Item property that the developer sets in Visual Studio's property sheet. The control's constructor defines the binding between this dependency property and the property sheet value ❷. The definition of this dependency property ❸ defines a *value callback* method called ComboDisplayItemChanged. This method calls the SetContentDataBinding ❺ method, which builds the display data template that defines each row in the ComboBox. Building this data template in code rather than statically defining it in XAML allows the control to change the contents at runtime. The next part of the code binds the selected item in the ComboBox to the value of the underlying data item ❻.

- **ComboBoxQueryProperty:** This dependency property stores the Combo Query property that the developer sets in Visual Studio's property sheet. This defines the name of a screen query that populates the ComboBox control's ItemsSource. The control's constructor defines the binding between this dependency property and the property sheet value ❶. The definition of this dependency property ❹ defines a *value callback* method called ComboQueryChanged. This method calls a method called SetComboContentDataBinding ❼ that binds the ItemsSource of the ComboBox to the screen query.

■ **Tip** Your ComboBox control will now compile and run. It's possible to now build and install this extension, but we'll carry on and extend the control further.

Finding the Summary Property for an Entity

When you're writing a details custom control, you might want to implement some functionality that uses the summary property of the entity that's bound to your control. For instance, you might want to know this so that you can show the summary property value on your control.

At present, the screen designer's properties sheet for the ComboBox control allows the developer to enter the display property that's shown in each row of the ComboBox. For example, the developer could enter **Surname**, and the ComboBox would display the surname value in each ComboBox row. You'll now modify your control so that if a developer doesn't supply a display property, the control uses the summary property. The purpose of this example is to teach you how to determine the summary property for an entity, and here's an overview of the steps that you'll carry out to add this feature to your ComboBox control extension:

1. In your custom control code, create a dependency property that binds to the data context of your control. This allows you to access the entity that your custom control binds to, and it allows you to determine its data type. In Listing 12-10, you'll notice that you've already done this by creating a dependency property called ContentItemProperty.

2. Write a method that accepts an entity type as an input and returns the summary property.

3. Modify the UI on your custom control so that it uses the summary property if the developer hasn't supplied a display property through the properties sheet.

Creating a Helper Class

To begin, let's create a helper class to help you with this task. The helper class defines methods that you'll reuse later in this chapter. The helper methods that you'll add to this class are:

- **GetSummaryProperty:** This method returns the summary property for an entity.

- **GetFirstEntityProperty:** The developer might not have defined a summary property for an entity. This method returns the first property.

- **IsTextProperty:** This method accepts a property and returns true if you can represent it as a string. For example, if you pass in a binary property, this method returns false.

- **GetBaseSystemType:** This method supports the IsTextProperty method. It's designed to return the underlying data type of a business type.

- **GetTextPropertiesForEntity:** This method returns a list of text properties for an entity.

To create this class, add a new class called CustomEditorHelper to your Common project and enter the code that's shown in Listing 12-11.

Listing 12-11. CustomEditorHelper

VB:
File: ApressExtensionVB\ApressExtensionVB.Common\CustomEditorHelper.vb

```vb
Imports System.Linq
Imports Microsoft.LightSwitch.Model

Public Module CustomEditorHelper

    ' This method returns the summary property
    Public Function GetSummaryProperty(
        entityType As IEntityType) As IEntityPropertyDefinition

        Dim attribute As ISummaryPropertyAttribute =
            entityType.Attributes.OfType(
                Of ISummaryPropertyAttribute)().FirstOrDefault()

        If attribute IsNot Nothing AndAlso
           attribute.Property IsNot Nothing Then
                Return attribute.Property
        End If

        ' There's no summary property - return the first property
        Return GetFirstEntityProperty(entityType)

    End Function

    Private Function GetFirstEntityProperty(
        entityType As IEntityType) As IEntityPropertyDefinition

        'Simple type properties are non business types/ non navigation properties
        Dim simpleTypeProperties As IEnumerable(Of IEntityPropertyDefinition) =
            entityType.Properties.Where(
                Function(p) TypeOf p.PropertyType Is ISimpleType)

        ' Find the first string property, or the first one that can
        ' be represented as a string
        Dim defaultSummaryProperty As IEntityPropertyDefinition =
            simpleTypeProperties.FirstOrDefault(
                Function(p) GetBaseSystemType(p.PropertyType) Is GetType(String))

        If defaultSummaryProperty Is Nothing Then
            simpleTypeProperties.FirstOrDefault(Function(p) IsTextProperty(p))
        End If

        Return defaultSummaryProperty

    End Function

    ' This returns true if a property can be represented by a string
    Public Function IsTextProperty(
        propertyDefinition As IPropertyDefinition) As Boolean
```

```vb
        Dim dataType As ISimpleType =
            TryCast(propertyDefinition.PropertyType, ISimpleType)
        If dataType IsNot Nothing Then
            Dim clrType As Type = GetBaseSystemType(dataType)
            Return clrType IsNot Nothing AndAlso
                clrType IsNot GetType(Byte())
        End If
        Return False
    End Function


    ' This returns the underlying type of a business type
    Public Function GetBaseSystemType(dataType As ISimpleType) As Type
        While dataType IsNot Nothing
            If TypeOf dataType Is IPrimitiveType Then
                ' Primitive types are foundation LightSwitch data types like:
                    String/Int32/Decimal/Date/...
                Return DirectCast(dataType, IPrimitiveType).ClrType
            ElseIf TypeOf dataType Is INullableType Then
                ' NullableType represents a Nullable version of
                    any primitive or semantic (business) type.
                dataType = DirectCast(dataType, INullableType).UnderlyingType
            ElseIf TypeOf dataType Is ISemanticType Then
                dataType = DirectCast(dataType, ISemanticType).UnderlyingType
            End If
        End While
        Return Nothing
    End Function


    ' This returns a collection of properties for an entity
    Public Function GetTextPropertiesForEntity(
        dataType As IDataType) As IEnumerable(Of IPropertyDefinition)

        If dataType IsNot Nothing Then
            Return dataType.Properties _
                .Where(Function(p) CustomEditorHelper.IsTextProperty(p)) _
                .Cast(Of IPropertyDefinition)()
        End If
        Return Enumerable.Empty(Of IPropertyDefinition)()

    End Function

End Module
```

C#:
File: ApressExtensionCS\ApressExtensionCS.Common\CustomEditorHelper.cs

```csharp
using System;
using System.Linq;
using Microsoft.LightSwitch.Model;
using System.Collections.Generic;
```

```csharp
public static class CustomEditorHelper
{
    // This method returns the summary property
    private static IEntityPropertyDefinition GetSummaryProperty(
        IEntityType entityType)
    {
        ISummaryPropertyAttribute attribute =
            entityType.Attributes.OfType
            <ISummaryPropertyAttribute>().FirstOrDefault();

        if (attribute != null && attribute.Property != null)
        {
            return attribute.Property;
        }

        // There's no summary property - return the first property
        return GetFirstEntityProperty(entityType);
    }

    private static IEntityPropertyDefinition GetFirstEntityProperty(
        IEntityType entityType)
    {
        // Simple types are non business types/ non navigation properties
        IEnumerable<IEntityPropertyDefinition> simpleTypeProperties =
            entityType.Properties.Where(p => p.PropertyType is ISimpleType);

        // Find the first string property, or the first one that can
        // be represented as a string
        IEntityPropertyDefinition defaultSummaryProperty =
            simpleTypeProperties.FirstOrDefault(
                p => CustomEditorHelper.GetBaseSystemType(
                    (ISimpleType)p.PropertyType) == typeof(string)) ??
            simpleTypeProperties.FirstOrDefault(
                p => CustomEditorHelper.IsTextProperty(p));

        return defaultSummaryProperty;
    }

    // This returns true if a property can be represented by a string
    public static bool IsTextProperty(IPropertyDefinition propertyDefinition)
    {
        ISimpleType dataType =
            propertyDefinition.PropertyType as ISimpleType;
        if (dataType != null)
        {
            Type clrType = GetBaseSystemType(dataType);
            return clrType != null &&
                !object.ReferenceEquals(clrType, typeof(byte[]));
        }
        return false;
    }
```

```
// This returns the underlying type of a business type
public static Type GetBaseSystemType(ISimpleType dataType)
{
    while (dataType != null)
    {
        if (dataType is IPrimitiveType)
        {
            // Primitive types are foundation LightSwitch data types like:
            // String/Int32/Decimal/Date/...
            return ((IPrimitiveType)dataType).ClrType;
        }
        else if (dataType is INullableType)
        {
            // NullableType represents a Nullable version of
            // any primitive or semantic (business) type.
            dataType = ((INullableType)dataType).UnderlyingType;
        }
        else if (dataType is ISemanticType)
        {
            dataType = ((ISemanticType)dataType).UnderlyingType;
        }
    }
    return null;
}

// This returns a collection of properties for an entity
public static IEnumerable<IPropertyDefinition>
    GetTextPropertiesForEntity(IDataType dataType)
{
    if (dataType != null)
    {
        return dataType.Properties.Where(
            p => CustomEditorHelper.IsTextProperty(p)
        ).Cast<IPropertyDefinition>();
    }
    return Enumerable.Empty<IPropertyDefinition>();
}
}
```

One of the benefits of a reusable helper class is that you can reuse it in other projects in your LightSwitch Extension library. You created the CustomEditorHelper class in your Common project, and to use the helper class from your Client project (the project where your Silverlight ComboBox control belongs), you'll need to add a link to this class from your Client project.

To do this, right-click your Client project and choose the Add Existing Item option. When the File Browser dialog appears, select the CustomEditorHelper file from your Common project. Expand the drop-down list next to the Add button, and choose Add As Link (as shown in Figure 12-13).

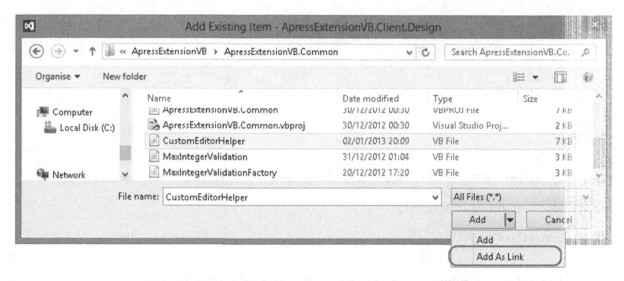

Figure 12-13. *Linking to your CustomEditorHelper class*

The final step is to modify the SetContentDataBinding method in your ComboBox control, as shown in Listing 12-12.

Listing 12-12. ComboBox Control Code

VB:
File: ApressExtensionVB\ApressExtensionVB.Client\Presentation\Controls\ComboBox.xaml.vb

```vb
Private Sub SetContentDataBinding()
    If ContentItem IsNot Nothing Then

        Dim entityType As IEntityType = ContentItem.ResultingDataType

        If entityType IsNot Nothing Then

            Dim displayProperty As String = Me.ComboDisplayItem

            If String.IsNullOrEmpty(displayProperty) Then            ❶
                displayProperty =
                    CustomEditorHelper.GetSummaryProperty(entityType).Name   ❷
            End If

            If Not String.IsNullOrEmpty(displayProperty) Then
                Dim str = "<DataTemplate
 xmlns=""http://schemas.microsoft.com/winfx/2006/xaml/presentation"">
  <TextBlock Text=""{Binding " & displayProperty &
 "}"" /> </DataTemplate>"

                Combo.ItemTemplate =
                    CType(XamlReader.Load(str), DataTemplate)

                Dim selectedBinding As New Data.Binding("Value")
                selectedBinding.Mode = BindingMode.TwoWay
```

```
                    Combo.SetBinding(
                        System.Windows.Controls.ComboBox.SelectedValueProperty,
                        selectedBinding)

                End If
            End If

        End If
    End Sub
```

C#:
File: ApressExtensionCS\ApressExtensionCS.Client\Presentation\Controls\ComboBox.xaml.cs

```
private void SetContentDataBinding()
{
    if (ContentItem != null)
    {

        IEntityType entityType = ContentItem.ResultingDataType as IEntityType;
        if (ContentItem != null)
        {
            string displayProperty = ComboDisplayItem;
            if (string.IsNullOrEmpty(displayProperty))                      ❶
            {
                displayProperty =                                           ❷
                    CustomEditorHelper.GetSummaryProperty(entityType).Name;
            }

            if (!string.IsNullOrEmpty(displayProperty))
            {
                string str = @"<DataTemplate
                        xmlns=""http://schemas.microsoft.com/winfx/2006/xaml/presentation"">
                        <TextBlock Text=""{Binding " +
                    displayProperty + @"}"" /> </DataTemplate>";

                Combo.ItemTemplate = (DataTemplate)XamlReader.Load(str);

                Binding selectedBinding = new Binding("Value");
                selectedBinding.Mode = BindingMode.TwoWay;
                Combo.SetBinding(
                    System.Windows.Controls.ComboBox.SelectedValueProperty,
                    selectedBinding);
            }
        }
    }
}
```

The changes that you've applied to the SetContentDataBinding method in Listing 12-12 (compared to Listing 12-10) are as follows. The code checks whether the developer has specified a display property in Visual Studio's property sheet ❶. If the developer hasn't specified a display property, the code calls your helper class's GetSummaryProperty method ❷ to return the summary property of the entity that's bound to your custom control.

Creating Custom Property Editors

Your ComboBox control is starting to take shape. You've added a feature that allows developers to configure the display property that's shown in each row of the ComboBox. And if your developer hasn't supplied a display property, your control uses the summary property of the underlying entity instead. Although the control works well, there's still room for further improvement. At the moment, developers must use a text box to enter the display property (as shown in Figure 12-14). This method of entering a display property name is difficult because developers have to remember and enter the exact property names. Worst of all, if the developer makes a mistake, your custom control will throw an exception at runtime and break your application.

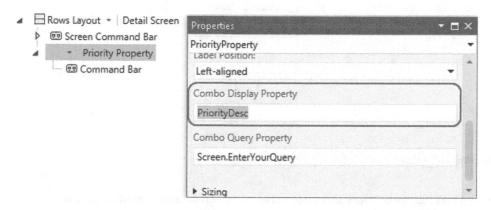

Figure 12-14. *By default, developers must use a text box to alter the display property*

In this section, you'll learn how to customize Visual Studio's properties sheet by modifying the Combo Display Property data entry control so that it uses a drop-down box, instead of a text box. There are two parts to this piece of work. In the first part, you'll customize the Combo Display Property entry control in Visual Studio's property sheet. However, remember that LightSwitch also allows developers to customize controls through the runtime screen designer. So, in part two, you'll learn how to apply the same customization to LightSwitch's Silverlight runtime designer.

Customizing Visual Studio's Property Editor

When Microsoft released Visual Studio 2010, it wanted to demonstrate its confidence in Windows Presentation Foundation (WPF) and, as a result, much of Visual Studio is built with WPF. This includes the *window management system* that includes the toolbars, context menus, and status bar areas of the IDE. Therefore, the method of extending Visual Studio's properties sheet involves building a WPF user control.

As you've seen, the LSML file for your custom control contains the definition for your custom Combo Display Property, along with the definition of any other custom properties that you've created. The LSML file also allows you to specify the control that developers would use to edit your Combo Display Property in the properties sheet. To use a custom editor, you'd specify the name of an *editor class* in your LSML file. (In the example that follows, you'll name your editor class EntityPropertyDropdownEditor.) This is a class that implements an interface called IPropertyValueEditorProvider and provides an implementation of a method called GetEditorTemplate.

Now imagine that you've installed your control extension and have added the ComboBox control to a screen. You're in the screen designer, you've selected an instance of your ComboBox, and you open your properties sheet. At this point, Visual Studio builds the property sheet, and it does this by searching your ComboBox control's LSML file to work out what custom properties there are and what editor control it should use. By using the LSML metadata, Visual Studio finds out that your ComboBox control's Combo Display Property is associated with the EntityPropertyDropdownEditor class. With this knowledge, Visual Studio calls the EntityPropertyDropdownEditor class's GetEditorTemplate method, which returns a WPF control that plugs into Visual Studio's property sheet.

This WPF control contains a ComboBox that displays a list of properties for the underlying entity. The WPF control binds to an object that represents the property value, which is an object that implements the IBindablePropertyEntry interface. Figure 12-15 illustrates the process in the form of a diagram.

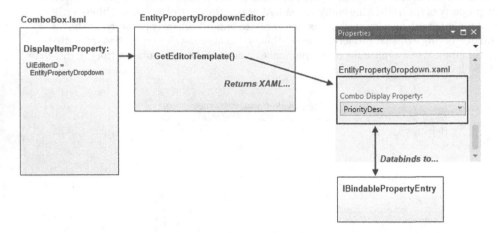

Figure 12-15. *Building the properties sheet*

Now that you understand how this works, here's an overview of how you'd create a custom editor for your ComboBox control's Combo Display Property:

1. Set the target .NET Framework version of your project to version 4.5, and add the required references.

2. Create a link to the CustomEditorHelper class from your Design project.

3. Create the WPF user control that contains the drop-down list of properties.

4. Create a supporting editor class for your control (EntityPropertyDropdownEditor).

5. Add value converters to assist with data binding.

Preparing Your Project

There are a few tasks that you need to carry out before you begin. First, you'll need to set the .NET Framework versions of your LSPKG and Design projects to .NET 4.5. To do this, right-click your project and use the Target Framework drop-down menu that you'll find in the Application tab.

Next, you'll need to add a reference to the Microsoft.LightSwitch.Design.Designer.dll file from your Design project. You'll find this file in Visual Studio's private assembly folder. On a 64-bit computer, the default location of this folder is

```
C:\Program Files (x86)\Microsoft Visual Studio 11.0\Common7\IDE\PrivateAssemblies
```

The code for your custom editor control uses the methods that are in your helper class. Therefore, you'll need to add a link to the CustomEditorHelper class from your Design project, in the same way you did for your Client project.

Creating a Custom Control Editor

Let's begin by creating the WPF editor control that plugs into Visual Studio's property sheet. To do this, create a new folder in your Design project and call it Editors. Create a WPF User Control in this folder, and name it EntityPropertyDropdown. Modify the contents of this file as shown in Listing 12-13.

Listing 12-13. Editor Control XAML

File: ApressExtensionVB\ApressExtensionVB.Design\Editors\EntityPropertyDropdown.xaml

```
<UserControl x:Class="Editors.EntityPropertyDropdown"                          ❶
    xmlns="http://schemas.microsoft.com/winfx/2006/xaml/presentation"
    xmlns:x="http://schemas.microsoft.com/winfx/2006/xaml"
    xmlns:mc="http://schemas.openxmlformats.org/markup-compatibility/2006"
    xmlns:d="http://schemas.microsoft.com/expression/blend/2008"
    mc:Ignorable="d"
    xmlns:e="clr-namespace:ApressExtensionVB.Editors">                          ❷

    <UserControl.Resources>
        <e:GetAllEntityPropertiesConverter
            x:Key="GetAllEntityPropertiesConverter" />
        <e:AppendColonConverter x:Key="AppendColonConverter" />
        <e:EmptyStringToSummaryConverter x:Key="EmptyStringToSummaryConverter" />
    </UserControl.Resources>

    <!--3 Set fonts -->                                                         ❸
    <Grid TextBlock.FontSize="{DynamicResource DesignTimeFontSize}"
        TextBlock.FontFamily="{DynamicResource DesignTimeFontFamily}">
        <Grid.RowDefinitions>
            <RowDefinition Height="Auto" />
            <RowDefinition Height="Auto" />
        </Grid.RowDefinitions>

        <!-- 4  This shows the Property Label -->                               ❹
        <TextBlock x:Name="ComboBoxLabel"
            Text="{Binding Entry.DisplayName, Mode=OneWay,
                Converter={StaticResource AppendColonConverter}}"
            TextWrapping="WrapWithOverflow"
            ToolTip="{Binding Entry.Description, Mode=OneWay}"
            Margin="0,0,0,2"/>

        <!-- 5 This is the ComboBox -->                                         ❺
        <ComboBox x:Name="ComboBox"
            Grid.Row ="1"
            SelectedItem="{Binding Entry.PropertyValue.Value}"
            ItemsSource="{Binding Entry.PropertyValue.ModelItem,
                Mode=OneWay,
                Converter={StaticResource GetAllEntityPropertiesConverter}}">

            <ComboBox.ItemTemplate>
                <DataTemplate>
                    <!-- 6 This shows the ComboBox data items-->                ❻
```

343

```
            <TextBlock Text="{Binding Converter=
                {StaticResource EmptyStringToSummaryConverter}}"/>
        </DataTemplate>
    </ComboBox.ItemTemplate>

    </ComboBox>
</Grid>

</UserControl>
```

In the XAML code, set the parent namespace of your control to `Editors` ❶. Add an XML reference to the `Editors` namespace as shown in ❷. (Make sure to replace `ApressExtensionVB` with the correct namespace for your extension project.)

The initial part of the code ❸ defines the font attributes that the editor control uses. So that your editor control doesn't look out of place, it's important to use fonts that are consistent with the rest of the Visual Studio IDE. `DesignTimeFontSize` and `DesignTimeFontFamily` are design-time public resource items that allow you to reference the font settings that the developer chooses in Visual Studio's Tools ➤ Option menu.

`ComboBoxLabel` ❹ defines the label that shows your property name. In this example, your label would show the text "Combo Display Property." Visual Studio binds your editor control to an `IBindablePropertyEntry` object. `Entry.DisplayName` is the binding path that allows you to show the property name.

`ComboBox` ❺ defines the drop-down box that will show the entity's properties, and the `ComboBox` object's `ItemTemplate` ❻ defines the content that's shown on each row of the `ComboBox`.

This code data binds to the `IBindablePropertyEntry` object with the help of the following three value converters:

- **GetAllEntityPropertiesConverter:** This returns a list of properties for an entity, and its purpose is to fill the `ComboBox`.

- **AppendColonConverter:** This appends a colon to the end of the display name label.

- **EmptyStringToSummaryConverter:** This sets the display text of the empty string that appears at the top of the `ComboBox` to *<Summary >*.

The next step is to create the .NET code for your custom editor control as shown in Listing 12-14.

Listing 12-14. Custom Editor Control Code

VB:
File: ApressExtensionVB\ApressExtensionVB.Design\Editors\EntityPropertyDropdown.xaml.vb

```
Imports System.Windows.Controls
Namespace Editors                                               ❶
    Public Class EntityPropertyDropdown
        Inherits UserControl

        Public Sub New()
            InitializeComponent()
        End Sub

    End Class
End Namespace
```

C#:

File: ApressExtensionCS\ApressExtensionCS.Design\Editors\EntityPropertyDropdown.xaml.cs

```csharp
using System.Windows.Controls;

namespace Editors                                                    ❶
{
    public partial class EntityPropertyDropdown : UserControl
    {
        public EntityPropertyDropdown()
        {
            InitializeComponent();
        }
    }
}
```

The code in Listing 12-14 contains the standard code that you'd find in any user control. The only change that you'd make to this code is to change the namespace to Editors ❶. The next step is to add the code that contains the value converters. To do this, create a new class in your Editors folder called CustomEditorValueConverters, and add the code that's shown in Listing 12-15.

Listing 12-15. Value Converter Code

VB:

File: ApressExtensionVB\ApressExtensionVB.Design\Editors\CustomEditorValueConverters.vb

```vb
Imports System
Imports System.Globalization
Imports System.Windows.Data
Imports Microsoft.LightSwitch.Model

Namespace Editors

    ' This appends ':' to the end of the property name label
    Public Class AppendColonConverter
        Implements IValueConverter

        Public Function Convert(value As Object, targetType As System.Type,
            parameter As Object, culture As System.Globalization.CultureInfo)
                As Object Implements System.Windows.Data.IValueConverter.Convert

            If value IsNot Nothing Then
                Return String.Format(CultureInfo.CurrentCulture, "{0}:", value)
            End If
            Return String.Empty

        End Function

        Public Function ConvertBack(value As Object, targetType As System.Type,
            parameter As Object, culture As System.Globalization.CultureInfo)
                As Object Implements System.Windows.Data.IValueConverter.ConvertBack
                Throw New NotSupportedException()
        End Function

    End Class
```

```vb
' This gets a collection of property names for an entity type and the result
' includes an entry that contains an empty string.
' The return value fills the values in the ComboBox.
Public Class GetAllEntityPropertiesConverter
    Implements IValueConverter

    Public Function Convert(value As Object, targetType As System.Type,
        parameter As Object, culture As System.Globalization.CultureInfo) As
            Object Implements System.Windows.Data.IValueConverter.Convert

        Dim textProperties As List(Of String) = New List(Of String)()

        textProperties.Add(String.Empty)

        Dim contentItemDefinition As IContentItemDefinition =
          TryCast(value, IContentItemDefinition)
        If contentItemDefinition IsNot Nothing Then
            Dim entityType As IEntityType =
                TryCast(contentItemDefinition.DataType, IEntityType)
            If entityType IsNot Nothing Then
                For Each p As IPropertyDefinition In
                    CustomEditorHelper.GetTextPropertiesForEntity(entityType)
                        textProperties.Add(p.Name)
                Next
            End If
        End If
        Return textProperties

    End Function

    Public Function ConvertBack(value As Object, targetType As System.Type,
        parameter As Object, culture As System.Globalization.CultureInfo) As
            Object Implements System.Windows.Data.IValueConverter.ConvertBack
            Throw New NotSupportedException()
    End Function

End Class

' If the developer hasn't entered a display name, this converts the display
' text of the empty value to '<Summary>'
Public Class EmptyStringToSummaryConverter
    Implements IValueConverter

    Public Function Convert(value As Object, targetType As System.Type,
        parameter As Object, culture As System.Globalization.CultureInfo) As
            Object Implements System.Windows.Data.IValueConverter.Convert

        If TypeOf value Is String AndAlso
            String.IsNullOrEmpty(DirectCast(value, String)) Then
                Return "<Summary>"
        End If
        Return value

    End Function
```

```vb
        Public Function ConvertBack(value As Object, targetType As System.Type,
            parameter As Object, culture As System.Globalization.CultureInfo) As
                Object Implements System.Windows.Data.IValueConverter.ConvertBack
            Throw New NotSupportedException()
        End Function

    End Class

End Namespace
```

C#:
File: ApressExtensionCS\ApressExtensionCS.Design\Editors\CustomEditorValueConverters.cs

```csharp
using System;
using System.Globalization;
using System.Windows.Data;
using Microsoft.LightSwitch.Model;
using System.Collections.Generic;

namespace ApressExtensionCS.Editors
{
    //This appends ':' to the end of the property name label
    public class AppendColonConverter : IValueConverter
    {
        public object Convert(object value, System.Type targetType,
            object parameter, System.Globalization.CultureInfo culture)
        {
            if (value != null)
            {
                return string.Format(CultureInfo.CurrentCulture, "{0}:", value);
            }
            return string.Empty;
        }

        public object ConvertBack(object value, System.Type targetType,
            object parameter, System.Globalization.CultureInfo culture)
        {
            throw new NotSupportedException();
        }
    }

    // This gets a collection of property names for an entity type and the result
    // includes an entry that contains an empty string.
    // The return value fills the values in the ComboBox.
    public class GetAllEntityPropertiesConverter : IValueConverter
    {
        public object Convert(object value, System.Type targetType,
            object parameter, System.Globalization.CultureInfo culture)
        {
            List<string> textProperties = new List<string>();

            textProperties.Add(string.Empty);
```

```
            IContentItemDefinition contentItemDefinition =
                value as IContentItemDefinition;
            if (contentItemDefinition != null)
            {
                IEntityType entityType =
                    contentItemDefinition.DataType as IEntityType;
                if (entityType != null)
                {
                    foreach (IPropertyDefinition p in
                        CustomEditorHelper.GetTextPropertiesForEntity(entityType))
                    {
                        textProperties.Add(p.Name);
                    }
                }
            }
            return textProperties;
        }

        public object ConvertBack(object value, System.Type targetType,
            object parameter, System.Globalization.CultureInfo culture)
        {
            throw new NotSupportedException();
        }
    }

    // If the developer hasn't entered a display name, this converts the display
    // text of the empty value to '<Summary>'
    public class EmptyStringToSummaryConverter : IValueConverter
    {
        public object Convert(object value, System.Type targetType,
            object parameter, System.Globalization.CultureInfo culture)
        {
            if (value is string && string.IsNullOrEmpty((string)value))
            {
                return "<Summary>";
            }
            return value;
        }
        public object ConvertBack(object value, System.Type targetType,
            object parameter, System.Globalization.CultureInfo culture)
        {
            throw new NotSupportedException();
        }
    }
}
```

The next step is to create the class that returns your WPF user control to Visual Studio. In the Editors folder of your Design project, create the EntityPropertyDropdownEditorProvider class, and add the code that's shown in Listing 12-16.

Listing 12-16. EntityPropertyDropdownEditorProvider Class

VB:
File: ApressExtensionVB\ApressExtensionVB.Design\Editors\
        EntityPropertyDropdownEditorProvider.vb

```vb
Imports System.ComponentModel.Composition
Imports System.Windows
Imports System.Windows.Markup
Imports Microsoft.LightSwitch.Designers.PropertyPages
Imports Microsoft.LightSwitch.Designers.PropertyPages.UI

Namespace ApressExtensionVB.Editors

    <Export(GetType(IPropertyValueEditorProvider))>
    <PropertyValueEditorName("EntityPropertyDropdown")>          ❷
    <PropertyValueEditorType("System.String")>
    Public Class EntityPropertyDropdownEditorProvider            ❶
        Implements IPropertyValueEditorProvider

        Public Function GetEditor(entry As IPropertyEntry) As
            IPropertyValueEditor Implements IPropertyValueEditorProvider.GetEditor
            Return New Editor()
        End Function

        Private Class Editor
            Implements IPropertyValueEditor

            ' The screen designer calls this method to create the UI control on
            ' the property sheet. Note that you should define the
            ' GetEditorTemplate and Context declarations in a single line.
            Public Function GetEditorTemplate(entry As IPropertyEntry) As     ❸
                System.Windows.DataTemplate Implements
                 IPropertyValueEditor.GetEditorTemplate
                  Return XamlReader.Parse(
                     EntityPropertyDropdownEditorProvider.ControlTemplate)
            End Function

            Public ReadOnly Property Context As Object Implements            ❹
                IPropertyValueEditor.Context
                  Get
                      Return Nothing
                  End Get
            End Property

        End Class

#Region "Constants"
        Private Const ControlTemplate As String =                           ❺
            "<DataTemplate" +
        " xmlns=""http://schemas.microsoft.com/winfx/2006/xaml/presentation""" +
        " xmlns:x=""http://schemas.microsoft.com/winfx/2006/xaml""" +
        " xmlns:editors=""clr-namespace:ApressExtensionVB.Editors;
```

```
                assembly=ApressExtensionVB.Design"">" +
         "    <editors:EntityPropertyDropdown/>" +
         "</DataTemplate>"
#End Region

    End Class

End Namespace
```

C#:
File: ApressExtensionCS\ApressExtensionCS.Design\Editors\
        EntityPropertyDropdownEditorProvider.cs

```csharp
using System.ComponentModel.Composition;
using System.Windows;
using System.Windows.Markup;
using Microsoft.LightSwitch.Designers.PropertyPages;
using Microsoft.LightSwitch.Designers.PropertyPages.UI;

namespace ApressExtensionCS.Editors
{

    [Export(typeof(IPropertyValueEditorProvider))]
    [PropertyValueEditorName("EntityPropertyDropdown")]                  ❷
    [PropertyValueEditorType("System.String")]
    public class EntityPropertyDropdownEditorProvider                    ❶
        : IPropertyValueEditorProvider
    {
        public IPropertyValueEditor GetEditor(IPropertyEntry entry)
        {
            return new Editor();
        }

        private class Editor : IPropertyValueEditor
        {
            // The screen designer calls this method to create the UI control on
            //  the property sheet.

            public DataTemplate GetEditorTemplate(IPropertyEntry entry)  ❸
            {
                return XamlReader.Parse(ControlTemplate) as DataTemplate;
            }

            public object Context                                        ❹
            {
                get
                {
                    return null;
                }
            }
        }
    }
```

```
    #region Constants

    private const string ControlTemplate =                              ⑤
        "<DataTemplate" +
        " xmlns=\"http://schemas.microsoft.com/winfx/2006/xaml/presentation\"" +
        " xmlns:x=\"http://schemas.microsoft.com/winfx/2006/xaml\"" +
        " xmlns:editors=\"clr-namespace: Editors;assembly=ApressExtensionCS.Design\">" +
        "   <editors:EntityPropertyDropdown/>" +
        "</DataTemplate>";

    #endregion
  }
}
```

EntityPropertyDropdownEditorProvider ❶ is the component that allows Visual Studio to create a custom property editor. Make a note of the PropertyValueEditorName ❷ attribute that you specify here. This is the unique "key" that associates this component with your custom property.

When Visual Studio builds the property sheet for your custom control, it calls the GetEditorTemplate method ❸ to generate the UI for your custom property. This method returns the contents of the ControlTemplate variable ❺, a string constant that defines the XAML for the WPF control (EntityPropertyDropdown) that you defined in Listing 12-13. If you named your WPF control differently, you'll need to amend the contents of the ControlTemplate variable to take account of this. It's important that you get this correct because if you make a mistake, Visual Studio will freeze when a developer opens the property sheet for your control.

When you're extending Visual Studio's property sheet, IBindablePropertyEntry's EditorContext member allows you to access an additional Context object ❹. This allows the property editor to store and access additional data. However, the Silverlight runtime designer doesn't support the Context object, so it remains unused in this example. But if you want to find out more, Chapter 13 shows how you can use the Context object to extend the property sheet for the table designer.

Linking Your Property with the Editor

Your WPF editor control is now complete, so the final step is to associate it with your custom control's ComboDisplayItemProperty property. To make this association, open your custom control and edit the UIEditorId attribute as shown in Listing 12-17.

Listing 12-17. Linking Your Property with Your Custom Editor

File: ApressExtensionVB\ApressExtensionVB.Common\Metadata\Controls\ComboBox.lsml

```
<Control.Properties>
    <ControlProperty Name="ComboDisplayItemProperty"
        PropertyType=":String"
        CategoryName="Appearance"
        UIEditorId="EntityPropertyDropdown"                             ❶
        EditorVisibility="PropertySheet">
```

The UIEditorId attribute ❶ allows you to specify the control that Visual Studio uses to present your property. The value that's used here (EntityPropertyDropdown) matches the PropertyValueEditorName value that you defined in your EntityPropertyDropdownEditorProvider class. (See Listing 12-16.) If you omit this attribute, Visual Studio chooses the most suitable property editor for the data type of your property.

You'll find a list of editors that you can use in the `Microsoft.LightSwitch.Designers.PropertyPages.UI.CommonPropertyValueEditorNames` class, and the list below shows some of the choices.

- `BooleanEditor`
- `CheckBoxEditor`
- `CiderStringEditor`
- `CodeCollectionEditor`
- `CodeRuleLinkEditor`
- `CollectionEditor`
- `ColorEditor`
- `DesignerCommandLinkEditor`

Customizing the Runtime Designer

Customizing Visual Studio's property sheet is just one half of the story. Developers can also set property values by using the Silverlight runtime designer, so it's equally important to apply the same customization to this part of your application. Fortunately, the steps that you'll need to carry out are similar to the previous example, and you can also reuse the code that you've already written. You'll carry out all of your work in the `ClientDesign` project. This is the project that allows you to customize the Silverlight runtime designer. Here's an overview of what you'll need to do:

1. Create a link to your `Common` project's `CustomEditorHelper` class from your `ClientDesign` project.

2. Create a link to your `Design` project's `CustomEditorValueConverters` file from your `Design` project.

3. Create a Silverlight user control that contains your custom editor control.

4. Create a supporting editor class that returns your Silverlight editor control to the runtime designer.

Once you've linked to the `CustomEditorHelper` and `CustomEditorValueConverters` classes from your `ClientDesign` project, create a new folder in your `ClientDesign` project called `Editors` and add a Silverlight User Control named `SilverlightEntityPropertyDropdown.xaml`. Now modify the contents of this file, as shown in Listing 12-18.

Listing 12-18. Silverlight Custom Editor Control

VB:
File: ApressExtensionVB\ApressExtensionVB.Client.Design\Editors\
     SilverlightEntityPropertyDropdown.xaml

```
<UserControl x:Class="ApressExtensionVB.Editors.SilverlightEntityPropertyDropdown"
    xmlns="http://schemas.microsoft.com/winfx/2006/xaml/presentation"
    xmlns:x="http://schemas.microsoft.com/winfx/2006/xaml"
    xmlns:d="http://schemas.microsoft.com/expression/blend/2008"
    xmlns:mc="http://schemas.openxmlformats.org/markup-compatibility/2006"
    xmlns:e="clr-namespace:ApressExtensionVB.Editors;
            assembly=ApressExtensionVB.Client.Design"        ❶
    mc:Ignorable="d">
```

```xml
<UserControl.Resources>
    <e:GetAllEntityPropertiesConverter
        x:Key="GetAllEntityPropertiesConverter" />
    <e:AppendColonConverter x:Key="AppendColonConverter" />
    <e:EmptyStringToSummaryConverter x:Key="EmptyStringToSummaryConverter" />
</UserControl.Resources>

<Grid>
    <Grid.RowDefinitions>
        <RowDefinition Height="Auto" />
        <RowDefinition Height="Auto" />
    </Grid.RowDefinitions>

    <!-- 2  This shows the Property Label -->                       ❷
    <TextBlock x:Name="EditorLabel"
        Text="{Binding Path=DisplayName,
        Converter={StaticResource AppendColonConverter}}"/>

    <!-- 3 This is the ComboBox -->                                 ❸
    <ComboBox Margin="0,1,0,0" Grid.Row="1"
        ItemsSource="{Binding Path=PropertyValue.ModelItem,
            Converter={StaticResource GetAllEntityPropertiesConverter}}"
        SelectedItem="{Binding Path=PropertyValue.Value, Mode=TwoWay}"
        AutomationProperties.LabeledBy="{Binding ElementName=EditorLabel}"
        HorizontalAlignment="Stretch">
        <ComboBox.ItemTemplate>
            <DataTemplate>
                <!-- 4 This shows the ComboBox data items-->        ❹
                <TextBlock Text="{Binding
                Converter={StaticResource EmptyStringToSummaryConverter}}" />
            </DataTemplate>
        </ComboBox.ItemTemplate>
    </ComboBox>
</Grid>
</UserControl>
```

When you added a custom editor to Visual Studio's property sheet, you did this by adding a WPF user control. Customizing the runtime designer involves adding a custom Silverlight control instead, and you'll notice that the code in Listing 12-18 looks almost identical to the code in Listing 12-13.

Listing 12-18 defines a custom editor that includes a TextBlock and a ComboBox. Your Silverlight editor control binds to an IPropertyEntry object, and you can reuse the value converters that you created in the previous example. Because you've added a link to the CustomEditorValueConverters, which belongs in your Design project, you'll need to add a namespace reference to this project ❶.

The TextBlock ❷ control shows the custom property's display name and uses the AppendColonConverter value converter to append a colon to the end of the text (for example, ComboBox Display Property:). The ComboBox ❸ uses the GetAllEntityPropertiesConverter to display the valid choices, and uses the data-binding path of PropertyValue.Value to set the selected item. In the markup for your ComboBox, it's very important to specify the ItemsSource property before the SelectedItem property. If you don't do this, your control won't correctly show the selected item.

The next step is to create the .NET code for your Silverlight editor control as shown in Listing 12-19.

Listing 12-19. SilverlightEntityPropertyDropdown Code

VB:
File: ApressExtensionVB\ApressExtensionVB.Client.Design\Editors\
          SilverlightEntityPropertyDropdown.xaml.vb

```
Namespace Editors                                                          ❶
    Partial Public Class SilverlightEntityPropertyDropdown
        Inherits UserControl
        Public Sub New()
            InitializeComponent()
        End Sub
    End Class
End Namespace
```

C#:
File: ApressExtensionCS\ApressExtensionCS.Client.Design\Editors\
          SilverlightEntityPropertyDropdown.xaml.cs

```
using System.Windows;
using System.Windows.Controls;

namespace ApressExtensionCS.Editors                                        ❶
{
    public partial class SilverlightEntityPropertyDropdown : UserControl
    {
        public SilverlightEntityPropertyDropdown()
        {
            InitializeComponent();
        }
    }
}
```

The code in Listing 12-19 contains the Silverlight equivalent of the code from Listing 12-14. Once again, the important point is to set the namespace of the control to Editors ❶. Now create a new code file in the Editors folder of your Client. Design project, and add the SilverlightEntityPropertyDropdownEditor class that's shown in Listing 12-20.

Listing 12-20. SilverlightEntityPropertyDropdownEditor Class

VB:
File: ApressExtensionVB\ApressExtensionVB.Client.Design\Editors\
          SilverlightEntityPropertyDropdownEditor.vb

```
Imports System.ComponentModel.Composition
Imports System.Windows
Imports System.Windows.Markup
Imports Microsoft.LightSwitch.Designers.PropertyPages
Imports Microsoft.LightSwitch.RuntimeEdit

Namespace ApressExtensionVB.Editors

    <Export(GetType(IPropertyValueEditorProvider))>
    <PropertyValueEditorName("EntityPropertyDropdown")>                    ❶
```

```vb
<PropertyValueEditorType("System.String")>
Public Class SilverlightEntityPropertyDropdownEditor
    Implements IPropertyValueEditorProvider

    Public Function GetEditor(entry As IPropertyEntry) As
        IPropertyValueEditor Implements IPropertyValueEditorProvider.GetEditor
            Return New Editor()
    End Function

    Private Class Editor
     Implements IPropertyValueEditor
        Public Function GetEditorTemplate(entry As IPropertyEntry)
            As DataTemplate Implements IPropertyValueEditor.GetEditorTemplate
            Return XamlReader.Load(
                SilverlightEntityPropertyDropdownEditor.ControlTemplate)
        End Function

    End Class

    Private Const ControlTemplate As String =
     "<DataTemplate" +
     " xmlns=""http://schemas.microsoft.com/winfx/2006/xaml/presentation""" +
     " xmlns:x=""http://schemas.microsoft.com/winfx/2006/xaml""" +
     " xmlns:editors=""clr-namespace:ApressExtensionVB.Editors;
         assembly=ApressExtensionVB.Client.Design"">" +
     "       <editors:SilverlightEntityPropertyDropdown/>" +
     "</DataTemplate>"

  End Class
End Namespace
```

C#:
File: ApressExtensionCS\ApressExtensionCS.Client.Design\Editors\
        SilverlightEntityPropertyDropdownEditor.cs

```csharp
using System.ComponentModel.Composition;
using System.Windows;
using System.Windows.Markup;
using Microsoft.LightSwitch.Designers.PropertyPages;
using Microsoft.LightSwitch.RuntimeEdit;

namespace ApressExtensionCS.Editors
{
    [Export(typeof(IPropertyValueEditorProvider))]
    [PropertyValueEditorName("EntityPropertyDropdown")]          ❶
    [PropertyValueEditorType("System.String")]
    public class SilverlightEntityPropertyDropdownEditor
        : IPropertyValueEditorProvider
    {
        public IPropertyValueEditor GetEditor(IPropertyEntry entry)
        {
            return new Editor();
        }
```

```
        private class Editor : IPropertyValueEditor
        {
            public DataTemplate GetEditorTemplate(IPropertyEntry entry)
            {
                return (DataTemplate)XamlReader.Load(ControlTemplate);
            }
        }

        #region Constants

        private const string ControlTemplate =
          "<DataTemplate" +
          " xmlns=\"http://schemas.microsoft.com/winfx/2006/xaml/presentation\"" +
          " xmlns:x=\"http://schemas.microsoft.com/winfx/2006/xaml\"" +
          " xmlns:editors=\"clr-namespace:ApressExtensionCS.Editors;
                assembly=ApressExtensionCS.Client.Design\">" +
          "        <editors:SilverlightEntityPropertyDropdown/>" +
          "</DataTemplate>";

        #endregion
    }
}
```

SilverlightEntityPropertyDropdownEditor is the component that's used by the run-time designer to load your custom editor. Once again, you need to set your PropertyValueEditorName ❶ so that it matches the UIEditor choice that you specified in your LSML file—this setting was shown in Listing 12-17.

This completes the runtime designer example. When you install and run your extension, you'll be able to modify your ComboBox control's display property in the runtime designer, as shown in Figure 12-16.

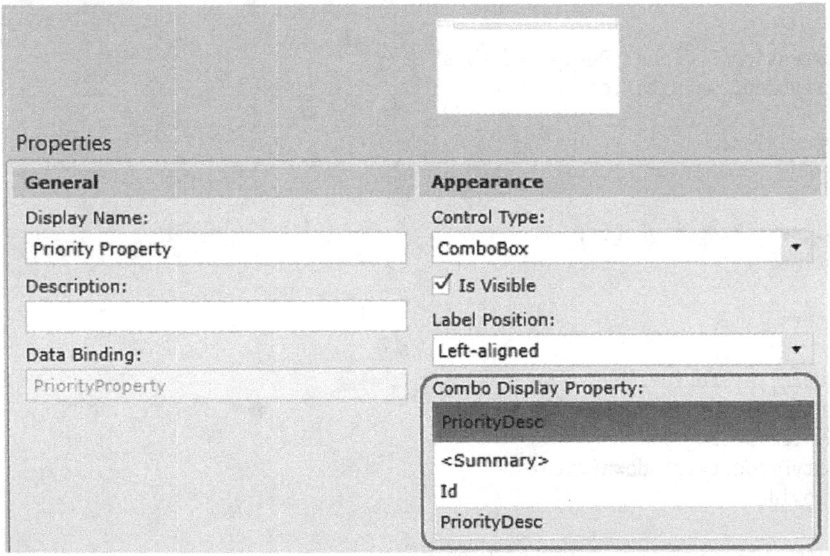

Figure 12-16. *Silverlight runtime designer*

Creating a Group Control Extension

The built-in group controls that you'll find in LightSwitch include Rows Layout and Columns Layout. Group control extensions allow you to create controls that arrange child items in a custom way. You can build a group control only through an extension.

To demonstrate how to create a group control, this section shows you how to create a control that includes a Show/Hide button. When the user clicks on this button, the control toggles the visibility of the data items that are shown inside the control. Here are the steps to create this control:

1. Right-click your LSPKG project, create a new Control item, and name it ToggleControl.xaml.

2. In your Client project, add a reference to the Microsoft.LightSwitch.Client.Internal assembly. The default location of this file on a 64-bit computer is C:\Program Files (x86)\Microsoft Visual Studio 11.0\Common7\IDE\LightSwitch\Client. This reference is needed to support the ContentItemPresenter control that you'll add to your custom control.

3. Modify your ToggleControl.xaml file by adding the contents from Listing 12-21.

Listing 12-21. XAML for ToggleControl Control

File: ApressExtensionVB\ApressExtensionVB.Client\Presentation\Controls\ToggleControl.xaml

```xml
<UserControl
    x:Class="ApressExtensionVB.Presentation.Controls.ToggleControl"
    xmlns="http://schemas.microsoft.com/winfx/2006/xaml/presentation"
    xmlns:framework ="clr-namespace:Microsoft.LightSwitch.Presentation.Framework;
        assembly=Microsoft.LightSwitch.Client"
    xmlns:x="http://schemas.microsoft.com/winfx/2006/xaml">
    <StackPanel>

        <StackPanel  Orientation="Horizontal" >
            <TextBlock Text="{Binding DisplayName}"></TextBlock>          ❶
            <Button Name="ToggleButton" Content="Hide"                   ❷
                Click="ToggleButton_Click"/>
        </StackPanel>

        <StackPanel Name="ContentPanel">                                 ❸
            <!-- ItemsControl binds to the child items of your control-->
            <ItemsControl ItemsSource="{Binding ChildItems}" >

                <!-- This arranges your child items in a rows layout fashion -->
                <ItemsControl.ItemsPanel>                                ❹
                    <ItemsPanelTemplate>
                        <StackPanel Orientation="Vertical" />
                    </ItemsPanelTemplate>
                </ItemsControl.ItemsPanel>

                <!-- ContentItemPresenter chooses the most suitable control
                    for your data item -->
                <ItemsControl.ItemTemplate>
                    <DataTemplate>
```

```
            <framework:ContentItemPresenter                          ❺
                ContentItem="{Binding}"  Margin="4"/>
            </DataTemplate>
          </ItemsControl.ItemTemplate>
        </ItemsControl>
      </StackPanel>
    </StackPanel>
  </UserControl>
```

4. Set the SupportedContentItemKind to Group in your control's LSML file, and remove the Supported Data Types element.

This control consists of two main parts:

- Logic that defines the Show/Hide button
- Logic that arranges the child data items that the developer adds to the control

The first part of the XAML defines a TextBlock control that shows the Display Name ❶. This allows the developer to set a title for the group control, and can help users to identify the purpose of the controls that are shown within the control. The next line of code defines a button called ToggleButton ❷. This button toggles the visibility of a StackPanel called ContentPanel ❸. This panel acts as the parent container for the child items that are shown in the control.

The ContentPanel control contains an ItemsControl. This is a Silverlight control that binds to a data source, and it allows you to customize the appearance of each data item by defining a layout in an ItemTemplate. You'll notice that the ItemsControl defines a data source that specifies a binding string of ChildItems. This is because the underlying IContentitem object that the toggle control (and all other custom group controls) binds to exposes the child data items through a collection called ChildItems.

ItemsControl.ItemsPanel ❹ allows you to define the parent control that contains the ItemsControl. ItemTemplate contents. The ItemsPanelTemplate element contains a StackPanel with its orientation set to vertical. This means that the toggle control displays the child items in Rows Layout style (that is, vertically stacked). If you want to lay out the child items differently, you can use a different layout control here.

The controls that have been described so far define the *framework* for you control. But you still need to define the controls that render your child data items. One way not to do this is to specify a TextBox control in your ItemsControl.ItemTemplate. Although this can work, a TextBox control isn't the best control to display every single data item type. For example, your users won't be impressed if your group control uses a TextBox to display an image. So a much better approach is to use a special control called a ContentItemPresenter ❺. This control renders the most suitable UI control for the bound data item.

The final task is to add the .NET code that toggles the visibility of ContentPanel, and this is shown in Listing 12-22.

Listing 12-22. Group Control Code

VB:
File: ApressExtensionVB\ApressExtensionVB.Client\Presentation\Controls\ToggleControl.xaml.vb

```
Private Sub ToggleButton_Click(sender As Object, e As RoutedEventArgs)
    If ContentPanel.Visibility = Windows.Visibility.Visible Then
        ContentPanel.Visibility = Windows.Visibility.Collapsed
        ToggleButton.Content = "Show"
    Else
        ContentPanel.Visibility = Windows.Visibility.Visible
        ToggleButton.Content = "Hide"
    End If
End Sub
```

C#:
File: ApressExtensionCS\ApressExtensionCS.Client\Presentation\Controls\ToggleControl.xaml.cs

```csharp
private void ToggleButton_Click(object sender, RoutedEventArgs e)
{
    if (ContentPanel.Visibility == Visibility.Visible)
    {
        ContentPanel.Visibility = Visibility.Collapsed;
        ToggleButton.Content = "Show";
    }
    else
    {
        ContentPanel.Visibility = Visibility.Visible;
        ToggleButton.Content = "Hide";
    }
}
```

Setting the Visibility of Labels

By default, LightSwitch displays a label next to any control that you add to a screen. Although this is very useful for controls such as text boxes and labels, you generally don't want labels to appear next to group or custom controls. LightSwitch controls the label settings in the LSML file for your control, as shown in Listing 12-23.

Listing 12-23. LSML Changes

File: ApressExtensionVB\ApressExtensionVB.Common\Metadata\Controls\ToggleControl.lsml

```xml
<?xml version="1.0" encoding="utf-8" ?>
<ModelFragment
  xmlns="http://schemas.microsoft.com/LightSwitch/2010/xaml/model"
  xmlns:x="http://schemas.microsoft.com/winfx/2006/xaml">

  <Control Name="ToggleControl"
    SupportedContentItemKind="Group"                                          ❶
    DesignerImageResource="ApressExtensionVB.ToggleControl::ControlImage"
            AttachedLabelSupport="DisplayedByControl">                        ❷
    <Control.Attributes>
      <DisplayName Value="Toggle Layout" />
    </Control.Attributes>
    <Control.PropertyOverrides>
      <!-- Override AttachedLabelPosition to allow it to be shown on the
           property sheet. -->
      <ControlPropertyOverride                                               ❸
          Property=":RootControl/Properties[AttachedLabelPosition]"
          EditorVisibility="PropertySheet">
      </ControlPropertyOverride>
    </Control.PropertyOverrides>
  </Control>
</ModelFragment>
```

Before you begin to modify the label properties, you should set the `SupportedContentItemKind` attribute to Group ❶ (to identify your custom control as a group control).

LightSwitch determines the label and other property settings by using Property Value Inheritance. The "Creating a Dependency Property" section in Chapter 11 describes how this works. If a developer doesn't set an Attached Label Position, LightSwitch uses the setting that's assigned to the parent control. If an Attached Label Position isn't set at that level, the resolution system carries on searching parent items until it finds a value. The default attached label position of a screen is *left aligned*. Unless a developer manually sets the Attached Label Position, your group control will most likely inherit the default label position of *left aligned*.

To prevent LightSwitch from displaying a label next to your group control, set the `AttachedLabelSupport` setting to `DisplayedByControl` ❷. (The other valid setting is `DisplayedByContainer`.) Although this switches off the label that appears next to your group control, you'll still want labels to appear next to child items that are shown inside your control. To do this, the LSML defines a `ControlPropertyOverride` element ❸ to make certain that Visual Studio includes the Attached Label Position control in the properties sheet for your group control. By allowing developers to set your group control's Attached Label Position, Silverlight's Property Value Inheritance behavior will apply the label position to your group control's child items.

This completes the example, and you can now build and run your extension. Figure 12-17 shows screenshots of the final control at design time, and run time.

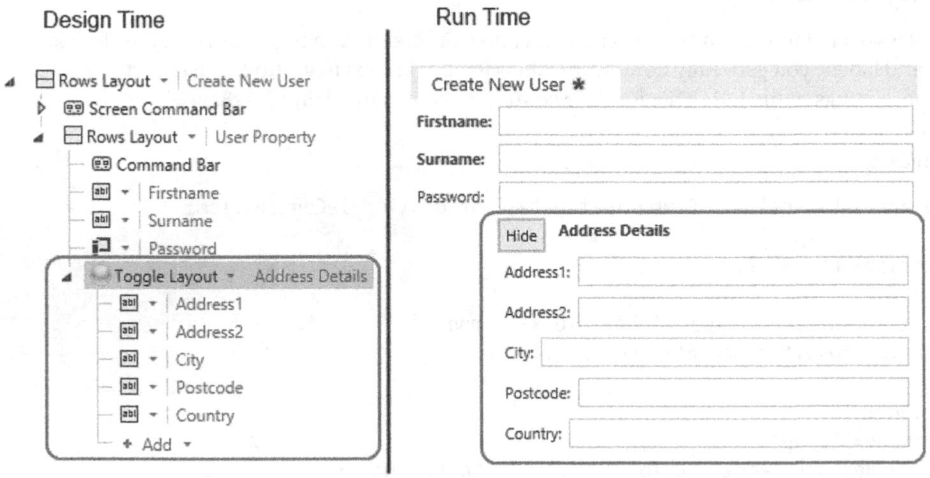

Figure 12-17. *Toggle layout control*

In Figure 12-17, you'll notice that your custom control doesn't left align the address labels, and because of this, the appearance of this control looks a bit jagged. If you don't like this appearance, you can resolve this by creating a Rows Layout beneath your Toggle Layout control and adding your data controls beneath your Rows Layout.

Creating a Command Control Extension

The final control extension that I'll show you in this chapter is a command extension. To demonstrate how to create a command extension, this example shows you how to create a customized button that includes a green background. This control functions in the same way as the custom button that you created in Chapter 11. However, the big advantage of the command extension is that it provides a much better implementation. The custom button in Chapter 11 contains a hard-coded reference to the screen method that the button calls. This imposes a dependency between the custom control and screen, and it results in an approach that isn't very extensible. By creating an extension, developers can data bind your custom button to the underlying screen method. This allows you to implement custom commands in the way that the LightSwitch designers at Microsoft intended it to work.

Here are the steps to carry out this example:

1. Right-click your LSPKG project, create a new Control item, and name it HighlightButton.xaml.

2. Modify your HighlightButton.xaml file by adding the contents from Listing 12-24.

Listing 12-24. Custom Button Code

File: ApressExtensionVB\ApressExtensionVB.Client\Presentation\Controls\HighlightButton.xaml

```
<UserControl x:Class="ApressExtensionVB.Presentation.Controls.HighlightButton"
    xmlns="http://schemas.microsoft.com/winfx/2006/xaml/presentation"
    xmlns:x="http://schemas.microsoft.com/winfx/2006/xaml">

    <Button Content="{Binding DisplayName}" Foreground="White"                    ❶
        Width="{Binding Properties[Microsoft.LightSwitch:RootControl/Width]}"
        Height="{Binding Properties[Microsoft.LightSwitch:RootControl/Height]}"
        MinWidth="{Binding Properties[Microsoft.LightSwitch:RootControl/MinWidth]}"
        MaxWidth="{Binding Properties[Microsoft.LightSwitch:RootControl/MaxWidth]}"
        MinHeight=
            "{Binding Properties[Microsoft.LightSwitch:RootControl/MinHeight]}"
        MaxHeight=
            "{Binding Properties[Microsoft.LightSwitch:RootControl/MaxHeight]}"
        Click="CustomButton_Click" >
        <Button.Template>
            <ControlTemplate TargetType="Button">
                <Border x:Name="Border" CornerRadius="4">
                    <Border.Background>                                            ❷
                        <LinearGradientBrush EndPoint="0.5,1" StartPoint="0.5,0">
                            <GradientStop Color="#FF294008" Offset="0"/>
                            <GradientStop Color="#FF74BB20" Offset="1"/>
                        </LinearGradientBrush>
                    </Border.Background>
                    <ContentPresenter VerticalAlignment="Center"
                        HorizontalAlignment="Center" />
                </Border>
            </ControlTemplate>
        </Button.Template>
    </Button>
</UserControl>
```

3. Set the SupportedContentItemKind to Command in your control's LSML file, remove the Supported Data Types settings, and modify the default label settings.

This XAML defines a normal Silverlight button ❶. This custom control allows the developer to set the dimensions of control by binding the presentation attributes such as Width and Height to the property sheet values. The button template code allows you to specify the look of your control, and defines the gradient green background color ❷. The next step is to add the CustomButton_Click method to your CustomButton class, as shown in Listing 12-25.

Listing 12-25. Custom Button Code

VB:
File: ApressExtensionVB\ApressExtensionVB.Client\Presentation\Controls\
      HighlightButton.xaml.vb

```vb
Private Sub CustomButton_Click(sender As Object, e As RoutedEventArgs)
    Dim cmd As Microsoft.LightSwitch.IExecutable =
        CType(Me.DataContext, IContentItem).Details
    If cmd IsNot Nothing AndAlso cmd.CanExecuteAsync Then
        cmd.ExecuteAsync()                                          ❶
    End If
End Sub
```

C#:
File: ApressExtensionCS\ApressExtensionCS.Client\Presentation\Controls\
      HighlightButton.xaml.cs

```csharp
using Microsoft.LightSwitch;

private void CustomButton_Click(object sender, RoutedEventArgs e)
{
    IExecutable cmd = (IExecutable)((IContentItem)this.DataContext).Details;
    if (cmd != null && cmd.CanExecuteAsync)
    {
        cmd.ExecuteAsync();                                         ❶
    }
}
```

The Details member of the IContentItem object that's bound to your control allows you to access the underlying screen method—this is an object that implements the IExecutable interface. You can simply call the ExecuteAsync method ❶ to asynchronously call the method that's defined on the LightSwitch screen. The next step is to make the necessary changes to your LSML file, as shown in Listing 12-26.

Listing 12-26. Custom Button LSML File

File: ApressExtensionVB\ApressExtensionVB.Common\Metadata\Controls\HighlightButton.lsml

```xml
<?xml version="1.0" encoding="utf-8" ?>
<ModelFragment
  xmlns="http://schemas.microsoft.com/LightSwitch/2010/xaml/model"
  xmlns:x="http://schemas.microsoft.com/winfx/2006/xaml">
  <Control Name="CustomButton"
    SupportedContentItemKind="Command"                              ❶
    DesignerImageResource="ApressExtensionVB.CustomButton::ControlImage"
    AttachedLabelSupport="DisplayedByControl">                      ❷
    <Control.Attributes>
      <DisplayName Value="Highlight Button" />
    </Control.Attributes>
  </Control>
</ModelFragment>
```

This code sets the SupportedContentItemKind to Command ❶ to identify the control as a command control. Just like the preceding group control example, you'll want to hide the default label that LightSwitch displays to the left of your custom button. This is achieved by setting the AttachedLabelSupport attribute to DisplayedByControl ❷.

This completes the custom button control sample. Figure 12-18 shows screenshots of the final control at design time and run time.

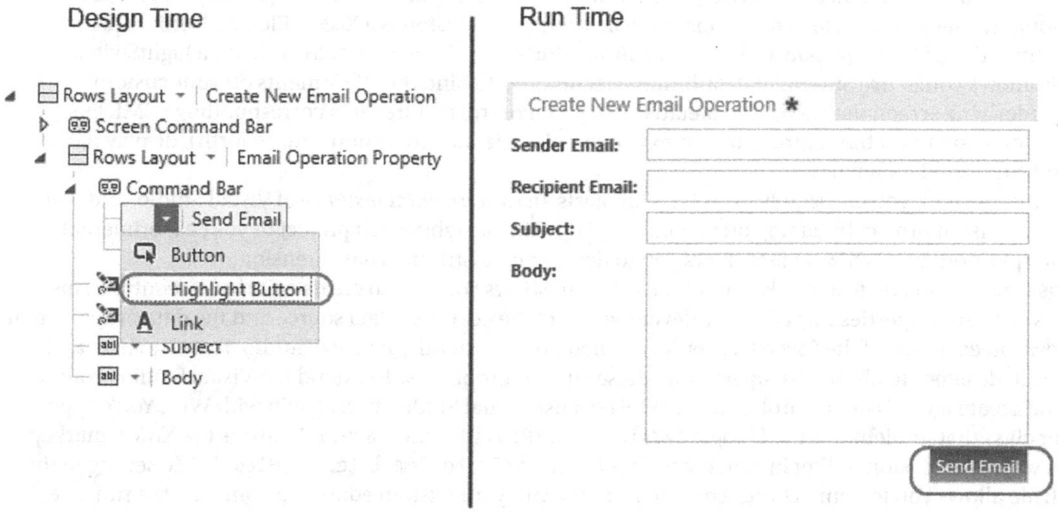

Figure 12-18. *Custom button*

Summary

Extensions are components that can extend the Visual Studio IDE and allow you to add extra capabilities to your Silverlight LightSwitch applications. To use an extension, the first step is to install it in Visual Studio. Extensions are packaged into files with a VSIX extension. To install an extension, simply run the VSIX file. When the installation completes, your extension will appear in Visual Studio's Extensions And Updates dialog. This dialog allows you to manage and uninstall extensions from Visual Studio. Before you can use an extension in a LightSwitch project, you have to first enable it through the properties window of your LightSwitch project. LightSwitch provides six extensibility types: business types, controls, data sources, screen templates, shells, and themes. This chapter concentrated on how to create control extensions, and the next chapter (Chapter 13) shows you how to create the remaining extension types.

Instead of directly using Silverlight controls as I showed you in Chapter 11, developers can more easily work with controls that are installed as an extension. If a developer wants to use a control extension on a LightSwitch screen, there's no need to select the control assembly from a separate dialog and write custom data-binding code. Developers can simply use the data item's drop-down menu to select the custom control and they're done. Another benefit of control extensions is that they support layout controls that can't be implemented in any other way (like RowsLayout and ColumnsLayout). When you're writing a custom control extension, you can create custom properties that developers can set through Visual Studio's properties sheet.

There are five types of control extension that you can create: value, details, command, collection, and group. You'll already be familiar with these control types because you'll have used controls that match these control types in your day-to-day use of LightSwitch. For instance, a value control displays a single value—just like a text box or label. A details control displays an entity—just like an autocomplete box or model window picker.

To create extensions, you need to install the Visual Studio SDK and the Microsoft LightSwitch Extensibility Toolkit. You can download these components free of charge from the Microsoft web site. Once you've set up your computer, you can add an Extension Library Project by using Visual Studio's Add New dialog. An Extension Library Project contains seven individual projects, one of which is an LSPKG project. The LSPKG project allows you to create one of the six extension items.

The first step in creating a control extension is to right-click your LSPKG project and select the New Item option. This creates all of the files that are needed. To complete your control extension, you can simply flesh out these files with the functionality that you want to add. The main file in a control extension is a XAML file (a Silverlight user control) that defines the UI for your control. A custom control binds to an IContentItem object on a LightSwitch screen, and this allows you to use Silverlight data-binding techniques to bind the UI elements on your custom control to the underlying screen data item. The metadata for your control is stored in a corresponding LSML file. This metadata allows you to set the control type (for example, value, details, collection, and so forth), display name, description, and supported data types.

To debug an extension, you can simply press F5. This starts an *experimental instance* of Visual Studio, and you can debug your extension project by adding breakpoints and opening a LightSwitch project in your experimental instance. The output from your VSIX project allows you to deploy and distribute your extension.

To demonstrate how to create a details control, this chapter shows you how to create a ComboBox control. This control includes custom properties that allow the developer to set the ComboBox data source and the data property that the control shows on each row of the ComboBox. You've learned how to extend the Visual Studio property sheet and Silverlight runtime designer to allow developers to set these custom properties. To extend the Visual Studio property sheet, you would create a WPF user control. You use WPF because Visual Studio itself is built with WPF. You'd then create an editor class that implements the IPropertyValueEditorProvider interface and returns the XAML markup that represents your WPF custom editor in a method that's called GetEditorTemplate. The UIEditorId setting in the control's LSML file allows you to connect your custom property with your custom editor. Customizing the runtime designer uses a very similar process, except that you create a Silverlight user control rather than a WPF user control.

This chapter has showed you the code that allows you to access the summary property. You've learned how to encapsulate this code in a helper class and to include logic that returns the first text property, or a property that can be represented as a string if the developer hasn't defined a summary property.

Group control extensions allow you to develop controls that arrange child items in a custom way. You've learned how to build a group control that includes a button to allow the user to toggle the visibility of the items that are shown in the control. The XAML for a group control contains an ItemsControl. This is Silverlight control that allows you to bind to data and to customize the appearance of each data item by defining a layout in an ItemTemplate. The ItemTemplate contains a ContentItemPresenter control. This control allows LightSwitch to render the child data items by using the Silverlight control that most suits the data type of the bound item.

Finally, this chapter has showed you how to create a command control Extension that features a button with a green background. A command control is designed to bind to a LightSwitch screen method. Within your Command Control, you can call the underlying screen method by using the Details member of an IContentItem object that's bound to your control. The Details member exposes an IExecutable object that allows you to run the underlying screen method by calling the IExecutable object's ExecuteAsync method.

■ ■ ■

CHAPTER 13

Creating Data and Presentation Extensions

Now that you understand the principles of how to build an extension project, this chapter focuses on how to build other LightSwitch extension types. In this chapter, you'll learn how to

- Create business type and data source extensions
- Create screen template extensions
- Create shell and theme extensions

In this chapter, you'll learn how to build a business type that stores time durations and incorporates the Duration Editor control that you created in Chapter 12. You'll learn how to *skin* your application with a custom look and feel by creating shell and theme extensions. If you find yourself carrying out repetitive tasks in the screen designer, you can automate your process by creating a custom screen template extension. You'll learn how to create a template that creates screens for both adding and editing data. Finally, you'll learn how to create a data source extension that allows you to connect to the Windows event log.

Creating a Business Type Extension

Business types are special types that are built on top of the basic LightSwitch data types. The business types that come with LightSwitch include phone number, money, and web address. The advantage of creating a business type is that it allows you to build a data type that incorporates validation and custom data entry controls, and it allows you to package it in such a way that you can reuse it in multiple projects and share it with other developers.

To show you how to build a business type, you'll learn how to create a business type that stores time durations. This example reuses the Duration Editor control and includes some additional validation. If a developer creates a table and adds a field that uses the "duration type," the validation allows the developer to specify the maximum duration that users can enter into the field, expressed in days. Here's an overview of the steps that you'll carry out to create this example:

1. Create a new business type, and set the underlying data type.
2. Create and/or associate custom controls with your business type.
3. Create an attribute that stores the maximum duration.
4. Write the validation logic in the Common project.

To begin, right-click your LSPKG project, select "New Item," and create a new business type called DurationType. When you do this, the business type template does two things. First, it creates an LSML file that allows you to define your business type and second, it creates a new custom control for your business type.

Your duration type uses the integer data type as its underlying storage type. This is defined in your business type's lsml file, which you'll find in your Common project. To define the underlying storage type, open the DurationType.lsml file in the Common project, and modify the UnderlyingType setting, as shown in Listing 13-1 ❶.

Listing 13-1. Creating a Business Type

VB:
File: ApressExtensionVB\ApressExtensionVB.Common\Metadata\Types\DurationType.lsml.vb

```
<SemanticType Name="DurationType"
  UnderlyingType=":Int32">                          ❶
  <SemanticType.Attributes>
    <DisplayName Value="Duration Type" />           ❷
  </SemanticType.Attributes>
</SemanticType>
..............

<DefaultViewMapping
  ContentItemKind="Value"
  DataType="DurationType"
  View="DurationTypeControl"/>                       ❸
```

The UnderlyingType values that you can specify include :Int32, :String, and :Double. Appendix B shows a full list of acceptable values that you can use. The DisplayName property ❷ specifies the name that identifies your business type in the table designer. Toward the bottom of your LSML file, you'll find a DefaultViewMapping ❸ element. This allows you to specify the default control that a business type uses to render your data. By default, the template sets this to the custom control that it automatically creates. So, in this case, it sets it to DurationTypeControl.

Although there's still much more functionality that you can add, you've now completed the minimum steps that are needed for a functional business type. If you want to, you can compile and install your extension.

Associating Custom Controls with Business Types

By now, you'll know that LightSwitch associates business types with custom controls. For instance, if you're in the screen designer and add a property that's based on the "phone number" business type, LightSwitch gives you the choice of using the "Phone Number Editor," "Phone Number Viewer," TextBox, or Label controls.

Strictly speaking, you don't configure a business type to work with specific set of controls. The relationship actually works in the other direction—you define custom controls to work with business types by adding data to the custom control's metadata.

When you create a business type, the template generates an associated control that you'll find in your Client project's Controls folder (for example, ApressExtensionVB.Client\Presentation\Controls\DurationTypeControl.xaml). This automatically provides you with a custom control that accompanies your business type.

Because you've already created a duration control, you can save yourself some time by associating it with your business type. The association between custom controls and business types is defined in your custom control's LSML file. To associate the Duration Editor control (discussed in Chapter 12) with your duration business type, open the LSML file for your control. You'll find this file in the Metadata ➤ Controls folder of your Common project. Find the Control.SupportedDataTypes node, add a SupportedDataType element, and set its DataType attribute to DurationType (as shown in Listing 13-2). DurationType refers to the name of your business type, as defined in the LSML file of your business type.

Listing 13-2. Specifying Control Data Types

File: ApressExtensionVB\ApressExtensionVB.Common\Metadata\Controls\DurationEditor.lsml

```
<Control.SupportedDataTypes>
    <SupportedDataType DataType="DurationType"/>
    <SupportedDataType DataType=":Int32"/>
</Control.SupportedDataTypes>
```

The code in Listing 13-2 specifies that the Duration Editor control supports integer and duration data types. You can add additional SupportedDataType entries here if you want your Duration Editor Control to support extra data types.

Enforcing Validation

The big advantage of business type validation is that LightSwitch applies your validation logic, irrespective of the control that you use on your screen. Business type validation runs on both the client and server and therefore, any validation code that you write must be added to your Common project. In this section, you'll create a validation rule that allows developers to specify the maximum duration in days that users can enter.

You can allow developers to control the behavior of your business type by creating attributes that LightSwitch shows in the table designer. Custom attributes are defined in a business type's LSML file, and you'll now create an attribute that allows developers to specify the maximum duration that an instance of your business type can store. Open the LSML file for your business type, and add the parts that are shown in Listing 13-3.

Listing 13-3. Extending the Metadata to Support a Maximum Duration

File: ApressExtensionVB\ApressExtensionVB.Common\Metadata\Types\DurationType.lsml

```
<?xml version="1.0" encoding="utf-8" ?>
<ModelFragment
  xmlns="http://schemas.microsoft.com/LightSwitch/2010/xaml/model"
  xmlns:x="http://schemas.microsoft.com/winfx/2006/xaml">

  <!--1 - Add the AttributeClass Element-->
  <AttributeClass Name="MaxIntegerValidationId">                    ❶
    <AttributeClass.Attributes>
      <Validator />                                                 ❷
      <SupportedType Type="DurationType?" />                        ❸
    </AttributeClass.Attributes>

    <AttributeProperty Name="MaxDays" MetaType="Int32">             ❹
      <AttributeProperty.Attributes>                                ❺
        <Category Value="Validation" />
        <DisplayName Value="Maximum Days" />
        <UIEditor Id="CiderStringEditor"/>
      </AttributeProperty.Attributes>
    </AttributeProperty>
  </AttributeClass>

  <SemanticType Name="DurationType"
    UnderlyingType=":Int32">
    <SemanticType.Attributes>
```

```
            <DisplayName Value="DurationType" />
            <!--2 - Add the Attribute Element-->
            <Attribute Class="@MaxIntegerValidationId">              ❻
               <Property Name="MaxDays" Value="0"/>                  ❼
            </Attribute>
         </SemanticType.Attributes>
      </SemanticType>

      <DefaultViewMapping
         ContentItemKind="Value"
         DataType="DurationType"
         View="DurationTypeControl"/>
</ModelFragment>
```

The code in Listing 13-3 defines two things. It associates validation logic with your business type, and it defines an attribute that allows developers to specify the maximum duration that an instance of your business type can store. Let's now look at this code in more detail.

Associating Validation Logic with a Business Type

To associate your business type with validation logic, there are two tasks that you need to carry out in your LSML file. The first is to define an AttributeClass, and the second is to apply the class to your business type.

The code in Listing 13-3 defines an AttributeClass ❶ that includes the Validator attribute ❷. It includes an attribute that defines the data type that the validation applies to ❸, and the value that you specify here should match the name of your business type. After you define your AttributeClass, you need to define an Attribute for your business type ❻.

When you're writing this code, there are two important naming rules that you must adhere to:

- Your AttributeClass name ❶ must match your Attribute's Class value ❻.

- Your Attribute's Class value ❻ must be preceded with @ symbol.

If you don't abide by these naming conventions, your validation simply won't work. You'll notice that the name of the class is MaxIntegerValidationId, and by the end of this section, you'll notice that you don't write any .NET code that creates an instance of the MaxIntegerValidationId class. Technically, MaxIntegerValidationId is a class that exists in the model's conceptual space rather than in the .NET code space. In practice, it's easier to think of MaxIntegerValidationId as a string identifier, and for this reason, this example names the class with an Id suffix to allow you to more easily follow its usage in the proceeding code files.

Defining Property Sheet Attributes

The code in Listing 13-3 defines an attribute that controls the maximum duration that an instance of your business type can store. To define an attribute, you need to add an AttributeProperty ❹ to your AttributeClass. Once you do this, you can define additional attributes ❺ that control the way that your attribute appears in the table designer. These attributes include

- **DisplayName:** Defines the label text that appears next to your property.

- **Category:** Specifies the group that your property appears in.

- **UIEditor:** Defines the editor that allows users to modify your property value. Chapter 12 contains a list of valid UIEditor choices.

Once you've defined your `AttributeProperty`, you'll also need to define a `Property` ❼ that's associated with your business type's `Attribute`. This `Property` specifies the default value that your business type applies if the developer hasn't set a value through the properties sheet.

Figure 13-1 illustrates how this property appears in the table designer at runtime.

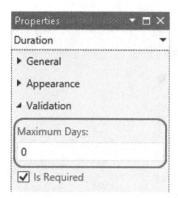

Figure 13-1. *Maximum Days attribute, as shown in the properties sheet*

Applying Validation Logic

Now that you've set up your LSML file to support custom validation, let's take a closer look at how business type validation works. In the LSML for your business type, you used the identifier `MaxIntegerValidationId`. This identifier ties your business type with a validation factory. When LightSwitch needs to validate the value of a business type, it uses this identifier to determine the factory class that it should use. The factory class then returns an instance of a validation class that contains the validation logic for your business type. In our example, we've named our validation class `MaxIntegerValidation`. This class implements the `IAttachedPropertyValidation` interface and a method called `Validate`. This is the method that LightSwitch calls to validate the value of your business type. Figure 13-2 illustrates this process.

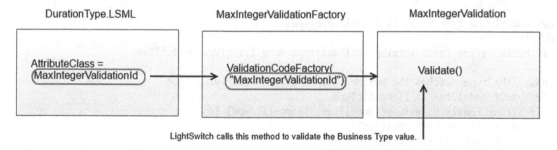

Figure 13-2. *Applying validation logic*

To apply this validation to your business type, let's create the factory and validation classes. Create a new class file in your `Common` project, and name it `MaxIntegerValidationFactory`. Now add the code that's shown in Listing 13-4.

Listing 13-4. Creating the Validation Factory Code

VB:
File: ApressExtensionVB.Common\MaxIntegerValidationFactory.vb

```vb
Imports System.ComponentModel.Composition
Imports Microsoft.LightSwitch.Runtime.Rules
Imports Microsoft.LightSwitch.Model

<Export(GetType(IValidationCodeFactory))>
<ValidationCodeFactory("ApressExtensionVB:@MaxIntegerValidationId")>     ❶
Public Class MaxIntegerValidationFactory
    Implements IValidationCodeFactory

    Public Function Create(
        modelItem As Microsoft.LightSwitch.Model.IStructuralItem,
        attributes As System.Collections.Generic.IEnumerable(
          Of Microsoft.LightSwitch.Model.IAttribute)) As
        Microsoft.LightSwitch.Runtime.Rules.IAttachedValidation Implements
        Microsoft.LightSwitch.Runtime.Rules.IValidationCodeFactory.Create

        ' Ensure that the data type is a positive integer semantic
        ' type (or nullable positive integer)
        If Not IsValid(modelItem) Then
            Throw New InvalidOperationException("Unsupported data type.")
        End If
        Return New MaxIntegerValidation(attributes)
    End Function

    Public Function IsValid(modelItem As
        Microsoft.LightSwitch.Model.IStructuralItem) As Boolean Implements
        Microsoft.LightSwitch.Runtime.Rules.IValidationCodeFactory.IsValid
        Dim nullableType As INullableType = TryCast(modelItem, INullableType)

        ' Get underlying type if it is a INullableType.
        modelItem =
          If(nullableType IsNot Nothing, nullableType.UnderlyingType, modelItem)

        ' Ensure the type matches the business type, or the underlying type
        While TypeOf modelItem Is ISemanticType
            If String.Equals(DirectCast(modelItem, ISemanticType).Id,
              "ApressExtensionVB:DurationType",                           ❷
                StringComparison.Ordinal) Then
                    Return True
            End If
            modelItem = DirectCast(modelItem, ISemanticType).UnderlyingType
        End While
        ' Don't apply the validation if the conditions aren't met
        Return False

    End Function
End Class
```

C#:
File: ApressExtensionCS.Common\MaxIntegerValidationFactory.cs

```csharp
using System;
using System.Collections.Generic;
using System.ComponentModel.Composition;
using System.Linq;
using Microsoft.LightSwitch;
using Microsoft.LightSwitch.Model;
using Microsoft.LightSwitch.Runtime.Rules;

namespace ApressExtensionCS
{
    [Export(typeof(IValidationCodeFactory))]
    [ValidationCodeFactory("ApressExtensionCS:@MaxIntegerValidationId")]        ❶
    public class MaxIntegerValidationFactory : IValidationCodeFactory
    {
        public IAttachedValidation Create(IStructuralItem modelItem,
            IEnumerable<IAttribute> attributes)
        {
            // Ensure that the data type is a positive integer semantic
            // type (or nullable positive integer)
            if (!IsValid(modelItem))
            {
                throw new InvalidOperationException("Unsupported data type.");
            }
            return new MaxIntegerValidation (attributes);
        }

        public bool IsValid(IStructuralItem modelItem)
        {
            INullableType nullableType = modelItem as INullableType;

            // Get underlying type if it is an INullableType.
            modelItem =
                null != nullableType ? nullableType.UnderlyingType : modelItem;

            // Ensure the type matches the business type,
            // or the underlying type
            while (modelItem is ISemanticType)
            {
                if (String.Equals(((ISemanticType)modelItem).Id,
                    "ApressExtensionCS:DurationType",                           ❷
                    StringComparison.Ordinal))
                {
                    return true;
                }
                modelItem = ((ISemanticType)modelItem).UnderlyingType;
            }
```

```
            //Don't apply the validation if the conditions aren't met
            return false;
        }
    }
}
```

The first part of this code contains the identifier (`AttributeClass`) that links your validation factory to your LSML file ❶. The syntax that you use is particularly important. You need to prefix the identifier with the namespace of your project, followed by the : symbol and the @ symbol.

The remaining code in the validation factory performs validation to ensure that the data type of the model item matches your business type, and returns a new instance of your `MaxIntegerValidation` validation class if the test succeeds. In the code that carries out this test, it's important to specify your business type identifier ❷ in the correct format. It should contain the namespace of your project, followed by the : symbol, followed by the business type name.

At this point, you'll see compiler errors because the `MaxIntegerValidation` class doesn't exist. So the next step is to create a new class in your `Common` project, name it `MaxIntegerValidation`, and add the code that's shown in Listing 13-5.

Listing 13-5. Creating the Validation Class

VB:
File: ApressExtensionVB\ApressExtensionVB.Common\MaxIntegerValidation.vb

```
Imports System
Imports System.Collections.Generic
Imports System.ComponentModel.Composition
Imports System.Linq
Imports Microsoft.LightSwitch
Imports Microsoft.LightSwitch.Model
Imports Microsoft.LightSwitch.Runtime.Rules

Public Class MaxIntegerValidation
    Implements IAttachedPropertyValidation

    Public Sub New(attributes As IEnumerable(Of IAttribute))
        Me.attributes = attributes
    End Sub

    Private attributes As IEnumerable(Of IAttribute)

    Public Sub Validate(value As Object,                                    ❶
        results As IPropertyValidationResultsBuilder) Implements
          Microsoft.LightSwitch.Runtime.Rules.IAttachedPropertyValidation.Validate
        If value IsNot Nothing Then

            ' Ensure the value type is integer.
            If GetType(Integer) IsNot value.GetType() Then
                Throw New InvalidOperationException("Unsupported data type.")
            End If

            Dim intValue As Integer = DirectCast(value, Integer)
```

```vb
        Dim validationAttribute As IAttribute =                    ❷
            Me.attributes.FirstOrDefault()
        If validationAttribute IsNot Nothing AndAlso
           validationAttribute.Class IsNot Nothing AndAlso
           validationAttribute.Class.Id =
              "ApressExtensionVB:@MaxIntegerValidationId" Then       ❸

            Dim intMaxDays =
                DirectCast(validationAttribute("MaxDays"), Integer)

            'There are 1440 minutes in a day
            If intMaxDays > 0 AndAlso intValue > (intMaxDays * 1440) Then
                results.AddPropertyResult(
                   "Max value must be less than " &
                    intMaxDays.ToString & " days", ValidationSeverity.Error)
            End If
        End If
    End If
    End Sub
End Class
```

C#:
File: ApressExtensionCS\ApressExtensionCS.Common\MaxIntegerValidation.cs

```csharp
using System;
using System.Collections.Generic;
using System.ComponentModel.Composition;
using System.Linq;
using Microsoft.LightSwitch;
using Microsoft.LightSwitch.Model;
using Microsoft.LightSwitch.Runtime.Rules;

public class MaxIntegerValidation : IAttachedPropertyValidation
{
    public MaxIntegerValidation (IEnumerable<IAttribute> attributes)
    {
        _attributes = attributes;
    }

    private IEnumerable<IAttribute> _attributes;

    public void Validate(object value,                              ❶
        IPropertyValidationResultsBuilder results)
    {
        if (null != value)
        {
            // Ensure the value type is integer.
            if (typeof(Int32) != value.GetType())
            {
                throw new InvalidOperationException("Unsupported data type.");
            }
```

```
                IAttribute validationAttribute = _attributes.FirstOrDefault();      ❷
                if (validationAttribute != null &&
                    validationAttribute.Class != null &&
                    validationAttribute.Class.Id ==
                        "ApressExtensionCS:@MaxIntegerValidationId")                 ❸
                {

                    int intValue = (int)value;
                    int intMaxDays = (int)validationAttribute["MaxDays"];

                    //There are 1440 minutes in a day
                    if (intMaxDays > 0 && intValue > (intMaxDays * 1440))
                    {
                        results.AddPropertyResult(
                            "Max value must be less than " + intMaxDays.ToString() +
                            " days", ValidationSeverity.Error);
                    }
                }
            }
        }
    }
}
```

The code in Listing 13-5 defines a class that implements the Validate method ❶. LightSwitch calls this method each time it needs to validate the value of your business type. This method allows you to retrieve the data value from the value parameter, apply your validation rules, and return any errors through the results parameter. The validation code retrieves the MaxDays attribute by querying the collection of attributes ❷ that are supplied to the validation class by the factory. The code retrieves the first attribute and checks that it relates to your duration type. In the test that the code carries out, notice the syntax of the class Id ❸. It should contain the namespace of your project, followed by the : symbol, followed by the @ symbol, followed by the validation identifier that you specified in your LSML file.

Creating Custom Property Editor Windows

By default, the "Maximum Day" attribute that you added to your business type shows up as a TextBox in the table designer's property sheet. In this section, you'll learn how to create a popup window that allows developers to edit custom attribute values. The phone number business type provides a great example of a business type that works just like this. As you'll recall from Chapter 2 (Figure 2-8), this business type allows developers to define phone number formats through a popup "Phone Number Formats" dialog. The advantage of a popup window is that it gives you more space and allows you to create a richer editor control that can contain extra validation or other neat custom features. In this section, you'll find out how to create an editor window that allows developers to edit the MaxDay attribute. The custom editor window will allow developers to set the value by using a slider control.

Chapter 12 showed you how to customize the screen designer's properties sheet, and this example works in a similar fashion. When you're in the table designer and Visual Studio builds the property sheet for an instance of your business type, it uses the LSML metadata to work out what custom attributes there are and what editor control it should use.

The LSML file allows you to specify a UIEditor for each custom attribute that you've added. The value that you specify provides an identifier that allows you to associate an attribute with a factory class. When Visual Studio builds the property sheet, it uses this identifier to find a matching factory class. It then uses the factory class to return an editor class that implements the IPropertyValueEditor interface. The editor class implements a method called GetEditorTemplate that returns the XAML that plugs into Visual Studio's property sheet. To create a custom popup property editor, you'd return a piece of XAML that contains a hyperlink control that opens your custom property editor in a new window. Figure 13-3 illustrates this process.

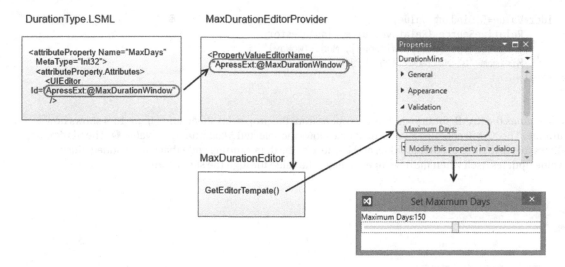

Figure 13-3. *Creating a popup custom editor window*

You'll remember from Chapter 12 that Visual Studio is built with WPF, so creating a pop up window that integrates with the IDE will involve writing a custom WPF user control. Just like the other examples in this book that extend the Visual Studio IDE, you'll carry out this work in your Design project.

To create the custom editor window, right-click your Design project, click Add ➤ New Item, and select "User Control (WPF)." As a prerequisite, you'll need to make sure that your LSPKG and Design projects are set to .NET 4.5. (You may have done this already in Chapter 12.) In your Design project, you'll need to add a reference to the Microsoft.LightSwitch.Design.Designer.dll file. You'll find this file in Visual Studio's private assembly folder. On a 64-bit computer, the default location of this folder is: C:\Program Files (x86)\Microsoft Visual Studio 11.0\Common7\IDE\ PrivateAssemblies.

Once your control opens in Visual Studio, modify the XAML for your user control as shown in Listing 13-6.

Listing 13-6. Creating a Custom Property Editor

File: ApressExtensionVB\ApressExtensionVB.Design\MaxIntegerEditorDialog.xaml

```
<Window x:Class="MaxIntegerEditorDialog"
        xmlns="http://schemas.microsoft.com/winfx/2006/xaml/presentation"
        xmlns:x="http://schemas.microsoft.com/winfx/2006/xaml"
        WindowStartupLocation="CenterOwner"
        ShowInTaskbar="False" ResizeMode="NoResize"
        Title="Set Maximum Days" Height="100" Width="300">
    <StackPanel>

        <StackPanel Orientation="Horizontal" >
            <TextBlock  Text="Maximum Days:" />
            <TextBlock Text="{Binding Value,
                RelativeSource={RelativeSource FindAncestor,
                AncestorType={x:Type Window}}, Mode=TwoWay}" />         ❶
        </StackPanel>
```

```
        <Slider Value="{Binding Value,                                    ❷
                RelativeSource={RelativeSource FindAncestor,
                AncestorType={x:Type Window}}, Mode=TwoWay}"
                Minimum="0" Maximum="300" Width="300" />
    </StackPanel>
</Window>
```

This code defines the XAML for the window that opens from the properties sheet, and Figure 13-4 shows how it looks at runtime. The XAML contains a TextBlock that shows the selected Maximum Days value ❶. The Slider control ❷ allows the developer to edit the value, and because of the data-binding code that you've added, the TextBlock value updates itself when the developer changes the value through the slider control.

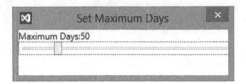

Figure 13-4. *The popup window that allows users to set maximum days*

■ **Caution**   If you copy and paste the XAML in a WPF user control, your code might fail to compile due to a missing InitializeComponent method. See here for more details: http://stackoverflow.com/questions/954861/why-can-visual-studio-not-find-my-wpf-initializecomponent-method

---

Once you've added your WPF user control, add the code that's shown in Listing 13-7.

Listing 13-7. Creating a Custom Property Editor

VB:
File: ApressExtensionVB\ApressExtensionVB.Design\MaxIntegerEditorDialog.xaml.vb

```
Imports System.Windows

Public Class MaxIntegerEditorDialog
    Inherits Window                                                        ❶

    Public Property Value As Nullable(Of Integer)
        Get
            Return MyBase.GetValue(MaxIntegerEditorDialog.ValueProperty)
        End Get
        Set(value As Nullable(Of Integer))
            MyBase.SetValue(MaxIntegerEditorDialog.ValueProperty, value)
        End Set
    End Property
```

```
    Public Shared ReadOnly ValueProperty As DependencyProperty =           ❷
        DependencyProperty.Register(
            "Value",
            GetType(Nullable(Of Integer)),
            GetType(MaxIntegerEditorDialog),
            New UIPropertyMetadata(0))

    Public Sub New()
        InitializeComponent()
    End Sub

End Class
```

C#:
File: ApressExtensionCS\ApressExtensionCS.Design\MaxIntegerEditorDialog.xaml.cs
```
using System.Windows;

public partial class MaxIntegerEditorDialog : Window                       ❶
{
    public MaxIntegerEditorDialog()
    {
        InitializeComponent();
    }
    public int? Value
    {
        get { return (int?)GetValue(ValueProperty); }
        set { SetValue(ValueProperty, value); }
    }
    public static readonly DependencyProperty ValueProperty =              ❷
        DependencyProperty.Register("Value", typeof(int?),
        typeof(MaxIntegerEditorDialog), new UIPropertyMetadata(0));
}
```

The code in Listing 13-7 sets up your control so that it inherits from the Window class ❶. By default, your WPF control would inherit from the UserControl class. This code contains a dependency property called ValueProperty, which is of data type integer ❷. This property allows the window to share the selected value with the code in the properties sheet that opens the window.

■ **Caution** When you create dependency properties, make sure to pass the correct value to the UIPropertyMetadata constructor. For example, if you define a decimal dependency property and you want to set the default value to 0, use the syntax UIPropertyMetadata (0d). If you set default values that don't match the data type of your dependency property, you'll receive an obscure error at runtime that can be difficult to decipher.

You've now created the window that allows the developer to edit the MaxDays attribute, so the next step is to define the UI that contains the hyperlink that opens this window. Create a new "User Control (WPF)" called EditorTemplates.xaml in your Design project, and add the code that's shown in Listing 13-8.

Listing 13-8. Adding the UI That Opens the Custom Window

File: `ApressExtensionVB\ApressExtensionVB.Design\EditorTemplates.xaml`

```xaml
<ResourceDictionary
    xmlns="http://schemas.microsoft.com/winfx/2006/xaml/presentation"
    xmlns:x="http://schemas.microsoft.com/winfx/2006/xaml"
    xmlns:self="clr-namespace:ApressExtensionVB">                    ❶
    <DataTemplate x:Key="MaxIntegerEditorTemplate">                   ❷
        <Label>
            <Hyperlink
                Command="{Binding EditorContext}"
                ToolTip="{Binding Entry.Description}">
                <Run
                    Text="{Binding Entry.DisplayName, Mode=OneWay}"
                    FontFamily="{DynamicResource DesignTimeFontFamily}"
                    FontSize="{DynamicResource DesignTimeFontSize}"
                    />
            </Hyperlink>
        </Label>
    </DataTemplate>
</ResourceDictionary>
```

The code in Listing 13-8 defines a resource dictionary that contains a single data template called `MaxIntegerEditorTemplate` ❷. Using a resource dictionary gives you the ability to add additional templates at a later point in time. You should make sure to configure the `xmlns:self` value ❶ so that it points to the namespace of your extension project. When you add a WPF User Control, the template creates a .NET code file that corresponds with your XAML file. Because this code isn't necessary, you can simply delete this file.

The next step is to create your editor class. Create a new class called `MaxIntegerEditor` in your `Design` project, and add the code that's shown in Listing 13-9.

Listing 13-9. Creating a Custom Property Editor

VB:
File: `ApressExtensionVB\ApressExtensionVB.Design\MaxIntegerEditor.vb`

```vb
Imports System
Imports System.ComponentModel.Composition
Imports System.Runtime.InteropServices
Imports System.Windows
Imports System.Windows.Input
Imports System.Windows.Interop
Imports Microsoft.LightSwitch.Designers.PropertyPages
Imports Microsoft.LightSwitch.Designers.PropertyPages.UI


Public Class MaxIntegerEditor
    Implements IPropertyValueEditor

    Public Sub New(entry As IPropertyEntry)
        Me.command = New EditCommand(entry)
    End Sub

    Private command As ICommand
```

```vbnet
    Public ReadOnly Property Context As Object
      Implements IPropertyValueEditor.Context
        Get
            Return Me.command
        End Get
    End Property

    Public Function GetEditorTemplate(entry As IPropertyEntry) As DataTemplate ❸
        Implements IPropertyValueEditor.GetEditorTemplate
        Dim dict As ResourceDictionary = New ResourceDictionary()
        dict.Source =
            New Uri("ApressExtensionVB.Design;component/EditorTemplates.xaml",
                UriKind.Relative)
        Return dict("MaxIntegerEditorTemplate")
    End Function

    Private Class EditCommand
        Implements ICommand

        Public Sub New(entry As IPropertyEntry)
            Me.entry = entry
        End Sub

        Private entry As IPropertyEntry

        Public Function CanExecute(parameter As Object) As Boolean
            Implements ICommand.CanExecute
                Return True
        End Function

        Public Event CanExecuteChanged(sender As Object,
            e As System.EventArgs) Implements ICommand.CanExecuteChanged

        Public Sub Execute(parameter As Object) Implements ICommand.Execute      ❹

            Dim dialog As MaxIntegerEditorDialog = New MaxIntegerEditorDialog()
            dialog.Value = Me.entry.PropertyValue.Value
            ' Set the parent window of your dialog box to the IDE window;
            ' this ensures the win32 window stack works correctly.
            Dim wih As WindowInteropHelper = New WindowInteropHelper(dialog)
            wih.Owner = GetActiveWindow()
            dialog.ShowDialog()
            Me.entry.PropertyValue.Value = dialog.Value

        End Sub

        'GetActiveWindow is a Win32 method; import the method to get the
        ' IDE window
        Declare Function GetActiveWindow Lib "User32" () As IntPtr

    End Class

End Class
```

```vbnet
<Export(GetType(IPropertyValueEditorProvider))>
<PropertyValueEditorName(                                                    ❶
    "ApressExtension:@MaxDurationWindow")>
<PropertyValueEditorType("System.String")>
Friend Class MaxIntegerEditorProvider
    Implements IPropertyValueEditorProvider

    Public Function GetEditor(entry As IPropertyEntry) As IPropertyValueEditor
        Implements IPropertyValueEditorProvider.GetEditor
            Return New MaxIntegerEditor(entry)                               ❷
    End Function

End Class
```

C#:
File: ApressExtensionCS\ApressExtensionCS.Design\MaxIntegerEditor.cs

```csharp
using System;
using System.ComponentModel.Composition;
using System.Runtime.InteropServices;
using System.Windows;
using System.Windows.Input;
using System.Windows.Interop;
using Microsoft.LightSwitch.Designers.PropertyPages;
using Microsoft.LightSwitch.Designers.PropertyPages.UI;

namespace ApressExtensionCS
{
    internal class MaxIntegerEditor : IPropertyValueEditor
    {
        public MaxIntegerEditor(IPropertyEntry entry)
        {
            _editCommand = new EditCommand(entry);
        }
        private ICommand _editCommand;

        public object Context
        {
            get { return _editCommand; }
        }

        public DataTemplate GetEditorTemplate(IPropertyEntry entry)          ❸
        {
            ResourceDictionary dict = new ResourceDictionary() {
            Source = new
            Uri("ApressExtensionCS.Design;component/EditorTemplates.xaml",
            UriKind.Relative)};
            return (DataTemplate)dict["MaxIntegerEditorTemplate"];
        }
```

```
    private class EditCommand : ICommand
    {
        public EditCommand(IPropertyEntry entry)
        {
            _entry = entry;
        }

        private IPropertyEntry _entry;

        #region ICommand Members

        bool ICommand.CanExecute(object parameter)
        {
            return true;
        }

        public event EventHandler CanExecuteChanged { add { } remove { } }

        void ICommand.Execute(object parameter)                        ❹
        {
            MaxIntegerEditorDialog dialog = new MaxIntegerEditorDialog() {
                Value = (int?)_entry.PropertyValue.Value };
          //Set the parent window of your dialog box to the IDE window;
          //this ensures the win32 window stack works correctly.
            WindowInteropHelper wih = new WindowInteropHelper(dialog);
            wih.Owner = GetActiveWindow();
            dialog.ShowDialog();
            _entry.PropertyValue.Value = dialog.Value;
        }

        #endregion
        //GetActiveWindow is a Win32 method; import the method to get the
        //IDE window

        [DllImport("user32")]
        public static extern IntPtr GetActiveWindow();
    }
}

[Export(typeof(IPropertyValueEditorProvider))]
[PropertyValueEditorName(                                              ❶
    "ApressExtension:@MaxDurationWindow")]
[PropertyValueEditorType("System.String")]
internal class MaxIntegerEditorProvider : IPropertyValueEditorProvider
{
    public IPropertyValueEditor GetEditor(IPropertyEntry entry)
    {
        return new MaxIntegerEditor(entry);                           ❷
    }
}
}
```

Listing 13-9 defines the factory class that specifies the `PropertyValueEditorName` attribute ❶. The value of this attribute identifies your custom editor control, and this is the value that you specify in your business type's LSML file to link an attribute to a custom editor.

When the LightSwitch table designer needs to display a custom editor, it uses the factory class to create an instance of a `MaxIntegerEditor` object ❷. The table designer calls the `GetEditorTemplate` ❸ method to retrieve the UI control to display on the property sheet. This UI control binds to an `ICommand` object, and the UI control can access this object through the `EditorContext` property (see listing 13-8). This UI control shows a hyperlink on the properties sheet, and when the developer clicks the on the link, it calls the code in the `Execute` method ❹, which opens the dialog. This allows the developer to set the "Max Days" attribute, and once the developer enters the value, the code sets the underlying property value using the value that was supplied through the dialog.

The next step is to link your custom editor class to your custom attribute. To do this, open the LSML file for your business type, find the section that defines the `UIEditor`, and modify it as shown in Listing 13-10.

Listing 13-10. Creating a Custom Property Editor

File: ApressExtensionVB\ApressExtensionVB.Common\Metadata\Types\DurationType.lsml

```
<AttributeProperty Name="MaxDays" MetaType="Int32">
   <!--Attribute Properties 3-->
   <AttributeProperty.Attributes>
      <Category Value="Validation" />
      <DisplayName Value="Maximum Days" />
      <UIEditor Id="ApressExtension:@MaxDurationWindow"/>            ❶
   </AttributeProperty.Attributes>
</AttributeProperty>
```

Listing 13-10 shows the snippet of XML that links the custom editor to the `MaxDays` attribute. The important amendment here is to make sure that the `UIEditor` ❶ value matches the `PropertyValueEditorName` value that you set in Listing 13-9.

Using Your Business Type

The duration business type is now complete, and you're now ready to build and use it. To demonstrate how to use the business type that you've created, open the `TimeTracking` table and select the `DurationMins` property. You'll now find that you can change the data type from `Integer` to `Duration`, and when you open the properties sheet, you'll find a "Maximum Days" link that allows you to open the dialog that contains the slider control (Figure 13-5).

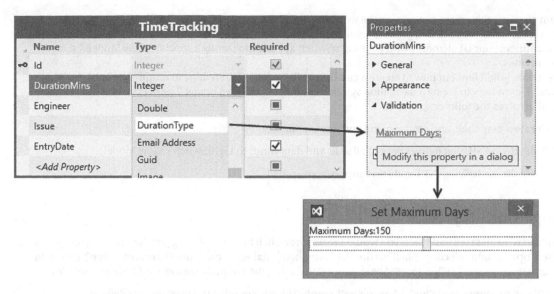

Figure 13-5. *The new slider control that appears in the properties sheet*

Figure 13-6 shows a screen at runtime. The Maximum Days setting for the `DurationMins` property is set to two days, and the screenshot shows the error message that appears when you try to enter a duration that's greater than two days. Notice how the control type for `DurationMins` is set to a `TextBox` rather than the default Duration Editor control. This emphasizes that LightSwitch applies your business type validation, irrespective of the control type that you choose.

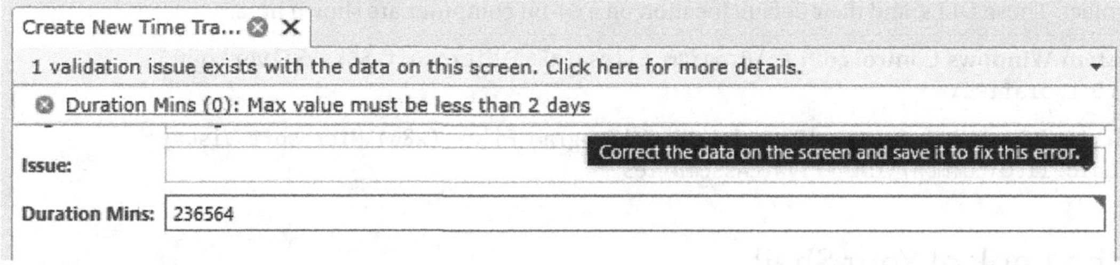

Figure 13-6. *Business type validation at runtime*

Creating a Custom Shell Extension

By creating a LightSwitch shell, you can radically change the appearance of your application. A custom shell allows you to change the position of where the command menu, navigation items, and screens appear.

When you add a new shell, the template creates a blank canvas that allows you to add as little or as much as you like. So if for some reason you don't want to include a navigation menu, that's no problem—you can simply choose not to implement that functionality. Some developers have created bare shells and used custom controls to achieve an appearance that looks nothing like a LightSwitch application. Custom shells, therefore, allow you to carry out extreme modification to your application's UI.

A custom shell is a Silverlight concept, so the work that you'll carry out takes place in your Client project. A LightSwitch shell consists of a XAML file that defines the layout and UI elements of your shell. Data binding then allows you to connect your UI elements with your LightSwitch application through special "View Models" that LightSwitch provides.

In this section, you'll find out how to create a custom shell. To demonstrate how to modify the behavior of your shell, you'll learn how to create a navigation system that uses drop-down boxes. The overview of how to create a custom shell involves the following:

1. Create a new shell, and set the name and description.

2. Write the XAML that defines your shell's UI, and data-binds to LightSwitch's View Models.

3. Write the underlying .NET code that supports your shell.

Preparing Your Project

Just as you would with all extension types, you would create a new shell by right-clicking your LSPKG project, choosing the Add ➤ New option, and selecting "Shell" in the "Add New Item" dialog. To carry out the example that's shown in this section, create a new shell called ApressShell. Once you do this, the template creates the following two files:

- **Client\Presentation\Shells\ApressShell.xaml:** This file contains the markup that defines the presentation and UI elements for your shell.

- **Client\Presentation\Shells\Components\ApressShell.vb:** This .NET code file contains the implementation code that allows your shell to work with MEF (Managed Extensibility Framework), and includes properties that identify your shell.

A large part of the shell development process involves rewriting parts of LightSwitch that you probably take for granted. A new shell provides you with a UI that's completely blank, and in this section, you'll find out how to re-create the tab controls that allow users to switch screens. This functionality relies on a couple of DLLs that you need to add to your Client project. These DLLs, and their default location on a 64-bit computer are shown here:

- **System.Windows.Controls.dll:** C:\Program Files (x86)\Microsoft SDKs\Silverlight\ v5.0\Libraries\

- **Microsoft.LightSwitch.ExportProvider.dll:** C:\Program Files (x86)\Microsoft Visual Studio 11.0\Common7\IDE\PrivateAssemblies.

Defining the Look of Your Shell

The key part about shell design is to work out how you want your shell to look. In this example, you'll create a shell that stacks the UI elements from top to bottom. Figure 13-7 shows the proposed layout of this shell.

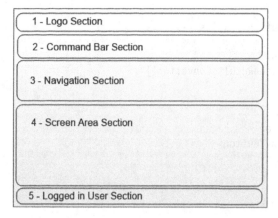

Figure 13-7. *The proposed layout for your Shell*

The code in Listing 13-11 contains the XAML that achieves the look that's shown in Figure 13-7. Take a look at this code but *don't* add it to your `ApressShell.xaml` file yet. It won't compile because it depends on some components that you haven't yet defined.

Listing 13-11. Shell UI Code

File: ApressExtensionVB\ApressExtensionVB.Client\Presentation\Shells\ApressShell.xaml

```
<UserControl
    x:Class="ApressExtensionVB.Presentation.Shells.ApressShell"              ❽
    xmlns="http://schemas.microsoft.com/winfx/2006/xaml/presentation"
    xmlns:x="http://schemas.microsoft.com/winfx/2006/xaml"
    xmlns:controls="clr-namespace:System.Windows.Controls;
        assembly=System.Windows.Controls"
    xmlns:ShellHelpers=
        "clr-namespace:Microsoft.LightSwitch.Runtime.Shell.Helpers;
        assembly=Microsoft.LightSwitch.Client"
    xmlns:local="clr-namespace:ApressExtensionVB.Presentation.Shells">       ❽

    <UserControl.Resources>                                                  ❶
        <local:WorkspaceDirtyConverter x:Key="WorkspaceDirtyConverter" />
        <local:ScreenHasErrorsConverter x:Key="ScreenHasErrorsConverter" />
        <local:ScreenResultsConverter x:Key="ScreenResultsConverter" />
        <local:CurrentUserConverter x:Key="CurrentUserConverter" />

        <!-- O Template that is used for the header of each tab item -->
        <DataTemplate x:Key="TabItemHeaderTemplate">
            <Border>
                <StackPanel Orientation="Horizontal">
                    <TextBlock Text="{Binding DisplayName}" />
                    <!-- This TextBlock shows ! when the screen is dirty -->
                    <TextBlock  Text="!"
                        Visibility="{Binding ValidationResults.HasErrors,
                        Converter={StaticResource ScreenHasErrorsConverter}}"
                        Margin="5, 0, 5, 0" Foreground="Red" FontWeight="Bold">
```

```xml
                    <ToolTipService.ToolTip>
                        <!-- This tooltip shows validation results -->
                        <ToolTip Content=
                            "{Binding ValidationResults,
                        Converter={StaticResource ScreenResultsConverter}}"/>
                    </ToolTipService.ToolTip>
                </TextBlock>
                <Button Height="16" Width="16"
                        Padding="0" Margin="5, 0, 0, 0"
                        Click="OnClickTabItemClose">X</Button>
            </StackPanel>
        </Border>
    </DataTemplate>
</UserControl.Resources>

<StackPanel>                                                          ❷

    <!-- 1 Logo Section -->
    <Image  Source="{Binding Logo}"                                   ❸
        ShellHelpers:ComponentViewModelService.ViewModelName=
        "Default.LogoViewModel"/>

    <!-- 2 Command Bar Section -->
    <ListBox x:Name="CommandPanel"                                    ❹
            ShellHelpers:ComponentViewModelService.ViewModelName=
            "Default.CommandsViewModel"
            ItemsSource="{Binding ShellCommands}"
            Background="{StaticResource RibbonBackgroundBrush}">

        <ListBox.ItemsPanel>
            <ItemsPanelTemplate>
                <StackPanel Orientation="Horizontal" />
            </ItemsPanelTemplate>
        </ListBox.ItemsPanel>
        <ListBox.ItemTemplate>
            <DataTemplate>
                <StackPanel Orientation="Horizontal">
                    <Button Click="GeneralCommandHandler"
                            IsEnabled="{Binding IsEnabled}"
                            Style="{x:Null}"Margin="1">
                        <Grid>
                            <Grid.RowDefinitions>
                                <RowDefinition Height="32" />
                                <RowDefinition MinHeight="24"
                                            Height="*" />
                            </Grid.RowDefinitions>
                            <Image Source="{Binding Image}"
                                    Grid.Row="0" Margin="0"
                                    Width="32" Height="32"
                                    Stretch="UniformToFill"
                                    VerticalAlignment="Top"
                                    HorizontalAlignment="Center" />
```

```
                    <TextBlock Grid.Row="1"
                            Text="{Binding DisplayName}"
                            TextAlignment="Center"
                            TextWrapping="Wrap"
                            MaxWidth="64" />
                </Grid>
            </Button>
        </StackPanel>
    </DataTemplate>
</ListBox.ItemTemplate>
</ListBox>
<!-- 3 Navigation Section -->
<StackPanel>                                                        ❺
    <ComboBox  ShellHelpers:ComponentViewModelService.ViewModelName=
        "Default.NavigationViewModel"
            ItemsSource="{Binding NavigationItems}"
            Name="navigationGroup"
            SelectionChanged="navigationGroup_SelectionChanged" >
        <ComboBox.ItemTemplate>
            <DataTemplate>
                <TextBlock Text="{Binding DisplayName}" />
            </DataTemplate>
        </ComboBox.ItemTemplate>
    </ComboBox>
    <ComboBox  ShellHelpers:ComponentViewModelService.ViewModelName=
        "Default.NavigationViewModel"
            Name="navigationItems"
            SelectionChanged="navigationItems_SelectionChanged" >
        <ComboBox.ItemTemplate>
            <DataTemplate>
                <TextBlock Text="{Binding DisplayName}" />
            </DataTemplate>
        </ComboBox.ItemTemplate>
    </ComboBox>
</StackPanel>

<!-- 4 Screen Area Section -->                                      ❻
<controls:TabControl x:Name="ScreenArea"
        SelectionChanged="OnTabItemSelectionChanged">
</controls:TabControl>

<!-- 5 Logged in User Section -->                                   ❼
<TextBlock ShellHelpers:ComponentViewModelService.ViewModelName=
    "Default.CurrentUserViewModel"
        Name="LoggedInUser"
        Text="{Binding CurrentUserDisplayName,
                Converter={StaticResource CurrentUserConverter}}" />
    </StackPanel>
</UserControl>
```

CHAPTER 13 ■ CREATING DATA AND PRESENTATION EXTENSIONS

The comments in Listing 13-11 allow you to match the code blocks with the screen sections that are shown in Figure 13-7. The first part of this code ❶ defines several supporting resources. This includes the value converters to support the shell's functionality and a template that defines the tab headings that appear above each screen. The tab heading includes the screen name and elements that indicate whether the screen is dirty or contains validation errors.

The next part of the XAML ❷ defines the parent StackPanel that arranges the contents of your shell in a top-to-bottom manner. The first control inside the StackPanel displays the application logo ❸, and the next control is a ListBox control ❹ that binds to the screen commands in your application. The standard commands that LightSwitch shows on each screen include "Save" and "Refresh." The next section contains a pair of ComboBox controls ❺ that you'll customize to allow users to navigate your application. The final part of the XAML contains the tab control ❻ that contains the screen area and a TextBlock ❼ that displays the currently logged-in user. In the sections of this chapter that follow, we'll refer back to this XAML and describe the code that's shown in further detail.

When you add this XAML to your project later, make sure to set the two namespace references that are indicated in ❽ to the name of your project.

Binding Data to Your Shell

LightSwitch exposes shell-related data through six view models, which are shown in Table 13-1.

Table 13-1. *Shell View Models*

Name	View Model ID	Description
Navigation	NavigationViewModel	Provides access to navigation groups and screens.
Commands	CommandsViewModel	Provides access to the commands that are normally shown in the command section.
Active Screens	ActiveScreensViewModel	Provides access to the active screens in your application (that is, the screens that your user has opened).
Current User	CurrentUserViewModel	Provides information about the current logged-on user.
Logo	LogoViewModel	Provides access to the image that's specified in the application's logo property.
Screen Validation	ValidationViewModel	Provides access to the validation information.

LightSwitch provides a Component View Model Service that allows you to bind UI elements to view models by simply adding one line of code against the control that you want to data-bind. The Component View Model Service uses MEF to find and instantiate a view model and to set it as the data context for the specified control. The advantage is that it makes it really simple for you to consume the data from the view models. To demonstrate how this works, let's take a closer look at the XAML that shows the screen commands (Listing 13-12).

Listing 13-12. Command Bar Section

File: ApressExtensionVB\ApressExtensionVB.Client\Presentation\Shells\ApressShell.xaml

```
<!-- 2 Command Bar Section -->
<ListBox x:Name="CommandPanel"
    ShellHelpers:ComponentViewModelService.ViewModelName=
        "Default.CommandsViewModel"                              ❶
    ItemsSource="{Binding ShellCommands}"                        ❷
    Background="{StaticResource RibbonBackgroundBrush}">
```

```
        <ListBox.ItemsPanel>
            <ItemsPanelTemplate>
                <StackPanel Orientation="Horizontal" />          ❸
            </ItemsPanelTemplate>
        </ListBox.ItemsPanel>

        <ListBox.ItemTemplate>
            <DataTemplate>
                <StackPanel>
                    <Button Click="GeneralCommandHandler"
                            IsEnabled="{Binding IsEnabled}">      ❹
                        <Image Source="{Binding Image}"/>         ❺
                        <TextBlock Text="{Binding DisplayName}"/> ❻
                    </Button>
                </StackPanel>
            </DataTemplate>
        </ListBox.ItemTemplate>
</ListBox>
```

Listing 13-12 is a simplified version of the code from Listing 13-11 that highlights the parts that are specific to data binding. The first section of this code defines a `ListBox` control. If you're not very familiar with Silverlight, it's useful to understand that the `ListBox` control isn't only just designed to display simple lists of text data. It allows you to bind to a data source and to render each data item using rich data controls that can include images and other Silverlight controls. The initial part of `ListBox` control defines the "parent" container for your list items. This code renders the child items horizontally by defining an `ItemsPanelTemplate` element that contains a `StackPanel` with its `Orientation` set to `Horizontal` ❸.

The definition of the `ListBox` control uses the Component View Model Service to bind it to the Commands View Model. It does this by applying the following line of code:

```
ShellHelpers:ComponentViewModelService.ViewModelName="Default.CommandsViewModel"
```

The Component View Model Service requires you to supply a view model name. The name that you provide should begin with `Default`, followed by the view model ID that's shown in Table 13-1. The code that's shown in ❶ sets the data context of your `ListBox` to the Commands View Model. The Commands View Model exposes the individual commands through a collection called `ShellCommands`, and the next line of code data-binds the `ItemsSource` of the `ListBox` control to this collection ❷.

The `DataTemplate` section presents each data item in your `ListBox` as a button. Each button is bound to an `IShellCommand` object, and you can use the properties of this object to control the enabled status ❹, Image ❺, and display name ❻ of each command item.

When a user clicks on one of these buttons, LightSwitch won't automatically execute the command. You'll need to write custom code that executes the command, and you'll find out how to do this shortly.

Displaying Your Application's Logo

The top section of your shell displays the logo that's defined in the properties of the LightSwitch application. You can show the application logo by using the Component View Model Service to bind an image control to the Logo View Model.

Listing 13-13 illustrates the code that you would use, and it provides another example of how to use the Component View Model Service.

Listing 13-13. Displaying a Logo

File: ApressExtensionVB\ApressExtensionVB.Client\Presentation\Shells\ApressShell.xaml

```
<Image
    ShellHelpers:ComponentViewModelService.ViewModelName="Default.LogoViewModel"
    Source="{Binding Logo}"/>
```

Adding Code That Supports our Custom Shell

Up till now, I've shown you plenty of XAML that defines the appearance of your Shell. Although the big advantage of custom shells is that they allow you to carry out extreme UI customization, the side effect is that you need to implement a lot of the functionality that you would take for granted in LightSwitch. This includes writing the code that executes command items, manages screens, and enables navigation. To support the XAML that you've created so far, you'll now add the following code to your shell:

- **ApressShell.xaml.vb or ApressShell.xaml.cs:** This defines the .NET code behind your XAML file and contains the logic that enables your custom shell to open and close screens and respond to user-initiated actions.

- **ScreenWrapper class:** LightSwitch's screen object doesn't contain any properties that allow you to determine if a screen is dirty or contains validation errors. This object extends LightSwitch's IScreenObject and provides these extra functions.

- **Value Converters:** The shell that you've created includes UI elements that indicate whether the screen is dirty or contains validation errors. These value converters help to convert the property results from your screen object into types that your UI controls can consume.

Let's begin by creating your ScreenWrapper class. Add a new class in your Client project's Presentation ➤ Shells folder and call it ScreenWrapper. Now add the code that's shown in Listing 13-14.

Listing 13-14. ScreenWrapper Object

VB:
File: ApressExtensionVB\ApressExtensionVB.Client\Presentation\Shells\ScreenWrapper.vb

```
Imports System
Imports System.Collections.Generic
Imports System.ComponentModel
Imports System.Linq
Imports System.Windows

Imports Microsoft.LightSwitch
Imports Microsoft.LightSwitch.Client
Imports Microsoft.LightSwitch.Details
Imports Microsoft.LightSwitch.Details.Client
Imports Microsoft.LightSwitch.Utilities

Namespace Presentation.Shells

    Public Class ScreenWrapper
        Implements IScreenObject
        Implements INotifyPropertyChanged
```

```vb
Private screenObject As IScreenObject
Private dirty As Boolean
Private dataServicePropertyChangedListeners As List(
    Of IWeakEventListener)

Public Event PropertyChanged(sender As Object,
    e As PropertyChangedEventArgs) Implements
        INotifyPropertyChanged.PropertyChanged

' 1.  REGISTER FOR CHANGE NOTIFICATIONS
Friend Sub New(screenObject As IScreenObject)
    Me.screenObject = screenObject
    Me.dataServicePropertyChangedListeners =
        New List(Of IWeakEventListener)

    ' Register for property changed events on the details object.
    AddHandler CType(screenObject.Details,
        INotifyPropertyChanged).PropertyChanged,
        AddressOf Me.OnDetailsPropertyChanged

    ' Register for changed events on each of the data services.
    Dim dataServices As IEnumerable(Of IDataService) =
        screenObject.Details.DataWorkspace.Details.Properties.All().OfType(
            Of IDataWorkspaceDataServiceProperty)().Select(
                Function(p) p.Value)

    For Each dataService As IDataService In dataServices
        Me.dataServicePropertyChangedListeners.Add(
            CType(dataService.Details, INotifyPropertyChanged).CreateWeakPropertyChangedListener(
                Me, AddressOf Me.OnDataServicePropertyChanged))
    Next
End Sub

Private Sub OnDetailsPropertyChanged(sender As Object,
    e As PropertyChangedEventArgs)
    If String.Equals(e.PropertyName,
        "ValidationResults", StringComparison.OrdinalIgnoreCase) Then
        RaiseEvent PropertyChanged(
            Me, New PropertyChangedEventArgs("ValidationResults"))
    End If
End Sub

Private Sub OnDataServicePropertyChanged(sender As Object,
    e As PropertyChangedEventArgs)
    Dim dataService As IDataService =
        CType(sender, IDataServiceDetails).DataService
    Me.IsDirty = dataService.Details.HasChanges
End Sub
```

```vb
' 2.  EXPOSE AN ISDIRTY PROPERTY
Public Property IsDirty As Boolean
    Get
        Return Me.dirty
    End Get
    Set(value As Boolean)
        Me.dirty = value
        RaiseEvent PropertyChanged(
                Me, New PropertyChangedEventArgs("IsDirty"))
    End Set
End Property

' 3.  EXPOSE A VALIDATION RESULTS PROPERTY
Public ReadOnly Property ValidationResults As ValidationResults
    Get
        Return Me.screenObject.Details.ValidationResults
    End Get
End Property

' 4.  EXPOSE UNDERLYING SCREEN PROPERTIES
Public ReadOnly Property CanSave As Boolean
  Implements IScreenObject.CanSave
    Get
        Return Me.screenObject.CanSave
    End Get
End Property

Public Sub Close(promptUserToSave As Boolean)
  Implements IScreenObject.Close
    Me.screenObject.Close(promptUserToSave)
End Sub

Friend ReadOnly Property RealScreenObject As IScreenObject
    Get
        Return Me.screenObject
    End Get
End Property

Public Property Description As String
 Implements IScreenObject.Description
    Get
        Return Me.screenObject.Description
    End Get
    Set(value As String)
        Me.screenObject.Description = value
    End Set
End Property

Public ReadOnly Property Details As IScreenDetails
  Implements IScreenObject.Details
    Get
        Return Me.screenObject.Details
    End Get
End Property
```

```vb
        Public Property DisplayName As String
            Implements IScreenObject.DisplayName
            Get
                Return Me.screenObject.DisplayName
            End Get
            Set(value As String)
                Me.screenObject.DisplayName = value
            End Set
        End Property

        Public ReadOnly Property Name As String Implements IScreenObject.Name
            Get
                Return Me.screenObject.Name
            End Get
        End Property

        Public Sub Refresh() Implements IScreenObject.Refresh
            Me.screenObject.Refresh()
        End Sub

        Public Sub Save() Implements IScreenObject.Save
            Me.screenObject.Save()
        End Sub

        Public ReadOnly Property Details1 As IBusinessDetails
            Implements IBusinessObject.Details
            Get
                Return CType(Me.screenObject, IBusinessObject).Details
            End Get
        End Property

        Public ReadOnly Property Details2 As IDetails
            Implements IObjectWithDetails.Details
            Get
                Return CType(Me.screenObject, IObjectWithDetails).Details
            End Get
        End Property

        Public ReadOnly Property Details3 As IStructuralDetails
            Implements IStructuralObject.Details
            Get
                Return CType(Me.screenObject, IStructuralObject).Details
            End Get
        End Property
    End Class

End Namespace
```

C#:
File: ApressExtensionCS\ApressExtensionCS.Client\Presentation\Shells\ScreenWrapper.cs

```csharp
using System;
using System.Collections.Generic;
using System.ComponentModel;
```

```
using System.Linq;
using System.Windows;

namespace ApressExtensionCS.Presentation.Shells
{
    using Microsoft.LightSwitch;
    using Microsoft.LightSwitch.Client;
    using Microsoft.LightSwitch.Details;
    using Microsoft.LightSwitch.Details.Client;
    using Microsoft.LightSwitch.Utilities;

    public class ScreenWrapper : IScreenObject, INotifyPropertyChanged
    {
        private IScreenObject screenObject;
        private bool dirty;
        private List<IWeakEventListener> dataServicePropertyChangedListeners;

        public event PropertyChangedEventHandler PropertyChanged;

        // 1.  REGISTER FOR CHANGE NOTIFICATIONS
        internal ScreenWrapper(IScreenObject screenObject)
        {
            this.screenObject = screenObject;
            this.dataServicePropertyChangedListeners =
                new List<IWeakEventListener>();

            // Register for property changed events on the details object.
            ((INotifyPropertyChanged)screenObject.Details).PropertyChanged +=
                this.OnDetailsPropertyChanged;

            // Register for changed events on each of the data services.
            IEnumerable<IDataService> dataServices =
                screenObject.Details.DataWorkspace.Details.Properties.All().OfType<
                IDataWorkspaceDataServiceProperty>().Select(p => p.Value);

            foreach (IDataService dataService in dataServices)
                this.dataServicePropertyChangedListeners.Add(
                    ((INotifyPropertyChanged)dataService.Details).CreateWeakPropertyChangedListener(
                        this, this.OnDataServicePropertyChanged));
        }

        private void OnDetailsPropertyChanged(
            object sender, PropertyChangedEventArgs e)
        {
            if (String.Equals(
                e.PropertyName, "ValidationResults", StringComparison.OrdinalIgnoreCase))
            {
                if (null != this.PropertyChanged)
                    PropertyChanged(
                        this, new PropertyChangedEventArgs("ValidationResults"));
            }
        }
```

```csharp
private void OnDataServicePropertyChanged(
    object sender, PropertyChangedEventArgs e)
{
    IDataService dataService = ((IDataServiceDetails)sender).DataService;
    this.IsDirty = dataService.Details.HasChanges;
}

// 2.  EXPOSE AN ISDIRTY PROPERTY
public bool IsDirty
{
    get{return this.dirty; }
    set
    {
        this.dirty = value;
        if (null != this.PropertyChanged)
            PropertyChanged(
              this, new PropertyChangedEventArgs("IsDirty"));
    }
}


// 3.  EXPOSE A VALIDATION RESULTS PROPERTY
public ValidationResults ValidationResults
{
    get {return this.screenObject.Details.ValidationResults;}
}

// 4.  EXPOSE UNDERLYING SCREEN PROPERTIES
public IScreenDetails Details
{
    get {return this.screenObject.Details; }
}
internal IScreenObject RealScreenObject
{
    get {return this.screenObject; }
}

public string Name
{
    get {return this.screenObject.Name; }
}

public string DisplayName
{
    get {return this.screenObject.DisplayName; }
    set {this.screenObject.DisplayName = value; }
}

public string Description
{
    get {return this.screenObject.Description; }
    set {this.screenObject.Description = value; }
}
```

```csharp
public bool CanSave
{
    get {return this.screenObject.CanSave; }
}

public void Save()
{
    this.screenObject.Save();
}

public void Refresh()
{
    this.screenObject.Refresh();
}

public void Close(bool promptUserToSave)
{
    this.screenObject.Close(promptUserToSave);
}

IBusinessDetails IBusinessObject.Details
{
    get {return ((IBusinessObject)this.screenObject).Details; }
}

IStructuralDetails IStructuralObject.Details
{
    get {return ((IStructuralObject)this.screenObject).Details; }
}

IDetails IObjectWithDetails.Details
{
    get{return ((IObjectWithDetails)this.screenObject).Details;}
}
    }
}
```

When you create a custom shell, it's important to be able to access screens in code, and the ScreenWrapper object allows you to do this. It provides a thin wrapper around the IScreenObject object and exposes properties you use to determine if a screen is dirty or contains validation errors. The code in Listing 13-14 includes the following features:

- **1 - Change Notification:** This class implements the INotifiedPropertyChanged interface and the PropertyChanged event. This allows the ScreenWrapper object to raise a notification if the underlying data becomes dirty or invalid. Ultimately, this allows you to build a UI that shows an indication as soon as a user makes a change or enters invalid data.

- **2 - Exposes an IsDirty Property:** This class allows you to determine whether the user has made any data changes by providing an IsDirty property. This returns true if the screen contains changes.

- • **3 - Exposes a ValidationResults Property:** This class exposes a public property called ValidationResults that allows you to access any underlying validation errors.

- • **4 - Implements Underlying Screen Properties:** The class implements the underlying properties of IScreenObject and allows you to access the screen's name, display name, and description in code. It also exposes methods such as Save and Refresh, which allow you to call these methods in code.

Once you've added the ScreenWrapper class, the next step is to create the helper class that contains the value converters. To do this, add a new class in your Client project's Presentation ➤ Shells folder and call it ShellHelper. Now modify your code, as shown in Listing 13-15.

Listing 13-15. ShellHelper (Value Converter) Code

VB:
File: ApressExtensionVB\ApressExtensionVB.Client\Presentation\Shells\ShellHelper.vb

```vb
Imports System.Windows.Data
Imports System.Globalization
Imports Microsoft.LightSwitch
Imports System.Text

Namespace Presentation.Shells

Public Class WorkspaceDirtyConverter
    Implements IValueConverter

    Public Function Convert(value As Object, targetType As Type,
        parameter As Object, culture As CultureInfo) As Object
            Implements IValueConverter.Convert
                Return If(CType(value, Boolean),
                    Visibility.Visible, Visibility.Collapsed)
    End Function

    Public Function ConvertBack(value As Object, targetType As Type,
        parameter As Object, culture As CultureInfo) As Object
            Implements IValueConverter.ConvertBack
                Throw New NotSupportedException()
    End Function

End Class

Public Class ScreenHasErrorsConverter
    Implements IValueConverter

    Public Function Convert(value As Object, targetType As Type,
        parameter As Object, culture As CultureInfo) As Object
            Implements IValueConverter.Convert
                Return If(CType(value, Boolean),
                    Visibility.Visible, Visibility.Collapsed)
    End Function
```

```vbnet
        Public Function ConvertBack(value As Object, targetType As Type,
            parameter As Object, culture As CultureInfo) As Object
                Implements IValueConverter.ConvertBack
                    Throw New NotSupportedException()
        End Function

End Class

Public Class ScreenResultsConverter
    Implements IValueConverter

    Public Function Convert(value As Object, targetType As Type,
        parameter As Object, culture As CultureInfo) As Object
            Implements IValueConverter.Convert

        Dim results As ValidationResults = value
        Dim sb As StringBuilder = New StringBuilder()
        For Each result As ValidationResult In results.Errors
            sb.Append(String.Format("Errors: {0}", result.Message))
        Next
        Return sb.ToString()
    End Function

    Public Function ConvertBack(value As Object, targetType As Type,
        parameter As Object, culture As CultureInfo) As Object
            Implements IValueConverter.ConvertBack
                Throw New NotSupportedException()
    End Function

End Class

Public Class CurrentUserConverter
    Implements IValueConverter

    Public Function Convert(value As Object, targetType As Type,
        parameter As Object, culture As CultureInfo) As Object
            Implements IValueConverter.Convert
        Dim currentUser As String = value

        If currentUser Is Nothing OrElse currentUser.Length = 0 Then
            Return "Authentication is not enabled."
        End If

        Return currentUser
    End Function

    Public Function ConvertBack(value As Object, targetType As Type,
        parameter As Object, culture As CultureInfo) As Object
            Implements IValueConverter.ConvertBack
            Throw New NotSupportedException()
    End Function

End Class

End Namespace
```

C#:
File: ApressExtensionCS\ApressExtensionCS.Client\Presentation\Shells\ShellHelper.cs

```csharp
using Microsoft.LightSwitch;
using System;
using System.Globalization;
using System.Text;
using System.Windows;
using System.Windows.Data;

namespace ApressExtensionCS.Presentation.Shells
{
public class WorkspaceDirtyConverter : IValueConverter
{
    public object Convert(object value, Type targetType,
        object parameter, CultureInfo culture)
    {
        return (bool)value ? Visibility.Visible : Visibility.Collapsed;
    }

    public object ConvertBack(object value, Type targetType,
        object parameter, CultureInfo culture)
    { throw new NotSupportedException();}
}

public class ScreenHasErrorsConverter : IValueConverter
{
    public object Convert(object value, Type targetType,
        object parameter, CultureInfo culture)
    {
        return (bool)value ? Visibility.Visible : Visibility.Collapsed;
    }

    public object ConvertBack(object value, Type targetType,
        object parameter, CultureInfo culture)
    { throw new NotSupportedException();}
}

public class ScreenResultsConverter : IValueConverter
{
    public object Convert(object value, Type targetType,
        object parameter, CultureInfo culture)
    {
        ValidationResults results = (ValidationResults)value;
        StringBuilder sb = new StringBuilder();

        foreach (ValidationResult result in results.Errors)
            sb.AppendLine(String.Format("Error: {0}", result.Message));
        return sb.ToString();
    }
```

```
      public object ConvertBack(object value, Type targetType,
         object parameter, CultureInfo culture)
      { throw new NotSupportedException();}
}

public class CurrentUserConverter : IValueConverter
{
      public object Convert(object value, Type targetType,
         object parameter, CultureInfo culture)
      {
         string currentUser = (string)value;

         if ((null == currentUser) || (0 == currentUser.Length))
             return "Authentication is not enabled.";

         return currentUser;
      }

      public object ConvertBack(object value, Type targetType,
         object parameter, CultureInfo culture)
      { throw new NotSupportedException();}
}

}
```

This code defines the following four value converters, and you'll notice references to these converters in the XAML code that's shown in Listing 13-11 The following list describes how these value converters apply to the XAML:

- **WorkspaceDirtyConverter:** The template for the screen tab title includes a text block that shows the value "*" —this symbol indicates to the user that the screen is dirty. The Visibility property of this text block is data-bound to the ScreenWrapper object's IsDirty property. The WorkspaceDirtyConverter converts the Boolean IsDirty property to the visibility values of either Visible or Collapsed. Setting the visibility of a Silverlight control to Collapsed hides the control completely. The other visibility value that you can you set is Hidden. The difference between Hidden and Collapsed is that Hidden hides the control, but displays white space in its place instead.

- **ScreenHasErrorsConverter:** The screen tab title includes a text block that shows the value "!" —this symbol indicates to the user that the screen contains validation errors. The Visibility property of this text block is data-bound to the ScreenWrapper object's ValidationResults.HasErrors property. The ScreenHasErrorsConverter converts the Boolean result to a visibility value of either Visible or Collapsed.

- **ScreenResultsConverter:** The tooltip property of the screen tab is bound to the ScreenWrapper's ValidationResults property. This allows the user to hover their mouse over a screen tab and to see a summary of any validation errors. ValidationResults returns a collection of errors, and the purpose of ScreenResultsConverter is to concatenate the individual error messages into a single string.

- **CurrentUserConverter:** The TextBlock in the bottom part of the shell displays the name of the currently logged-on user. The data context of this control is the CurrentUserViewModel, and the TextBlock binds to the CurrentUserDisplayName property. If authentication isn't enabled in the LightSwitch application, CurrentUserConverter returns a string that indicates this condition, which is friendlier than showing nothing at all.

Now compile your project so that the value converter code becomes available. You can now add the XAML for your shell, which was shown in Listing 13-11, and you can also add the .NET "code behind" that's shown in Listing 13-16.

Listing 13-16. XAML Code-Behind Logic

VB:
File: ApressExtensionVB\ApressExtensionVB.Client\Presentation\Shells\ApressShell.xaml.vb

```
Imports Microsoft.VisualStudio.ExtensibilityHosting
Imports Microsoft.LightSwitch.Sdk.Proxy
Imports Microsoft.LightSwitch.Runtime.Shell
Imports Microsoft.LightSwitch.BaseServices.Notifications
Imports Microsoft.LightSwitch.Client
Imports Microsoft.LightSwitch.Runtime.Shell.View
Imports Microsoft.LightSwitch.Runtime.Shell.ViewModels.Commands
Imports Microsoft.LightSwitch.Runtime.Shell.ViewModels.Navigation
Imports Microsoft.LightSwitch.Threading


Namespace Presentation.Shells

Partial Public Class ApressShell
    Inherits UserControl

    Private weakHelperObjects As List(Of Object) =
        New List(Of Object)()

    'Declare the Proxy Object
    Private serviceProxyCache As IServiceProxy
    Private ReadOnly Property ServiceProxy As IServiceProxy
        Get
            If Me.serviceProxyCache Is Nothing Then
                Me.serviceProxyCache =
                    VsExportProviderService.GetExportedValue(Of IServiceProxy)()
            End If
            Return Me.serviceProxyCache
        End Get
    End Property

    ' SECTION 1 - Screen Handling Code
    Public Sub New()
        InitializeComponent()
        ' Subscribe to ScreenOpened,ScreenClosed, ScreenReloaded notifications
        Me.ServiceProxy.NotificationService.Subscribe(
            GetType(ScreenOpenedNotification), AddressOf Me.OnScreenOpened)
        Me.ServiceProxy.NotificationService.Subscribe(
            GetType(ScreenClosedNotification), AddressOf Me.OnScreenClosed)
        Me.ServiceProxy.NotificationService.Subscribe(
            GetType(ScreenReloadedNotification), AddressOf Me.OnScreenRefreshed)
    End Sub
```

```vb
Public Sub OnScreenOpened(n As Notification)
    Dim screenOpenedNotification As ScreenOpenedNotification = n

    Dim screenObject As IScreenObject =
        screenOpenedNotification.Screen

    Dim view As IScreenView =
        Me.ServiceProxy.ScreenViewService.GetScreenView(
            screenObject)

    ' Create a tab item from the template
    Dim ti As TabItem = New TabItem()
    Dim template As DataTemplate = Me.Resources("TabItemHeaderTemplate")
    Dim element As UIElement = template.LoadContent()

    'Wrap the underlying screen object in a ScreenWrapper object
    ti.DataContext = New ScreenWrapper(screenObject)
    ti.Header = element
    ti.HeaderTemplate = template
    ti.Content = view.RootUI

    ' Add the tab item to the tab control.
    Me.ScreenArea.Items.Add(ti)
    Me.ScreenArea.SelectedItem = ti

    ' Set the currently active screen in the active screens view model.
    Me.ServiceProxy.ActiveScreensViewModel.Current = screenObject

End Sub

Public Sub OnScreenClosed(n As Notification)
    Dim screenClosedNotification As ScreenClosedNotification = n
    Dim screenObject As IScreenObject =
        screenClosedNotification.Screen

    For Each ti As TabItem In Me.ScreenArea.Items
        ' Get the real IScreenObject from the instance of the ScreenWrapper.
        Dim realScreenObject As IScreenObject =
            CType(ti.DataContext, ScreenWrapper).RealScreenObject
        ' Remove the screen from the tab control
        If realScreenObject Is screenObject Then
            Me.ScreenArea.Items.Remove(ti)
            Exit For
        End If
    Next

    ' Switch the current tab and current screen
    Dim count As Integer = Me.ScreenArea.Items.Count
    If count > 0 Then
        Dim ti As TabItem = Me.ScreenArea.Items(count - 1)
        Me.ScreenArea.SelectedItem = ti
```

```vbnet
            Me.ServiceProxy.ActiveScreensViewModel.Current =
                CType(ti.DataContext, ScreenWrapper).RealScreenObject
        End If
    End Sub

    Public Sub OnScreenRefreshed(n As Notification)
        Dim srn As ScreenReloadedNotification = n
        For Each ti As TabItem In Me.ScreenArea.Items
            Dim realScreenObject As IScreenObject =
                CType(ti.DataContext, ScreenWrapper).RealScreenObject
            If realScreenObject Is srn.OriginalScreen Then
                Dim view As IScreenView =
                    Me.ServiceProxy.ScreenViewService.GetScreenView(
                        srn.NewScreen)

                ti.Content = view.RootUI
                ti.DataContext = New ScreenWrapper(srn.NewScreen)
                Exit For
            End If
        Next
    End Sub

    Private Sub OnTabItemSelectionChanged(sender As Object,
        e As SelectionChangedEventArgs)
        If e.AddedItems.Count > 0 Then
            Dim selectedItem As TabItem = e.AddedItems(0)

            If selectedItem IsNot Nothing Then
                Dim screenObject As IScreenObject =
                    CType(selectedItem.DataContext,
                        ScreenWrapper).RealScreenObject

                Me.ServiceProxy.ActiveScreensViewModel.Current =
                    screenObject
            End If
        End If
    End Sub

    Private Sub OnClickTabItemClose(sender As Object, e As RoutedEventArgs)
        Dim screenObject As IScreenObject =
            TryCast(CType(sender, Button).DataContext, IScreenObject)

        If screenObject IsNot Nothing Then
            screenObject.Details.Dispatcher.EnsureInvoke(
                Sub()
                    screenObject.Close(True)
                End Sub)
        End If
    End Sub
```

```vb
' SECTION 2 - Command Button Handling Code
Private Sub GeneralCommandHandler(sender As Object, e As RoutedEventArgs)
    Dim command As IShellCommand = CType(sender, Button).DataContext
    command.ExecutableObject.ExecuteAsync()
End Sub

' SECTION 3 - Screen Navigation Code
Private Sub navigationGroup_SelectionChanged(sender As Object,
    e As SelectionChangedEventArgs) Handles navigationGroup.SelectionChanged
    navigationItems.ItemsSource =
        (navigationGroup.SelectedItem).Children
End Sub

Private Sub navigationItems_SelectionChanged(sender As Object,
    e As SelectionChangedEventArgs) Handles navigationItems.SelectionChanged
    Dim screen As INavigationScreen =
        TryCast((navigationItems.SelectedItem), INavigationScreen)
    If screen IsNot Nothing Then
        screen.ExecutableObject.ExecuteAsync()
    End If
End Sub


End Class


End Namespace
```

C#:
File: ApressExtensionCS\ApressExtensionCS.Client\Presentation\Shells\ApressShell.xaml.cs

```csharp
using Microsoft.VisualStudio.ExtensibilityHosting;
using Microsoft.LightSwitch.Sdk.Proxy;
using Microsoft.LightSwitch.Runtime.Shell;
using Microsoft.LightSwitch.Runtime.Shell.View;
using Microsoft.LightSwitch.Runtime.Shell.ViewModels.Commands;
using Microsoft.LightSwitch.Runtime.Shell.ViewModels.Navigation;
using Microsoft.LightSwitch.BaseServices.Notifications;
using Microsoft.LightSwitch.Client;
using Microsoft.LightSwitch.Threading;
using System.Windows.Controls;
using System.Collections.Generic;
using System.Windows;
using System;

namespace ApressExtensionCS.Presentation.Shells
{
public partial class ApressShell : UserControl
{
    private IServiceProxy serviceProxy;
    private List<object> weakHelperObjects = new List<object>();
```

```
// Declare the Proxy Object
private IServiceProxy ServiceProxy
{
    get
    {
        if (null == this.serviceProxy)
            this.serviceProxy =
          VsExportProviderService.GetExportedValue<IServiceProxy>();
        return this.serviceProxy;
    }
}


// SECTION 1 - Screen Handling Code
public ApressShell()
{
    InitializeComponent();
    // Subscribe to ScreenOpened,ScreenClosed, ScreenReloaded notifications
    this.ServiceProxy.NotificationService.Subscribe(
        typeof(ScreenOpenedNotification), this.OnScreenOpened);
    this.ServiceProxy.NotificationService.Subscribe(
        typeof(ScreenClosedNotification), this.OnScreenClosed);
    this.ServiceProxy.NotificationService.Subscribe(
        typeof(ScreenReloadedNotification), this.OnScreenRefreshed);
}

public void OnScreenOpened(Notification n)
{
    ScreenOpenedNotification screenOpenedNotification =
        (ScreenOpenedNotification)n;
    IScreenObject screenObject = screenOpenedNotification.Screen;
    IScreenView view =
         this.ServiceProxy.ScreenViewService.GetScreenView(screenObject);

    // Create a tab item from the template
    TabItem ti = new TabItem();
    DataTemplate template =
        (DataTemplate)this.Resources["TabItemHeaderTemplate"];
    UIElement element = (UIElement)template.LoadContent();

    // Wrap the underlying screen object in a ScreenWrapper object
    ti.DataContext = new ScreenWrapper(screenObject);
    ti.Header = element;
    ti.HeaderTemplate = template;
    ti.Content = view.RootUI;

    // Add the tab item to the tab control.
    this.ScreenArea.Items.Add(ti);
    this.ScreenArea.SelectedItem = ti;
```

```
        // Set the currently active screen in the active screens view model.
        this.ServiceProxy.ActiveScreensViewModel.Current = screenObject;
}

public void OnScreenClosed(Notification n)
{
    ScreenClosedNotification screenClosedNotification =
        (ScreenClosedNotification)n;
    IScreenObject screenObject = screenClosedNotification.Screen;

    foreach (TabItem ti in this.ScreenArea.Items)
    {
        // Get the real IScreenObject from the instance of the ScreenWrapper
        IScreenObject realScreenObject =
            ((ScreenWrapper)ti.DataContext).RealScreenObject;
        // Remove the screen from the tab control
        if (realScreenObject == screenObject)
        {
            this.ScreenArea.Items.Remove(ti);
            break;
        }
    }

    // Switch the current tab and current screen
    int count = this.ScreenArea.Items.Count;
    if (count > 0)
    {
        TabItem ti = (TabItem)this.ScreenArea.Items[count - 1];

        this.ScreenArea.SelectedItem = ti;
        this.ServiceProxy.ActiveScreensViewModel.Current =
            ((ScreenWrapper)(ti.DataContext)).RealScreenObject;
    }
}

public void OnScreenRefreshed(Notification n)
{
    ScreenReloadedNotification srn = (ScreenReloadedNotification)n;
    foreach (TabItem ti in this.ScreenArea.Items)
    {
        IScreenObject realScreenObject =
            ((ScreenWrapper)ti.DataContext).RealScreenObject;
        if (realScreenObject == srn.OriginalScreen)
        {
            IScreenView view =
                this.ServiceProxy.ScreenViewService.GetScreenView(
                    srn.NewScreen);
            ti.Content = view.RootUI;
            ti.DataContext = new ScreenWrapper(srn.NewScreen);
            break;
        }
    }
}
```

```csharp
private void OnTabItemSelectionChanged(object sender,
    SelectionChangedEventArgs e)
{
    if (e.AddedItems.Count > 0)
    {
        TabItem selectedItem = (TabItem)e.AddedItems[0];
        if (null != selectedItem)
        {
            IScreenObject screenObject =
                ((ScreenWrapper)selectedItem.DataContext).RealScreenObject;
            this.ServiceProxy.ActiveScreensViewModel.Current = screenObject;
        }
    }
}


private void OnClickTabItemClose(object sender, RoutedEventArgs e)
{
    IScreenObject screenObject =
        ((Button)sender).DataContext as IScreenObject;
    if (null != screenObject)
    {
        screenObject.Details.Dispatcher.EnsureInvoke(() =>
        {
            screenObject.Close(true);
        });
    }
}
```

```csharp
//SECTION 2 - Command Button Handling Code
private void GeneralCommandHandler(object sender, RoutedEventArgs e)
{
    IShellCommand command = (IShellCommand)((Button)sender).DataContext;
    command.ExecutableObject.ExecuteAsync();
}
```

```csharp
// SECTION 3 - Screen Navigation Code
private void navigationGroup_SelectionChanged(object sender,
    SelectionChangedEventArgs e)
{
    navigationItems.ItemsSource =
                ((INavigationGroup)(navigationGroup.SelectedItem)).Children;
}

private void navigationItems_SelectionChanged(object sender,
    SelectionChangedEventArgs e)
{
    INavigationScreen screen =
        (INavigationScreen) navigationItems.SelectedItem ;
```

```
        if (screen != null){
            screen.ExecutableObject.ExecuteAsync();
        }
    }

    }
}
```

Although Listing 13-16 contains a lot of code, you can split the logic into three distinct sections:

- Section 1 – Screen Handling Code
- Section 2 – Command Button Handling Code
- Section 3 – Screen Navigation Code

In the sections that follow, I'll explain this code in more detail.

Managing Screens

The LightSwitch API provides an object called INavigationScreen. This object represents a screen navigation item and provides a method that you can call to open the screen that it represents. The Navigation View Model gives you access to a collection of INavigationScreen objects and, in general, you would bind this collection to a control that allows the user to select a screen. INavigationScreen provides an executable object that you can call to open a screen. But when you call this method, LightSwitch doesn't show the screen to the user. The runtime simply "marks" the screen as open, and you'll need to carry out the work that shows the screen UI to the user.

To work with screens, you'll need to use an object that implements the IServiceProxy interface. This allows you to set up notifications that alert you whenever the runtime opens a screen, and you can use these notifications to add the code that shows the screen UI to the user. In Listing 13-16, the shell's constructor uses the IServiceProxy to subscribe to the ScreenOpened, ScreenClosed, and ScreenRefreshed notifications. The code that you'll find in "Section 1 – Screen Handling Code" defines the following methods:

- **OnScreenOpened:** Your shell calls this method when the runtime opens a screen. It creates a tab item and sets the contents of the tab to the UI of the newly opened screen. Screen objects expose their UI contents via a property called RootUI. The code creates a ScreenWrapper object from the underlying IScreenObject object and sets the data context of the tab item to the ScreenWrapper object.

- **OnScreenClosed:** This method executes when the runtime closes a screen, and removes it from the application's collection of active screens. This custom method removes the tab item that displayed this screen, sets the selected tab to the last tab in the tab control, and sets the current screen to the screen that's contained in that tab.

- **OnScreenRefreshed:** When a user refreshes a screen, the runtime actually creates a new IScreenObject and discards the old one. This code replaces the data context of the tab item that contains the screen with a ScreenWrapper object that represents the new IScreenObject instance.

- **OnTabItemSelectionChanged:** This method handles the SelectionChanged event of the tab control. The XAML for the tab control (Listing 13-11) defines OnTabItemSelectionChanged as the method that handles the SelectionChanged event. When a user switches tabs, this code uses the proxy to set the active screen. It's important that you do this because it causes the commands view model to update itself to reflect the commands of the new screen.

Executing Commands

The custom shell includes a command bar section that renders your screen commands using buttons. Typically, every screen includes save and refresh commands, in addition to any other commands that the developer might add through the screen designer.

Technically, the shell implements the command bar section through a list control that data binds to the Commands View Model (Listing 13-11). The list control's data template defines a button control that represents each command data item.

The data context of each button control is an object that implements the IShellCommand interface. The IShellCommand object exposes a member called ExecutableObject. This object represents the logic that's associated with the command item.

So to make the buttons on your command bar work, you need to handle the Click event of the button, retrieve the IShellCommand object that's bound to the button, and call the IShellCommand object's ExecutableObject's ExecuteAsync method. This code is shown in the GeneralCommandHandler method, in Listing 13-16 (Section 2—Command Button Handling Code).

Performing Navigation

Your custom shell includes a pair of ComboBoxes that allow your users to navigate your application. The first ComboBox displays a list of navigation groups. When the user selects a navigation group, the second ComboBox populates itself with a list of screens that belong to the selected navigation group.

The first navigation group ComboBox binds to the Navigation View Models NavigationItems collection. When a user selects a navigation group by using the first ComboBox, the shell runs the code in the navigationGroup_SelectionChanged method and sets the data source of the second ComboBox to the Children collection of the NavigationGroup. This binds the second ComboBox to a collection of INavigationScreen objects.

When the user selects an item from the second ComboBox, the shell executes the navigationItems_SelectionChanged method. The code in this method retrieves the INavigationScreen object that's bound to the selected item in the ComboBox. Just like the IShellCommand object, the INavigationScreen object exposes an ExecutableObject. The code then calls the ExecutableObject.ExecuteAsync method. This causes the runtime to open the screen, and triggers the code that's defined in your OnScreenOpened method. The code in the OnScreenOpened method creates a new screen tab, and carries out the remaining actions that are needed to show the screen UI to the user. Figure 13-8 illustrates this process.

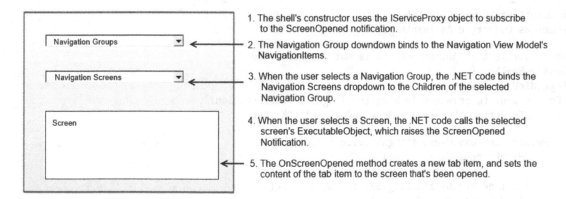

Figure 13-8. *Custom navigation process*

Persisting User Settings

The IServiceProxy object includes a user settings service that allows you to persist user settings, such as the position of screen elements. For example, if you create a shell with a splitter control that allows users to apportion the visible screen area between the navigation and screen areas, you can save the screen sizing details when the user closes your application and restore the settings when your user next opens your application.

To demonstrate the user settings service, we'll add a feature to the shell that allows the user to hide the "logged-in user" section if authentication isn't enabled in the application. When the user closes an application that doesn't have authentication enabled, you'll display a confirmation dialog that allows the user to permanently hide the "logged-in user" section. Listing 13-17 shows the code that adds this feature.

Listing 13-17. Saving User Preferences

VB:
File: ApressExtensionVB\ApressExtensionVB.Client\Presentation\Shells\ApressShell.xaml.vb

```vb
Public Sub New()
   InitializeComponent()

   ' Append this code to the end of the constructor...
   AddHandler Me.ServiceProxy.UserSettingsService.Closing,          ❶
      AddressOf Me.OnSettingsServiceClosing

   Dim hideLoggedInUser As Boolean =
      Me.ServiceProxy.UserSettingsService.GetSetting(Of Boolean)(    ❷
          "HideLoggedInUser")

   If hideLoggedInUser Then
      LoggedInUser.Visibility = Windows.Visibility.Collapsed
   Else
       LoggedInUser.Visibility = Windows.Visibility.Visible
   End If

 End Sub

Public Sub OnSettingsServiceClosing(
        sender As Object, e As EventArgs)

   If LoggedInUser.Text = "Authentication is not enabled." Then
      If MessageBox.Show(
         LoggedInUser.Text,
         "Do you want to permanently hide the logged in user section?",
         MessageBoxButton.OKCancel) = MessageBoxResult.OK Then

          Me.ServiceProxy.UserSettingsService.SetSetting(            ❸
              "HideLoggedInUser", True)
      Else
          Me.ServiceProxy.UserSettingsService.SetSetting(
              "HideLoggedInUser", False)
      End If
  End If

End Sub
```

C#:
File: ApressExtensionCS\ApressExtensionCS.Client\Presentation\Shells\ApressShell.xaml.cs

```csharp
public ApressShell()
{
    InitializeComponent();
    // Append this code to the end of the constructor...

    this.ServiceProxy.UserSettingsService.Closing +=              ❶
        this.OnSettingsServiceClosing;

    bool hideLoggedInUser =
      this.ServiceProxy.UserSettingsService.GetSetting<bool>(
        "HideLoggedInUser");

    if (hideLoggedInUser)                                         ❷
    {
        this.LoggedInUser.Visibility = Visibility.Collapsed;
    }
    else
    {
        this.LoggedInUser.Visibility = Visibility.Visible;
    }
}

public void OnSettingsServiceClosing(object sender, EventArgs e)
{
    if(this.LoggedInUser.Text == "Authentication is not enabled." ){

        if(MessageBox.Show(
            LoggedInUser.Text,
            "Do you want to permanently hide the logged in user section?",
            MessageBoxButton.OKCancel) == MessageBoxResult.OK ){

                this.ServiceProxy.UserSettingsService.SetSetting(   ❸
                    "HideLoggedInUser", true);
        }
        else
        {
                this.ServiceProxy.UserSettingsService.SetSetting(
                    "HideLoggedInUser", false);
        }
    }
}
```

The code in the constructor adds an event handler for the user settings service's Closing event ❶. LightSwitch raises this event when the user closes your application. The user settings service exposes two methods: GetSetting and SaveSetting. The SaveSetting method allows you to persist a setting by supplying a name/value pair as shown in ❸. When your application loads, the code in the constructor hides the LoggedInUser TextBlock if the value of the HideLoggedInUser setting is true ❷.

411

Setting the Name and Description

The name and description for your shell are defined in the LSML file for your shell. Developers can view these details through the properties window of their LightSwitch solution. To set these details, modify the DisplayName and Description attributes as shown in Listing 13-18.

Listing 13-18. Setting the Name and Description

File: ApressExtensionVB\ApressExtensionVB.Common\Metadata\Shells\ApressShell.lsml

```xml
<?xml version="1.0" encoding="utf-8" ?>
<ModelFragment
  xmlns="http://schemas.microsoft.com/LightSwitch/2010/xaml/model"
  xmlns:x="http://schemas.microsoft.com/winfx/2006/xaml">

  <Shell Name="ApressShell">
    <Shell.Attributes>
      <DisplayName Value="ApressShell"/>
      <Description Value="ApressShell description"/>
    </Shell.Attributes>
  </Shell>

</ModelFragment>
```

Using Your Custom Shell

Your custom shell is now complete, and you can build and share it with other developers. Once a developer installs your extension, LightSwitch adds your custom shell to the list of available shells that it shows in the properties window of each application. A developer can apply your shell by selecting it from the list. Figure 13-9 shows the final appearance of your screen.

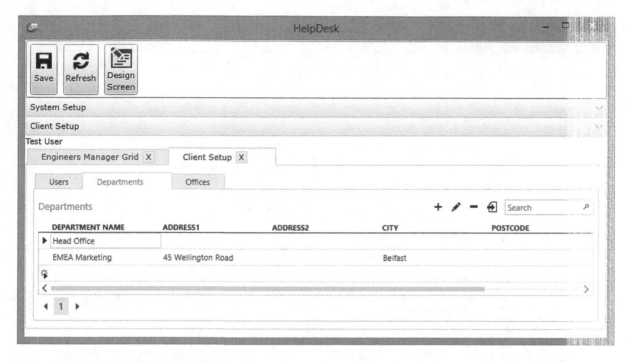

Figure 13-9. *Illustration of the final Shell*

Creating a Custom Theme Extension

Custom themes are the ideal companion to a custom shell. You can use themes to customize your application's font, color, and control styles. You'll be pleased to know that it's much simpler to create a theme, compared to some of the extension types that you've already created. The process involves

1. Creating a new theme, and setting the name and description.

2. Modifying the style information that's defined in the theme's XAML file.

To begin, right-click your LSPKG project, select "New Item," and create a new theme called ApressTheme. As soon as you do this, the template creates a XAML file in your Client project and opens this file in Visual Studio's XML text editor.

The template prepopulates this file with default fonts and colors. It groups the style definitions into well-commented sections. At this point, you could build and deploy your theme. But before you do this, let's modify the fonts and colors that your theme applies.

Applying a Different Font

The default theme that's created by the template uses the Segoe UI font, and you'll find references to this font throughout your theme file. Figure 13-10 shows a screenshot of the theme file in Visual Studio's editor. Notice how the file defines font styles, and notice how it sets the FontFamily value to "Segoe UI, Arial." This setting defines Segoe UI as the preferred font and Arial as the fallback font. This means that LightSwitch will apply the Arial font, only if the Segoe UI font isn't available on the end-user PC.

413

Figure 13-10. *The contents of your Theme file in Visual Studio*

To change the font, simply replace the references to "Segoe UI" with the name of the font that you want to use. For example, you could replace "Segoe UI" with "Times New Roman," Tahoma, or Verdana. To perform a global change, you can use Visual Studio's Find and Replace option. You can find a full list of font name values that you can use by visiting the following page on MSDN: http://msdn.microsoft.com/en-us/library/cc189010(v=vs.95).aspx

Setting Different Colors

Changing the colors in a style is just as easy. For an example, refer back to the command bar control that you added in the custom shell section. Listing 13-19 shows the code that defines the ListBox control that contains the command buttons. You'll notice that this code applies the static resource RibbonBackgroundBrush to the ListBox control's Background property ❶. RibbonBackgroundBrush defines a key that links a shell with a theme.

Listing 13-19. CommandPanel Section of Shell

File: ApressExtensionVB\ApressExtensionVB.Client\Presentation\Shells\ApressShell.xaml

```
<ListBox x:Name="CommandPanel"
  ShellHelpers:ComponentViewModelService.ViewModelName=
    "Default.CommandsViewModel"
  ItemsSource="{Binding ShellCommands}"
  Background="{StaticResource RibbonBackgroundBrush}">            ❶
```

If you now use the find feature in Visual Studio to search for the string RibbonBackgroundBrush in your theme file, you'll find an entry that relates to this style. To apply a different background style, you can modify this entry as appropriate. To demonstrate this, we'll modify the background style to apply a diagonal gradient background style that goes from white to black. To do this, modify the RibbonBackgroundBrush style in your theme as shown in Listing 13-20.

Listing 13-20. Setting the Theme Colors

File: ApressExtensionVB\ApressExtensionVB.Client\Metadata\Themes\ApressTheme.xaml

```
<!-- RibbonBackground - The background of the ribbon menu -->
<LinearGradientBrush x:Key="RibbonBackgroundBrush"
                     StartPoint="0,0" EndPoint="1,1">
    <GradientStop Color="White" Offset="0" />
    <GradientStop Color="#FFC7C7C7" Offset="0.769" />
    <GradientStop Color="#FF898989" Offset="0.918" />
    <GradientStop Color="#FF595959" Offset="1" />
</LinearGradientBrush>
```

Listing 13-20 defines the color codes that allow you to replicate this example. But rather than manually hand-code the styles in your theme, you can select a style entry and use the graphical designer that you'll find in the properties sheet to define your colors and gradient styles (Figure 13-11).

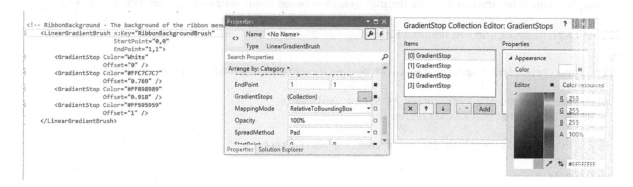

Figure 13-11. *The contents of your Theme file in Visual Studio*

To complete your theme, the final step is to specify a name and description. The LSML file for your theme allows you to define these settings. You'll find this file in your Common project, in the following location:

...Common\Metadata\Themes\ApressTheme.lsml

Once you build and install your theme extension, you can apply it to your LightSwitch application through the properties windows for your application. Figure 13-12 shows the Command Bar section of an application with the ApressTheme applied, and highlights the white-to-black gradient style that runs from the top left to bottom right.

Figure 13-12. *Applying a gradient background to the command bar*

Creating a Screen Template Extension

If you frequently create screens that contain common patterns, features, and code snippets, you can save yourself time by creating a custom screen template. In this section, you'll extend the example that you saw in Chapter 7 and learn how to create a template that creates a combined add and edit screen. As you found out in Chapter 7, creating a combined add and edit screen requires you to carry out several detailed steps. The advantage of using a screen template is that you can automate this process and save yourself from having to carry out the same repetitive tasks every time you want to create this type of screen. The process for creating a screen template is as follows:

1. Add a screen template item, and specify the template attributes.

2. Write code that generates the templated screen controls.

3. Write code that generates the templated .NET code.

To create this example, right-click your LSPKG project, select "New Item," and create a new screen template called AddEditScreenTemplate. After you do this, Visual Studio opens the code file for your template in the code editor.

Setting Template Properties

The first part of the code file enables you to set the properties of your template. You can set the name, description, and display name of the screens that your template generates by modifying your code as shown in Listing 13-21.

Listing 13-21. Creating a Screen Template Extension

VB:
File: ApressExtensionVB\ApressExtensionVB.Design\ScreenTemplates\AddEditScreenTemplate.vb

```
Public ReadOnly Property Description As String Implements
   IScreenTemplateMetadata.Description
   Get
       Return "This template creates a combined Add/Edit screen."
   End Get
End Property

Public ReadOnly Property DisplayName As String Implements
   IScreenTemplateMetadata.DisplayName
   Get
       Return "Add/Edit Screen Template"
   End Get
End Property

Public ReadOnly Property ScreenNameFormat As String Implements
   IScreenTemplateMetadata.ScreenNameFormat
   Get
       Return "{0}AddEditScreen"
   End Get
End Property
```

```vb
Public ReadOnly Property RootDataSource As RootDataSourceType Implements
    IScreenTemplateMetadata.RootDataSource
    Get
        Return RootDataSourceType.ScalarEntity
    End Get
End Property

Public ReadOnly Property SupportsChildCollections As Boolean
    Implements IScreenTemplateMetadata.SupportsChildCollections
    Get
        Return True
    End Get
End Property
```

C#:
File: ApressExtensionCS\ApressExtensionCS.Design\ScreenTemplates\AddEditScreenTemplate.cs

```csharp
public string Description
{
    get { return "This template creates a combined Add/Edit screen"; }
}

public string DisplayName
{
    get { return "Add/Edit Screen Template"; }
}

public string ScreenNameFormat
{
    get { return "{0}AddEditScreen"; }
}

public RootDataSourceType RootDataSource
{
    get { return RootDataSourceType.ScalarEntity; }
}

public bool SupportsChildCollections
{
    get { return true; }
}
```

You'll find several more properties that you can set. These include the images that are associated with your template, the root data source, and whether or not your template supports child data items. The SupportsChildCollection property controls the visibility of the "Additional Data to Include" check boxes, and LightSwitch exposes many other of these properties through the "Add New Screen" dialog, as shown in Figure 13-13.

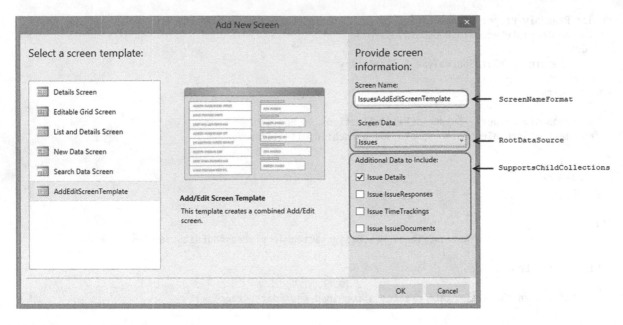

Figure 13-13. *Add New Screen dialog*

Defining the Data Source Type

By now, you'll be familiar with the "Add New Screen" dialog and understand how the "Screen Data" drop-down shows different data, depending on the template that you choose. When you build a screen template, you can define the data that appears in the "Screen Data" drop-down by setting the RootDataSource property. Table 13-2 shows the four values that you can set for this property.

Table 13-2. *Query Types*

RootDataSource value	Description
Collection	Allows the developer to select collections or multiple result queries.
ScalarEntity	Allows the developer to select a single entity type or queries that return one item.
NewEntity	Used for screens that are intended to create new entities.
None	Used for screens in which no data needs to be selected.

In your example template, set the RootDataSource property to ScalarEntity to configure the "Screen Data" drop-down to show singleton queries when a developer selects your screen template.

Generating Screen Controls

The most important part of designing a template is to work out the screen components that you want to add to your template. The best way to do this is to create a normal screen and use that to work out your requirements. Figure 13-14 shows the add/edit screen from Chapter 7, and highlights the steps that you would carry out in the screen designer to create this screen.

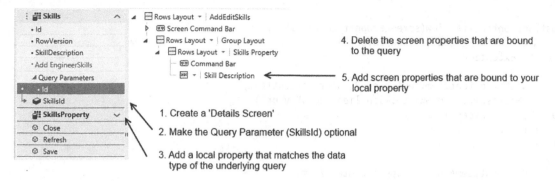

Figure 13-14. *Screen requirements*

Once you've established the items that you want to add to your template, you'll need to translate these tasks into code. The screen template produces screens by calling a method called Generate, and Listing 13-22 shows the code that you'd add to this method to create the screen that's shown in Figure 13-14.

Listing 13-22. Creating a Screen Template Extension

VB:
File: ApressExtensionVB\ApressExtensionVB.Design\ScreenTemplates\AddEditScreenTemplate.vb

```vb
Public Sub Generate(host As IScreenTemplateHost) Implements
    IScreenTemplate.Generate

    Dim screenBase =
        DirectCast(host.PrimaryDataSourceProperty, ScreenPropertyBase)          ❶

    Dim groupLayout1 As ContentItem =
        host.AddContentItem(host.ScreenLayoutContentItem,
          "GroupLayout1", ContentItemKind.Group)                                ❷

    Dim entityTypeFullName As String =
        CType(host.PrimaryDataSourceProperty, ScreenProperty).PropertyType
    Dim entityTypeName As String =
        CType(host.PrimaryDataSourceProperty,
          ScreenProperty).PropertyType.Split(":").LastOrDefault()
    Dim screenProperty1 As ScreenProperty =
        host.AddScreenProperty(entityTypeFullName, entityTypeName + "Property") ❸

    'make the default id parameter not required
    Dim idParameter =
        host.PrimaryDataSourceParameterProperties().FirstOrDefault()
    CType(idParameter, ScreenProperty).PropertyType =
        "Microsoft.LightSwitch:Int32?"                                          ❹

    'This creates an AutoCompleteBox for the item
    Dim screenPropertyContentItem =
        host.AddContentItem(groupLayout1, "LocalProperty", screenProperty1)     ❺
```

```vbnet
            Try
                host.SetContentItemView(screenPropertyContentItem,
                    "Microsoft.LightSwitch:RowsLayout")                    ❻
            Catch ex As Exception
                Try
                    host.SetContentItemView(screenPropertyContentItem,
                        "Microsoft.LightSwitch.RichClient:RowsLayout")
                Catch ex2 As Exception
                    Throw ex2
                End Try
            End Try
            host.ExpandContentItem(screenPropertyContentItem)
            'Code Generation
            Dim codeTemplate As String = ""
            If _codeTemplates.TryGetValue(
                host.ScreenCodeBehindLanguage, codeTemplate) Then

                host.AddScreenCodeBehind(String.Format(codeTemplate,
                    Environment.NewLine,
                    host.ScreenNamespace,
                    host.ScreenName,
                    screenBase.Name,
                    idParameter.Name,
                    screenProperty1.Name,
                    entityTypeName))
            End If

End Sub
```

C#:
File: ApressExtensionCS\ApressExtensionCS.Design\ScreenTemplates\AddEditScreenTemplate.cs

```csharp
public void Generate(IScreenTemplateHost host)
{
    var screenBase = (ScreenPropertyBase)host.PrimaryDataSourceProperty;     ❶

    ContentItem groupLayout1 =
        host.AddContentItem(host.ScreenLayoutContentItem,
            "GroupLayout1", ContentItemKind.Group);                          ❷

    string entityTypeFullName =
        ((ScreenProperty)host.PrimaryDataSourceProperty).PropertyType;

    var entityTypeName =
        ((ScreenProperty)host.PrimaryDataSourceProperty).PropertyType.Split(
            ":".ToArray()).LastOrDefault();

    ScreenProperty screenProperty1 =
        (ScreenProperty)host.AddScreenProperty(entityTypeFullName,
            entityTypeName + "Property");                                    ❸
```

```
//make the default id parameter not required
var idParameter = host.PrimaryDataSourceParameterProperties.FirstOrDefault();
((ScreenProperty)idParameter).PropertyType =
    "Microsoft.LightSwitch:Int32?";                                          ❹

//This creates an AutoCompleteBox for the item
var screenPropertyContentItem = host.AddContentItem(
    groupLayout1, " LocalProperty", screenProperty1);                        ❺
try
{
    host.SetContentItemView(
        screenPropertyContentItem, "Microsoft.LightSwitch:RowsLayout");   ❻
}
catch (Exception ex)
{
    try
    {
        host.SetContentItemView(screenPropertyContentItem,
            @"Microsoft.LightSwitch.RichClient:RowsLayout");
    }
    catch (Exception ex2)
    {
        throw ex2;
    }
}

host.ExpandContentItem(screenPropertyContentItem);

string codeTemplate = "";
if (codeTemplates.TryGetValue(
    host.ScreenCodeBehindLanguage , out codeTemplate ))
{
    host.AddScreenCodeBehind(String.Format(codeTemplate,
        Environment.NewLine,
        host.ScreenNamespace,
        host.ScreenName,
        screenBase.Name,
        idParameter.Name,
        screenProperty1.Name,
        entityTypeName));
}
}
```

The following list highlights the actions that you'd carry out in the screen designer if you created the screen manually, and identifies the code in Listing 13-22 that carries out the corresponding task.

- **Creating a Details Screen and Query.** The add/edit screen is based on a query that returns a single record by Id value. The good news is that you don't need to write any specific code to create the screen's underlying query. The screen template automatically creates a query when you set the RootDataSource to ScalarEntity. You can use the syntax host.PrimaryDataSourceProperty ❶ to access the query that LightSwitch generates.

If you set the `RootDataSource` to `NewEntity` instead, the `PrimaryDataSourceProperty` object would be a property that matches the data type the developer chooses in the "Add New Screen" dialog. And if you set the `RootDataSource` to `Collection`, the `PrimaryDataSource` would be a collection of entities (that is, a Visual Collection).

- **Adding Group Layouts:** Let's imagine that you select a node in the screen designer's tree view and click on the "Add" drop-down button. The code equivalent that performs this action is the `AddContentItem` method. This method requires you to supply the content item type that you want to add and the name that you want to give your new data item. The code in Listing 13-22 adds a new group layout by specifying the content item kind of `ContentItemKind.Group` ❷.

- **Adding a Local Property that matches the underlying query's data type:** In the screen designer, you'd add a new local property by opening the "Add Data Item" dialog and choosing the radio option to add a local property. In code, you'd carry out this action by calling the `AddScreenProperty` method ❸. As with the "Add Data Item" dialog, you need to supply a name and data type to create a new local property. The code uses the `PrimaryDataSourceProperty` object to determine the data type of the underlying screen object and names the property after the entity type name, but with the word "Property" appended to the end. Another useful method is the `AddScreenMethod` method. This is the code equivalent of creating a screen method through the "Add Data Item" button.

- **Making the Query Parameter Optional:** To allow your screen to work in "New Data" entry mode, the Id parameter on your screen must be set to optional. You might expect to find a Boolean property that allows you to set the optional status of a parameter to `false`, but interestingly, no such property exists. So to make a parameter optional, you need to carry out a step that might seem unusual. To make a parameter optional, you'd change the underlying data type from an integer to a nullable integer, as shown in ❹.

- **Deleting the Screen properties that are bound to the query:** If you create an add/edit screen manually through the screen designer, you'd need to delete the data items that are bound to the underlying query. You don't need to carry out this action when you create a screen template in code. The screen that the screen generator creates includes only the root element and doesn't include any extra content that you need to delete.

- **Add the screen properties that are bound to your local entity property:** If you create an add/edit screen manually through the screen designer, the final step is to drag your local property onto your screen and to add data items that are bound to your local property's data items. The `AddContentItem` method ❺ allows you to add the local property onto your screen in code. If you carried out this task in the screen designer, LightSwitch would render your local property as an autocomplete box. In code, the `AddContentItem` method does the same—it'll add the local screen property as an autocomplete box. To change the autocomplete box to a Rows Layout in code, you'd call the `SetContentItemView` method. This method accepts a reference to the content item and a `ViewID` that identifies a `RowsLayout`.

The `SetContentItemView` method is a versatile method, and Appendix C shows a full list of `ViewID`s that you can use. Unfortunately, the `ViewID`s are different in projects that have been upgraded to support the HTML client. If a developer attempts to run your screen template on a project with the HTML client installed, the screen template will fail with an exception. The `Try Catch` block attempts to correct this error condition if it occurs.

Another useful method that you can call is `ExpandContentItem`. This method expands a content item by adding child items that represent each property in the entity. This method mimics the use of the reset button in the LightSwitch screen designer.

Generating Screen Code

It's highly likely that any screen that you want to generate from a template requires some sort of custom code, and the add/edit screen is no exception. This screen requires code in its loaded method to create a new instance of your local screen property and to set the value of the local screen property to the results of the underlying screen query.

The final part of Listing 13-22 creates the screen's .NET code by calling the AddScreenCodeBehind method. A developer can call your screen template from either a VB or C# application. The host.ScreenCodeBehindLanguage property returns the language of the target application, and you can use this information to build your screen's source code in the correct language. The code retrieves a language specific template from a Dictionary called _codeTemplates. It then uses .NET's String.Format method to substitute the required values into the template (Listing 13-23). The aim of this code is to create the code that was shown in Chapter 7 (Listing 7-14).

Listing 13-23. Creating Screen Template Code

VB:
File: ApressExtensionVB\ApressExtensionVB.Design\ScreenTemplates\AddEditScreenTemplate.vb

```
Private Shared _codeTemplates As Dictionary(Of CodeLanguage, String) =
    New Dictionary(Of CodeLanguage, String)() From
{
    {CodeLanguage.CSharp, _
        "" _
        + "{0}namespace {1}" _
        + "{0}{{" _
        + "{0}    public partial class {2}" _
        + "{0}    {{" _
        + "{0}" _
        + "{0}        partial void {5}_Loaded(bool succeeded)" _
        + "{0}        {{" _
        + "{0}            if (!this.{4}.HasValue){" _
        + "{0}                this.{5} = new {6}();" _
        + "{0}            }else{" _
        + "{0}                this.{5}  = this.{3};" _
        + "{0}            }" _
        + "{0}            this.SetDisplayNameFromEntity(this.{5});" _
        + "{0}        }}" _
        + "{0}" _
        + "{0}    }}" _
        + "{0}}}"
    }, _
    {CodeLanguage.VB, _
        "" _
        + "{0}Namespace {1}" _
        + "{0}" _
        + "{0}    Public Class {2}" _
        + "{0}" _
        + "{0}        Private Sub {5}_Loaded(succeeded As Boolean)" _
        + "{0}            If Not Me.{4}.HasValue Then" _
        + "{0}                Me.{5} = New {6}()" _
        + "{0}            Else" _
        + "{0}                Me.{5} = Me.{3}" _
```

```
        + "{0}              End If" _
        + "{0}              Me.SetDisplayNameFromEntity(Me.{5})" _
        + "{0}          End Sub" _
        + "{0}" _
        + "{0}    End Class" _
        + "{0}" _
        + "{0}End Namespace" _
    }
}
```

C#:
File: ApressExtensionCS\ApressExtensionCS.Design\ScreenTemplates\AddEditScreenTemplate.cs

```
private static Dictionary<CodeLanguage, String> codeTemplates =
    new Dictionary<CodeLanguage, String>()
    {
        {CodeLanguage.CSharp,
            ""
            + "{0}namespace {1}"
            + "{0}{{"
            + "{0}    public partial class {2}"
            + "{0}    {{"
            + "{0}"
            + "{0}        partial void {5}Loaded(bool succeeded)"
            + "{0}        {{"
            + "{0}            if (!this.{4}.HasValue){"
            + "{0}                this.{5} = new {6}();"
            + "{0}            }else{"
            + "{0}                this.{5} = this.{3};"
            + "{0}            }"
            + "{0}            this.SetDisplayNameFromEntity(this.{5});"
            + "{0}        }}"
            + "{0}"
            + "{0}    }}"
            + "{0}}}"
        },
        {CodeLanguage.VB,
            ""
            + "{0}Namespace {1}"
            + "{0}"
            + "{0}    Public Class {2}"
            + "{0}"
            + "{0}        Private Sub {5}Loaded(succeeded As Boolean)"
            + "{0}            If Not Me.{4}.HasValue Then"
            + "{0}                Me.{5} = New {6}()"
            + "{0}            Else"
            + "{0}                Me.{5} = Me.{3}"
            + "{0}            End If"
            + "{0}            Me.SetDisplayNameFromEntity(Me.{5})"
            + "{0}        End Sub"
```

```
            + "{0}"
            + "{0}     End Class"
            + "{0}"
            + "{0}End Namespace"
    }
};
```

Another way to generate code is to use .NET's Code Document Object Model (CodeDOM). CodeDOM is specially designed for this purpose, and you can read more about it on the following Microsoft web page: http://msdn.microsoft.com/en-us/library/650ax5cx.aspx. However, this example uses string substitution because it's simple to understand and saves you the small task of having to learn a new API.

Creating More Complex Screen Templates

Your add/edit screen template is now complete, and you can now build and deploy your extension. The template generation host allows you to do much more than this chapter shows—for example, you can add query parameters, related collections, and entity properties to your screen. You can use Visual Studio's IntelliSense to work out the purpose of the host generation methods, so designing more complex screens shouldn't be difficult.

If you need to create screen templates that are more complex, the best advice is to create your screen as normal in your LightSwitch application. If you then examine the LSML file that LightSwitch produces in the Common folder, you'll be able to work out how to construct the same output in a screen template. This technique is particularly useful in helping you work out the correct ViewIDs to use (especially when you're using custom controls) and building the ChainExpressions that you need to access the selected item in a collection.

Creating a Data Source Extension

In the final part of this chapter, I'll show you how to create a data source extension. Data source extensions allow developers to consume data sources that are not natively supported. Although there are several other ways to connect to external data, which include RIA Services and OData, the advantage of a data source extension is that it allows you to more easily package and share the code that consumes a data source. In this section, you'll learn how to create a data source extension that connects to the Windows event log on the server. The purpose of this example is twofold. First, it demonstrates how to connect to a slightly unusual data source, and the second reason is slightly more practical. It allows you to display your server's event log from within your application so that, once you deploy your application, developers or support staff can view the errors that have been generated by your application, without needing access rights to log on to the server. Here's an overview of the steps that are needed to create the Windows event log data source extension:

1. Create a new data source extension, and name it WindowsEventLog. To do this, right-click your LSPKG project, select "New Item," and choose the "Data Source" option.

2. Add entity classes to represent event sources and event log entries.

3. Add the RIA Services code that retrieves the event log data.

Creating an Entity Class

Just as in the RIA services code from Chapter 9, you need to define entity classes to enable LightSwitch to consume your data. So to carry out this example, you'll need to create a pair of entity classes: a class that represents an event log entry, and a class that represents an event log source. An event log source represents a group of event log entries. (The Application, System, and Security logs in the Windows Event Log are examples of sources.) To add these classes, create a new class file in your Server project, name it EventLogEntityClasses, and add the code that's shown in Listing 13-24.

Listing 13-24. Entity Class for Event Log

VB:
File: ApressExtensionVB\ApressExtensionVB.Server\EventLogEntityClasses.vb

```vb
Imports System.Collections.Generic
Imports System.Linq
Imports System.Text
Imports System.ComponentModel
Imports System.ComponentModel.DataAnnotations

Public Class LogEntry

    <Key()> _
     <[ReadOnly](True)> _
     <Display(Name:="Log Entry ID")> _
     <ScaffoldColumn(False)> _
    Public Property LogEntryID As Integer

    <Required()> _
    <Display(Name:="Message")> _
    Public Property Message() As String

    <Display(Name:="Source Name")> _
    Public Property SourceName As String

    <Association("EventLog_EventEntry",
        "SourceName", "SourceName", IsForeignKey:=True)> _
    <Display(Name:="Source")> _
    Public Property EventSource As LogSource

    <Display(Name:="Event DateTime")> _
    Public Property EventDateTime() As DateTime

End Class

Public Class LogSource

    <Key()> _
     <[ReadOnly](True)> _
     <Display(Name:="Source Name")> _
     <ScaffoldColumn(False)> _
     <Required()> _
    Public Property SourceName As String

    <Association("EventLog_EventEntry", "SourceName", "SourceName")> _
    <Display(Name:="EventLogEntries")> _
    Public Property EventEntries As ICollection(Of LogEntry)

End Class
```

C#:
File: ApressExtensionCS\ApressExtensionCS.Server\EventLogEntityClasses.cs

```csharp
using System;
using System.Collections.Generic;
using System.ComponentModel.DataAnnotations;

namespace ApressExtensionCS
{
    public class LogEntry
    {
        [Key(), Editable(false), ScaffoldColumn(false),
            Display(Name = "Log Entry ID")]
        public int LogEntryID { get; set; }

        [Required(), Display(Name = "Message")]
        public string Message { get; set; }

        [Display(Name = "Source Name")]
        public string SourceName { get; set; }

        [Association("EventLog_EventEntry", "SourceName", "SourceName",
            IsForeignKey = true)]
        public LogSource EventSource { get; set; }

        [Required(), Display(Name = "Event DateTime")]
        public DateTime EventDateTime { get; set; }
    }

    public class LogSource
    {
        [Key(), Editable(false), ScaffoldColumn(false),
            Required() ,  Display(Name = "Source Name")]
        public string SourceName { get; set; }

        [Association("EventLog_EventEntry", "SourceName", "SourceName"),
            Display (Name="EventLogEntries")]
        public ICollection<LogEntry> EventEntries { get; set; }
    }

}
```

In the code that's shown in Listing 13-24, notice how the primary-key property is decorated with the key attribute, and how it's also decorated with the Editable attribute with the value set to false. LightSwitch uses these attributes to prevent users from editing the ID property and to render it on screens by using read-only controls.

The Required attribute allows you to define mandatory properties. You can also use the StringLength attribute to specify the maximum length of a property. Both these attributes allow LightSwitch to apply its built-in validation, and prevent users from saving data that violates the rules that you've specified.

A highlight of this code is that it defines a relationship between the LogSource and LogEntry entities. A single LogSource record can be associated with many LogEntry entries, and the Association attribute allows you to define this relationship between the two entities.

Creating the Data Service Class

The next step is to write the code in your domain service class. Just like the RIA service example, this class contains the logic that adds, updates, retrieves, and deletes the data from your underlying data source. The data source template creates a domain service class called WindowsEventLog. So now add the code that's shown in Listing 13-25.

Listing 13-25. Domain Service Code for Accessing Data

VB:
File: ApressExtensionVB\ApressExtensionVB.Server\DataSources\WindowsEventLog.vb

```vb
Imports System
Imports System.Collections.Generic
Imports System.ComponentModel
Imports System.ComponentModel.DataAnnotations
Imports System.Linq
Imports System.ServiceModel.DomainServices.Server

Imports System.Configuration
Imports System.Web.Configuration
Imports System.Diagnostics.EventLog

Namespace DataSources

    <Description("Enter your server path.")> _
    Public Class WindowsEventLog
        Inherits DomainService

        Private _serverName As String

        Public Overrides Sub Initialize(context As DomainServiceContext)
            MyBase.Initialize(context)
        End Sub

        Public Overrides Function Submit(changeSet As ChangeSet) As Boolean
            Dim baseResult As [Boolean] = MyBase.Submit(changeSet)
            Return True
        End Function

#Region "Queries"

        Protected Overrides Function Count(Of T)(query As IQueryable(Of T))
          As Integer
             Return query.Count()
        End Function

        <Query(IsDefault:=True)> _                                              ❶
        Public Function GetEventEntries() As IQueryable(Of LogEntry)

            Dim idCount As Integer = 0
            Dim eventLogs As New List(Of LogEntry)()
            Dim logSource As LogSource
```

```vb
    For Each eventSource In EventLog.GetEventLogs(".")

        logSource = New LogSource
        logSource.SourceName = eventSource.Log

        Try
            For Each eventEntry As System.Diagnostics.EventLogEntry
                In eventSource.Entries
                    Dim newEntry As New LogEntry
                    newEntry.LogEntryID = idCount

                    newEntry.EventDateTime = eventEntry.TimeWritten
                    newEntry.Message = eventEntry.Message
                    newEntry.Message = eventEntry.Source
                    newEntry.SourceName = eventSource.Log
                    newEntry.EventSource = logSource
                    eventLogs.Add(newEntry)

                    idCount += 1
                    If idCount > 200 Then
                        Exit For
                    End If

            Next

        Catch ex As System.Security.SecurityException
            'User doesn't have access to view the log
            'Move onto the next log
        End Try
    Next

    Return eventLogs.AsQueryable
End Function

<Query(IsDefault:=True)> _
Public Function GetEventLogTypes() As IQueryable(Of LogSource)

    Dim eventLogs As New List(Of LogSource)()
    For Each elEventEntry In System.Diagnostics.EventLog.GetEventLogs

        Dim event1 As New LogSource
        event1.SourceName = elEventEntry.Log
        eventLogs.Add(event1)
    Next

    Return eventLogs.AsQueryable
End Function

Public Sub InsertLogEntry(entry As LogEntry)
    Try
        Using applicationLog As New
          System.Diagnostics.EventLog("Application", ".")
            applicationLog.Source = "Application"
```

```
                    applicationLog.WriteEntry(
                        entry.Message, EventLogEntryType.Warning)
                End Using

            Catch ex As Exception
                Throw New Exception("Error writing Event Log Entry" & ex.Message)
            End Try
        End Sub

        Public Sub UpdateLogEntry(entry As LogEntry)
        End Sub

        Public Sub DeleteLogEntry(entry As LogEntry)
        End Sub

#End Region

    End Class

End Namespace
```

C#:
File: ApressExtensionCS\ApressExtensionCS.Server\DataSources\WindowsEventLog.cs

```csharp
using System;
using System.Collections.Generic;
using System.ComponentModel.DataAnnotations;
using System.Linq;
using System.ServiceModel.DomainServices.Server;
using System.Diagnostics;

namespace ApressExtensionCS.DataSources
{
    public class WindowsEventLog : DomainService
    {

        private string _serverName;
        public override void Initialize(DomainServiceContext context)
        {
            base.Initialize(context);
        }

        public override bool Submit(ChangeSet changeSet)
        {
            Boolean baseResult = base.Submit(changeSet);
            return true;
        }

        protected override int Count<T>(IQueryable<T> query)
        {
            return query.Count();
        }
```

```
[Query(IsDefault = true)]                                              ❶
public IQueryable<LogEntry> GetEventEntries()
{

    int idCount = 0;
    List<LogEntry> eventLogs = new List<LogEntry>();
    LogSource logSource = default(LogSource);

    foreach (var eventSource in EventLog.GetEventLogs("."))
    {
        logSource = new LogSource();
        logSource.SourceName = eventSource.Log;

        try
        {
            foreach (System.Diagnostics.EventLogEntry eventEntry
                in eventSource.Entries)
            {
                LogEntry newEntry = new LogEntry();
                newEntry.LogEntryID = idCount;
                newEntry.EventDateTime = eventEntry.TimeWritten;
                newEntry.Message = eventEntry.Message;
                newEntry.Message = eventEntry.Source;
                newEntry.SourceName = eventSource.Log;
                newEntry.EventSource = logSource;
                eventLogs.Add(newEntry);
                idCount += 1;
                if (idCount > 200)
                {
                    break;
                }
            }

        }
        catch (System.Security.SecurityException ex)
        {
            //User doesn't have access to view the log
            //Move onto the next log
        }
    }

    return eventLogs.AsQueryable();
}

[Query(IsDefault = true)]
public IQueryable<LogSource> GetEventLogTypes()
{

    List<LogSource> eventLogs = new List<LogSource>();
```

```csharp
        foreach (var elEventEntry in
            System.Diagnostics.EventLog.GetEventLogs())
        {
            LogSource event1 = new LogSource();
            event1.SourceName = elEventEntry.Log;
            eventLogs.Add(event1);
        }

        return eventLogs.AsQueryable();
    }

    public void InsertLogEntry(LogEntry entry)
    {
        try
        {
            using (System.Diagnostics.EventLog applicationLog =
                new System.Diagnostics.EventLog("Application", "."))
            {
                applicationLog.Source = "Application";
                applicationLog.WriteEntry(
                    entry.Message, EventLogEntryType.Warning);
            }
        }
        catch (Exception ex)
        {
            throw new Exception(
                "Error writing Event Log Entry" + ex.Message);
        }
    }

    public void UpdateLogEntry(LogEntry entry)
    {}

    public void DeleteLogEntry(LogEntry entry)
    {}
    }
}
```

This code relies on the methods in the System.Diagnostics namespace to retrieve the event log messages. It decorates the GetEventEntries method with the Query(IsDefault=true) attribute ❶. This indicates that LightSwitch should use it as the default method for returning a collection. This code includes logic that limits that number of entries to return to 200, and it also includes an error trap that allows the code to skip over event sources that it can't access because of insufficient permissions. In practice, you can modify this code so that it better handles these conditions.

Because the Windows Event Log doesn't allow you to update or delete individual entries, notice that the code doesn't implement the UpdateLogEntry and DeleteLogEntry methods.

Using the Data Source Extension

You've now completed all of the code that's needed to build and use your data source extension. Once you've installed your extension, you can use it by going to Solution Explorer in your LightSwitch project, selecting the right-click "Add Data Source" option, and choosing "WCF RIA Service." In the next dialog that appears, you'll find an entry for the Windows Event Log service in the "Available WCF RIA Service classes" list box, as shown in Figure 13-15.

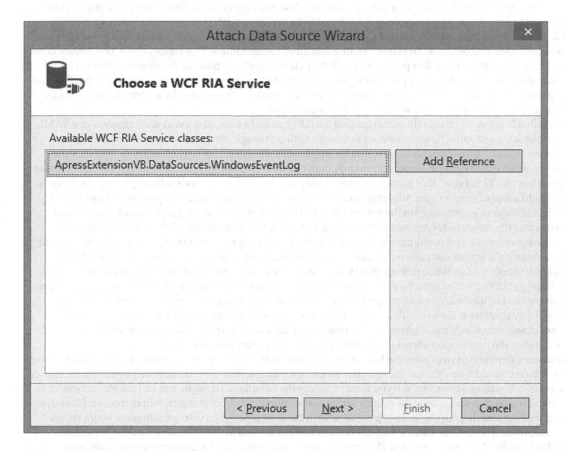

Figure 13-15. *Using the Data Source Extension*

Select the Windows Event Log service, and carry out the remaining steps in the "Attach Data Source Wizard." Once you've completed the Wizard, you'll be able to consume the Windows Event Log in your application, just as you would for any other data source.

Summary

In this chapter, you learned how to create business type, shell, theme, and data source extensions. Business types allow you to define rich data types that contain validation and are associated with custom controls that allow users to work with your data. They're based on primitive, basic LightSwitch types, and an advantage of using them is that LightSwitch applies business type validation, irrespective of the screen control you use. LightSwitch stores business type definitions in an LSML file. This file allows you to specify the underlying data type, any custom validation that you want to apply, and the attributes that you want to expose through the table designer. To associate your business type with custom validation, you'd specify the name of a validation factory class in your business type's LSML file. When LightSwitch needs to validate the value of a business type, the factory class returns an instance of a custom validation class that contains your validation logic. The validation code that you write belongs in your Common project, because this allows LightSwitch to carry out validation on both the server and the client.

You can define custom attributes to allow developers to control the behavior of your business type. An example of this is the list of valid phone number formats that you'll find in LightSwitch's Phone Number business type. LightSwitch allows you to edit this list by opening a pop-up window from the table designer's property sheet. This chapter shows you how to create an editor control that behaves in the same way. This technique relies on a WPF control that defines your pop-up editor control. To link this control with an attribute, you specify an attribute in your business type's LSML file and define a "UI Editor" setting that links the attribute with a factory class. The factory class returns an instance of an editor class that produces the UI that Visual Studio displays in the property sheet. This UI may contain controls that allow the developer to edit your attribute, but in this case, it simply returns a hyperlink that opens the pop-up window. Once the developer edits the value, the editor class updates the underlying attribute by using an IPropertyEntry object that was supplied by the factory class.

Custom shells allow you to modify the structure and overall layout of an application. A shell consists of a XAML file that defines the layout of your UI, and also contains controls that manage commands, navigation, and screen interaction. "View Models" allow your UI to consume the application data that LightSwitch exposes. The six view models allow you to access navigation items, commands, active screens, and validation details. LightSwitch includes a "Component View Model Service" that provides you with easy access to the view models through your XAML code. You can simply add a line of code in your Silverlight control that references the service and pass in a View Model Id. This sets the data context of your control to the view model, and you can data-bind the properties of your control to the properties that the view model exposes. A custom shell requires you to write the .NET code that executes commands, manages screens, and performs navigation. This chapter has shown you how to create a ScreenWrapper object that determines if a screen contains data changes or validation errors. You've also found out how to build custom navigation by using a ComboBox control that allows users to open screens. This ComboBox data-binds to a collection of INavigationScreen objects by using the navigation view model. When a user selects a screen, it triggers code that prompts the LightSwitch runtime to open the selected screen. Although the runtime opens the screen, it doesn't display any content to the user—this is something that you need to manage yourself. To do this, you'd use a ServiceProxy object that notifies you whenever the runtime opens a screen. In the example that you've seen, the code that handles the notification shows the screen by adding the content to a tab control.

Custom themes allow you to customize the font, color, and styles that a shell applies. The styles in a theme are defined in a XAML file. When you add a new theme, the template creates a working theme that contains well-commented sections that describe each style setting. For example, if you want to change the command bar style, you can use the comments to find the command bar section and amend the entries within that section to modify the colors, font names, and font styles.

If you find yourself carrying out the same repetitive tasks in the screen designer, you can automate your process by creating a custom screen template extension. Screen templates are defined in .NET files in your Design project. The template file includes .NET properties that allow you to specify attributes such as the name, description, and importantly, the root data source type. The root data source type allows you to define the data that fills the "Screen Data" drop-down in the "Add New Screen" dialog. Screen templates create screens by calling a method called Generate. This method allows you to build screens in code by calling the methods that are provided by a screen generator host. This host object includes methods that you can call to carry out the same tasks that you'd perform in the screen designer. For example, you can use the host to create local screen properties, add content items, and change the control that renders a data item. The host generator also includes a method that allows you to add .NET code to your screen. When you create a screen template, you'll need to create code templates that define both the VB and C# versions of your code.

Finally, data source extensions allow you to write an extension that connects to a data source. This process uses a domain service class, so the code that you need looks very similar to the RIA service code from Chapter 9. This chapter has shown you how to create a data source extension that connects to the Windows Event Log. To create a data source extension, you need to add entity classes that describes the data that your extension returns. You can also create Associations that enable you to define relations between the entity classes that you've defined. The code in your domain service class includes methods to retrieve, add, update, and delete the data from your data source. Just as if you were writing an RIA service, you need to define a default method that returns a collection of data. You'd do this by decorating a "get" method with the Query(IsDefault=true) attribute.

CHAPTER 14

∎∎∎

Creating Reports

Although LightSwitch doesn't include a built-in report generator, you can build reports by using other products and integrate the results into your LightSwitch application. In this chapter, you'll learn how to

- Create reports using ASP.NET and SQL Server Reporting Services

- Link and display reports from within your LightSwitch application

- Create documents using Microsoft Word, and generate PDF output

This chapter shows you how to extend the HelpDesk application to include reports. You'll find out how to create ASP.NET pages to show timesheet entries for an engineer and create charts that summarize the status of the issues that have been recently added. You'll learn how to use SQL Server Reporting Services to list the issues that have been assigned to an engineer, and you'll find out how to use Microsoft Word's mail-merge feature to generate letters to departments that have raised a high number of issues.

Choosing a Reporting Option

Microsoft SQL Server Reporting Services and Microsoft ASP.NET are great choices for reporting because you can obtain them free of charge, they're well supported by Microsoft, and they integrate well with LightSwitch. Both products share one thing in common: they're capable of producing output that you can access through a web address. This chapter shows you how to produce reports by using both of these products, and it teaches you a common technique that links web-based reports with your LightSwitch application.

Accessing Microsoft Word through COM automation is a technique that you can use in desktop applications. By using COM, you can also generate PDF reports on the client by using Silverlight PDF libraries. If you're looking for report generators that integrate well with LightSwitch and are prepared to pay, there are third-party controls that you can buy that are specifically built for LightSwitch. Table 14-1 summarizes the reporting techniques that this chapter teaches you.

Table 14-1. *Reporting Techniques*

Technique	Desktop Application	Web Application
Use Reporting Services	✓	✓
Automate Microsoft Word	✓	
Create PDF files on the client	✓	
Use third-party controls	✓	✓

This chapter focuses mainly on the Silverlight client for two reasons. The first reason is that, for web-based applications (Silverlight and the HTML client), users can print the page that they're viewing through their web browser. So in web applications, you can produce printable output by creating a screen that contains the data that your users want to print. If you need to aggregate your data so that it includes counts and averages, you can use the query techniques that you learned in Chapter 4 to produce this output. Second, HTML client applications are targeted toward mobile and tablet devices. Someone who's using a mobile device is less likely to want to print and generate reports, compared to someone who's sitting in front of a desktop application at an office.

Although web users can use the built-in printing feature that their web browser offers, the printed output might contain content that the user doesn't want, such as navigation items, tab headings, and commands. The ASP.NET and Reporting Services examples solve this problem by producing output that doesn't contain any extraneous content. Unlike browser applications, desktop applications don't include any printing support, which is why there's a greater need to add reporting functionality to Silverlight desktop applications.

Using ASP.NET to Create Reports

A simple method of producing printable output is to create an ASP.NET web site that contains web pages that are populated with data. In this section, you'll learn how to create a simple ASP.NET web project that includes some simple data-driven web pages. This is a fairly basic overview of ASP.NET; if you want to find out more, the official ASP.NET web site (http://www.asp.net/) is a great resource.

Creating an ASP.NET Project

The first step is to create an ASP.NET web site. You can reuse the HelpDeskPortal project from Chapter 10 or create a new project. To make it easier for you to work with both your ASP.NET and LightSwitch projects, you can add your ASP.NET project into the same solution as your LightSwitch project (as shown in Figure 14-1).

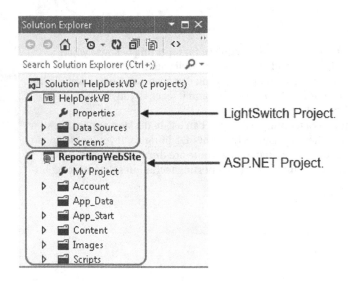

Figure 14-1. *The web site as it appears in Solution Explorer*

To create a new ASP.NET web site in your existing HelpDesk application, right-click your solution and choose the Add ➤ New Web Site option. This opens the Add New Web Site dialog and from here, you can select the ASP.NET Web Forms Application template. If you want to add your existing ASP.NET project from Chapter 10, you can choose the Add ➤ Existing Web Site option instead.

Adding an ASP.NET Page

Once you've created a Web Site project, you can add web pages that contain the data that you want to show. To demonstrate this, this section shows you how to create a web page that allows managers to view the issues that have been allocated to an engineer. Here are the steps that you'll need to carry out:

1. Right-click your Web Site project in Solution Explorer and select the Add ➤ Web Form option. When the Specify Name For Item dialog appears, name your Web Form IssuesByEngineer.aspx.

2. Place your page in either Split or Design view (as shown in Figure 14-2). Drag a SqlDataSource object from your toolbox onto your Web Form.

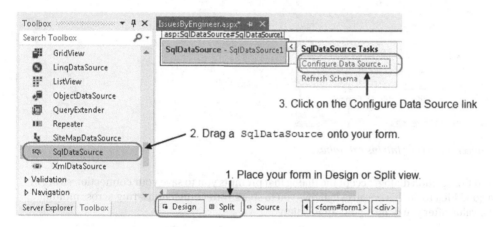

Figure 14-2. *Adding a SQL Server data source*

3. Select the SqlDataSource, and click the Configure Data Source link.

The Configure Data Source link opens a wizard that allows you to create a connection to your database. (See Figure 14-3.) Most likely, you'll want to deploy your LightSwitch application so that it creates a SQL Server database that you can work against. (See Chapter 18.) Alternatively, you could also work against your Intrinsic development database. To do this, click on the Change button that appears next to the Data Source label and choose the Microsoft SQL Server Database File option. This modifies the Add Connection dialog by providing a text box that allows you to enter the path to your ApplicationDatabase.mdf file.

Figure 14-3. *Adding a connection to your Intrinsic database*

When you exit the Add Connection dialog, accept the dialog that prompts you to save your connection string in the web.config file. It's a good idea to do this because it allows you to share your connection string across multiple web pages and change the value after you deploy your application.

Specifying the Data Source and Defining Parameters

Now that you've specified your connection string, the next step is to build a query that retrieves your data. This involves creating a parameter that filters your issue data by engineer. The Configure Data Source dialog should still be open at this point, so here are the remaining steps that you'll need to carry out in the wizard:

1. Carry on through the initial pages, and when you reach the Configure the Select Statement page, select the option to Specify A Custom SQL Statement Or Stored Procedure.

2. Use the Query Builder button to build a SELECT query based on the Issue table. Figure 14-4 shows the SQL statement that the Query Builder builds. This query retrieves timesheet entries for an engineer and includes a WHERE clause that filters the engineer column by a parameter called @Issue_Engineer.

Click a tab to create a SQL statement for that operation.

| SELECT | UPDATE | INSERT | DELETE |

◉ SQL statement:

```
SELECT Issues.Issue_Engineer, Issues.TargetEndDateTime, Issues.ProblemDescription, Issues.Id,
IssueStatusSet.StatusDescription, Issues.CreateDateTime, Issues.ClosedDateTime FROM Issues INNER JOIN
IssueStatusSet ON Issues.Issue_IssueStatus = IssueStatusSet.Id
WHERE (Issues.Issue_Engineer = @Issue_Engineer)
```

Query Builder...

Figure 14-4. *Defining a SELECT statement*

3. When you move to the next screen, the wizard recognizes that you've defined a parameter (@Issue_Engineer) and allows you to specify how this parameter value should be set. In our example, we want to supply the Issue_Engineer value through the web address. To do this, set the Parameter Source option to QueryString (shown in Figure 14-5) and name your QueryStringField EngineerId.

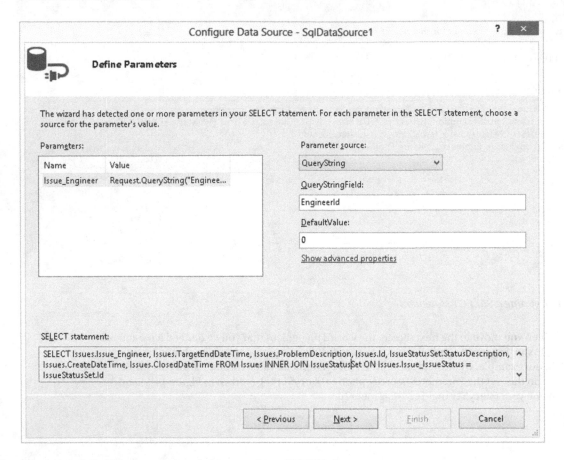

Figure 14-5. Defining parameters that are used in a WHERE clause

---

■ **Tip** This example prompts you to choose a SQL Server data source and create custom SQL commands to query your data. The benefit of this approach is that you can use it to access your raw data and to run fast-performing aggregate queries. Another approach is to use an `ObjectDataSource` that connects to your application's OData end point. And for more complex queries, you can use an `ObjectDataSource` that connects to custom data you exposed with the help of the Service Context API (which is described in Chapter 15). If you're unfamiliar with SQL, this provides a more familiar and integrated approach for querying your data and also allows you to apply any security access rules you added to the query pipeline.

Displaying your Data in a Grid and Viewing your Page

After you create your data source, the last step is to bind your data to a screen control. The easiest way to do this is to use a `GridView` control. This control allows you to show a tabular view of data. To use this control, drag an instance of a `GridView` control from the Data section of your toolbox onto your Web Form. Next, use the `GridView` Tasks panel to set the data source to your `SqlDataSource` (shown in Figure 14-6), and use the Auto Format link to style your grid more attractively.

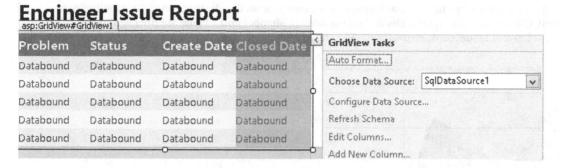

Figure 14-6. *Setting the data source of your* GridView

If you now run your ASP.NET project, Visual Studio opens your web page in a new browser window. You can specify which engineer you want to view by appending the EngineerId in the address (for example, http://localhost:1767/IssuesByEngineer.aspx?EngineerId=8). (See Figure 14-7.)

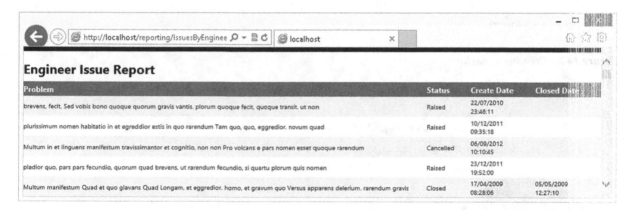

Figure 14-7. *The final report*

Creating Charts

ASP.NET 4 includes a Chart control that allows you to visualize your data. It includes all the usual chart types, such as pie, area, range, point, circular, and accumulation. This example shows you how to create a pie chart that summarizes issues by status code.

Create a new web page called StatusChart.aspx, and in the same way as the previous example, add a SqlDataSource. When you reach the Configure The Select Statement page, select the option to Specify A Custom SQL Statement Or Stored Procedure. In the wizard page shown, enter the SELECT statement shown in Listing 14-1.

Listing 14-1. Counting Issues Created Within the Last Seven Days, Grouped by Status

```
SELECT iss.StatusDescription, COUNT(i.id) AS IssueCount
FROM Issues i
JOIN IssueStatusSet iss
ON i.Issue_IssueStatus = iss.Id
WHERE  i.CreateDateTime >=DATEADD(DAY,DATEDIFF(DAY,0,GETDATE())- 7,0)
GROUP BY iss.StatusDescription
```

After you complete the steps in the wizard, drag a Chart control from the Data section of your toolbox onto your Web Form. Change the chart type to Pie, and set the X Value Member and Y Value Member settings to StatusDescription and IssueCount, respectively. (See Figure 14-8.)

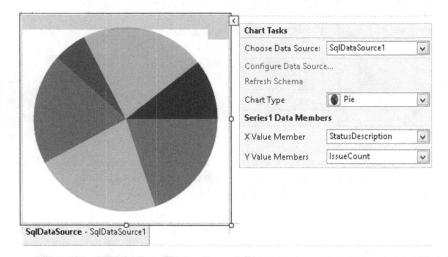

Figure 14-8. *Creating a pie chart*

When you run the page, the pie chart appears, as shown in Figure 14-9.

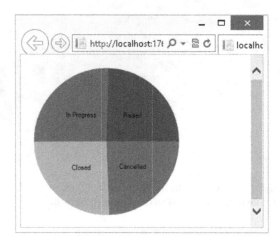

Figure 14-9. *ASP.NET page showing a pie chart*

Securing Reports

One problem with allowing users to connect to your data outside of LightSwitch is that it might expose information that some users shouldn't see. To address this problem, you can deny access to particular users by writing code in the load method of your ASP.NET page. Listing 14-2 shows the code that denies access to the user Tim, or to anyone who belongs in the Engineers group.

Listing 14-2. Securing Access to Reports

VB:
File: HelpDeskPortalVB\StatusChart.aspx.vb

```vb
Imports System.Security

Protected Sub Page_Load(ByVal sender As Object, ByVal e As System.EventArgs) Handles Me.Load
    If User.Identity.Name = "Tim" Then
        Throw New SecurityException("Access Denied to Tim")
    End If
    If User.IsInRole("Engineers") Then
        Throw New SecurityException(
            "Access Denied to users in the Engineers group")
    End If
End Sub
```

C#:
File: HelpDeskPortalCS\StatusChart.aspx.cs

```csharp
using System.Security;

protected void Page_Load(object sender, EventArgs e)
{
    if (User.Identity.Name == "Tim")
    {
        throw new SecurityException("Access Denied to Tim");
    }
    if (User.IsInRole("Engineers"))
    {
        throw new SecurityException(
            "Access Denied to users in the Engineers group");
    }
}
```

You can configure both your ASP.NET and LightSwitch applications to share the same authentication database. Chapter 16 describes how you would do this.

Instead of adding code to every web page that you create, another option is to specify your access rights declaratively in your web.config file. You'll find this file in the root folder of your ASP.NET project, and Listing 14-3 shows the code that you would add to your web.config file.

Listing 14-3. Securing Access via the web.config File

```xml
<system.web>
  <authorization>
      <deny role="Technicians"/>          ❶
      <deny users="Tim"/>                 ❷
      <deny users="?"/>                   ❸
      <allow users="*"/>                  ❹
  </authorization>
```

ASP.NET iterates through the entries in the authorization element and applies the first matching rule. In this example, the application denies access to users in the Technicians role ❶ and the Tim user ❷. Next, it denies access to all unauthenticated users (indicated by the ? entry) ❸. Finally, all remaining users (indicated by the * entry) will reach the allow rule ❹ and are subsequently granted access.

Deploying Your ASP.NET Application

To access the web pages that you've created outside of Visual Studio's development environment, you'll need to deploy your web project to an Internet Information Services (IIS) web server.

In this section, you'll find out how to deploy your ASP.NET project to an instance of IIS that's running locally on your computer. The first step is to install IIS and ASP.NET on your machine (if you haven't done so already). Chapter 18 includes a section that shows you how to do this. Once you've installed IIS, here are the main steps that you'll need to follow to get your application installed.

1. By default, IIS installs itself into the folder C:\inetpub\wwwroot. Create a new folder here called Reporting.

2. Build your ASP.NET project, and copy your project files into the folder C:\inetpub\wwwroot\Reporting.

3. Open IIS Manager—you'll find this in Control Panel ➤ Administrative Tools. Right-click the Reporting folder that's shown in the tree view, and choose the Convert To Application option. (See Figure 14-10.)

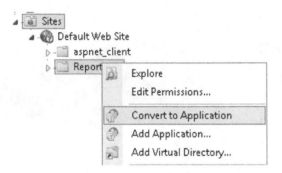

Figure 14-10. *Setting up an IIS web application*

This completes the steps that are necessary to set up your machine. You should be able to view the first page that you created by opening a browser and navigating to the URL http://localhost/IssuesByEngineer.aspx?EngineerId=8. The process of setting up a web server can be quite complex, and there might be variations to the steps that are shown here that depend on your operating system and the way that you've set up your machine. But this gives you the gist of what you need to do to install your web application locally on your machine. If you want to find out more, you'll find plenty of articles on the Web—a great place to start is the official ASP.NET web site (http://www.asp.net/web-forms/tutorials/deployment).

EXERCISE 14.1 – CREATING REPORTS

Choose one of the other tables in the HelpDesk application, and try to create an ASP.NET report. For example, try creating a report that shows a list of issue responses for a selected issue, and sort the results in date descending order. Rather than use a SQL Server data source, try to use an object data source and connect to your application's Issue Response table via the OData end point.

Using Microsoft SQL Server Reporting Services

Microsoft SQL Server Reporting Services provides a reporting environment that's more powerful than what you can achieve by using simple ASP.NET pages. Additional features in Reporting Services include subscription notifications and the ability to export data in formats such as Microsoft Word and Adobe PDF.

The example in this section shows you how to create a report that returns the number of issues raised by each department during the past six months.

Installing Reporting Services

SQL Server Reporting Services comes as part of SQL Server. Although it's not included in the basic version of SQL Server Express that's installed by Visual Studio, you can get it for free by installing SQL Server Express with Advanced Services. You can upgrade your basic instance of SQL Server Express to the Advanced Services version by installing the setup package that you can download from the official Microsoft SQL Server web site (http://www.microsoft.com/en-gb/download/details.aspx?id=29062).

Creating Reports

The tool that allows you to create, design, and edit reports is called SQL Server Data Tools (SSDT)—you can download this from http://msdn.microsoft.com/en-gb/data/tools.aspx. If you've used Reporting Services in the past, you'll recognize that the previous incarnation of SSDT was called Business Intelligence Development Studio (BIDS).

Reporting Services allows you to define and save reports in Report Definition Language (RDL) files. To create a report that returns HelpDesk issues by department, start SSDT and create a new Reporting Services project. Right-click the project menu, and choose the Add New Item option. From here, you can either create a blank report or use the wizard. For simplicity, I'll show you how to create a report by using the wizard. The first stage of the wizard prompts you to enter a data source. As with the ASP.NET example, you can specify a connection to a deployed version of your SQL Server database or your Intrinsic database.

When the wizard prompts you to enter a query, type in the SQL that's shown in Listing 14-4.

Listing 14-4. SQL to Return a List of Issues by Department

```
SELECT DepartmentName, COUNT(i.Id) AS 'DeptIssueCount' FROM Departments d
JOIN Users u
ON d.id = u.User_Department
JOIN Issues i
ON i.Issue_User = u.Id
WHERE  i.CreateDateTime >=DATEADD(MONTH, DATEDIFF(MONTH, 0, GETDATE())- 6,0)
GROUP by d.DepartmentName
```

The next dialog box prompts you to select a report type. The available options that you can choose include Tabular, Matrix, and Tablix. Select the tabular report option, and complete the remaining steps in the wizard. The last page in the wizard allows you to name your report—give it the name of IssuesByDepartment.rdl. This completes your report. You can test it by clicking the Preview tab that you'll find along the top of the report designer.

Using the Report Designer

Although you now have a functioning report, let's take a look at the report designer and explore some of the features that you'll find in SSDT. (See Figure 14-11.) On the left side of the designer, you'll find a Report Data pane—if it doesn't appear, you can open it by choosing the View ➤ Report Data option from the top-level menu. You'll also find a Toolbox pane on the left part of the designer. This allows you to add additional components to your report, including text boxes, lines, and subreports.

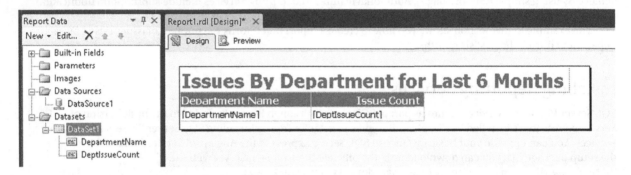

Figure 14-11. *The SSDT report design surface*

The rest of this section will show you how to add additional data sources, add data controls, and write code.

Managing and Adding Data Sources

The 'Report Data' pane allows you to manage the data items in your report. With it, you can add images, parameters, or built-in fields (for example, page numbers) to your report.

The Datasets folder allows you manage the table data that your report shows. It's important to understand that a Dataset in Reporting Services isn't the same as the DataSet object that you'll find when you're writing ADO.NET code.

You can use the right-click context menu on the Datasets folder to add additional DataSets. For example, if you want to add a drop-down box that allows your report to be filtered, you add an additional DataSet here to populate the choices that you want to show in your drop-down box.

Using the Report Design Surface

When you click the Design tab, SSDT shows a graphical designer that allows you to edit and design reports. If you examine the issues report that you've created, the body of the report contains a table. A table is a control that allows you to show data in rows and columns. This control is an example of a *data region*. Other data regions include the list, matrix, and tablix controls.

The list control allows you to show individual data items by using text boxes. The list control is more flexible than the table control because you can position the text boxes anywhere inside the row section.

The matrix control displays data grouped by row and column. This allows you to produce reports that are similar to cross tabs and pivot tables.

446

Writing Code

A great feature in Reporting Services is the ability to customize your reports through code. By doing this, you can apply custom logic to style and format your reports more attractively. With Reporting Services, you can add custom code in two ways: you can either use code from a .NET assembly, or you can embed code into your report. Here are the characteristics of these two options:

- **Use code from a .NET assembly:** This option is ideal if you want to use your logic in multiple reports. You can take advantage of the classes in the .NET Framework, such as the string formatting and math functions.

- **Embed custom code:** You can create custom methods in each report by right-clicking your report in Design view and choosing Report Properties ➤ Code. The advantage of embedded code is that it's quick and easy to use understand—there's no need to mess about compiling your .NET code assembly in a separate project before you can use it in your report.

Embedded code allows you to do something that's very powerful: set the value of a report property to an expression. For example, you can apply alternate row coloring in table rows by simply writing one line of code:

```
IIf(RowNumber(Nothing) Mod 2 = 0, "Silver", "Transparent")
```

This expression uses the IIf (conditional If) function. This function accepts three arguments: a test, the return value if the test is true, and the return value if the test is false. Figure 14-12 shows how you apply this expression to the BackgroundColor property of a table row.

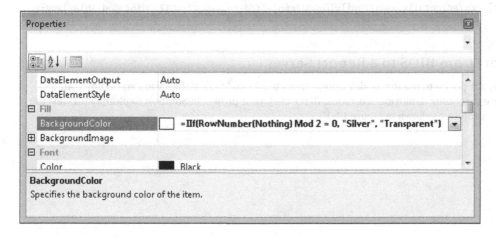

Figure 14-12. *Setting property values by using expressions*

Although this technique is very powerful, it's also quite easy to overlook. When you click your mouse into the BackgroundColor property, SSDT shows a drop-down box that allows you to choose a color. The presence of this drop-down box might make you forget that you can type code expressions into this control. Many of the other properties in the property sheet also include custom renderers, so this behavior applies not just to the BackgroundColor property.

Creating Drill-Through Reports

Drill-through reports allow users to click on a link to view additional details or related data. In the example that you've just created, you could modify the report so that it opens a child report of department issues when the user clicks on a department name. The key to creating a drill-through report is to set the Action property of your TextBox control. The properties sheet contains a button that's next to the Action property. When you click on this button, SSDT opens a dialog that allows you to choose what happens when the user clicks on the TextBox control. You can either open a subreport, go to a different URL, or jump to a predefined bookmark on your report.

Deploying Reports

Reporting Services uses a web-based report server and allows users to access reports through a web address. There are a couple of ways in which you can deploy your reports to your report server. You can deploy reports directly from SSDT, or you can upload your RDL files through a web-based Report Manager.

If you don't have a report server, you can host your RDL report through an ASP.NET page that contains a ReportViewer control. The advantages of this method are that it removes the dependency on the report server and saves you the trouble of having to set up a report server. The disadvantage is that you won't be able to take full advantage of all the features that are in Reporting Services, such as email notifications.

■ **Note**   When you deploy your Reporting Services solution into IIS, you must install the Reporting Services Redistributable package on your server. You can download this from the following URL: www.microsoft.com/downloads/en/details.aspx?FamilyID=a941c6b2-64dd-4d03-9ca7-4017a0d164fd&displaylang=en.

Deploying a Report from BIDS to a Report Server

The easiest way to deploy a report is to use the deploy option that's built into SSDT. Before you can deploy your report, you'll need to configure some deployment options. Right-click your project in Solution Explorer, and view the property window for your project, as shown in Figure 14-13.

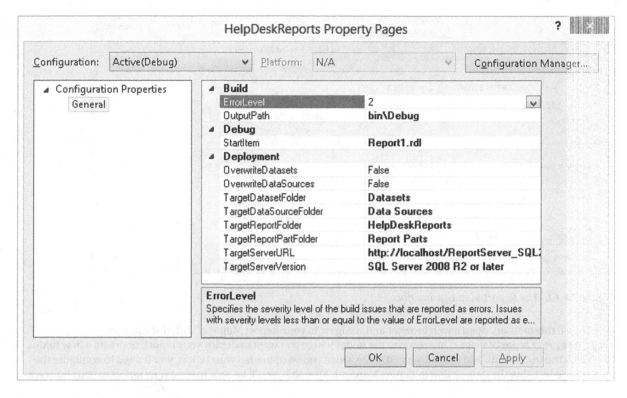

Figure 14-13. The properties of a Reporting Services project

You'll need to set the following items:

- **TargetReportFolder:** Enter the folder on the report server where you want to publish your reports.

- **TargetDataSourceFolder:** This specifies the folder where SSDT saves your Data Source files. If you leave this option blank, SSDT will publish your data sources in the `TargetReportFolder`.

- **TargerServerURL:** This field is mandatory if you wish to publish reports. Enter the path to the virtual directory of your report server (for example, `http://server/reportserver` or `https://server/reportserver`), rather than the URL of Report Manager. (Report Manager is the web application that allows you to manage Reporting Services.)

After you enter these details, you can deploy your reports by using the right-click Deploy option in Solution Explorer.

Importing a Report from Report Manager

Another way to deploy a report is to import your RDL file in Report Manager, shown in Figure 14-14. This option is ideal if you're unable to deploy from SSDT. An example of where this might apply is if your development computer isn't connected to the same domain or network as your target report server.

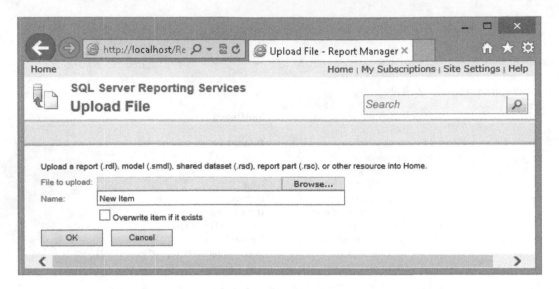

Figure 14-14. *The Report Manager interface*

To use this method, open a web browser and navigate to your Report Manager URL (for example, http://server/reportmanager). Navigate to the folder where you want to deploy your report, or create a new folder.

Click the Import link and upload your RDL file. Once you've uploaded your report, you'll need to configure the data source by using the data option in Report Manager. After that, you'll be able to view your report in your browser.

Hosting a Report on an ASP.NET Page

If you don't have access to a report server, you can still use reports by creating an ASP.NET web page that includes a Report Viewer control. The Report Viewer control can display reports from a report server, or it can process reports locally without needing a report server. When you set the Report Viewer control to Local Processing mode, it expects to process Report Definition Language Client-side (RDLC) files. These are cut-down versions of RDL files. You can create them in your ASP.NET project by using the File ➤ New menu option. If you created an RDL report in SSDT and want to use the Report Viewer control to process it locally, you need to first convert it to the RDLC format. Fortunately, this is quite an easy task. To carry out the conversion, you can simply rename your RDL file with an .rdlc extension. After you do this, return to your ASP.NET project and import your report by choosing the Add Existing Item option from your project menu. This process will convert your RDL file to RDLC format.

To show you how to use the Report Viewer control, here's how to display the Issue Report By Department report you created earlier in this chapter. The first steps are to create a new page in your ASP.NET project and set up the data source for your report:

1. Right-click your ASP.NET project in Solution Explorer, and select the Add ➤ New Item option. When the Add New Item dialog appears, go to the Data group that appears in the left pane and select DataSet. Name your object ReportingDataSet.xsd.

2. When the Dataset designer opens, choose the right-click Add ➤ TableAdapter option. This starts the TableAdapter Configuration Wizard. The first page prompts you to specify a connection to your SQL Server database. The next page asks you how the TableAdapter should access the database. Choose Use SQL Statements and in the next page, enter the SQL that's shown in Listing 14-4. Now build your project.

After you've set up your `DataSet`, import the `IssuesByDepartment.rdl` report from earlier in this chapter. If you didn't create this report, you can create a new RDLC report in your ASP.NET project. To create an RDLC report, select the Add ➤ New Item option in Solution Explorer. When the Add New Item dialog appears, go to the Reporting group that appears in the left pane and select `Report`. Name your object `IssuesByDepartment.rdlc`. Now carry out the following two steps:

1. In the designer for your report, right-click the `DataSets` folder and choose Add DataSet. This opens the DataSet Properties dialog. In the Data Source drop-down box select the `ReportingDataSet` that you've just created.

2. From the toolbox, drag a Table control onto your report. Use the designer to add the `DepartmentName` and `DeptIssueCount` fields to your table control.

Here's how to create a new web page that uses the Report Viewer control:

1. Add a new Web Form to your ASP.NET project, and call it `IssuesByDepartment.aspx`.

2. Switch your page to Design View, and drag a `ReportViewer` control from the Reporting section of the toolbar onto your page.

3. In the smart tag for the `ReportViewer` control, choose the `IssuesByDepartment.rdlc` report.

4. Click on the Choose Data Sources option. When the Choose Data Sources dialog appears, use the drop-down box to select the `ReportingDataSet` Departments DataSet. (See Figure 14-15.)

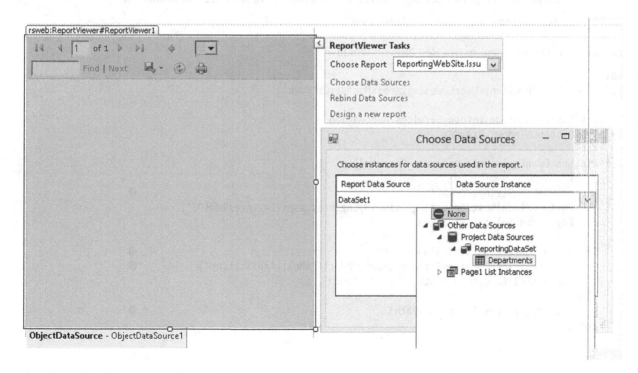

Figure 14-15. *Adding the Report Viewer control onto a web page*

This completes the design of your web page. You're now ready to run your page.

Linking Reports to LightSwitch

Once you've created a web-based report in ASP.NET or Reporting Services, the next step is to link it to your LightSwitch application. This section shows you how to

- Open your web report in a new browser window
- Display a web report inside a LightSwitch screen

Opening Reports in a New Browser Window

To open a report (or web page) in a new browser window, you can either *shell* an instance of your browser (in a desktop application) or use Silverlight's HtmlPage class (in a browser application).

In this example, you'll create a screen that shows a list of engineers in a data grid. You'll add a link on each row that opens the IssuesByEngineer report that you created earlier. To create this example, carry out the following steps:

1. Switch your LightSwitch project to File View, and add a reference to the System.Windows.Browser assembly in your Client project.

2. Create an Editable Grid Screen screen that's based on the Engineer table, and name your screen EngineersManagerGrid. (You might have already created this screen from Chapter 7.)

3. In the command bar for the data grid, add a new button called OpenEngineerIssueReport. If you created some of the earlier exercises, you'll already have some buttons here. You can optionally change the OpenEngineerIssueReport button to a link once you've added it.

4. Add the code that's shown in Listing 14-5.

Listing 14-5. Opening Reports in a New Browser Window

VB:
File: HelpDeskVB\Client\UserCode\EngineersManagerGrid.vb

```
Imports System.Runtime.InteropServices.Automation
Imports System.Windows.Browser

Private Sub OpenEngineerIssueReport_Execute()

    Dim urlPath = String.Format(                                    ❶
        "http://localhost/Reporting/IssuesByEngineer.aspx?EngineerId={0}",
        Engineers.SelectedItem.Id)

    If AutomationFactory.IsAvailable Then                           ❷
        Dim shell = AutomationFactory.CreateObject("Shell.Application")  ❸
        shell.ShellExecute(urlPath, "", "", "open", 1)
    Else
        HtmlPage.Window.Invoke(urlPath)                            ❹
    End If

End Sub
```

C#:
File: HelpDeskCS\Client\UserCode\EngineersManagerGrid.cs

```csharp
using System.Runtime.InteropServices.Automation;
using System.Windows.Browser;

partial void OpenEngineerIssueReport_Execute()
{
    string urlPath = string.Format(                                    ❶
            "http://localhost/IssuesByEngineer.aspx?EngineerId={0}",
            Engineers.SelectedItem.Id);

    if (AutomationFactory.IsAvailable)                                 ❷
    {
        var shell = AutomationFactory.CreateObject("Shell.Application"); ❸
        shell.ShellExecute(urlPath, "", "", "open", 1);
    }
    else
    {
        HtmlPage.Window.Invoke(urlPath);                               ❹
    }
}
```

The first part of this code builds the URL to the ASP.NET web page that you created earlier and appends the Id of the engineer that the user has selected in the data grid ❶. Although the root part of the URL is hard-coded in this example, it would be wise to retrieve this from a table or a place that you can modify after you deploy your application. The next part of the code detects your application type ❷. If youve created a desktop application, the code displays your report by using COM automation to *shell* an instance of your browser ❸. If you've created a browser application, the code uses the Silverlight HtmlPage class instead ❹.

When you now run your application, you'll be able to view the engineer issue report by clicking the button that appears against each engineer record (as shown in Figure 14-16).

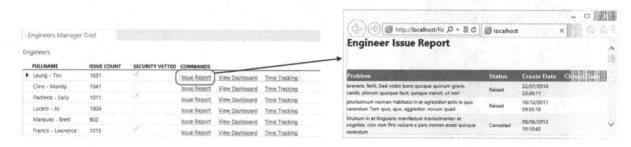

Figure 14-16. *Clicking a button in the grid opens the report in a new window*

Displaying Reports Inside a LightSwitch Screen

Rather than opening web pages in a new browser window, you can show reports inside your LightSwitch screen by using the Silverlight WebBrowser control. A slight disadvantage is that browser applications don't support this control, so this method works only in desktop applications.

Showing Reports in a Details Screen

To demonstrate how to display a web page on a screen, this example adds the ASP.NET pie chart of issue statuses to a screen that allows managers to see an overview of issues. To create this example, carry out the following steps:

1. Open the IssuesManagerGrid screen from Chapter 7, or alternatively create a new screen. The screen doesn't need to be based on any particular screen template or table.

2. Click the Add Data Item button, and add a new string property called ReportProperty. Make sure that you've unchecked the Is Required check box.

3. Drag ReportProperty onto your screen, and change the control type from a text box to a custom control. You can add this control to a new tab layout to keep it separate from the existing items on your screen.

4. In the properties sheet for ReportProperty, click on the Change link and set the control type to System.Windows.Controls.WebBrowserControl. (Refer to Chapter 11 for more details.)

5. In the properties sheet for ReportProperty, set the Min Width and Min Height values to 300. Your web page won't show if you leave the Width and Height properties set to Auto.

6. Append the code that's shown in Listing 14-6 to the Created method of your screen.

This completes your screen. Figure 14-17 shows how it looks at runtime.

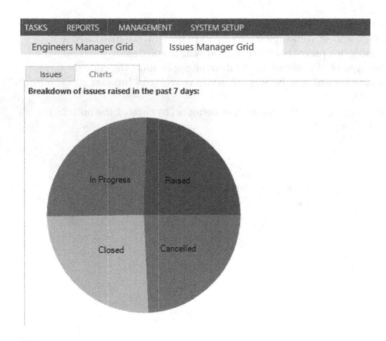

Figure 14-17. *Report shown inside a LightSwitch screen*

Listing 14-6. Showing a Web Page on a LightSwitch Details Screen

VB:
File: HelpdeskVB\Client\UserCode\IssuesManagerGrid.vb

```vb
Imports System.Windows.Controls

Private Sub IssuesManagerGrid_Created()
    Dim control = Me.FindControl("ReportProperty")
    AddHandler control.ControlAvailable,
        Sub(send As Object, e As ControlAvailableEventArgs)
            DirectCast(e.Control, WebBrowser).Navigate(
                New Uri("http://localhost/reporting/IssuesByStatus.aspx"))
        End Sub
End Sub
```

C#:
File: HelpdeskCS\Client\UserCode\IssuesManagerGrid.cs

```csharp
using System.Windows.Controls;

partial void IssuesManagerGrid_Created()
{
    var control = this.FindControl("ReportProperty");
    control.ControlAvailable += (sender, e) => ((WebBrowser)e.Control).Navigate(
        new Uri("http://localhost/reporting/IssuesByStatus.aspx"));
}
```

■ **Caution** The WebBrowser control belongs in a different windowing plane, and odd things can therefore happen when you resize or scroll your screens. The WebBrowser control also appears on top of all other controls on your screen, and it won't honor any z-order values that you might try to apply. If you place an AutoCompleteBox control above the WebBrowser control, for example, the drop-down contents will appear behind the WebBrowser control. There isn't any easy way to fix this behavior. Therefore, you should thoroughly test any screens that use the WebBrowser control.

Showing Reports in a List Screen

Another way to use the WebBrowser control is to apply it on a screen that contains a data list or data grid. As the user changes the selected record through the list or grid, the page that's shown in the WebBrowser control will automatically update itself.

In this example, you'll create a screen that allows managers to view the IssuesByEngineer report. But unlike the earlier example that opened the report in a new browser window (as shown in Figure 14-16), you'll display the report in a WebBrowser control. The WebBrowser control will belong on a screen that shows a list of engineers. When the manager selects an engineer from the list, the WebBrowser control will update itself to show the details for the selected engineer. Here are the steps to build this example:

1. Build the WebBrowser custom control from Chapter 11. (See Listing 11-9.)

2. In your LightSwitch project, create a new List And Details screen based on the Engineer table. Name your screen EngineerListReport.

3. Delete the engineer fields that you don't want to show from the Engineer Details section of your screen. Add the Id property to the Engineer Details section of your screen. Change the control type from a label to a custom control.

4. In the properties sheet, click on the Change button and open the Add Custom Control dialog. Use the browse button to select your ApressControls.dll file from Chapter 11, and set the custom control type to ApressControls.WebBrowser. To further improve the presentation of your screen, set the Min Width and Min Height to 300. You can also set the Label Style to Collapsed, and the horizontal and vertical alignments to Stretch.

5. Add the code to the Created method of your screen, as shown in Listing 14-7.

Listing 14-7. Showing a Web Page on a LightSwitch List and Details Screen

VB:
File: HelpDeskVB\Client\UserCode\EngineerListReport.vb

```
Imports System.Windows.Controls
Imports System.Windows.Data

Private Sub EngineerListReport_Created()
    Dim control = Me.FindControl("Id")
    Dim converter As New IdToReportUrlConverter()
    control.SetBinding(                                          ❶
        ApressControlsVB.WebBrowser.URIProperty,
        "Value", converter, BindingMode.OneWay)
End Sub

'Add this after the 'End Class' for your 'EngineerListReport' Class
Public Class IdToReportUrlConverter                             ❷
    Implements IValueConverter

    Public Function Convert(
    value As Object,
    targetType As System.Type,
    parameter As Object,
    culture As System.Globalization.CultureInfo
) As Object Implements System.Windows.Data.IValueConverter.Convert

        If value IsNot Nothing Then
            Return New Uri(                                      ❸
                "http://localhost/Reporting/IssuesByEngineer.aspx?EngineerId=" &
                    value.ToString)
        Else
            Return New Uri("")
        End If
    End Function

    Public Function ConvertBack(
    value As Object,
    targetType As System.Type,
    parameter As Object,
```

```
        culture As System.Globalization.CultureInfo
) As Object Implements System.Windows.Data.IValueConverter.ConvertBack

        Return New NotImplementedException
    End Function

End Class
```

C#:
File: HelpDeskCS\Client\UserCode\EngineerListReport.cs

```csharp
using System.Windows.Controls;
using System.Windows.Data;

partial void EngineerListReport_Created()
{
    IdToReportUrlConverter converter = new IdToReportUrlConverter();
    var control = this.FindControl("id");
    control.SetBinding(ApressControlsCS.WebBrowser.URIProperty,        ❶
        "Value", converter, BindingMode.OneWay);
}

// Add this code after your 'EngineerListReport' class
public class IdToReportUrlConverter : IValueConverter                 ❷
{
    public object Convert(object value, Type targetType,
        object parameter, System.Globalization.CultureInfo culture)
    {
        if (value != null){
        return new Uri(                                               ❸
            @"http://localhost/Reporting/IssuesByEngineer.aspx?EngineerId=" +
                value.ToString());
        }
        else{
            return null;
        }
    }

    public object ConvertBack(object value, Type targetType,
        object parameter, System.Globalization.CultureInfo culture)
    {
        return new NotImplementedException();
    }
}
```

6. This code uses a value converter called IdToReportUrlConverter. Create this class immediately after your EngineerListReport class. Listing 14-7 shows the code that you'll need to add.

This completes the screen design tasks. You're now ready to run your application.

This code uses the WebBrowser custom control that you created in Chapter 11. This custom control exposes a dependency property called URIProperty. Whenever this property changes, the control will navigate to the value of the URIProperty.

This example adds an Id property to your screen and changes the control type to the custom WebBrowser control. This means that the underlying data context of the WebBrowser control is the numeric Id value. The SetBinding method ❶ binds the numeric Id to the custom web control's URIProperty. But the URIProperty must be supplied in the format of a web address. Therefore, the IdToReportUrlConverter value converter ❷ takes the numeric ID and returns a web address that builds the Id value into the address ❸.

Printing Reports

An important requirement in many business applications is the ability to print documents. Unfortunately, LightSwitch doesn't include any built-in support for printing. But with a small modification to your ASP.NET reports, you can call some JavaScript that opens the web browser's print dialog. This would allow the user to send the contents of the web page to the printer. To demonstrate this, you'll now modify your IssuesByEngineer report so that it includes a print button. To create this example, carry out the following steps:

1. Open your ASP.NET project, and open the IssuesByEngineer.aspx page.

2. Switch your page to Source View. Just above the GridView control, add the following line of code:

```
<input type="button" value="Print"
    onclick="javascript:window.print()" />
```

3. Redeploy this page to your web server.

The line of code that you've added creates a print button. When the user clicks on this button, it triggers a piece of JavaScript that opens the browser's print dialog. Figure 14-18 shows what this button looks like when you add it to the EngineerListReport screen that you created from the earlier example.

Figure 14-18. *Report shown inside a screen based on the List And Details Screen template*

■ **Tip** If you're using the WebBrowser control from the System.Windows.Controls namespace, a useful method that you can call from your C# or VB code is the WebBrowser.InvokeScript method. This allows you to call JavaScript functions that are defined on the web page that's shown in the control. For example, if you didn't want to include a print button on the actual web page, you could call the JavaScript Window.Print method by using the InvokeScript method.

Opening Reports in an HTML Client Application

So far, I've shown you how to link Silverlight applications to custom web pages that contain reports. As I mentioned earlier, the main focus of this chapter is Silverlight desktop applications because that's the platform where users are most likely to want to produce reports. If you're creating an HTML client application, you can still use the ASP.NET and Reporting Service techniques that I've showed you in this chapter.

A big advantage of HTML client applications is that it easily allows you to add hyperlinks to other web pages and resources. Let's suppose that your HTML client application includes a screen that shows engineers. If you want to add a link that opens the IssuesByEngineer report page, you can accomplish this by creating a custom control. The code in Chapter 8 demonstrates how to add a hyperlink in a custom control. If you want to show a web page inline with the rest of your screen, you can create a custom control that uses an iframe. An iframe is an HTML control that displays a web page inside another web page. Chapter 8 included an example of how to use an iframe to upload files.

Creating Reports with Microsoft Word

If you're writing a desktop application, you can create reports by accessing Microsoft Word through COM automation. The only prerequisite is that your users must have Microsoft Word installed on their computers. In this section, you'll learn how to write code that adds LightSwitch data into Word documents. You'll learn how to combine the contents of a single record into a document and also learn how to mail merge a collection of screen data into a Word document.

■ **Tip** Microsoft Excel is also a great tool for creating charts and reports. You can adapt the COM automation techniques that are described here to automate Excel rather than Word.

Performing Simple Automation

The first example shows you how to use Word automation to create a simple letter. This example will be based on a Details Screen for a department record. You'll add a button that opens an existing Microsoft Word template, retrieves the department details from the LightSwitch screen, and inserts the contents into bookmarks that you've pre-added to your Word template. This method of automating Word is well established, and you might already be familiar with this technique. Unlike some other methods that rely on generating XML, for example, there's no requirement to have a modern version of Word. This chapter uses Word 2013. If you have an earlier version of Word, some of the menu items and options that you'll see might belong in a different place.

Creating a Word Template

To create a Word template, first open Microsoft Word and enter the body of your letter. In our example letter, the top section contains the recipient's address and name. These bits of data will be retrieved from the LightSwitch screen, and you'll add Word bookmarks into these locations to allow a data substitution to take place.

To insert a bookmark, click the Insert menu and choose Bookmark, as shown in Figure 14-19. In the Bookmark dialog box that opens, enter a bookmark name and add the bookmark. For the purpose of this example, add a bookmark after the "Dear" part of your letter and name your bookmark DepartmentName.

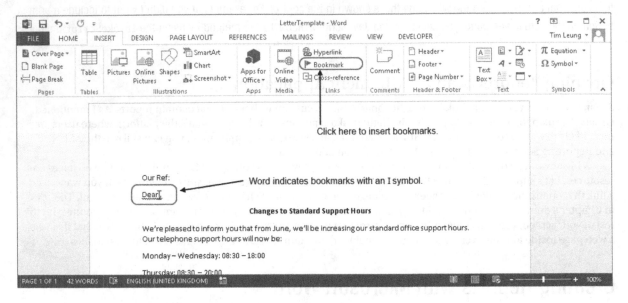

Figure 14-19. *Inserting a bookmark in a template*

Notice how Word identifies bookmarks with an I symbol. By default, Word doesn't show bookmarks, but you can make them visible by selecting the Show Bookmarks check box in the Word Options dialog box (shown in Figure 14-20). Enabling this option is useful because it allows you to see exactly where the data substitution takes place.

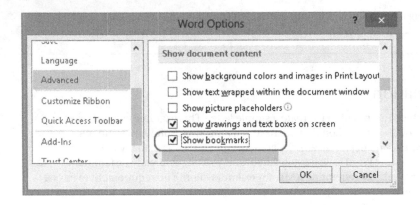

Figure 14-20. *Enabling the option to show bookmarks in Word*

Once you've finished your letter template, save your file as LetterTemplate.dotx.

Generating Word Documents

Having created your Word template, you can write code that produces your document and opens it in Word, or you can send the document directly to a printer without the user ever seeing Word appear on screen. This section will describe both techniques.

Generating and Showing Documents Onscreen in Word

In your LightSwitch application, create a Details Screen for the Department table, and name it DepartmentDetail. Add a button to your screen called CreateWordDoc, and enter the code that's shown in Listing 14-8. You'll need to add a reference to the System.Runtime.InteropServices.Automation namespace by using the imports or using statement.

Listing 14-8. Microsoft Word Automation Code

VB:
File: HelpDeskVB\Client\UserCode\DepartmentDetail.vb

```
Imports System.Runtime.InteropServices.Automation

Private Sub CreateWordDoc_Execute()
    If AutomationFactory.IsAvailable Then                                        ①
        Try
            Using wordApp = AutomationFactory.CreateObject("Word.Application")   ②
                Dim wordDoc = wordApp.Documents.Open(                            ③
                    "\\FileServer\Templates\LetterTemplate.dotx")
                wordDoc.Bookmarks("DepartmentName").Range.InsertAfter(           ④
                    Department.DepartmentName)
                wordApp.Visible = True                                          ⑤
            End Using
        Catch ex As Exception
            Throw New InvalidOperationException("Failed to create letter.", ex)
        End Try
    End If
End Sub
```

C#:
File: HelpDeskCS\Client\UserCode\DepartmentDetail.cs

```
using System.Runtime.InteropServices.Automation;

partial void CreateWordDoc_Execute()
{
    if (AutomationFactory.IsAvailable)                                          ①
    {
        try
        {
            using (dynamic wordApp =
                AutomationFactory.CreateObject("Word.Application"))             ②
            {
                dynamic wordDoc = wordApp.Documents.Open(                        ③
                    @"\\FileServer\Templates\LetterTemplate.dotx");
```

461

```
            wordDoc.Bookmarks("DepartmentName").Range.InsertAfter(        ❹
                Department.DepartmentName);
            wordApp.Visible = true;                                       ❺
        }
    }
    catch (Exception ex)
    {
        throw new InvalidOperationException("Failed to create letter.", ex);
    }
}
}
```

The first part of this code checks that your application is running on the desktop ❶. To improve this code, you could also add the same logic to the `CreateWordDoc` button's `CanExecute` method. This hides your button if your application runs in a browser, and it's a good idea to add this logic to the other examples in this chapter that are desktop specific. The next part of the code creates a COM reference to Word by calling the `AutomationFactory` class's `CreateObject` method ❷. The way that you instantiate a COM object is to supply a string argument that's known as a `ProgID`. This example supplies the `ProgID Application.Word`. But if you want to automate Excel instead, for example, you'd replace this with a `ProgID` of `Application.Excel`.

This technique of creating a COM object by passing in a `ProgID` string is known as *late binding*. The advantage of late binding is that it doesn't rely on any particular version of Word. As long as a version of Word exists on the client computer, your code will work. A major disadvantage, however, is that during design time, Visual Studio's code designer won't provide you with any IntelliSense. This means that you can easily write buggy and invalid code that you won't discover until run time.

The next part of the code opens your Word template document by calling the `Documents.Open` method ❸. In this example, the Word template file is held on a file share that's accessible through a UNC (Universal Naming Convention) file path. You'll need to modify this location so that it points to where you've saved your Word template. Storing your Word template in a local file share is ideal for applications that run on a local network, and you'll find out more about the pros and cons of using a local file share later in this section.

The next line of code uses the `Bookmarks` collection to locate the `DepartmentName` bookmark. It then inserts the screen entity's `DepartmentName` property after the bookmark location by calling the `Range.InsertAfter` method ❹. At the end of the process, the code shows the Word document to the user by setting the `visibility` property of the Word application to true ❺.

Sending Documents Directly to a Printer

Instead of showing the document to the user on the screen, you can send your Word document to a printer and discard it immediately afterward without saving changes. This allows you to easily send reports to a printer without any additional user intervention.

Listing 14-9 shows the code that allows you to accomplish this. The `Close` method allows you to pass an argument that forces Word to either discard or save changes, or prompts the user to save their changes. Because we want Word to quit without saving any changes, passing 0 into the `Close` method allows you to do this.

Listing 14-9. Printing and Closing a Word Document

VB:
File: HelpDeskVB\Client\UserCode\DepartmentDetail.vb

```
wordApp.PrintOut()
wordDoc.Close(0)
```

C#:
File: HelpDeskCS\Client\UserCode\DepartmentDetail.cs

```
wordApp.PrintOut();
wordDoc.Close(0);
```

Distributing the Template with the LightSwitch Client

The preceding automation example stores the Word template file in a file share that's available through a UNC file share. (Alternatively, you could have chosen to use a mapped drive.) The biggest disadvantages of this technique are that it works only on the internal network and it won't work in environments where Windows file sharing is disallowed.

You can overcome this problem by embedding your Word template in your application's XAP file. There are several other pros and cons of using this technique, and these are summarized in Table 14-2.

Table 14-2. *Template Distribution Techniques*

Distribution via a File Share	Distribution via the XAP File
This technique works only within your local network.	You can use this technique in applications that you deploy over the Internet.
You can easily update your file template after deploying your application.	You'll need to rebuild and redeploy your LightSwitch application if you want to make changes to your template file.
There isn't any impact on the load time of your application.	Adding your Word template to the XAP file makes it larger, which in turn makes your application slower to load.
This technique is more fragile because there's a dependency on a file outside of your application.	This technique is more robust because everything is self-contained.

You'll now find out how to modify the code from Listing 14-9 so that it retrieves the Word template from the XAP file rather than from a UNC file share. To add your LetterTemplate.dotx file to your XAP file, switch to File View and right-click your ClientGenerated project. Choose the Add Existing Item option, and use the Open File dialog to select your Word template file. Once you've added your template file, open the Properties sheet and set the Build Action property to Content. Note that if you've added an HTML client to your project, the ClientGenerated project will no longer exist. In this case, you'll need to add the Word template file to your Client project instead. The Resources folder is a good place to store your template file, as shown in Figure 14-21.

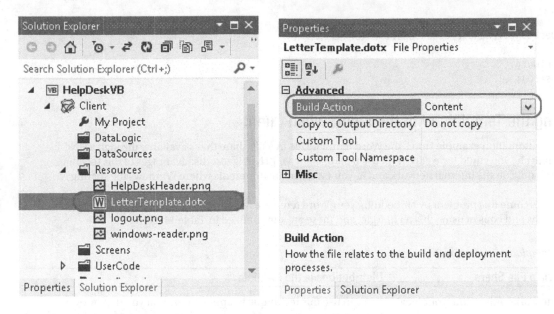

Figure 14-21. *Setting the build action to Content*

Listing 14-10 illustrates the code that extracts the template from your XAP package and saves it in the My Documents folder on the client computer. This code saves your template into the My Documents folder because security restrictions in Silverlight limit the places where you can save files on the local file system. You would add this code to Listing 14-8, just before the initial part that calls the CreateObject method to create a COM reference to Word.

Listing 14-10. Saving the Word Template to My Documents\LetterTemplate.dotx

VB:
File: HelpDeskVB\Client\UserCode\DepartmentDetail.vb

```
Dim resourceInfo = System.Windows.Application.GetResourceStream(        ❶
    New Uri("Resources/LetterTemplate.dotx", UriKind.Relative))

Dim path = Environment.GetFolderPath(
    Environment.SpecialFolder.MyDocuments) + "LetterTemplate.dotx"

Dim file = System.IO.File.Create(path)                                  ❷
file.Close()

'Write the stream to the file
Dim stream As System.IO.Stream = resourceInfo.Stream

Using fileStream = System.IO.File.Open(path,
    System.IO.FileMode.OpenOrCreate,
    System.IO.FileAccess.Write,
    System.IO.FileShare.None)
```

```
        Dim buffer(0 To stream.Length - 1) As Byte
        stream.Read(buffer, 0, stream.Length)
        fileStream.Write(buffer, 0, buffer.Length)          ❸
End Using
```

C#:
File: HelpDeskCS\Client\UserCode\DepartmentDetail.cs

```
var resourceInfo = System.Windows.Application.GetResourceStream(      ❶
    new Uri("Resources/LetterTemplate.dotx", UriKind.Relative));

dynamic path = Environment.GetFolderPath(
    Environment.SpecialFolder.MyDocuments) + "LetterTemplate.dotx";

dynamic file = System.IO.File.Create(path);                           ❷
file.Close();

//Write the stream to the file
System.IO.Stream stream = resourceInfo.Stream;

using (FileStream fileStream = System.IO.File.Open (path,
    System.IO.FileMode.OpenOrCreate,
    System.IO.FileAccess.Write,
    System.IO.FileShare.None)) {
        byte[] buffer = new byte[stream.Length];
        stream.Read(buffer, 0, int.Parse (stream.Length.ToString() ));
        fileStream.Write(buffer, 0, buffer.Length);                   ❸
}
```

The first part of this code calls the GetResourceStream method ❶. This method allows you to load resources that are embedded inside of your XAP file. The method expects you to supply a relative path that identifies your resource. This path doesn't require any leading slashes—if you add a leading slash, your code won't work. Also notice how the directory separator uses a forward slash (/) rather than a backslash. This line specifies a letter template that belongs in the Resources folder. But if you added the template file to the root of your project, the Uri string would simply be "LetterTemplate.dotx".

When the code obtains a resource stream, it creates a new file in the user's My Documents folder ❷. In practice, you'll most likely want to save the template in a more specific location and perform same basic error checking to see if a file of the same name already exists before creating it. Next, the code uses the methods in the System.IO.File namespace, and saves the contents of the embedded Word template in the new file that you've created ❸. This completes the extraction of the Word template file from the XAP file. To finish the code, you can modify the call to the wordApp.Documents.Open method in Listing 14-8 so that it opens the template from the My Documents folder rather than from the UNC file location.

■ **Note**   The main purpose of this example is to show you how to embed content in your LightSwitch application. If you need to access large resources in your application and discover that embedding resources in your XAP file slows down your application excessively, another option is to store your resources on a web server. You can then make a web request from the client to download the resource locally. If you apply this technique to this example, it would work well for Internet-deployed applications and allow you to change your Word template, without having to redeploy your application.

Performing Mail Merges with Word

Another common scenario in many business applications is the ability to perform mail merges. To show you how this works, this example shows you how to build a feature in the HelpDesk system to allow managers to generate letters to departments that have raised an excessive numbers of issues.

Creating a Mail Merge Word Template

The first step is to create a mail merge template in Word. From the ribbon in Word, select the Mailings group, click the Start Mail Merge button, and select the Letters option. Click the Select Recipients button, and choose the Type New List option. This opens the New Address List window, as shown in Figure 14-22.

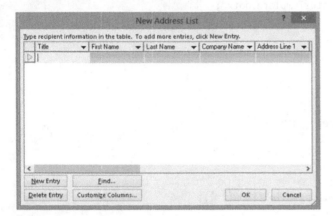

Figure 14-22. *Creating the mail-merge fields*

The New Address List window displays the mail-merge fields as columns in the grid. As you'll see, the default mail-merge fields include Title, FirstName, LastName, and several more.

You can add fields by clicking the Customize Columns button. For the purpose of this example, create three custom fields called DepartmentName, DepartmentManager, and Address1. When you click on the OK button, Word prompts you to save the list as a new Microsoft Office Address List file (or MDB file if you're using an earlier version of Word). Name this file MailMergeData and when the save operation completes, Word will enable the Insert Merge Field buttons on the ribbon. Although you'll no longer need to refer to this data file, you'll need to carry out these steps to create mail-merge fields that you can add to your template document.

The next step is to write the body of your letter. When you reach a point in a sentence or paragraph where you want to substitute a data value, use the Insert Merge Field to insert a merge field. (See Figure 14-22.) Once you've finished, save your template file as MailMergeTemplate.dotx.

Writing the Mail Merge Code

There are two ways to perform a mail merge. The first is to use the MailMergeTemplate.docx file that you've just created. Although this method works great and is relatively simple, the disadvantage is that both your letter text and mail-merge fields are hard-coded in your template file. This makes it more difficult if you want to dynamically generate your letter text, and to change the exact locations within your letter body where your mail-merge fields appear. The second method, therefore, relies on building your letter text in code. This allows you to change the content that's shown in your Word document based on some condition. This section shows you how to carry out a mail merge by using both techniques.

Using the Mail-Merge Fields Specified in the Word Template

Let's begin by creating a mail merge using the `MailMergeTemplate.docx` template. In this example, you'll create a screen that includes a list of departments and add a button that mail merges the screen data with your Word Template file. Here are the steps to carry out this example:

1. Create a query that returns departments that have raised a high number of HelpDesk issues. (Refer to Chapter 6 if you need help on this.) If you just want to run this example, you can skip this step and base the next step on the `Department` table rather than a custom query.

2. Create an editable grid screen that's based on this query, and name it `DepartmentsWithHighIssues`. The screen template creates a data grid of departments. Change the control from Data Grid to Data List.

3. Create a new `GroupBox` beneath the data list, and add a button to your screen. Name your button `DoMailMerge`. Figure 14-23 shows the design of your screen.

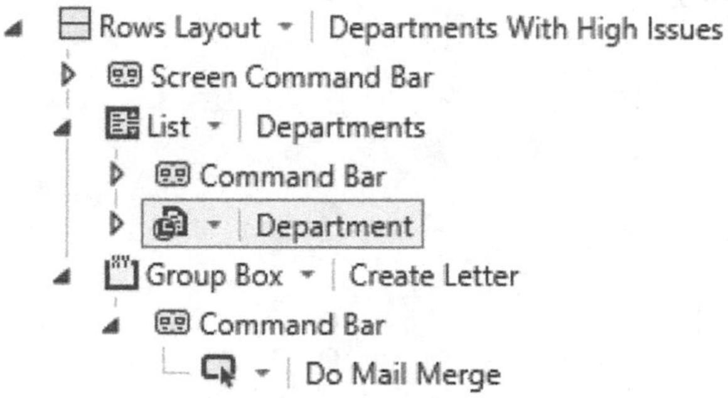

```
▲  ⊟ Rows Layout  ▾ │ Departments With High Issues
   ▷ ⊞ Screen Command Bar
   ▲ 🖺 List ▾ │ Departments
      ▷ ⊞ Command Bar
      ▷ 🗃 ▾ │ Department
   ▲ 🗔 Group Box ▾ │ Create Letter
      ▲ ⊞ Command Bar
         └ 🖵 ▾ │ Do Mail Merge
```

Figure 14-23. *Screen design*

4. Enter the code shown in Listing 14-11.

Listing 14-11. Mail-Merge Code

VB:
File: `HelpDeskVB\Client\UserCode\DepartmentsWithHighIssues.vb`

```vb
Imports System.Runtime.InteropServices.Automation
Imports System.Reflection

Namespace LightSwitchApplication

    Public Class DepartmentsWithHighIssues

        ' Declare Global Variables
        Private wordApp As Object
        Private wordDoc As Object
        Private missingValue As Object = System.Reflection.Missing.Value
```

```
    ' Here are the values of the WdMailMergeDestination Enum
    Const wdSendToNewDocument As Integer = 0
    Const wdSendToPrinter As Integer = 1
    Const wdSendToEmail As Integer = 2
    Const wdSendToFax As Integer = 3

    Private Sub DoMailMerge_Execute()                                    ❶
        Dim wordMailMerge As Object
        Dim wordMergeFields As Object

        ' Create an instance of Word  and make it visible.
        wordApp = AutomationFactory.CreateObject("Word.Application")
        wordApp.Visible = True

        ' Open the template file
        wordDoc = wordApp.Documents.Open(
            "\\Fileserver\Docs\MailMergeTemplate.dotx")                  ❷
        wordDoc.Select()

        wordMailMerge = wordDoc.MailMerge

        ' Create a MailMerge Data file.
        CreateMailMergeDataFile()                                        ❸

        wordMergeFields = wordMailMerge.Fields
        wordMailMerge.Destination = wdSendToNewDocument                  ❿
        wordMailMerge.Execute(False)                                     ❾

        ' Close the original form document.
        wordDoc.Saved = True
        wordDoc.Close(False, missingValue, missingValue)

        ' Release References.
        wordMailMerge = Nothing
        wordMergeFields = Nothing
        wordDoc = Nothing
        wordApp = Nothing

    End Sub
    Private Sub CreateMailMergeDataFile()

        Dim wordDataDoc As Object

        'Specify a Location with write access
        Dim fileName As Object = "\\Fileserver\Docs\DataDoc.doc"         ❹

        Dim header As Object =
            "DepartmentName, DepartmentManager, Address1"                ❻

        wordDoc.MailMerge.CreateDataSource(                              ❺
            fileName, missingValue, missingValue, header)
```

```vb
        ' Open the data document to insert data.
        wordDataDoc = wordApp.Documents.Open(fileName)

        ' Loop through the department screen collection
        ' Start at rowCount 2 because row 1 contains the column headers

        Dim rowCount As Integer = 2
        For Each d As Department In Departments                    ❼
            FillRow(wordDataDoc, rowCount,                         ❽
                d.DepartmentName, d.DepartmentManager, d.Address1)
            rowCount += 1
        Next

        ' Save and close the file.
        wordDataDoc.Save()
        wordDataDoc.Close(False)

    End Sub

    Private Sub FillRow(WordDoc As Object, Row As Integer,
        Text1 As String, Text2 As String, Text3 As String)

        If Row > WordDoc.Tables(1).Rows.Count Then
            WordDoc.Tables(1).Rows.Add()
        End If

        ' Insert the data into the table.
        WordDoc.Tables(1).Cell(Row, 1).Range.InsertAfter(Text1)
        WordDoc.Tables(1).Cell(Row, 2).Range.InsertAfter(Text2)
        WordDoc.Tables(1).Cell(Row, 3).Range.InsertAfter(Text3)

    End Sub

End Class

End Namespace
```

C#:
File: HelpDeskCS\Client\UserCode\DepartmentsWithHighIssues.cs

```csharp
using System.Runtime.InteropServices.Automation;
using System.Reflection;

namespace LightSwitchApplication
{
    public partial class DepartmentsWithHighIssues
    {

        dynamic wordApp;
        dynamic wordDoc;
        object missingValue = System.Reflection.Missing.Value;
```

```csharp
        // Here are the values of the WdMailMergeDestination Enum
        const int wdSendToNewDocument = 0;
        const int wdSendToPrinter = 1;
        const int wdSendToEmail = 2;
        const int wdSendToFax = 3;

        partial void DoMailMerge_Execute()                                      ❶
        {
            dynamic wordMailMerge;
            dynamic wordMergeFields;

            // Create an instance of Word  and make it visible.
            wordApp = AutomationFactory.CreateObject("Word.Application");
            wordApp.Visible = true;

            // Open the template file
            wordDoc =
                wordApp.Documents.Open(
                    @"\\Fileserver\Docs\MailMergeTemplate.dotx");            ❷
            wordDoc.Select();

            wordMailMerge = wordDoc.MailMerge;

            // Create a MailMerge Data file.
            CreateMailMergeDataFile();                                          ❸

            wordMergeFields = wordMailMerge.Fields;
            wordMailMerge.Destination = wdSendToNewDocument;                    ❿

            wordMailMerge.Execute(false);                                       ❾

            // Close the original form document.
            wordDoc.Saved = true;
            wordDoc.Close(false, ref missingValue, ref missingValue);

            // Release References.
            wordMailMerge = null;
            wordMergeFields = null;
            wordDoc = null;
            wordApp = null;

        }


        private void CreateMailMergeDataFile()
        {
            dynamic wordDataDoc;
            var fileName = @"\\Fileserver\Docs\DataDoc.doc";                    ❹
            var header = "DepartmentName, DepartmentManager, Address1";         ❻

            wordDoc.MailMerge.CreateDataSource(ref fileName, ref missingValue,  ❺
                ref missingValue, ref header);
```

```
        // Open the data document to insert data.
        wordDataDoc = wordApp.Documents.Open(ref fileName);

        // Loop through the customer screen collection
        // Start at rowCount 2 because row 1 contains the column headers
        int rowCount = 2;
        foreach (Department d in Departments )                          ❼
        {
            FillRow(                                                    ❽
              wordDataDoc, rowCount,
              d.DepartmentName , d.DepartmentManager , d.Address1 );
            rowCount++;
        }

        // Save and close the file.
        wordDataDoc.Save();
        wordDataDoc.Close(false, ref missingValue, ref missingValue);

    }

    private void FillRow(dynamic wordDoc, int Row,
        string Text1,string Text2, string Text3)

    {
        if (Row > wordDoc.Tables[1].Rows.Count)
        {
            wordDoc.Tables[1].Rows.Add();
        }
        // Insert the data into the table.
        wordDoc.Tables[1].Cell(Row, 1).Range.InsertAfter(Text1);
        wordDoc.Tables[1].Cell(Row, 2).Range.InsertAfter(Text2);
        wordDoc.Tables[1].Cell(Row, 3).Range.InsertAfter(Text3);
    }
  }
}
```

The high-level overview of the process that's shown in Listing 14-11 is as follows:

1. The code creates a Word document and populates it with data from your LightSwitch screen.

2. It uses your Word template file to create a new Word document, and sets the mail-merge data source to the document that you created earlier. It then carries out the actual mail merge.

The method that runs when the user clicks on the Mail Merge button is called DoMailMerge_Execute ❶. This method creates a Word document by opening your MailMergeTemplate.dotx template file ❷. It then calls a method called CreateMailMergeDataFile ❸. This creates a data document called DataDoc.doc and sets the data source of your Word document to this data document ❹. It does this by calling Word's CreateDataSource method ❺. This method expects you to supply the column headers for your data. The column names that you define must match the names of the mail-merge fields that you defined in the New Address List dialog. So in this example, these headings are called DepartmentName, DepartmentManager, and Address1 ❻. The remaining code in this method loops through the departments in the Departments collection ❼ and calls the FillRow ❽ method to populate the data document (DataDoc.doc).

Once the code populates the data document, the remaining code in the DoMailMerge_Execute method performs the mail merge by calling the Execute method on the wordMailMerge object ❾. This completes the mail merge, and the remaining code tidies up the objects that have been declared. You can optionally add some code here to delete the DataDoc.doc file if you want.

Prior to calling the Execute method, the code sets the Destination property ❿ of the wordMailMerge object to wdSendToNewDocument. This represents the numeric value of 0 and forces Word to show the document to the user. Table 14-3 shows the other acceptable values that you can set.

Table 14-3. *Constants That Are Used to Set the Mail Merge Destination*

Name of Constant	Value	Description
wdSendToNewDocument	0	Mail merge will be shown in the document.
wdSendToPrinter	1	Mail merge will be sent to the printer.
wdSendToEmail	2	Mail merge will be sent to your default email client.
wdSendToFax	3	Mail merge will be sent to a fax.

This mail-merge code populates your data document by using your screen's Departments collection. By default, this shows only 45 records at time. Therefore, you might want to increase this by changing the value of the No. Of Items To Display Per Page text box. If you want to mail merge all of the records in a table, you can modify your code so that it uses a query rather than a screen collection.

Creating Mail Merge Fields in Code

The preceding example relies on a static Word template file (MailMergeTemplate.dotx). If you want to dynamically change your letter body contents, you can use Word automation to create a blank Word document. You would then build the content and merge fields of your document in code before performing the mail merge.

To demonstrate this technique, this example customizes your screen to allow users to specify the first paragraph that appears in the letter, and also adds a check box that allows users to specify the level of formality of the letter. To create these screen controls, open your DepartmentsWithHighIssues screen, click on the Add Data Item button and create the following two local properties:

- **FirstParagraphProperty:** Data Type: String, Is Required: False
- **FormalityProperty:** Data Type: Boolean, Is Required: False

Now modify the contents of your DoMailMerge_Execute method, as shown in Listing 14-12.

Listing 14-12. Creating the Mail Merge Fields in Code

VB:
File: HelpDeskVB\Client\UserCode\DepartmentsWithHighIssues.vb

```
Private Sub DoMailMerge_Execute()

    Dim wordMailMerge As Object
    Dim wordMergeFields As Object

    ' Create an instance of Word  and make it visible.
    wordApp = AutomationFactory.CreateObject("Word.Application")
    wordApp.Visible = True
```

```vb
    ' Create a new file rather than open it from a template
    wordDoc = wordApp.Documents.Add()                                    ❶

    Dim wordSelection As Object
    wordSelection = wordApp.Selection
    wordMailMerge = wordDoc.MailMerge

    ' Create a MailMerge Data file.
    CreateMailMergeDataFile()                                            ❷

    wordMergeFields = wordMailMerge.Fields

    ' Type the salutation and add the 'DepartmentManager' merge field
    If FormalityProperty.GetValueOrDefault(False) Then                   ❸
        wordSelection.TypeText("Dear ")
    Else
        wordSelection.TypeText("Hi ")
    End If

    Dim wordRange As Object = wordSelection.Range

    wordMergeFields.Add(wordRange, "DepartmentManager")                  ❹
    wordSelection.TypeText(",")
    ' add the paragraph text that the user has entered
    wordSelection.TypeText(FirstParagraphProperty)                       ❺

    ' Perform mail merge.
    wordMailMerge.Destination = 0
    wordMailMerge.Execute(False)

    ' Close the original form document.
    wordDoc.Saved = True
    wordDoc.Close(False, missingValue, missingValue)

    ' Release References.
    wordMailMerge = Nothing
    wordMergeFields = Nothing
    wordDoc = Nothing
    wordApp = Nothing
End Sub
```

C#:
File: HelpDeskCS\Client\UserCode\DepartmentsWithHighIssues.cs

```csharp
private void DoMailMerge_Execute()
{
    dynamic wordMailMerge;
    dynamic wordMergeFields;
    dynamic wordSelection;
```

```
// Create an instance of Word and make it visible.
wordApp = AutomationFactory.CreateObject("Word.Application");
wordApp.Visible = true;

// Create a new file rather than open it from a template
wordDoc = wordApp.Documents.Add();                                    ❶

wordSelection = wordApp.Selection;
wordMailMerge = wordDoc.MailMerge;

// Create a MailMerge Data file.
CreateMailMergeDataFile();                                            ❷

wordMergeFields = wordMailMerge.Fields;

// Type the salutation and add the ' DepartmentManager' merge field
If(FormalityProperty.GetValueOrDefault(false))                        ❸
{
    wordSelection.TypeText("Dear ");
}
else
{
    wordSelection.TypeText("Hi ");
}


wordMergeFields.Add(wordSelection.Range, "DepartmentManager");        ❹
wordSelection.TypeText(",");
// add the paragraph text that the user has entered
wordSelection.TypeText(FirstParagraphProperty);                       ❺

// Perform mail merge.
wordMailMerge.Destination = 0;
wordMailMerge.Execute(false);

// Release References.
wordMailMerge = null;
wordMergeFields = null;
wordDoc = null;
wordApp = null;
}
```

This code works in much the same way as the preceding example. The first difference is that it creates a brand new Word document rather than creating one from a template ❶. It generates the data document just as before by calling the CreateMailMergeDataFile method ❷. If the user has checked the Formality check box ❸, the code sets the salutation of the letter to "Dear" Otherwise, it sets it to "Hi." This is a perfect example of the type of conditional logic that you couldn't apply if you used a static Word template. Immediately after the salutation text, the code adds the mail-merge field that allows the department manager name to be substituted in ❹. It then adds the paragraph text that's been added by the user ❺. Figure 14-24 shows how the final screen looks.

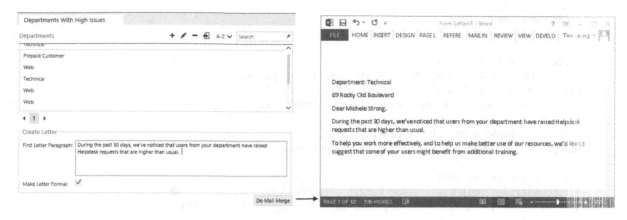

Figure 14-24. *Word mail-merge example*

Creating Adobe PDF Documents

Some organizations prefer to produce documents in PDF format, particularly for letters and documents that shouldn't be editable. The advantage of the PDF format is that it better preserves the layout and positioning of documents, and makes it more difficult for users to modify their contents.

There are several ways in which you can generate PDF documents. On the server, you can use Microsoft Reporting Services to export reports in PDF format. If your users use Microsoft Word 2007 or above, you could extend the Word automation code from earlier to save your output in PDF format rather than the default DOCX format.

In this section, you'll find out how to create a PDF document that summarizes the contents of an issue record. LightSwitch and Silverlight don't include built-in support for generating PDF files, but you'll find various third-party libraries that do allow you to create PDF documents. The one that we'll use is *silverPDF*—a free, open source library that you'll find at the CodePlex web site (`http://silverpdf.codeplex.com/`). This library is based on two other open source projects (iTextSharp and PDFsharp). If you've used any of these libraries before, the code here will be familiar to you.

To get started with silverPDF, download the `silverPDF.dll` file from the CodePlex web site. In your LightSwitch project, switch to File View and add a reference to the `silverPDF.dll` assembly in your `client` project. Open the `AddEditIssue` screen from Chapter 7, create a method called `OpenPDFReport`, and insert the code that's shown in Listing 14-13.

Listing 14-13. Programming silverPDF

VB:
File: HelpDeskVB\Client\UserCode\AddEditIssue.vb

```
Imports PdfSharp
Imports PdfSharp.Drawing
Imports PdfSharp.Pdf

Private Sub OpenPDFReport_Execute()

    Microsoft.LightSwitch.Threading.Dispatchers.Main.BeginInvoke(
    Sub()
        Dim document As New PdfDocument()                    ❶
        document.Info.Title = "Issue"
```

```vb
        ' Create an empty page
        Dim page As PdfPage = document.AddPage()                        ❷

        ' Create a set of  fonts                                        ❸
        Dim fontHeader1 As New XFont("Verdana", 18, XFontStyle.Bold)
        Dim fontHeader2 As New XFont("Verdana", 14, XFontStyle.Bold)
        Dim fontNormal As New XFont("Verdana", 12, XFontStyle.Regular)

        ' Get an XGraphics object for drawing
        Dim gfx As XGraphics = XGraphics.FromPdfPage(page)              ❹

        ' Create the report text
        gfx.DrawString("HelpDesk - Issue Detail", fontHeader1,          ❺
        XBrushes.Black, New XRect(10, 10, 200, 18), XStringFormats.TopLeft)

        gfx.DrawString("Issue Id:" & Issue.Id.ToString(), fontNormal,
            XBrushes.Black, New XRect(10, 30, 200, 18), XStringFormats.TopLeft)

        gfx.DrawString(Issue.Subject, fontHeader2,
        XBrushes.Black, New XRect(10, 50, 200, 18), XStringFormats.TopLeft)
        '.... create other Elements here

        ' Save the document here
        Dim myDocuments As String = Environment.GetFolderPath(
            Environment.SpecialFolder.MyDocuments)

        document.Save(myDocuments & "\IssueReport.pdf")

        'optionally 'shell' the native PDF application to view the file

    End Sub
    )

End Sub
```

C#:
File: HelpDeskCS\Client\UserCode\AddEditIssue.cs

```csharp
using PdfSharp;
using PdfSharp.Drawing;
using PdfSharp.Pdf;

partial void OpenPDFReport_Execute()
{
    Microsoft.LightSwitch.Threading.Dispatchers.Main.BeginInvoke(() =>
    {
        PdfDocument document = new PdfDocument();                       ❶
        document.Info.Title = "Issue";

        // Create an empty page
        PdfPage page = document.AddPage();                             ❷
```

```
    // Create a font                                             ❸
    XFont fontHeader1 = new XFont("Verdana", 18, XFontStyle.Bold);
    XFont fontHeader2 = new XFont("Verdana", 14, XFontStyle.Bold);
    XFont fontNormal = new XFont("Verdana", 12, XFontStyle.Regular );

    // Get an XGraphics object for drawing
    XGraphics gfx = XGraphics.FromPdfPage(page);                  ❹

    // Create the report text
    gfx.DrawString ("HelpDesk - Issue Detail " , fontHeader1,     ❺
    XBrushes.Black, new XRect(10, 10, 200, 18), XStringFormats.TopCenter );

    gfx.DrawString ("Issue Id: " + Issue.Id.ToString(), fontNormal ,
        XBrushes.Black, new XRect(10, 30, 200, 18), XStringFormats.TopLeft );

    gfx.DrawString (Issue.Subject, fontHeader2,
    XBrushes.Black, new XRect(10, 50, 200, 18), XStringFormats.TopLeft );

    //.... create other Elements here

    // Save the document here
    string myDocuments =
        Environment.GetFolderPath(Environment.SpecialFolder.MyDocuments);
    document.Save(myDocuments + "\\IssueReport.pdf");

    // optionally 'shell' the native PDF application to view the file

});

}
```

This code invokes the PDF creation code on the main UI dispatcher. This is required because the silverPDF library internally uses Silverlight methods that can be accessed only on the main UI thread.

Building a PDF document involves writing code that adds, configures, and lays out the items that you want to display. silverPDF doesn't include a graphical designer; despite this, it still works effectively.

The code in this method begins by creating a PDF document ❶, and then it adds a page to the document ❷. It then defines a set of fonts that are used in the document ❸. The XGraphics object ❹ allows you to add content to your PDF document. It exposes various Draw methods that allow you to create graphical elements, as shown in Figure 14-25. DrawString is the method that allows you to add text to your document, and the code calls this method several times, starting with a call that creates a piece of header text ❺. The DrawString method requires you to supply the font name, color, X-Y co-ordinates, sizing, and alignment details to properly display the text.

`gfx.draw`

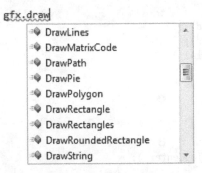

Figure 14-25. silverPDF `Draw` *methods*

The final part of the procedure saves the PDF file to the user's `My Documents` folder by calling the `PDFDocument` object's Save method. Figure 14-26 shows how the final report looks.

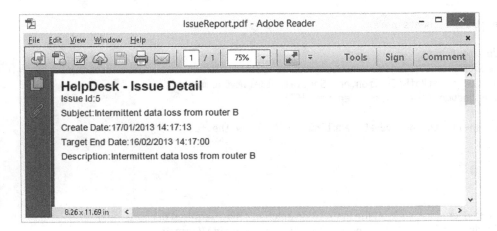

Figure 14-26. PDF output produced with silverPDF

Note that this code invokes the PDF creation logic on the main UI thread by calling the `BeginInvoke` method. An alternative, however, is to call the `Invoke` method instead. If you call the `Invoke` method, the logic thread waits while the PDF creation code runs on the UI thread. During this time, LightSwitch shows the hourglass and prevents the user from interacting with your application. The advantage of synchronously executing the PDF creation code with `Invoke` is that it makes it easier for you to handle and propagate any errors back to the logic thread. As discussed in Chapter 7, you need to add an `imports` or `using` statement that refers to the `Microsoft.LightSwitch.Threading` namespace to call the `Invoke` method.

■ **Tip** Microsoft Word 2010 allows you to natively save documents in PDF format. You can therefore create PDF files by using COM automation and the Word object model (in desktop applications). You create your PDF file by calling the Save method on your Word document and passing in the file format type of 17. (This relates to Word's `wdFormatPDF` enumeration value.) The C# code would look something like this: `myWordDoc.Save(17);`

Using Other Third-Party Solutions

Third-party tools provide you with another choice for reporting. Although you normally need to pay for these tools, they can simplify the report-writing process and offer an experience that's more integrated into the LightSwitch development environment. In addition to third-party controls that are specifically tailored for LightSwitch, you can also purchase Silverlight-specific controls and access their full functionality by wrapping them in your own custom controls. If you want to find out more about third-party controls, here are some products that you can explore:

- **ComponentOne (Studio for LightSwitch):** This product includes a FlexGrid control that includes print support and a PDF viewer that allows you to view PDFs from inside your application. You can find it at http://www.componentone.com.

- **DevExpress:** The XtraReports suite includes tools you can use to create custom reports. You can find it at http://www.devexpress.com/.

- **Infragistics:** The Netadvantage suite includes charting and a Pivot Grid control that allows you to visualize your data. You can find it at http://www.infragistics.com.

Summary

LightSwitch doesn't include any built-in reporting. However, there are several techniques that allow you to generate output from your LightSwitch application. This chapter showed you how to create reports by using ASP.NET and SQL Server Reporting Services. The benefit of both these products is that they're simple, low cost, and capable of producing output that you can access through a web URL. Once you create a web-based report, you can either display it inside a LightSwitch screen or provide a hyperlink that opens your report in a new browser window.

The advantage of ASP.NET is that it allows you to build web pages that include data or charts. If you want to filter the data that's shown to the user, you can build a web page that includes parameters and supply the parameter values from your LightSwitch application.

If you need to produce more powerful reports, you can use SQL Server Reporting Services. You can obtain Reporting Services free of charge as part of SQL Server Express with Advanced Services, and it's also included in higher editions of SQL Server. To author reports, you use a tool called SQL Server Data Tools (SSDT), which allows you to produce reports in a format called RDL (Report Definition Language).

The types of reports that you can create include Matrix and Tablix. Tablix reports allow you to produce tabular reports that show data in rows and columns, whereas Matrix reports produce cross-tab and pivot-table type reports. You can also create drill-through reports that allow users to view additional details by clicking on a link. Reporting Services allows you to customize your report by writing code. This can help you with operations such as styling and formatting.

Once you create a report by using ASP.NET or Reporting Services, you'll need a technique to link your report to your LightSwitch application. In a browser application, you can do this by creating a screen command that opens your report in a new browser window by using Silverlight's HtmlPage object. In a desktop application, you can open your report in a new browser instance by *shelling* your browser, or alternatively, you can show your report inside your LightSwitch screen using Silverlight's WebBrowser control.

Desktop applications allow you to integrate with other applications that are installed on the user's computer through COM automation. This allows you to integrate with applications such as Excel, Outlook, and Word. This chapter showed you how to generate letters and mail merges by automating Word.

The example code that you've seen uses *late binding*. This mechanism doesn't impose any dependency on any specific version of Word, so your code will work irrespective of the version of Word that's installed on the client. The first part of automating Word is to use Silverlight's AutomationFactory class to create an instance of a Word application object. This parent object allows you to use Word's API to create or open documents, as well as to insert text into your document. Using Word's API, you can save documents and even send documents to a printer without ever showing the Word application to the user.

To automate the creation of Word documents, you can create a Word template file that includes bookmarks, and you can add code to your LightSwitch application that inserts your data values into these bookmarks. This method relies on your application being able to access your Word template file. One way to do this is to deploy it through your application's XAP file. The advantage of this technique is that your Word template file becomes part of your Silverlight application, and therefore offers a robust way to deploy your application's resources. The disadvantages are that it makes your application larger and can slow down its load time.

To produce a mail merge, you can base your content on a static Word template file, or you can build your template in code if you need to dynamically adapt the contents of your Word document. The code that performs the mail merge extracts your LightSwitch data into a data document and merges this document with your template file.

If you want to create read-only documents that look consistent on all computers, the PDF format is ideal for you. You can create PDF files on a server by using Reporting Services or, alternatively, you can use COM automation on the client. This chapter showed you how to produce PDF documents on the client by using a third-party component called silverPDF.

Other options for reporting include using other third-party tools. These usually offer simplicity, and good integration with the Visual Studio IDE, but there'll often be a cost involved in buying these tools.

CHAPTER 15

■ ■ ■

Sending E-mail

One of the most important tools used by businesses today is e-mail. It provides a cheap and effective means of communication, and the whole world would struggle to function without it. If you want your application to communicate with outside users, send alerts, or perform some sort of mass communication, e-mail is the perfect tool.

In this chapter, you'll learn how to

- Send e-mails and alerts from the server
- Automate Microsoft Outlook
- Create draft messages by using the default e-mail program

In addition to teaching you about sending e-mail, this chapter also teaches you how to call web services from your Silverlight or HTML Client applications. In terms of the HelpDesk application, you'll learn how to automatically send alerts to users when an engineer closes the user's issue. You'll also find out how to send e-mails from screens, add file attachments, and integrate with Microsoft Outlook.

Choosing How to Send E-mail

Sending e-mail from LightSwitch might be more difficult than you first imagine. The challenge is that you can't send e-mail directly from the LightSwitch client. The Silverlight platform doesn't include the System.Net.Mail methods that would allow you to send e-mail from the client. E-mail support isn't much better in the HTMLClient because JavaScript doesn't include built-in e-mail support.

The solution to this problem is to write server-side code that sends the e-mail and to trigger this logic from the client. Because LightSwitch's middle tier uses ASP.NET, you can write code that uses the System.Net.Mail namespace from the server. If you prefer to send e-mail from the Silverlight client, you can automate Microsoft Outlook by using COM. Another way to send mail is to construct HTML hyperlinks that open the default e-mail client and pre-populate the message body. A slight disadvantage of this technique is that you can send e-mails only one at a time, rather than multiple e-mails in one go.

The final technique relies on calling a web service, and the advantage of this technique is that it's not just limited to sending e-mail. You can adapt the code that's shown in this chapter to call other types of web services, such as services that send SMS messages or services to retrieve addresses or stock prices.

Table 15-1 summarizes the options that you can use according to your application type. This chapter will show you how to implement all of these techniques.

Table 15-1. *E-mailing Techniques You Can Use, Listed by Application Type*

Technique	Silverlight Desktop Application	Silverlight/HTML Client Web Application
Send SMTP mail via server	✓	✓
Automate Microsoft Outlook	✓	
Use `mailto` links	✓	✓
Call Web Services	✓	✓

Sending E-mail by Using Server-Side Code

There's no built-in way to directly call a server method from the Silverlight LightSwitch client, so an effective work-around is to use the methods that you'll find in the save pipeline.

To use the `System.Net.Mail` objects to send an e-mail from the server, you'll need to apply your code to an entity event. These events occur when the save pipeline creates, inserts, deletes, or validates a record. (See Chapter 4, Figure 4-10 for further details.) If you want to send an e-mail when data changes in your application, the process is somewhat straightforward. For instance, if the status of an issue changes from open to closed, you can send a message that alerts the user by adding code to the `Issue` table's `Updated` method.

If you want to send an e-mail through a process that's disconnected from data, the procedure is more involved. An example of this could be a button that sends a message to a user, without saving any of the other data on the screen. One way to implement this functionality is to create an *operation table*. This is designed as a temporary table that gives you access to data source events and allows you to call custom server-side code. Having to create a table just to call some server-side code can be quite convoluted. Later in this chapter, you'll learn how to use a different technique that relies on web service calls.

Figure 15-1 illustrates how the two "save pipeline" techniques work.

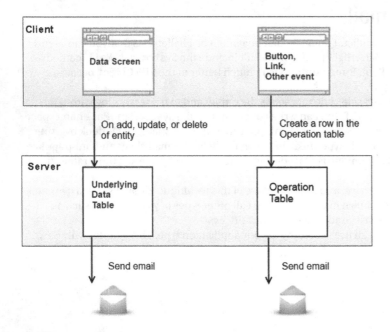

Figure 15-1. *Sending an e-mail by using server-side code*

Sending E-mail When Data Changes

Let's begin by looking at how to send a message when an engineer closes an issue. This method requires you to write code in your Issue entity's Updated method.

To carry out this example, open the Issue table in the table designer. Click on the "Write Code" button, and select the Updated method. Now enter the code that's shown in Listing 15-1.

Listing 15-1. Sending E-mail When Users Update Data

VB:
File: HelpDeskVB\Server\UserCode\ApplicationDataService.vb

```vb
Imports System.Net.Mail

Private Sub Issues_Updated(entity As Issue)

    ' 1 Test if the issue has changed to a closed status              ❶
    If entity.Details.Properties.IssueStatus.OriginalValue IsNot Nothing AndAlso
        (Not entity.Details.Properties.IssueStatus.OriginalValue.StatusDescription
            = "Closed") AndAlso
        entity.IssueStatus IsNot Nothing AndAlso
        (entity.IssueStatus.StatusDescription = "Closed") Then

        Dim message As New MailMessage()                             ❷
        message.From = New MailAddress("admin@lsfaq.com")
        message.To.Add(entity.User.Email)                            ❸
        message.Subject = "Issue Updated"
        message.Body =
            "The status of your Issue has changed. Issue ID " & entity.Id    ❹

        Dim client As New SmtpClient("relay.yourmailserver.net", 25)  ❺

        'Set the details below if you need to send credentials
        'client.Credentials =
            ' new System.Net.NetworkCredential("yourUsername", "yourPassword")
        'client.UseDefaultCredentials = false
        client.Send(message)                                          ❻

    End If

End Sub
```

C#:
File: HelpDeskCS\Server\UserCode\ApplicationDataService.cs

```csharp
using System.Net.Mail;

partial void Issues_Updated(Issue entity)
{
    //1 Test if the issue has changed to a closed status              ❶
    if (entity.Details.Properties.IssueStatus.OriginalValue !=null &&
        entity.Details.Properties.IssueStatus.OriginalValue.StatusDescription
```

```
            != "Closed" &&
        entity.IssueStatus != null &&
        entity.IssueStatus.StatusDescription == "Closed")
    {
        MailMessage message = new MailMessage();                          ❷
        message.From = new MailAddress("admin@lsfaq.com");
        message.To.Add(entity.User.Email);                                ❸
        message.Subject = "Issue Updated";
        message.Body =
            "The status of your Issue has changed. Issue ID " +
                entity.Id.ToString();                                     ❹

        SmtpClient client = new SmtpClient("relay.yourmailserver.net", 25);   ❺

        //Set the details below if you need to send credentials
        //client.Credentials = new System.Net.NetworkCredential(
        //    "yourusername", "yourpassword");
        //client.UseDefaultCredentials = false;
        client.Send(message);                                             ❻
    }
}
```

The first part of the code checks if the user has changed the issue status to closed ❶. It does this by checking that the original status isn't "closed," and then tests whether or not the new status is "closed." Next, the code uses the following objects in the System.Net.Mail namespace to send the e-mail message:

- MailMessage ❷: This object represents an e-mail message. It allows you to set e-mail properties like the recipient address, subject, and message body. This code retrieves the e-mail address of the user that's been assigned to the issue ❸, and it appends the issue id to the message body ❹.

- SmtpClient ❺: This class represents the object that sends the e-mail. You must initialize this object with the SMTP Server URL and port number. You can optionally set authentication credentials if your server requires this. For the SMTP Server setting, you can supply either a server name or an IP address. The method that allows you to send the e-mail is called Send ❻. There's also a method called SendAsync that allows you to send your message asynchronously.

The MailMessage object includes several extra properties that you can set. For example, you can CC additional recipients by using a property called CC. Table 15-2 shows a full list of properties that you can use.

Table 15-2. *MailMessage Object Properties*

Name	Description
Attachments	Gets the collection used for storing file attachments
Bcc	Gets a collection of blind carbon copy (BCC) recipients
CC	Gets a collection of carbon copy (CC) recipients
DeliveryNotificationOptions	Gets or sets the delivery notifications
From	Gets or sets the *from* address
IsBodyHtml	Gets or sets a value that indicates whether the message body is in HTML format
Priority	Gets or sets the message priority
ReplyToList	Gets or sets the list of *reply to* addresses
Sender	Gets or sets the sender's e-mail address

■ **Tip** If the attempt to send your e-mail fails, there are a few simple things that you can check. First, are there any firewalls or antivirus applications that are blocking your SMTP traffic? Some antivirus programs protect against mass-mailing worms by blocking all outgoing SMTP traffic. Second, e-mail servers such as Microsoft Exchange might require you to configure relay settings in order for you to make a connection.

Making Your E-mail Code Reusable

If you want to send e-mail from several places in your application, a helper class saves you from having to duplicate your code. To create a helper class, switch your LightSwitch project to File View and create a new class in your Server project. A good place to create this class is in your UserCode folder. Name your class SMTPMailHelper, and add the code that's shown in Listing 15-2.

Listing 15-2. SMTP Mail Helper Class and Method

VB:
File: HelpDeskVB\Server\UserCode\SMTPMailHelper.vb

```
Imports System.Net
Imports System.Net.Mail
Imports System.IO

Public Module SmtpMailHelper
    Const SMTPServer As String = "relay.yourmailserver.net"
    Const SMTPUserId As String = "myUsername"
    Const SMTPPassword As String = "myPassword"
    Const SMTPPort As Integer = 25

    Public Sub SendMail(sendFrom As String,              ❶
      sendTo As String,
      subject As String,
```

```vb
    body As String,
    attachment As Byte(),
    filename As String)

    Dim fromAddress As New MailAddress(sendFrom)
    Dim toAddress As New MailAddress(sendTo)
    Dim mail As New MailMessage()                                    ❷

    mail.From = fromAddress
    mail.To.Add(toAddress)
    mail.Subject = subject
    mail.Body = body
    If body.ToLower().Contains("<html>") Then                        ❸
        mail.IsBodyHtml = True                                       ❹
    End If

    Dim smtp As New SmtpClient(SMTPServer, SMTPPort)

    If attachment IsNot Nothing AndAlso                              ❺
      Not String.IsNullOrEmpty(filename) Then
        Using ms As New MemoryStream(attachment)
            mail.Attachments.Add(New Attachment(ms, filename))
            smtp.Send(mail)
        End Using
    Else
        smtp.Send(mail)
    End If

    End Sub

End Module
```

C#:
File: HelpDeskCS\Server\UserCode\SMTPMailHelper.cs

```csharp
using System.Net;
using System.Net.Mail;
using System.Configuration;
using System.IO;

namespace LightSwitchApplication.UserCode
{
    public static class SmtpMailHelper
    {
        const string SMTPServer = "relay.yourmailserver.net";
        const string SMTPUserId = "myUsername";
        const string SMTPPassword = "myPassword";
        const int SMTPPort = 25;

        public static void SendMail(string sendFrom,                 ❶
          string sendTo,
          string subject,
```

```
        string body,
        byte[] attachment,
        string filename)
    {
        MailAddress fromAddress = new MailAddress(sendFrom);
        MailAddress toAddress = new MailAddress(sendTo);
        MailMessage mail = new MailMessage();                           ❷

        mail.From = fromAddress;
        mail.To.Add(toAddress);
        mail.Subject = subject;
        mail.Body = body;
        if (body.ToLower().Contains("<html>"))                          ❸
        {
            mail.IsBodyHtml = true;                                     ❹
        }

        SmtpClient smtp = new SmtpClient(SMTPServer, SMTPPort);

        if (attachment != null && !string.IsNullOrEmpty(filename))      ❺
        {
            using (MemoryStream ms = new MemoryStream(attachment))
            {
                mail.Attachments.Add(new Attachment(ms, filename));
                smtp.Send(mail);
            }
        }
        else
        {
            smtp.Send(mail);
        }
    }
}
}
```

This class defines a method called SendMail ❶ that contains the logic that sends an SMTP mail message. You'll find out how to call this method in Listing 15-4.

This first part of this code creates a new message by creating a new instance of a MailMessage object ❷. It then sets the value of the sender, recipient, subject, and e-mail body properties.

The next part of the code checks if the message body contains an HTML tag ❸. If so, it sets the format of your e-mail message to HTML ❹. This line of code allows you to author HTML e-mails, simply by including an HTML tag at the start of your message body. The advantage of HTML is that it allows you to apply additional formatting, such as font sizes, boldification, and coloration to your e-mail message.

The code then checks if you've supplied a file name and attachment ❺. If you have done so, it attaches the file to your e-mail message. The final part of this code sends your message by calling the SmtpClient object's Send method.

If you want to use this code in multiple LightSwitch projects, you can reuse the helper class by compiling it into a separate DLL and adding a reference to it in your Server project.

■ **Tip** If you choose to use the SMTP service that's provided by Google's Gmail, here are some tips to make your code work. First, you should set the `DeliveryMethod` attribute of your `SmtpClient` to `SmtpDeliveryMethod.Network`. Second, make sure to set the `SmtpClient` credentials property with the credentials of your Gmail account. At the time of this writing, the port number that Google uses is 465 rather than the standard SMTP port of 25.

Using Configuration Settings to Save Credentials

The code in Listing 15-2 hard-codes the e-mail settings such as the SMTP server, authentication credentials, and port number. These details can change over time, so it makes good sense to save these settings in a place that you can easily modify after deployment. One option is to store these settings is in a user-defined table. The AppOption table that you saw in Chapter 7 is specifically designed for this purpose. But because you've already seen plenty of examples of how to retrieve data from tables, you'll now see a different approach for storing configuration settings. This method uses custom Application Settings that are defined in your Server project. After you deploy your application, you can set these values by editing your application's `Web.config` file. You'll find the `Web.config` file in the root of your published application.

To create these Application Settings, right-click your Server project and open the properties window for your project. Switch to the `Settings` tab, and create a set of *application-scoped* settings to store your e-mail credentials, as shown in Figure 15-2.

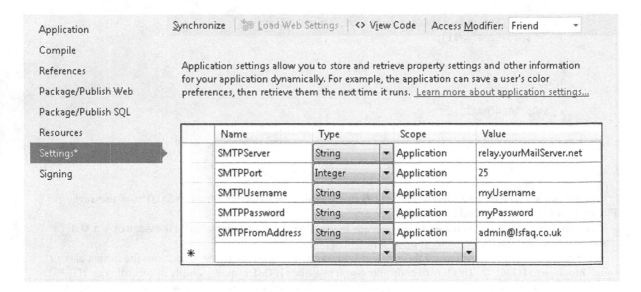

Figure 15-2. *Creating configuration settings in the server project*

You can now modify the code in your helper class to use these configuration settings. Listing 15-3 highlights the changes that you would make to your `SmtpMailHelper` class.

Listing 15-3. Configuration Settings Code

VB:
File: HelpDeskVB\Server\UserCode\SMTPMailHelper.vb

```vb
Imports System.Configuration

Private ReadOnly SMTPServer As String = My.Settings.SMTPServer
Private ReadOnly SMTPUserId As String = My.Settings.SMTPUsername
Private ReadOnly SMTPPassword As String = My.Settings.SMTPPassword
Private ReadOnly SMTPPort As Integer = My.Settings.SMTPPort
```

C#:
File: HelpDeskCS\Server\UserCode\SMTPMailHelper.cs

```csharp
using System.Configuration;

private static readonly string SMTPServer =
        LightSwitchApplication.Properties.Settings.Default.SMTPServer;
private static readonly string SMTPUserId =
        LightSwitchApplication.Properties.Settings.Default.SMTPUsername;
private static readonly string SMTPPassword =
        LightSwitchApplication.Properties.Settings.Default.SMTPPassword;
private static readonly int SMTPPort =
        LightSwitchApplication.Properties.Settings.Default.SMTPPort;
```

This code uses the functionality that's provided by .NET's System.Configuration namespace to retrieve the application setting values. Unlike C#, VB makes it slightly easier for you to access your configuration settings by exposing your values through an object called My.Settings.

■ **Caution**   If you modify your "application setting" values by editing the web.config file in an application that you've deployed in IIS, IIS will restart your application. There'll be a performance hit as your application restarts, and if you've written any custom server code that uses session objects, you'll lose that data (unless you've chosen to persist your session data in SQL Server or State Server).

Triggering Server E-mail from an Onscreen Button on the Client

If you want to send an e-mail from a client method that's unrelated to data, the way to do this is to create an "operation table" that allows you to mimic the steps that you performed in the earlier example. This would allow you to create a button or a link on your screen that triggers an e-mail.

The first step is to create the table that's shown in Figure 15-3. This table contains the fields that are needed to send an e-mail, such as the recipient e-mail address, e-mail body, and subject.

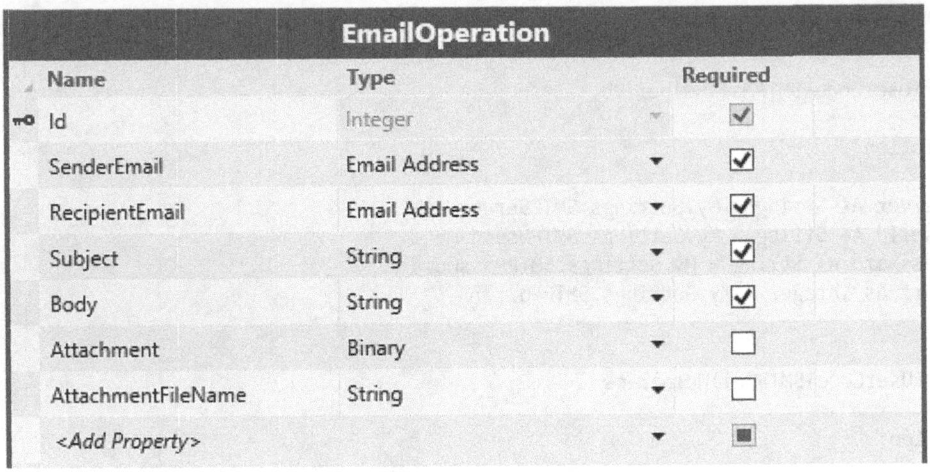

EmailOperation			
Name	Type		Required
Id	Integer		☑
SenderEmail	Email Address	▼	☑
RecipientEmail	Email Address	▼	☑
Subject	String	▼	☑
Body	String	▼	☑
Attachment	Binary	▼	☐
AttachmentFileName	String	▼	☐
<Add Property>		▼	■

Figure 15-3. The layout of the EmailOperation table

When you insert a row into this table, the code in the Inserting method sends the e-mail, just like the previous example. You can therefore send a message by simply adding rows to this table. Listing 15-4 shows the code that you'll need to add to the Inserting method for this table. This code takes advantage of the SmtpMailHelper class that you created in Listing 15-2.

Listing 15-4. Sending E-mail by Inserting Records into the EmailOperation Table

VB:
File: HelpDeskVB\Server\UserCode\ApplicationDataService.vb

```
Private Sub EmailOperations_Inserting(entity As EmailOperation)

    SmtpMailHelper.SendMail(
        entity.SenderEmail,
        entity.RecipientEmail,
        entity.Subject,
        entity.Body,
        entity.Attachment,
        entity.AttachmentFileName)
End Sub
```

C#:
File: HelpDeskCS\Server\UserCode\ApplicationDataService.cs

```
partial void EmailOperations_Inserting (EmailOperation entity)
{
    LightSwitchApplication.UserCode.SmtpMailHelper.SendMail(
    entity.SenderEmail,
    entity.RecipientEmail,
    entity.Subject,
    entity.Body
```

```
        entity.Attachment,
        entity.AttachmentFileName);
}
```

Triggering Server Email from the Silverlight Client

Once you've added your entity code, the next step is to create a screen that allows your users to send e-mails. This section shows you how to add e-mail composition controls to a user detail screen in your Silverlight client to allow engineers to send messages to users. Here are the steps that you'll need to carry out:

1. Create a Detail Screen that's based on the User table. Name your screen UserDetail.

2. Use the "Add Data" button to add two local string properties. Name these properties SubjectProperty and BodyProperty.

3. Add a new group beneath the root control of your screen, and set the control type to Group Box. Drag SubjectProperty and BodyProperty into this group. Set the display name of your Group Box control to "Contact the User." Open the properties sheet for your BodyProperty and set the lines property to a value greater than 1. This allows the user to enter multiline text.

4. Right-click your Group Box control, and choose the option to "Add Button." When the Add Button dialog appears, select the "Write My Own Method" radio button and name your method SendEmail. Figure 15-4 shows what your screen now looks like.

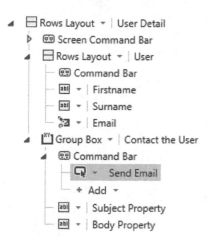

Figure 15-4. *Screen layout*

Select the SendEmail method from the screen members list, and choose the right-click option to "Edit Execute Code." Now add the code that's shown in Listing 15-5.

Listing 15-5. Button Code for Sending E-mail

VB:
File: HelpDeskVB\Client\UserCode\UserDetail.vb

```
Private Sub SendEmail_Execute()
```

```vbnet
    Using tempWorkspace As New DataWorkspace()                                    ❶
        Dim newEmail =
            tempWorkspace.ApplicationData.EmailOperations.AddNew()                ❷
        With newEmail
            .RecipientEmail = User.Email
            .SenderEmail = "admin@lsfaq.com"
            .Subject = SubjectProperty
            .Body = BodyProperty
        End With

        Try
            tempWorkspace.ApplicationData.SaveChanges()                           ❸

            ' If you want, you can write some code here to create a record in an audit table
            newEmail.Delete()                                                     ❹
            tempWorkspace.ApplicationData.SaveChanges()
            ShowMessageBox("Your email has been sent")

        Catch ex As Exception
            ShowMessageBox(ex.Message)
        End Try

    End Using
End Sub
```

C#:
File: HelpDeskCS\Client\UserCode\UserDetail.cs

```csharp
partial void SendEmail_Execute()
{
    using (var tempWorkspace = new DataWorkspace())                              ❶
    {
        EmailOperation newEmail =
            tempWorkspace.ApplicationData.EmailOperations.AddNew();             ❷

        newEmail.RecipientEmail = User.Email;
        newEmail.SenderEmail = "admin@lsfaq.com";
        newEmail.Subject = SubjectProperty;
        newEmail.Body = BodyProperty;

        try
        {
            tempWorkspace.ApplicationData.SaveChanges();                         ❸

            //If you want, you can write some code here to create a record in an audit table
            newEmail.Delete();                                                   ❹
            tempWorkspace.ApplicationData.SaveChanges();
            this.ShowMessageBox("Your email has been sent");
```

```
        }
        catch (Exception ex)
        {
            this.ShowMessageBox(ex.Message);
        }
    }
}
```

The first part of this code creates a temporary data workspace ❶ and uses it to create a new EmailOperation record ❷. This temporary data workspace allows your code to save the EmailOperation record, without saving any of the other data on the screen. The next section of code sets the e-mail properties, which include the subject, body text, and sender and recipient addresses.

The code then calls the SaveChanges method on the temporary workspace ❸. This, in turn, triggers the EmailOperations_Inserting method (shown in Listing 15-4), which performs the actual sending of the e-mail. At the end of the procedure, the code deletes the record from the EmailOperation table ❹. But if you want to maintain an audit trail of sent items, you could add some extra code here to create a record in an audit table. Figure 15-5 shows how the final screen appears at runtime.

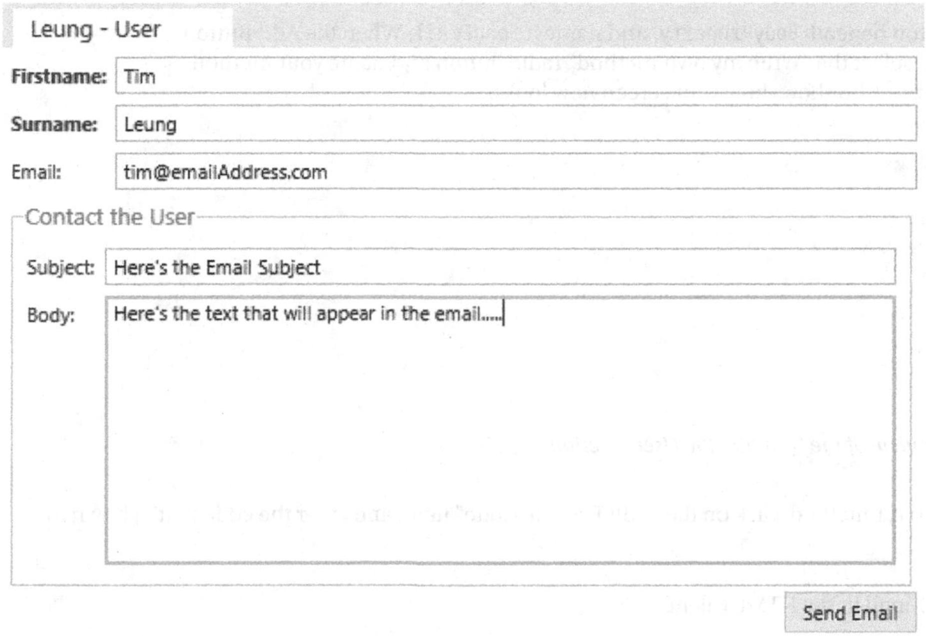

Figure 15-5. *E-mail composition screen at runtime*

Triggering server e-mail from the HTML Client

If you want to use this technique in an HTML client application, the screen design process is very similar. This section shows you a couple of HTML screen design methods that you've not yet seen. It shows you how to use the JavaScript API to create a new data workspace and to add records, and it also describes a "best-practices" pattern that allows you to call asynchronous methods. To create this example, open your HTML client project and carry out the following steps:

1. Create an "Add/Edit Details Screen" that's based on the User table, and name your screen AddEditUser.

2. Use the "Add Data" button to add two local string properties. Name these properties SubjectProperty and BodyProperty. Uncheck the "Is Required" check box for both properties.

3. Add a Tab beneath the root control of your screen. Set the display name of your Tab control to "Contact User." Drag SubjectProperty and BodyProperty into this tab. Change the control type of BodyProperty to a TextArea to allow the user to enter multiline text. Set the "Display Name" of SubjectProperty and BodyProperty to Subject and Body, respectively.

4. Add a new button beneath BodyProperty, and name it SendEmail. When the Add Button dialog appears, select the "Write my own method" radio button and name your method SendEmail. Figure 15-6 shows how your screen now looks.

Figure 15-6. *Screen design view of the "Contact the User" section*

Right-click your SendEmail method, click on the "Edit Execute Code" item, and enter the code that's shown in Listing 15-6.

Listing 15-6. Sending an E-mail in the HTML Client

File: HelpDeskVB\HTMLClient\UserCode\AddEditUser.js

```
myapp.AddEditUser.SendEmail_execute = function (screen) {

    var tempWorkspace = new msls.application.DataWorkspace();          ❶
    var newEmail = new myapp.EmailOperation(
        tempWorkspace.ApplicationData.EmailOperations);                ❷

    newEmail.RecipientEmail = screen.User.Email;                       ❸
    newEmail.SenderEmail = "admin@lsfaq.com";
    newEmail.Subject = screen.SubjectProperty;
    newEmail.Body = screen.BodyProperty;
```

```
    return tempWorkspace.ApplicationData.saveChanges().then(function () {        ❹
        newEmail.deleteEntity();
        return tempWorkspace.ApplicationData.saveChanges().then(function () {    ❺
            msls.showMessageBox("Your email has been sent");
        });
    });
}
```

The first part of this code uses the JavaScript API to add a new record to the EmailOperation table. It creates a temporary data workspace ❶ so that you can save your EmailOperation record, without saving any other data changes in the user's session. The next section contains the actual code that creates a new EmailOperation record ❷ in the temporary data workspace, and sets the e-mail properties that includes the subject, body text, and sender and recipient addresses ❸.

A key feature of this function is that it returns a promise object to the LightSwitch runtime ❹. Chapter 8 introduced the concept of promise objects, and showed you how to use promise objects to execute long running queries. The promise object allows LightSwitch to keep track of the asynchronous saveChanges operation. If the process appears to take a long time, LightSwitch automatically shows a progress indicator and blocks the user from doing anything else on the screen until the method completes. Importantly, using a promise object also allows LightSwitch to manage and return any errors to the user.

The promise object's then method allows you to specify the code that runs when the saveChanges operation succeeds. Although this example doesn't show it, the then method allows you to specify code that runs if the saveChanges operation fails. If the saveChanges method succeeds, the code deletes the newEmail entity and calls the saveChanges method again to commit the deletion ❺. The second call to saveChanges also returns a promise, and highlights a useful coding practice—that is, the ability to create chains of promises, by returning promises from child methods.

To illustrate why it's important to use this pattern, consider the following scenario. Let's say that you modify your code by replacing line ❹ with a straight call to saveChanges like so: tempWorkspace.ApplicationData.saveChanges();. Delete the code beneath that deletes the entity and calls saveChanges a second time, but keep the code that displays the confirmation message by calling the msls.showMessageBox method. Finally, delete the line of code above that sets the newEmail.Subject property (this property is defined as mandatory at the table level), and run your application. You'll find that the call to SaveChanges won't work because the record fails validation. But by not returning a promise object, the user incorrectly sees the dialog that's shown in Figure 15-7 rather than a validation warning. LightSwitch won't show any errors to the user and won't show any indication whatsoever that the operation has failed. For this reason, it's important to apply the pattern that's shown in this listing whenever you call asynchronous methods to allow the LightSwitch runtime to properly manage errors and to show the progress of an operation to the user.

Figure 15-7. *Sending an e-mail from the HTML Client*

Sending E-mails with File Attachments

The SendMail helper method that you created in Listing 15-2 allows you to include e-mail attachments. This section shows you how to modify the Silverlight UserDetail screen to allow users to add file attachments. This example uses the Silverlight File Open dialog. You'll remember from Chapter 7 that Silverlight file dialogs don't work well in browser applications. You can use a custom control to overcome this obstacle, and this section shows you how. Here are the steps to create this example:

1. Open your UserDetail screen.

2. Click on the "Add Data" button, and add a local string property called FileUploadButton. Make sure to uncheck the "Is Required" check box.

3. Drag your FileUploadButton property from the Screen Member list onto your screen. LightSwitch automatically creates a TextBox control for this property. Use the drop-down list to change the control type from a TextBox to a Custom Control.

4. Open the property sheet for the FileUploadButton control, and click on the "change" link to open the Add Custom Control dialog. Set the control type to System.Windows. Controls.Button. You can refer to Chapter 11 if you want to find out more about this process.

5. Click on the "Write Code" button, and select the UserDetail_InitializeDataWorkspace method. Now enter the code that's shown in Listing 15-7.

Listing 15-7. Screen Code to Send E-mail Attachments

VB:

File: HelpDeskVB\Client\UserCode\UserDetail.vb

```vb
Imports System.Runtime.InteropServices.Automation
Imports Microsoft.LightSwitch.Threading

Private Sub UserDetail_InitializeDataWorkspace(
    saveChangesTo As List(Of Microsoft.LightSwitch.IDataService))

    AddHandler Me.FindControl("FileUploadButton").ControlAvailable,       ❶
        Sub(sender As Object, e As ControlAvailableEventArgs)

            CType(e.Control, Button).Content = "Send Message With Attachment"   ❷

            AddHandler CType(e.Control, Button).Click,                    ❸
                Sub(sender2 As Object, e2 As RoutedEventArgs)

                    Dim dlg As New OpenFileDialog()                       ❹
                    If dlg.ShowDialog().GetValueOrDefault(False) = True Then
                        Dim data As Byte()
                        Using stream As FileStream = dlg.File.OpenRead()
                            data = New Byte(stream.Length - 1) {}
                            stream.Read(data, 0, data.Length)
                        End Using

                        Dim filename = dlg.File.Name

                        'send the email here
                        Me.Details.Dispatcher.BeginInvoke(                ❺
                            Sub()

                                Using dw As New DataWorkspace()

                                    Dim newEmail =
                                        dw.ApplicationData.EmailOperations.AddNew()
                                    With newEmail
                                        .RecipientEmail = User.Email
                                        .SenderEmail = "admin@lsfaq.com"
                                        .Subject = SubjectProperty
                                        .Body = BodyProperty
                                        .Attachment = data
                                        .AttachmentFileName = filename
                                    End With

                                    Try
                                        dw.ApplicationData.SaveChanges()
                                        ' If you want, you can write some code here to
                                        ' create a record in an audit table
                                        newEmail.Delete()
                                        dw.ApplicationData.SaveChanges()
```

```
                        Catch ex As Exception
                            ShowMessageBox(ex.Message)
                        End Try
                    End Using


                End Sub
            )

        End If
    End Sub
End Sub
End Sub
```

C#:
File: HelpDeskCS\Client\UserCode\UserDetail.cs

```csharp
using Microsoft.LightSwitch.Threading;
using System.Windows.Controls;
using System.Windows;

partial void UserDetail_InitializeDataWorkspace(
    List<IDataService> saveChangesTo)
{
    var control = this.FindControl("FileUploadButton");

    control.ControlAvailable +=                                         ❶
    (object sender, ControlAvailableEventArgs e) =>
    {
        var fileButton = (Button)e.Control;
        fileButton.Content = "Send Message With Attachment";           ❷

        fileButton.Click +=                                            ❸
            (object sender2, RoutedEventArgs e2) =>
            {
                OpenFileDialog dlg = new OpenFileDialog();             ❹
                if (dlg.ShowDialog().GetValueOrDefault(false) == true)
                {
                    byte[] data;
                    using (FileStream stream = dlg.File.OpenRead())
                    {
                        data = new byte[stream.Length];
                        stream.Read(data, 0, data.Length);
                    }

                    string filename = dlg.File.Name;
                    //send the email here
                    this.Details.Dispatcher.BeginInvoke(() =>          ❺
                    {
                        using (var dw = new DataWorkspace())
                        {
                            EmailOperation newEmail =
```

```
            dw.ApplicationData.EmailOperations.AddNew();
        newEmail.RecipientEmail = User.Email;
        newEmail.SenderEmail = "admin@lsfaq.com";
        newEmail.Subject = SubjectProperty;
        newEmail.Body = BodyProperty;
        newEmail.Attachment = data;
        newEmail.AttachmentFileName = filename;
        try
        {
            dw.ApplicationData.SaveChanges();
            //If you want, you can write some code here to
            //create a record in an audit table
            newEmail.Delete();
            dw.ApplicationData.SaveChanges();
        }
        catch (Exception ex)
        {
            this.ShowMessageBox(ex.Message);
        }
    }
    });
        };
    };
    };
}
```

Chapter 7 showed you how to open Silverlight file dialogs from a button on a desktop application's screen. LightSwitch executes command code on the screen's logic thread, but the code that opens the file dialog needs to run on the UI thread. This is because file dialogs are UI elements that interact with the user. In a desktop application, you can open the Silverlight file dialogs by invoking your code on the UI thread. But for browser applications that don't run with "elevated trust," this technique won't work. However, in the case of a custom Silverlight button, LightSwitch executes the code that handles the click event on the UI thread. This characteristic allows you to open Silverlight file dialogs by adding your code to the method that handles your custom button's click event.

The code in this listing accesses the underlying Silverlight custom button by obtaining an IContentItem reference and handling the ControlAvailable event ❶. Once the code obtains a reference to the Silverlight button, it sets the button's text ❷ and adds the code that handles the button's click event ❸.

The code that handles the button's click event opens the Silverlight file open dialog ❹ and reads the content of the selected file into a byte array. The next part of the code creates a new record in the EmailOperation table, and calls the SaveChanges method to call the code that sends the e-mail. Because SaveChanges is a data operation that could take a long time to complete, the code invokes this logic on the screen's logic thread ❺ to prevent the process from locking up the UI.

Creating Mail in a Pickup Folder

If you're unable to send e-mail by using the preceding techniques (for example, if you're unable to establish an SMTP connection on port 25), another option is to configure a *pickup folder*. Most SMTP servers, including Microsoft Exchange, allow you to configure such a folder. Rather than directly sending your e-mail, you would create a plain-text message in the pickup folder. The mail service then processes any file that you save here as an outbound e-mail. The snippet in Listing 15-8 illustrates the format that you should use to create files in this folder.

Listing 15-8. Mail Pickup Text File Format

```
to:tim.leung@hotmail.com
from: admin@lsfaq.com
subject:This is where you put the email subject.
this is the body of the email.
```

Sending Mail via Outlook by Using COM Automation

Another option for desktop applications is to automate Microsoft Outlook. This technique is entirely client based, and unlike the previous example, it requires no server-side coding. The obvious requirement is that Microsoft Outlook must be installed on the end-user computers, so this technique might be more suitable for corporate environments where you can more easily mandate the software that's installed on the clients.

To send e-mail from Outlook, add the helper class that's shown in Listing 15-9 to your client project.

Listing 15-9. Client-Side COM Code to Create an Outlook Message

VB:
File: HelpDeskVB\Client\UserCode\OutlookMailHelper.vb

```vbnet
Option Strict Off

Imports System.Runtime.InteropServices.Automation

Public Module OutlookMailHelper
    Const olMailItem As Integer = 0
    Const olFormatPlain As Integer = 1
    Const olFormatHTML As Integer = 2

    Public Sub CreateEmail(toAddress As String,
        subject As String, body As String)                           ❶
        Try
            Dim outlook As Object = Nothing

            If AutomationFactory.IsAvailable Then                    ❷
                Try                                                  ❸
                    'Get the reference to the open Outlook App
                    outlook = AutomationFactory.GetObject("Outlook.Application")
                Catch ex As Exception
                    'Outlook isn't open, therefore try and open it
                    outlook =
                        AutomationFactory.CreateObject("Outlook.Application")
                End Try
                If outlook IsNot Nothing Then

                    Dim mail = outlook.CreateItem(olMailItem)        ❹
                    If body.ToLower().Contains("<html>") Then        ❺
                        mail.BodyFormat = olFormatHTML
                        mail.HTMLBody = body
                    Else
                        mail.BodyFormat = olFormatPlain
```

```
                mail.Body = body
            End If

            mail.Recipients.Add(toAddress)
            mail.Subject = subject

            mail.Save()                                                    ❻
            mail.Display()                                                 ❼
            'uncomment this code to send the email immediately
            'mail.Send()
        End If

    End If
Catch ex As Exception
    Throw New InvalidOperationException("Failed to create email.", ex)
End Try
    End Sub
End Module
```

C#:
File: HelpDeskCS\Client\UserCode\OutlookMailHelper.cs

```csharp
using System;
using System.Runtime.InteropServices.Automation;

namespace LightSwitchApplication.UserCode
{
    public static class OutlookMailHelper
    {
        const int olMailItem = 0;
        const int olFormatPlain = 1;
        const int olFormatHTML = 2;

        public static void CreateEmail(
            string toAddress, string subject, string body)          ❶
        {
            try
            {
                dynamic outlook = null;

                if (AutomationFactory.IsAvailable)                  ❷
                {
                    Try
                    {
                        //Get the reference to the open Outlook App    ❸
                        outlook =
                            AutomationFactory.GetObject("Outlook.Application");
                    }
                    catch (Exception ex)
```

```
            {
                //Outlook isn't open, therefore try and open it
                outlook =
                  AutomationFactory.CreateObject("Outlook.Application");
            }

            if (outlook != null)
            {
                //Create the email
                dynamic mail = outlook.CreateItem(olMailItem);         ❹
                if (body.ToLower().Contains("<html>"))                  ❺
                {
                    mail.BodyFormat = olFormatHTML;
                    mail.HTMLBody = body;
                }
                else
                {
                    mail.BodyFormat = olFormatPlain;
                    mail.Body = body;
                }
                mail.Recipients.Add(toAddress);
                mail.Subject = subject;

                mail.Save();                                           ❻
                mail.Display();                                        ❼
                //uncomment this code to send the email immediately
                //mail.Send()
            }
        }

    }
    catch (Exception ex)
    {
        throw new InvalidOperationException(
          "Failed to create email.", ex);
    }
  }
}


}
```

This class defines a method called CreateEmail ❶. This is the method that you would call to create an Outlook message. COM automation works only in desktop applications, so the first part of the code checks that your application is indeed running on a desktop ❷.

The next part of the code obtains a reference to the Outlook application ❸. If Outlook is already open, it uses COM's GetObject method to obtain a reference to the existing Outlook application. Otherwise, it uses the CreateObject method to create a new instance of Outlook.

The next part of the code calls the Outlook API's CreateItem method to create a new mail message ❹. Just like the SMTP helper method that you created in Listing 15-2, this code tests for the existence of an HTML tag ❺. If it finds this tag, the code sets the format of your mail message to HTML. The next section of code sets the message body, subject, and recipient address. Finally, the code saves the e-mail message ❻ and calls the Display method to open the message in a new Outlook message window ❼.

At this point, the user can review the message and manually click on the message window's send button to complete the send. If you want to send the e-mail without any user intervention, you can do this by deleting the call to the Display method, and call the message object's Send method instead.

The final step that remains is to call your CreateEmail method from a screen. To show you how to do this, open your UserDetail screen and add a button called SendWithOutlook. Now add the code that's shown in Listing 15-10.

Listing 15-10. Screen Code to Create an Outlook Message

VB:
File: HelpDeskVB\Server\UserCode\UserDetail.vb

```
Imports System.Runtime.InteropServices.Automation

Private Sub SendWithOutlook_Execute()
   OutlookMailHelper.CreateEmail(User.Email,
   SubjectProperty, BodyProperty)                              ❶
End Sub

Private Sub SendWithOutlook_CanExecute(ByRef result As Boolean)
   result = AutomationFactory.IsAvailable                      ❷
End Sub
```

C#:
File: HelpDeskCS\Server\UserCode\UserDetail.cs

```
using System.Runtime.InteropServices.Automation;

partial void SendWithOutlook_Execute()
{
    LightSwitchApplication.UserCode.OutlookMailHelper.CreateEmail(
        User.Email,
        SubjectProperty,
        BodyProperty);                                         ❶
}

partial void SendWithOutlook_CanExecute(ref bool result)       ❷
{
    result = AutomationFactory.IsAvailable;
}
```

The code in the SendWithOutlook method calls the CreateEmail method and supplies the e-mail address, subject, and message body values that the user has entered on the screen ❶. This code also implements the SendWithOutlook_CanExecute method ❷. The purpose of this code is to disable the SendWithOutlook button if the application isn't running on the desktop. You'll find out more about CanExecute methods in Chapter 17. Figure 15-8 shows how your screen looks at runtime.

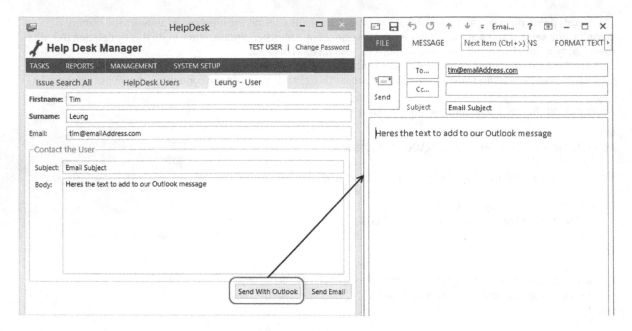

Figure 15-8. *Clicking the "Send With Outlook" button opens Outlook*

■ **Tip** Although this chapter focuses on how to send e-mail, you can automate Outlook in many other ways. By using similar code, you can create powerful applications that create Outlook appointments, contacts, or tasks via your LightSwitch application.

Opening the Default Mail Program

This section shows you how to open the default mail client by creating a `mailto` hyperlink. You can use this technique in both desktop and browser applications. It works by opening the user's default e-mail program (if one exists). This might be Outlook, Outlook Express, Windows Live Mail, or any other e-mail client that the user has installed.

You can set the recipient e-mail address, subject, and body of your message by supplying arguments to the `mailto` hyperlink. It's very likely that you've encountered these links when browsing the Web, and web developers will be familiar with this technique. The syntax of a simple `mailto` link is as follows:

```
mailto:recipient1@hotmail.com
```

If you want to send an e-mail to multiple recipients, you can specify a comma-separated list of e-mail addresses in the following way:

```
mailto:recipient1@hotmail.com,recipient2@hotmail.com
```

After the recipient details, you can use the ? character to supply additional arguments. For example, you can use the following syntax to specify an e-mail subject:

```
mailto:recipient1@hotmail.com,recipient2@hotmail.com?subject=Email Subject
```

If you want to supply multiple arguments, separate the arguments by using the & symbol. Here's an example link that specifies both an e-mail subject and body:

```
mailto:recipient1@hotmail.com, recipient2@hotmail.com?
    subject=Email Subject&Body=Here is the body of the email.
```

Table 15-4 shows the list of available parameters.

Table 15-4. *mailto Parameters*

Function	mailto **Parameter**
Set the e-mail subject	subject
CC a recipient (copy)	cc
BCC as recipient (blind carbon copy)	bcc
Set the body text	body

Using *mailto* in a Silverlight Client

Once you've built a mailto hyperlink, you can call it from a Silverlight application's screen command.

To see this in action, switch your project to File View and add a reference to the System.Windows.Browser.dll assembly in your Client project. Open the UserDetail screen, and add the code that's shown in Listing 15-11.

Listing 15-11. Sending E-mail by Using a mailto Hyperlink

VB:
File: HelpDeskVB\Client\UserCode\UserDetail.vb

```
Public Sub OpenDefaultMailClient(
   ByVal toAddress As String,
   ByVal subject As String,
   ByVal body As String)                                              ❶

   subject = System.Uri.EscapeDataString(subject)                     ❷
   body = System.Uri.EscapeDataString(body)

   Dim url As String = String.Format(
      "mailto:{0}?subject={1}&body={2}", toAddress, subject, body)    ❸
   Dim uri As Uri = New Uri(url)

   If AutomationFactory.IsAvailable Then                              ❹
      Dim shell = AutomationFactory.CreateObject("Shell.Application")
      'shell.ShellExecute(url) if Option Strict is Off
      CompilerServices.Versioned.CallByName(
         shell, "ShellExecute", CallType.Method, url)                 ❺
   Else
      Microsoft.LightSwitch.Threading.Dispatchers.Main.BeginInvoke(
         Sub()
```

```
            System.Windows.Browser.HtmlPage.Window.Navigate(
                uri, "_blank")                                      ❻
        End Sub
      )
    End If
End Sub
```

C#:
File: HelpDeskCS\Client\UserCode\UserDetail.cs

```
public static void OpenDefaultMailClient (
    string toAddress, string subject, string body)              ❶
{
    subject = Uri.EscapeDataString(subject);                    ❷
    body = Uri.EscapeDataString(body);

    string url = string.Format(
        "mailto:{0}?subject={1}&body={2}", toAddress, subject, body);   ❸
    Uri uri = new Uri(url);

    if (AutomationFactory.IsAvailable)                          ❹
    {
        var shell = AutomationFactory.CreateObject("Shell.Application");
        shell.ShellExecute(url);                                ❺
    }
    else
    {
        Microsoft.LightSwitch.Threading.Dispatchers.Main.BeginInvoke(() =>
        {
            System.Windows.Browser.HtmlPage.Window.Navigate(
                uri, "_blank");                                 ❻
        });
    }
}
```

This code defines a method called OpenDefaultMailClient ❶ that allows you to open the mail client that's installed on the client. If you want to call this code from multiple places, you can create a helper class in your Client project, and create the OpenDefaultMailClient method as a shared/static method within this class, just like the OutlookMailHelper class from Listing 15-9.

The OpenDefaultMailClient method allows you to supply the subject, body, and recipient address to add to your message.

When you send e-mails using this technique, you need to encode any special characters that might appear in your hyperlink. For example, the & symbol needs to be replaced with %25 because & is the character that separates the arguments in the mailto string. The code toward the top of the method encodes the Subject and Body values by calling the Uri.EscapeDataString method ❷. The next part of the code builds the content of the mailto link ❸.

The next line of code checks where your application is running ❹. If it's running on the desktop, the code uses the shell command to open the default e-mail client ❺. Otherwise, it uses the HtmlPage object from the System.Windows.Browser namespace instead ❻. This code needs to be invoked on the main UI thread.

The final step is to call your OpenDefaultMailClient method from a screen. To do this, add a button to your UserDetail screen and name it SendByDefaultClient. Once you've created this button, add the code that's shown in Listing 15-12.

Listing 15-12. Screen Code to Use the Default Client

VB:
File: HelpDeskVB\Client\UserCode\UserDetail.vb

```
Private Sub SendByDefaultClient_Execute()
    OpenDefaultMailClient(User.Email,
    SubjectProperty, BodyProperty)                              ❶
End Sub
```

C#:
File: HelpDeskCS\Client\UserCode\UserDetail.cs

```
partial void SendByDefaultClient_Execute()
{
    OpenDefaultMailClient(
        User.Email,
        SubjectProperty,
        BodyProperty);                                          ❶
}
```

This code in the SendByDefaultClient method calls the OpenDefaultMailClient method, and supplies the e-mail address, subject, and message body values that are shown on the screen ❶. This completes this code sample, and you can now run your screen.

Using *mailto* in the HTML Client

The mailto technique also works in HTML client applications. In this section, you'll find out how to apply this method to a screen that's designed to show information about your application, such as version numbers and contact details. First, create a Browse Data Screen and leave the screen data drop-down set to "None." Name your screen About, and add a new button to your screen. When the "Add Button" dialog appears, select the radio option to "Write my own method" and name your method EmailAdministrator. Figure 15-9 shows how your screen now looks.

Figure 15-9. Screen at design time

Now right-click your EmailAdministrator method, click on the "Edit Execute Code" option, and add the JavaScript that's shown in Listing 15-13.

Listing 15-13. Sending E-mail by Using a mailto Hyperlink

File: HelpDeskVB\HTMLClient\UserCode\About.js

```
myapp.About.EmailAdministrator_execute = function (screen) {
    var emailTo = "administrator@lsfaq.com";                    ❶
    var subject = "Helpdesk Mobile App Enquiry";
    var body  = "I have an enquiry about the Helpdesk App.";

    var url = "mailto:" + emailTo +
        "?subject=" + encodeURIComponent(subject) +            ❷
        "&body=" + encodeURIComponent(body);

    document.location.href = url;                              ❸
};
```

The first part of this code creates variables to store the recipient ❶, subject, and body values of your e-mail. In practice, you could set these values from data or local properties. The next part of the code builds the mailto URL. Notice how it calls JavaScript's encodeURLComponent function ❷ to encode any special characters in the subject or body parts of your URL. Although there aren't any special characters in this example, the listing includes the encodeURLComponent call to demonstrate how to carry out this task. The final piece of this code opens the URL by setting the address of the current browser page to the mailto address ❸.

Figure 15-10 shows how the screen looks on an Android device, and illustrates how the Android mail client opens when you click on the "Email Administrator" button. It's useful to note that this technique may not work on all mobile devices or browsers, so it's important to test your application on your intended device.

Figure 15-10. *Opening mailto links on a mobile Android device*

Calling External Resources from LightSwitch Clients

Sending e-mail is really just one example of calling an external resource from a LightSwitch client. In reality, there are many other reasons why you'd want to consume external web-based resources. Examples include calling SMS gateways to send text messages, looking up online stock quotes, calling mapping services, or looking up addresses based on postal codes.

Consuming these types of services usually requires you to make some sort of web service call. This section shows you how to accomplish this by making an AJAX call from an HTML application or consuming a web service from a Silverlight application. In keeping with the theme of this chapter and to provide examples that you can easily re-create, this section remains on the topic of sending e-mail.

Using AJAX from the HTML Client

The first part of this section shows you how to make AJAX (Asynchronous JavaScript and XML) calls from HTML client applications. This technique allows you to call many different types of web resources and create much more versatile applications. To demonstrate this technique, this example shows you how to create an ASP.NET handler that sends an e-mail. This handler allows you to supply e-mail address, subject, and body values. Once you've added your handler, the second part of this example shows you how to call it from your LightSwitch application.

To create the server-side part of this example, switch your project to "File View." Navigate to your Server project, right-click your Web project, and add a new "Generic Handler." Name your handler SendMail.ashx. This creates a code file that includes a method stub for the ProcessRequest method. Modify the code in this method, as shown in Listing 15-14.

Listing 15-14. SendMail Handler Code

VB:
File: HelpDeskVB\Server\Web\SendMail.ashx.vb

```
Sub ProcessRequest(ByVal context As HttpContext) Implements
  IHttpHandler.ProcessRequest
    '1 Is the user authenticated? Does he belong in the Manager Role?      ❶
    'context.User.Identity.IsAuthenticated
    'context.User.IsInRole("Manager")

  If context.Request.Params("emailTo") IsNot Nothing AndAlso              ❷
      context.Request.Params("subject") IsNot Nothing AndAlso
      context.Request.Params("body") IsNot Nothing Then
      Try
          Dim senderEmail As String = "admin@lsfaq.com"
          SmtpMailHelper.SendMail(senderEmail,                            ❸
              context.Request.Params("emailTo").ToString(),
              context.Request.Params("subject").ToString(),
              context.Request.Params("body").ToString(), Nothing, Nothing)
          context.Response.Write("Email Sent")
      Catch ex As Exception
          context.Response.Write(ex.Message)                             ❹
      End Try
  Else
      context.Response.Write("EmailTo, Subject, and Body required")
  End If
End Sub
```

C#:
File: HelpDeskCS\Server\Web\SendMail.ashx.cs

```csharp
public void ProcessRequest(HttpContext context)
{
    //1 Is the user authenticated? Does he belong in the Manager Role?        ❶
    //context.User.Identity.IsAuthenticated
    //context.User.IsInRole("Manager")

    if (context.Request.Params["emailTo"] != null &&                          ❷
        context.Request.Params["subject"] != null &&
        context.Request.Params["body"] != null)
    {
        try
        {
            string senderEmail = "admin@lsfaq.com";
            LightSwitchApplication.UserCode.SmtpMailHelper.SendMail(          ❸
                senderEmail,
                context.Request.Params["emailTo"].ToString(),
                context.Request.Params["subject"].ToString(),
                context.Request.Params["body"].ToString(), null, null);
            context.Response.Write("Email Sent");
        }
        catch (Exception ex)
        {
            context.Response.Write(ex.Message);                              ❹
        }
    }
    else
    {
        context.Response.Write("EmailTo, Subject, and Body required");
    }
}
```

This code uses the SMTPMailHelper class that's shown in Listing 15-2, so you'll need to create this class if you haven't done so already.

The first part of this code includes a comment that contains the syntax that allows you to find out whether the user is authenticated or belongs in a user-defined role called "Manager" ❶. It's a good idea to include some access-control checks, and you'll find more about this in Chapters 16 and 17. The next part of the code checks that the request includes the recipient e-mail address, subject, and body ❷. If any of this data is missing, the code returns a message to the caller. Otherwise, the code sends the e-mail by calling the SMTPMailHelper class's SendMail method ❸. If an error occurs, the catch block ❹ returns the error to the caller.

This completes the server side code. To create the client-side code that carries out the AJAX request, open the AddEditUser screen that you created earlier. Right-click your SendEmail method, click on the "Edit Execute Code" option, and replace the code from the earlier example with the code that's shown in Listing 15-15.

Listing 15-15. Calling the SendEmail Handler Page via AJAX

File: HelpDeskVB\HTMLClient\UserCode\AddEditUser.js

```
myapp.AddEditUser.SendEmail_execute = function (screen) {

    return new msls.promiseOperation(function (operation) {             ❶
        var emailTo = screen.User.Email;
        var mailUrl = "../Web/SendMail.ashx" +                          ❷
            "?emailTo=" + emailTo +
            "&subject=" + encodeURIComponent(screen.SubjectProperty) +
            "&body=" + encodeURIComponent(screen.BodyProperty);

        $.ajax({                                                        ❸
            type: 'post',
            data: {},
            url: mailUrl,
            success: function success(result) {
                operation.complete();                                   ❹
                msls.showMessageBox(result);                            ❺
            },
            error: function err(jqXHR, textStatus, errorThrown) {       ❻
                operation.error(errorThrown);                           ❼
            }
        });
    });
}
```

The function that's shown in this listing returns a promise object. It does this by wrapping the logic in a call to the msls.promiseOperation method ❶. The promise object enables the LightSwitch runtime to place the screen into a "busy" mode, as shown in the screenshot on the left in Figure 15-11. If you didn't wrap your code inside a call to msls. promiseOperation, your application wouldn't show any progress indication.

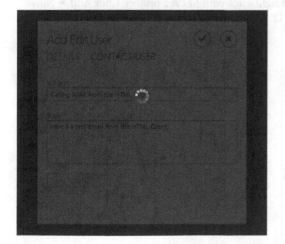

Figure 15-11. Sending an e-mail via an AJAX call

The next part of this code creates the URL that points to your e-mail handler and sets the emailTo, subject, and body arguments ❷. The next line of code calls this URL by calling jQuery's ajax method. This method allows you to supply a function that runs when the AJAX request succeeds. The code in this function calls the operation parameter's complete method ❹, and then and calls the showMessageBox ❺ method to show the result from the server. If the server returns a "404 not found," or if the process encounters some other type of error, you can handle this condition by supplying an error function to your jQuery's ajax call ❻. The definition of this function contains three parameters. In the event of an error, the third parameter, errorThrown, allows you to access the textual part of the HTTP status such as "Internal Server Error" or "Not found." The code in the error function calls the operation parameter's error method ❼ to allow the LightSwitch runtime to manage the error condition.

Note that your code must call either the operation.complete or operation.error method. If you don't do this, LightSwitch never closes the blacked-out "busy" screen and prevents your user from carrying out any further actions in your application.

This example shows you the general pattern that allows you to make an AJAX call. To find out more, take a look at the ajax method documentation that you'll find on the jQuery web site http://api.jquery.com/jQuery.ajax/.

Calling Web Services from the Silverlight Client

Calling web services from your Silverlight client allows you to extend the capabilities of your application. In addition to calling services that other companies or developers have created, you can also call web services to execute custom server-side code that you've written yourself. To demonstrate how this works, this section shows you how to create a WCF web service that sends e-mail. You'll then learn how to consume this service from your Silverlight client.

It's important to note that in the case of browser applications, Silverlight's default security policy prevents it from communicating with web services that are hosted on servers other than the server from which your application originated from. To save you from having to make additional configuration changes to run your code, the following example shows you how to add a WCF web service to your application's existing ASP.NET middle tier.

Hosting a WCF Service in your LightSwitch server

To develop this example in Visual Studio, you'll need to set up your project to use IIS Express. LightSwitch does this automatically for any projects that you've upgraded. So if you've not done so, you'll need to install "Visual Studio 2012 Update 2" and select the right-click "Upgrade" option that you'll find in Solution Explorer. To add a WCF web service to your existing application, switch your project to "File View" and right-click your Server project. Click Add ➤ New Item, and select the "WCF Service" option, as shown in Figure 15-12. Name your service MailService.svc.

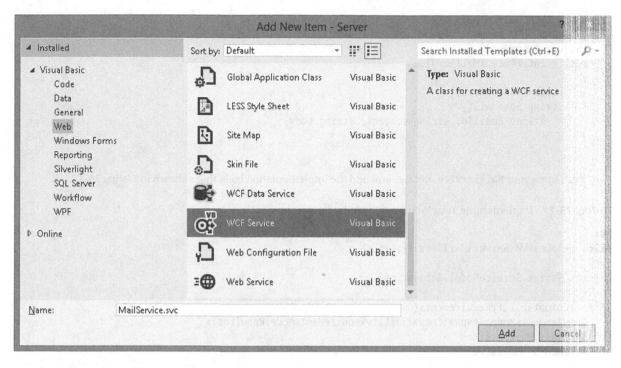

Figure 15-12. *Adding a new WCF Web Service*

After you add a WCF Service, Visual Studio creates two files: IMailService.vb and MailService.svc.vb for VB, or IMailService.cs and MailService.svc.cs for C#. The IMailService file defines your service's interface, and the MailService file contains the implementation. Open your IMailService file, and modify it as shown in Listing 15-16.

Listing 15-16. Defining the Interface for Your Web Service

VB:
File: HelpDeskVB\Server\IMailService.vb

```
Imports System.ServiceModel

<ServiceContract()>
Public Interface IMailService

    <OperationContract()>
    Function SendMail(
        emailTo As String, subject As String, body As String) As String

End Interface
```

C#:
File: HelpDeskCS\Server\IMailService.cs

```
using System.ServiceModel;
```

```
namespace LightSwitchApplication
{
    [ServiceContract]
    public interface IMailService
    {
        [OperationContract]
        string SendMail(
            string emailTo, string subject, string body);
    }
}
```

Next, open your `MailService.svc` file, and add the implementation code that's shown in Listing 15-17.

Listing 15-17. Implementing Your Web Service Method

VB:
File: HelpDeskVB\Server\MailService.svc.vb

```
Imports System.ServiceModel.Activation

<AspNetCompatibilityRequirements(                                              ❶
    RequirementsMode:=AspNetCompatibilityRequirementsMode.Required)> _
Public Class MailService
    Implements IMailService

    Public Function SendMail (
        emailTo As String, subject As String, body As String
          ) As String Implements IMailService.SendMail
        Try
            Dim senderEmail As String = "admin@lsfaq.com"
            SmtpMailHelper.SendMail(                                           ❷
                senderEmail, emailTo, subject, body,
                Nothing, Nothing) ' optional - add email attachment here...
            Return ("Email Sent")
        Catch ex As Exception
            Return ex.Message
        End Try
    End Function

End Class
```

C#:
File: HelpDeskCS\Server\MailService.svc.cs

```
using System;
using System.ServiceModel.Activation;

namespace LightSwitchApplication
{
    [AspNetCompatibilityRequirements(                                         ❶
        RequirementsMode = AspNetCompatibilityRequirementsMode.Allowed)]
```

```
public class MailService : IMailService
{
    public string SendMail(
        string emailTo, string subject, string body)
    {
        try
        {
            string senderEmail = "admin@lsfaq.com";
            LightSwitchApplication.UserCode.SmtpMailHelper.SendMail(    ❷
                senderEmail, emailTo, subject, body,
                null, null); // optional - add email attachment here...
            return ("Email Sent");
        }
        catch (Exception ex)
        {
            return ex.Message;
        }
    }
}
```

The first part of this code sets the AspNetCompatibilityRequirements mode to allowed ❶. By setting this attribute, you'll be able to test your web service by calling it from a web browser. You'll need to add an import or using statement for System.ServiceModel.Activation in order to apply this attribute. The next part of this code calls the SendMail helper method ❷ that you created at the start of this chapter.

Next, you'll need to modify some of the settings beneath the system.serviceModel section of your web.config file as shown in Listing 15-18.

Listing 15-18. Changes to the web.config File

File: HelpDeskVB\Server\Web.config

```
<system.serviceModel>

  <serviceHostingEnvironment
    aspNetCompatibilityEnabled="true"
    multipleSiteBindingsEnabled="true" />
  <behaviors>
    <serviceBehaviors>
      <behavior>
        <dataContractSerializer maxItemsInObjectGraph="6553600" />
        <serviceMetadata httpGetEnabled="true" />                    ❶
      </behavior>
    </serviceBehaviors>
  </behaviors>
  <bindings>
    <webHttpBinding>
      <binding maxReceivedMessageSize="6553600" >
      </binding>
    </webHttpBinding>
    <basicHttpBinding>                                               ❷
      <binding name="MailServiceBinding" >
```

```
          <security mode="TransportCredentialOnly">
            <transport clientCredentialType="Windows" />
          </security>
        </binding>
      </basicHttpBinding>
    </bindings>

    <services>
      <service name="LightSwitchApplication.MailService">                    ❸
        <endpoint address="MailService.svc"
            binding="basicHttpBinding"
            bindingConfiguration="MailServiceBinding"
            contract="LightSwitchApplication.IMailService" />
      </service>
    </services>

</system.serviceModel>
```

First, you'll need to enable metadata publishing ❶ by setting the httpGetEnabled attribute to true. This allows you to add a reference to your web service from Visual Studio at a later stage. The other changes that you'll need to make to this file are to define a binding ❷ and endpoint ❸. The binding that you create here specifies Windows authentication, so you'll need to confirm that you've enabled Windows Authentication in your project. Figure 15-13 shows the section in the property sheet for your server project that allows you to set this. If your project isn't set to use IIS Express, you'll find a right-click option on your server project that allows you to enable IIS Express.

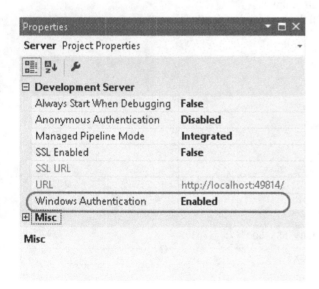

Figure 15-13. *Configuring development server authentication settings*

Now run your LightSwitch application by pressing F5, and stop it when it loads. After you stop your application, IIS Express should still be running in the background. Click the IIS Express icon that appears on the Windows taskbar (next to the clock) to find out the root URL of your application. (See Figure 15-14.)

Figure 15-14. *Adding a new WCF Web Service*

Now create a web address by appending MailService.svc to the end of your root URL (for example,
http://localhost:49814/MailService.svc), and open your address in a web browser. If you see the page that's
shown in Figure 15-15, you've successfully created your service. If not, you'll probably see an error page that contains
exception details. You can use the exception details to fix your code, although any errors that you might encounter will
typically be due to incorrect security or service settings that you've defined in your web.config file.

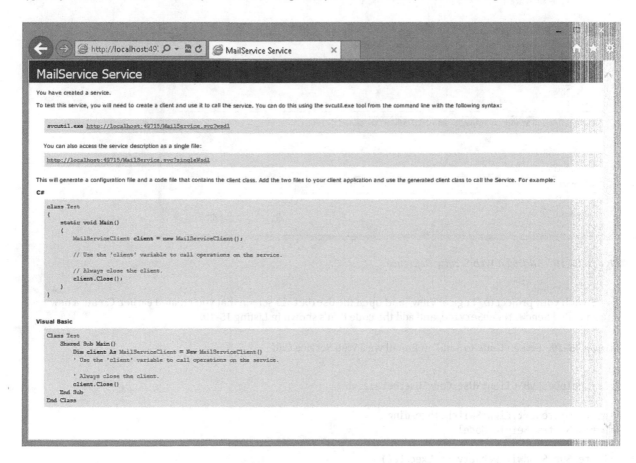

Figure 15-15. *Opening your service in a web browser*

Consuming a Web Service from your LightSwitch Client

Now that you've created your web service, here's how to call it from your Silverlight client. Switch your project to "File View," right-click your Client project, and select the "Add Service Reference" option. When the "Add Service Reference" dialog opens, enter the URL to your web service and click on the Go button. This populates the Services and Operations boxes that are shown in Figure 15-16. Set the value of the Namespace text box to MailService, and click on the OK button.

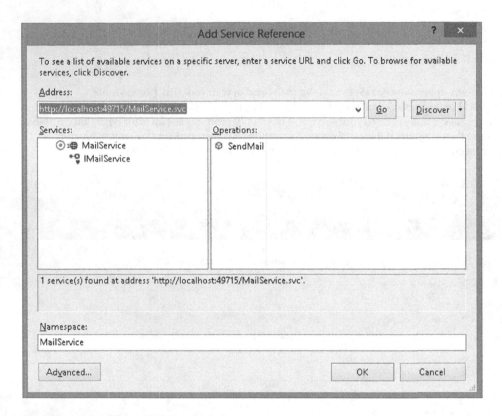

Figure 15-16. *Adding a Web Service Reference*

Switch your project to "Logical View," and open the UserDetail screen that you created earlier. Create a new button called SendWithWebService, and add the code that's shown in Listing 15-19.

Listing 15-19. Screen Code to Send an E-mail via a Web Service Call

VB:
File: HelpDeskVB\Client\UserCode\UserDetail.vb

```
Imports Microsoft.LightSwitch.Threading
Imports System.ServiceModel

Private Sub SendWithWebService_Execute()
```

```vb
    Microsoft.LightSwitch.Threading.Dispatchers.Main.BeginInvoke(
        Sub()
            Dim serverUrl As Uri = System.Windows.Application.Current.Host.Source        ❶

            Details.Dispatcher.BeginInvoke(
                Sub()
                    'serverUrl.AbsoluteUri returns a URL like this:
                    '    http://localhost:49715/Client/Web/HelpDesk.Client.xap
                    Dim rootUrl =                                                        ❷
                            serverUrl.AbsoluteUri.Substring(
                            0, serverUrl.AbsoluteUri.IndexOf("/Client/Web/"))

                    Dim binding = New System.ServiceModel.BasicHttpBinding()

                    'example endPoint url:
                    '  endPoint http://localhost:49715/MailService.svc
                    Dim endPoint =                                                       ❸
                        New EndpointAddress(rootUrl + "/MailService.svc ")

                    Dim proxy As MailService.MailServiceClient =                         ❹
                        New MailService.MailServiceClient(binding, endPoint)

                    AddHandler proxy.SendMailCompleted,                                  ❺
                        Sub(sender As Object, e As MailService.SendMailCompletedEventArgs)
                            Me.Details.Dispatcher.BeginInvoke(
                                Sub()
                                    ShowMessageBox(e.Result.ToString())
                                End Sub
                            )
                        End Sub

                    proxy.SendMailAsync(User.Email, SubjectProperty, BodyProperty)       ❻

                End Sub
            )
        End Sub
    )
End Sub
```

C#:
File: HelpDeskCS\Client\UserCode\UserDetail.cs

```csharp
using System.ServiceModel;
using Microsoft.LightSwitch.Threading;

partial void SendWithWebService_Execute()
{
    Microsoft.LightSwitch.Threading.Dispatchers.Main.BeginInvoke(() =>
    {
        Uri serverUrl = System.Windows.Application.Current.Host.Source;                 ❶
```

```
        this.Details.Dispatcher.BeginInvoke(() =>
        {
            //serverUrl.AbsoluteUri returns a URL like this:
            //    http://localhost:49715/Client/Web/HelpDesk.Client.xap
            string rootUrl =                                                    ❷
                serverUrl.AbsoluteUri.Substring(
                    0, serverUrl.AbsoluteUri.IndexOf("/Client/Web/"));

            var binding = new System.ServiceModel.BasicHttpBinding();
            //example endPoint url:
            //    http://localhost:49715/MailService.svc/MailService.svc
            var endPoint =                                                      ❸
                new EndpointAddress(rootUrl + "/MailService.svc/MailService.svc");

            MailService.MailServiceClient proxy =                               ❹
                new MailService.MailServiceClient(binding, endPoint);

            proxy.SendMailCompleted +=                                          ❺
                (object sender, MailService.SendMailCompletedEventArgs e) =>
                {
                    this.Details.Dispatcher.BeginInvoke(() =>
                    {
                        this.ShowMessageBox(e.Result.ToString());
                    });
                };

            proxy.SendMailAsync(User.Email, SubjectProperty, BodyProperty);      ❻

        });
    }
);
}
```

To simplify the process of deployment, this code sets your web service's endpoint address in code. This means that if you deploy your application and later move it to a different server, there'll be no need for you to reconfigure your client. The code accomplishes this by finding the address of your XAP file ❶ and stripping off the trailing part of the address that contains Client/Web/HelpDesk.Client.xap ❷. It then uses the root part of the URL to build an address that points to your MailService.svc endpoint ❸. The next line declares a proxy to your web service ❹. If your code fails to connect to your web service at runtime, try creating your proxy by calling the non-overloaded constructor (for example, New MailService.MailServiceClient()). This applies the endpoint address that you specified in the "Add Service Reference" dialog, and it can help you diagnose the problem that prevents you from establishing a connection. The next block of code contains the logic that handles the completion of your web service call ❺. Finally, the line toward the end of the method contains the code that asynchronously calls your web service's SendMail method ❻.

This completes your screen, and you can now run your application. When you open the user detail screen and click on the "Send With Web Service" button, your application will send your e-mail by calling your web service method.

EXERCISE 15.1 – CALLING WEB SERVICES

There are many public web services that you can call. Try finding some by Googling "Free WebService." Alternatively, you can visit http://www.webservicex.net/ws/default.aspx to find a list of open web services. There, you'll find web services that allow you to convert currencies, find out the weather, verify addresses, and many more. Find a web service that interests you, and try to call the service from your client application. Just like the example in this section, you'll need to add a service reference and write code in your client application to consume the service.

Summary

This chapter showed you several ways to add e-mail support to your LightSwitch application. You've learned how to send e-mail alerts when data changes, how to allow users to send e-mails from screens, create e-mails with file attachments, and integrate with Microsoft Outlook. You've also learned how to send e-mail by calling web services.

This chapter began by showing you how to send SMTP messages from the server. This approach uses the methods in the System.Net.Mail namespace, and the advantage of server-side e-mail is that it works for both web and desktop applications. Microsoft Outlook integration, for example, works only in desktop applications. The data source events in the save pipeline enable you to send e-mail when your application creates, updates, or deletes entities. This allows you to send e-mail messages based conditionally on data changes or data values. The SmtpClient and MailMessage objects in the System.Net.Mail namespace provide the mechanism that sends the actual e-mail. If you want to apply custom fonts and colors to your message, you can accomplish this by composing your e-mail content in HTML format. To maximize code reusability, you can create an SMTP helper class that enables you to call your e-mail logic from multiple places.

If you don't want to send e-mail only when data changes, you can create an EmailOperation table for the sole purpose of sending e-mails. The EmailOperation table contains fields such as recipient address, subject, and body. Any row that you add to this table triggers an e-mail by using the data that you've entered into the table. The code sample shows you how to add a row to this table by using a temporary data workspace. This allows you to send ad-hoc e-mails from your screens, without forcing the user to save other changes that they've made on the screen.

The MailMessage object allows you to add file attachments to your e-mail. If you've created a Silverlight browser application, security restrictions prevent you from adding button code that opens the Silverlight file dialogs. You can work around this restriction by adding a custom "button" control and adding the logic that opens the file dialog in the code that handles the button's click event.

If your users use Microsoft Outlook and you've created a desktop application, automating Outlook is another option that you can choose. You've seen sample code that shows you how to create an Outlook message from a LightSwitch screen by using COM automation.

If Microsoft Outlook is not available, an alternative is to create a mailto hyperlink. This technique allows you to compose a draft message that includes the "to address," subject, and body. You can then add a command on your LightSwitch screen that opens the message in the user's default mail program. This might be Outlook, Outlook Express, Windows Live Mail, or any other e-mail client that the user has installed.

In the last part of this chapter, you've found out how to send an e-mail by calling a web service from your LightSwitch client. The benefit of this approach is that you can easily adapt the code in this section to call other web-based resources, such as SMS gateways or mapping services.

From an HTML client application, you can use jQuery's ajax method to call external web resources. By wrapping the asynchronous AJAX call in a promise object, you can take advantage of LightSwitch's progress indication and error-handling capabilities.

Finally, you've seen how to add a WCF web service to your LightSwitch application's logic tier. The WCF service in this chapter sends an e-mail, but once again, you could adapt the code in this section to carry out different tasks. An advantage of adding a web service to your application's logic tier is that you can consume the service from a Silverlight browser application, without having to make tricky changes to your security settings. To call your web service from a Silverlight client, you'd switch your project to File View and add a "Service Reference" to your service's endpoint. Once you do this, you can write .NET code in your client project that consumes your web service.

CHAPTER 16

■ ■ ■

Authenticating Your Users

The next two chapters show you how to secure your application. You'll begin by learning about *authentication*— the process that determines the identity of your user. Once you identify your user, you can control the screens that they can see, and functions that they can perform, in your application. You'll find out how to implement this type of access control in Chapter 17.

In this chapter, you'll learn how to

- Choose an authentication method that suits your application type

- Apply Windows or Forms authentication in your LightSwitch application

- Share authentication credentials with other applications

By the end of this chapter, you'll understand how to enable authentication in the HelpDesk application. You'll also find out how to force users to enter a user name and password at login by enabling Forms authentication.

Choosing an Authentication Method

LightSwitch supports two authentication methods: Windows and Forms. When you enable Windows authentication, LightSwitch identifies the logged-in user by examining the credentials that they've used to log in to their Windows computer.

Forms authentication identifies a user by forcing them to enter a user name and password when the application starts up.

Your application type helps you choose the most appropriate type of authentication. Table 16-1 summarizes the recommended options.

Table 16-1. *Recommended Authentication Methods by Application Type*

Application Type	None	Windows	Forms
Two-Tier Desktop App – Deployed on an Internal Network	✓	✓	
Three-Tier Desktop or Web App – Deployed on an Internal Network		✓	✓
Three-Tier Desktop or Web App – Deployed on the Internet or Azure			✓

The most secure choice for a two-tier desktop application is Windows authentication. In a two-tier application, the connection string to your membership database is stored in clear text inside your application's web.config file, which is held on the client's machine. If a malicious user discovers this connection string, they could tamper with your membership data outside of LightSwitch.

If you want to make your application available via the Internet (or you want to deploy to Azure), Windows authentication isn't really a viable choice. Forms authentication is the recommended choice in this scenario.

In a three-tier local network deployment (with the LightSwitch server components hosted in IIS), you have a choice of either Windows or Forms authentication. Table 16-2 summarizes some of the features of these two authentication types and explains when you should use each type.

Table 16-2. *When to Use Each Type of Authentication*

Windows	Forms
Use Windows authentication if all your users belong in the same domain	Use Forms authentication if you don't have a Windows domain—for example, if you're using a workgroup or Novell network.
Use Windows authentication if you don't want to have an extra login screen. With Windows authentication, your users won't need to enter a user name and password when they run your application.	Use Forms authentication if you want your users to enter a user name and password when they run your application. You might choose to do this to enforce an extra layer of security.
	Forms authentication is ideal if you want to share authentication details with other applications, perhaps with an existing ASP.NET web site.

Disabling Authentication

The Access Control tab in the properties of your application allows you to manage authentication. By default, LightSwitch disables authentication in all new projects that you create. (See Figure 16-1.)

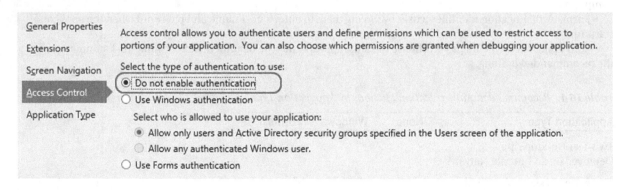

Figure 16-1. *Default authentication option*

You would leave authentication disabled if you have no need to know who your users are. This choice is suitable if you want to give users open access to your application and have no need to control access to specific parts of your application.

Enabling Windows Authentication

To enable Windows authentication, select the Use Windows Authentication radio button. (See Figure 16-2.) This enables an additional set of radio buttons that allows you to choose who can run your application.

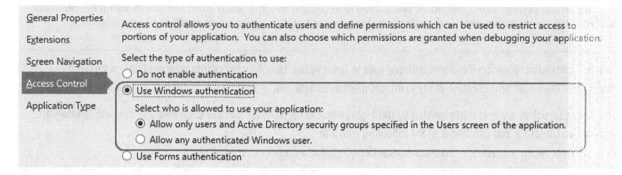

Figure 16-2. Allow any authenticated Windows user

The first option requires you to enter each Windows user who wants to access your application. You would do this at runtime by using the Users screen. (See Figure 16-3.)

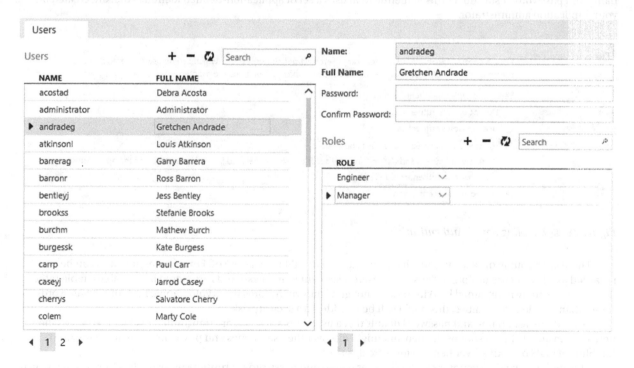

Figure 16-3. Specifying users through the users screen at runtime

The second option (Allow Any Authenticated Windows User) allows all users who have been authenticated by Windows to run your application. This option is ideal if you want to identify your users without going through the time-consuming process of adding each user to your application. If you enable this option, you can still restrict the tasks that individual users can carry out in your application by specifying their login names in the Users screen. Chapter 17 covers this in greater depth.

When you deploy your application, you'll need to designate an application administrator by using the publish wizard. Chapter 18 shows you the specific steps that you would follow to set up an application administrator.

■ **Tip** Instead of requiring the administrative user to enter Active Directory users into your application by hand, make their life easier and create a utility to import them automatically.

The Active Directory sample that's written by the LightSwitch team provides sample code that you can use to integrate with Active Directory. You can find it at the following web site:

http://code.msdn.microsoft.com/windowsdesktop/LightSwitch-Active-5092eaa8

Enabling Forms Authentication

When you choose Use Forms Authentication (shown in Figure 16-4), your application prompts the user for a user name and password at startup. Forms authentication uses a set of application-defined identities that are created by your application administrator.

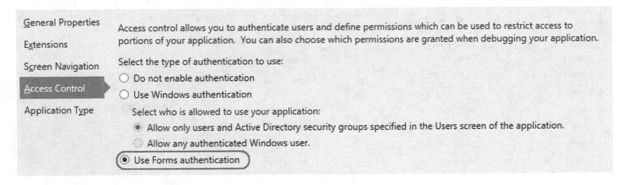

Figure 16-4. Enabling Forms Authentication

There are a couple of security considerations that you should to be aware of. Forms authentication can be regarded as a less secure option, because your users' user names and passwords are stored in a database table rather than being securely maintained by Windows. Although LightSwitch stores the cryptographic hash of the passwords rather than the clear-text values, this might still be considered a security risk.

Second, the user name and password details that a user enters at logon are transmitted in clear text across the network. An attacker who snoops the network might discover the user names and passwords that are being used. Enabling HTTPS on your server helps to mitigate this risk.

The application administrator creates the user names and passwords at runtime by using the Users screen, which was shown in Figure 16-3. The administrator can also use this screen to delete users or reset passwords.

If users want to change their password, they can do so by using an option that's shown by LightSwitch. (See Figure 16-5.) The location of the control that opens the Change Password dialog depends on the shell that you've chosen. In the Standard shell, the control appears in the bottom right part of the application.

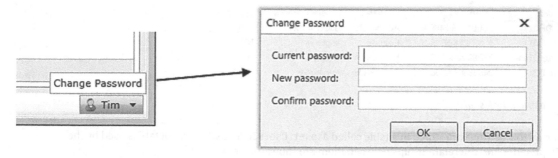

Figure 16-5. *Changing a password*

■ **Caution**   If you enable Forms authentication, you should configure Secure Sockets Layer (SSL) when you deploy your application. (See Chapter 18.) This secures any user login credentials that are transmitted over the network.

Understanding Where User Details Are Stored

When you enable authentication, LightSwitch uses the ASP.NET membership provider to manage your users. This provider stores your users in a table called aspnet_Users in your Intrinsic database. Figure 16-6 shows a screenshot of this table that's taken from SQL Server Management Studio. The primary key field is called UserId and is of data type GUID. The user names that you specify are stored in a field called UserName.

	ApplicationId	UserId	UserName	LoweredUserName	MobileAlias	IsAnony...	LastActivityDate
1	9B6DE0DF-314...	1444C4BA...	AcostaD	acostad	NULL	0	2013-01-14 10:55:17.227
2	9B6DE0DF-314...	57CC02E9...	administrator	administrator	NULL	0	2013-01-14 10:55:17.230
3	9B6DE0DF-314...	8013EC73-..	AndradeG	andradeg	NULL	0	2013-01-14 10:55:17.230
4	9B6DE0DF-314...	EAD9A8D...	AtkinsonL	atkinsonl	NULL	0	2013-01-14 10:55:17.230
5	9B6DE0DF-314...	1857547F-..	BarreraG	barrerag	NULL	0	2013-01-14 10:55:17.233

Figure 16-6. *aspnet_Users table*

The provider stores any roles that you define in a table called aspnet_Roles. This is shown in Figure 16-7.

	ApplicationId	RoleId	RoleName	LoweredRoleName	Description
1	9B6DE0DF-314A-...	7DEB15F8-748F-41...	Administrator	administrator	NULL
2	9B6DE0DF-314A-...	A3999CF6-5B38-4E...	Engineer	engineer	NULL
3	9B6DE0DF-314A-...	7FD8D708-7596-45...	Manager	manager	NULL
4	9B6DE0DF-314A-...	34B5890B-C79D-46...	TeamLeader	teamleader	NULL

Figure 16-7. aspnet_Roles table

The user-to-role settings are stored in a table called `aspnet_UsersInRoles`. The set of tables used by the membership provider and the relationships between them are shown in Figure 16-8.

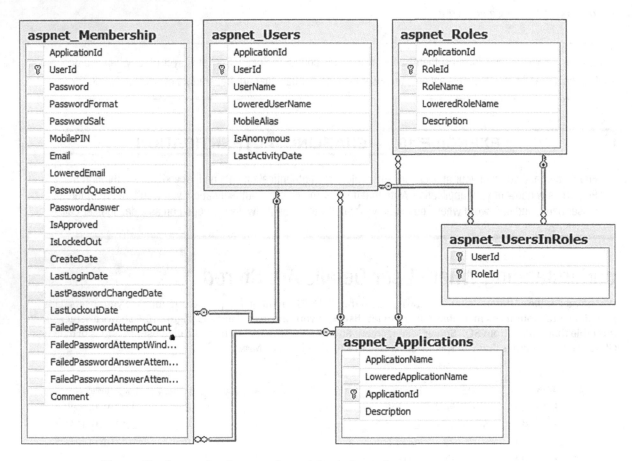

Figure 16-8. Tables used by the membership provider and their relationships

It's useful to understand the tables that the membership provider uses because this knowledge can help you to create and retrieve user accounts outside of LightSwitch. If you're familiar with SQL Server, you can manually create users by calling the `aspnet_Membership_CreateUser` and `aspnet_Profile_SetProperties` stored procedures.

Changing the Password Complexity Rules

When you enable Forms authentication, the membership provider enforces a password-complexity rule that helps to keep your application secure. By default, passwords must be eight characters in length and contain a non-alphanumeric character. An example of a valid (but absurdly weak) password is pass@word1.

The default rule provides a good level of security, but some users might find it too restrictive and you might prefer to weaken the rule. Alternatively, you might even want to strengthen the password-complexity rule to force users to use passwords that are even more complex.

After you deploy your application, you can change the password-complexity rule by modifying a setting in your web.config file. When you deploy your application in Internet Information Services (IIS), you'll find the web.config file in the root folder of your LightSwitch application. As mentioned earlier, Forms authentication isn't recommended for two-tier applications; therefore, this section applies only to three-tier IIS deployments.

Once you find your web.config file, open it in a text editor and search for the ASPNetSQLMembershipProvider element. The membership provider controls the password complexity through the minRequiredPasswordLength and minRequiredNonalphanumericCharacters attributes (shown in Figure 16-9). If these two attributes don't exist, you can simply add them in.

```xml
<?xml version="1.0" encoding="utf-8"?>
<configuration>
  <configSections>...</configSections>
  <appSettings>...</appSettings>
  <runtime>...</runtime>
  <connectionStrings>...</connectionStrings>
  <system.web>
    <!-- LightSwitch trace.axd handler -->
    <trace enabled="true" localOnly="false" requestLimit="40" writeToDiagnosticsTrace="false" traceMode="Sort
    <httpHandlers>...</httpHandlers>
    <httpModules>...</httpModules>
    <compilation targetFramework="4.0">...</compilation>
    <authentication mode="Forms">...</authentication>
    <pages validateRequest="false">...</pages>
    <!-- Setting maxRequestLength to be much greater than default 4096 so that large data may be uploaded e.g
    <httpRuntime requestPathInvalidCharacters="" requestValidationMode="2.0" maxRequestLength="102400" />
    <membership defaultProvider="AspNetMembershipProvider">
      <providers>
        <clear />
        <add name="AspNetMembershipProvider" type="System.Web.Security.SqlMembershipProvider"
             connectionStringName="_IntrinsicData"
             applicationName="HelpDesk"
             requiresUniqueEmail="false"
             requiresQuestionAndAnswer="false"

             minRequiredPasswordLength="1"
             minRequiredNonalphanumericCharacters="0"     ◄── These attributes control the password strength.
             passwordFormat="Hashed"
             maxInvalidPasswordAttempts="5"
             passwordAttemptWindow="10"
             passwordStrengthRegularExpression=""

        />
      </providers>
    </membership>
```

Figure 16-9. *Changing the password-complexity rules in the web.config file*

Changing Password-Encryption Settings

By default, LightSwitch saves the hashes of the user passwords rather than the clear-text password. This is controlled by the `passwordFormat` attribute in the `AspNetSqlMembershipProvider` element of your `web.config` file (which you also can see in Figure 16-9). There are three choices that you can enter here:

- `Hashed`

- `Encrypted`

- `Clear`

`Hashed` is the default value and the most secure. When you choose this option, LightSwitch uses a one-way hash algorithm and a randomly generated salt value to encrypt the passwords that it stores in the database. When a user enters a user name and password at logon, LightSwitch hashes the password that is entered and compares it to the value that's stored in the database.

It's impossible for you to retrieve the plain-text password values when `passwordFormat` is set to `Hashed`. If you want your user passwords to be stored in plain text inside your `aspnet_users` table, change the `passwordFormat` setting to `Clear`. This is obviously less secure because anyone who can access the `aspnet_users` table can see all your passwords.

Although this is less secure, there are a couple of reasons why you might choose this option:

- You might want to build some mechanism outside of LightSwitch to remind users of their actual password.

- During the initial setup of your application, you might want to pre-load users and known passwords by manually populating the `aspnet_users` table. Maintaining clear-text passwords simplifies this process and saves you from having to create some additional process to work out the hash or encrypted value.

Sharing Forms Authentication Data with ASP.NET

Let's imagine that you have an existing ASP.NET web site that uses Forms authentication. Because your web site already contains a set of users, you might want to share these existing credentials with your LightSwitch application. You can set up your LightSwitch application to share Forms authentication details with existing ASP.NET web sites by modifying your `web.config` file.

To do this, deploy your LightSwitch application to IIS and open the `web.config` file in a text editor. (See Chapter 18 for more help on deployment.) You'll need to make the following changes to this file:

- Create a new connection string that points to the authentication database that your existing ASP.NET application uses.

- Update the membership, role, and profile provider strings to reference the connection string that you've created.

- Ensure that the same `ApplicationName` is specified in the provider strings in both your LightSwitch and ASP.NET applications.

- Specify the same machine key setting for both of your applications.

To create a new connection string that references the authentication database that your existing ASP.NET application uses, search for the `connectionStrings` element. Beneath the `_IntrinsicData` connection string that's created by LightSwitch, create a new connection string that points to your existing authentication database (highlighted in Figure 16-10). The new connection string in this example is called `_AuthData`.

```
<?xml version="1.0" encoding="utf-8"?>
<configuration>
  <configSections>...</configSections>
  <appSettings>...</appSettings>
  <runtime>...</runtime>
  <connectionStrings>
    <add name="_IntrinsicData"
         connectionString="Data Source=MyDBServer1;Database=HelpDesk;User ID=Sqllogin1;Password=somepassword1;" />

    <add name="_AuthData" connectionString="Data Source=MyDBServer2;
    Initial Catalog=MyAuthDB;Integrated Security=False;
    User ID=Sqllogin2;Password=somepassword2;
    Pooling=True;Connect Timeout=30;User Instance=False" />
```

◄— Add your new connection string here.

Figure 16-10. *Creating a new connection string in your LightSwtich application's web.config file*

Now search for the AspNetMembershipProvider, AspNetRoleProvider, and AspNetProfileProvider entries in the web.config file of your LightSwitch application. By default, the connectionStringName setting for each entry is set to _IntrinsicData by default. Change this to _AuthData (as shown in Figure 16-11).

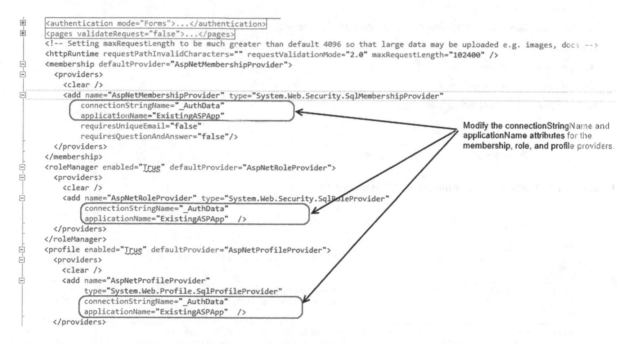

```
<authentication mode="Forms">...</authentication>
<pages validateRequest="false">...</pages>
<!-- Setting maxRequestLength to be much greater than default 4096 so that large data may be uploaded e.g. images, docs -->
<httpRuntime requestPathInvalidCharacters="" requestValidationMode="2.0" maxRequestLength="102400" />
<membership defaultProvider="AspNetMembershipProvider">
  <providers>
    <clear />
    <add name="AspNetMembershipProvider" type="System.Web.Security.SqlMembershipProvider"
        connectionStringName="_AuthData"
        applicationName="ExistingASPApp"
        requiresUniqueEmail="false"
        requiresQuestionAndAnswer="false"/>
  </providers>
</membership>
<roleManager enabled="True" defaultProvider="AspNetRoleProvider">
  <providers>
    <clear />
    <add name="AspNetRoleProvider" type="System.Web.Security.SqlRoleProvider"
        connectionStringName="_AuthData"
        applicationName="ExistingASPApp"  />
  </providers>
</roleManager>
<profile enabled="True" defaultProvider="AspNetProfileProvider">
  <providers>
    <clear />
    <add name="AspNetProfileProvider"
        type="System.Web.Profile.SqlProfileProvider"
        connectionStringName="_AuthData"
        applicationName="ExistingASPApp"  />
  </providers>
```

Modify the connectionStringName and applicationName attributes for the membership, role, and profile providers.

Figure 16-11. *Modify the connection string and application name settings*

Open the web.config file for your *existing* ASP.NET application, and search for the AspNetMembershipProvider entry. Find the applicationName that this uses. In this example, let's assume that the applicationName value is set to ExistingASPApp.

Make sure that the three provider strings in the web.config file for your LightSwitch application specify the applicationName of ExistingASPApp.

You need to have the same machine key defined in both of your applications. Because passwords are hashed (or encrypted), identical machine keys allow both applications to encrypt and decrypt passwords in the same exact way.

If a machine key isn't specified in the web.config file of your existing application, you'll need to generate a new key. IIS Manager includes a feature that generates machine keys for you. (See Figure 16-12.) Alternatively, you can search the Web to find online web sites that can generate keys for you. Once you've decided on a key, add the machine key entry to the <system.web> section in both of your web.config files. Figure 16-13 shows how this looks.

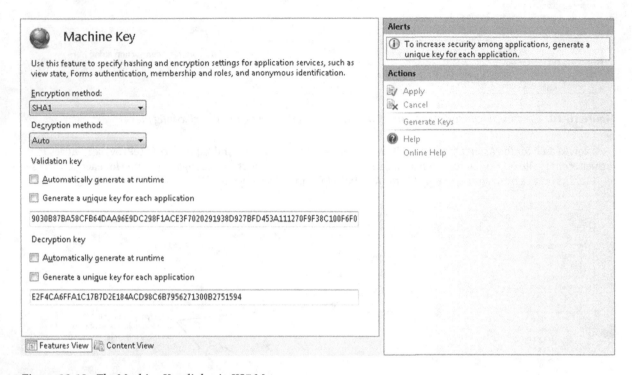

Figure 16-12. *The Machine Key dialog in IIS7 Manager*

Figure 16-13. *Add identical key values to both of your web.config files*

Allowing Users to Log Out of Web Applications

Silverlight LightSwitch browser applications don't include a Logout button, so the only way for a user to log out of a Forms authenticated application is to close their browser.

This behavior isn't convenient for someone who wants to quit their session and log in as a different user. This example shows you how to add a Logout button to save your users the trouble of closing and reopening their browser.

This technique uses an ASP.NET page to kill the current session, and reloads the web page that hosts your LightSwitch application.

First of all, you'll need to deploy your application into IIS. (Refer to Chapter 18 for details.) Create a new text file in the web-site folder that contains your LightSwitch application. Now add the content that's shown in Listing 16-1, and rename your file to LogOff.aspx.

Listing 16-1. Logoff.aspx Code-Behind

VB:
File: HelpDeskVB\Server\Logoff.aspx
```
<%@ Page Language="vb" %>
<%
System.Web.Security.FormsAuthentication.SignOut()
Response.Redirect("default.htm")
%>
```

C#:
File: HelpDeskCS\Server\Logoff.aspx
```
<%@ Page Language="C#" %>
<%
System.Web.Security.FormsAuthentication.SignOut();
Response.Redirect("default.htm");
%>
```

To call this web page, create a button called Logout on your Engineer Dashboard screen and add the code shown in Listing 16-2. You can use the Properties sheet to set an icon for your button. For the code to work, you'll need to switch to File view and add a reference to the System.Windows.Browser assembly in your Client project. You'll also need to include the imports or using statements shown in the listing.

Listing 16-2. Execution Code for the Logout Button

VB:
File: HelpDeskVB\Client\UserCode\EngineerDashboard.vb

```
Imports Microsoft.LightSwitch.Threading
Imports System.Windows.Browser
Imports Microsoft.LightSwitch.Security

Private Sub Logout_Execute()
   Dispatchers.Main.Invoke(
      Sub()
         HtmlPage.Window.Navigate(
            New Uri("LogOff.aspx", UriKind.Relative))          ❶
      End Sub)
End Sub

Private Sub Logout_CanExecute(ByRef result As Boolean)

   Dim logoutCanExecute As Boolean
   Dispatchers.Main.Invoke(
      Sub()
```

```
        logoutCanExecute =
            (System.Windows.Application.Current.IsRunningOutOfBrowser =
                False) AndAlso
              (Application.Current.User.AuthenticationType =
                  AuthenticationType.Forms)
      End Sub)

    result = logoutCanExecute                                    ❷
End Sub
```

C#:
File: HelpDeskCS\Client\UserCode\EngineerDashboard.cs

```csharp
using Microsoft.LightSwitch.Threading;
using System.Windows.Browser;
using Microsoft.LightSwitch.Security;

partial void Logout_Execute()
{
    Dispatchers.Main.Invoke(() =>
    {
        HtmlPage.Window.Navigate(
            new Uri("LogOff.aspx", UriKind.Relative));      ❶
    });
}

partial void Logout_CanExecute(ref bool result)
{
    bool logoutCanExecute = false;
    Dispatchers.Main.Invoke(() =>
    {
        logoutCanExecute =
            (System.Windows.Application.Current.IsRunningOutOfBrowser == false)
                && (Application.Current.User.AuthenticationType ==
                    AuthenticationType.Forms);
    });

    result = logoutCanExecute;                                   ❷
}
```

The code in the Logout_Execute method navigates the user to the LogOff.aspx page ❶. This page contains the logic that signs out the user. The code in the Logout_CanExecute method ❷ hides the Logout button if you haven't enabled Forms authentication or if your application isn't running in a browser.

When the user now runs your application, they'll be able to log out of your application by clicking on the Logout button. (See Figure 16-14.)

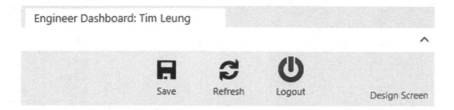

Figure 16-14. Logout button on the command bar

If you want to show a logout command that appears throughout your application, you can attach the logout code to a navigation menu rather than to a button. To do this, you would create a dummy screen and add code to its _CanRun method. The "Opening Screens Conditionally at Login" section in Chapter 17 demonstrates this technique.

Summary

Authentication allows you to determine the identity of your user, and thus control what the user can do in your application.

There are two types of authentication that you can use: Forms authentication and Windows authentication. Windows authentication is the most secure method for a two-tier desktop application.

Windows authentication uses the credentials that your user uses to log into their Windows computer. The advantage of using Windows authentication is that your users don't need to supply additional credentials when they start your application.

Forms authentication is perfect for Internet applications or for environments that don't have a Windows domain. If you enable Forms authentication, LightSwitch prompts the user to supply a user name and password at login.

For both types of authentication, the administrator enters the user data through a screen that's provided by LightSwitch.

LightSwitch uses the ASP.NET membership provider to manage your users. This stores your user data using tables that belong in your Intrinsic database.

If you choose Forms authentication, your passwords must be eight characters in length and contain a non-alphanumeric character. You can change this rule by amending your web.config file. This file also allows you to change how the membership provider encrypts the password values in your database.

You can share your Forms authentication credentials with other LightSwitch or ASP.NET applications by modifying your web.config file. This would permit users to log in to different applications using the same user name and password. To set this up, you would need to amend the user, role, and profile providers in all systems to use the same authentication database and machine key.

Silverlight LightSwitch web applications don't include a Logout button. If you want to add this ability, you can create a web page that logs off your user and then create a command in your LightSwitch application that calls this web page.

CHAPTER 17

■ ■ ■

Authorizing Your Users

Security can be extremely important in a business application. Fortunately, LightSwitch allows you to carry out access control in a granular fashion. Using LightSwitch, you can restrict access to screens, screen commands, entities, and queries.

In this chapter, you'll learn how to

- Define permissions and roles

- Set up an administrator, and allocate users to roles

- Restrict access to resources based on role membership

This chapter extends the HelpDesk application by including access-control rules. You'll find out how to apply entity (table) level permissions to prevent engineers from updating, inserting, or deleting engineer records. You'll also find out how to prevent engineers from updating an issue's problem-description field, but still allow the other fields in the table to be updatable.

You'll learn how to prevent an engineer from opening screens that are used by managers and to how to disable the autocomplete box on the issue screen that controls who the issue is assigned to. Finally, you'll find out how to stop all users (regardless of role membership) from using the system between midnight and 3 a.m. You'll also learn how to open different screens at startup depending on role membership.

Applying Permissions

The way to secure a LightSwitch application is to create permissions at design time. Permissions define what your users can do. Permissions are defined in your application's metadata in the same way that screens and entities are defined by your application. Therefore, LightSwitch stores your permission definitions in your application's LSML file.

At run time, the system administrator creates roles and assigns permissions to those roles. Roles allow you to group together permissions, and you can assign the same permission to multiple roles. At runtime, the system administrator creates users and assigns the roles to users. Each user can belong to one or more roles. Figure 17-1 illustrates this relationship.

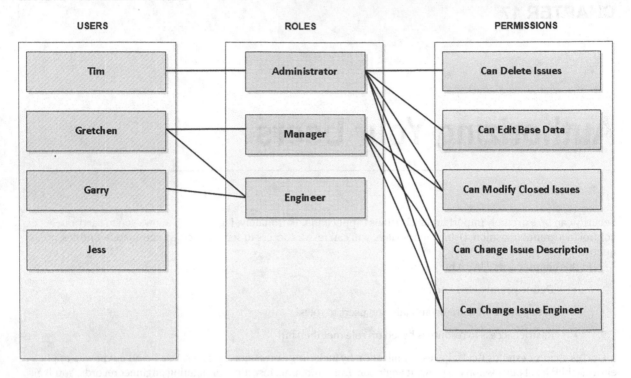

Figure 17-1. Permissions get assigned to roles, and roles get assigned to users

To restrict access to screens and data, you write code that checks whether the logged-in user belongs in a role that has been assigned the required permission.

Unlike permissions, roles and users are defined outside of your application. Therefore, a user of the application with appropriate permissions can create users and roles, but cannot define permissions. Figure 17-2 illustrates where permissions, roles, and users are defined.

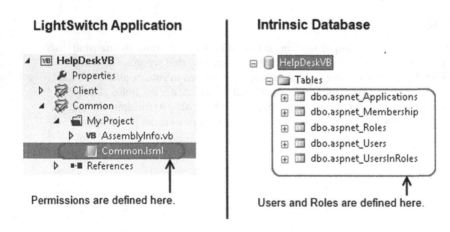

Figure 17-2. This is where permissions, roles, and users are defined

Defining Permissions

Permissions are defined through the permissions grid in the Access Control tab of your project's properties.

Figure 17-3 shows the permissions that exist in the HelpDesk application and demonstrates the types of permissions that you could create.

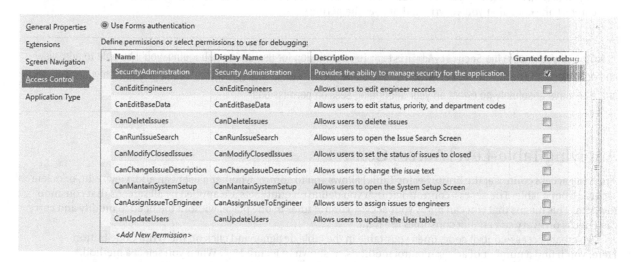

Figure 17-3. *Adding permissions in the Access Control tab*

In this application, only managers can add, edit, or update engineers. Therefore, the application defines a permission called CanEditEngineers that helps to enforce this rule. Also, only managers can edit application data such as priority and status codes. This will be controlled by a permission called CanEditBaseData.

■ **Note**　Either Windows Authentication or Forms Authentication must be selected. Otherwise, the Define Permissions grid will be disabled.

Setting Up Administrators Who Can Manage Users

Every LightSwitch application has a built-in permission called SecurityAdministration. Users who belong in roles that have been assigned this permission can add, edit, and maintain users and roles.

By default, LightSwitch also creates a role called Administrator that includes the built-in SecurityAdministration permission. So to create an administrator who can manage and create other users, you should create a user and add that user to the Administrator role.

Administrators maintain users and roles by using screens that are shown in a navigation menu group called Administration (although you can change the name of this navigation group if you prefer, just as with any other navigation group).

Debugging Permissions

When you debug a LightSwitch application, you won't be prompted to log in, even if you've enabled authentication. So to test that your application works as expected, you can assign yourself permissions at debug time by checking the Granted For Debug check box, which appears next to each permission row (as shown in Figure 17-3).

If you tick this check box, you'll be granted the permission while you're debugging. With this option selected, you can test any code that you've written that uses the permission.

■ **Note**   If you enable the `SecurityAdministration` permission for use during debugging, you'll be able to add, view, and edit roles and users. However, any roles or users that you add while debugging won't be deployed with your application, and they have absolutely no effect on your debugging session permissions.

Applying Table-Level Access Control

Applying access control at the Entity Set (or Table) allows you to control whether a user can add, view, edit, or delete records from a table. The access-control logic that you define on entity sets are applied by all screens that consume the data. This means that you can apply your access-control rules in one place, without the need to modify and carry out checks on every screen that consumes the data.

To create access-control code, open your table in the table designer and click on the Write Code button. Here, you'll find a number of access-control methods, as shown in Figure 17-4. When you select a method, LightSwitch opens the code editor and creates a code stub in your data service class (that is: `Server\UserCode\ApplicationDataService.vb`, or the equivalent data service file).

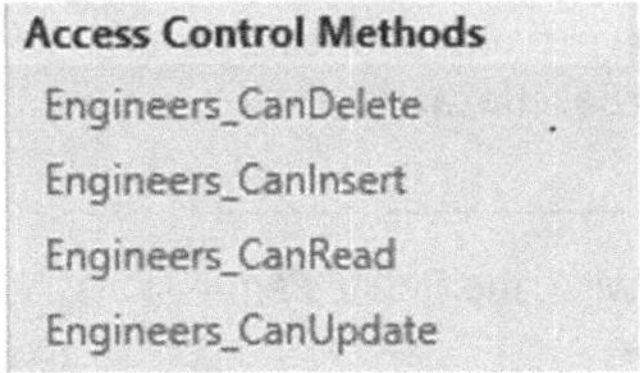

Access Control Methods
Engineers_CanDelete
Engineers_CanInsert
Engineers_CanRead
Engineers_CanUpdate

Figure 17-4. *Entity set access-control methods*

LightSwitch executes the access-control logic on the server. An advantage of this is that if a user attempts to read or update data outside of a screen (via the OData end point, for example), LightSwitch still enforces your access-control rules.

To prevent the current user from a performing an action, set the result of the relevant access-control method to `false`. For example, to prevent the current user from deleting engineers, set the return value of the `Engineers_CanDelete` method to `false`. The rest of this section shows you exactly how to prevent users from editing, reading, and saving data.

■ **Tip**   You can refer to the Save Pipeline flowchart (in Chapter 4, Figure 4-10) to remind yourself how the `_Can` methods fit into the server-side save process.

Restricting users from editing data

In the HelpDesk application, only users who belong in roles that have been granted the CanEditEngineers permission can add, update, and delete engineer records. All other users can view engineers, but not edit any of their details.

To apply this rule, you'll need to create code in the Engineer_CanDelete, Engineer_CanInsert, and Engineer_CanUpdate methods. Open the Engineer table in the table designer, click on the Write Code button, and create code in the three _Can methods that have been outlined. Amend your code as shown in Listing 17-1.

Listing 17-1. Setting Access-Control Permissions

VB:
File: HelpDeskVB\Server\UserCode\ApplicationDataService.vb

```
Private Sub Engineers_CanDelete(ByRef result As Boolean)
    result = Application.User.HasPermission(
        Permissions.CanEditEngineers)
End Sub

Private Sub Engineers_CanInsert(ByRef result As Boolean)
    result = Application.User.HasPermission(
        Permissions.CanEditEngineers)
End Sub

Private Sub Engineers_CanUpdate(ByRef result As Boolean)
    result = Application.User.HasPermission(
        Permissions.CanEditEngineers)
End Sub
```

C#:
File: HelpDeskCS\Server\UserCode\ApplicationDataService.cs

```
private void Engineers_CanDelete(ref bool result)
{
    result = Application.User.HasPermission(
        Permissions.CanEditEngineers);
}

private void Engineers_CanInsert(ref bool result)
{
    result = Application.User.HasPermission(
        Permissions.CanEditEngineers);
}

private void Engineers_CanUpdate(ref bool result)
{
    result = Application.User.HasPermission(
        Permissions.CanEditEngineers);
}
```

LightSwitch exposes a Permissions class that allows you to refer to each permission that you've defined in your application. With this class, you can refer to the CanEditEngineers permission by using the syntax Permissions.CanEditEngineers.

The HasPermission method accepts a permission and returns a Boolean result that indicates whether the logged-in user is assigned to a role that contains the permission that you've supplied. The code uses the return value to set the result of the _CanDelete, _CanInsert, and _CanUpdate methods.

If you've created access-control code that prevents a user from deleting, inserting, or updating records, LightSwitch automatically disables any built-in buttons (in data grids, for example) that carry out these functions. But if you've created your own screen command (for example, a button or link) to perform a data operation that's disallowed, LightSwitch won't automatically disable it. You'll need to write code in the screen command's _CanExecute method to perform this task.

An important point when you're writing authentication code is that you should not perform access-control checks based on role membership. Because roles are defined by the administrator at runtime, you can't guarantee that the role will exist. Therefore, always check against permissions, and leave the task of managing roles and role permissions to the application's administrative user.

■ **Note** It might seem strange that the access-control methods set the result through the method's parameter rather than returning a Boolean result. This behavior is consistent with how LightSwitch exposes other entry points that return values. The primary reason is because LightSwitch often uses partial methods and partial methods can't return values.

Restricting Users from Reading Data

You can prevent users from reading data by setting the result of the entity set's CanRead method to false. LightSwitch executes this method before it reads any data.

If a user tries to load a search or editable grid screen that uses a table where the CanRead method returns false, the data grid will display nothing except a red X. This behavior isn't user friendly, so it's good practice to also apply access-control checks at the screen level.

Using the CanRead method is very valuable, particularly if your table contains sensitive data. If you deny access to a table by using the CanRead method, those records are also hidden in the server pipelines. This means that your data cannot be exposed in any way (for example, via the OData end point).

If your server-side business logic requires access to data that the current user doesn't have, you can override the restrictions by granting the necessary permissions in code. You would use the method Application.Current.User. AddPermissions.

■ **Note** Unfortunately, you can call AddPermissions only from code in the save pipeline. If you try calling this method from any of the methods in the query pipeline (for example, PreProcessQuery), you'll receive an exception. This behavior prevents you from denying all users read access to a table and to allow access only through queries. (queries would include permission-elevation logic that depend on the identity of the logged-on user.)

Restricting Users from Saving All Data

You can stop users from saving data by setting the return value of the SaveChanges_CanExecute method to false.

LightSwitch executes this method on the server after a user attempts to save data. Unlike the earlier access-control methods, this method extends to all tables in the data source. If SaveChanges_CanExecute returns false, the user won't be able to save any data in any table at all.

The logic that you write in all the access-control methods that you've seen so far (for example, _CanRead or _CanUpdate) is not just restricted to permission checks. You can also deny access based on other business reasons. As an example, the code in Listing 17-2 shows how you can use this method to prevent users from updating the data in your application between the hours of midnight and 3 a.m.

Listing 17-2. Preventing Users from Saving Data

VB:
File: HelpDeskVB\Server\UserCode\ApplicationDataService.vb

```vb
Private Sub SaveChanges_CanExecute(ByRef result As Boolean)
    'System is down for daily maintenance from midnight to 3am
    If Now.TimeOfDay.Hours >= 0 AndAlso
        Now.TimeOfDay.Hours <= 3 Then
        result = False
    Else
        result = True
    End If
End Sub
```

C#:
File: HelpDeskCS\Server\UserCode\ApplicationDataService.cs

```csharp
partial void SaveChanges_CanExecute(ref bool result)
{
    //System is down for daily maintenance from midnight to 3am
    if (DateTime.Now.TimeOfDay.Hours >= 0 &&
        DateTime.Now.TimeOfDay.Hours <= 3)
    {
        result = false;
    }
    else
    {
        result = true;
    }
}
```

Restricting Users from Editing a Property

In addition to implementing table-level access control, you can prevent users from editing a property by setting the result of the property's _IsReadOnly method to false (as shown in Figure 17-5).

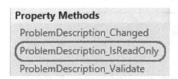

Figure 17-5. IsReadOnly *method*

As an example, the HelpDesk system allows all users to view issues. But only users who belong in roles that have been granted the CanChangeIssueDescription permission can modify the problem description. If a user hasn't been granted this permission, the problem-description property should always be read only. Listing 17-3 shows the code that performs this access-control check.

Listing 17-3. Setting a Property's IsReadOnly Method

VB:
File: HelpDeskVB\Common\UserCode\Issue.vb

```vb
Private Sub ProblemDescription_IsReadOnly(ByRef result As Boolean)
    If Id = 0 Then                                                        ❶
        result = False
    Else
        result =
            (Not Current.User.HasPermission(
             Permissions.CanChangeIssueDescription))                      ❷
    End If
End Sub
```

C#:
File: HelpDeskCS\Common\UserCode\Issue.cs

```csharp
partial void ProblemDescription_IsReadOnly(ref bool result)
{
    if (Id == 0)                                                          ❶
    {
        result = false;
    }
    else
    {
        result =
            !Application.User.HasPermission(
                Permissions.CanChangeIssueDescription);                   ❷
    }
}
```

This code checks whether the user is adding a new issue by testing for an Id value of 0 ❶. If the user is adding a new record, the code returns false to allow the user to create the problem description. Otherwise, it returns a result based on whether the logged-on user has the CanChangeIssueDescription permission ❷.

■ **Note**   The IsReadOnly method is run on the tier where the method's result is being checked.

Applying Screen-Level Access Control

By applying screen-level access control, you can create rules to prevent certain users from opening screens. If you've granted a user access to a screen, you can control the buttons and commands that the user can execute.

However, your access-control logic can be based on any condition, not just conditions that are permissions related. For example, you can disable the Logout button you created in Chapter 16 if your application isn't using Forms authentication and running in a browser.

Restricting Users from Opening Screens

To control access to a screen, open your screen in the designer, click on the Write Code button, and select the screen's _CanRun method. This generates a method stub in LightSwitch's client Application class. To prevent users from opening a screen, set the result of the _CanRun method to false.

The HelpDesk application allows only users who belong in roles that have been assigned the CanEditEngineers permission to open the engineer management screen (from Chapter 9).

To apply this rule, open the screen in the designer and use the Write Code button to add the code shown in Listing 17-4.

Listing 17-4. Setting a Screen's CanRun Method

VB:
File: HelpDeskVB\Client\UserCode\Application.vb

```
Private Sub EngineersManagerGrid_CanRun(ByRef result As Boolean)
    result =
        Application.Current.User.HasPermission(
            Permissions.CanEditEngineers)
End Sub
```

C#:
File: HelpDeskCS\Client\UserCode\Application.cs

```
partial void EngineersManagerGrid_CanRun(ref bool result)
{
    result =
        Application.Current.User.HasPermission(
            Permissions.CanEditEngineers);
}
```

If a user attempts to open a screen (for example, from a user-defined method) where the result of the _CanRun method returns false, the screen will not open.

To help keep things tidy, LightSwitch automatically filters the screens that are shown in the navigation menu. If a user doesn't have rights to open a screen, LightSwitch hides the screen in the navigation menu.

EXERCISE 17.1 – AUTHORIZING USERS

Re-create the preceding example that prevents users without the CanEditEngineers permission from opening the Engineer Management screen. Test your code by enabling the CanEditEngineers permission's Granted For Debug check box in your application property's Access Control tab. When you run your application, you'll be able to open the Engineer Management screen. Now uncheck the check box and rerun your application. Notice that LightSwitch hides the option to open your screen in the navigation panel.

Restricting Users from Clicking Links/Buttons

Screen buttons and links are bound to screen commands that are shown in the Screen Member list of the screen designer. To prevent a user from executing a command, set the result of the command's _CanExecute method to false. You can open the code editor by clicking the link that you'll find in the command's Properties sheet (shown in Figure 17-6).

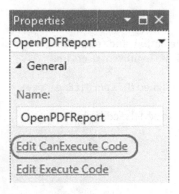

Figure 17-6. Securing screen commands

If a user doesn't have sufficient permissions to execute a command, LightSwitch automatically hides any buttons or links that are bound to that command.

In this example, the add/edit issue detail screen (from Chapter 14) includes a link that opens a PDF report. This link should be visible only if the user belongs in a role that's been assigned the CanViewReport permission. Listing 17-5 shows the code that carries out this rule.

Listing 17-5. Editing a Command's CanExecute Method

VB:
File: HelpDeskVB\Client\UserCode\AddEditIssue.vb

```
Private Sub OpenPDFReport_CanExecute(
   ByRef result As Boolean)
    result = Application.User.HasPermission(Permissions.CanViewReport)
End Sub
```

C#:
File: HelpDeskCS\Client\UserCode\AddEditIssue.cs

```
partial void OpenPDFReport_CanExecute(ref bool result)
{
    result = Application.User.HasPermission(Permissions.CanViewReport);
}
```

■ **Tip**   Remember that although we've used the CanRun method to enforce permissions, you can use this method to guard screen commands based on other conditions. Let's suppose you've created a method that generates Microsoft Word documents by using COM automation. If your application runs as a browser application (rather than a desktop application), you can hide the button that carries out the Word automation by writing code in the CanRun method that checks AutomationFactory.IsAvailable.

Applying Query-Level Permissions

There's only one method that's related to query-level access control: the CanExecute method. (See Figure 17-7.) The query pipeline calls this method prior to actually executing the query, and allows you to check the current user's permissions. Just like entity set validation, LightSwitch will always execute the code in the query's CanExecute method, even if a user calls the query from outside of a screen.

Access Control Methods

IssuesWithHighestFeedback_CanExecute

Figure 17-7. *A query's CanExecute method*

Earlier in the book, you saw a query that allows managers to find the issues with the highest feedback ratings. To allow only the users with the CanViewReport permission to execute this query, add the code shown in Listing 17-6 to the query's CanExecute method.

Listing 17-6. Editing a Query's CanExecute Method

VB:
File: HelpDeskVB\Server\UserCode\ApplicationDataService.vb

```
Private Sub IssuesWithHighestFeedback_CanExecute(ByRef result As Boolean)
    result =
        Application.User.HasPermission(Permissions.CanViewReport)
End Sub
```

C#:
File: HelpDeskCS\Server\UserCode\ApplicationDataService.cs

```
partial void IssuesWithHighestFeedback_CanExecute(ref bool result)
{
    result =
        Application.User.HasPermission(Permissions.CanViewReport);
}
```

Specifying the Application Administrator

When you publish an application for the first time (which is discussed in Chapter 18), you need to specify the details of a user who will be the administrator of the program. The administrator needs to run the application before anyone else does, because the administrator needs to add roles, decide which permissions need to be added to those roles, and decide which roles are assigned to which users.

■ **Note** If you've chosen Forms authentication as your authentication method, the first user who logs on needs to use the user name and password that you entered into the publishing wizard when you published the application.

Creating and Managing Roles

To create and manage roles, log in to your application with an account that belongs in a role that's been granted the SecurityAdministration permission.

By default, you'll find a link to the Roles screen (see Figure 17-8) in the Administration section of the navigation menu. This screen allows you to create roles and assign permissions to those roles. You can also use it to assign users to roles.

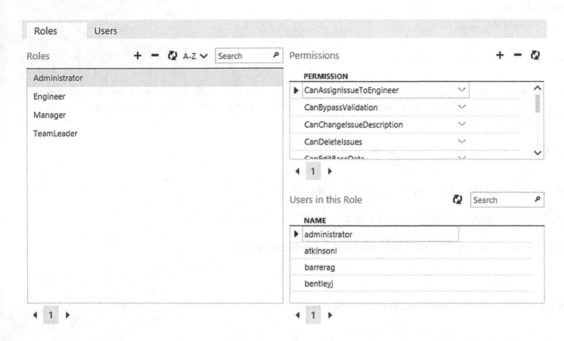

Figure 17-8. *Roles screen*

Custom Authorization Examples

Now that you understand how authorization works, this section demonstrates some practical examples of security and access control.

Associating Logins with Your Data

The HelpDesk application stores engineer details in a user-defined table that we've created ourselves. When a user logs in to a LightSwitch application using either Windows or Forms authentication, it's simple enough to write code that determines the login name of the authenticated user.

But to allow login names to be associated with engineer records, you'll need to create a field in your engineer table that stores the engineer's login name.

If you know the engineer who is logged in, you can tailor your application to better suit the needs of your user. For example, you can set default values or open screens at startup depending on the data that you've stored in the Engineer table.

To allow administrators to assign login names to engineers, you'll need to create a control that shows a list of available login names. Use the following steps to create a `ComboBox` picker that shows a list of login names:

1. Open the `Engineer` table in the designer, and add a string property called `LoginName`.

2. Open your engineer details screen.

3. Use the Add Data button to add a new string property called `LoginNameProperty`. Uncheck the Is Required check box.

4. Create a Rows Layout control, and name it `LoginNameGroup`. Set the Label Position value of this group to Collapsed.

5. Within `LoginNameGroup`, add the engineer's `LoginName` property and change the control type to a Label. Next, add a modal window and name it `LoginPicker`. Set the display name of your modal window to '...'.

6. Drag `LoginNameProperty` into your `LoginNameGroup` modal window, and change the control type to a custom control. Set the custom control type to a `System.Windows.Controls.ComboBox`.

7. Add two buttons to your `LoginNameGroup` modal window, and name them `CloseModalWindow` and `OkModalWindow`.

8. Add the code shown in Listing 17-7.

Listing 17-7. Adding a Username ComboBox

VB:
File: `HelpDeskVB\Client\UserCode\EngineerDetail.vb`

```
Imports System.Windows.Controls

Private cbo As ComboBox

Private Sub EngineerDetail_InitializeDataWorkspace(
    saveChangesTo As List(Of Microsoft.LightSwitch.IDataService))

    'Set assigned login details
    Dim items = DataWorkspace.SecurityData.UserRegistrations.Cast(
      Of Microsoft.LightSwitch.Security.UserRegistration)().ToList        ❶

    AddHandler FindControl("LoginNameProperty").ControlAvailable,
      Sub(sender As Object, e As ControlAvailableEventArgs)
        cbo = CType(e.Control, ComboBox)

        Microsoft.LightSwitch.Threading.Dispatchers.Main.BeginInvoke(
          Sub()
            cbo.ItemsSource = items                                       ❷
            cbo.DisplayMemberPath = "FullName"
          End Sub)
      End Sub

End Sub
```

```vb
Private Sub OkModalWindow_Execute()
   Microsoft.LightSwitch.Threading.Dispatchers.Main.BeginInvoke(
      Sub()
         Engineer.LoginName = cbo.SelectedItem.ToString          ❸
      End Sub)
End Sub

Private Sub CloseModalWindow_Execute()
   Me.CloseModalWindow("LoginPicker")                            ❹
End Sub
```

C#:
File: HelpDeskCS\Client\UserCode\EngineerDetail.cs

```csharp
using System.Windows.Controls;

private ComboBox cbo;

partial void EngineerDetail_InitializeDataWorkspace(
   List<IDataService> saveChangesTo)
{
   var items =
      DataWorkspace.SecurityData.UserRegistrations.Cast<
         Microsoft.LightSwitch.Security.UserRegistration>().ToList();     ❶

   this.FindControl("LoginNameProperty").ControlAvailable +=
      (object sender, ControlAvailableEventArgs e) =>
        {

           ComboBox cbo = (ComboBox)e.Control;
           Microsoft.LightSwitch.Threading.Dispatchers.Main.BeginInvoke(() =>
              {
                 cbo.ItemsSource = items;                        ❷
                 cbo.DisplayMemberPath = "FullName";
              }
           );
        };
}

partial void OkModalWindow_Execute()
{
   Microsoft.LightSwitch.Threading.Dispatchers.Main.BeginInvoke(()=>
      {Engineer.LoginName = cbo.SelectedItem.ToString();});     ❸
}

partial void CloseModalWindow_Execute()
{
   this.CloseModalWindow("LoginPicker");                        ❹
}
```

Figure 17-9 shows how your screen now looks.

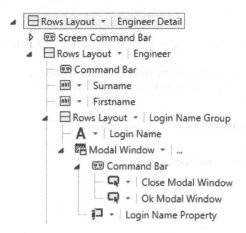

Figure 17-9. Login name picker screen

The code shown in Listing 17-7 produces a list of logins by querying LightSwitch's `DataWorkspace.SecurityData` data source ❶. It then sets the data source of the `ComboBox` control to this list ❷. (If you need some help with this code, you can refer to the "Handling Silverlight Control Events" section in Chapter 7.)

At runtime, the user can open the modal window by clicking on the button that appears next to the login name. The modal window contains the `ComboBox` that allows the user to choose a login. When the user clicks on the OK button, the code assigns the login that's selected in the `ComboBox` to the engineer's `LoginName` property ❸. The Close button calls code that closes the modal window without setting the `LoginName` property ❹. Figure 17-10 shows how your screen looks at runtime.

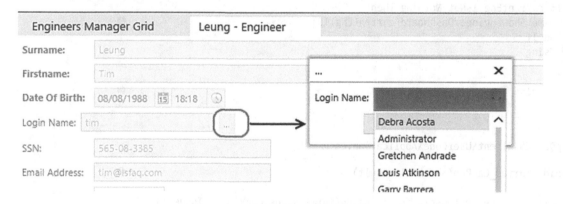

Figure 17-10. Opening the modal window with a login name drop-down list

Opening Screens Conditionally at Login

Now that you know how to determine the logged-in engineer, you can use this to customize the startup routine of your application.

When an engineer logs in to the HelpDesk application, the application opens the Engineer Dashboard page. If the engineer belongs in a role that has been assigned the CanViewAllIssues permission, the Manager Dashboard page opens instead. To create this example, carry out the following steps:

1. Create a new screen by using the New Data Screen template, and call it StartUp. Leave the Screen Data drop-down list blank.

2. Click the Write Code button, select the Startup_CanRun method, and add the code shown in Listing 17-8.

Listing 17-8. Opening Screens Conditionally

VB:
File: HelpDeskVB\Client\UserCode\Application.vb

```
Private Sub Startup_CanRun(ByRef result As Boolean)                              ❶

    If Application.Current.User.HasPermission(Permissions.CanViewAllIssues) Then
        Me.ShowEngineersManagerGrid()                                           ❷
    Else
        Using dw As DataWorkspace = Me.CreateDataWorkspace                       ❸
            Dim currentEng As Engineer =
                dw.ApplicationData.Engineers.Where(
                    Function(eng) eng.LoginName =
                        Application.Current.User.Name).FirstOrDefault()
            If currentEng IsNot Nothing Then
                Me.ShowEngineerDashboard(currentEng.Id)                          ❹
            End If
        End Using
    End If

    result = False                                                              ❺
End Sub
```

C#:
File: HelpDeskCS\Client\UserCode\Application.cs

```
partial void Startup_CanRun(ref bool result)                                     ❶
{
    if (Application.Current.User.HasPermission(Permissions.CanViewAllIssues))
    {
        this.ShowEngineersManagerGrid();                                         ❷
    }
    else
    {
        using (DataWorkspace dw = this.CreateDataWorkspace())                    ❸
        {
            Engineer currentEng =
                dw.ApplicationData.Engineers.Where(
                    eng => eng.LoginName ==
                        Application.Current.User.Name).FirstOrDefault();
```

```
        if (currentEng != null)
        {
            this.ShowEngineerDashboard(currentEng.Id);          ❹
        }
        result = false;                                          ❺
    }
  }
}
```

3. Open the properties of your application, and use the option in the Screen Navigation tab to set your startup screen to StartUp.

Notice how this code uses the screen's CanRun method ❶ rather than the IntializeDataWorkspace or Activated method of the screen. If you used one of these screen methods, the user would see the startup screen appear, prior to the desired screen appearing.

If the user has the CanViewAllIssues permission ❷, the code opens the manager screen. If not, it looks up the engineer ID that relates to the logged-in user ❸. Because the code runs outside the context of a screen object, it needs to create a data workspace to perform this query. If it finds the engineer, it opens the Engineer Dashboard screen for the engineer ❹. Finally, the code sets the return value of the CanRun method to false ❺ to cancel the opening of the Startup screen.

Restricting Row-Level Access to Data

Engineers should be able to view only the issues that have been assigned to them. The safest way to enforce this rule is to apply your access-control check on the default All query. Any query that returns issues ultimately calls the default All query. Therefore, LightSwitch executes any code that you add here every time you return issue records from the server.

To apply this example, open the issue table in the table designer. Click the Write Code button, and select the Issues_Filter option. Add the code shown in Listing 17-9.

Listing 17-9. Restricting Row-Level Access to Data

VB:
File: HelpDeskVB\Server\UserCode\ApplicationDataService.vb

```vb
Private Sub Issues_Filter(
   ByRef filter As System.Linq.Expressions.Expression(
     Of System.Func(Of Issue, Boolean)))

   If Not Application.User.HasPermission(Permissions.CanViewAllIssues) Then
     Dim currentUser As String = Application.User.Name

     Dim currentEng As Engineer =
         DataWorkspace.ApplicationData.Engineers.Where(
             Function(eng) eng.LoginName = currentUser).FirstOrDefault     ❶

     If currentEng IsNot Nothing Then
         filter = Function(e) e.AssignedTo.Id = currentEng.Id              ❷
     End If
   End If

End Sub
```

C#:
File: HelpDeskCS\Server\UserCode\ApplicationDataService.cs

```csharp
partial void Issues_Filter(ref Expression<Func<Issue, bool>> filter)
{
    if (!Application.User.HasPermission(Permissions.CanViewAllIssues))
    {
        string currentUser = Application.User.Name;

        Engineer currentEng =
            DataWorkspace.ApplicationData.Engineers.Where(
                eng => eng.LoginName == currentUser).FirstOrDefault();        ❶

        if (currentEng != null)
        {
            filter = e => e.AssignedTo.Id == currentEng.Id;                   ❷
        }
    }
}
```

The code shown here obtains the currently logged-in engineer ❶ and applies the filter ❷ to the entity set that the query returns. If the code doesn't find an engineer record for the currently logged-in user, it doesn't apply a filter and allows the user to see all issues. You might choose to change this behavior and prevent the query from returning any records.

It's important to note that if an engineer retrieves issues via a navigation property, the data-retrieval process bypasses the default All query. If an engineer is allowed to view other engineer records on a screen that shows related issues, the engineer will be able to view issues that should not be visible.

Another important point is that if an engineer updates a record that has been updated by someone else, the concurrency error window that appears could contain data that shouldn't be seen by the engineer.

■ **Caution**   If you need to restrict the data that a user can see, make sure to test your application to make sure that data leakage doesn't occur in the way that was described earlier.

Setting Screen Control Properties by Permission

By testing for permissions, you can conditionally hide screen controls depending on the logged-in user.

The issue search screen allows users to filter issues by using multiple criteria options, including the engineer that's assigned to the issue. If an engineer performs a search, the engineer should not be able to search issues that have been assigned to a different engineer.

To set the engineer autocomplete box to the logged-in engineer and make the autocomplete box read-only, open the Issue Search All screen, click on the Write Code button and select the InitializeDataWorkspace method. Enter the code that's shown in Listing 17-10.

Listing 17-10. Modifying Screen Controls by Permission

VB:
File: HelpDeskVB\Client\UserCode\IssueSearchAll.vb

```vb
Private Sub IssueSearchAll_InitializeDataWorkspace(
    saveChangesTo As List(Of Microsoft.LightSwitch.IDataService))
```

```
If Not Application.User.HasPermission(Permissions.CanViewAllIssues) Then
    Dim currentEng As Engineer =
        DataWorkspace.ApplicationData.Engineers.Where(
            Function(eng) eng.LoginName = Application.User.Name).FirstOrDefault    ❶

    If currentEng IsNot Nothing Then
        EngineerSelectionProperty = currentEng
        Me.FindControl("EngineerSelectionProperty").IsEnabled = False              ❷
    End If
End If

End Sub
```

C#:
File: HelpDeskCS\Client\UserCode\IssueSearchAll.cs

```
partial void IssueSearchAll_InitializeDataWorkspace(
    List<IDataService> saveChangesTo)
{
    if (!Application.User.HasPermission(Permissions.CanViewAllIssues))
    {
        Engineer currentEng =
            DataWorkspace.ApplicationData.Engineers.Where(
                eng => eng.LoginName == Application.User.Name
                    ).FirstOrDefault();                                            ❶

        if (currentEng != null)
        {
            EngineerSelectionProperty = currentEng;
            this.FindControl("EngineerSelectionProperty").IsEnabled = false;       ❷
        }
    }
}
```

If the user doesn't have the CanViewAllIssues permission, the code obtains the currently logged-in engineer ❶. It then sets the value of the AutoCompleteBox by setting the value of the underlying property and disables the control by setting the IsEnabled property to false ❷.

Allowing Users to Bypass Validation

To allow certain users to bypass custom validation, you can add conditional logic so that LightSwitch applies validation rules only according to the permissions of the logged-on user.

To save you from having to modify every validation rule that you've defined in a table, you can simplify the task by writing code in the _AllowSaveWithErrors method. If you want to enable users to save records, even though they contain validation errors, set the return value of this method to true.

In the HelpDesk system, users who have the Can Bypass Validation permission can save engineer records without adhering to the validation rules. To implement this rule, open the Engineer table, click the Write Code button, and select the Engineer_AllowSaveWithErrors method. Enter the code as shown in Listing 17-11.

Listing 17-11. Bypassing Validation

VB:
File: HelpDeskVB\Common\UserCode\Engineer.vb

```
Private Sub Engineer_AllowSaveWithErrors(ByRef result As Boolean)
    result =
        Application.User.HasPermission(Permissions.CanBypassValidation)
End Sub
```

C#:
File: HelpDeskCS\Client\UserCode\Engineer.cs

```
partial void Engineer_AllowSaveWithErrors(ref bool result)
{
    result = Application.User.HasPermission(Permissions.CanBypassValidation);
}
```

Although this code allows the user to bypass any custom validation that you've written, LightSwitch still honors any validation rules that are enforced by your data layer (for example, SQL Server check constraints).

Summary

LightSwitch allows you to define access-control rules on screens, screen commands, entities, and queries. LightSwitch authorization uses permissions, roles, and users. Permissions are defined by the developer and are stored in your application's LSML file.

Roles and users and are created at runtime and stored in your Intrinsic database. At runtime, an administrator allocates permissions to roles and allocates users to roles. Each user can belong to one or more roles.

Entities, queries, screens, and commands expose _Can methods that allow you to write code to define access-control rules. To deny a user access to a resource, you would set the return value of the _Can method to false. The LightSwitch API includes methods that allow you to determine whether the logged-in user has been allocated a specific permission.

You've seen some examples of how to apply authorization code to the HelpDesk application. You also saw how to add a ComboBox control that allows managers to associate logins with engineer records. The code you saw populates the ComboBox control by calling methods in LightSwitch's DataWorkspace.SecurityData data source.

You can perform conditional logic when a user starts your application by writing code in your application startup screen's CanRun method.

To secure all access to a table, you can apply rules in the default All query for your table by writing code in the Filter method. Every LightSwitch query uses the entity set's All query as the underlying data source, and any rules that you apply in the Filter method will be applied to child queries. The code that you add to the Filter method doesn't apply to navigation properties, so it's important to exercise some caution when you use this method.

Finally, you can allow users to bypass all of a table's validation rules by setting the result of the entity set's AllowSaveWithErrors method to true. The example in this chapter shows you how to create and grant a permission that allows a user to override all validation rules.

CHAPTER 18

■ ■ ■

Deploying Your Application

The last chapter of this book focuses on deployment. I'll show you how to allow users to access your application, and you'll finally get the chance to show off all the hard work that you've carried out on your LightSwitch project. With all the tips and tricks that you've learned, your users will surely be impressed. In this chapter, you'll find out how to

- Use the Publish Wizard to deploy both desktop and web applications

- Set up and configure a web server

- Publish your applications onto Windows Azure

There are many ways for you to deploy an application, and the method that you choose depends on your application type and infrastructure. This chapter explains all the possible options and shows you exactly how to carry out a deployment.

Getting Started with Deployment

LightSwitch allows you to create HTML Client or Silverlight applications that can run on either the desktop or web. It also relies on the application services that can run on a server, Azure, or the client workstation (in the case of a desktop application). This combination results in several distinct deployment scenarios, each with a unique set of installation tasks. Figure 18-1 highlights your choices in the form of a flow diagram and shows you the main tasks that you'd need to carry out. You can use this diagram to help you identify the sections in this chapter that you can skip over. For example, you can ignore the sections on setting up Internet Information Services (IIS) and ASP.NET if you want to deploy a desktop application and install your application services on the workstation.

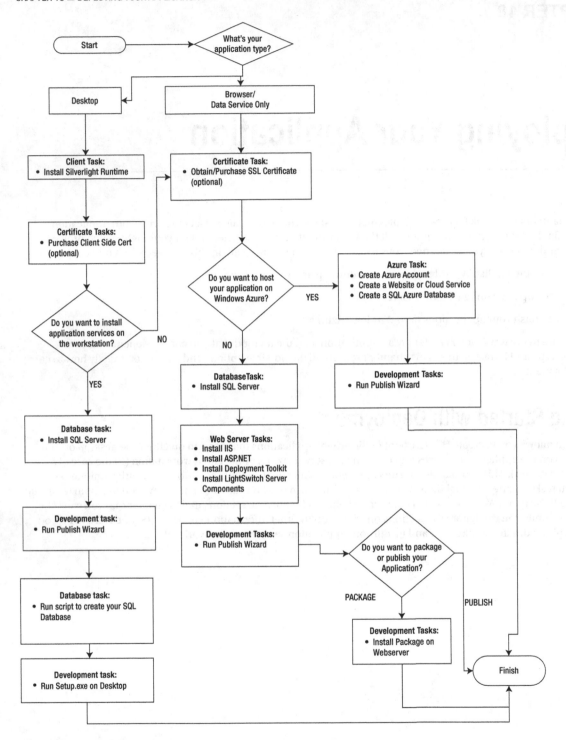

Figure 18-1. *Deployment steps*

The rest of this chapter is arranged as follows. I'll begin by explaining some of the underlying principles of deployment, and then show you how the Publish Wizard works. If you're publishing a web application, you'll need to set up a web server before you run the Publish Wizard. The next part of this chapter shows you how to install IIS, and then shows you how to work with the output that's generated by the Publish Wizard.

Choosing an Application Topology

LightSwitch relies on application services that can run in IIS, Windows Azure, or the end user's machine. If you're deploying a web application (either Silverlight or HTML client), your application services must be hosted in IIS or Windows Azure. But if you're deploying a Silverlight desktop application, you can choose to host the application services on the local machine, and this is a configuration that's called a "two-tier" setup. The advantage of running the services locally is that it's easier to set up. Unlike a "three-tier" setup, you don't need to go through the tricky process of setting up a web server, or understanding how Windows Azure works. But the disadvantage is that you'll need to install the services on every machine that you want to run your application. Two-tier applications are therefore more suitable for single-user applications or applications that don't have many users. In this type of deployment, you can also choose to install the database on the end-user machine by using a local instance of SQL Server or SQL Express. This means that you can run your entire application from a single machine.

Choosing Whether to Publish or Package

If you want to host your application services in IIS, you can choose to either publish or to package your application (Figure 18-2).

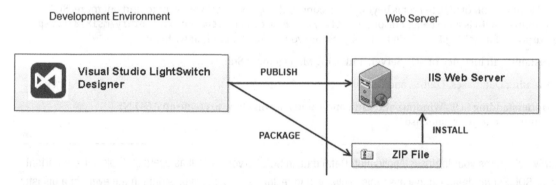

Figure 18-2. Publishing vs. packaging

If you choose to publish your application, LightSwitch deploys it directly from Visual Studio onto your IIS server. It's very easy to publish an application, but you'll need to carry out more work to prepare your IIS server beforehand. The operating systems that support publishing are Windows Server 2003 or above, and Windows 7 or above.

The second option is to package your application. Packaging produces a set of install files that you would manually copy and install on your server. Packaging an application is easier than publishing. There are fewer tasks to carry out on your web server, and you don't need to struggle to make Visual Studio talk to IIS. For example, your application will fail to publish if a firewall blocks the ports that are required for publishing to work (port 8172 by default). If you're developing your application on a machine that isn't on the same domain as the server that you want to deploy to, packaging is a good choice.

Setting Up Your Workstations

In order to set up a workstation to run LightSwitch, there are actually very few tasks for you to carry out. HTML client applications require only a web browser, so in almost all cases, you don't need to carry out any additional work. Silverlight applications require the Silverlight 4 runtime. If a user doesn't have the runtime installed and attempts to run a Silverlight browser application, the application displays a web page that prompts the user to download the Silverlight runtime from the Microsoft web site. If you're in a corporate environment, you can distribute the Silverlight runtime by using group policy, SMS (Microsoft Systems Management Server), or some other software distribution mechanism. Some companies have policies in place that block Silverlight or Adobe Flash. If you have a policy like this in place, your Silverlight LightSwitch application will simply not work.

Setting Up SQL Server

In all deployment scenarios, you'll need a database server with SQL Server 2005 or above to host your application. If you're deploying your application into Windows Azure, you'd create a SQL Azure database rather than carry out an "on premises" installation of SQL Server. If you're building a two-tier desktop application, you can install SQL Server Express on the client and run your entire application on the workstation. This type of setup is ideal for single-user or stand-alone applications. SQL Server Express is a free edition of SQL Server, and it's perfect if you don't have a license for a higher, paid-for edition of SQL. A disadvantage of SQL Server Express is that it limits performance by placing restrictions on the amount of memory and CPU cores that the database engine can use. You can find out more and download SQL Express from the following web site:

http://www.microsoft.com/en-us/sqlserver/editions/2012-editions/express.aspx

A detailed explanation of SQL Server is beyond the scope of this book, but if you want to find out more, SQL Server Books Online (BOL) is an excellent resource: http://msdn.microsoft.com/en-us/library/ms187875.aspx
For the purpose of installing LightSwitch, the topics that you should be familiar with are

- Installing an instance of SQL Server, and using Management Studio

- Creating Databases, Logins, and Users

- Understanding SQL/Windows authentication, and knowing how to create an ADO.NET connection to your database

---

■ **Tip**   LightSwitch stores your Intrinsic (Application Data) data in SQL Server, as well as users and roles. It's important to back up your SQL Server database, because this allows you to restore your application's data in the event of a disaster. You can refer to Books Online to find out more about backing up and restoring databases.

Using the Publish Wizard

The Publish Wizard is a tool that guides you step by step through the deployment process. You can use the wizard to package or publish your application onto IIS or to publish your application into Windows Azure. To begin the Publish Wizard, right-click your project in Solution Explorer and select the Publish menu option. The first page prompts you to choose the type of application that you want to install (Figure 18-3). Notice how the wizard shows a warning message if you've set your active configuration to *Debug*. When you publish an application, you should set the active configuration of your application to *Release* by using the drop-down menu that appears in Visual Studio's toolbar.

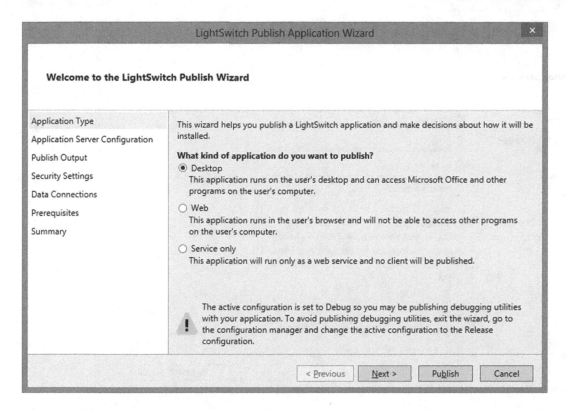

Figure 18-3. *Choosing your application type*

The wizard allows you to publish a Desktop or Web application. But in addition to this, you can also choose to publish only the LightSwitch data service. This option is ideal if you've written a non LightSwitch application that consumes your LightSwitch data via the OData protocol. If you've installed the HTML client, you'll see two options only on this page: the option to install the "Complete Application," and an option to install the "Service Only." If you choose "Complete Application," LightSwitch publishes all of the clients (Silverlight and HTML client) that exist in your project.

The second page in the wizard allows you to specify where you want to host your server components, as shown in Figure 18-4. As mentioned earlier, you can host your application services in IIS or Azure. But in the case of a Desktop application, you'll also have the option of hosting your application services locally. If you've upgraded your LightSwitch project to include an HTML client, you'll no longer have the option to deploy your application services locally. So make sure not to add an HTML Client to your project if you want to run your application services locally.

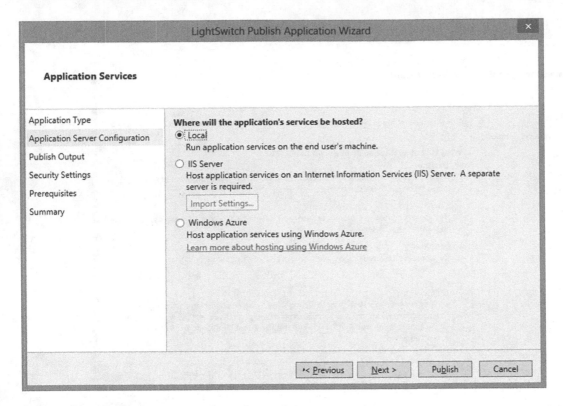

Figure 18-4. *Choosing where to host the application's services*

The remaining steps in the wizard are all fairly intuitive, and I'll now explain these in more detail.

■ **Caution**   If you've installed the HTML client components, some of the screens that you'll find in the wizard might look a bit different. For example, the wizard adds the "Certificate" details into a "Security" page rather than show it on a separate page. However, all of these changes are cosmetic, and the concepts that I'll show you all still apply.

Data Connections Page

If you choose to publish your application, the wizard shows the "Database Connections" page that's illustrated in Figure 18-5. This page prompts you for two connection strings. The first connection string specifies the connection that LightSwitch uses to connect to your Intrinsic database at runtime. The wizard uses the second connection string during the publishing stage to create and/or update your Intrinsic database. The buttons next to the connection string text boxes open a dialog that helps you to build a connection string.

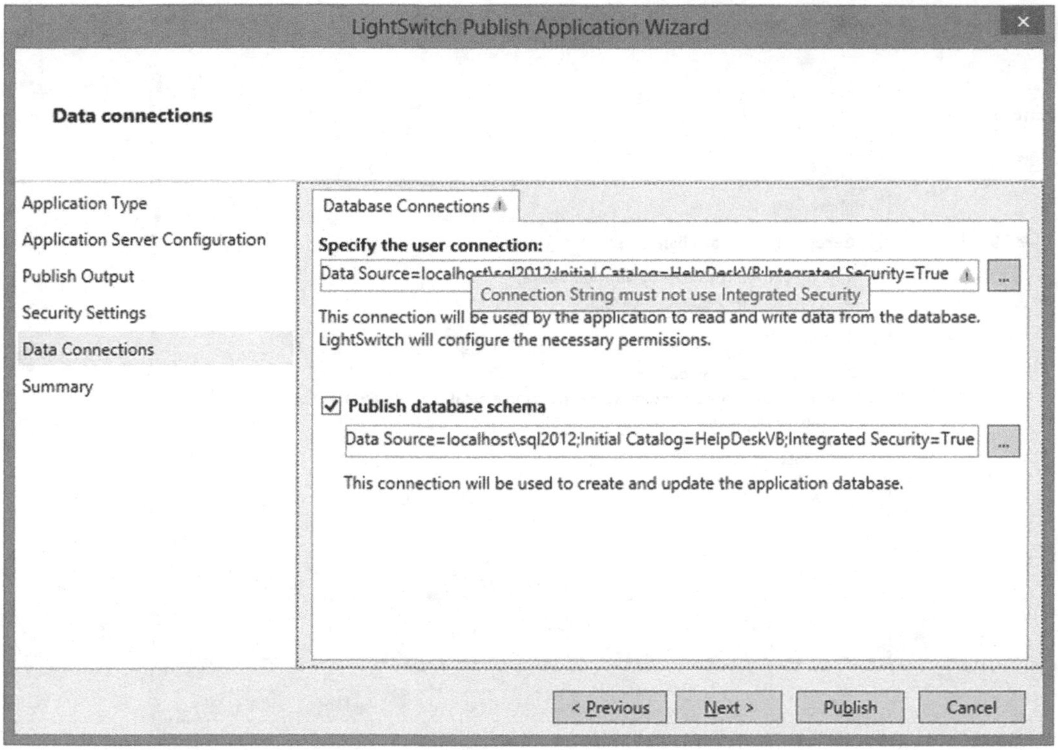

Figure 18-5. *Specifying Database Connection dialog*

Figure 18-5 highlights the warning that the wizard shows when you enter a connection string that uses integrated security. The Publish Wizard allows you to specify only connection strings that use SQL Server authentication. If you're not happy with this type of authentication, you'll find out how to manually set up your application so that it uses integrated security later in this chapter.

If you choose to package your application, rather than publish it, the wizard shows the page that's shown in Figure 18-6. This page allows you to create a new Intrinsic database or to update an existing database.

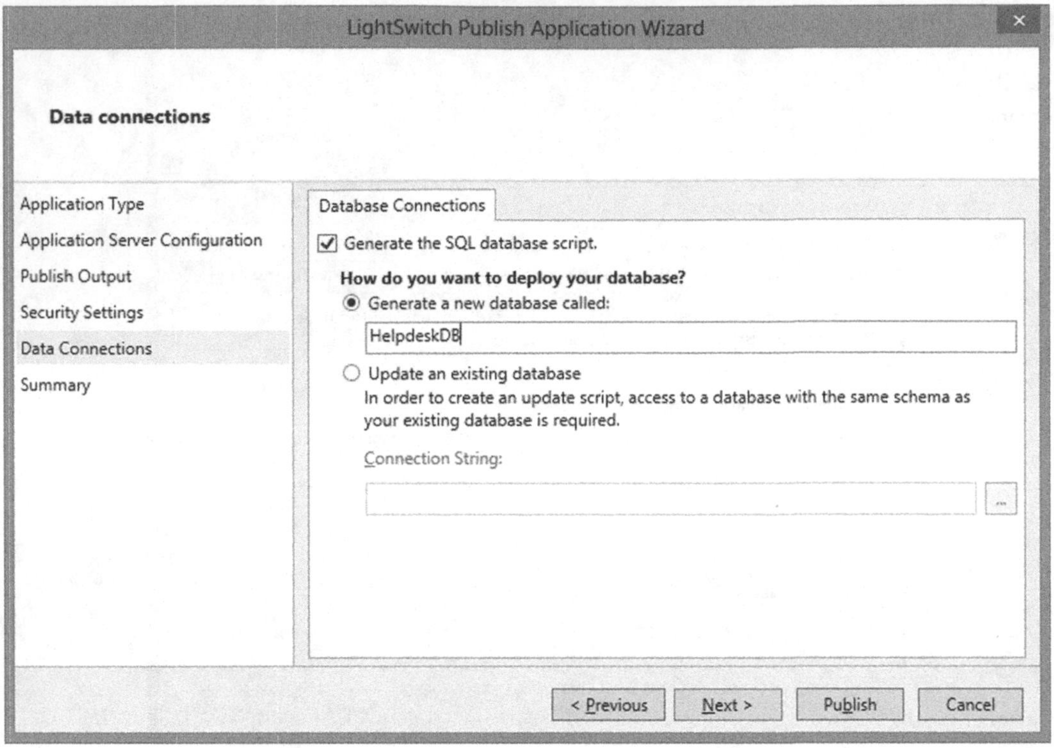

Figure 18-6. *Database Configuration dialog*

You'd typically update an existing database if you're updating an application that you've already deployed. When you choose this option, you'll need to provide a connection string. This allows the wizard to compare your database schema against the existing database and to create an update script.

You might wonder why the wizard doesn't prompt you to supply database credentials at this point. This is because LightSwitch asks you for the credentials when you actually install the package, and by doing this, it avoids persisting your sensitive credentials in a package file that someone else could get hold of.

Prerequisites Page

If you deploy a two-tier desktop application, you can specify your application's dependencies by using the page that's shown in Figure 18-7. By default, your setup package includes the LightSwitch prerequisite component. This component allows LightSwitch to host your application services without IIS being available.

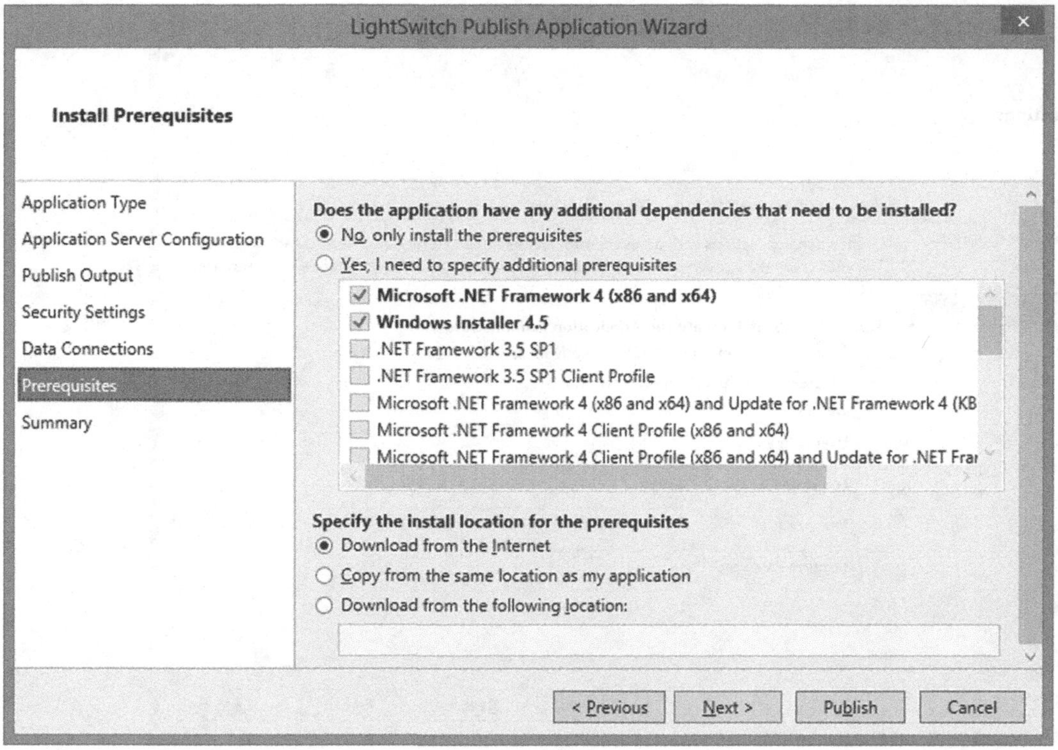

Figure 18-7. *Install Prerequisites dialog*

In addition to the LightSwitch prerequisites, you can also specify additional prerequisites by choosing the "Yes" radio button and using the check boxes to select the items that you want to include. When you do this, the wizard automatically includes the .NET 4 Framework and Windows Installer 4.5 packages. LightSwitch requires the .NET 4 Framework to run, and Windows needs the Windows Installer to install the .NET 4 Framework. The final set of radio buttons allows you to specify the install location for your prerequisites. You can select the option that prompts the user to download the prerequisites from the Internet if you want to reduce the file size of your setup package.

The LightSwitch wizard doesn't allow you to include your own prerequisites. For example, the wizard allows you to add Microsoft SQL Server Express 2008 R2 and 2012. But if Microsoft releases a newer version of SQL Server or if there are any other components that you want to include, there isn't any option for you to add them to this list.

Security Page

If you've enabled authentication in your application, the Application Administrator tab allows you to specify your application administrator. As I showed you in Chapter 16, authentication allows you to determine the identity of the logged-in user and to secure your application by specifying users, groups, and permissions.

Figure 18-8 shows the page that appears when you enable Forms authentication in the properties of your LightSwitch project. If you enable Windows authentication, the Wizard doesn't show the full name and password text boxes; it'll prompt you to enter only a domain user name. In the case of Windows authentication, make sure that you enter your administrator's user name in a format that includes your domain (for example, DOMAIN\TIM). If you leave out the domain specifier, LightSwitch assumes that you're referring to a local Windows user on your database server.

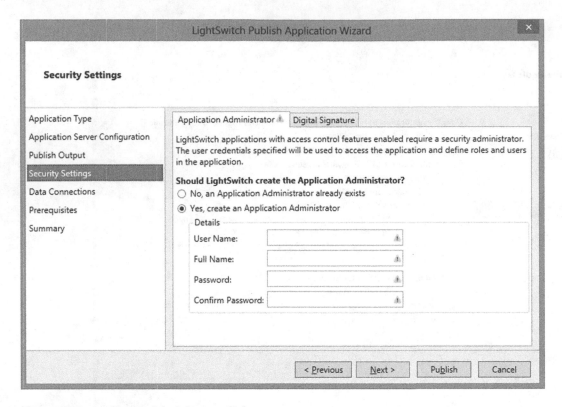

Figure 18-8. *Application Administrator dialog*

If you're updating an application that you've already deployed, you'd choose the radio option that specifies that an application administrator already exists.

■ **Caution**   Remember that if you're deploying a two-tier desktop application, Forms authentication isn't secure because a hacker can use the connection string that's stored locally on your client workstation to connect to SQL Server behind the scenes. For two-tier deployments, I recommend that you use Windows authentication instead.

Digital Signature/Certificate Page

When you deploy a Silverlight application, you can optionally specify a certificate. But what's the purpose of a certificate, and why would you want to add one? A digital certificate allows you to sign your application's XAP file—this is the compiled Silverlight application that runs on the end-user's machine. Signing a XAP file verifies the authenticity of your application and makes it difficult for a hacker to tamper with your application without it being noticed.

If you don't sign your application, Windows shows a warning when the user installs your application. This warning states that Windows can't verify the publisher and that your application might be harmful (Figure 18-9). Your users might be scared by this warning, so it's a good idea to prevent it from showing by signing your application with a certificate.

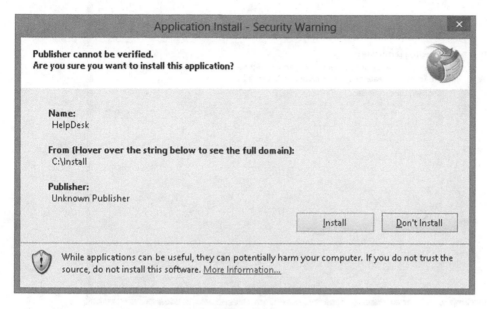

Figure 18-9. *Warning Dialog shown during installation*

Figure 18-10 illustrates the page that allows you to specify a certificate and sign your application. To obtain a certificate, you can purchase one from a third-party company such as VeriSign or use an internal certificate server if your company has one in place. If you want test the process of signing an application, you can generate a self-signed certificate by using a utility called makecert. You can read more about this and find out the command-line switches that you can use by visiting the following MSDN page:
http://msdn.microsoft.com/en-us/library/bfsktky3%28v=vs.80%29.aspx

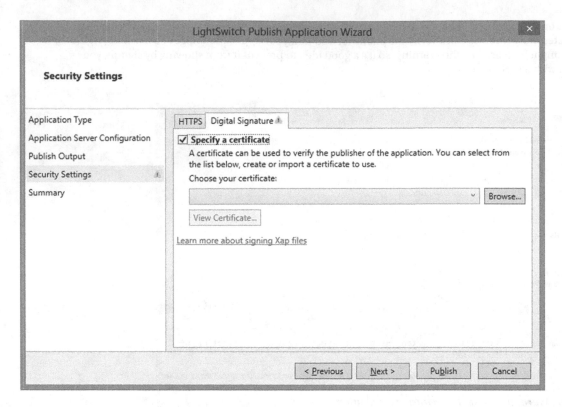

Figure 18-10. *Dialog for specifying a certificate*

This next page in the wizard is the summary page. This allows you to review your settings and carry on to publish or package your application.

EXERCISE 18.1 – USING THE PUBLISH WIZARD

Open an existing project, and start the Publish Wizard. Work your way through each page in the wizard, and examine the options that you can choose. Pay attention to how the options that the wizard shows changes, depending on the choices that you make earlier in the wizard.

Setting Up Your Web Server

Now that you understand how the Publish Wizard works, this section shows you how to set up and configure a web server. A web server is necessary for browser applications and requires you to carry out the following tasks, which I'll fully describe in this section:

1. Install the IIS web server.

2. Install ASP.NET 4.

3. Install LightSwitch prerequisites and the Web Deploy Tool.

4. Configure Application Pools.

5. Optionally, set up SSL.

The version of IIS that you'll set up depends on your server's operating system, and in this section, you'll find out how to install LightSwitch on Windows 2003 through to Windows 2012.

Setting Up IIS on Windows Server 2008/2012

Windows 2008 comes with IIS7, whereas Windows 2012 includes IIS8. Both of these operating systems allow you to set up IIS by using the "Server Manager" application. Once you open Server Manager, go to the Roles Summary group, and click on the *Add Roles* link (shown in Figure 18-11). This opens the "Add Roles Wizard," and you'll find a page in this wizard that allows you to select the *Web Server (IIS)* server role.

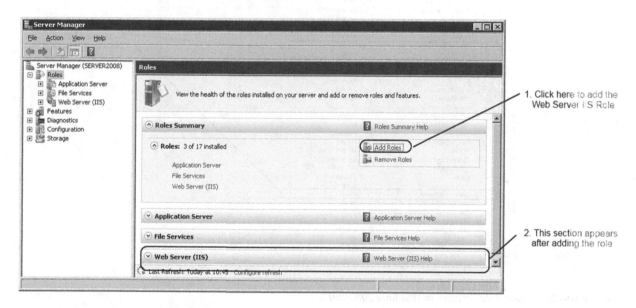

Figure 18-11. *Adding the IIS Server Role*

Once you complete the "Add Roles Wizard," Server Manager adds a "Web Server (IIS)" section inside the Roles group as shown in Figure 18-12.

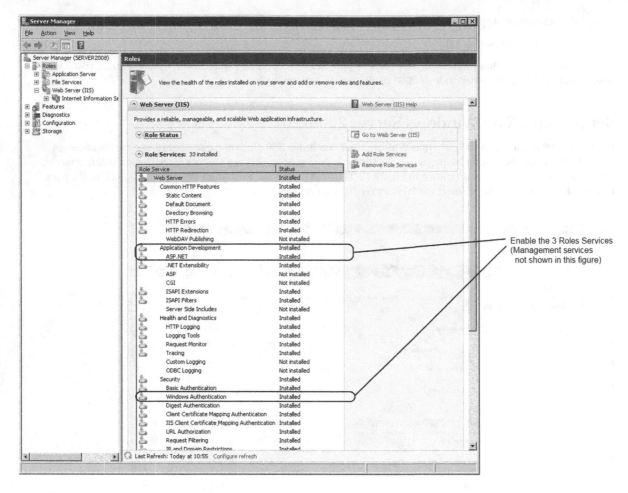

Figure 18-12. Adding Role Services in Windows 2008/2012

In the Role Services pane, enable the following three Role Services, as highlighted in Figure 8-12:

- Management Service
- Application Development ➤ ASP.NET
- Security ➤ Windows Authentication

Setting Up IIS on Windows 8, 7, or Vista

To set up IIS on a client operating system, you'll need to enable IIS in Windows Control Panel rather than add the "Web Server Role" as in the case of a server operating system. When you open Control Panel, select "Programs and Features" and choose the option to "Turn Windows features on or off." When the Windows Features dialog opens (Figure 18-13), select the options "Management Service," Application Development Features ➤ ASP.NET, and Security ➤ Windows Authentication.

Figure 18-13. *Turning Windows features on or off in Control Panel*

Setting Up IIS 6 on Windows 2003

To set up IIS6 on Windows 2003, you'll need to install it by using the "Add/Remove Windows Components" option that you'll find in Windows Control Panel. When the "Windows Component Wizard" dialog opens, select "Application Server" and click on the Details button to open up the dialog that's shown in Figure 18-14. When you click on the OK button, Windows might ask you to insert the Windows 2003 CD that matches the exact edition of Windows 2003 that you're using. For example, if your server runs "Windows 2003 Standard, Volume License Edition, with SP2," you'll need the CAB file from that specific CD, and a CAB file from a different edition might not work. It might be difficult to locate the correct CD, particularly if the person who originally installed your server has now left, which is quite likely in a case of an operating system that's now 10 years old. If this is the case, we wish you good luck in finding your installation CD!

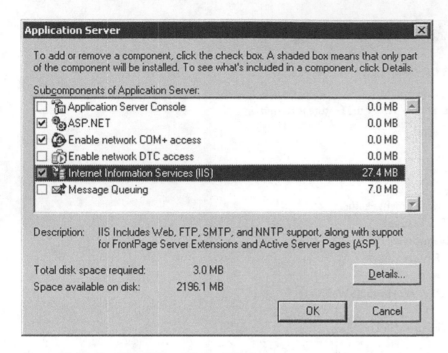

Figure 18-14. *Enabling IIS6 on Windows 2003*

After you've installed IIS6, you'll need to install ASP.NET and the LightSwitch prerequisites. (I'll explain how to do this very shortly.) Once you've installed ASP.NET 4, it's important to make sure that it's enabled in the "Web Service Extensions" section of Internet Information Services (IIS) Manager, as shown in Figure 18-15.

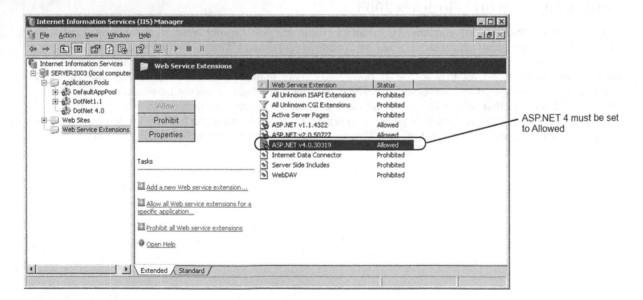

Figure 18-15. *Enable the ASP.NET v4 Web Service Extension*

Setting Up IIS Application Pools

Application pools improve the reliability of your web server by isolating the applications that run in IIS. If a web site in an application pool crashes, it won't bring down the other web sites that run in other application pools. It therefore makes good sense to deploy each LightSwitch application into its own separate application pool.

Each application pool also runs under a specific security context, and this enables you to configure your application services to connect to your SQL Server database through Windows Authentication. Figure 18-16 illustrates this concept.

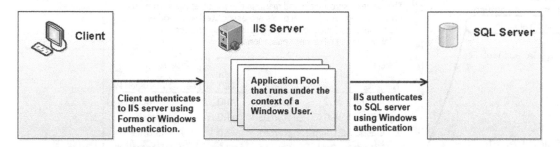

Figure 18-16. Set up an Application Pool to Windows Authenticate to SQL Server

To create a new application pool, open Internet Information Services (IIS) Manager and right-click the Application Pools node on the navigation menu on the left. You'll find a right-click context menu option that allows you to create a new application pool, as shown in Figure 18-17. It's important to set up your Application Pool to use version 4 of the .NET Framework.

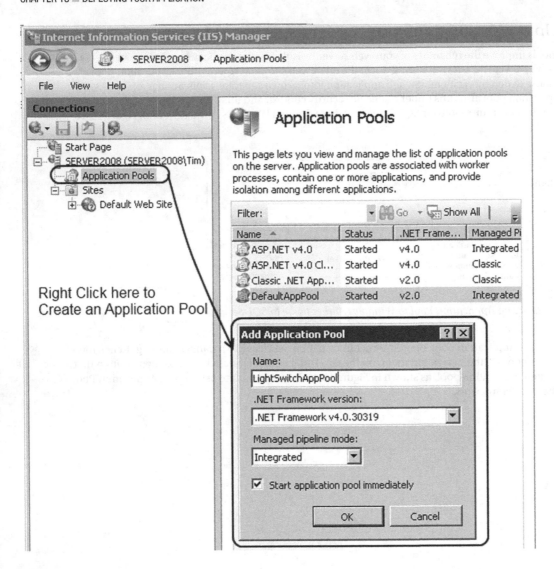

Figure 18-17. *Creating an Application Pool in IIS7*

In IIS7 and above, it is also preferable to choose the Integrated Managed Pipeline Mode, as opposed to Classic Mode. Classic mode is primarily designed for legacy code that might not run properly in integrated mode. Your LightSwitch server runs more efficiently when you set the pipeline mode to integrated.

After you deploy your web site, you can configure it to use the Application Pool that you've added by modifying the web-site properties in IIS Manager.

Configuring SQL Server Windows Authentication

Your LightSwitch application services can authenticate onto SQL Server by using two types of authentication: SQL Server authentication or Windows authentication. SQL Server authentication uses SQL Server to store and manage the login and password credentials. If you use SQL Server authentication, you'll need to hard-code your SQL server login and password in the connection string that LightSwitch uses to connect to your database. Because your login name and password are hard-coded in a plain text file, some IT departments regard SQL Server authentication as less secure than Windows authentication. If you want to read more about the pros and cons of SQL Server authentication vs. Windows authentication, you can find out more in the following TechNet article http://technet.microsoft.com/en-us/library/ms144284.aspx.

To use Windows authentication, you'll need to first create a Windows domain user. If your IIS server and SQL Server are on the same machine, you might find it easier to create a local Windows user rather than a domain user (particularly if you don't have sufficient permissions to create new domain users).

Select the application pool that your application uses, and open the "Advanced Settings" dialog. Open the "Application Pool Identity" dialog by clicking the button that you'll find next to the Process Model ➤ Identity text box. When the dialog opens, choose the "custom account" radio button (Figure 18-18), and use the "Set" button to specify the Windows user who you want to use.

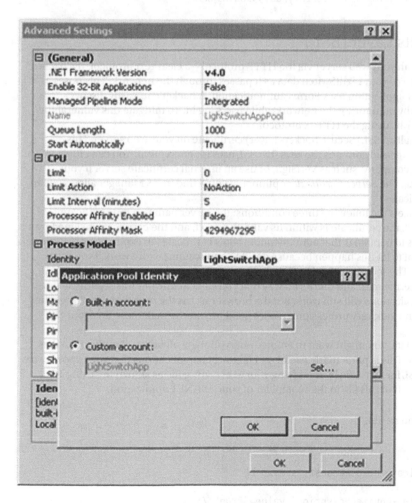

Figure 18-18. *Changing the Application Pool Identities*

The Windows user who you specify needs to have NTFS read permissions on the folders where you've installed your LightSwitch application. You should also add the user to the local IIS_IUSRS group in order to grant access to the ASP.NET resources that are needed.

The last step is to make sure that you add a SQL Server login for your Windows user by using SQL Server Management Studio. You'll also need to grant access permissions to the tables in your application and grant access rights to the tables that the ASP.NET membership provider uses. The quickest way to do this is to add your user into the following database roles:

- `aspnet_Membership*`
- `aspnet_Roles*`
- `db_datareader`
- `db_datawriter`
- `public`

Windows authentication should now work, but if it doesn't, you might need to configure the NTLM provider or carry out some extra steps to configure Kerberos authentication. The following TechNet article will help you if you run into problems: `http://technet.microsoft.com/en-us/library/dd759186.aspx`.

Configuring Secure Sockets Layer (SSL)

The LightSwitch client communicates with your web server via the HTTP protocol—a clear text protocol. If a hacker monitors your network, they'll be able to see your LightSwitch data as it passes through the network. This poses a security vulnerability, particularly if your application uses Forms authentication. A hacker can easily discover user-name and password combinations by monitoring the network while users log in. To mitigate this vulnerability, you'd encrypt your data over the network by using the HTTPS protocol.

To set up HTTPS, you'll need to install an SSL (Secure Sockets Layer) certificate on your web server. This certificate verifies the identity of your server and contains the keys that SSL uses for encryption. You can either purchase a certificate from a third-party company, such as VeriSign, or use an internal certificate server if your company has such infrastructure in place. The *Server Certificates* option that you'll find in IIS Manager allows you to request, install, and configure SSL certificates.

An SSL certificate is valid when it meets the following three conditions: the server name on the certificate matches the server on which it's installed, the certificate is within its validity period, and the certificate is signed by a trusted Certificate Authority. What tends to happen is that administrators allow certificates to expire by not renewing them in sufficient time. It's important not to let this happen because desktop applications won't work if your web server's SSL certificate becomes invalid. The security model in Silverlight prevents LightSwitch applications from connecting to web servers with invalid certificates, and there's no way that you can circumvent this security feature. Silverlight browser and HTML client applications will still work, but the browser warns the user that they "might be visiting a dangerous website." This doesn't look very professional, so it's good practice to make sure that your SSL certificates don't lapse.

If your application stores sensitive data, you might want to enforce encryption on all network traffic that takes place between your client and the server. This is particularly useful on LightSwitch applications that you expose over the public Internet. You can mandate SSL for all traffic by modifying your `web.config` file as shown in Listing 18-1. When you deploy your application, you'll find this file in the root folder of your ASP.NET application.

Listing 18-1. Web.config Setting to Mandate SSL

```
<configuration>
  <appSettings>
    <!-- A value of true will indicate http requests should be
         re-directed to https -->
    <add key="Microsoft.LightSwitch.RequireEncryption" value="true" />
```

■ **Note** You can find out more about setting up SSL on the official IIS and Microsoft TechNet web sites:

http://learn.iis.net/page.aspx/144/how-to-set-up-ssl-on-iis/
http://www.microsoft.com/technet/prodtechnol/WindowsServer2003/Library/IIS/
56bdf977-14f8-4867-9c51-34c346d48b04.mspx.

Microsoft Web Platform Installer

After you install IIS, the Web Platform Installer (or *Web PI*) is the easiest way to install the remaining components on your server. You can obtain Web PI from the following web site:
http://www.microsoft.com/web/downloads/platform.aspx

Once you install and start Web PI, you can use the search feature to find and install "ASP.NET 4.5" (Figure 18-19). Once you've installed ASP.NET, do a search on "LightSwitch" to find the server configuration components. You'll find a couple of search results for LightSwitch 2012: a Server Configuration package that includes SQL Express, and a package that doesn't. If you already have a SQL Server that you can use, you can choose the package without SQL Express.

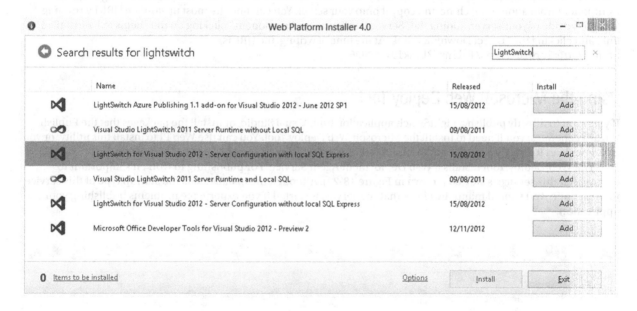

Figure 18-19. *Installing the prerequisites using Web PI*

Note that you must install ASP.NET or .NET 4.5 in order for the LightSwitch 2012 Server Configuration options to appear in Web PI.

ASP.NET Configuration

Although Web PI provides an easy way for you to set up your server, some companies might have policies that stop you from installing tools like Web PI on production servers. Another reason that can prevent you from installing Web PI is that your server might not have Internet access—this isn't unusual on servers in locked-down, secure environments. In these circumstances, you can install ASP.NET by downloading the full Microsoft .NET 4 Framework redistributable from the Microsoft web site: http://www.microsoft.com/download/en/details.aspx?id=17718

ASP.NET might not work if .NET 4 already exists on your server and you install IIS afterward. In this situation, ASP.NET might not be registered correctly, but you can correct this by opening a command prompt and running the aspnet_regiis.exe command. You can find this utility in the following folder:

- On a 32-bit server: `<WindowsDir>\Microsoft.NET\Framework\v4.0.30319\`

- On a 64-bit server: `<WindowsDir>\Microsoft.NET\Framework64\v4.0.30319\`

Once you've navigated to the correct folder, run the command with the i switch (that is, `aspnet_regiis.exe -i`) to re-register ASP.NET. You can also use the same process to reinstall or repair ASP.NET.

Installing the LightSwitch Server Components

If you're unable to install Web PI on your server, you can download the LightSwitch 2012 Server Configuration Component from another machine and copy it onto your server. You can find the most up-to-date URL by running Web PI outside of your server, adding the "Server Configuration Component," clicking on the "Items to be Installed" link, and clicking the "Direct Download" link. At the time of writing, the URL is http://go.microsoft.com/fwlink/?LinkID=213906

Using the Microsoft Web Deploy Tool

If you want to directly publish a LightSwitch application from Visual Studio, or install the packages that the Publish Wizard generates, you'll need to install the Microsoft Web Deploy Tool. You can use Web PI to install this utility, or you can download it directly from the Microsoft IIS web site (http://www.iis.net/download/WebDeploy).

The Web Deploy Tool installs a Web Deployment Agent Service. For publishing to work, it's important to ensure that this service is started (shown in Figure 18-20). Although the installer sets the startup type of this service to Automatic, you should manually check that the service is started if you experience problems publishing your application.

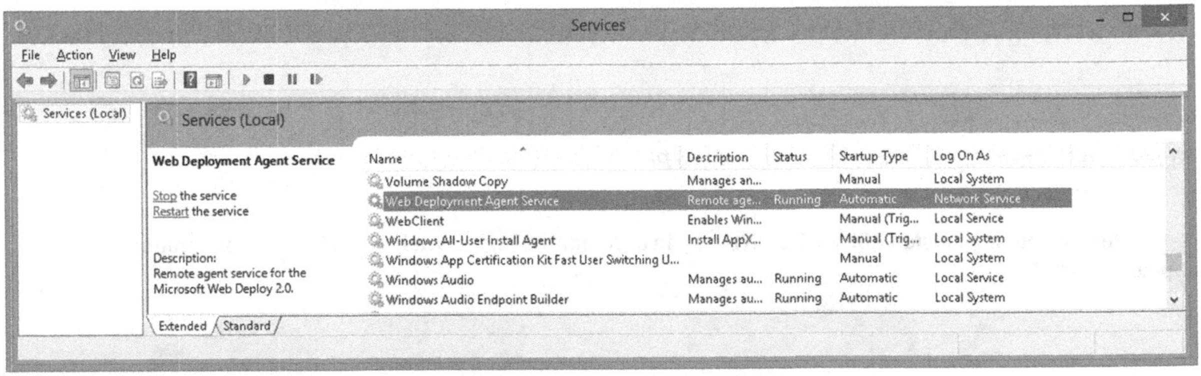

Figure 18-20. *The Web Deployment Agent Service must be started*

Installing the Packages

Now that you know how to build a web server with all the necessary components, this section shows you how to install the packages that you created with the Publish Wizard.

Installing a Two-Tier Desktop Application

When you use the Publish Wizard to build a two-tier desktop application, the wizard produces a set of installation files in the output folder that you specified in the wizard. The publish output includes a file called Setup.exe, and this is the application that you would run on the client workstation to install your application. If you've specified any prerequisites in the Publish Wizard (such as the .NET 4.5 Framework), Setup.exe will install these components too. But before you run Setup.exe, you'll need to carry out the following data tasks:

1. Create your SQL Server Database.

2. Modify your application's database connection string.

Installing Your SQL Database

The output from the Publish Wizard produces a SQL script called <YourApplication>.sql (where <YourApplication> is the name of your LightSwitch application). This script creates the database, tables, stored procedures, and other database objects that support your application. You'll need to execute this script on your database server, either by using the sqlcmd command-line tool or SQL Server Management Studio.

If you've installed a basic instance of SQL Server Express without the Management Tools, sqlcmd is the method that you would use. The default location of this utility on a 64-bit machine is

```
Program Files(x86)\Microsoft SQL Server\100\Tools\Binn
```

To use sqlcmd, open an elevated command prompt, navigate to the directory where it's installed, and run the following command:

```
sqlcmd.exe -i Helpdesk.sql -S .\SQLExpress
```

You'll need to replace the arguments that you supply to sqlcmd.exe as follows:

- **-i Helpdesk.sql:** This specifies the SQL file that you want to execute. Replace this with the name of the SQL file in your publish folder.

- **-S .\SQLExpress:** This specifies the name of your database server and SQL Server instance.

- **-U <username> -P <password>:** If you don't specify the –U and –P switches, sqlcmd connects to your SQL Server instance using Windows authentication. These switches allow you to supply a user name and password if you want to use SQL authentication instead.

If you choose to install the SQL Script by using SQL Server Management Studio, make sure to place your query window into SQLCMD Mode by using the option that you'll find under the Query menu. Your script won't run correctly if you don't do this.

Setting the Database Connection String

If you specify a correct and valid connection string in the Publish Wizard, you can skip this step. But if not, you'll need to modify your application's connection string so that it points to the database that you've installed. The publish output contains an "Application Files" subdirectory that includes a file called web.config. Open this file in Notepad, and edit the connection string value in the <connectionStrings> section like so:

```
<add name="_IntrinsicData" connectionString="Data Source=SERVERNAME\SQLEXPRESS;
   Initial Catalog=HelpDeskDB;Integrated Security=True;Pooling=True;
   Connect Timeout=30;User Instance=False" />
```

Replace SERVERNAME\SQLEXPRESS with the name of your database server and instance, and replace HelpDeskDB with the name of your database. If you've defined additional data sources in your application, you'll find the connection strings in the same section of the web.config file, and you can modify them as appropriate.

If you've enabled authentication in your application, you will have defined your application's administrator in the Publish Wizard. You'll find the settings that relate to your application's administrator in the web.config file, and you can also modify the values manually if needed.

Once you configure these data tasks, you'll be able to successfully run setup.exe on your client workstation. This creates a shortcut on the desktop, and the user can use this to start your application.

▪ **Note**   LightSwitch 2011 included a utility called Microsoft.LightSwitch.SecurityAdmin.exe that helped you set up Administrators. LightSwitch 2012 no longer includes this utility.

Installing a Three-Tier Browser and Desktop Applications

When you use the Publish Wizard to create a three-tier browser or desktop application, the wizard produces a single zip file rather than a set of files that includes an installer, as in the case of a two-tier application. The wizard names your zip file after your application (for example, HelpDesk.zip). This zip file is the package that the "IIS installer" consumes, and to use it, you'll need to install the "Web Deploy Tool," as I explained earlier.

To install the package, copy the zip file onto your server. Open IIS Manager, use the panel on the left to navigate to your web server, and select the right-click *Install* option. This opens the "Import Application Package" wizard, and the first page will prompt you to enter the path to your zip file. The next page shows you the package contents and allows you to review the items that the wizard will install (Figure 18-21). The default items include the SQL Script that defines your Intrinsic database, the option to create an IIS application, and the option to install the actual web files. You'll want to select all of these options.

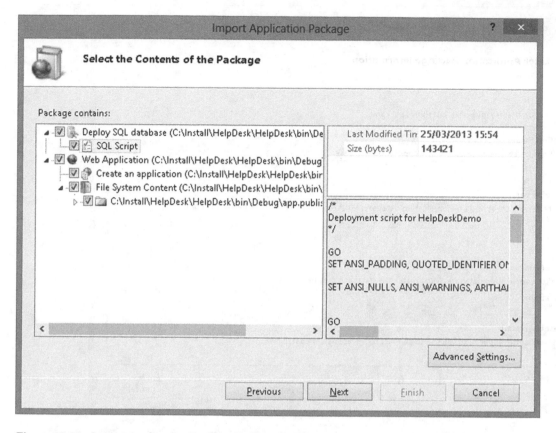

Figure 18-21. Import Application Package dialog—first page

The next page (shown in Figure 18-22) allows you to specify your database connection strings. The first "Connection String" text box specifies the connection string that the wizard uses to install or update your Intrinsic database. The next text box allows you to specify the connection that IIS uses at runtime to connect to your Intrinsic database. The wizard provides DatabaseUserName and DatabaseUserPassword text boxes because it expects you to use SQL Server authentication. If you want to use Windows authentication, you'll need to manually modify your web.config file after the import tool finishes and set up an application pool in IIS, as described earlier.

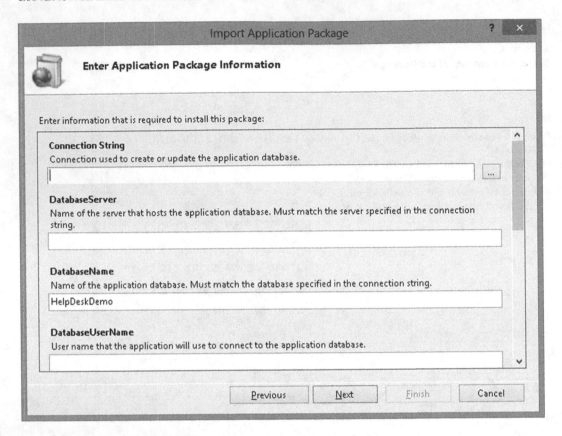

Figure 18-22. Import Application Package—database connection strings

Once you complete all the steps in the "Import Application Package" wizard, your application will be installed. If everything has worked correctly, you'll be able to open a web browser and navigate to the URL where you've installed your application.

In the case of a desktop application, you'll see an installation page like the one that's shown in Figure 18-23. When the user clicks on the "Install HelpDesk" button, the "Click Once" installer installs your desktop application and creates a desktop icon.

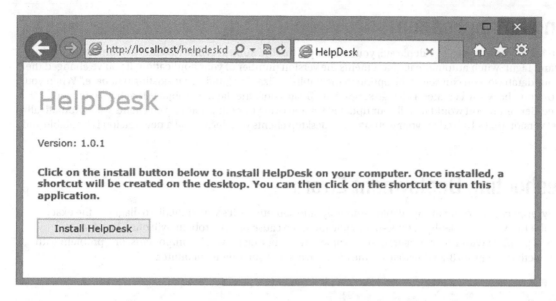

Figure 18-23. *Out-of-browser application install page*

Three-Tier Manual Deployment

Although the wizard provides a rich graphical way for you to deploy an application, you can just as easily deploy your three-tier application manually rather than create a zip file and use the Web Deploy Tool. If you're a traditional developer and like working in the "old school" way, this technique will suit you well. If you know what you're doing, it's quicker than using IIS's "Import Application Package" wizard and working through each page one by one.

The server-side part of your LightSwitch application is simply an ASP.NET web site. Instead of relying on the "Import Application Package" wizard to create your web site, you can create one manually by using IIS Manager. You would then need to use the option in IIS Manager to create an application and configure it to use an application pool that targets the .NET 4 Framework.

To publish your application, you'll still need to use the Publish Wizard from within LightSwitch. Once you've completed the wizard, you'll find your published files in the folder bin\Release\app.publish. You can now simply copy the contents of this folder into the folder for your web site. Before you run your application, you might need to modify the database connection strings in your web.config file so that they point to the right data source.

Deploying Data

When you were writing your application, you might have added records into your Intrinsic database that you now want to deploy. Although the Publish Wizard deploys the schema of your database, it won't deploy the data that you entered at design time.

You know that the Publish Wizard creates a SQL Script that contains the schema of your database, so the easiest way to deploy your data during the setup process is to add SQL INSERT statements to the end of this script file.

If you want to retrieve the data that you entered into your design-time database, you can attach your database's .MDF file by using SQL Server Management Studio. Management Studio includes a feature that allows you to script the data in your tables. To use this feature, right-click your database in Object Explorer and start the "Script Wizard" by selecting Tasks ➤ Generate Scripts. When you reach the options page, set the "Script Data" option to true. When the wizard completes, you can copy the SQL INSERT statements that the Script Wizard creates into the clipboard and paste them to the end of your deploy script.

Updating an Application

To update an application that you've deployed, you can simply run the Publish Wizard again. Each time you use the Publish Wizard, LightSwitch automatically increments the version number of your application. If you've changed the schema of your database, you can select the option in the Publish Wizard to "update an existing database." When you choose this option, the wizard creates a change script that updates only the database objects that have changed.

In a three-tier setup, you would install your updated version over your old version. Web clients will automatically run the latest version that's hosted on your web site, and desktop clients will detect that a new version is available and install it.

Troubleshooting Deployment Errors

Unfortunately, applications don't always deploy smoothly, and sometimes it's very difficult to diagnose the exact cause of a problem. When you deploy a three-tier application, the cause of any problem will often be down to three reasons: a problem with IIS's configuration, a problem with your LightSwitch components, or a problem with database connectivity. Figure 18-24 illustrates some of the errors that you might encounter.

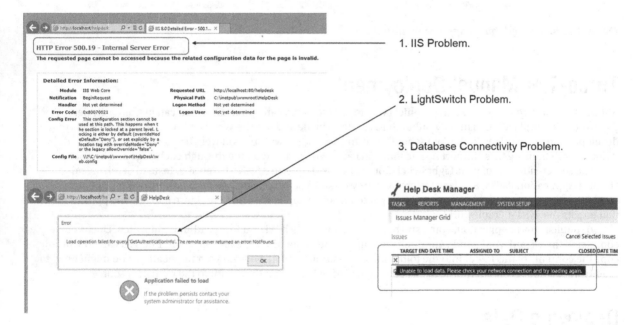

Figure 18-24. *LightSwitch deployment errors*

The first error in Figure 18-24 shows an IIS error. If your browser returns an HTTP error code that's generated by IIS, it means that you have some sort of IIS misconfiguration. This could be due to permissions or application pool settings. In the case of an IIS error, you can use the HTTP error code to diagnose your problem, and you should also check the Windows Event Log for additional details. Instead of an IIS error, you might encounter what's known as the "yellow screen of death"—this is a reference to the error page that ASP.NET generates. If this happens, it suggests that you've configured IIS and ASP.NET correctly, but there's some problem that's caused by the way that your application is set up in IIS. The error message that ASP.NET returns should hopefully help you diagnose the exact cause of the problem.

The second screenshot in Figure 18-24 illustrates a case where the Silverlight client loads successfully, but the application doesn't load any further. GetAuthenticationInfo is the first server method that your Silverlight Client calls, and because of this, it's common to see error messages that refer to this method. But deceptively, your problem might have nothing to do with authentication, and the best way to diagnose this problem is to trace your application. (The next section shows you how to do this.)

The final type of problem that you might encounter is the dreaded "red X" problem. This is a condition where your application loads successfully, but red crosses appear instead of data. Usually, this indicates a database or network connectivity problem. A classic symptom is that your screen shows the spinning hourglass for 30 seconds before it fails and shows the "red X." This 30-second period corresponds with SQL Server's default connection-timeout period of 30 seconds, and it highly suggests a database connection problem. If you see a "red X" on your screen, try opening a screen that contains a custom screen query that you've written in code. When a LightSwitch control such as DataGrid experiences a data problem, it "swallows" the exception and displays a "red X." But when a code query experiences a problem, it'll raise an unhandled exception, and LightSwitch will open the exception details in a dialog box. The error message that you'll see includes the exact exception (for example, SQL Exception Timeout Exception), and you can use this to confirm whether or not you have a general database connectivity problem.

Tracing Your Application

LightSwitch includes a diagnostic subsystem that integrates with ASP.NET's tracing functionality. You can use this feature to help you diagnose errors, resolve configuration issues, or work out why a query has failed. The trace messages that LightSwitch produces include the server request, the server response, and an error description.

For performance and security reasons, LightSwitch turns off tracing by default. To turn it on, you'll need to make some changes to your web.config file. Listing 18-2 shows the sections in your web.config file that apply to tracing.

Listing 18-2. Trace Settings in Web.Config

```
<appSettings>
  <!-- A value of true will enable diagnostic logging on the server -->
  <add key="Microsoft.LightSwitch.Trace.Enabled" value="true" />        ❶
  <!-- A value of true only lets local access to Trace.axd -->
  <add key="Microsoft.LightSwitch.Trace.LocalOnly" value="true" />      ❷
  <!-- The valid values for the trace level are: None, Error, Warning,
       Information, Verbose -->
  <add key="Microsoft.LightSwitch.Trace.Level" value="Information" />   ❸
  <!-- A value of true will indicate that logging sensitive information is ok -->
  <add key="Microsoft.LightSwitch.Trace.Sensitive" value="false" />     ❹
  <!-- The semi-colon separated list of categories that will be enabled at the
       specified trace level -->
    <add key="Microsoft.LightSwitch.Trace.Categories"
      value="Microsoft.LightSwitch" />
  <!-- Other web.config details here…… -->

<system.web>
    <!-- LightSwitch trace.axd handler -->
    <trace enabled="true" localOnly="false" requestLimit="40"          ❺
      writeToDiagnosticsTrace="false"
      traceMode="SortByTime" mostRecent="true" />
```

Let's take a closer look at some of these settings:

- **Enabled** - **❶:** You need to set this value to true to turn on tracing.

- **LocalOnly** - **❷:** When you set this to true, you can view trace messages only when you're logged on to your web server. If you set this to false, you'll be able to view the trace data from outside of your server, but note that this is a less secure setting.

- **Level** - **❸:** This setting allows you to specify the amount of information that LightSwitch logs. For diagnostic purposes, I recommend setting this to verbose. This is the setting that retrieves the maximum amount of information.

- **Sensitive** - **❹:** This setting controls whether or not LightSwitch can include your table data in its trace output. If you set this to true, LightSwitch may write sensitive data (for example, addresses, balances, prices) into the trace log.

The final change that you need to make is to enable ASP.NET's trace.axd handler **❺**. You'll find this setting lower down in the file, inside the system.web group.

Once you modify your web.config file, you can view your application's trace by opening a browser and navigating to your web site's trace.axd page (for example, http://MyWebServer/MyApp/trace.axd). When this page opens, you'll be able to view a list of trace messages, and you can view additional details by clicking on the *View Details* link. Figure 18-25 shows an example of the trace output that LightSwitch produces. Notice how the trace records all calls to the data service, and entries 5 and 6 in Figure 18-25 highlight calls to the data service's Engineers and Issues methods.

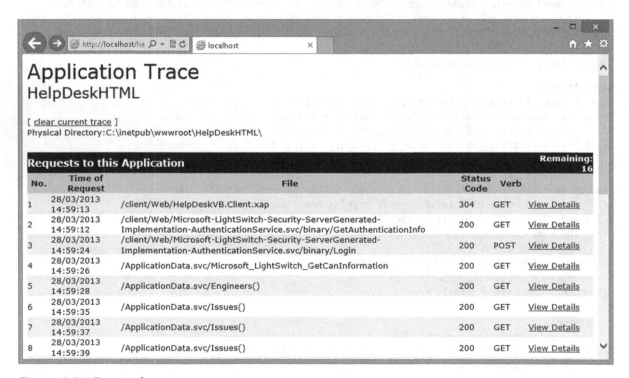

Figure 18-25. *Trace.Axd page*

Deploying to Azure

A great feature of LightSwitch is that you can easily deploy applications to Windows Azure—an Internet cloud-based platform. An excellent use-case scenario is to build an HTML client application and to host your application services in Azure. This allows your users to access your application "on the road" by using a mobile phone or tablet device that connects to the Internet via a cellular connection. Other advantages of Azure include simplicity, easier maintainability, and scalability.

Earlier in this chapter, you learned how to set up IIS and, hopefully, this hasn't been too difficult for you. Unfortunately, setting up a web server can be quite tricky, particularly if you don't have much experience of IIS. To make your application work, you need to install all the necessary components, configure permissions correctly, and make sure that you don't have firewall or antivirus rules that block your HTTP traffic. If you get this wrong, you can find yourself fighting with errors that can be quite obscure—Azure saves you from all of this trouble.

Another benefit of Windows Azure is that it's easier to maintain your underlying infrastructure. If you (rather than someone else in your company) are responsible for managing your own web server, you'll appreciate Azure much more. You'll no longer need stay at work late every "patch Tuesday" to install Windows Updates, struggle to work out why your server suddenly starts performing sluggishly, or end up being forced to replace a failed hard disk at the most inconvenient moment.

Azure also provides scalability. If you need more performance during busy times, you can simply use the web portal to provision more resources (and pay more money, of course). When demand goes down, you can scale back down again.

To get started, you'll need to log in to the Windows Azure web site (http://www.microsoft.com/windowsazure/) and sign up for an account. Windows Azure is priced on a "pay as you go" basis, so it's a good idea to study the pricing details that you'll find on the web site before you carry on. If you're new to Windows Azure, Microsoft provides a free 90-day trial. This is a great way to test out the service. When you sign up to the service, you'll need to enter a credit card number so that Microsoft can bill you after the initial 90-day period. If you intend only to try the service, remember to cancel your subscription before your trial period expires.

Once you've created an account, you'll find it surprising easy to publish to Azure. You simply choose the "Azure" option in the Publish Wizard and allow the wizard to guide you through the process, step by step. Let's now examine the publishing process by walking through the steps that you'll find in the wizard.

Connecting Visual Studio to Azure

Once you start the Publish Wizard, the second page prompts you to choose where to host your application's services—select the Windows Azure option. If you've installed the HTML client, the wizard prompts you to download and install the latest "Windows Azure SDK." Once you've installed this SDK, you can resume the wizard and enter your Azure details. This page will prompt you to create a new "publish setting" entry. When you choose this option, the wizard opens the dialog that's shown in Figure 18-26.

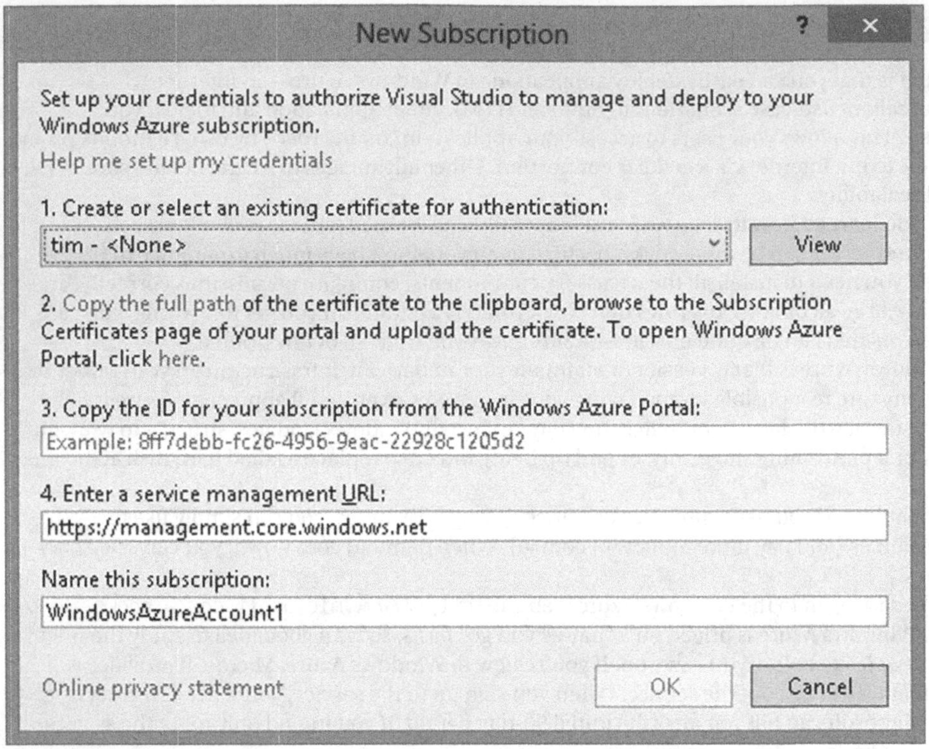

Figure 18-26. *New Subscription dialog*

The first drop-down box allows you to create or select an authentication certificate. Once you select a certificate, click on the "Copy the full path" link to copy the file location of your certificate onto the Windows clipboard.

You'll now need to move away from the wizard by logging in to the Azure Portal. Go to the Settings section, and click on the option to "Upload a Management Certificate" (Figure 18-27). While you're in the Azure Portal, make a note of your Azure Subscription ID, which you'll find in the accounts section. Your subscription ID is a GUID that uniquely identifies your Azure account. Once you've made a note of this, you can return to the wizard and enter this value into the third text box in the "New Subscription" dialog. Once you've entered all of the details that are shown in this dialog, Visual Studio is authorized to publish your application to your Azure account.

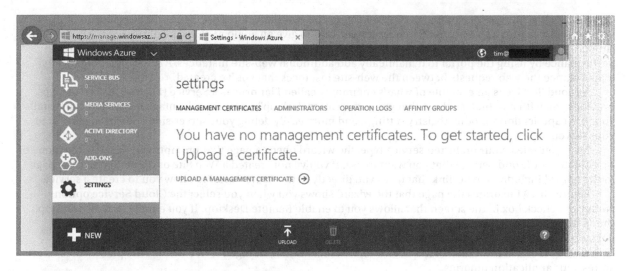

Figure 18-27. *Installing a new management certificate*

Choosing an Azure Service Type

The next step in the wizard prompts you to choose a service type, and there are two types that you can choose from: a Web Site Service or Cloud Service (Figure 18-28).

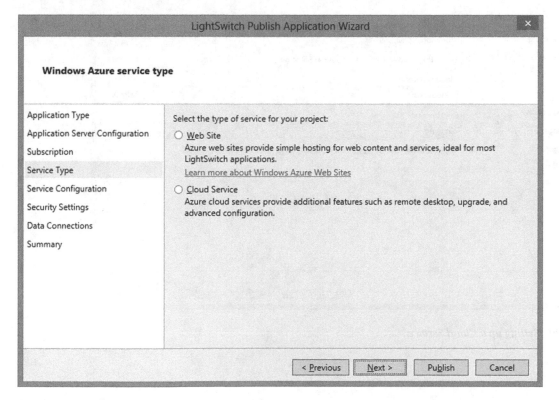

Figure 18-28. *Choosing a Service Type*

Azure's Web Site service provides simple hosting and is suitable for most LightSwitch applications. The Web Site service provides a hosted IIS environment, and to give an analogy, this type of service competes with services that are generally offered by web-hosting companies. Once you create a web site, you can increase performance by using the portal to dynamically add additional web-site instances. Azure will automatically load-balance the web requests between the web-site instances that you've created.

A Cloud Service is an example of what's commonly called Platform as a Service (PaaS). This service type provides you with a virtual machine that you can "remote desktop" onto. The advantage is that you can install your own applications, modify registry settings, and more easily debug your server-side code by logging in to your server.

After you select your preferred service type, the wizard opens a page that prompts you to select the name of the Web Site or Cloud Service that you want to use. If you've not created a Web Site or Cloud Service, the page in the wizard includes a hyperlink that takes you directly to the Azure Portal to allow you to create a service.

Figure 18-29 illustrates the page that the wizard shows you when you select the Cloud Service option. Notice the check box in the screen that allows you to enable Remote Desktop. If you enable Remote Desktop, the "Settings" link allows you to define the user name and password credentials for establishing a remote desktop connection. If you select the Cloud Service option, you'll need to specify a storage service in the "Advanced" tab, and the Azure Portal allows you to create this. A storage service defines the place where Azure stores your application binaries.

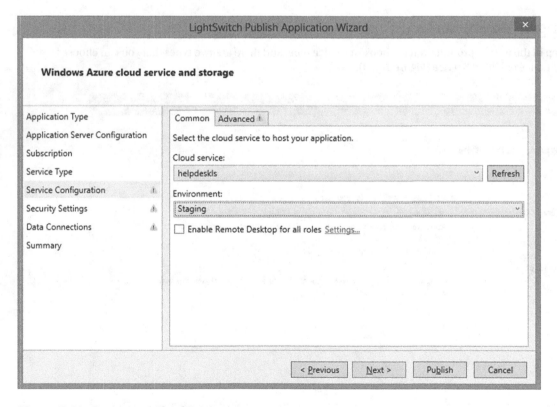

Figure 18-29. *Setting up a Cloud Service*

Creating a Database

After setting up the "application hosting" part of your application, the next step is to create the database that supports your application. Figure 18-30 shows the page in the wizard that prompts you to specify your Database connection. You'll notice that the page includes a link that allows you to "Provision a database at the Azure Portal." This link opens the Azure Portal in a new web browser window, and you can navigate to the "SQL Databases" part of the portal to create a new Azure database.

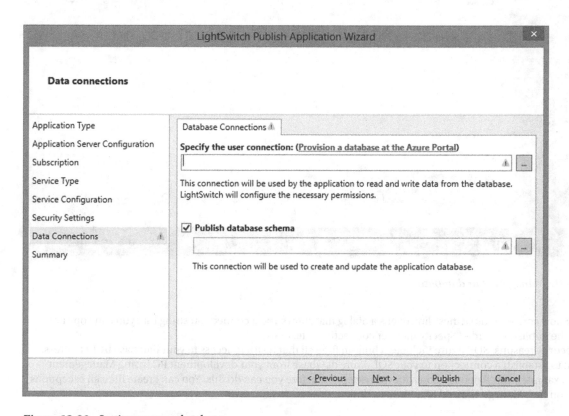

Figure 18-30. *Setting up your database*

When you add a new SQL database, you'll need to define an administrative user name and password, specify a database name, and set the maximum size of your database in gigabytes. The size that you choose partly determines the price that you'll need to pay for the Azure service.

After you've created your database, Figure 18-31 shows a screenshot of your database's "Dashboard" in the Azure portal. In the "quick glance" section that appears toward the bottom right, you'll see two useful links: Show connections strings, and Manage allowed IP addresses.

Figure 18-31. *Managing your database*

The "Show connections strings" link opens a dialog that shows you a connection string that you can copy and paste into the Publish Wizard's "Specify the user connections" text box.

For security reasons, SQL Azure includes a built-in firewall that restricts access to your database by IP address. If you want to establish a connection to your SQL Azure database from your development PC (using Management Studio, for example), you'll need to add a firewall exception before you can do this. You can create firewall exceptions by clicking on the "Manage allowed IP addresses" link.

Completing the Publishing Process

The remaining steps in the wizard allow you to specify an HTTPS certificate and to sign your XAP file with a digital certificate (in the case of a Silverlight application). Once you've completed all the steps in the wizard, you can click on the "Publish" button and complete the deployment of your application to the Azure platform. Hopefully, this section highlights how easy it is to deploy your applications to Windows Azure.

If you want to expose your application over the Internet, Windows Azure is a great choice, but it isn't the only option. You shouldn't overlook the services that web-hosting companies offer. The web-hosting market is competitive, and there are many companies that can host your LightSwitch application for a cheaper price.

You should also consider the security and privacy implications of exposing your application over the Internet. If you expose your application over the Internet, it's up to you to review the sensitivity of your data and to risk-assess the impact that a data breach could have on your business.

With Windows Azure, you should also be aware that because Microsoft is a US company, any data that you store in Azure might be subject to interception by US authorities. You won't be too shocked by this if you live in the US, but if you live in Europe (for example), you might want to do an Internet search on "US PATRIOT Act" to read more about the impact of choosing to use a US firm for processing and storing your data.

Publishing to SharePoint

Visual Studio 2012 Update 2 introduces the option to host your Silverlight or HTML client applications in SharePoint 2013 or Office 365.

Hosting your application in SharePoint 2013 can be beneficial if your organization already uses SharePoint. One advantage is that you can customize your LightSwitch application so that it integrates more closely with your SharePoint system. For example, you can implement authentication using SharePoint identities and permissions, or create list items, create workflows, or add images to SharePoint picture libraries.

The SharePoint client object model (CSOM) is the API you use to write code that integrates your LightSwitch application with SharePoint. You can find out more about CSOM on the help page: http://go.microsoft.com/fwlink/?LinkId=285361.

The quickest way to get started is to create a SharePoint developer site on Office 365. You can find out how to do this by visiting the following web page: http://go.microsoft.com/fwlink/?LinkId=263490.

Once you've prepared your SharePoint or Office 365 web site, the first step is to enable the SharePoint feature in your LightSwitch project. You'll need to upgrade your project, and once you do this, your application's properties will include a SharePoint tab (Figure 18-32). When you click on the "Enable SharePoint" button, LightSwitch prompts you to download and install the "Microsoft Office Developer Tools for Visual Studio" package.

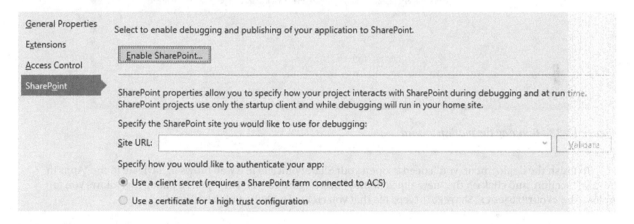

Figure 18-32. *Enabling SharePoint*

Clicking the "Enable SharePoint" button prompts you to enter the URL and security credentials for your Office 365 or SharePoint site. Once you do this, LightSwitch adds a new project into your solution, and it also adds references to several supporting assemblies.

If you now debug your application, LightSwitch uses SharePoint to provide authentication, and then it redirects you to an instance of your application that's hosted locally in IIS Express. When you debug your application for the first time, LightSwitch prompts you to install a self-signed certificate to support SSL.

To deploy your application to SharePoint, simply run the LightSwitch Publish Wizard. You'll notice that the wizard now shows only one page. The instructions in the wizard describe how the process works (Figure 18-33), and it provides you with the following two hosting options: Autohosted or Provider-hosted. When you deploy an autohosted application in Office 365, the process automatically hosts your application in Windows Azure and hosts your Intrinsic database in SQL Azure. When you complete the Publish Wizard, LightSwitch generates a file called <YourProject>.SharePoint.app.

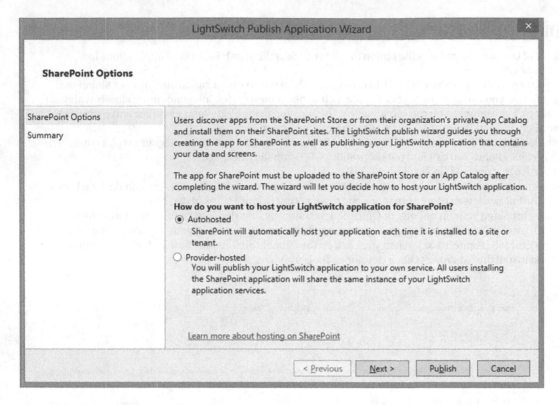

Figure 18-33. Running the publish wizard

To finish the deployment, you'll need to open your SharePoint site in a web browser, navigate to the "Apps in Testing" section, and click on the "new app to deploy" link (Figure 18-34). This opens a dialog that allows you to upload the <YourProject>.SharePoint.app file that you created with the Publish Wizard.

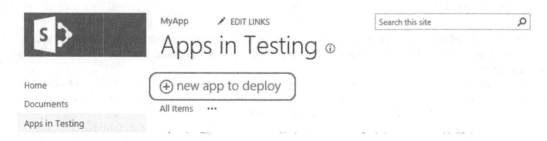

Figure 18-34. Uploading your app

After you upload your application, you'll see another dialog that prompts you to deploy your application. After you click on the deploy button, you'll be able to run your application by clicking the link that appears in the "Apps in Testing" section.

Summary

This chapter has showed you how to deploy LightSwitch applications. It's possible to create many different types of applications, which results in several distinct deployment combinations. LightSwitch applications depend on application services that you can install on an IIS server, on Azure, or on the client workstation. You can install your application services on the client only if you're building a desktop application. This deployment scenario is ideal for stand-alone applications or applications that do not have many users. However, there's a larger deployment overhead because you'll need to install the application services on each workstation that needs to access to your application.

If you're building a browser application, you must host your application services in IIS or Windows Azure. If you choose to host your application in IIS, there are several setup tasks that you need to carry out. First, you need to install IIS, and the exact way to do this depends on your server's operating system. A tool called Web Platform Installer (Web PI) allows you to download and install the remaining components that are required to host a LightSwitch application. You can download Web PI from the Microsoft web site. The items that you'll need to install on your server are ASP.NET 4, the "LightSwitch 2012 Server Configuration" component, and the Web Deploy Tool. If you're unable to install Web PI on your web server, you can download the components on a separate computer and copy them onto your server.

Other relevant IIS settings include setting up SSL and adding application pools. SSL makes your application more secure by encrypting the data between your LightSwitch client and server. Application pools improve reliability by isolating the applications that run on your web server. If a web application crashes, it won't bring down other web applications that run in other application pools. Application pools also allow you to set up your data service to use Windows authentication with your SQL Server instance.

LightSwitch includes a "Publish Wizard" that allows you to deploy your application. This contains a series of screens that guide you step by step through the deployment process. If you're deploying an application to IIS, you can choose to either package or publish your application. The difference between publishing and packaging is that publishing deploys an application immediately to your IIS server, whereas packaging produces setup files that you need to manually install afterward. In the case of Silverlight applications, the Publish Wizard allows you to digitally sign your XAP file. If you don't do this, Windows shows a dialog when your user installs your application that warns that your application might be dangerous. You can prevent this warning by signing your application with a digital certificate.

If you choose to deploy a three-tier application, the Publish Wizard either publishes your application or produces a deployment zip file. If you create a package, you can use IIS's "Import Application Package" wizard to install your package. This wizard takes care of setting up your application service's web site and creating the SQL Server database that supports your application. Once you've added your application to IIS, your users can run your browser application or install your desktop application by navigating to your application's URL through a web browser.

In the case of a two-tier desktop application, the Publish Wizard produces a file called Setup.exe, along with a script that creates your database and supporting database objects. To install your application, you'll need to run the script against your database server and run the setup.exe file on the client workstation.

To update an existing application, you can simply re-run the wizard. The Publish Wizard can analyze your existing database and produce a SQL script that applies the incremental schema changes that you've made.

The Publish Wizard also allows you to deploy your application to Windows Azure. Azure is a cloud service that you can use to publish applications that users can access through the Internet. The service works on a "pay as you go" basis, and the cost depends on the resource and network utilization of your application. To use Azure, you'll need to set up an account by using the Azure web portal. You can host your application by using either a "Web Site," or Cloud service. An Azure "Web Site" provides simple hosting, whereas the Cloud service provides an environment that supports "remote desktop" and allows you to install custom software. The publishing process requires you to authorize your copy of Visual Studio with your Azure account by adding a management certificate through the Azure Portal web site. You also need to provision a "Web Site" or Cloud service and a SQL Azure database. You can carry out both these tasks through the Azure Portal.

Finally, you can host your application in SharePoint or Office 365 by installing Visual Studio 2012 Update 2. One of the advantages of hosting your application in SharePoint is that you can integrate your application with lists, libraries, and other SharePoint assets.

Sadly, this brings us to the end of the book. I hope that you've found it useful; well done for persevering through all 18 chapters! You're now capable of building some excellent LightSwitch applications, and I wish you the very best of luck in all of your future LightSwitch projects.

APPENDIX A

■ ■ ■

Culture Names

Chapter 2 showed you how to apply the Money Business Type to a property. This Business Type allows you to set the currency code of your property, and Table A-1 shows a list of the most popular currency codes.

Table A-1. *Currency Symbols*

Code	Description
USD	US Dollar
GBP	British Pound
EUR	Euro (European Currency Unit)
AUD	Australian Dollar
CHF	Swiss Franc
JPY	Japanese Yen
NZD	New Zealand Dollar
CAD	Canadian Dollar

If you're building an application that supports multiple languages, it's useful to understand the culture names that you can use. Table A-2 shows you a list of culture names. The culture name is a combination of an ISO 639 two-letter culture code that describes the language and an ISO 3166 two-letter uppercase subculture code that identifies the country or region. For the name to be valid, the culture part must be in lowercase and the country/region part in uppercase.

Table A-2. *Culture Names*

Code	Description
af	Afrikaans
ar-AE	Arabic (U.A.E.)
ar-BH	Arabic (Bahrain)
ar-DZ	Arabic (Algeria)
ar-EG	Arabic (Egypt)
ar-IQ	Arabic (Iraq)
ar-JO	Arabic (Jordan)
ar-KW	Arabic (Kuwait)
ar-LB	Arabic (Lebanon)
ar-LY	Arabic (Libya)
ar-MA	Arabic (Morocco)
ar-OM	Arabic (Oman)
ar-QA	Arabic (Qatar)
ar-SA	Arabic (Saudi Arabia)
ar-SY	Arabic (Syria)
ar-TN	Arabic (Tunisia)
ar-YE	Arabic (Yemen)
be	Belarusian
bg	Bulgarian
ca	Catalan
cs	Czech
da	Danish
de	German (Standard)
de-AT	German (Austria)
de-CH	German (Switzerland)
de-LI	German (Liechtenstein)
de-LU	German (Luxembourg)
el	Greek
en	English
en-AU	English (Australia)
en-BZ	English (Belize)
en-CA	English (Canada)

(*continued*)

Table A-2. (*continued*)

Code	Description
en-GB	English (United Kingdom)
en-IE	English (Ireland)
en-JM	English (Jamaica)
en-NZ	English (New Zealand)
en-TT	English (Trinidad)
en-US	English (United States)
en-ZA	English (South Africa)
es	Spanish (Spain)
es-AR	Spanish (Argentina)
es-BO	Spanish (Bolivia)
es-CL	Spanish (Chile)
es-CO	Spanish (Colombia)
es-CR	Spanish (Costa Rica)
es-DO	Spanish (Dominican Republic)
es-EC	Spanish (Ecuador)
es-GT	Spanish (Guatemala)
es-HN	Spanish (Honduras)
es-MX	Spanish (Mexico)
es-NI	Spanish (Nicaragua)
es-PA	Spanish (Panama)
es-PE	Spanish (Peru)
es-PR	Spanish (Puerto Rico)
es-PY	Spanish (Paraguay)
es-SV	Spanish (El Salvador)
es-UY	Spanish (Uruguay)
es-VI	Spanish (Venezuela)
et	Estonian
eu	Basque
fa	Farsi
fi	Finnish
fo	Faeroese
fr	French (Standard)

(*continued*)

Table A-2. (*continued*)

Code	Description
fr-BE	French (Belgium)
fr-CA	French (Canada)
fr-CH	French (Switzerland)
fr-LU	French (Luxembourg)
ga	Irish
gd	Gaelic (Scotland)
he	Hebrew
hi	Hindi
hr	Croatian
hu	Hungarian
id	Indonesian
is	Icelandic
it	Italian (Standard)
it-CH	Italian (Switzerland)
ja	Japanese
ji	Yiddish
ko	Korean
ko	Korean (Johab)
lt	Lithuanian
lv	Latvian
mk	Macedonian (FYROM)
ms	Malaysian
mt	Maltese
nl	Dutch (Standard)
nl-BE	Dutch (Belgium)
no	Norwegian
pl	Polish
pt	Portuguese (Portugal)
pt-BR	Portuguese (Brazil)
rm	Rhaeto-Romanic
ro	Romanian
ru	Russian
ru-MO	Russian (Republic of Moldova)

(continued)

Table A-2. (*continued*)

Code	Description
sb	Sorbian
sk	Slovak
sl	Slovenian
sq	Albanian
sr	Serbian
sr-Cyrl-CS	Serbian (Cyrillic, Serbia and Montenegro)
sr-Latn-CS	Serbian (Latin, Serbia and Montenegro)
sv	Swedish
sv-FI	Swedish (Finland)
sx	Sutu
sz	Sami (Lappish)
th	Thai
tn	Tswana
tr	Turkish
ts	Tsonga
uk	Ukrainian
ur	Urdu
ve	Venda
vi	Vietnamese
xh	Xhosa
zh-CN	Chinese (Simplified, PRC)
zh-HK	Chinese (Traditional, Hong Kong SAR)
zh-SG	Chinese (Simplified, Singapore)
zh-TW	Chinese (Traditional, Taiwan)
zu	Zulu

APPENDIX B

■ ■ ■

Data Type Identifiers

Several places in this book require you to specify a data type by providing a string. This table contains a list of valid identifiers that you can use.

LightSwitch Data Types

:Binary

:Boolean

:Byte

:DateTime

:Date

:Decimal

:Double

:Guid

:Int16

:Int32

:Int64

:SByte

:Single

:String

:TimeSpan

LightSwitch Extension Data Types

Microsoft.LightSwitch.Extensions:EmailAddress

Microsoft.LightSwitch.Extensions:Image

Microsoft.LightSwitch.Extensions:Money

Microsoft.LightSwitch.Extensions:Percent

Microsoft.LightSwitch.Extensions:PhoneNumber

Microsoft.LightSwitch.Extensions:WebAddress

Chapter 6 showed you how to create a Global Query Value that you can use in your queries. You learned how to create a Global Query Value called "7 Days Ago" that allows you to filter your data by using an operator (e.g., Greater Than/Less Than) and the "7 Days Ago" Global Query Value. This requires you to specify the Global Query Value return type in your LSML file by using the format :DateTime. If you were creating a different Global Query Value and needed to specify a different return type, the table shows the list of acceptable values that you can use.

The LightSwitch Data Types that begin with : and aren't preceded with a namespace refer to types that belong to the Microsoft.LightSwitch namespace.

Chapter 12 includes an example that creates a custom value control, and another example that extends Visual Studio's property sheet. Both of these examples require you to edit the contents of an LSML file and choose a data type value from the table in this appendix.

Chapter 13 shows you how to create a Business Type. When you create a business type, you must define the underlying data type that your business type uses in its LSML file. Once again, you'd use one of the choices that are shown in this table.

APPENDIX C

■ ■ ■

Using Properties in Custom Controls

When you're writing a custom Silverlight control extension, you can bind the attributes of UI elements to the values that a developer enters in the Visual Studio screen designer (Figure C-1).

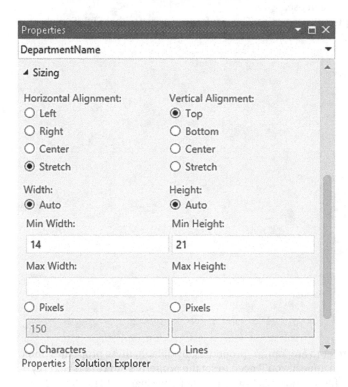

Figure C-1. *Property values that developers can modify*

Chapter 12 (Listing 12-7) highlights a piece of XAML that includes a custom control that consumes the values from the property sheet. An excerpt of this code is shown in Listing C-1.

Listing C-1. Using Property Names

```
<StackPanel
   Width="{Binding Properties[Microsoft.LightSwitch:RootControl/Width]}"
   Height="{Binding Properties[Microsoft.LightSwitch:RootControl/Height]}"
   VerticalAlignment ="{Binding
      Properties[Microsoft.LightSwitch:RootControl/VerticalAlignment]}">

   <TextBlock
           Text="{Binding Value, Mode=OneWay,
               Converter={StaticResource formatter}}"
           TextAlignment="{Binding
               Properties[Microsoft.LightSwitch:RootControl/TextAlignment]}">
```

The data Binding syntax that's shown here includes the property names Width, Height, TextAlignment, and VerticalAlignment. You can use these property names in your XAML and .NET code, and the purpose of this appendix is to show you a list of property names that you can use.

These appearance properties are examples of "opt-out" properties. These refer to properties that LightSwitch automatically shows in the property sheet:

- AttachedLabelPosition

- HeightSizingMode

- WidthSizingMode

- MinHeight

- MaxHeight

- MinWidth

- MaxWidth

- Height

- Width

- Rows

- Characters

- VerticalAlignment

- HorizontalAlignment

The other group of property names that you can refer to are "opt-in" properties. By default, these properties don't show up in Visual Studio's property sheet. To make them appear, you'll need to set the property's EditorVisibility value to PropertySheet in your custom control's LSML file, as shown in Listing C-2. Refer to Chapter 12 (Listing 12-23) to see a full example of a custom control's LSML file.

Listing C-2. Showing Properties in Visual Studio's Property Sheet

```
<Control.PropertyOverrides>
     <!-- Support Show As Link property -->
     <ControlPropertyOverride
        Property=":RootControl/Properties[ShowAsLink]"
        EditorVisibility="PropertySheet"/>
</Control.PropertyOverrides>
```

The two EditorVisibility values that you can set are

- NotDisplayed

- PropertySheet

Here's a full list of opt-in properties that you can use:

- ShowAsLink

- FontStyle

- TextAlignment

- BrowseOnly

- Image

To see an example of two of these properties, you can look at the Label control, which is a built-in LightSwitch control that applies the ShowAsLink and FontStyle properties. To see screenshots of these properties, refer to Figure 3-29 and Figure 3-26, respectively.

■ ■ ■

Custom Screen Template View IDs

When you're writing a custom screen template (as discussed in Chapter 13), you can call the host generator methods to add content items onto your screen. Once you've done this, you can call the SetContentItemView method to change the control that renders your data item. In effect, the SetContentItemView method provides the code equivalent of you using the drop-down box that appears next to a data item in the screen designer to select a different control type. Let's say that you've added a local screen property called screenPropertyContentItem and want to change the control type from an autocomplete box (the default control) to a Rows Layout, here's the code that you would use:

```
host.SetContentItemView(screenPropertyContentItem, "Microsoft.LightSwitch:RowsLayout");
```

"Microsoft.LightSwitch:RowsLayout" is the ViewID that identifies the RowsLayout control type. When you're writing a custom screen template, you'll need to know what ViewIDs to use, and this is summarized in the following table. The ViewIDs that you need to use will vary depending on whether the user has upgraded their project to use the HTML client, and this is shown in the following table.

Control Type	ViewID String (Project that hasn't been upgraded with the HTML client)	ViewID String (Project that has been upgraded with the HTML client)
Collection Controls		
DataGrid	Microsoft.LightSwitch:DataGrid	Microsoft.LightSwitch.RichClient:DataGrid
DataGrid	Microsoft.LightSwitch:DataGrid	Microsoft.LightSwitch.RichClient:DataGrid
Command Controls		
Button	Microsoft.LightSwitch:Button	Microsoft.LightSwitch.RichClient:Button
Link	Microsoft.LightSwitch:Link	Microsoft.LightSwitch.RichClient:Link
ShellButton	Microsoft.LightSwitch:ShellButton	Microsoft.LightSwitch.RichClient:ShellButton
CollectionButton	Microsoft.LightSwitch:CollectionButton	Microsoft.LightSwitch.RichClient:CollectionButton
Details Controls		
Summary	Microsoft.LightSwitch:Summary	Microsoft.LightSwitch.RichClient:Summary

(*continued*)

Control Type	ViewID String (Project that hasn't been upgraded with the HTML client)	ViewID String (Project that has been upgraded with the HTML client)
Details Picker Controls		
ModalWindowPickerDetails	Microsoft.LightSwitch:Modal WindowPickerDetails	Microsoft.LightSwitch.RichClient: ModalWindowPickerDetails
DetailsAutoCompleteBox	Microsoft.LightSwitch: DetailsAutoCompleteBox	Microsoft.LightSwitch.RichClient: DetailsAutoCompleteBox
Value Picker Controls		
ModalWindowPickerValue	Microsoft.LightSwitch: ModalWindowPickerValue	Microsoft.LightSwitch.RichClient: ModalWindowPickerValue
ValueAutoCompleteBox	Microsoft.LightSwitch: ValueAutoCompleteBox	Microsoft.LightSwitch. RichClient:ValueAutoCompleteBox
Group Controls		
ModalWindow	Microsoft.LightSwitch: ModalWindow	Microsoft.LightSwitch. RichClient:ModalWindow
RowsLayout	Microsoft.LightSwitch: RowsLayout	Microsoft.LightSwitch. RichClient:RowsLayout
ColumnsLayout	Microsoft.LightSwitch: ColumnsLayout	Microsoft.LightSwitch. RichClient:ColumnsLayout
TableLayout	Microsoft.LightSwitch: TableLayout	Microsoft.LightSwitch. RichClient:TableLayout
TableColumnLayout	Microsoft. LightSwitch:TableColumnLayout	Microsoft.LightSwitch. RichClient:TableColumnLayout
TabsLayout	Microsoft.LightSwitch:TabsLayout	Microsoft.LightSwitch. RichClient:TabsLayout
DataGridRow	Microsoft.LightSwitch:DataGridRow	Microsoft.LightSwitch. RichClient:DataGridRow
PictureAndText	Microsoft.LightSwitch:PictureAndText	Microsoft.LightSwitch. RichClient:PictureAndText
TextAndPicture	Microsoft.LightSwitch:TextAndPicture	Microsoft.LightSwitch. RichClient:TextAndPicture
GroupBox	Microsoft.LightSwitch:GroupBox	Microsoft.LightSwitch. RichClient:GroupBox
AddressViewerSmartLayout	Microsoft.LightSwitch.Extensions: AddressViewerSmartLayout	Microsoft.LightSwitch.Extensions: AddressViewerSmartLayout
AddressEditorSmartLayout	Microsoft.LightSwitch.Extensions: AddressEditorSmartLayout	Microsoft.LightSwitch.Extensions: AddressEditorSmartLayout
WebLink	Microsoft.LightSwitch. Extensions:WebLink	Microsoft.LightSwitch. Extensions:WebLink
WebAddressEditor	Microsoft.LightSwitch. Extensions:WebAddressEditor	Microsoft.LightSwitch. Extensions:WebAddressEditor

(continued)

Control Type	ViewID String (Project that hasn't been upgraded with the HTML client)	ViewID String (Project that has been upgraded with the HTML client)
Screen Controls		
Screen	Microsoft.LightSwitch:Screen	Microsoft.LightSwitch.RichClient:Screen
Value and Picker Controls		
TextBox	Microsoft.LightSwitch:TextBox	Microsoft.LightSwitch.RichClient:TextBox
Label	Microsoft.LightSwitch:Label	Microsoft.LightSwitch.RichClient:Label
CheckBox	Microsoft.LightSwitch:CheckBox	Microsoft.LightSwitch.RichClient:CheckBox
DateTimePicker	Microsoft.LightSwitch:DateTimePicker	Microsoft.LightSwitch.RichClient:DateTimePicker
DateTimeViewer	Microsoft.LightSwitch:DateTimeViewer	Microsoft.LightSwitch.RichClient:DateTimeViewer
DatePicker	Microsoft.LightSwitch:DatePicker	Microsoft.LightSwitch.RichClient:DatePicker
DateViewer	Microsoft.LightSwitch:DateViewer	Microsoft.LightSwitch.RichClient:DateViewer
StaticImage	Microsoft.LightSwitch:StaticImage	Microsoft.LightSwitch.RichClient:StaticImage
StaticLabel	Microsoft.LightSwitch:StaticLabel	Microsoft.LightSwitch.RichClient:StaticLabel
EmailAddressViewerControl	Microsoft.LightSwitch.Extensions:EmailAddressViewerControl	Microsoft.LightSwitch.Extensions:EmailAddressViewerControl
EmailAddressEditorControl	Microsoft.LightSwitch.Extensions:EmailAddressEditorControl	Microsoft.LightSwitch.Extensions:EmailAddressEditorControl
ImageViewerControl	Microsoft.LightSwitch.Extensions:ImageViewerControl	Microsoft.LightSwitch.Extensions:ImageViewerControl
ImageEditorControl	Microsoft.LightSwitch.Extensions:ImageEditorControl	Microsoft.LightSwitch.Extensions:ImageEditorControl
MoneyViewerControl	Microsoft.LightSwitch.Extensions:MoneyViewerControl	Microsoft.LightSwitch.Extensions:MoneyViewerControl
MoneyEditorControl	Microsoft.LightSwitch.Extensions:MoneyEditorControl	Microsoft.LightSwitch.Extensions:MoneyEditorControl
PhoneNumberViewerControl	Microsoft.LightSwitch.Extensions:PhoneNumberViewerControl	Microsoft.LightSwitch.Extensions:PhoneNumberViewerControl
PhoneNumberEditorControl	Microsoft.LightSwitch.Extensions:PhoneNumberEditorControl	Microsoft.LightSwitch.Extensions:PhoneNumberEditorControl
PercentViewerControl	Microsoft.LightSwitch.Extensions:PercentViewerControl	Microsoft.LightSwitch.Extensions:PercentViewerControl
PercentEditorControl	Microsoft.LightSwitch.Extensions:PercentEditorControl	Microsoft.LightSwitch.Extensions:PercentEditorControl

■ ■ ■

HelpDesk Tables

Throughout this book, you've seen examples from the HelpDesk sample application. Chapter 2 describes the main tables and relationships that the application uses. This appendix summarizes the remaining tables that belong in this application.

HelpDesk Tables

This section shows you the tables in the Intrinsic database, organized in alphabetical order.

AppOption			
Name	Type		Required
⊶ Id	Integer	▼	☑
AuditChangesOn	Boolean	▼	☑
SendEmailOn	Boolean	▼	☑
SMTPServer	String	▼	☐
SMTPPort	Integer	▼	☐
SMTPUsername	String	▼	☐
SMTPPassword	String	▼	☐
ReportWebSiteRootURL	String	▼	☐
<Add Property>		▼	☐

User

Department

∞

Department

Name	Type	Required
Id	Integer	☑
DepartmentName	String ▼	☑
DepartmentManager	String ▼	☐
Address1	String ▼	☐
Address2	String ▼	☐
City	String ▼	☐
Postcode	String ▼	☐
Country	String ▼	☐
Users	User Collection ▼	☐
<Add Property>	▼	☐

0..1

EmailOperation

Name	Type	Required
Id	Integer	☑
SenderEmail	Email Address ▼	☑
RecipientEmail	Email Address ▼	☑
Subject	String ▼	☑
Body	String ▼	☑
Attachment	Binary ▼	☐
AttachmentFileName	String ▼	☐
<Add Property>	▼	☐

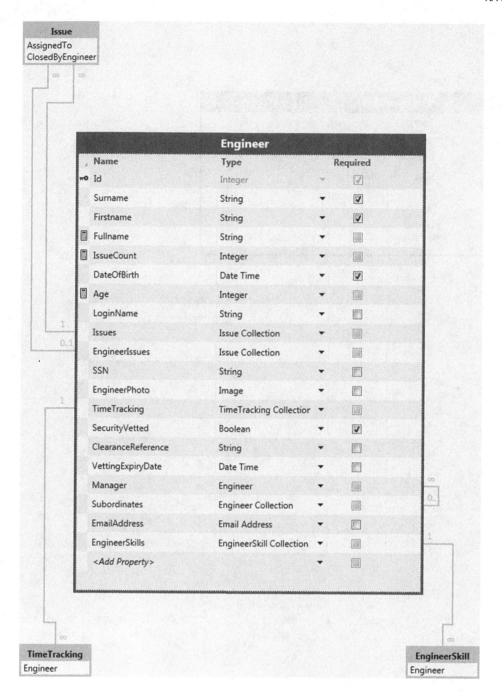

Issue
AssignedTo
ClosedByEngineer

Engineer		
Name	**Type**	**Required**
Id	Integer	✓
Surname	String	✓
Firstname	String	✓
Fullname	String	
IssueCount	Integer	
DateOfBirth	Date Time	✓
Age	Integer	
LoginName	String	
Issues	Issue Collection	
EngineerIssues	Issue Collection	
SSN	String	
EngineerPhoto	Image	
TimeTracking	TimeTracking Collection	
SecurityVetted	Boolean	✓
ClearanceReference	String	
VettingExpiryDate	Date Time	
Manager	Engineer	
Subordinates	Engineer Collection	
EmailAddress	Email Address	
EngineerSkills	EngineerSkill Collection	
<Add Property>		

TimeTracking
Engineer

EngineerSkill
Engineer

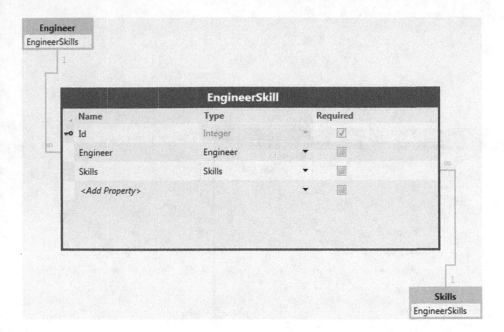

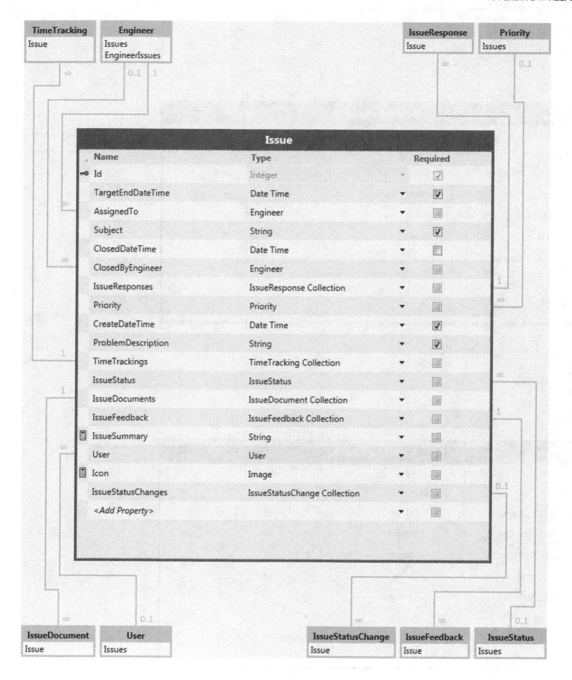

TimeTracking	Engineer
Issue	Issues
	EngineerIssues

IssueResponse	Priority
Issue	Issues

Issue

Name	Type		Required
Id	Integer		☑
TargetEndDateTime	Date Time	▼	☑
AssignedTo	Engineer	▼	☐
Subject	String	▼	☑
ClosedDateTime	Date Time	▼	☐
ClosedByEngineer	Engineer	▼	☐
IssueResponses	IssueResponse Collection	▼	☐
Priority	Priority	▼	☐
CreateDateTime	Date Time	▼	☑
ProblemDescription	String	▼	☑
TimeTrackings	TimeTracking Collection	▼	☐
IssueStatus	IssueStatus	▼	☐
IssueDocuments	IssueDocument Collection	▼	☐
IssueFeedback	IssueFeedback Collection	▼	☐
IssueSummary	String	▼	☐
User	User	▼	☐
Icon	Image	▼	☐
IssueStatusChanges	IssueStatusChange Collection	▼	☐
<Add Property>		▼	☐

IssueDocument	User
Issue	Issues

IssueStatusChange	IssueFeedback	IssueStatus
Issue	Issue	Issues

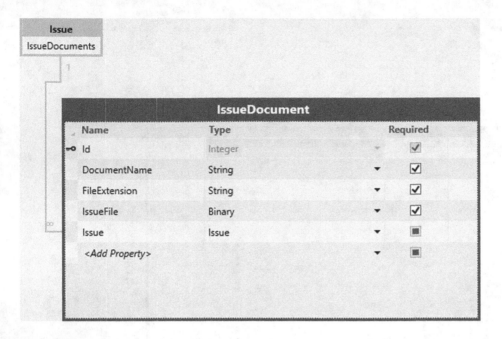

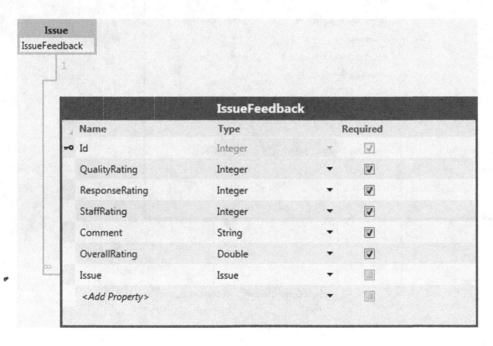

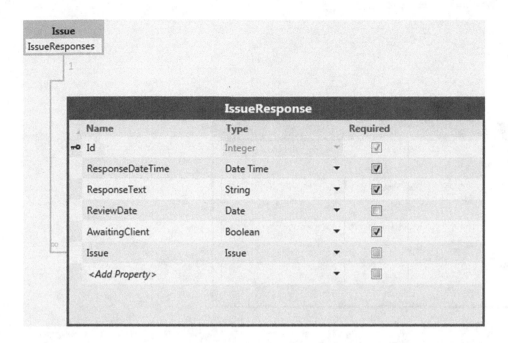

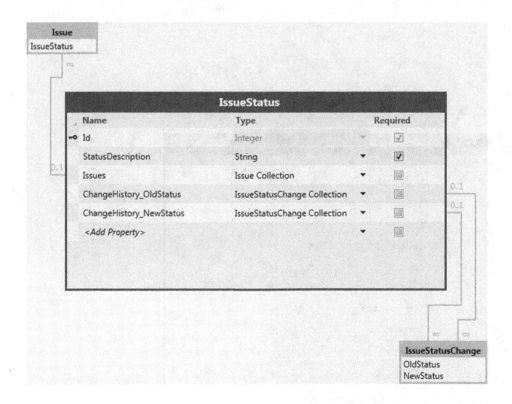

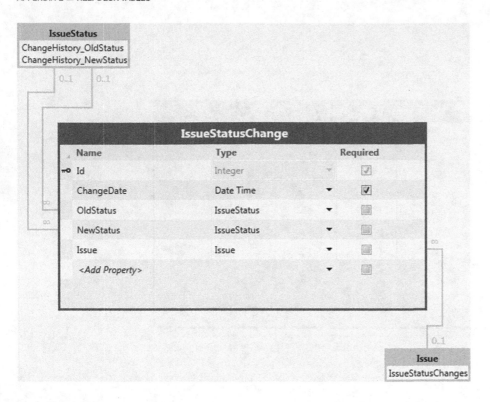

IssueStatus
ChangeHistory_OldStatus
ChangeHistory_NewStatus

0..1   0..1

IssueStatusChange

Name	Type		Required
Id	Integer	▼	✓
ChangeDate	Date Time	▼	✓
OldStatus	IssueStatus	▼	☐
NewStatus	IssueStatus	▼	☐
Issue	Issue	▼	☐
<Add Property>		▼	☐

∞

0..1

Issue
IssueStatusChanges

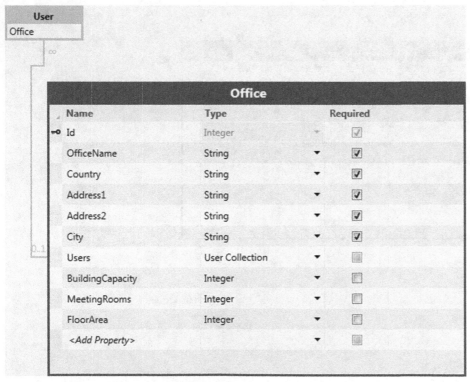

User
Office

∞

Office

Name	Type		Required
Id	Integer	▼	✓
OfficeName	String	▼	✓
Country	String	▼	✓
Address1	String	▼	✓
Address2	String	▼	✓
City	String	▼	✓
Users	User Collection	▼	☐
BuildingCapacity	Integer	▼	☐
MeetingRooms	Integer	▼	☐
FloorArea	Integer	▼	☐
<Add Property>		▼	☐

0..1

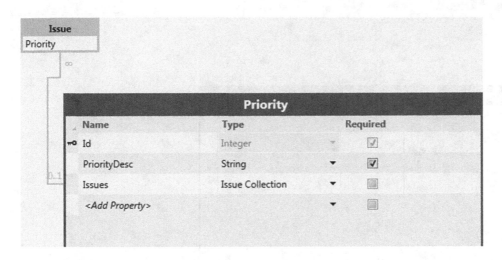

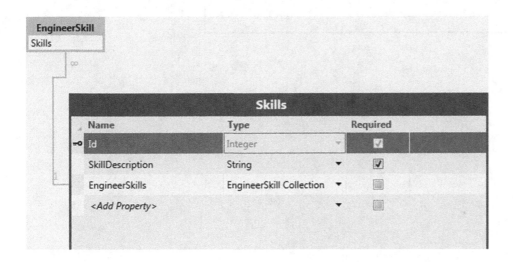

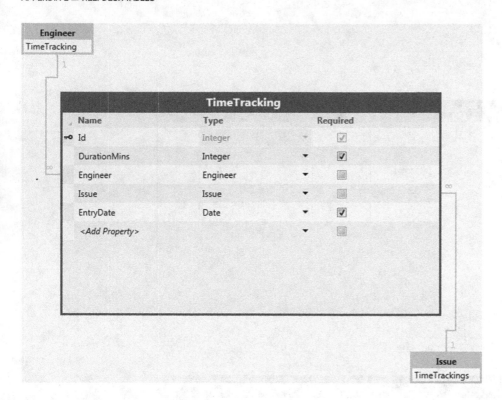

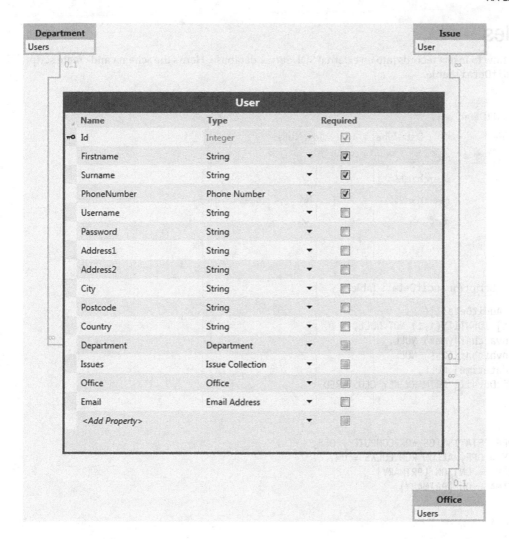

External Tables

Chapter 4 showed you how to insert records into an external SQL Server database. Here's the schema and create script (Listing E-1) for the AuditDetail table.

HelpDeskAudit - dbo.AuditDetail		▼ ☐ ✕
Column Name	**Data Type**	**Allow Nulls**
▶🔑 AuditID	int	☐
AuditDesc	nvarchar(MAX)	☑
LoginName	nvarchar(255)	☑
AuditDate	datetime	☑
		☐

Listing E-1. SQL Create Script for AuditDetail Table

```
CREATE TABLE [dbo].[AuditDetail](
      [AuditID] [int] IDENTITY(1,1) NOT NULL,
      [AuditDesc] [nvarchar](max) NULL,
      [LoginName] [nvarchar](255) NULL,
      [AuditDate] [datetime] NULL,
 CONSTRAINT [PK_AuditDetail] PRIMARY KEY CLUSTERED
(
      [AuditID] ASC
)
WITH (PAD_INDEX = OFF, STATISTICS_NORECOMPUTE = OFF,
      IGNORE_DUP_KEY = OFF, ALLOW_ROW_LOCKS = ON,
      ALLOW_PAGE_LOCKS = ON) ON [PRIMARY]
) ON [PRIMARY] TEXTIMAGE_ON [PRIMARY]
```

Database Diagram

The following two diagrams show the relationships between tables in SQL Server after the Intrinsic database has been deployed.

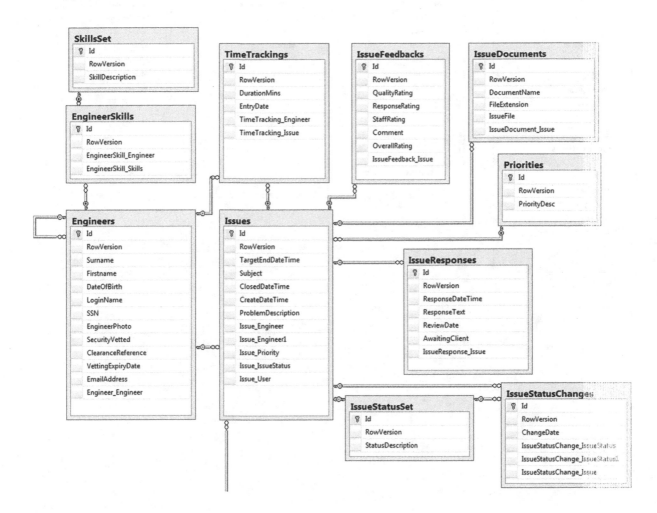

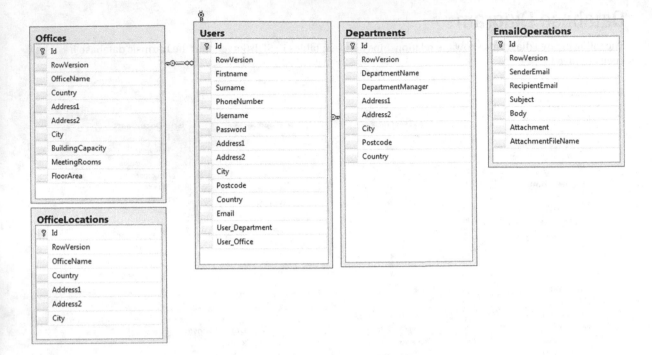

Index

■ D, E

Data and presentation extensions, 365.
  See also Business type extension
  custom theme extension
    different font, 413
    process, 413
    setting different colors, 414–415
  data source
    attach data file, 433
    data service class, 428–432
    entity class, 425–427
    steps, 425
  screen template extension
    add/edit screen template, 425
    data source type, 418
    new screen dialog, 418
    process, 416
    screen code generation, 423, 425
    screen controls, 418–422
    template properties, 416–417
Data Grid control
  add-new row properties, 49
  command bar buttons, 50
  details screen, 47
  header buttons, 50
  hiding existing records, 49
  paging, sorting and searching options, 48
  properties, 49
Data, LightSwitch, 11
  business types
    Email addresses, 17
    meaning, 16
    Money values, 17–18
    phone numbers, 18–19
    web addresses and
      percentage values, 19
  choice lists
    vs. related tables, 21
    reorder items, 20–21
  computed properties
    calculate dates, 32
    child records, 33
    images, 33–34
    meaning, 30
    sort and filter, 34
    summary properties, 31
  entities and properties, 12
  existing data source
    attachment, 27
    connect to MySQL data source, 27
    DataTime offset, 30
    delete, 30
    missing tables, 28
    refresh data sources, 29–30
    SharePoint data, 30

fields creation (properties)
    changing data types, 16
    ensuring unique values, 16
    formatting numeric fields, 14–15
    image type, 16
    storing number
      (double and decimal types), 14
    string data types, 13
  relationships
    child records deletion, 26
    many-to-many relationships, 25–26
    one-to-many relationships, 22–23
    self-referencing/recursive relationships, 24–25
    SQL server, 24
  SQL Server database, 19–20
  storing data, 11
  table creation (entities), 12–13
Data List control
  configuration, 48–49
  details screen, 47
Data-picker controls, 195
Data type identifiers, 603
Data validation. *See also* Custom validation
  access validation results, 110–111
  client validation works, 90–91
  database validation
    check constraint, 111
    constraint violation error, 111–112
    unique index, 111
  deletions
    DeleteIssue_Execute
      and Issue_Validate code, 106–107
    server, 107–109
    tasks, 105–106
  errors, 90
  HelpDesk application, 89
  predefined validation, 93
  rules declaration
    data types, 92
    properties, 91–92
  screen validation
    creation, 104
    and entity validation, 90
    screen-level validation, 105
  storage layer, 89
  table designer, 89
  type, 90
  validation summary control, 91
  workflow, 90
Dependency properties, Custom controls
  data context, 298–299
  dynamic value resolution, 292
  local value, 292
  new control and dependency properties
    behavior, 298
    code-behind, 294–296